Microsoft® SQL Server® 2012 Analysis Services: The BISM Tabular Model

Marco Russo
Alberto Ferrari
Chris Webb

Published with the authorization of Microsoft Corporation by:
O'Reilly Media, Inc.
1005 Gravenstein Highway North
Sebastopol, California 95472

ISBN: 978-0-7356-5818-9

1 2 3 4 5 6 7 8 9 M 7 6 5 4 3 2

Printed and bound in the United States of America.

Microsoft Press books are available through booksellers and distributors worldwide. If you need support related to this book, email Microsoft Press Book Support at *mspinput@microsoft.com*. Please tell us what you think of this book at *http://www.microsoft.com/learning/booksurvey*.

Acquisitions and Developmental Editor: Russell Jones

Production Editor: Holly Bauer

Editorial Production: nSight, Inc.

Technical Reviewers: Darren Gosbell and John Mueller

Copyeditor: Kerin Forsyth / Ann Weaver

Indexer: Nancy Guenther

Cover Design: Twist Creative • Seattle

Cover Composition: Karen Montgomery

Illustrator: nSight, Inc.

To the many BI communities that have supported me in the last years.

—Marco Russo

I dedicate this book to Caterina, Lorenzo, and Arianna: my family.

—Alberto Ferrari

I dedicate this book to my wife, Helen, and my two daughters, Natasha and Mimi. Thank you for your love, understanding, and patience.

—Chris Webb

Contents at a Glance

Contents

Chapter 1 Introducing the Tabular Model   1

What do you think of this book? We want to hear from you!

Microsoft is interested in hearing your feedback so we can continually improve our
books and learning resources for you. To participate in a brief online survey, please visit:

microsoft.com/learning/booksurvey

What do you think of this book? We want to hear from you!

Microsoft is interested in hearing your feedback so we can continually improve our
books and learning resources for you. To participate in a brief online survey, please visit:

microsoft.com/learning/booksurvey

Foreword

I have known Marco Russo, Alberto Ferrari, and Chris Webb for many years through my work on the Analysis Services product team. Early on, these authors were among the first to embrace multidimensional modeling and offered their insights and suggestions as valued partners to help us make the product even better. When we introduced tabular modeling in SQL Server 2012, the authors were on board from the start, participating in early reviews and applying their substantial skills to this new technology. Marco, Alberto, and Chris have been instrumental in helping to shape the product design and direction, and we are deeply grateful for their contributions.

The authors are truly among the best and brightest in the industry. Individually and collectively, they have authored many books. *Expert Cube Development with Microsoft SQL Server 2008 Analysis Services* notably stands out as a must-have book for understanding multidimensional modeling in Analysis Services. In addition to writing amazing books, you can often find Marco, Alberto, and Chris speaking at key conferences, running training courses, and consulting for companies who are applying business intelligence to improve organizational performance. These authors are at the top of their field; their blogs come up first in the search list for almost any query you might have related to building business intelligence applications.

The book you have in your hands describes ways to build business intelligence applications in detail, using DAX and tabular models. But what truly sets this book apart is its practical advice. This is a book that only seasoned BI practitioners could write. It is a great blend of the information you need the most: an all-up guide to tabular modeling, balanced with sensible advice to guide you through common modeling decisions. I hope you enjoy this book as much as I do. I'm sure it will become an essential resource that you keep close at hand whenever you work on tabular models.

Edward Melomed
Program Manager
SQL Server Analysis Services

Introduction

When we, the authors of this book, first learned what Microsoft's plans were for Analysis Services in the SQL Server 2012 release, we were not happy. Analysis Services hadn't acquired much in the way of new features since 2005, even though in the meantime it had grown to become the biggest-selling OLAP tool. It seemed as if Microsoft had lost interest in the product. The release of PowerPivot and all the hype surrounding self-service Business Intelligence (BI) suggested that Microsoft was no longer interested in traditional corporate BI, or even that Microsoft thought professional BI developers were irrelevant in a world where end users could build their own BI applications directly in Excel. Then, when Microsoft announced that the technology underpinning PowerPivot was to be rolled into Analysis Services, it seemed as if all our worst fears had come true: the richness of the multidimensional model was being abandoned in favor of a dumbed-down, table-based approach; a mature product was being replaced with a version 1.0 that was missing a lot of useful functionality. Fortunately, we were proven wrong and as we started using the first CTPs of the new release, a much more positive—if complex—picture emerged.

SQL Server 2012 is undoubtedly a milestone release for Analysis Services. Despite all the rumors to the contrary, we can say emphatically that Analysis Services is neither dead nor dying; instead, it's metamorphosing into something new and even more powerful. As this change takes place, Analysis Services will be a two-headed beast—almost two separate products (albeit ones that share a lot of the same code). The Analysis Services of cubes and dimensions familiar to many people from previous releases will become known as the "Multidimensional Model," while the new, PowerPivot-like flavor of Analysis Services will be known as the "Tabular Model." These two models have different strengths and weaknesses and are appropriate for different projects. The Tabular Model (which, from here onward, we'll refer to as simply Tabular) does not replace the Multidimensional Model. Tabular is not "better" or "worse" than Multidimensional. Instead, the Tabular and Multidimensional models complement each other well. Despite our deep and long-standing attachment to Multidimensional, Tabular has impressed us because not only is it blindingly fast, but because its simplicity will bring BI to a whole new audience.

In this book we'll be focusing exclusively on Tabular for two reasons. First, there's not much that's new in the Multidimensional Model, so books written for previous versions of Analysis Services will still be relevant. Second, if you're using Analysis Services on a project, you'll have to make a decision early on about which of the two models to use—and it's very unlikely you'll use both. That means anyone who decides to use Tabular is unlikely to be interested in reading about the Multidimensional Model anyway. One of the first things we'll do in this book is to give you all the information you need to make the decision about which model to use.

We have enjoyed learning about and writing about Tabular and we hope you enjoy reading this book.

Who Should Read This Book

This book is aimed at professional Business Intelligence developers: consultants or members of in-house BI development teams who are about to embark on a project using the Tabular Model.

Assumptions

Although we're going to start with the basics of Tabular—so in a sense this is an introductory book—we're going to assume that you already know certain core BI concepts such as dimensional modeling and data warehouse design. Some previous knowledge of relational databases, and especially SQL Server, will be important when it comes to understanding how Tabular is structured and how to load data into it and for topics such as DirectQuery.

Previous experience with Analysis Services Multidimensional isn't necessary, but because we know most readers of this book will have some we will occasionally refer to its features and compare them with equivalent features in Tabular.

Who Should Not Read This Book

No book is suitable for every possible audience, and this book is no exception. Those without any existing business intelligence experience will find themselves out of their depth very quickly, as will managers who do not have a technical background.

Organization of This Book

This book is organized as follows: In the first chapter we will introduce the Tabular Model, what it is and when it should (and shouldn't) be used. In Chapters 2 and 3 we will cover the basics of building a Tabular Model. In Chapters 4 through 8 we'll introduce DAX, its concepts, syntax and functions, and how to use it to create calculated columns, measures, and queries. Chapters 9 through 16 will deal with numerous Tabular design topics such as hierarchies, relationships, many-to-many, and security. Finally, Chapters 17 and 18 will deal with operational issues such as hardware sizing and configuration, optimization, and monitoring.

Conventions and Features in This Book

This book presents information using conventions designed to make the information readable and easy to follow:

- Boxed elements with labels such as "Note" provide additional information or alternative methods for completing a step successfully.

- Text that you type (apart from code blocks) appears in bold.

- A plus sign (+) between two key names means that you must press those keys at the same time. For example, Press Alt+Tab means that you hold down the Alt key while you press the Tab key.

- A vertical bar between two or more menu items (for example, File | Close), means that you should select the first menu or menu item, then the next, and so on.

System Requirements

You will need the following hardware and software to install the code samples and sample database used in this book:

- Windows Vista SP2, Windows 7, Windows Server 2008 SP2, or greater. Either 32-bit or 64-bit editions will be suitable.

- At least 4 GB of free space on disk.

- At least 4 GB of RAM.

- A 2.0GHz x86 or x64 processor or better.

- An instance of SQL Server Analysis Services 2012 Tabular plus client components. Full instructions on how to install this are given in Chapter 2, "Getting Started with the Tabular Model."

Code Samples

The database used for examples in this book is based on Microsoft's Adventure Works 2012 DW sample database. Because there are several different versions of this database in existence, all of which are slightly different, we recommend that you download the database from the link below rather than use your own copy of Adventure Works if you want to follow the examples.

All sample projects and the sample database can be downloaded from the following page:

http://go.microsoft.com/FWLink/?Linkid=254183

Follow the instructions to download the BismTabularSample.zip file and the sample database.

Installing the Code Samples

Follow these steps to install the code samples on your computer so that you can follow the examples in this book:

1. Unzip the samples file onto your hard drive.

2. Restore the two SQL Server databases from the .bak files that can be found in the Databases directory. Full instructions on how to do this can be found here: *http://msdn.microsoft.com/en-us/library/ms177429.aspx.*

3. Restore the Adventure Works Tabular database to Analysis Services from the .abf file that can also be found in the Databases directory. Full instructions on how to do this can be found here: *http://technet.microsoft.com/en-us/library/ ms174874.aspx.*

4. Each chapter has its own directory containing code samples. In many cases this takes the form of a project, which that must be opened in SQL Server Data Tools. Full instructions on how to install SQL Server Data Tools are given in Chapter 2, "Getting Started With the Tabular Model."

Acknowledgments

We'd like to thank the following people for their help and advice: Akshai Mirchandani, Amir Netz, Ashvini Sharma, Brad Daniels, Cristian Petculescu, Dan English, Darren Gosbell, Dave Wickert, Denny Lee, Edward Melomed, Greg Galloway, Howie Dickerman,

Hrvoje Piasevoli, Jeffrey Wang, Jen Stirrup, John Sirmon, John Welch, Kasper de Jonge, Marius Dumitru, Max Uritsky, Paul Sanders, Paul Turley, Rob Collie, Rob Kerr, TK Anand, Teo Lachev, Thierry D'Hers, Thomas Ivarsson, Thomas Kejser, Tomislav Piasevoli, Vidas Matelis, Wayne Robertson, Paul te Braak, Stacia Misner, Javier Guillen, Bobby Henningsen, Toufiq Abrahams, Christo Olivier, Eric Mamet, Cathy Dumas, and Julie Strauss.

Errata & Book Support

We've made every effort to ensure the accuracy of this book and its companion content. Any errors that have been reported since this book was published are listed on our Microsoft Press site at oreilly.com:

http://go.microsoft.com/FWLink/?Linkid=254181

If you find an error that is not already listed, you can report it to us through the same page.

If you need additional support, email Microsoft Press Book Support at *mspinput@microsoft.com*.

Please note that product support for Microsoft software is not offered through the addresses above.

We Want to Hear from You

At Microsoft Press, your satisfaction is our top priority and your feedback our most valuable asset. Please tell us what you think of this book at:

http://www.microsoft.com/learning/booksurvey

The survey is short, and we read every one of your comments and ideas. Thanks in advance for your input!

Stay in Touch

Let's keep the conversation going! We're on Twitter: *http://twitter.com/MicrosoftPress*

Introducing the Tabular Model

The purpose of this chapter is to introduce Analysis Services 2012, provide a brief overview of what the Tabular model is, and explore its relationship to the Multidimensional model, to Analysis Services 2012 as a whole, and to the wider Microsoft business intelligence (BI) stack. This chapter will also help you make what is probably the most important decision in your project's life cycle: whether you should use the Tabular model.

The Microsoft BI Ecosystem

In the Microsoft ecosystem, BI is not a single product; it's a set of features distributed across several products, as explained in the following sections.

What Is Analysis Services and Why Should I Use It?

Analysis Services is an online analytical processing (OLAP) database, a type of database that is highly optimized for the kinds of queries and calculations that are common in a business intelligence environment. It does many of the same things that a relational database can do, but it differs from a relational database in many respects. In most cases, it will be easier to develop your BI solution by using Analysis Services in combination with a relational database such as Microsoft SQL Server than by using SQL Server alone. Analysis Services certainly does not replace the need for a relational database or a properly designed data warehouse.

One way of thinking about Analysis Services is as an extra layer of metadata, or a semantic model, that sits on top of a data warehouse in a relational database. This extra layer contains information about how fact tables and dimension tables should be joined, how measures should aggregate up, how users should be able to explore the data through hierarchies, the definitions of common calculations, and so on. This layer includes one or more models containing the business logic of your data warehouse—and end users query these models rather than the underlying relational database. With all this information stored in a central place and shared by all users, the queries that users need to write become much simpler: All a query needs to do in most cases is describe which columns and rows are required, and the model applies the appropriate business logic to ensure that the numbers that are returned make sense. Most important, it becomes impossible to write a query that returns "incorrect" results due to a mistake by end users, such as joining two tables incorrectly or summing a column that cannot be summed. This, in turn, means that end-user reporting and analysis tools must do much less work and can provide a clearer visual interface for end users to build queries. It also means that different tools can connect to the same model and return consistent results.

Another way of thinking about Analysis Services is as a kind of cache that you can use to speed up reporting. In most scenarios in which Analysis Services is used, it is loaded with a copy of the data in the data warehouse. Subsequently, all reporting and analytic queries are run against Analysis Services rather than against the relational database. Even though modern relational databases are highly optimized and contain many features specifically aimed at BI reporting, Analysis Services is a database specifically designed for this type of workload and can, in most cases, achieve much better query performance. For end users, optimized query performance is extremely important because it allows them to browse through data without waiting a long time for reports to run and without any breaks in their chain of thought.

For the IT department, the biggest benefit of all this is that it becomes possible to transfer the burden of authoring reports to the end users. A common problem with BI projects that do not use OLAP is that the IT department must build not only a data warehouse but also a set of reports to go with it. This increases the amount of time and effort involved, and can be a cause of frustration for the business when it finds that IT is unable to understand its reporting requirements or to respond to them as quickly as is desirable. When an OLAP database such as Analysis Services is used, the IT department can expose the models it contains to the end users and enable them to build reports themselves by using whatever tool with which they feel comfortable. By far the most popular client tool is Microsoft Excel. Ever since Office 2000, Excel PivotTables have been able to connect directly to Analysis Services cubes and Excel 2010 has some extremely powerful capabilities as a client for Analysis Services.

All in all, Analysis Services not only reduces the IT department's workload but also increases end user satisfaction because users now find they can build the reports they want and explore the data at their own pace without having to go through an intermediary.

A Short History of Analysis Services

SQL Server Analysis Services—or OLAP Services, as it was originally called when it was released with SQL Server 7.0—was the first foray by Microsoft into the BI market. When it was released, many people commented that this showed that BI software was ready to break out of its niche and reach a mass market, and the success of Analysis Services and the rest of the Microsoft BI stack over the past decade has proved them correct. SQL Server Analysis Services 2000 was the first version of Analysis Services to gain significant traction in the marketplace; Analysis Services 2005 quickly became the biggest-selling OLAP tool not long after its release, and, as Analysis Services 2008 and 2008 R2 improved scalability and performance still further, more and more companies started to adopt it as a cornerstone of their BI strategy. Terabyte-sized cubes are now not uncommon, and the famous example of the 24-TB cube Yahoo! built shows just what can be achieved. Analysis Services today is an extremely successful, mature product that is used and trusted in thousands of enterprise-level deployments.

The Microsoft BI Stack Today

The successes of Analysis Services would not have been possible if it had not been part of an equally successful wider suite of BI tools that Microsoft has released over the years. Because there are so many of these tools, it is useful to list them and provide a brief description of what each does.

The Microsoft BI stack can be broken up into two main groups: products that are part of the SQL Server suite of tools and products that are part of the Office group. As of SQL Server 2012, the SQL Server BI-related tools include:

- **SQL Server relational database** The flagship product of the SQL Server suite and the platform for the relational data warehouse. *http://www.microsoft.com/sqlserver/en/us/default.aspx*

- **SQL Azure** The Microsoft cloud-based version of SQL Server, not commonly used for BI purposes at the moment, but, as other cloud-based data sources become more common in the future, it will be used more and more. *https://www.windowsazure.com/en-us/home/features/sql-azure*

- **Parallel Data Warehouse** A highly specialized version of SQL Server, aimed at companies with multiterabyte data warehouses, which can scale out its workload over many physical servers. *http://www.microsoft.com/sqlserver/en/us/solutions-technologies/data-warehousing/pdw.aspx*

- **SQL Server Integration Services** An extract, transform, and load (ETL) tool for moving data from one place to another. Commonly used to load data into data warehouses. *http://www.microsoft.com/sqlserver/en/us/solutions-technologies/business-intelligence/integration-services.aspx*

- **Apache Hadoop** The most widely used open-source tool for aggregating and analyzing large amounts of data. Microsoft has decided to support it explicitly in Windows and provide tools to help integrate it with the rest of the Microsoft BI stack. *http://www.microsoft.com/bigdata*

- **SQL Server Reporting Services** A tool for creating static and semistatic, highly formatted reports and probably the most widely used SQL Server BI tool of them all. *http://www.microsoft.com/sqlserver/en/us/solutions-technologies/business-intelligence/reporting-services.aspx*

- **SQL Azure Reporting** The cloud-based version of SQL Server Reporting Services, in beta at the time of writing. *http://msdn.microsoft.com/en-us/library/windowsazure/gg430130.aspx*

- **Power View** A powerful new data visualization and analysis tool, available through Microsoft SharePoint, which acts as a front end to Analysis Services. *http://www.microsoft.com/sqlserver/en/us/future-editions/SQL-Server-2012-breakthrough-insight.aspx*

- **StreamInsight** A complex event-processing platform for analyzing data that arrives too quickly and in too large a volume to persist in a relational database. *http://www.microsoft.com/sqlserver/en/us/solutions-technologies/business-intelligence/complex-event-processing.aspx*

- **Master Data Services**   A tool for managing a consistent set of master data for BI systems. *http://www.microsoft.com/sqlserver/en/us/solutions-technologies/business-intelligence/ master-data-services.aspx*

- **Data Quality Services**   A data quality and cleansing tool. *http://msdn.microsoft.com/en-us/ library/ff877917(v=sql.110).aspx*

- **PowerPivot**   A self-service BI tool that enables users to construct their own reporting solutions in Excel and publish them in SharePoint. It is very closely related to Analysis Services and will be discussed in greater detail in the following section, "Self-Service BI and Corporate BI."

BI tools developed by the Office group include:

- **SharePoint 2010**   The Microsoft flagship portal and collaboration product. In the view of Microsoft, SharePoint is where all your BI reporting should be surfaced, through Excel and Excel Services, Reporting Services, Power View, or PerformancePoint. It also serves as the hub for sharing PowerPivot models by using PowerPivot for SharePoint.

- **PerformancePoint Services**   A tool for creating BI dashboards inside SharePoint.

- **Excel 2010**   The venerable spreadsheet program and probably the most widely used BI tool in the world, Excel has long been able to connect directly to Analysis Services through pivot tables and cube formulas. Now, with the release of PowerPivot (which is an Excel add-in), it is at the center of the Microsoft self-service BI strategy.

It is also worth mentioning that Microsoft makes various experimental BI tools available on its SQL Azure Labs site (*http://www.microsoft.com/en-us/sqlazurelabs/default.aspx*), which include the projects code-named "Social Analytics" and "Data Explorer." In addition, a large number of third-party software vendors make valuable contributions to the Microsoft BI ecosystem; for example, by building client tools for Analysis Services.

Self-Service BI and Corporate BI

One of the most significant trends in the BI industry over the last few years has been the appearance of so-called self-service BI tools such as QlikView and Tableau. These tools aim to give power users the ability to create small-scale BI solutions with little or no help from IT departments. In a sense, Analysis Services has always been a kind of self-service BI tool in that it enables end users to build their own queries and reports, but it still requires an IT professional to design and build the Analysis Services database and the underlying data warehouse. This means that it is usually grouped with other, more traditional corporate BI tools, where the design of databases and reporting of and access to data is strictly controlled by the IT department. In many organizations, however, especially smaller ones, the resources simply do not exist to undertake a large-scale BI project; even when they do, the failure rate for this type of project is often very high, hence the appeal to a certain class of users of self-service BI tools that enable them to do everything themselves.

The quickest way to start an argument between two BI professionals is to ask them what they think of self-service BI. On one hand, self-service BI makes BI development extremely business-focused, responsive, and agile. On the other hand, it can amplify the problems associated with the persistence of out-of-date data, poor data quality, lack of integration between multiple source systems, and different interpretations of how data should be modeled, especially because self-service BI proponents often claim that the time-consuming step of building a data warehouse is unnecessary. Whatever the advantages and disadvantages of self-service BI, it is a fast-growing market and one that Microsoft, as a software company, could not ignore, so in 2010 it released its own self-service BI tool called PowerPivot.

PowerPivot is essentially a desktop-based version of Analysis Services, but it takes the form of a free-to-download add-in for Excel 2010. (See *www.powerpivot.com* for more details.) It makes it very easy for Excel power users to import data from a number of sources, build their own models, and then query them using pivot tables. The PowerPivot database runs in-process inside Excel; all the imported data is stored there and all queries from Excel go against it. Excel users can work with vastly greater data volumes than they ever could before if they were storing the data directly inside an Excel worksheet, and they can still get lightning-fast query response times. When the Excel workbook is saved, the PowerPivot database and all the data in it is saved inside the workbook; the workbook can then be copied and shared like any regular Excel workbook, although any other user wishing to query the data held in PowerPivot must also have PowerPivot installed on his or her PC. To share models and reports between groups of users more efficiently, PowerPivot for SharePoint, a service that integrates with Microsoft SharePoint 2010 Enterprise edition, is required. With PowerPivot for SharePoint, it becomes possible to upload a workbook containing a PowerPivot database into SharePoint, enabling other users to view the reports in the workbook over the web by using Excel Service or to query the data held in PowerPivot on the server by using Excel or any other Analysis Services client tool on the desktop.

The release of PowerPivot does not mean that the Microsoft commitment to corporate BI tools has diminished. No single type of tool is appropriate in every situation, and it is to the credit of Microsoft that it not only sells both self-service and corporate BI tools but also has a coherent story for how both types of tools should coexist inside the same organization. Microsoft foresees a world in which IT departments and power users live in harmony, where IT-led projects use corporate BI tools and push data down from a central data warehouse out to the masses through reports and Analysis Services cubes, but where power users are also free to build their own self-service models in PowerPivot, share them with other people, and, if their models are popular, see them handed over to the IT department for further development, support, and eventual incorporation into the corporate model. PowerPivot for SharePoint provides a number of dashboards that enable the IT department to monitor usage of PowerPivot models that have been uploaded to SharePoint and, in Analysis Services 2012, it is possible to import a model created in PowerPivot into Analysis Services. It is likely that future releases will include features that help bridge the gap between the worlds of self-service and corporate BI.

Analysis Services 2012 Architecture: One Product, Two Models

This section explains a little about the architecture of Analysis Services, which in SQL Server 2012 is split into two models.

The first and most important point to make about Analysis Services 2012 is that it is really two products in one. Analysis Services in the SQL Server 2008 R2 release and before is still present, but it is now called the Multidimensional model. It has had a few improvements relating to performance, scalability, and manageability, but there is no new major functionality. Meanwhile, there is a new version of Analysis Services that closely resembles PowerPivot—this is called the Tabular model. The Tabular model is the subject of this book.

When installing Analysis Services, you must choose between installing an instance that runs in Tabular mode and one that runs in Multidimensional mode; more details on the installation process will be given in Chapter 2, "Getting Started with the Tabular Model." A Tabular instance can support only databases containing Tabular models, and a Multidimensional instance can support only databases containing Multidimensional models. Although these two parts of Analysis Services share much of the same code underneath, in most respects they can be treated as separate products. The concepts involved in designing the two types of model are very different, and you cannot convert a Tabular database into a Multidimensional database, or vice versa, without rebuilding everything from the beginning. That said, it is important to emphasize the fact that, from an end user's point of view, the two models do almost the same things and appear almost identical when used through a client tool such as Excel.

The following sections compare the functionality available in the Tabular and Multidimensional models and define some important terms that are used throughout the rest of this book.

The Tabular Model

A *database* is the highest-level object in the Tabular model and is very similar to the concept of a database in the SQL Server relational database. An instance of Analysis Services can contain many databases, and each database can be thought of as a self-contained collection of objects and data relating to a single business solution. If you are writing reports or analyzing data and find that you need to run queries on multiple databases, you have probably made a design mistake somewhere because everything you need should be contained in a single database.

Tabular models are designed by using *SQL Server Data Tools* (*SSDT*), and a project in SSDT maps onto a database in Analysis Services. After you have finished designing a project in SSDT, it must be *deployed* to an instance of Analysis Services, which means SSDT executes a number of commands to create a new database in Analysis Services or alters the structure of an existing database. *SQL Server Management Studio (SSMS)*, a tool that can be used to manage databases that have already been deployed, can also be used to write queries against databases.

Databases are made up of one or more *tables* of data. Again, a table in the Tabular model is very similar to a table in the relational database world. A table in Tabular is usually loaded from a single table in a relational database or from the results of a SQL SELECT statement. A table has a fixed number of *columns* that are defined at design time and can have a variable number of rows, depending on the amount of data that is loaded. Each column has a fixed type, so for example, a single column could contain only integers, only text, or only decimal values. Loading data into a table is referred to as *processing* that table.

It is also possible to define *relationships* between tables at design time. Unlike in SQL, it is not possible to define relationships at query time; all queries must use these preexisting relationships. However, relationships between tables can be marked as *active* or *inactive*, and at query time it is possible to choose which relationships between tables are actually used. It is also possible to simulate the effect of relationships that do not exist inside queries and calculations. All relationships are one-to-many relationships and must involve just one column from each of two tables. It is not possible to define relationships that are explicitly one to one or many to many, although it is certainly possible to achieve the same effect by writing queries and calculations in a particular way. It is also not possible to design relationships that are based on more than one column from a table or recursive relationships that join a table to itself.

The Tabular model uses a purely memory-based engine and stores only a copy of its data on disk so that no data is lost if the service is restarted. Whereas the Multidimensional model, like most relational database engines, stores its data in a row-based format, the Tabular model uses a column-oriented database called the *xVelocity in-memory analytics engine*, which in most cases offers significant query performance improvements. (For more details on the column-based type of database, see *http://en.wikipedia.org/wiki/Column-oriented_DBMS*.)

Note The xVelocity analytics in-memory engine was known as the Vertipaq engine before the release of Analysis Services 2012. Many references to the Vertipaq name remain in documentation, blog posts, and other material online, and it even persists inside the product itself in property names and Profiler events. The name xVelocity is also used to refer to the wider family of related technologies, including the new column store index feature in the SQL Server 2012 relational database engine. For a more detailed explanation of this terminology, see *http://blogs.msdn.com/b/analysisservices/archive/2012/03/09/xvelocity-and-analysis-services.aspx*.

Queries and calculations in Tabular are defined in *Data Analysis eXpressions* (*DAX*), the native language of the Tabular model, and in PowerPivot. Client tools such as Power View can generate DAX queries to retrieve data from a Tabular model, or you can write your own DAX queries and use them in reports. It is also possible to write queries by using the *MDX* language that Multidimensional models use. This means that the Tabular model is backward compatible with the large number of existing Analysis Services client tools that are available from Microsoft, such as Excel and SQL Server Reporting Services, and tools from third-party software vendors.

Derived columns, called *calculated columns*, can be added to a table in a Tabular model; they use DAX expressions to return values based on the data already loaded in other columns in the same or other tables in the same Analysis Services database. Calculated columns are populated at processing time and, after processing has taken place, behave in exactly the same way as regular columns.

Measures can also be defined on tables by using DAX expressions; a measure can be thought of as a DAX expression that returns some form of aggregated value based on data from one or more columns. A simple example of a measure is one that returns the sum of all values from a column of data that contains sales volumes. *Key performance indicators (KPIs)* are very similar to measures, but are collections of calculations that enable you to determine how well a measure is doing relative to a target value and whether it is getting closer to reaching that target over time.

Most front-end tools such as Excel use a PivotTable-like experience for querying Tabular models: Columns from different tables can be dragged onto the rows axis and columns axis of a pivot table so that the distinct values from these columns become the individual rows and columns of the pivot table, and measures display aggregated numeric values inside the table. The overall effect is something like a Group By query in SQL, but the definition of how the data aggregates up is predefined inside the measures and is not necessarily specified inside the query itself. To improve the user experience, it is also possible to define *hierarchies* on tables inside the Tabular model, which create multi-level, predefined drill paths. *Perspectives* can hide certain parts of a complex model, which can aid usability, and security *roles* can be used to deny access to specific rows of data from tables to specific users. Perspectives should not be confused with security, however; even if an object is hidden in a perspective it can still be queried, and perspectives themselves cannot be secured.

The Multidimensional Model

At the highest level, the Multidimensional model is very similar to the Tabular model: Data is organized in databases, and databases are designed in SSDT (formerly BI Development Studio, or BIDS) and managed by using SQL Server Management Studio.

The differences become apparent below the database level, where multidimensional rather than relational concepts are prevalent. In the Multidimensional model, data is modeled as a series of *cubes* and *dimensions*, not tables. Each cube is made up of one or more *measure groups*, and each measure group in a cube is usually mapped onto a single fact table in the data warehouse. A measure group contains one or more *measures*, which are very similar to measures in the Tabular model. A cube also has two or more dimensions: one special dimension, the *Measures dimension*, which contains all the measures from each of the measure groups, and various other dimensions such as Time, Product, Geography, Customer, and so on, which map onto the logical dimensions present in a dimensional model. Each of these non-Measures dimensions consists of one or more *attributes* (for example, on a Date dimension, there might be attributes such as *Date*, *Month*, and *Year*), and these attributes can themselves be used as single-level hierarchies or to construct multilevel *user hierarchies*. Hierarchies can then be used to build queries. Users start by analyzing data at a highly aggregated level, such as a Year level on a Time dimension, and can then navigate to lower levels such as Quarter, Month, and Date to look for trends and interesting anomalies.

As you would expect, because the Multidimensional model is the direct successor to previous versions of Analysis Services, it has a very rich and mature set of features representing the fruit of more than a decade of development, even if some of them are not used very often. Most of the features available in the Tabular model are present in the Multidimensional model, but the Multidimensional model also has many features that have not yet been implemented in Tabular. A detailed feature comparison between the two models appears later in this chapter.

In terms of data storage, the Multidimensional model can store its data in three ways:

- *Multidimensional OLAP* (*MOLAP*), where all data is stored inside Analysis Services' own disk-based storage format.

- *Relational OLAP* (*ROLAP*), where Analysis Services acts purely as a metadata layer and where no data is stored in Analysis Services itself; SQL queries are run against the relational source database when a cube is queried.

- *Hybrid OLAP* (*HOLAP*), which is the same as ROLAP but where some pre-aggregated values are stored in MOLAP.

MOLAP storage is used in the vast majority of implementations, although ROLAP is sometimes used when a requirement for so-called real-time BI HOLAP is almost never used.

One particular area in which the Multidimensional and Tabular models differ is in the query and calculation languages they support. The native language of the Multidimensional model is MDX, and that is the only language used for defining queries and calculations. The MDX language has been successful and is supported by a large number of third-party client tools for Analysis Services. It was also promoted as a semiopen standard by a cross-vendor industry body called the XMLA Council (now effectively defunct) and, as a result, has also been adopted by many other OLAP tools that are direct competitors to Analysis Services. However, the problem with MDX is the same problem that many people have with the Multidimensional model in general: although it is extremely powerful, many BI professionals have struggled to learn it because the concepts it uses, such as dimensions and hierarchies, are very different from the ones they are accustomed to using in SQL.

In addition, Microsoft has publicly committed (in this post on the Analysis Services team blog and other public announcements at *http://blogs.msdn.com/b/analysisservices/archive/2011/05/16/ analysis-services-vision-amp-roadmap-update.aspx*) to support DAX queries on the Multidimensional model at some point after Analysis Services 2012 has been released, possibly as part of a service pack. This will allow Power View to query Multidimensional models and Tabular models, although it is likely that some compromises will have to be made and some Multidimensional features might not work as expected when DAX queries are used.

Why Have Two Models?

Why has this split happened? Although Microsoft does not want to make any public comments on this topic, there are a number of likely reasons.

- Analysis Services Multidimensional is getting old. It was designed in an age of 32-bit servers with one or two processors and less than a gigabyte of RAM, when disk-based storage was the only option for databases. Times have changed, and modern hardware is radically different; now a new generation of memory-based, columnar databases has set the standard for query performance with analytic workloads, and Analysis Services must adopt this new technology to keep up. Retrofitting the new xVelocity in-memory engine into the existing Multidimensional model was not, however, a straightforward job, so it was necessary to introduce the new Tabular model to take full advantage of xVelocity.

- Despite the success of Analysis Services Multidimensional, there has always been a perception that it is difficult to learn. Some database professionals, accustomed to relational data modeling, struggle to learn multidimensional concepts, and those that do find the learning curve is steep. Therefore, if Microsoft wants to bring BI to an ever-wider audience, it must simplify the development process—hence the move from the complex world of the Multidimensional model to the relatively simple and familiar concepts of the Tabular model.

- Microsoft sees self-service BI as a huge potential source of growth, and PowerPivot is its entry into this market. It is also important to have consistency between the Microsoft self-service and corporate BI tools. Therefore, if Analysis Services must be overhauled, it makes sense to make it compatible with PowerPivot, with a similar design experience so self-service models can easily be upgraded to full-fledged corporate solutions.

- Some types of data are more appropriately, or more easily, modeled by using the Tabular approach, and some types of data are more appropriate for a Multidimensional approach. Having different models gives developers the choice to use whichever approach suits their circumstances.

What Is the BI Semantic Model?

One term that has been mentioned a lot in the discussions about Analysis Services 2012 is the *BI Semantic Model* or *BISM*. This term does not refer to either the Multidimensional or Tabular models specifically but, instead, describes the function of Analysis Services in the Microsoft BI stack: the fact that it acts as a semantic layer on top of a relational data warehouse, adding a rich layer of metadata that includes hierarchies, measures, and calculations. In that respect, it is very similar to the term Unified Dimensional Model that was used around the time of the SQL Server 2005 launch. In some cases, the term BI Semantic Model has referred to the Tabular model only, but this is not correct. Because this book is specifically concerned with the Tabular model, we will not be using this term very often; nevertheless, we believe it is important to understand exactly what it means and how it should be used.

The Future of Analysis Services

Having two models inside Analysis Services, plus two query and calculation languages, is clearly not an ideal state of affairs. First and foremost, it means you have to choose which model to use at the start of your project, when you might not know enough about your requirements to know which one is appropriate—and this is the question we will address in the next section. It also means that anyone who decides to specialize in Analysis Services has to learn two technologies. Presumably, this state of affairs will not continue in the long term.

Microsoft has been very clear in saying that the Multidimensional model is not deprecated and that the Tabular model is not its replacement. It is likely that new features for Multidimensional will be released in future versions of Analysis Services. The fact that the Tabular and Multidimensional models share some of the same code suggests that some new features could easily be developed for both models simultaneously. The post on the Analysis Services blog previously referenced suggests that in time the two models will converge and offer much the same functionality, so the decision about which model to use is based on whether the developer prefers to use a multidimensional or relational way of modeling data. Support for DAX queries in the Multidimensional model, when it arrives, will represent one step in this direction.

One other thing is clear about the future of Analysis Services: It will be moving to the cloud. Although no details are publicly available at the time of writing, Microsoft has confirmed it is working on a cloud-based version of Analysis Services and this, plus SQL Azure, SQL Azure Reporting Services, and Office 365, will form the core of the Microsoft cloud BI strategy.

Choosing the Right Model for Your Project

It might seem strange to be addressing the question of whether the Tabular model is appropriate for your project at this point in the book, before you have learned anything about the Tabular model, but you must answer this question at an equally early stage of your BI project. At a rough guess, either model will work equally well for about 60 percent to 70 percent of projects, but for the remaining 30 percent to 40 percent, the correct choice of model will be vital.

As has already been stated, after you have started developing with one model in Analysis Services, there is no way of switching over to use the other; you have to start all over again from the beginning, possibly wasting much precious development time, so it is very important to make the correct decision as soon as possible. Many factors must be taken into account when making this decision. In this section we discuss all of them in a reasonable amount of detail. You can then bear these factors in mind as you read the rest of this book, and when you have finished it, you will be in a position to know whether to use the Tabular model or the Multidimensional model.

Licensing

Analysis Services 2012 is available in the following editions: SQL Server Standard, SQL Server Business Intelligence, and SQL Server Enterprise. In SQL Server Standard edition, however, only the Multidimensional model is available, and has the same features that were available in SQL Server Standard edition of previous versions of Analysis Services. This means that several important features needed for scaling up the Multidimensional model, such as partitioning, are not available in SQL Server Standard edition. SQL Server Business Intelligence edition contains both the Multidimensional and Tabular models, as does SQL Server Enterprise edition. In terms of Analysis Services functionality, these two editions are the same; the only difference between them is that SQL Server Business Intelligence edition licensing is based on buying a server license plus Client Access Licenses (CALs), whereas SQL Server Enterprise edition is licensed on a per-CPU core basis. (You can no longer license

SQL Server Enterprise edition on a server-plus-CALs basis as was possible in the past.) In SQL Server Business Intelligence and SQL Server Enterprise editions, both Tabular and Multidimensional models contain all available features and can use as many cores as the operating system makes available.

The upshot of this is that it could be more expensive in some situations to use Tabular than Multidimensional because Multidimensional is available in SQL Server Standard edition and Tabular is not. If you have a limited budget, already have existing Multidimensional skills, or are willing to learn them, and your data volumes mean that you do not need to use Multidimensional features such as partitioning, it might make sense to use Multidimensional and SQL Server Standard edition to save money. If you are willing to pay slightly more for SQL Server Business Intelligence edition or SQL Server Enterprise edition, however, then licensing costs should not be a consideration in your choice of model.

Upgrading from Previous Versions of Analysis Services

As has already been mentioned, there is no easy way of turning a Multidimensional model into a Tabular model. Tools undoubtedly will appear on the market that claim to make this transition with a few mouse clicks, but such tools could only ever work for very simple Multidimensional models and would not save much development time. Therefore, if you already have a mature Multidimensional implementation and the skills in house to develop and maintain it, it probably makes no sense to abandon it and move over to Tabular unless you have specific problems with Multidimensional that Tabular is likely to solve.

Ease of Use

In contrast, if you are starting an Analysis Services 2012 project with no previous Multidimensional or OLAP experience, it is very likely that you will find Tabular much easier to learn than Multidimensional. Not only are the concepts much easier to understand, especially if you are used to working with relational databases, but the development process is also much more straightforward and there are far fewer features to learn. Building your first Tabular model is much quicker and easier than building your first Multidimensional model. It can also be argued that DAX is easier to learn than MDX, at least when it comes to writing basic calculations, but the truth is that both MDX and DAX can be equally confusing for anyone used to SQL.

Compatibility with PowerPivot

The Tabular model and PowerPivot are almost identical in the way their models are designed; the user interfaces for doing so are practically the same and both use DAX. PowerPivot models can also be imported into SQL Server data tools to generate a Tabular model, although the process does not work the other way, and a Tabular model cannot be converted to a PowerPivot model. Therefore, if you have a strong commitment to self-service BI by using PowerPivot, it makes sense to use Tabular for your corporate BI projects because development skills and code are transferable between the two.

Query Performance Characteristics

Although it would be dangerous to make sweeping generalizations about query performance, it's fair to say that Tabular will perform at least as well as Multidimensional in most cases and will outperform it in some specific scenarios. Distinct count measures, which are a particular weakness of the Multidimensional model, perform extremely well in Tabular, for instance. Anecdotal evidence also suggests that queries for detail-level reports (for example, queries that return a large number of rows and return data at a granularity close to that of the fact table) will perform much better on Tabular as long as they are written in DAX and not MDX. When more complex calculations or modeling techniques such as many-to-many relationships are involved, it is much more difficult to say whether Multidimensional or Tabular will perform better, unfortunately, and a proper proof of concept will be the only way to tell whether the performance of either model will meet requirements.

Processing Performance Characteristics

Comparing the processing performance of Multidimensional and Tabular is also difficult. It might be a lot slower to process a large table in Tabular than the equivalent measure group in Multidimensional because Tabular cannot process partitions in the same table in parallel, whereas Multidimensional (assuming you are using SQL Server Business Intelligence or SQL Server Enterprise edition and are partitioning your measure groups) can process partitions in the same measure group in parallel. Disregarding the different, noncomparable operations that each model performs when it performs processing, such as building aggregations and indexes in the Multidimensional model, the number of rows of raw data that can be processed per second for a single partition is likely to be similar.

However, Tabular has some significant advantages over Multidimensional when it comes to processing. First, there are no aggregations in the Tabular model, and this means that there is one less time-consuming task to be performed at processing time. Second, processing one table in a Tabular model has no direct impact on any of the other tables in the model, whereas in the Multidimensional model, processing a dimension has consequential effects. Doing a full process on a dimension in the Multidimensional model means that you must do a full process on any cubes that dimension is used in, and even doing a process update on a dimension requires a process index on a cube to rebuild aggregations. Both of these can cause major headaches on large Multidimensional deployments, especially when the window available for processing is small.

Hardware Considerations

The Multidimensional and Tabular models also have very different hardware specification requirements. Multidimensional's disk-based storage means that high-performance disks plus plenty of space on those disks is important; it will cache data in memory as well, so having sufficient RAM for this is very useful but not essential. For Tabular, the performance of disk storage is much less of a priority because it is an in-memory database. For that very reason, though, it is much more important to have enough RAM to hold the database and to accommodate any spikes in memory usage that occur when queries are running or when processing is taking place.

Multidimensional's disk requirements will probably be easier to accommodate than Tabular's memory requirements. Buying a large amount of disk storage for a server is relatively cheap and straightforward for an IT department; many organizations have storage area networks (SANs) that, though they might not perform as well as they should, make providing enough storage space (or increasing that provision) very simple. However, buying large amounts of RAM for a server can be more difficult—you might find that asking for half a terabyte of RAM on a server raises some eyebrows—and if you find you need more RAM than you originally thought, increasing the amount that is available can also be awkward. Based on experience, it is easy to start with what seems like a reasonable amount of RAM and then find that, as fact tables grow, new data is added to the model, and queries become more complex, you start to encounter out-of-memory errors. Furthermore, for some extremely large Analysis Services implementations with several terabytes of data, it might not be possible to buy a server with sufficient RAM to store the model, so Multidimensional might be the only feasible option.

Real-Time BI

Although not quite the industry buzzword that it was a few years ago, the requirement for real-time or near-real-time data in BI projects is becoming more common. Real-time BI usually refers to the need for end users to be able to query and analyze data as soon as it has been loaded into the data warehouse, with no lengthy waits for the data to be loaded into Analysis Services.

The Multidimensional model can handle this in one of two ways: Either use MOLAP storage and partition your data so that all the new data in your data warehouse goes to one relatively small partition that can be processed quickly, or use ROLAP storage and turn off all caching so that Multidimensional issues SQL queries every time it is queried. The first of these options is usually preferred, although it can be difficult to implement, especially if dimension tables and fact tables change. Updating the data in a dimension can be slow and can also require aggregations to be rebuilt. ROLAP storage in Multidimensional can often result in very poor query performance if data volumes are large, so the time taken to run a query in ROLAP mode might be greater than the time taken to reprocess the MOLAP partition in the first option.

The Tabular model offers what are essentially the same two options but with fewer shortcomings than their Multidimensional equivalents. If data is being stored in the xVelocity in-memory engine, updating data in one table has no impact on the data in any other table, so processing times are likely to be faster and implementation much easier. If data is to remain in the relational engine, then the major difference is that the equivalent of ROLAP mode, called DirectQuery, will, it's hoped, perform much better than ROLAP. This is because in DirectQuery mode, Analysis Services tries to push all its query processing back to the relational database by translating the whole query it receives into SQL queries. (Multidimensional ROLAP mode does not do this; it translates some internal operations into SQL queries but will still do some work, such as evaluating calculations, by itself.) DirectQuery, however, also comes with a number of significant limitations: It can accept only DAX queries and not MDX when in DirectQuery mode, which means, for instance, that Excel users cannot see real-time data because Excel can generate only MDX queries; only SQL Server is supported as a data source; data security must be implemented in SQL Server and cannot be implemented in Analysis Services; and, finally, neither calculated columns nor many common DAX functions are supported, so only models with very simple DAX calculations can be used. A full description of how to configure DirectQuery mode is given in Chapter 9, "Understanding xVelocity and DirectQuery."

Client Tools

In many cases, the success or failure of a BI project depends on the quality of the tools that end users use to analyze the data being provided. Therefore, the question of which client tools are supported by which model is an important one.

Both the Tabular model and the Multidimensional model support MDX queries, so, in theory, most Analysis Services client tools should support both models. However, in practice, although some client tools such as Excel and SQL Server Reporting Services do work equally well on both, some third-party client tools might need to be updated to their latest versions to work, and some older tools that are still in use but are no longer supported might not work properly or at all.

At the time of writing, only the Tabular model supports DAX queries, although support for DAX queries in the Multidimensional model is promised at some point in the future. This means that, at least initially, Power View—the new, highly regarded Microsoft data visualization tool—will work only on Tabular models. Even when DAX support in Multidimensional models is released, it is likely that not all Power View functionality will work on it and, similarly, that not all Multidimensional functionality will work as expected when queried by using DAX.

Feature Comparison

One more thing to consider when choosing a model is the functionality present in the Multidimensional model that either has no equivalent or is only partially implemented in the Tabular model. Not all of this functionality is important for all projects, however, and it must be said that in many scenarios it is possible to approximate some of this Multidimensional functionality in Tabular by using some clever DAX in calculated columns and measures. In any case, if you do not have any previous experience using Multidimensional, you will not miss functionality you have never had.

Here is a list of the most important functionality missing in Tabular:

- **Writeback**, the ability for an end user to write values back to a Multidimensional database. This can be very important for financial applications in which users enter budget figures, for example.

- **Translations**, in which the metadata of a Multidimensional model can appear in different languages for users with different locales on their desktops. There is no way of implementing this in Tabular.

- **Dimension security on measures**, in which access to a single measure can be granted or denied.

- **Cell security**, by which access to individual cells can be granted or denied. Again, there is no way of implementing this in Tabular, but it is only very rarely used in Multidimensional.

- **Ragged hierarchies**, a commonly used technique for avoiding the use of a parent/child hierarchy. In a Multidimensional model, a user hierarchy can be made to look something like a parent/child hierarchy by hiding members if certain conditions are met; for example, if a member has the same name as its parent. This is known as creating a ragged hierarchy. Nothing equivalent is available in the Tabular model.

- **Role-playing dimensions**, designed and processed once, then appear many times in the same model with different names and different relationships to measure groups; in the Multidimensional model, this is known as using role-playing dimensions. Something similar is possible in the Tabular model, by which multiple relationships can be created between two tables (see Chapter 3, "Loading Data Inside Tabular," for more details on this), and although this is extremely useful functionality, it does not do exactly the same thing as a role-playing dimension. In Tabular, if you want to see the same table in two places in the model simultaneously, you must load it twice, and this can increase processing times and make maintenance more difficult.

- **Scoped assignments** and **unary operators**, advanced calculation functionality, is present in MDX in the Multidimensional model but is not possible or at least not easy to re-create in DAX in the Tabular model. These types of calculation are often used in financial applications, so this and the lack of writeback and true parent/child hierarchy support mean that the Tabular model is not suited for this class of application.

The following functionality can be said to be only partially supported in Tabular:

- **Parent/child hierarchy support** in Multidimensional is a special type of hierarchy built from a dimension table with a self-join on it by which each row in the table represents one member in the hierarchy and has a link to another row that represents the member's parent in the hierarchy. Parent/child hierarchies have many limitations in Multidimensional and can cause query performance problems. Nevertheless, they are very useful for modeling hierarchies such as company organization structures because the developer does not need to know the maximum depth of the hierarchy at design time. The Tabular model implements similar functionality by using DAX functions such as *PATH* (see Chapter 9 for details), but, crucially, the developer must decide what the maximum depth of the hierarchy will be at design time.

- **Support for many-to-many relationships** in the Multidimensional model is one of its most important features, and it is frequently used. (For some applications, see the white paper at *http://www.sqlbi.com/articles/many2many/*.) It is possible to re-create this functionality in Tabular by using DAX, as described in Chapter 12, "Using Advanced Tabular Relationships," but even though query performance is likely to be just as good if not better than Multidimensional when using this approach, it adds a lot of complexity to the DAX expressions used in measures. If a model contains a large number of many-to-many relationships or chained many-to-many relationships, this added complexity can mean that maintenance of the DAX used in measures is extremely difficult.

- **Drillthrough**, by which the user can click a cell to see all the detail-level data that is aggregated to return that value. Drillthrough is supported in both models but, in the Multidimensional model, it is possible to specify which columns from dimensions and measure groups are returned from a drillthrough. In the Tabular model, no interface exists in SQL Server data tools for doing this and, by default, a drillthrough returns every column from the underlying table. It is possible, though, to edit the XMLA definition of your model manually to do this, as described in the blog post at *http://sqlblog.com/blogs/marco_russo/ archive/2011/08/18/drillthrough-for-bism-tabular-and-attribute-keys-in-ssas-denali.aspx*. A user interface to automate this editing process is also available in the BIDS Helper add-in (*http://bidshelper.codeplex.com/*).

Summary

In this chapter, you have seen what the Tabular and Multidimensional models in Analysis Services 2012 are, what their strengths and weaknesses are, and when they should be used. The key point to remember is that the two models are very different—practically separate products—and that you should not make the decision to use the Tabular model on a project without considering whether it is a good fit for your requirements. In the next chapter, you will take a first look at how you can actually build Tabular models.

CHAPTER 2

Getting Started with the Tabular Model

Now that you have been introduced to the Microsoft Business Intelligence (BI) stack, Analysis Services 2012, and the Tabular model, this chapter shows you how to get started developing Tabular models yourself. You will discover how to install Analysis Services, how to work with projects in SQL Server Data Tools, what the basic building blocks of a Tabular model are, and how to build, deploy, and query a very simple Tabular model.

Setting Up a Development Environment

Before you can start working with the Tabular model, you must set up a development environment for yourself.

Components of a Development Environment

A development environment will have three logical components: a development workstation, a workspace server, and a development server. You may install each of these components on separate machines or on a single machine. Each component has a distinct role to play, and it is important for you to understand those roles.

Development Workstation

You will design your Tabular models on your development workstation. As you've just seen, Tabular models are designed by using SQL Server Data Tools (previously called BI Development Studio, or BIDS); this is Visual Studio 2010 plus a number of SQL Server–related project templates. No separate license for Visual Studio is required, and you can fully install SQL Server Data Tools by using the SQL Server installer. If you have purchased a license for the full version of Visual Studio 2010 to do .NET or other development work, then the SQL Server project templates will appear as additional options in the new project dialog box.

When you have finished designing your Tabular model in SQL Server Data Tools (SSDT), you must build and deploy your project. Building a project is similar to compiling code: The build process translates all the information stored in the files in your project into a data definition language called *XML for Analysis (XMLA)*. Deployment then involves executing this XMLA on the Analysis Services Tabular instance running on your development server. The result will either create a new database or alter an existing database.

Development Server

A development server is a server with an installed instance of Analysis Services running in Tabular mode that you can use to host your models while they are being developed. You deploy your project to the development server from your development workstation. A development server should be in the same domain as your development workstation. After your project has been deployed to your development server, you and anyone else you give permission will be able to see your Tabular model and query it. This will be especially important for any other members of your team who are building reports or other parts of your BI solution.

Your development workstation and your development server can be two machines, or you can use the same machine for both roles. It is best, however, to use a separate, dedicated machine as your development server for a number of reasons.

- It's likely that a dedicated server will have a much better hardware specification than a workstation, and—as you will soon see—the amount of available memory in particular can be very important when developing with Tabular. Memory requirements also mean that using a 64-bit operating system is important and, although this can almost be taken for granted on a server nowadays, many workstation PCs are still installed with 32-bit versions of Windows.

- Using a separate server will also make it easy for you to grant access to your Tabular models to other developers, testers, or users while you work. This enables them to run their own queries and build reports without disturbing you; some queries can be resource intensive, and you will not want your workstation grinding to a halt unexpectedly when someone else runs a huge query. Additionally, of course, no one would be able to run queries on your workstation if you have turned it off and gone home for the day.

- A dedicated server will also enable you to reprocess your models while you perform other work. Similar to the last point, reprocessing a large model will be very resource intensive and could last for several hours. As a result, if you try to do this on your own workstation, it is likely to stop you from doing anything else.

- A dedicated development server will also (probably) be backed up regularly, so it will reduce the likelihood that hardware failure will result in a loss of work or data.

Not having a separate development server should be considered only if you don't have sufficient hardware available, if you're not working on an official project, or perhaps if you're only evaluating Tabular or installing it so you can learn more about it.

Workspace Database Server

One way that Tabular aims to make development easier is by providing a WYSIWYG experience for working with models, so that whenever you change a model, that change is reflected immediately in the data you see in SSDT without you having to save or deploy anything. This is possible because SSDT has its own private Tabular database, called a workspace database, to which it can deploy automatically every time you make a change. You can think of this database as a kind of work-in-progress database.

It is important not to confuse a workspace database with a development database. A development database can be shared with the entire development team and might be updated only once or twice a day. In contrast, a workspace database should never be queried or altered by anyone or anything other than the instance of SSDT that you are using. Although the development database might not contain the full set of data you are expecting to use in production, it is likely to contain a representative sample that might still be quite large. The workspace database, because it must be changed so frequently, might contain only a very small amount of data. Finally, as we have already seen, there are many good reasons for putting the development database on a separate server; in contrast, there are, as we shall soon see, several good reasons for putting the workspace database server on the same machine as your development database.

Licensing

All the installations in the developer environment should use SQL Server Developer Edition. This edition has all of the functionality of Enterprise Edition but at a fraction of the cost; the only drawback is that the license cannot be used on a production server.

Installation Process

You now learn how to install the various components of a development environment.

Development Workstation Installation

On your development workstation, you need to install the following: SQL Server Data Tools and SQL Server Management Studio; the SQL Server documentation; a source control system; and other useful development tools such as BIDS Helper.

Development tools installation   You can install the components required for your development workstation from the SQL Server installer as follows:

1. Ensure that you are logged on as a user with administrator rights.

2. Double-click SETUP.EXE to start the SQL Server Installation Center.

3. Click Installation in the menu on the left side of the SQL Server Installation Center window, as shown in Figure 2-1.

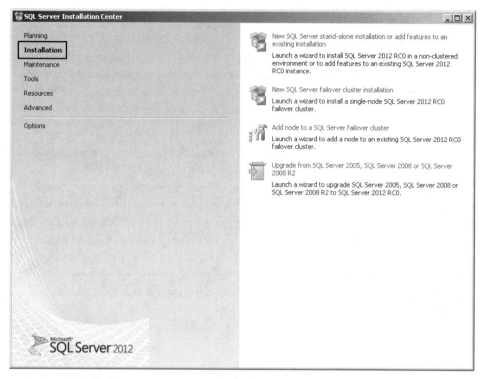

FIGURE 2-1 This is the SQL Server Installation Center page.

4. Click the first option on the right side, New SQL Server Stand-Alone Installation Or Add Features To An Existing Installation.

    The wizard checks SQL Server Support Rules to ensure that setup support files can be installed without any problems.

5. Assuming all these checks pass, click OK.

    The wizard checks for any SQL Server updates such as service packs that you might also want to install.

6. Assuming none are found, click Next, and the setup files will be installed.

    The wizard checks the Setup Support Rules, as shown in Figure 2-2, to see whether any conditions might prevent setup from succeeding. Failures must be addressed before installation can proceed. Warnings, as shown in Figure 2-2 by the items with warning triangle icons, may be ignored if you feel they are not relevant.

7. Click Next to continue.

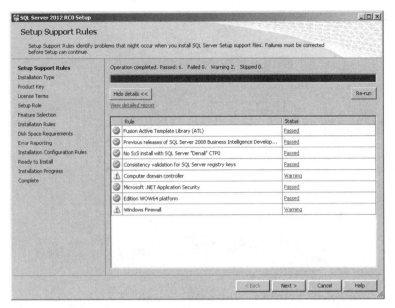

FIGURE 2-2 This is the Setup Support Rules page.

8. On the Installation Type page, make sure the Perform A New Installation Of SQL Server 2012 option button is selected and then click Next.

9. On the Product Key page, choose Enter A Product Key and enter the key for your SQL Server Developer Edition license.

10. On the License Terms page, select the I Accept The License Terms check box and then click Next.

11. On the Setup Role page, ensure that the SQL Server Feature Installation option button is selected and then click Next.

12. On the Feature Selection page, ensure that the check boxes for SSDT, Documentation Components, Management Tools – Basic, and Management Tools – Complete are selected, as shown in Figure 2-3.

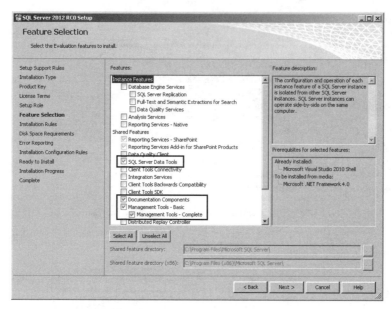

FIGURE 2-3 Select your features on the Feature Selection page.

 Important At this point, if you are installing a workspace database server on the same machine as your development workstation, start to follow the steps listed in the "Workspace Database Server Installation" section, too.

13. On the Installation Rules page, assuming all rules pass, click Next.

14. On the Disk Space Summary page, assuming you have sufficient disk space to continue, click Next.

15. On the Error Reporting page, click Next.

16. On the Installation Configuration Rules page, assuming all rules pass, click Next

17. On the Ready To Install page, click Install, and the installation starts.

18. After the installation has completed successfully, close the wizard.

SQL Server documentation installation   At this point, you have SSDT and SQL Server Management Studio installed but no local copy of the help and documentation. This ensures that whenever you need to use the documentation, you always see the latest version, but it also means that you cannot use it if you are not connected to the Internet. The first time you open SQL Server Documentation, you will see a dialog box like the one shown in Figure 2-4.

FIGURE 2-4 Choose the default settings for Help.

If you click Yes, your web browser will open, and you'll be directed to the SQL Server documentation on the MSDN website. However, if you expect to develop offline at any point, it can be helpful to switch to using offline help. You can do this by clicking Manage Help Settings, which you can find on the Start menu in Windows. Navigate to All Programs | Microsoft SQL Server 2012 | Documentation and Community | Manage Help Settings. This starts the Help Library application. To switch to using local Help, follow these steps:

1. Click Choose Online Or Local Help, as shown in Figure 2-5.

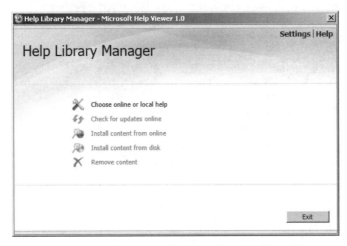

FIGURE 2-5 Choose Online Or Local Help on the Help Library Manager page.

2. Select the I Want To Use Local Help option button, as shown in Figure 2-6.

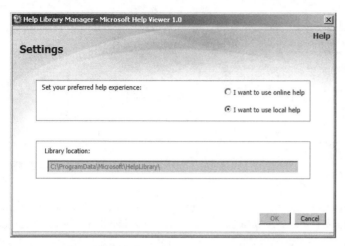

FIGURE 2-6 Choose local help.

3. Click OK to go back to the main menu and click Install Content From Online.

   This opens the Install Content From Online window.

4. Click Add for all three options listed underneath SQL Server 2012, as shown in Figure 2-7.

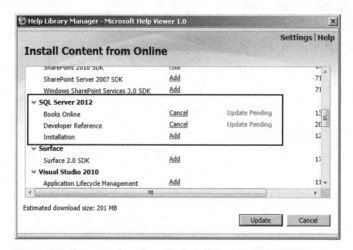

FIGURE 2-7 Choose options from the Install Content From Online page.

5. Click Update, and the help file packages will be downloaded to your workstation.

6. Click Finish and Exit.

Source control Ensure that you have some form of source control that integrates well with Visual Studio, such as Team Foundation Server, set up at this point so you can check any projects you create by using SSDT. Developing a BI solution for Analysis Services is no different from any other form of development, and it is vitally important that your source code, which is essentially what an SSDT project contains, is stored safely and securely and that you can roll back to previous versions after any changes have been made.

Other tools   You must also install Office 2010 on your development workstation so that you can browse your Tabular model after you have deployed it. You cannot browse a Tabular model inside SSDT after you have deployed it; as you'll see later in this chapter, SSDT will attempt to launch Microsoft Excel when you are ready to do this. The browser inside SQL Server Management Studio is very limited (it is based on the MDX query generator control in SQL Server Reporting Services) and, in fact, much worse than the cube browser that was available in earlier versions of SQL Server Management Studio.

In addition, you should install the following free tools on your development workstation at this point, which provide useful extra functionality and are referenced in upcoming chapters.

- **BIDS Helper**   An award-winning, free Visual Studio add-in developed by members of the Microsoft BI community to extend SSDT. Although most of its functionality is relevant only to the Multidimensional model, new functionality is being added for Tabular as well, such as the ability to define actions. It can be downloaded from *http://bidshelper.codeplex.com/*.

- **OLAP PivotTable Extensions**   An Excel add-in that adds extra functionality to PivotTables connected to Analysis Services data sources. Among other things, it enables you to see the MDX generated by the PivotTable. It can be downloaded from *http://olappivottableextend .codeplex.com/*.

- **DAX Editor for SQL Server**   A Visual Studio add-in from the Analysis Services development team that provides a full DAX editor inside SSDT. Note that this add-in, although developed by Microsoft employees, is not officially supported by Microsoft. It can be downloaded from *http://daxeditor.codeplex.com/*.

- **BISM Normalizer**   A tool for comparing and merging two Tabular models. This tool is particularly useful when trying to merge models created in PowerPivot with an existing Tabular model. You can download it from *http://visualstudiogallery.msdn.microsoft .com/5be8704f-3412-4048-bfb9-01a78f475c64*.

Development Server Installation

To install an instance of Analysis Services in Tabular mode on your development server, follow all the steps listed in the previous section on Development Workstation Installation up to step 11. Then do the following:

1. On the Feature Selection page, select the check box for Analysis Services, as shown in Figure 2-8.

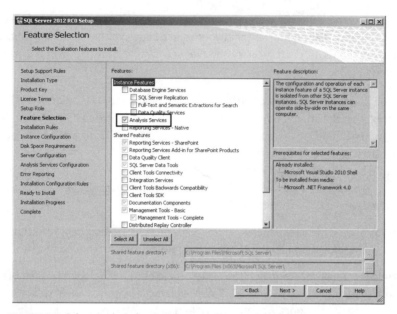

FIGURE 2-8 Select Analysis Services from the Feature Selection page.

2. On the Instance Configuration page, choose to install either a default instance or a named instance, as shown in Figure 2-9.

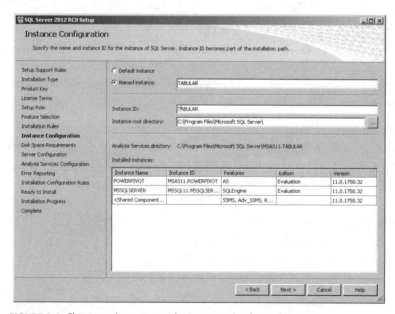

FIGURE 2-9 Choose an instance on the Instance Configuration page.

A named instance with a meaningful name (for example, Tabular) is preferable because if you subsequently decide to install another instance of Analysis Services but run it in

Multidimensional mode on the same server, it will be much easier to determine the instance to which you are connecting.

3. On the Disk Space Requirements page, assuming you have sufficient space to continue, click Next.

4. On the Server Configuration page, on the Service Accounts tab, enter the username and password under which the Analysis Services Windows service will run. This should be a domain account created especially for this purpose.

5. On the Collation tab, choose which collation you want to use. It is a good idea not to use a case-sensitive collation because this means you will not need to remember to use the correct case when writing queries and calculations. Click Next.

6. On the Analysis Services Configuration page, on the Server Configuration tab, select the Tabular Mode option button, as shown in Figure 2-10. Click either the Add Current User button or the Add button to add a user as an Analysis Services administrator. At least one user must be nominated here.

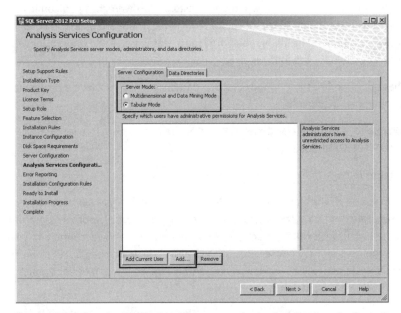

FIGURE 2-10 Select the Tabular Mode button on the Analysis Services Configuration page.

7. On the Data Directories tab, you can specify the directories Analysis Services will use for its Data, Log, Temp, and Backup directories.

   We recommend that you create new directories specifically for this and put them on a drive with a large amount of space available and not on the C drive. Doing this makes it easier to find these directories if you want to check their contents and size.

8. On the Error Reporting page, click Next.

9. On the Installation Configuration Rules page, assuming that all the rules have passed success-fully, click Next.

10. On the Ready To Install page, click Install, and the installation starts. After it finishes, close the wizard.

 Note It's very likely you will also need to have access to an instance of the SQL Server relational database engine for your development work; you might want to consider installing one on your development server.

Workspace Database Server Installation

Installing a workspace database server involves following similar steps as installing a development database server, but you must answer two important questions before you perform the install.

The first is to consider the physical machine on which to install your workspace database server. Installing it on its own dedicated server would be a waste of hardware, but you can install it on either your development workstation or on the development server. There are pros and cons to each option but, in general, we recommend installing your workspace database server on your development workstation when possible for the following reasons:

- SSDT has the option to back up a workspace database when you save a project (although this does not happen by default).

- It is possible to import data and metadata when creating a new Tabular project from an existing PowerPivot workbook.

- It is easier to import data from Excel, Microsoft Access, or text files.

The second question is which account you will use to run the Analysis Services service. In the previous section, a separate domain account was recommended for the development database installation; for the workspace database, it can be much more convenient to use the account with which you normally log on for the Analysis Services service. This will allow the workspace database instance access to all the same file system locations you can access and will make it much easier to back up workspace databases and import data from PowerPivot.

All these considerations are explored in much more detail in this post on Cathy Dumas's blog at *http://blogs.msdn.com/b/cathyk/archive/2011/10/03/configuring-a-workspace-database-server.aspx.*

Working with SQL Server Data Tools

After you set up the development environment, you can start using SQL Server Data Tools to perform several tasks.

Creating a New Project

With everything set up, you are now ready to start building a new Tabular model. To do this, you must create a new project in SSDT. That is what you learn in this section.

First, start SSDT. If this is the first time you have done this, you see the dialog box displayed in Figure 2-11, asking you to choose default environment settings; you should choose Business Intelligence Settings.

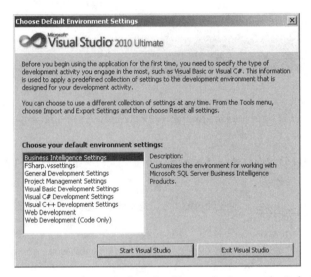

FIGURE 2-11 Choose Business Intelligence Settings on the Default Environment Settings page.

After the Start Page has appeared, choose New\Project from the File menu. The dialog box shown in Figure 2-12 will then be displayed. Click Analysis Services in the Installed Templates list on the left side to show the options for creating a new Analysis Services project.

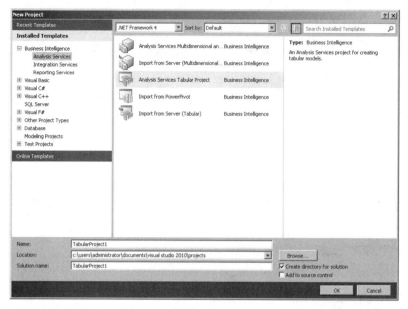

FIGURE 2-12 This is the New Project dialog box.

The first two options on the list displayed here are for creating projects for the Multidimensional model, so they can be ignored. That leaves the following three options:

- **Analysis Services Tabular Project** This creates a new, empty project for designing a Tabular model.

- **Import From PowerPivot** This enables you to import a model created by using PowerPivot into a new SSDT project.

- **Import From Server (Tabular)** This enables you to point to a model that has already been deployed to Analysis Services and import its metadata into a new project.

Click the Analysis Services Tabular Project option to create a new project; the other two options will be explored in more detail later in this chapter.

Editing Projects Online

Readers with experience in Analysis Services Multidimensional know that there is another option for working with Multidimensional models in SSDT: online mode. This enables you to connect to a Multidimensional database that has already been deployed and edit it live on the server, so every time you save, the changes are immediately made on the server. This option is not officially supported for Tabular models and does not work out of the box.

Configuring a New Project

Now that your new project has been created, the next thing to do is configure various properties inside it.

Default Properties Wizard

The first time you create a new Tabular project in SSDT, a wizard helps you set one important property for your projects: the server you wish to use as both the default workspace database server and the default development server, as shown in Figure 2-13.

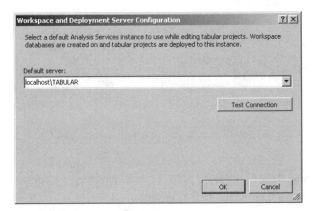

FIGURE 2-13 This is how to set the default workspace server.

It is possible, however, that you wish to use different servers for the workspace database and the development database; you can learn how to change these properties manually in the following sections.

Project Properties

Project properties can be set by right-clicking the name of the project in the Solution Explorer window and then selecting Properties on the right-click menu. The Project Properties dialog box shown in Figure 2-14 then appears.

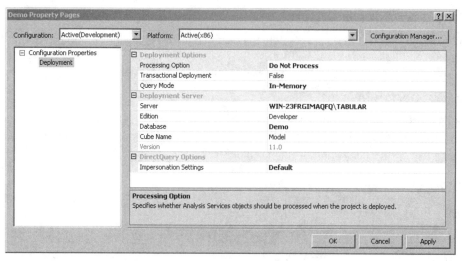

FIGURE 2-14 This is the Project Properties dialog box.

The properties that should be set now are as follows. (Some of the others will be dealt with later in this book.)

- **Deployment Options\Processing Option** This property controls which type of processing takes place after a project has been deployed to the development server; it controls if and how Analysis Services automatically loads data into your model when it has been changed. The default setting, Default, reprocesses any tables that are either not processed or where the alterations you are deploying would leave them in an unprocessed state. You can also choose Full, which means that the entire model is completely reprocessed. However, we recommend that you choose Do Not Process, so that no automatic processing takes place. This is because processing a large model can take a long time, and it is often the case that you will want to deploy changes without reprocessing or reprocessing only certain tables.

- **Deployment Server\Server** This property contains the name of the development server to which you wish to deploy. By default it is set to the value entered in the Default Properties Wizard. Even if you are using a local development server, you should still delete this and enter the full name of the development server here (in the format of servername\instancename) in case the project is ever used on a different workstation.

- **Deployment Server\Edition** This property enables you to set the edition of SQL Server that you are using on your production server and prevents you from developing by using any features that are not available in that edition. Because, at the moment, there are no feature differences between the Enterprise and Business Intelligence editions of SQL Server, the only two editions in which the Tabular model is available, setting this property is not very important, but it might be a good idea to set this property in case there are differences in functionality in the future.

- **Deployment Server\Database**   This is the name of the database to which the project will be deployed. By default, it is set to the name of the project, but because the database name will be visible to end users, you should check with them about what database name they would like to see.

- **Deployment Server\Cube Name**   This is the name of the cube that is displayed to all client tools that query your model in MDX, such as Excel. The default name is Model, but it is strongly recommended that you change it, again consulting your end users to see what name they would like to use.

Model Properties

There are also properties that should be set on the model itself. They can be found by right-clicking the Model.bim file in the Solution Explorer window and then choosing Properties to display the properties pane inside SSDT, as shown in Figure 2-15.

FIGURE 2-15 This is the Model Properties dialog box.

The properties that should be set here are as follows:

- **Data Backup**   This controls what happens to the workspace database when you close your project. The default setting is Do Not Back Up To Disk, which means that nothing is backed up when the project is closed. However, if you are working with a local workspace database server, if the instance on the workspace database server is running as an account with sufficient permissions to write to your project directory (such as your own domain account, as recommended earlier in this chapter), and if the data volumes in the workspace database are small, you might consider changing this property to Back Up To Disk. When you close your project, the workspace database is backed up to the same directory as your SSDT project. The reasons this could be useful are listed in the blog post at *http://blogs.msdn.com/b/cathyk/ archive/2011/09/20/working-with-backups-in-the-tabular-designer.aspx*, but they are not particularly compelling, and taking a backup increases the amount of time it takes to save a project.

- **File Name**   This sets the file name of the .bim file in your project; the "Contents of a Tabular Project" section later in this chapter explains exactly what this file is. Changing the name of the .bim file could be useful if you are working with multiple projects inside a single SSDT solution.

- **Workspace Retention**   When you close your project in SSDT, this property controls what happens to the workspace database (its name is given in the read-only Workspace Database property) on the workspace database server. The default setting is Unload From Memory. The database itself is detached, so it is still present on disk but not consuming any memory; it is, however, reattached quickly when the project is reopened. The Keep In Memory setting indicates that the database is not detached and nothing happens to it when the project closes. The Delete Workspace setting indicates that the database is completely deleted and must be re-created when the project is reopened. For projects with small datasets or for temporary projects created for testing and experimental purposes, we recommend using the Delete Workspace setting because otherwise you'll accumulate a large number of unused work-space databases that will clutter your server and use disk space. If you are working with only one project or are using very large data volumes, the Keep In Memory setting can be useful because it decreases the time taken to open your project.

- **Workspace Server**   This is the name of the Analysis Services 2012 Tabular instance you want to use as your workspace database server.

Options Dialog Box

Many of the default settings for the properties mentioned in the previous two sections can also be changed inside SSDT, so you do not need to reconfigure them for every new project you create. To do this, from the Tools menu, click Options to open the Options dialog box, as shown in Figure 2-16.

On the left side, choose Analysis Services\Data Modeling to set the default values for the Workspace Server, Workspace Retention, and Data Backup model properties. The Analysis Services\ Deployment page enables you to set the name of the deployment server you wish to use by default, and the Business Intelligence Designers\Analysis Services Designers\General page enables you to set the default value for the Deployment Server Edition property.

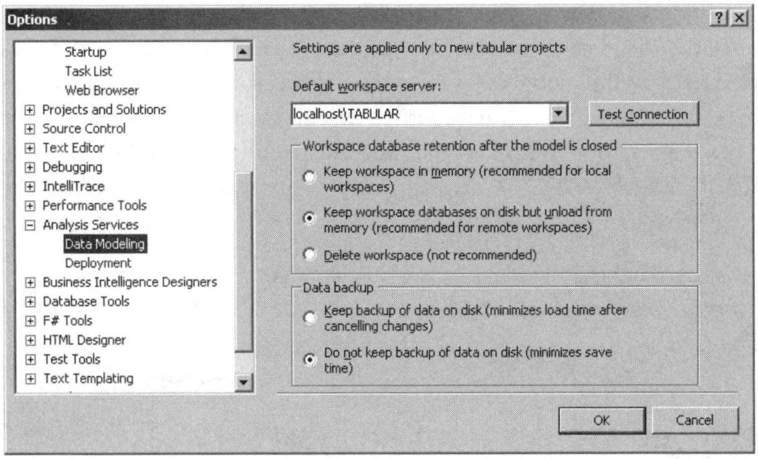

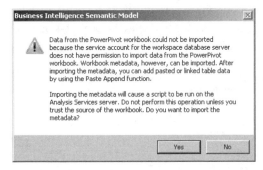

FIGURE 2-16 This is the Options dialog box.

Importing from PowerPivot

Instead of creating an empty project in SSDT, it is possible to import the metadata and, in some cases, the data of a model created in PowerPivot into a new project. To do this, create a new project and choose Import From PowerPivot in the New Project dialog box shown in Figure 2-12. Then choose the Excel workbook that contains the PowerPivot model that you want to import, and a new project containing a Tabular model identical to the PowerPivot model will be created.

If the service account you are using to run your workspace database server does not have read permissions on the file that you have just selected, the dialog box shown in Figure 2-17 will appear, indicating that only the metadata and not the data from the model will be imported.

FIGURE 2-17 This is the PowerPivot import warning dialog box.

Clicking Yes results in a project with no data being created. If all the data for the PowerPivot project came from external data sources, then reloading the data will be relatively straightforward. However, if some or all the data for the model came from the workbook itself, more work will be needed to reload the data, and it may be easier to grant the workspace database service account the appropriate permissions on the file. More details on this problem can be found in the blog post at *http://blogs.msdn.com/b/cathyk/archive/2011/08/22/recovering-from-cryptic-errors-thrown-when-importing-from-powerpivot.aspx*.

Information on what happens behind the scenes when a PowerPivot model is imported can be found in the blog post at *http://blogs.msdn.com/b/cathyk/archive/2011/08/15/what-does-import-from-powerpivot-actually-do.aspx*.

Importing a Deployed Project from Analysis Services

It is also possible to create a new project from an existing Analysis Services Tabular database that has already been deployed on a server. This can be useful if you must create a copy of a project quickly or if the project has been lost, altered, or corrupted, and you weren't using source control. To do this, choose Import From Server (Tabular) in the New Project dialog box, as shown in Figure 2-12. You are then asked to connect to the server and the database from which you wish to import, and a new project will be created.

Contents of a Tabular Project

It's important to be familiar with all the different files associated with a Tabular project in SSDT. You can see all the files associated with a new, blank project in the Solution Explorer pane, as shown in Figure 2-18.

At first glance, it seems as though the project contains only one file, the model.bim file. However, if you click the Show All Files button at the top of the Solution Explorer pane, you see there are several other files and folders there (some of which are only created the first time the project is built), as shown in Figure 2-19. It's useful to know what these are.

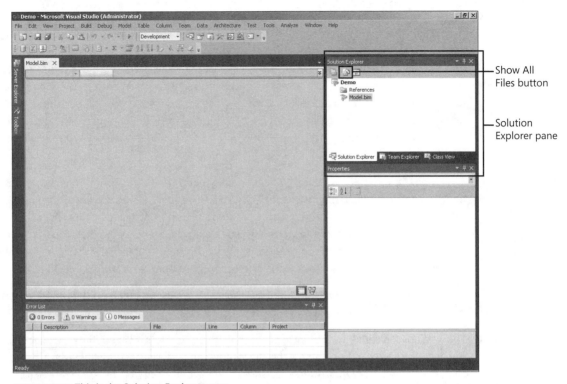

Show All Files button

Solution Explorer pane

FIGURE 2-18 This is the Solution Explorer pane.

FIGURE 2-19 These are the contents of a Tabular Project.

- Model.bim contains the metadata for the project plus any data that has been copied/pasted into the project. (More details on this will be given in Chapter 3, "Loading Data Inside Tabular.") This metadata takes the form of an XMLA alter command. (XMLA is the XML-based data definition language for Analysis Services.) Note that this metadata was used to create the workspace database; this is not necessarily the same as the metadata used when the project is deployed to the development server. If for any reason your Model.bim file becomes corrupted and will not open, it can be re-created by following the steps in the blog post at *http://blogs .msdn.com/b/cathyk/archive/2011/10/07/recovering-your-model-when-you-can-t-save-the-bim-file.aspx.*

- The .asdatabase, .deploymentoptions, and .deploymenttargets files contain the properties that might be different when the project is deployed to locations such as the development data-base server as opposed to the workspace database server. They include properties such as the server and the database name to which it will be deployed, and they are the properties that can be set in the Project Properties dialog box shown in Figure 2-14. More detail on what these files contain can be found at *http://msdn.microsoft.com/en-us/library/ms174530(v=SQL.110).aspx.*

- The .abf file contains the backup of the workspace database that is created if the Data Backup property on the Model.bim file is set to Back Up To Disk.

- The .settings file contains a few properties that are written to disk every time a project is opened; more information on how this file is used can be found at *http://blogs.msdn.com/b/ cathyk/archive/2011/09/23/where-does-data-come-from-when-you-open-a-bim-file.aspx/ BismData.* If you wish to make a copy of an entire SSDT project by copying and pasting its folder to a new location on disk, you must delete this file manually, as detailed in the blog post at *http://sqlblog.com/blogs/alberto_ferrari/archive/2011/09/27/creating-a-copy-of-a-bism-tabular-project.asp.*

- The .layout file contains information on the size, position, and state of the various windows and panes inside SSDT when a project is saved. More information about it can be found at *http://blogs.msdn.com/b/cathyk/archive/2011/12/03/new-for-rc0-the-layout-file.aspx.*

Building a Simple Tabular Model

To help you get your bearings in the SSDT user interface, and to help illustrate the concepts intro-duced in the preceding sections, this section walks through the process of creating and deploying a simple model. This is only a very basic introduction to the process and, of course, all these steps are dealt with in much more detail in the rest of this book. Before you start, make sure that you—and the accounts you have used to run instances of Analysis Services on your workspace and development servers—have access to an instance of SQL Server and the Adventure Works DW 2012 sample data-base on your development server. (You can download Adventure Works DW for SQL Server 2012 from *http://msftdbprodsamples.codeplex.com.*)

Loading Data into Tables

First, create a new Tabular project in SSDT; your screen should resemble the one shown in Figure 2-18 with the Model.bim file open. You now have an empty project, and the first thing you should do is load data into some tables. From the Model menu (which will be visible only if the Model.bim file is open) at the top of the screen, select Import From Data Source; the Table Import Wizard will start, as shown in Figure 2-20.

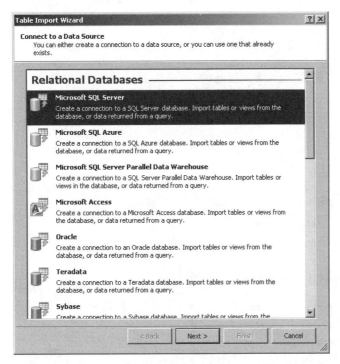

FIGURE 2-20 This is the first step of the Table Import Wizard.

Choose Microsoft SQL Server under Relational Databases and click Next. On the next page, connect to the Adventure Works DW 2012 database in SQL Server, as shown in Figure 2-21.

Click Next again. In the Impersonation Information step, configure how Analysis Services will connect to SQL Server to load data. At this point, the easiest thing to do is to choose Specific Windows User Name And Password and enter the username and password you're logged on as at the moment, as shown in Figure 2-22. A full explanation of this process is given in Chapter 3.

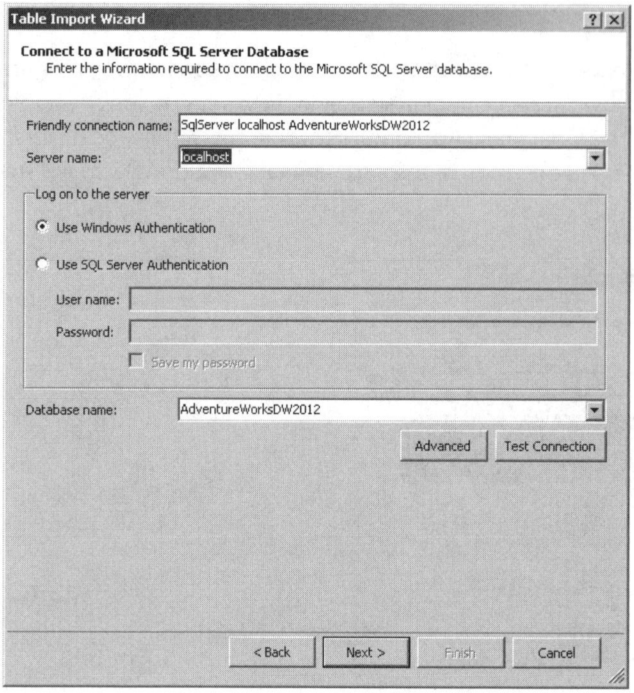

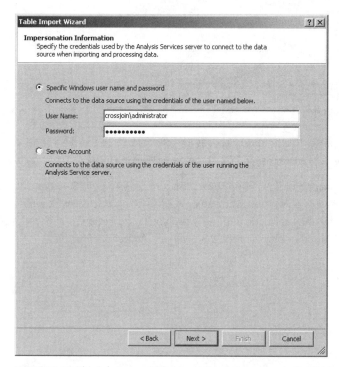

FIGURE 2-21 This is how to connect to SQL Server in the Table Import Wizard.

FIGURE 2-22 This is how to set impersonation information in the Table Import Wizard.

Click Next once more, ensure that Select From A List Of Tables And Views is selected, click Next again, and then, in Select Tables And Views, select the following tables, as shown in Figure 2-23: DimProduct, DimProductCategory, DimProductSubcategory, and FactInternetSales.

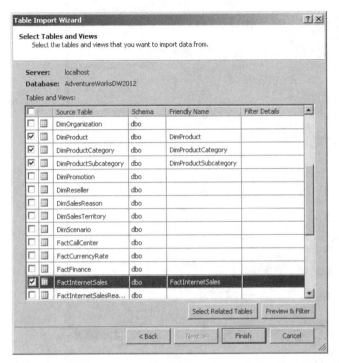

FIGURE 2-23 This is how to select tables and views in the Table Import Wizard.

Click Finish, and you will see data from these tables being loaded into your workspace database. This should take only a few seconds; if you encounter any errors here, the cause is likely that the Analysis Services instance you're using for your workspace database cannot connect to the SQL Server database. To fix this, repeat all the previous steps and, when you get to the Impersonation Information step, try a different username that has the necessary permissions or use the service account. If you are using a workspace server on a machine other than your development machine, check that firewalls are not blocking the connection from Analysis Services to SQL Server and that SQL Server is enabled to accept remote connections. Click Close to finish the wizard.

Working in the Grid View at this point, your screen should look something like the image shown in Figure 2-24, and you'll be able to see data in a table in the Grid View.

Column
drop-down

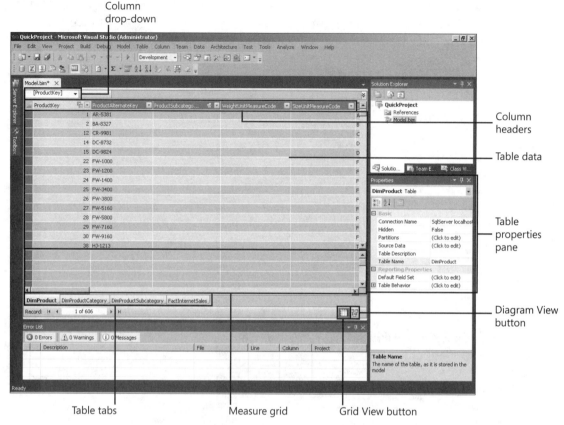

Column
headers

Table data

Table
properties
pane

Diagram View
button

Table tabs   Measure grid   Grid View button

FIGURE 2-24 This is the Grid View.

You can view data in different tables by clicking the tab with the name of that table on it. Selecting a table makes its properties appear in the Properties pane; some of the properties, plus the ability to delete a table and move it around in the list of tabs, can also be set by right-clicking the tab for the table.

Within a table, you can find an individual column by using the horizontal scrollbar immediately above the table tabs or by using the column drop-down list above the table. To explore the data within a table, you can click the down arrow next to a column header, as shown in Figure 2-25, and then sort the data in the table by the values in a column or filter it by selecting or clearing individual values or by using one of the built-in filtering rules. Note that this filters only the data displayed on the screen, not the data that is actually in the table itself.

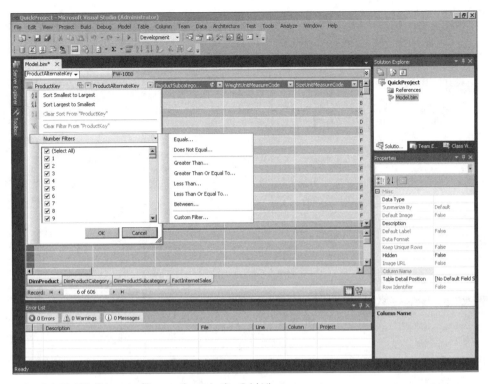

FIGURE 2-25 This is how to filter a column in the Grid View.

Right-clicking a column enables you to delete, rename, freeze (which means that wherever you scroll, the column will always be visible, similar to freezing columns in Excel), and copy the data from it.

Creating Measures

One of the most important tasks for which you'll use the Grid View is to create a measure. Measures, you remember, are predefined ways of aggregating the data in tables. The simplest ways to create a measure are either to click the Sum (Σ) button in the toolbar, as shown in Figure 2-26, and create a new measure that sums up the values in a column, or to click the drop-down arrow next to that button and choose another type of aggregation. In the model you have just created, find the *SalesAmount* column in the FactInternetSales table and create a sum measure from it.

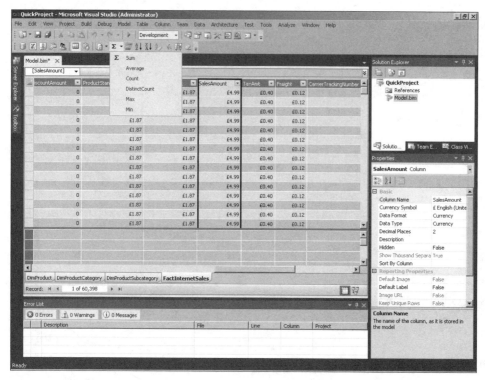

FIGURE 2-26 This is how to create a measure in the Grid View.

After you have created a measure, it appears in the measure grid underneath the highlighted column, as shown in Figure 2-27. The measure name and a sample output (which is the aggregated total of the rows that are currently being displayed) are shown in the measure grid, and clicking that cell in the measure grid displays the DAX definition of the measure in the formula bar, where it can be edited.

Although by default a measure appears in the measure grid underneath the column that was highlighted when it was created, its position in the measure grid is irrelevant and you might want to move it somewhere else. It's very easy to lose track of all the measures that have been created in a model, and it's a good idea to establish a standard location in which to keep your measures; for example, in the first column in the measure grid. To move a measure in the measure grid, right-click it, choose Cut, select the cell to which you want to move it, and then choose Paste.

Measure definition in the formula bar

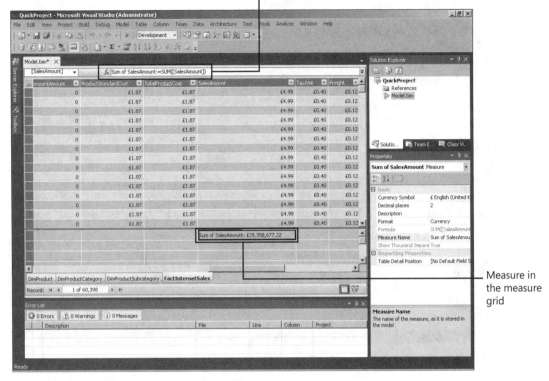

Measure in the measure grid

FIGURE 2-27 This is a measure in the measure grid.

Notice also that when a measure is selected in the measure grid, its properties are displayed in the Properties pane.

Measure definitions in the formula bar take the following form.

```
<Measure name> := <DAX definition>
```

Resizing the formula bar so that it can display more than a single line is usually a good idea when dealing with more complex measure definitions; you can insert a line break in your formulas by pressing Shift+Enter. To help you write your own DAX expressions in the formula bar, there is extensive IntelliSense for tables, columns, and functions, as shown in Figure 2-28. As you type, SSDT displays a list of all the objects and functions available in the current context in a drop-down list underneath the formula bar; selecting one item in this list and then pressing the Tab key on the keyboard results in that object or function being inserted into your expression in the formula bar.

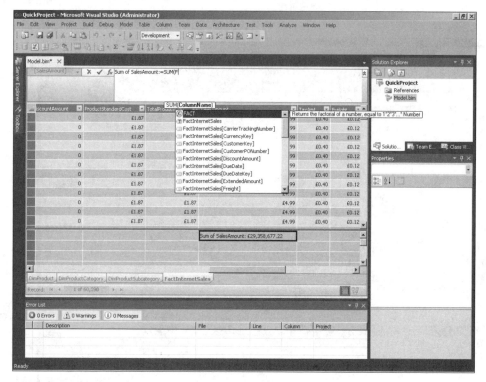

FIGURE 2-28 This shows how to use IntelliSense when defining a measure.

Creating Calculated Columns

Calculated columns can be created in two ways in the Grid View. The first method is to scroll to the far right of the table where a final column called Add Column is displayed, as shown in Figure 2-29. Selecting this column enables you to enter a new DAX expression for that column in the formula bar in the following format.

```
= <Dax definition>
```

Editing the DAX expression for a calculated column in the formula bar is done in the same way as editing the expression for a measure, but the name of a calculated column cannot be edited from within its own expression. IntelliSense works in exactly the same way as it does for measures.

After you have entered the DAX expression to be used for the calculated column and pressed Enter, a new calculated column is created with a name such as CalculatedColumn1. The calculated column can then be renamed to something more meaningful, either by double-clicking the column header and entering the new name or by editing the Column Name property in the Properties pane.

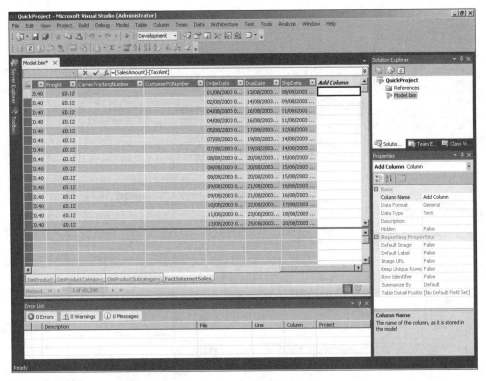

FIGURE 2-29 This figure shows how to create a calculated column.

The second method is to right-click an existing column and select Insert Column on the right-click menu. This creates a new calculated column next to the column you have just selected.

In your model, create a new calculated column called Sales After Tax with the following definition.

```
= [SalesAmount] - [TaxAmt]
```

Then create a new measure from it by using the Sum button in the same way you did in the previous section.

Working in the Diagram View

An alternative way of looking at a Tabular model can be found by clicking the Diagram View button at the bottom right corner of the measure grid (marked in Figure 2-30) to see the tables in your model laid out in a diagram with the relationships between them displayed. Clicking Diagram View for the model you have created in this section should show you something like what is displayed in Figure 2-30. It is also possible to switch to Diagram View by selecting Model View\Diagram View from the Model menu.

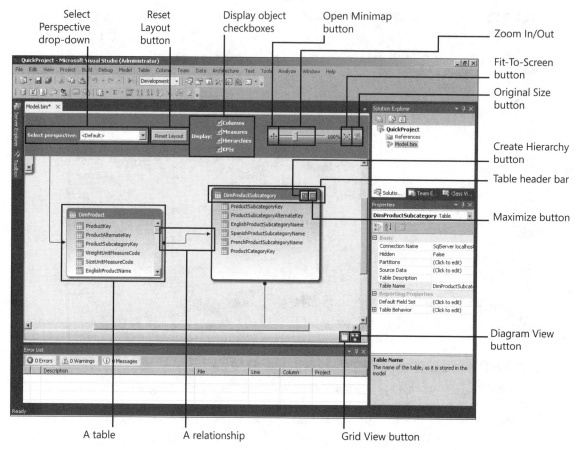

FIGURE 2-30 This is the Diagram View.

In the Diagram View, you can opt to display all the tables in your model or only the tables that are present in a particular perspective; you can also choose whether to display all object types or just the columns, measures, hierarchies, or KPIs associated with a table by selecting and clearing the boxes at the top center of the pane. You can automatically arrange the tables in the model by clicking the Reset Layout button, by arranging all the tables so they fit on one screen by clicking the Fit-To-Screen button, by zooming out to the default size by clicking the Original Size button, by zooming in and out by using the slider at the top-right edge of the pane, and by exploring a model that takes up more than one page by clicking the Crosshairs button next to the slider to open the minimap. Tables can be rearranged manually by dragging and dropping them if you left-click their blue table header bar. They can be resized by clicking their bottom-left corner, and they can be maximized so that all the columns in them are displayed by clicking the Maximize button in the right corner of the table header bar.

Creating Relationships

Relationships between tables can be created in the Grid View, but it's easier to create them in the Diagram View because they are actually visible there after you have created them. To create a relationship, click the column on the many side of the relationship (usually the *Dimension Key* column on the Fact table) and drag it onto the column on another table that will be on the one side of the relationship (for example, the column that will be the lookup column, usually the primary key column on a dimension table). As an alternative, select the table in the Diagram View and, from the Table menu at the top of the screen, select Create Relationship.

After a relationship has been created, you can delete it by clicking it to select it and pressing the Delete key. You can also edit it by double-clicking it or by selecting Manage Relationships from the Table menu; this shows the Manage Relationships dialog box, as shown in Figure 2-31, and a relationship can then be selected for editing, which in turn shows the Edit Relationship dialog box.

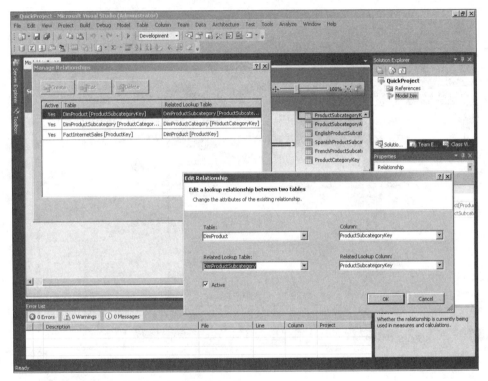

FIGURE 2-31 This is the Edit Relationship dialog box.

In the model you have been building, there should already be the following relationships:

- Between FactInternetSales and DimProduct based on the *ProductKey* column.

- Between DimProduct and DimProductSubcategory based on the *ProductSubcategoryKey* column.

- Between DimProductSubcategory and DimProductCategory based on the *ProductCategoryKey* column.

These relationships were created automatically because they were present as key relationships in the SQL Server database; if they do not exist in your model, create them.

Creating Hierarchies

Staying in the diagram view, the last task to complete before the model is ready for use is to create a hierarchy. Select the DimProduct table and click the Maximize button so as many columns as possible are visible. Then click the Create Hierarchy button on the table, and a new hierarchy will be created at the bottom of the list of columns; name it **Product by Color**. Drag the *Color* column down onto it—if you drag it to a point after the hierarchy, nothing will happen, so be accurate—to create the top level and drag the *EnglishDescription* column down to below the new Color level to create the bottom level, as shown in Figure 2-32. As an alternative, you can multiselect all these columns and then, on the right-click menu, select Create Hierarchy. Finally, click the Restore button (which is in the same place the Maximize button was) to restore the table to its original size.

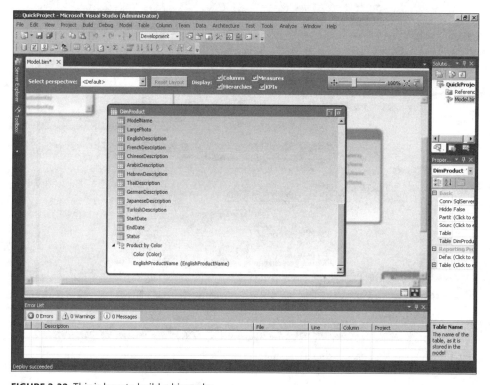

FIGURE 2-32 This is how to build a hierarchy.

Deployment

The simple model you have been building is now complete and must be deployed. To do this, from the Build menu, click Deploy. The metadata for the database is deployed to your development server, and then it is processed automatically if you have left the project's Processing Option property set to Default. If you have changed this property to Do Not Process, you must process your model by selecting Process\Process All from the Model menu. If you chose to use a Windows username on the Impersonation Information step of the Table Import Wizard for creating your data source, you might need to reenter the password for your username at this point. After processing has completed successfully, you should see a large green tick mark with the word Success, as shown in Figure 2-33.

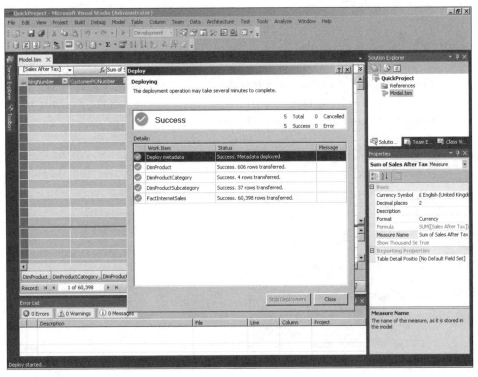

FIGURE 2-33 This shows the end of a successful deployment.

The model is now present on your development server and ready to be queried.

Querying a Tabular Model in Excel

Excel is the client tool your users are most likely to want to use to query your Tabular models. It's also an important tool for an Analysis Services developer. During development, you must browse the model you are building to make sure that it works in the way you expect. As a result, it's important to understand how to use the Excel built-in functionality for querying Analysis Services, and this section provides an introductory guide on how to do this, even though it is beyond the scope of this book to explore all the Excel BI capabilities.

This section focuses on Excel 2010 as a client tool. End users can use earlier versions of Excel but will not have the same functionality. Excel 2007 is very similar to Excel 2010, but Excel 2003 and earlier versions provide only basic support for querying Analysis Services and have not been fully tested with Analysis Services 2012.

Connecting to a Tabular Model

Before you can query a Tabular model in Excel, you must first open a connection to the model; there are several ways to do this.

Browsing a Workspace Database

While you are working on a Tabular model, you can check your work very easily by browsing your workspace database in Excel by choosing the Model menu and clicking Analyze In Excel. (You also see a button on the toolbar with an Excel icon on it that does the same thing.) Doing this opens the Analyze In Excel dialog box shown in Figure 2-34.

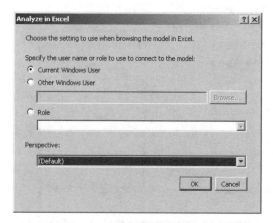

FIGURE 2-34 This is the Analyze In Excel dialog box.

The default option of Current Windows User enables you to connect to your workspace database as yourself and see all the data in there. The next two options, Other Windows User and Role, enable you to connect to the database as if you were another user to test security; these options are discussed in more detail in Chapter 15, "Security." The final option, Perspective, enables you to connect to a perspective instead of the complete model.

When you click OK, Excel opens, and a blank PivotTable connected to your database is created on the first worksheet in the workbook, as shown in Figure 2-35. Remember that this is possible only if you have Excel installed on your development workstation and there is no way of querying a Tabular model from within SSDT.

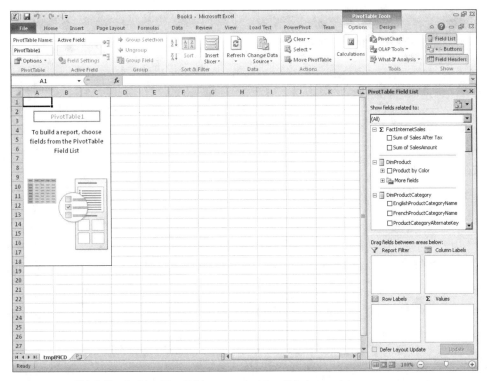

FIGURE 2-35 This is Excel with a PivotTable connected to a Tabular model.

Connecting to a Deployed Database

You can also connect to a Tabular model without using SSDT. This is how your end users will con-nect to your model. To do this, start Excel and, from the Data tab on the ribbon, click the From Other Sources button. Select From Analysis Services, as shown in Figure 2-36.

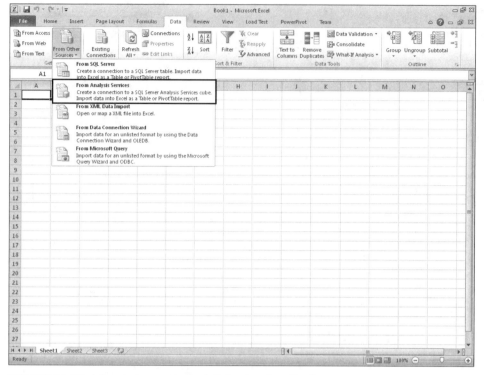

FIGURE 2-36 This is how to connect to Analysis Services from Excel.

This starts the Data Connection Wizard. On the first page, enter the name of the instance of Analysis Services to which you wish to connect and click Next; do not change the default selection of Use Windows Authentication for logon credentials. Choose the database to which you want to connect and the cube you want to query. (If you are connecting to your workspace database server, you'll probably see one or more workspace databases with long names incorporating GUIDS.) There are no cubes in a Tabular database, but because Excel 2010 predates the Tabular model and generates only MDX queries, it will see your model as a cube. Therefore, choose the item on the list that represents your model, which, by default, will be called Model, as shown in Figure 2-37. If you defined perspectives in your model, every perspective will be listed as a cube name in the same list.

Finally, click Next and then click Finish to save the connection and close the wizard. You will be asked whether you want to create a new PivotTable, a PivotTable and a pivot chart, or just a connection; if you are creating a PivotTable, you must choose where to put it. If you opt to create a new PivotTable and click OK, you arrive at the point shown in Figure 2-35.

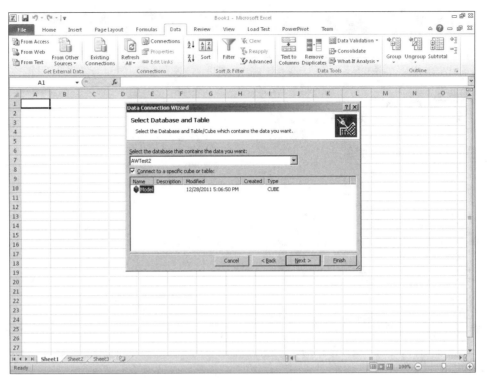

FIGURE 2-37 This is the Data Connection Wizard.

Using PivotTables

Building a basic PivotTable is very straightforward. In the PivotTable Field List on the right side of the screen is a list of measures grouped by table (there is a Σ before each table name, which shows these are lists of measures), followed by a list of columns and hierarchies, again grouped by table.

You can select measures either by choosing them in the Field List or dragging them down into the Values pane in the bottom right corner of the Field List pane. In a similar way, you can select columns either by choosing them or by dragging them to the Column Labels, Row Labels, or Report Filter panes in the bottom half of the Field List pane. Columns and hierarchies become rows and columns in the PivotTable, whereas measures display the numeric values inside the body of the PivotTable. The list of measures you have selected is, by default, displayed on the columns axis of the PivotTable, but it can be moved to rows by dragging the Values icon from the Column Labels pane to the Row Labels pane; it cannot be moved to the Report Filter pane, however. Figure 2-38 shows a PivotTable using the sample model you have built with two measures on columns, the Product By Color hierarchy on rows, and the *EnglishProductCategoryName* field on the filter.

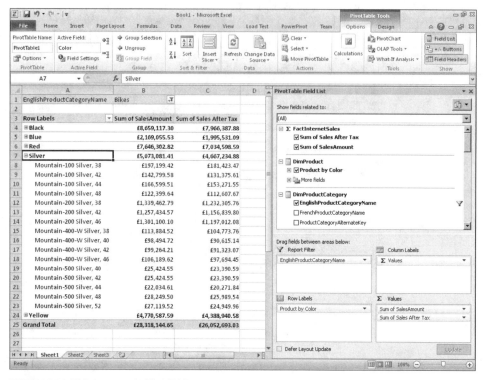

FIGURE 2-38 This is a sample PivotTable.

Using Slicers

A new feature in Excel 2010 that provides an alternative to the Report Filter box you've just seen is the slicer. Slicers are a much easier to use and more visually appealing way to filter the data that appears in a report. To create one, from the Insert tab on the ribbon, click the Slicer button and then, in the Insert Slicers dialog box, select the field you want to use, as shown in Figure 2-39.

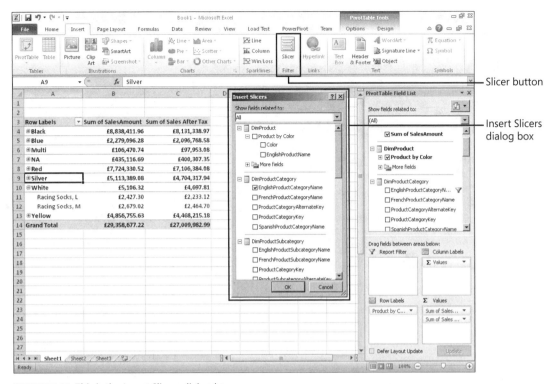

Slicer button

Insert Slicers
dialog box

FIGURE 2-39 This is the Insert Slicers dialog box.

Click OK, and the slicer is added to your worksheet; after it is created, the slicer can be dragged to wherever you want in the worksheet. You then only need to click one or more names in the slicer to filter your PivotTable; all filters can be removed by pressing the Clear Filter button in the top right corner of the slicer. Figure 2-40 shows the same PivotTable as Figure 2-38 but with the filter on EnglishProductCategoryName replaced with a slicer and with an extra slicer added based on EnglishProductSubcategoryName.

When there are multiple slicers, you might notice that some of the items in a slicer are shaded; this is because, based on the selections made in other slicers, no data would be returned in the PivotTable if you selected the shaded items. For example, in Figure 2-40, the Components item on EnglishProductCategoryName is shaded because no data exists for that selection. In the EnglishProductSubcategoryName slicer, all items except Mountain Bikes, Road Bikes, and Touring Bikes are shaded because these are the only three subcategories in the Bikes product category, which is selected in the other slicer.

Putting an attribute on a slicer enables you to use it on rows, columns, or filter area of the PivotTable. This is not the case of an attribute placed in the filter area, which cannot be used on rows and columns of the same PivotTable. You can also connect a single slicer to many PivotTables, so that the selections you make in it are applied to all those PivotTables simultaneously.

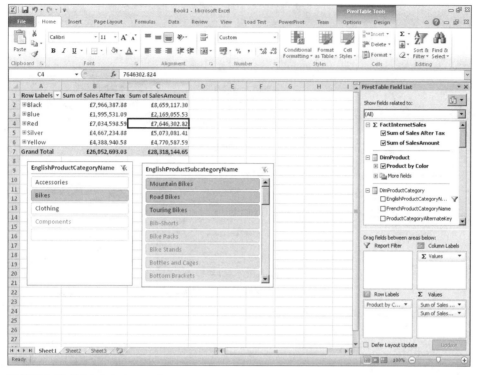

FIGURE 2-40 This is how to use slicers.

Sorting and Filtering Rows and Columns

When you first drag a field onto either the Row Labels or Column Labels pane, you see all the values in that field displayed in the PivotTable. However, you might want to display only some of these values and not others; there are a number of options for doing this.

When you click any field in the PivotTable Field List, or click on the drop-down arrow next to the Row Labels or Column Labels box in the PivotTable, you can choose individual items to display and apply sorting and filtering, as shown in Figure 2-41.

Selecting and clearing members in the list at the bottom of the dialog box selects and clears members from the PivotTable, and it is also possible to filter by the names of the items and by the value of a measure by using the Label Filters and Value Filters options.

If you need more control over which members are displayed and in which order they are shown, you must use a Named Set. To create a Named Set, from the PivotTable\Options tab on the ribbon, click the Calculations button, choose Fields, Items, and Sets and then select either Create Set Based On Row Items or Create Set Based On Column Items, as shown in Figure 2-42.

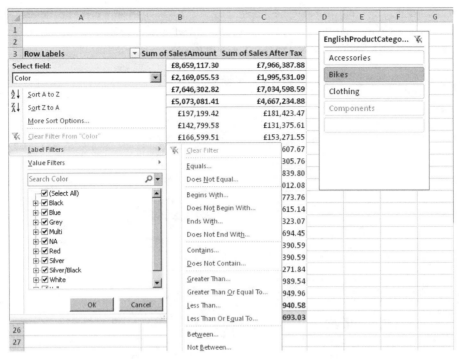

FIGURE 2-41 This is how to sort and filter in a PivotTable.

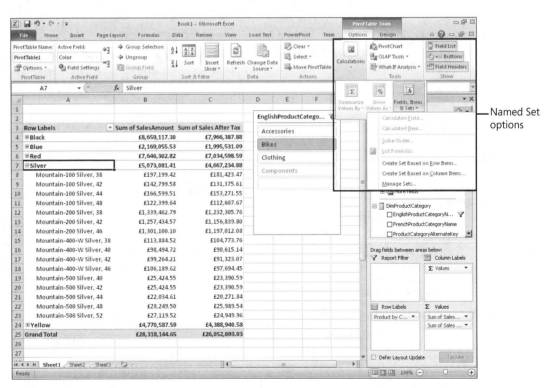

FIGURE 2-42 This is how to create a Named Set.

The New Set dialog box then appears, as shown in Figure 2-43, where you can add, delete, and move individual rows in the PivotTable. If you have some knowledge of MDX, you can also click the Edit MDX button and write your own MDX set expression to use.

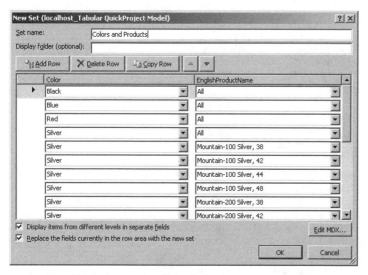

FIGURE 2-43 This is the New Set dialog box.

Clicking OK results in the creation of a new Named Set. You can think of a Named Set as being a predefined selection that is saved with the PivotTable but does not necessarily need to be used; after it has been created, it appears under a folder called Sets in the PivotTable Field List, as shown in Figure 2-44. As long as you leave the Replace The Fields Currently In The Row/Column Area With The New Set option selected in the New Set dialog box, your set will control what appears on rows in the PivotTable.

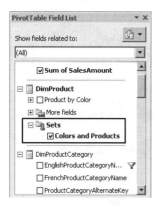

FIGURE 2-44 This shows sets in the PivotTable Field List.

Using Excel Cube Formulas

The last important bit of Analysis Services–related functionality to mention in Excel is the Excel cube formulas. These functions enable Excel to retrieve a single cell of data from a cube; for example, a reference to an individual item name or a measure value. The easiest way to understand how they work is to convert an existing PivotTable to cells containing formulas by clicking the PivotTable\Options tab on the ribbon, clicking the OLAP Tools button, and selecting Convert To Formulas from the drop-down box, as shown in Figure 2-45.

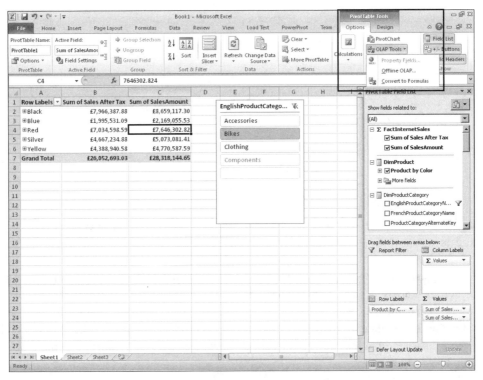

FIGURE 2-45 This is how to convert a PivotTable to formulas.

The result is shown in Figure 2-46; notice how the B3 cell that returns the value of the measure Sum Of Sales After Tax for blue products returns the value, but this value is returned now by the following formula.

```
=CUBEVALUE("localhost_Tabular QuickProject Model",$A3,B$1,Slicer_EnglishProductCategoryName)
```

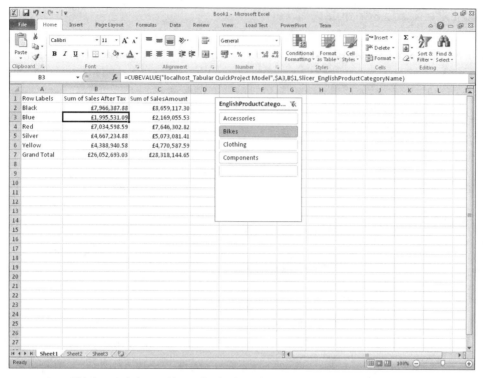

FIGURE 2-46 This is a worksheet with Excel cube formulas.

The four parameters used in the *CubeValue()* function here are as follows: the name of the Excel connection to Analysis Services; a cell reference to cell A3, which contains another function that returns the item name Blue; another cell reference to cell B1, which returns the measure Sum Of Sales Amount; and a reference to the slicer containing the product category names. As a result, this cell returns the value from the cube for the Sum Of Sales Amount, Blue products, and the product category Bikes.

Cube formulas are a very powerful way of displaying free-form reports in Excel and allow much greater flexibility in layout and formatting than PivotTables. Their one drawback is that they do not allow as much interactivity as PivotTables; users can no longer change what appears on rows and columns by dragging and dropping, and they can no longer navigate down through hierarchies (although slicers and report filters still work as expected).

It is beyond the scope of this book to provide a full description of what Excel cube formulas can do, but the Excel help, found at *http://office.microsoft.com/en-us/excel-help/cube-functions-reference-HA010342384.aspx*, is a good place to start if you would like to learn more about them.

Querying a Tabular Model in Power View

Apart from Excel, another tool you might want to use to query your Tabular model is Power View, the new Microsoft data visualization tool. As with Excel, it's beyond the scope of this book to provide more than a basic introduction to Power View, but this section should give you an idea of the capabilities of this powerful tool. Power View is part of SQL Server 2012 features provided in Microsoft SharePoint 2010 Enterprise edition when you install SQL Server 2012 Reporting Services with SharePoint integration. Describing the setup for this tool is beyond the scope of this book.

Creating a Connection to a Tabular Model

Before you can create a new Power View report, you must create a new Power View connection to your Tabular model inside SharePoint. To do this, open a SharePoint document library and, from Library Tools\Documents on the ribbon, click the New Document drop-down and select BI Semantic Model (BISM) Connection, as shown in Figure 2-47.

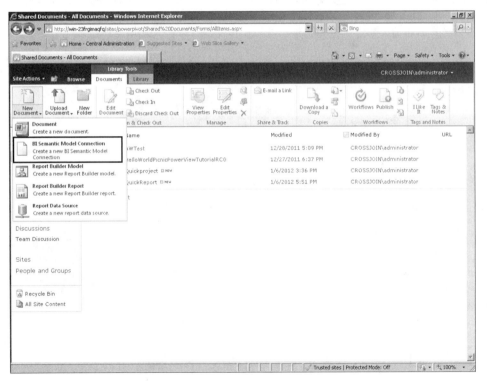

FIGURE 2-47 This is how to create a new BISM Connection.

Note The option to create a BISM Connection is available only if you have installed PowerPivot for SharePoint on your SharePoint server farm. SharePoint administrators can also control which content types are available to users, so if you can't see the BISM Connection type, consult your SharePoint administrator.

This displays the New BI Semantic Model Connection page, as shown in Figure 2-48. Fill in a name for this connection in the File Name box and enter the name of your development server instance in the Workbook URL or Server Name box and the name of the database you have just created in the Database box. Click OK.

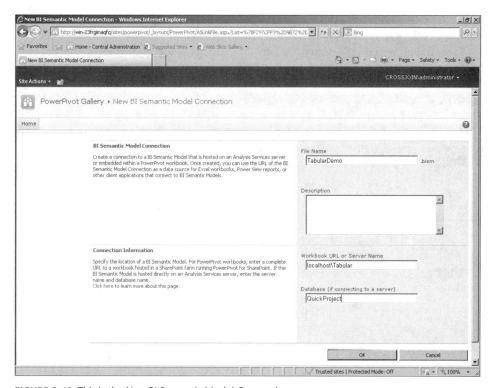

FIGURE 2-48 This is the New BI Semantic Model Connection page.

Building a Basic Power View Report

With the connection created, you can either click the connection in the document library or click the down arrow next to it and select Create Power View Report to open Power View with a new report, as shown in Figure 2-49. A report consists of one or more views, which are similar to slides in a Microsoft PowerPoint deck; what you see on the screen is a new blank view in your report.

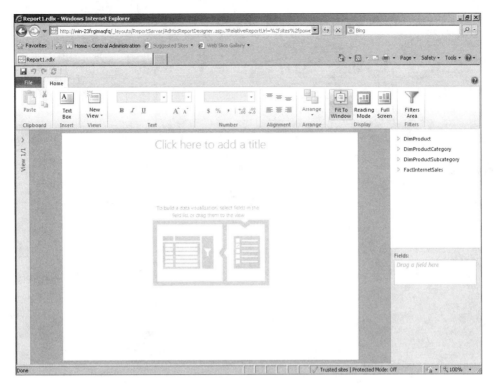

FIGURE 2-49 This is a blank view in a Power View report.

On the right side of the screen in Figure 2-49, you can see a list of the tables in the model you created earlier; clicking the arrows next to the names shows the columns and measures in each table. Drag the *EnglishProductSubCategoryName* column from DimProductSubcategory into the Fields pane on the bottom right side, drag the Sum Of Sales Amount measure down after it, and then drag the *EnglishProductCategoryName* column into the Tile By pane that appears above the Field pane. This creates a new table in the view. In fact, the table is inside a new tile control that enables you to filter the contents of the table by Product Category by clicking the category names at the top of it. Resize both the table and the tile control by clicking their bottom-left edges and expanding them so all the data is visible. Also, enter an appropriate title at the top of the view in the Click Here To Add A Title section. The result should look like the view shown in Figure 2-50.

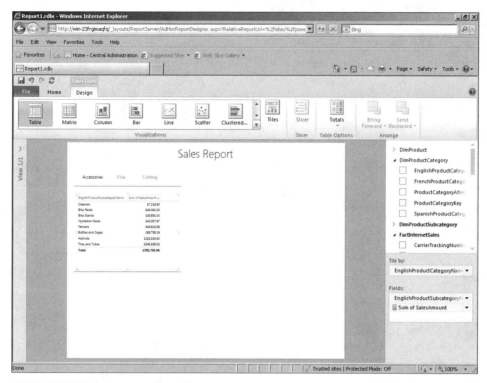

FIGURE 2-50 This is a report with a table.

Adding Charts and Slicers

To turn a table into a chart, you just must click somewhere inside the table and then, on the Design tab in the ribbon, select a chart type such as Bar. You can then go to the Layout tab on the ribbon and click Chart Title\None to remove the chart title to improve its appearance.

You can also add a slicer inside the view to provide another way of filtering the chart you have just created. Drag the *Color* column from the DimProduct table into the empty space to the right of the chart to create a new table; click inside the table and, on the Design tab of the ribbon, click the Slicer button to turn the table into a slicer. In addition to resizing the controls, you can also move them around to improve the layout of the view by hovering over the top right side of a control until the mouse turns into a figure icon and then dragging it. Selecting a color name inside the slicer filters the values that are used in the chart.

One of the coolest visualizations available in Power View is the animated scatter chart. To create one on your report, drag the *EnglishProductCategoryName* column into the empty space at the bottom of the report to create a new table. Then drag the *OrderDate* column from FactInternetSales next to it and drag in the Sum Of SalesAmount measure. Click inside the table and change it to be a scatter chart and resize it. Then drag the *OrderQuantity* column into the Y Value pane in the bottom-right corner (Sum Of SalesAmount is in the X Value pane). Finally, drag the *ProductStandardCost* column into the Size pane, click the down arrow next to it, and select Average. This creates a new measure just for this report that returns the average cost of products in each category. Remove the chart title again and then, still on the Layout tab in the ribbon, click Data Labels\Right. The view should now look like the one shown in Figure 2-51. Last, click the Save button in the top-left corner to save the report.

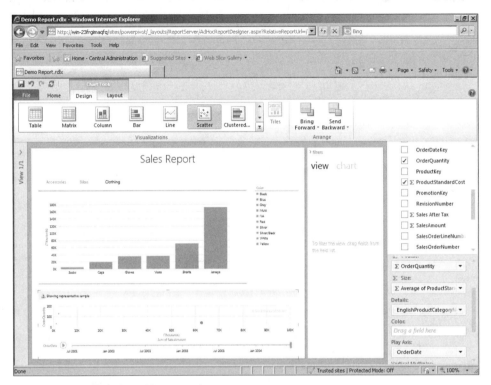

FIGURE 2-51 This is a view with scatter chart.

Interacting with a Report

To give you as much screen surface as possible to view a report, click the Home tab in the ribbon and click the Full Screen button to show the report in a full screen. Because the scatter chart still doesn't have much space, click the Pop-Out button in the top-left corner of the chart to expand it to the full screen, as shown in Figure 2-52. Then press the Play button in the bottom-left corner to show an animation of how the sales of the three product categories, their order volumes, and their average product costs change over time. To return the scatter chart to its original size, click the Pop-In button in the top right-hand corner.

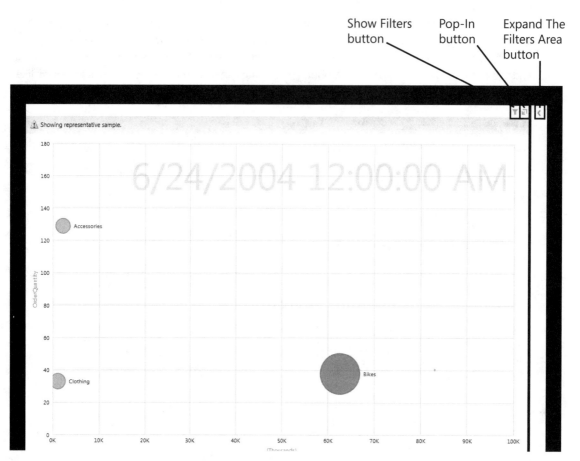

FIGURE 2-52 This is an example of a full-screen scatter chart.

Click the Expand The Filters Area button in the top-right corner to show the Filters area, where you can apply filters either to individual charts or (if you have created any) the whole view, as shown in Figure 2-53.

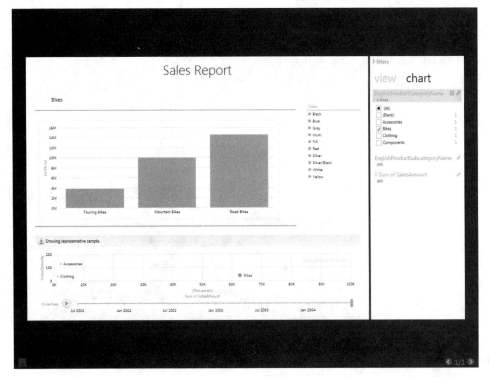

FIGURE 2-53 This is the Filters area.

 More Info For more information about how to use Power View, see the documentation on TechNet at *http://technet.microsoft.com/en-us/library/hh213579(SQL.110).aspx*.

Working with SQL Server Management Studio

The last tool with which you need to familiarize yourself is SQL Server Management Studio (usually abbreviated to SSMS), which you use to manage Analysis Services instances and databases that have already been deployed. To connect to an instance of Analysis Services, open SSMS and, in the Connection dialog box that appears, choose Analysis Services in the Server Type drop-down box and enter your instance name in the Server Name box, as shown in Figure 2-54. Click Connect.

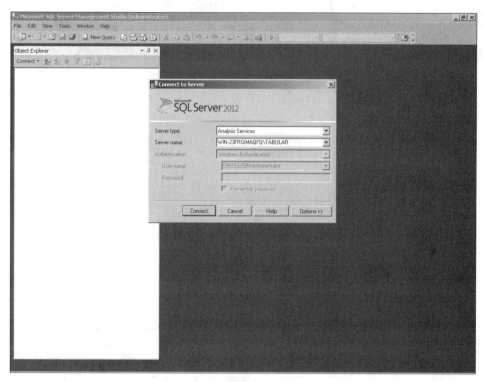

FIGURE 2-54 Connect to Analysis Services in SSMS.

This opens a new connection to Analysis Services in the Object Explorer pane, and expand-ing all available nodes on a Tabular instance should show something similar to what is displayed in Figure 2-55, which shows the database you created and deployed earlier in this chapter.

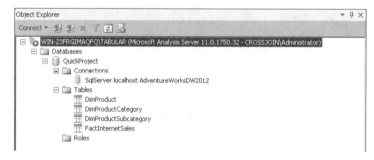

FIGURE 2-55 This is the Object Explorer pane in SSMS.

At the top of the pane is the Instance node, showing the name of the instance, the version number, and your username. Underneath that is a folder containing a list of databases; inside each database, you can see the connections, tables, and security roles inside that database. Right-clicking any of these objects enables you to view and edit their properties; in the case of the instance, this is the only place in which Analysis Services server properties can be edited in a user interface. In addition, databases and individual tables can be processed, and objects can be scripted out to XMLA. All this functionality is covered in more detail in Chapter 17, "Tabular Deployment."

It is also possible to execute both DAX and MDX queries against a Tabular model in SSMS. Although confusing, both must be executed through an MDX query window; to open one, you can either click the New MDX Query button on the toolbar or right-click a database in the Object Explorer and then select New Query\MDX. In the former case, the same Connection dialog box appears as when you opened a connection in Object Explorer; in the latter case, you are connected directly to the database you have clicked, but you can always change the database to which you are connected by using the Database drop-down box in the toolbar. After you have connected, your new MDX query window appears, and you can enter your MDX or DAX query, as shown in Figure 2-56. Clicking the Execute button on the toolbar or pressing F5 runs the query; a query can be canceled during execution by clicking the red Cancel button next to the Execute button. You can try this yourself by running the following DAX query against the model you have built, which returns all of the FactInternetSales table.

```
evaluate FactInternetSales
```

The subject of writing DAX queries is dealt with in detail in Chapter 6, "Querying Tabular."

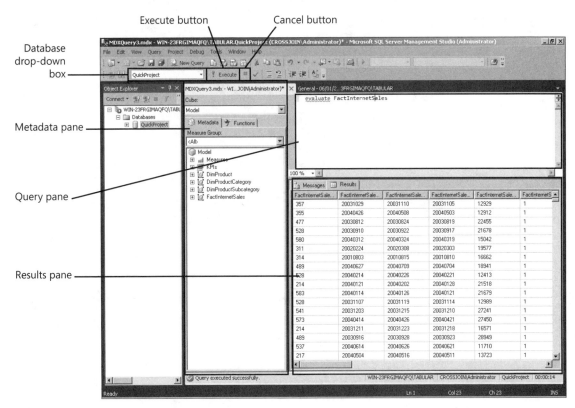

FIGURE 2-56 How to execute a DAX query.

Summary

In this chapter, you saw how to set up a development environment for Analysis Services 2012 Tabular and had a whirlwind tour of the development process and the tools you use, such as SQL Server Data Tools, Excel, and SQL Server Management Studio. You should now have a basic understanding of how a Tabular model works and how you build one. In the rest of the book you will learn about loading data (Chapter 3), DAX, and model design in detail.

Loading Data Inside Tabular

As you learned in Chapter 2, "Getting Started with the Tabular Model," the key to producing a Tabular model is to load data from one or many sources integrated in the analysis data model that enables users to create their reports by browsing the Tabular database on the server. This chapter describes the data-loading options available in Tabular. You have already used some of the loading features to prepare the examples of the previous chapters. Now, you move a step further and examine all options for loading data so that you can determine which methods are the best for your application.

Understanding Data Sources

In this section, you learn the basics of data sources, the interfaces between SQL Server Analysis Services (SSAS) and databases. They provide the abstraction layer Analysis Services needs to communicate with different sources of data. Analysis Services provides several kinds of data sources, which can be divided into the following categories:

- **Relational databases** Analysis Services can load data hosted in relational databases such as Microsoft Access, Microsoft SQL Server, Oracle, and many other relational databases. You can load tables, views, and queries from the server with the data sources in this category.

- **Multidimensional sources** You can load data in Tabular model from an Analysis Services Multidimensional model by using these data sources. Currently, SQL Server Analysis Services is the only multidimensional database for which there is an available data source. The same data source can also load data from queries issued to PowerPivot data contained in a Microsoft Excel workbook published on Microsoft SharePoint or from a Tabular data model hosted on a server.

- **Data feeds** This category of data sources enables you to load data from dynamic feeds such as Open Data Protocol (OData) feeds from the Internet or data feeds tied to reports stored in Reporting Services.

- **Text files** Data sources in this category can load data that is stored in comma-separated text files, Excel, fixed-length files, or any other file format that can be interpreted by Analysis Services.

- **Other sources**   Data can be loaded from the Clipboard or from XML information hosted inside the SQL Server Data Tools (SSDT) solution.

In a Tabular data model, you can freely mix different data sources to load data from various media. It is important to remember that data, after it's loaded, must be refreshed by the server on a scheduled basis, depending on your needs, during the database processing.

If you want to see the complete list of all the data sources available in Tabular, you can open the Table Import Wizard (see Figure 3-1), which you can find by selecting Import From Data Source from the Model menu.

FIGURE 3-1 The Table Import Wizard shows all the available data sources.

The first page of the Table Import Wizard lists all the data sources available in Tabular. Each data source has specific parameters and dialog boxes, which we will not cover in detail; the details necessary for connecting to the specialized data sources can be provided by your local administrator, and they are outside of the scope of this book. It is interesting to look at the differences between loading from a text file or from a SQL Server query, but it is of little use to investigate the subtle differences between Microsoft SQL Server and Oracle, which are both relational database servers and behave in much the same way.

Understanding Impersonation

Whenever Analysis Services loads information from a data source, it must use the credentials of a Windows account so that security can be applied and data access granted. Stated more technically, SSAS impersonates a user when opening a data source. The credentials used for impersonation might be different from both the credentials of the user currently logged on—that is, from the user's credentials—and the ones running the SSAS service.

For this reason, it is very important to decide which user will be impersonated by SSAS when accessing a database. If you fail to provide the correct set of credentials, SSAS cannot correctly access data, and the server will raise errors during processing.

Moreover, it is important to understand that impersonation is different from SSAS security. Impersonation is related to the credentials the service uses to refresh data tables in the database. In contrast, SSAS security secures the cube after it has been processed to present different subsets of data to different users. Impersonation comes into play during processing; security during querying.

Impersonation is defined on the Impersonation Information page of the Table Import Wizard, which is described later, from which you can choose one of two options:

- Specific Windows user

- Service Account

If you use a specific Windows user, you must provide the credentials of a user who will be impersonated by SSAS. If, however, you choose Service Account, SSAS presents itself to the data source by using the same account that runs SSAS (which you can change by updating the service parameters in the server by using SQL Server Configuration Manager).

Impersonation is applied to each data source. Whether you must load data from SQL Server or from a text file, impersonation is always something you must use and understand to smooth the process of data loading. Each data source can have different impersonation parameters.

It is important, at this point, to digress a bit about the Workspace Server. As you might recall from Chapter 2, the workspace server hosts the workspace database, which is the temporary database SSDT uses when developing a Tabular solution. If you choose to use Service Account as the user running SSAS, you must pay attention to whether this user might be different in the workspace server and in the production server, leading to processing errors. You might find that the workspace server processes the database smoothly, whereas the production server fails.

Understanding Server-Side and Client-Side Credentials

Up to now, you have learned that SSAS impersonates a user when it accesses data. Nevertheless, when you are authoring a solution in SSDT, some operations are executed by the server and others are executed by SSDT on your local machine. Operations executed by the server are called *server-side operations*, whereas the ones executed by SSDT are called *client-side operations*.

Even if they appear to be executed in the same environment, client and server operations are, in reality, executed by different software and therefore might use different credentials. An example might clarify the scenario.

When you import data from SQL Server, you follow the Table Import Wizard, by which you can choose the tables to import; you can preview and filter data and then, when the selection is concluded, you have loaded data from the database into the Tabular model.

The Table Import Wizard runs inside SSDT and is executed as a client-side operation, which means that it uses the credentials specified for client-side operations—that is, the credentials of the current user. The final data loading process, instead, is executed by the workspace server by using the workspace server impersonation settings, and it is a server-side operation.

Thus, in the same logical flow of an operation, you end up mixing client-side and server-side operations, which might lead to different users being impersonated by different layers of the software.

Note In a common scenario that leads to misunderstanding, you specify Service Account for impersonation and try to load some data. If you follow the default installation of SQL Server, the account used to execute SSAS does not have access to the SQL engine, whereas your personal account should normally be able to access the databases. Thus, if you use the Service Account impersonation mode, you can follow the wizard up to when data must be loaded (for example, you can select and preview the tables). At that point, the data loading starts and, because this is a server-side operation, Service Account cannot access the database; this final phase raises an error.

Although the differences between client-side and server-side credentials are difficult to understand, it is important to understand how connections are established. To understand the topic, consider that these are the components involved when establishing a connection:

- The connection can be initiated by an instance of SSAS or SSDT. You refer to server and client operations, respectively, depending on who initiated the operation.

- The connection is established by using a connection string, defined in the first page of the wizard.

- The connection is started by using the impersonation options, defined on the second page of the wizard.

When the server is trying to connect to the database, it checks whether it should use impersonation. Thus, it looks at what you have specified on the second page and, if requested, impersonates the desired Windows user. The client does not perform this step; it operates under the security context of the current user running SSDT.

After this first step, the data source connects to the server by using the connection string specified in the first page of the wizard, and impersonation is no longer used at this stage.

Thus, the main difference between client and server operations is that the impersonation options are not relevant to the client operations; they only open a connection by using the current user.

This is important for some data sources such as the Access data source. If the Access file is in a shared folder, this folder must be accessible by both the user running SSDT, to let client side operations to be executed, and the user impersonated by SSAS when processing the table on both the workspace and the deployment servers. If opening the Access file requires a password, both the client and the server use the password stored in the connection string to obtain access to the content of the file.

Working with Big Tables

In a Tabular project, SSDT shows data from the workspace database in the model window, and you have already learned that the workspace database is a physical database that can reside on your workstation or on a server on the network. Wherever this database is, it occupies memory and resources and needs CPU time whenever it is processed.

Processing the production database is a task that can take minutes if not hours. The workspace database, however, should be kept as small as possible to avoid wasting time whenever you must update it, something that happens quite often during development.

To reduce time, avoid processing the full tables when working with the workspace database. You can follow some of these hints:

- Build a development database that contains a small subset of the production data so that you can work on the development database and then, when the project is deployed, change the connection strings to make them point to the production database.

- When loading data from a SQL Server database, you can create views that restrict the number of returned rows and later change them to retrieve the full set of data when in production.

- If you have SQL Server Enterprise edition, you can rely on partitioning to load a small subset of data in the workspace database and then rely on the creation of new partitions in the production database to hold all the data. You can find further information about this technique at *http://blogs.msdn.com/b/cathyk/archive/2011/09/01/importing-a-subset-of-data-using-partitions-step-by-step.aspx*.

Your environment and your experience might lead you to different mechanisms to handle the size of the workspace database. In general, it is good practice to think about this aspect of development before you start building the project to avoid problems later due to the increased size of the workspace model.

Loading from SQL Server

The first data source is SQL Server. To start loading data from SQL Server, choose Import From Data Source from the Model menu to open the Table Import Wizard. If you select Microsoft SQL Server, the Table Import Wizard asks you the parameters by which to connect to SQL Server, which you can see in Figure 3-2.

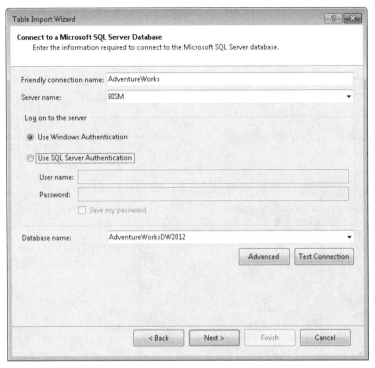

FIGURE 3-2 The Table Import Wizard asks you for the parameters by which to connect to SQL Server.

The Table Import Wizard guides you step by step during the whole loading process, asking for just a few parameters in each dialog box. These are the important parameters you must complete in this first dialog box:

- **Friendly Connection Name** This is a name that you can assign to the connection to recall it later. We suggest overriding the default name that SSDT suggests because a meaningful name will be easier to remember later.

- **Server Name** This is the name of the SQL Server instance to which you want to connect.

- **Log On To The Server** This option enables you to choose the method of authentication to use when connecting to SQL Server. You can choose between Windows Authentication (which uses the account of the user running SSDT to provide the credentials for SQL Server) and SQL Server Authentication. (In this case, you must provide username and password in this dialog box.)

- **Database Name** In this box, you must specify the name of the database to which you want to connect.

The next step of the wizard requires you to specify the impersonation options, shown in Figure 3-3.

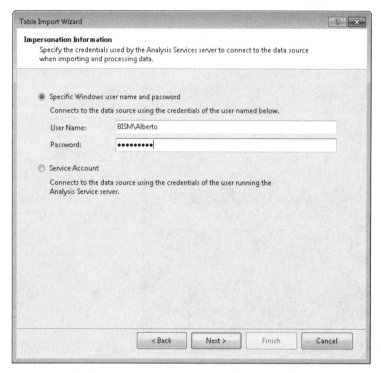

FIGURE 3-3 The Impersonation page enables you to choose the impersonation method.

From this dialog box, you can choose whether SSAS must impersonate a specific user when it tries to access the database or whether it will use the service account.

On the next page of the wizard (see Figure 3-4), you decide whether you want to load data directly from tables or views or to write a SQL query to perform the data loading.

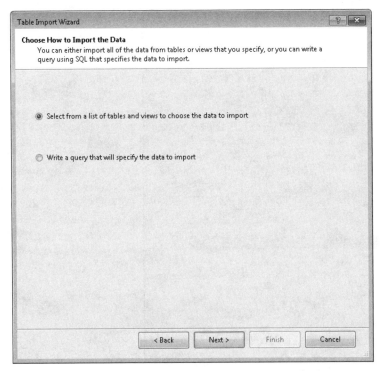

FIGURE 3-4 Choose the correct loading method.

The wizard continues differently, depending on which option is chosen. This is explored in the following sections.

Loading from a List of Tables

If you choose to select the tables from a list, the next page shows the list of tables and views available in the database and offers choices of which to load, as shown in Figure 3-5.

When you select a table for import, you can give it a friendly name, which is the name that SSAS uses for the table after it has been imported. You can change the table name later if you forget to set it here. If needed, you can click the Preview & Filter button to preview the data, set a filter on which data is imported, and select which columns to import (see Figure 3-6).

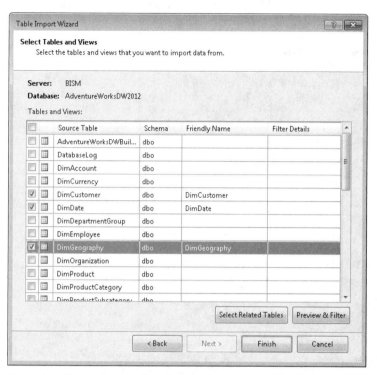

FIGURE 3-5 Choose from the list of tables to import.

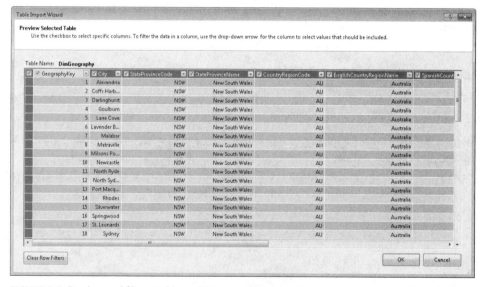

FIGURE 3-6 Preview and filter a table on this page of the wizard.

To limit the data in a table, you can apply two kinds of filters:

- **Column filtering** You can select or clear column choices of the table by using the check box that appears before each column title in the grid. This is convenient when the source table contains technical columns, which are not useful in your data model, to save memory space and achieve quicker processing.

- **Data filtering** You can also choose to load only a subset of the rows of the table, specifying a condition that filters out the unwanted rows. In Figure 3-7, you can see the data-filtering dialog box open for the *Name* column.

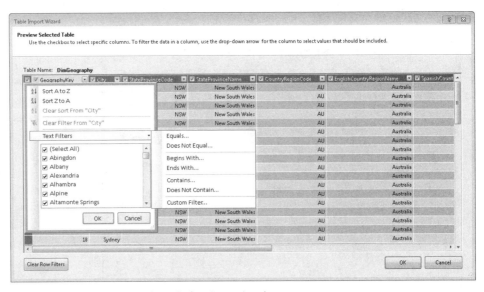

FIGURE 3-7 Filter values in a column before importing data.

Data filtering is powerful and easy to use. You can use the list of values automatically provided by SSDT or, if there are too many values, use Text Filters and provide a set of rules in the forms greater than, less than, equal to, and so on. There are various filter options for several data types such as date filters, which enables you to select previous month, last year, and other specific, date-related filters.

Both column and data filters are saved in the table definition so that when you process the table on the server, they are applied again.

Note Pay attention to the date filters. The query they generate is always relative to the creation date and not to the execution date. Thus, if you select Last Month, December 31, you will always load the month of December, even if you run the query on March. To create queries relative to the current date, rely on views or author-specific SQL code.

Loading Relationships

When you finish selecting and filtering the tables, clicking OK makes SSDT process the tables in the workspace model, which in turn fires the data-loading process. During table processing, the system detects whether any relationships are defined in the database among the tables currently being loaded and, if so, the relationships are loaded inside the data model. The relationship detection occurs only when you load more than one table.

At the end of the Work Item list in the Table Import Wizard, shown in Figure 3-8, you can see an additional step, called Data Preparation, which indicates that relationship detection has occurred.

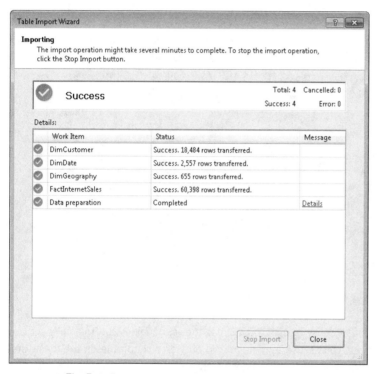

FIGURE 3-8 The Data Preparation step of the Table Import Wizard shows that relationships have been loaded.

If you want to see more details about the found relationships, you can use the Details hyperlink to open a small window that summarizes the relationships created.

Selecting Related Tables

Another feature in the Table Import Wizard is the Select Related Tables button. By clicking the button, the wizard automatically includes all tables that are directly related to the ones already selected. Although it might save some time during the model definition, it is always better to spend some time to decide which tables to load and avoid loading useless tables that will later be deleted, a common scenario that might arise by using this feature.

Loading from a SQL Query

In the previous sections, you completed the process of loading data from a SQL Server database. On the first step of the Table Import Wizard, you chose to select some tables, and then you followed all the steps to the end. However, as you have seen before, there is another option: Write A Query That Will Specify The Data To Import (see Figure 3-4).

If you choose the latter option, you can write the query in a simple text box (in which you normally paste it from a SQL Server Management Studio [SSMS] window in which you have already developed it) or, if you are not familiar with SQL Server, you can rely on the Query Editor for help building the query. You can see the Query Editor in Figure 3-9.

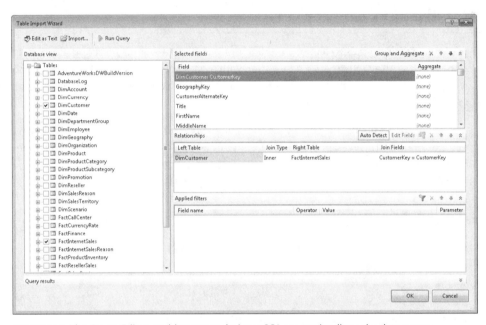

FIGURE 3-9 The Query Editor enables you to design a SQL query visually as the data source.

Loading from Views

Because you have more than one option by which to load data (Table or SQL Query), it is useful to have guidance on which method is the best one. The answer is often neither of these methods.

Linking the data model directly to a table creates an unnecessary dependence between the Tabular data model and the database structure. In the future, it will be harder to make any change to the physical structure of the database. However, writing a SQL query hides information about the data source within the model. Neither of these options seems the right one.

It turns out, as in the case of Multidimensional solutions, that the best choice is to load data from views instead of from tables. You gain many advantages by using views, which are outside the scope of this book. The advantages can be summarized in this way:

- Decoupling of the physical database structure from the Tabular data model

- Declarative description in the database of the tables involved in the creation of a Tabular entity

- The ability to add hints such as NOLOCK to improve processing performance

Thus, we strongly suggest spending some time defining views in your database, each of which will describe one entity in the Tabular data model and then load data directly from those views. By using this technique, you will get the best of both worlds: the full power of SQL to define the data to be loaded without hiding SQL code in the model definition.

Opening Existing Connections

In the preceding section, you saw all the steps and options of data loading, creating a connection from the beginning. After you create a connection with a data source, it is saved in the data model so you can open it again without providing the connection information again. This option is located in the Model menu in Existing Connections.

Choosing this option opens the Existing Connection dialog box shown in Figure 3-10, in which you can select the connections saved in the model. From this window, you can decide to use connection to load data from other tables, edit the connection parameters, delete the connection, or process all the tables linked to that connection.

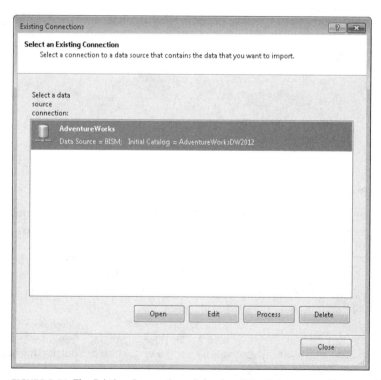

FIGURE 3-10 The Existing Connections dialog box lists all the connections saved in the project.

Note It is very important to become accustomed to reopening existing connections whenever you must import more tables from the same database because, if you create a new connection each time you intend to load data, you create many connections in the same model. If you have many connections and you need to modify some of the connection parameters, you will have extra work to update all the connections.

Loading from Access

Now that you have seen all the ways data can be loaded from relational databases, you can examine other data sources, the first of which is the Access data source.

When you open the Table Import Wizard by using the Access data source, the connection parameters are different because Access databases are stored in files on disk instead of being hosted in server databases. In Figure 3-11, you can see the Table Import Wizard asking for an Access file.

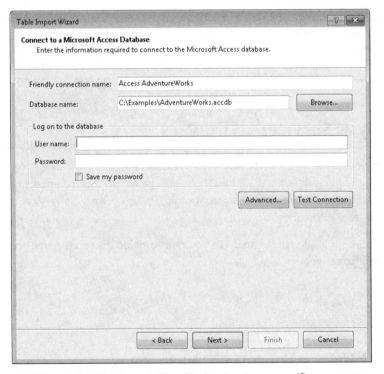

FIGURE 3-11 The Table Import Wizard is showing Access-specific parameters.

There is no practical difference between Access and any other relational database in loading tables, but be aware that the server uses the 64-bit Access Database Engine (ACE) driver, whereas in SSDT, you are using the 32-bit version. It is worth noting that the SQL Server designer of Access is limited because it does not offer a visual designer for the SQL query. When you query Access, you must write the query in a plain text editor.

Because the Table Import Wizard for Access has no query designer, if you must load data from Access and need help with SQL, it might be better to write the query by using the query designer from inside Access. Then, after the query has been built in Access, you can load the data from that query. By doing so, you add an abstraction layer between the Access database and the Tabular data model, which is always a best practice to follow.

Pay attention, when using an Access data source, to these points:

- The file path should point to a network location the server can access when it processes the data model.

- The user impersonated by the SSAS engine when processing the table should have enough privileges to be able to access that folder.

- The workspace database uses the ACE driver installed on that server, so be aware of the bit structure of SSAS versus the bit structure of Office.

If the file is password protected, the password should be entered on the first page of the wizard and saved in the connection string so that the SSAS engine can complete the processing without errors.

Loading from Analysis Services

In the preceding sections, you learned how to load data from relational databases. Different relational data sources might have some slight differences among them, but the overall logic of importing from a relational database remains the same. You now learn about the SQL Server Analysis Services data source, which has some unique features.

In the Table Import Wizard for SSAS (see Figure 3-12), you must provide the server name and the database to which you want to connect.

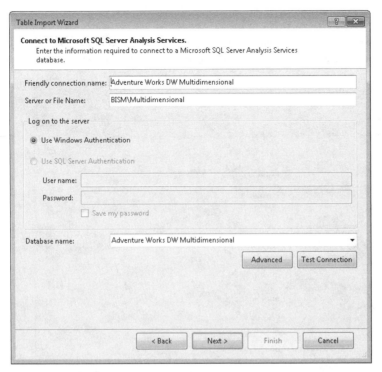

FIGURE 3-12 Connect to an Analysis Services database.

Click Next on this first page to proceed to the MDX query editor. The MDX editor is similar to the SQL editor and contains a simple text box, but the language you must use to query the database is not SQL but MDX. You can write MDX code in the text box or paste it from an SSMS window in which you have already developed and tested it.

As with the SQL editor, you do not need to know the language to build a simple query; SSDT contains an advanced MDX query designer, which you can open by clicking the Design button.

Note As you might have already noticed, you cannot import tables from an Analysis Services database; the only way to load data from an Analysis Services database is to write a query. The reason is very simple: Online analytical processing (OLAP) cubes do not contain tables, so there is no option for table selection. OLAP cubes are composed of measure groups and dimensions, and the only way to retrieve data from these is to create an MDX query that creates a dataset to import.

Using the MDX Editor

Using the MDX editor (see Figure 3-13) is as simple as dragging measures and dimensions into the result panel and is very similar to querying a Multidimensional cube by using Excel.

FIGURE 3-13 You can use the MDX editor when loading from an OLAP cube.

After you have designed the query and clicked OK, the user interface returns to the query editor, showing the complex MDX code that executes the query against the server.

Because this book is not about MDX, it does not include a description of the MDX syntax or MDX capabilities. The interested reader can find several good books about the topic from which to start learning MDX.

Note A good reason to study MDX is the option, in the MDX editor, to define new calculated members that might help you loading data from the SSAS cube. A calculated member is similar to a SQL calculated column, but it uses MDX and is used in an MDX query.

Loading from a Tabular Database

As you have learned, you can use the SSAS data source to load data from a Multidimensional database. An interesting and, perhaps, not so obvious feature is that you can use the same data source to load data from a Tabular data model. The Tabular model can be either a Tabular database in SSAS or a PowerPivot workbook hosted in PowerPivot for SharePoint.

To load data from Tabular, you connect to a Tabular database in the same way you connect to a Multidimensional one. The MDX editor shows the Tabular database as if it were a Multidimensional one, exposing the data in measure groups and dimensions even if no such concept exists in a Tabular model. In Figure 3-14, you can see the MDX editor open over the Tabular version of the Adventure Works SSAS database.

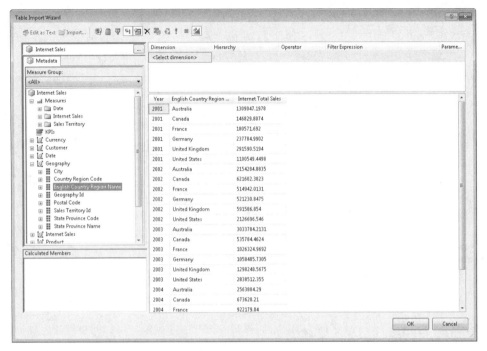

FIGURE 3-14 The MDX editor can also browse Tabular models.

You might be wondering, at this point, whether a Tabular database can be queried by using DAX. After all, DAX is the native language of Tabular, and it seems odd to be able to load data from Tabular by using MDX only. It turns out that this feature, although well hidden, is indeed available.

The MDX editor is not capable of authoring or understanding DAX queries. Nevertheless, because the SSAS server in Tabular mode understands both languages, you can write a DAX query directly in the Table Import Wizard in place of an MDX statement, as you can see in Figure 3-15.

The query of DAX syntax shown in Figure 3-15 is a very simple one; it loads the sales aggregated by year and model name, and you learn later in this book how to use DAX to author complex queries.

Authoring the DAX query inside the small text box provided by the Table Import Wizard is not very convenient. Nevertheless, you can prepare the DAX query inside SQL Server Management Studio and then paste it inside the text box.

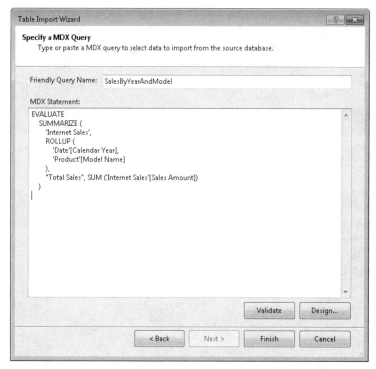

FIGURE 3-15 You can use DAX instead of MDX when querying a Tabular data model.

Column Names in DAX Queries

When using DAX to query the Tabular data model, the column names assigned by the data source contain the table name as a prefix if they come from a table. They represent the full name if they are introduced by the query. For example, the query in Figure 3-15 produces the result shown in Figure 3-16.

DateCalendar Year	ProductModel Name	Total Sales
2003	Sport-100	92583.54
2004	Sport-100	132752.06
2003	Cycling Cap	7956.15
2004	Cycling Cap	11731.95
2003	Long-Sleeve Logo Jersey	34143.17
2004	Long-Sleeve Logo Jersey	52639.47
2001	Road-150	2601402.29
2002	Road-150	2948494.48

FIGURE 3-16 The column names from the result of DAX queries must be adjusted after data loading.

The *Calendar Year* and *Model Name* columns must be adjusted later, but the *Total Sales* column is already correct.

Loading from an Excel File

In this section, you learn how to load data inside SSAS Tabular from an Excel source. It happens often that data such as budgets or predicted sales is hosted inside Excel files. In such a case, you can load data directly from the Excel workbook into the Tabular data model.

It might be worthwhile to write an Integration Services package to load that Excel workbook into a database and keep historical copies of it. Tabular models are intended for corporate business intelligence (BI), so you do not need the practice that self-service users do. Loading data from Excel is fraught with possible problems. If you are loading from a range in which the first few rows are numeric, but further rows are strings, the driver might interpret those rows as numeric and return the string values as null. However, if you insist on loading from Excel, read on.

Let us suppose that you have an Excel workbook containing some predicted sales in an Excel table named PredictedSales, as shown in Figure 3-17.

Year	Model	Amount
2005	Mountain-500	196558.94
2005	Mountain-400-W	323185.8
2005	Road-750	566314.51
2005	Road-350-W	1299131.1
2005	Touring-3000	296940
2005	Touring-1000	2416851
2005	Touring-2000	320416.69
2005	Touring Tire	21090.225
2005	HL Road Tire	18867.25
2005	ML Road Tire	16649.588

FIGURE 3-17 This sample Excel table containing predicted sales can be loaded in Tabular.

To begin the loading process, open the Table Import Wizard and select the Excel data source, which opens the window shown in Figure 3-18.

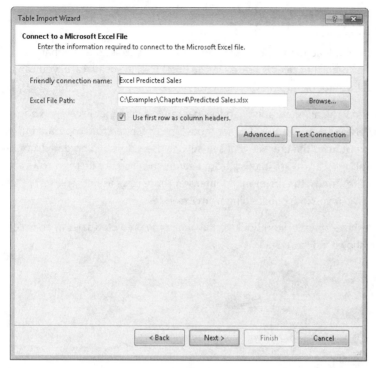

FIGURE 3-18 The Table Import Wizard shows options for the Excel file loading.

Provide the file path of the file containing the data. An important check box is Use First Row As Column Headers. If your table contains column names in the first row (as is the case in the example), you must select this check box so that SSDT automatically detects the column names of the table.

You can proceed to the Impersonation options and then move forward to the Select Tables And Views page (Figure 3-19), from which you can define the ranges to load inside the data model.

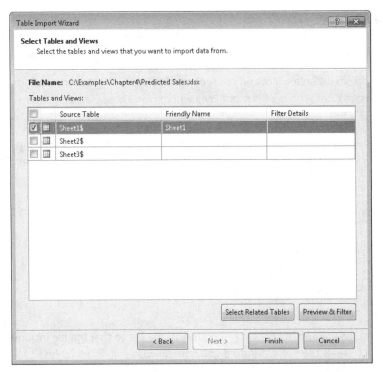

FIGURE 3-19 You can choose the worksheet to import from an Excel workbook.

Important Only worksheets are imported from an external Excel workbook. If multiple tables are defined on a single sheet, they are not considered. For this reason, it is better to have only one table for each worksheet and no other data in the same worksheet. SSDT cannot detect single tables in a workbook. The wizard automatically removes blank space around your data.

After you select the worksheet to import, the wizard loads data into the workspace data model. You can use the Preview & Filter button to look at the data before the data loads, and you can apply filtering, if you like, as you have already learned to do with relational tables.

As happens for Access files, you must specify a file path that will be available to the server when processing the table, so you should not use local resources (such as the C drive), and you must check that the account impersonated by SSAS has enough privileges to reach the network resource in which the Excel file is located.

Loading from a Text File

A common data format from which to load is text files.

Data in text files often comes in the form of comma separated values (CSV), a common format by which each column is separated from the previous one by a comma, and a newline character is used as the row separator.

If you have a CSV file containing some data, you can import it into the data model by using the text file data source. If your CSV file contains the special offers planned for the year 2005, it might look like this.

```
Special Offer,Start,End,Category,Discount
Christmas Gifts,12/1/2005,12/31/2005,Accessory,25%
Christmas Gifts,12/1/2005,12/31/2005,Bikes,12%
Christmas Gifts,12/1/2005,12/31/2005,Clothing,24%
Summer Specials,8/1/2005,8/15/2005,Clothing,10%
Summer Specials,8/1/2005,8/15/2005,Accessory,10%
```

Usually, CSV files contain the column header in the first row of the file so that the file includes the data and the column names. This is the same standard you normally use with Excel tables.

To load this file, choose the Text File data source. The Table Import Wizard for text files (see Figure 3-20) contains the basic parameters used to load from text files.

You can choose the column separator, which by default is a comma, from a list that includes colon, semicolon, tab, and several other separators. The correct choice depends on the column separator used in the text file.

Handling More Complex CSV Files

You might encounter a CSV file that contains fancy separators and find that the Table Import Wizard cannot load it correctly because you cannot choose the necessary characters for the separators. It might be helpful, in such a case, to use the schema.ini file, in which you can define advanced properties of the comma separated file. Read *http://msdn.microsoft.com/en-us/library/ms709353(VS.85).aspx* to learn this advanced technique for loading complex data files.

At the same link, you'll find information about how to load text files that do not follow the CSV schema but use a fixed width instead.

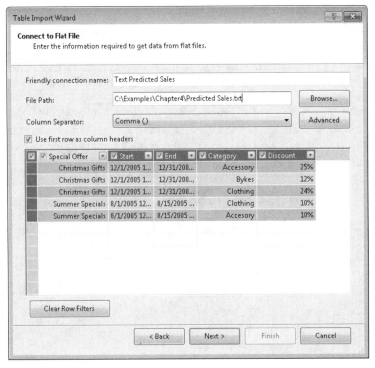

FIGURE 3-20 The Table Import Wizard for CSV contains the basic parameters for CSV.

The Use First Row As Column Headers check box indicates whether the first row of the file contains the column names and works the same as the Excel data source. By default, this check box is cleared even if the majority of the CSV files follow this convention and contain the column header.

As soon as you fill the parameters, the grid shows a preview of the data. You can use the grid to select or clear any column and to set row filters, as you can do with any other data source you have seen. When you finish the setup, click Finish to start the loading process.

After the loading is finished, you must check whether the column types have been detected correctly. CSV files do not contain, for instance, the data type of each column, so SSDT tries to determine the types by evaluating the file content. Clearly, as with any guess, it might fail to detect the correct data type.

In the example, SSDT detected the correct type of all the columns except the *Discount* column because the flat file contains the percentage symbol after the number, so SSDT treats it as a character string and not as a number. If you must change the column type, you can do that later by using SSDT or, in a case like the example, by using a calculated column to get rid of the percentage sign.

Loading from the Clipboard

You now learn about the Clipboard data-loading feature. It is a peculiar method of loading data inside Tabular that has some unique behavior that must be well understood because it does not rely on a data source.

If you open the workbook of Figure 3-17 and copy the Excel table content into the Clipboard, you can then go back to SSDT and choose Edit | Paste from inside a Tabular model. SSDT analyzes the content of the Clipboard and, if it contains valid tabular data, shows the Paste Preview dialog box (Figure 3-21), showing the Clipboard as it will be loaded inside a Tabular table.

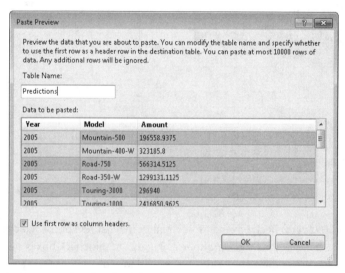

FIGURE 3-21 Loading from the Clipboard opens the Paste Preview dialog box.

By using the Paste Preview dialog box, you can give the table a meaningful name and preview the data before you import it into the model. Click OK to end the loading process and place the table in the data model.

The same process can be initiated by copying a selection from a Word document or from any other software that can copy data in tabular format to the Clipboard.

How will the server be able to process such a table if no data source is available? Even if data can be pushed inside the workspace data model from SSDT, when the project is deployed to the server, Analysis Services will reprocess all the tables, reloading data inside the model. It is clear that the Clipboard content will not be available to SSAS. Thus, it is interesting to understand how the full mechanism works in the background.

If you deploy this project and open it by using SSMS, you can see that, under the various connections for the project, there is one that seems not to be related to any data-loading operation, which is highlighted. (In Figure 3-22, you can see many connections used to load data from various sources up to now.)

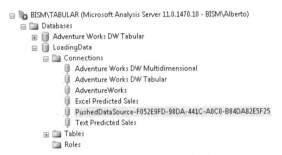

FIGURE 3-22 Clipboard data is loaded from a special system-created connection.

If the Tabular project contains data loaded from the Clipboard, this data is saved inside the project file and then published to the server with a special data source created by the system, the name of which always starts with PushedDataSource followed by a GUID to create a unique name.

This special data source is not tied to any server, folder, or other real source. It is fed by data present in the project file and, if processed, reloads data from a special store, which lives within the deployed database, into the server data files.

Note The same technique is used to push data to the server when you have created an SSDT solution starting from a PowerPivot workbook containing linked tables. Linked tables, in SSDT, are treated much the same way as the Clipboard is treated, saving the data in the project file and pushing them to the server by using this technique. This means that linked tables cannot be refreshed when the Excel workbook is promoted to a fully featured BISM Tabular solution.

Note that in a Tabular data model, some other paste features are available. You can use Paste Append and Paste Replace, which append data or replace data, respectively, into a table starting from the Clipboard content.

If, for example, you choose Paste Append on the same table with the same content, you see the Paste Preview dialog box (Figure 3-23).

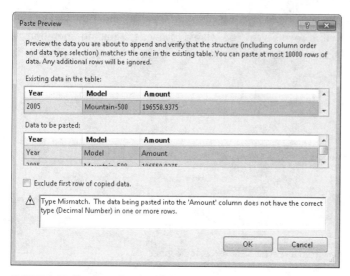

FIGURE 3-23 The Paste Preview dialog box shows that data will be pasted in the model.

You can see that the dialog box contains a warning message because by copying the table content, you have copied the column header too, and both the *Year* and the *Amount* columns contain string values in the first row, whereas in the data model, they should be saved as numeric values.

To resolve the warning, select Exclude First Row Of Copied Data, which makes SSDT ignore the first row containing the column headers; then try appending the remaining rows to the table, as you can see in Figure 3-24.

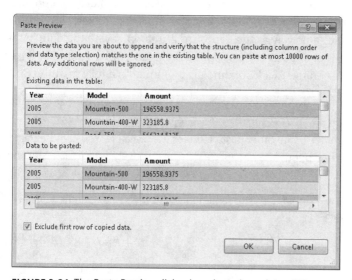

FIGURE 3-24 The Paste Preview dialog box shows how data will be merged.

After data is appended, the new table is saved in the model file and refreshed with the special data source.

 Note If you are interested in looking at how data is saved in the model file, you can open the source of the model, which is an XML file; you will find the data source definition and, later in the file, all the rows coming from the copied data. This technique works well with small amounts of data. Saving millions of rows of data in an XML format is definitely not a good idea.

Although this feature looks like a convenient way of pushing data inside a Tabular data model, there is no way, apart from manually editing the XML content of the project, to update this data later. Moreover, there is absolutely no way to understand, later on, the source of this set of data. Using this feature is not a good practice in a Tabular solution that must be deployed on a production server, because all the information about this data source is very well hidden inside the project. A much better solution is to perform the conversion from the Clipboard to a table when outside of SSDT, creating a table inside SQL Server (or Access if you want users to be able to update it easily) and then loading data inside Tabular from that table.

We strongly discourage any serious BI professional to use this feature, apart from prototyping, when it might be convenient to load data quickly inside the model to make some test. Nevertheless, Tabular prototyping is usually carried out by using PowerPivot for Excel, and there you might copy the content of the Clipboard inside an Excel table and then link it inside the model. Never confuse prototypes with production projects; in production, you must avoid any hidden information to save time later when you will probably need to update some information.

Loading from a Reporting Services Report

When you work for a company, you are likely to have many reports available to you. You might want to import part or all of the data of an existing report into your model. You might be tempted to import such data by copying it manually or by using copy and paste techniques. However, these methods mean that you always load the final output of the report and not the original data that has been used to make the calculations. Moreover, if you use the copy and paste technique, you often have to delete formatting values from the real data, such as separators, labels, and so on. In this way, building a model that can automatically refresh data extracted from another report is difficult, if not impossible, and most of the time you end up repeating the import process of copying data from your sources.

If you are using reports published by SQL Server Reporting Services 2008 R2 and later, SSAS can connect directly to the data the report uses. In this way, you have access to a more detailed data model, which can also be refreshed. Furthermore, you are not worried by the presence of separators or other decorative items that exist in the presentation of the report. You get only the data; in fact, you can use a report as a special type of data feed, a more general type of data source described in the next section. Because this is a particular case of data feed, there is a dedicated user interface to select data coming from a Reporting Services report.

Look at the report shown in Figure 3-25; the URL points to a sample Reporting Services report. (The URL can be different, depending on the installation of Reporting Services sample reports, which you can download from *http://msftrsprodsamples.codeplex.com/*.)

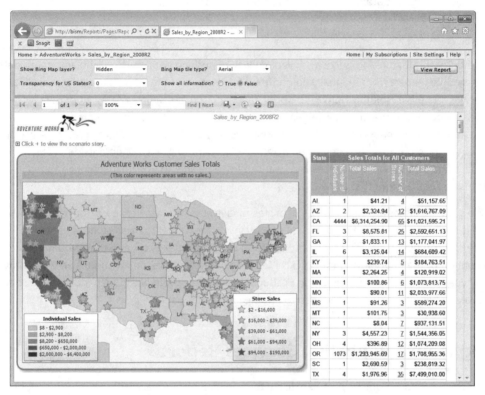

FIGURE 3-25 This report shows Sales By Region from Reporting Services 2008 R2.

This report shows the sales divided by region and by individual stores by using a chart and a table. If you click the Number Of Stores number of a state, the report scrolls down to the list of shops in the corresponding state so you see another table, not visible in Figure 3-25, which appears when you scroll down the report.

You can import data from a report inside SSDT by using the Report data source. The Table Import Wizard asks you for the Report Path, as you can see in Figure 3-26.

When you click the Browse button, you can choose the report to use, as shown in Figure 3-27.

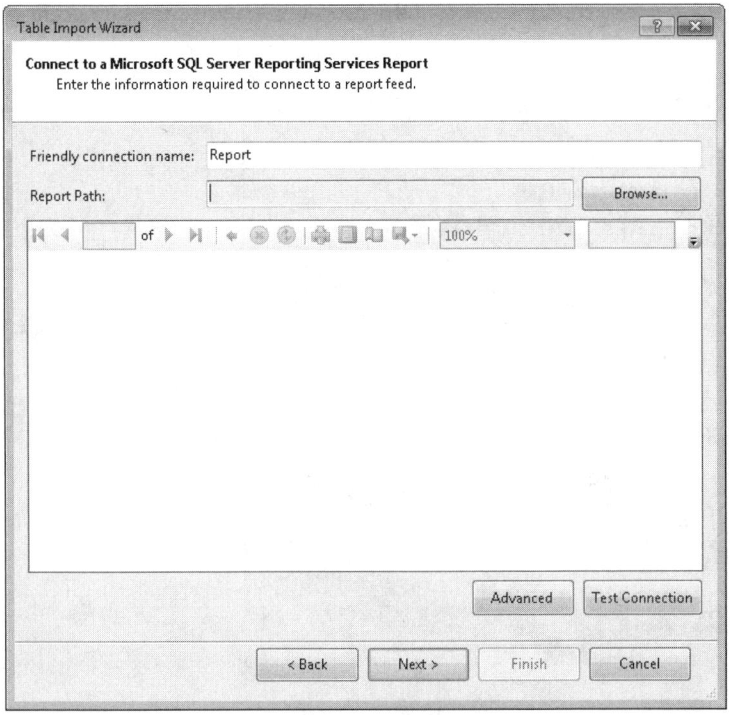

FIGURE 3-26 The Table Import Wizard is importing data from a report.

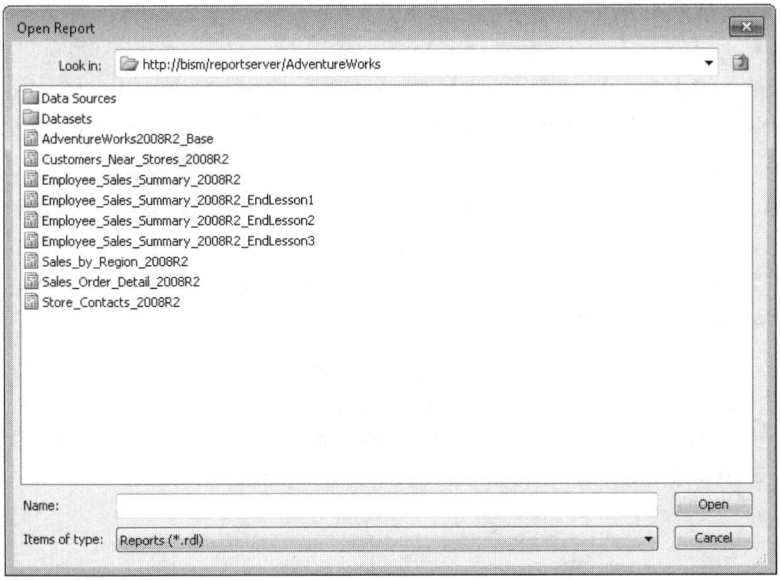

FIGURE 3-27 The Table Import Wizard shows the available reports on the server.

When you click Open, the selected report appears in the Table Import Wizard, as you can see in Figure 3-28.

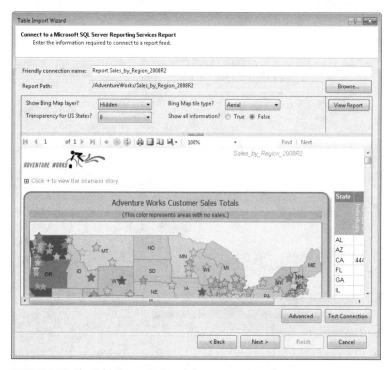

FIGURE 3-28 The Table Import Wizard shows a preview of a report.

You can just change the friendly connection name for this connection and then click Next to set up the impersonation options. Click Next again to choose which data table to import from the report, as you can see in Figure 3-29.

The report contains four data tables. The first two contain information about the graphical visualization of the map on the left side of the report. The other two are more interesting: Tablix1 is the source of the table on the right side, which contains sales divided by state, and tblMatrix_ StoresbyState contains the sales of each store for each state.

The first time you import data from a report, you might not know the content of each of the available data tables; in this case, you can use the preview features available in the Table Import Wizard or import everything and then remove all the tables and columns that do not contain useful data. You can see this in Figure 3-30, which shows the first few rows of the Tablix1 table.

FIGURE 3-29 Select tables to import from a data feed.

Note You can see in Figure 3-30 that the last two columns do not have meaningful names. These names depend on the discipline of the report author and, because they usually are internal names not visible in a report, it is common to have such nondescriptive names. In such cases, you should rename these columns before you use these numbers in your data model.

Distance	ShowBingMaps	BingMapTileType	USState.Transparency	ShowAll	StateProvinceCode	CustomerID	TotalDue	Textbox9	Textbox18
50	Hidden	Aerial	0	FALSE	AL	1	41.2055	4	51157.6464
50	Hidden	Aerial	0	FALSE	AZ	2	2324.9417	12	1616767.085
50	Hidden	Aerial	0	FALSE	CA	4444	6314254.9032	65	11021595.2057
50	Hidden	Aerial	0	FALSE	FL	3	8575.8053	25	2592651.1315
50	Hidden	Aerial	0	FALSE	GA	3	1833.1067	13	1177041.9682
50	Hidden	Aerial	0	FALSE	IL	6	3125.0391	14	684609.4209
50	Hidden	Aerial	0	FALSE	KY	1	239.7408	5	184763.5116

FIGURE 3-30 Here you can see some sample rows imported from the report.

Now that you have imported report data into the data model, each time you reprocess it, the report is queried again and updated data is imported to the selected tables, overriding previously imported data.

Loading Reports by Using Data Feeds

You have seen how to load data from a report by using the Table Import Wizard for the Report data source. There is another way to load data from a report, which is by using data feeds.

If you look at the report, as shown in Explorer using the web interface of Reporting Services, you will notice the Export To Data Feed icon that is highlighted in Figure 3-31. Click it, and your browser asks you whether to open or save a file with a name that has the .atomsvc extension.

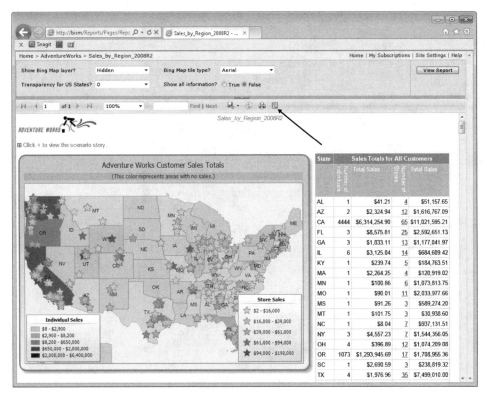

FIGURE 3-31 The Reporting Services web interface shows the Export To Data Feed icon.

Note The .atomsvc file contains technical information about the source data feeds. This file is a data service document in an XML format that specifies a connection to one or more data feeds.

If you choose to save this file, you get an .atomsvc file that can be used to load data inside Tabular by using the Data Feed data source. The Table Import Wizard for Data Feed asks you the URL of a data feed and, by clicking Browse, you can select the .atomsvc file downloaded, as you can see in Figure 3-32.

Click Next on this page to follow the same procedure you used when loading data from the report. In fact, the two connections work exactly the same way; it is up to you to choose the one that fits your needs best. Note that, after the .atomsvc file has been used to grab the metadata information, you can safely remove it from your computer because SSDT does not use it anymore.

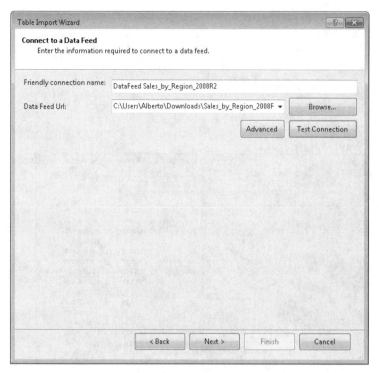

FIGURE 3-32 In the Table Import Wizard for Data Feeds, you must provide the path to the .atmosvc file.

Loading from a Data Feed

In the previous section, you saw how to load a data feed exported by Reporting Services in Tabular. In fact, Reporting Services makes data available to PowerPivot by exporting it as a data feed. However, this technique is not exclusive to Reporting Services and can be used to get data from many other services, including Internet sources that support the Open Data Protocol (see *www.odata.org* for more information) and data exported as a data feed by SharePoint 2010 and later, which is described in the next section.

The Table Import Wizard dialog box displayed in Figure 3-33 asks for the data feed URL. You saw this dialog box in Figure 3-32 when you were getting data from a report. This time, however, the Data Feed URL text box can be modified and does not have a fixed value provided by the report itself.

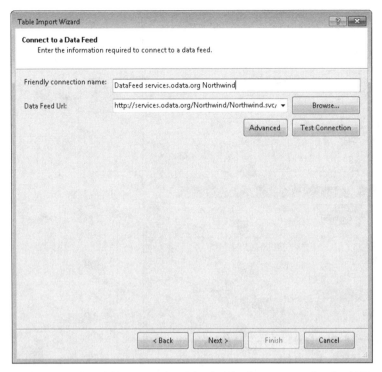

FIGURE 3-33 The Table Import Wizard for data feeds requests a data feed URL.

You can use the following URL to test this data source.

http://services.odata.org/Northwind/Northwind.svc/

After you click Next, you can select the tables to import (see Figure 3-34) and then follow a standard table-loading procedure.

After you click Finish, the selected tables are imported into the data model. This operation can take a long time when you have a high volume of data to import and the remote service providing data has a slow bandwidth.

FIGURE 3-34 You can select tables to load from a data feed URL.

Loading from SharePoint

SharePoint 2010 might contain several instances of data you would like to import into your data model. There is no specific data source dedicated to importing data from SharePoint. Depending on the type of data or the document you want to use, you must choose one of the methods already shown.

A list of the most common data sources you can import from SharePoint includes:

- **Report** A report generated by Reporting Services can be stored and displayed in SharePoint. In this case, you follow the same procedure described in the "Loading from a Reporting Services Report" section of this chapter by providing the report pathname or by using OData.

- **Excel workbook** You can import data from an Excel workbook saved in SharePoint the same way you would if it were saved on disk. You can refer to the "Loading from an Excel File" section of this chapter and use the path to the library that contains the Excel file that you want.

- **PowerPivot model embedded in an Excel workbook** If an Excel workbook contains a PowerPivot model and is published in a PowerPivot folder, you can choose to extract data from the model by querying it. To do that, you can follow the same steps described in the

"Loading from Analysis Services" section earlier in this chapter, with the only difference being that you use the complete path to the published Excel file instead of the name of an Analysis Services server. (You do not have a Browse help tool; you probably need to copy and paste the complete URL from a browser.)

- **SharePoint list**   Any data included in a SharePoint list can be exported as a data feed, so you can use the same instructions described in the preceding "Loading from a Reporting Services Report" and "Loading from a Data Feed" sections later in this chapter.

In Figure 3-35, you see an example of the user interface that enables you to export a SharePoint list as a data feed. The Export As Data Feed button is highlighted. When you click it, an .atomsvc file is downloaded and you see the same user interface previously shown for reports.

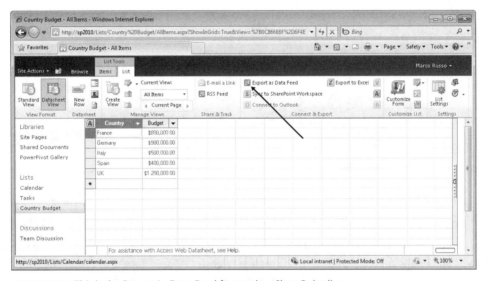

FIGURE 3-35 This is the Export As Data Feed feature in a SharePoint list.

Loading from the Windows Azure DataMarket

Another very powerful OData producer is the Windows Azure Marketplace. The Windows Azure Marketplace is an online market for buying and selling finished Software as a Service (SaaS) applications and premium datasets. On the Azure Marketplace, you can find both paid and free data sources that can be loaded inside your Tabular database to expand your analytics opportunities.

To browse the Azure Marketplace, you can go to *https://datamarket.azure.com*, where you must log on using a Windows Live account. You can browse many data sources without being logged on, but to subscribe to any data feed, you must log on and create an account key. You can also start to browse the Azure DataMarket by starting the Table Import Wizard using the Azure DataMarket data source, which opens the window shown in Figure 3-36.

FIGURE 3-36 You can use the Table Import Wizard to load data from the Azure DataMarket.

By using View Available Azure DataMarket Datasets, you can open the home page of the Azure DataMarket, from which you can search interesting datasets (see Figure 3-37).

An interesting available OData is DateStream, which provides a simple yet effective table containing dates and many interesting columns to create a calendar table in your data model. By clicking a data source, you get a description of the data source and, most important, the service root URL, which you can see in Figure 3-38 (bottom line).

To use a data feed, you must subscribe to it, and then you can copy the service root URL in the Table Import Wizard, shown in Figure 3-36. Finally, you must provide your service key (hidden in Figure 3-36).

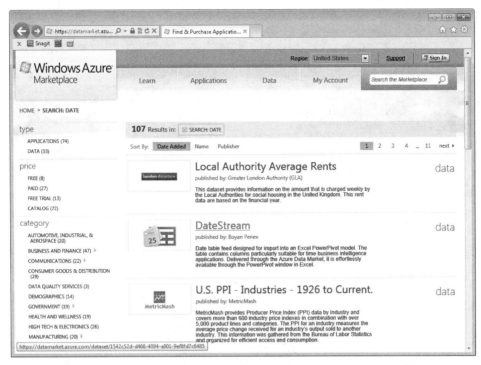

FIGURE 3-37 The home page of the Windows Azure DataMarket lists many sources of data.

FIGURE 3-38 The DateStream feed is available on the DataMarket.

Clicking Next gets the list of available tables, as you can see in Figure 3-39. From that point, the data-loading process is the same as for all other data sources, but each time the data source is refreshed, it will load data from the DataMarket.

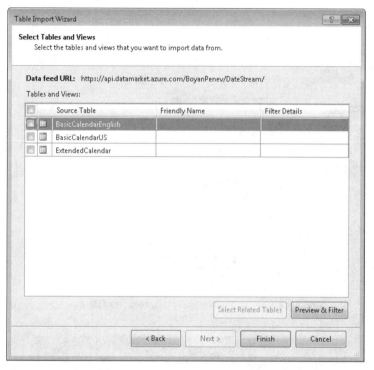

FIGURE 3-39 The Table Import Wizard shows some of the tables available for the DateStream data source.

 Warning Be aware that many of the sources on the DataMarket are not free, and refreshing the table means being charged the amount indicated in the data source page. It is a good idea to cache this data on SQL Server tables and then refresh a Tabular model from there to avoid paying high bills for the same data again and again.

Choosing the Right Data-Loading Method

SSDT makes many data sources available, each one with specific capabilities and scenarios of usage. Nevertheless, because the authors are seasoned BI professionals, we think it is important to warn our readers about some issues they can encounter during the development of a Tabular solution if they use all these data sources without carefully thinking about the consequences.

The problems with the Clipboard method of loading data were discussed earlier; the fact that it is not reproducible should discourage you from adopting it in a production environment. Nevertheless, other data sources should be used only with great care.

Whenever you develop a BI solution that must be processed by SSAS, you must use data sources that are:

- **Well typed**   Each column should have a data type clearly indicated by the source system. Relational databases normally provide this information, whereas other sources, such as CSV files, Excel workbooks, and the Clipboard, do not provide this kind of information. SSDT infers this information by analyzing the first few rows of data and takes them for granted, but it might be the case that later rows will contain different data types, and this will make the loading process fail.

- **Coherent**   The data types and the columns should not change over time. If you use, for example, an Excel workbook as the data source and let users freely update the workbook, you might encounter a situation in which the workbook contains wrong data or the user has moved one column before another one by editing the workbook. SSAS will crash, and the data loading will not be successful.

- **Time predictable**   Some data sources, such as the OData on the Windows Azure DataMarket, might take a very long time to execute, and this time varies depending on the network bandwidth available and problems with the Internet connection. This might make the processing time quite variable or create problems due to timeouts.

- **Verified**   If the user can freely update data, as is the case in Excel workbooks, wrong data might enter your Tabular data model and produce unpredictable results. Data entering Analysis Services should always be double-checked by some kind of software that ensures its correctness.

For these reasons, we discourage our readers from using these data sources:

- **Excel**   Not verified, not coherent, not well typed

- **Text file**   Not well typed

- **OData**   Not time predictable when data comes from the web

For all these kinds of data sources, a much better solution is to create some kind of extract, transform, and load (ETL) that loads data from these sources, cleans the data, and verifies that the data is valid and available and puts all the information inside SQL Server tables, from which you can feed the Tabular data model.

> ### Using DirectQuery Requires SQL Server as a Data Source
>
> Another excellent reason to use SQL Server to hold all the data that feeds your data model is that if data is stored inside SQL Server, you always have the freedom to activate DirectQuery mode, which is prevented if you decide to load data directly from the various data sources.

It is important always to remember that having the option to do something does not mean that you must do it. SSAS Tabular offers many options to load data, but, although we feel that all these options are relevant and important for PowerPivot for Excel or PowerPivot for SharePoint, we think that corporate BI, addressed by SSAS Tabular running in Server mode, has different needs, and you can avoid using these data sources.

We are not saying to avoid using these features; we are saying that you must use them with care, understanding the pros and cons of your choice.

Understanding Why Sorting Data Is Important

The last topic of this chapter is sorting. Although it might seem unusual to speak about sorting in a chapter about data loading, you learn that—for Tabular databases—sorting plays an important role when loading data.

As you learned in Chapter 2, Tabular uses the xVelocity (VertiPaq) technology to store data in a powerful and highly compressed columnar database. In xVelocity, the spaces used for each column depend on the number of distinct values of that column. If a column has only three values, it can be compressed to a few bits. If, however, the column has many values (as happens, for example, for identity values), then the space used will be much higher.

The exact application of this scenario is a bit more complicated than this. To reduce memory pressure, xVelocity does not load the whole table before starting to compress it. It processes the table in segments of eight million rows each. Thus, a table with 32 million rows is processed in four segments, each counting eight million rows.

For this reason, the number of distinct values is not to be counted for the whole table but for each segment. Each segment is processed and compressed individually. Smaller tables (up to eight million rows) will always fit a single segment, whereas bigger ones can span several segments.

Before processing a segment, xVelocity uses a highly sophisticated algorithm to find the best way to sort the rows so that similar ones appear near each other in the sequence. Improving homogeneity reduces the distribution of distinct values and greatly improves the compression of the segment, resulting in less memory usage and better performance during queries. Thus, sorting a segment is not useful because xVelocity reverts sorting due to its internal consideration.

Nevertheless, sorting the whole table, when it is bigger than a single segment, can reduce the number of distinct values for some columns inside a segment. (If, for example, you have a mean of four million rows for each date, sorting by date reduces the number of distinct dates to two for each segment.) A sorted table creates homogeneous segments that xVelocity can better compress. Both the size of the database and the query speed of the Tabular model benefit from this.

Because all these considerations apply to big tables, it is clear that a careful study of the best clustered index to use for the table is highly recommended because issuing an *ORDER BY* over a table by using keys that do not match the clustered index slows the processing due to SQL Server using the TempDB.

Summary

In this chapter, you were introduced to all of the various data-loading capabilities of Tabular. You can load data from many data sources, which enables you to integrate data from the different sources into a single, coherent view of the information you must analyze.

The main topics you must remember are:

- **Impersonation**   SSAS can impersonate a user when opening a data source, whereas SSDT always uses the credentials of the current user. This can lead to server-side and client-side operations that can use different accounts for impersonation.

- **Working with big tables**   Whenever you are working with big tables, because data need to be loaded in the workspace database, you must limit the number of rows SSDT reads and processes in the workspace database so that you can work safely with your solution.

- **Data sources**   There are many data sources to connect to different databases; choosing the right one depends on your source of data. That said, if you must use one of the discouraged sources, remember that storing data in SQL Server before moving it into Tabular permits data quality control, data cleansing, and more predictable performances.

- **Sorting**   Data can be sorted outside SSAS to provide homogeneous chunks of data to SSAS when it processes the table. This reduces the memory footprint of the project and query execution time.

CHAPTER 4

DAX Basics

Now that you have seen the basics of SQL Server Analysis Services (SSAS) Tabular, it is time to learn the fundamentals of Data Analysis Expressions (DAX) expressions. DAX has its own syntax for defining calculation expressions; it is somewhat similar to a Microsoft Excel expression, but it has specific functions that enable you to create more advanced calculations on data stored in multiple tables.

Understanding Calculation in DAX

Any calculation in DAX begins with the equal sign, which resembles the Excel syntax. Nevertheless, the DAX language is very different from Excel because DAX does not support the concept of cells and ranges as Excel does; to use DAX efficiently, you must learn to work with columns and tables, which are the fundamental objects in the Tabular world.

Before you learn how to express complex formulas, you must master the basics of DAX, which include the syntax, the different data types that DAX can handle, the basic operators, and how to refer to columns and tables. In the next few sections, we introduce these concepts.

DAX Syntax

A relatively simple way to understand how DAX syntax works is to start with an example. Suppose you have loaded the FactInternetSales table in a Tabular project. In Figure 4-1, you can see some of its columns.

FIGURE 4-1 Here you can see the FactInternetSales table in a Tabular project.

You now use this data to calculate the margin, subtracting the TotalProductCost from the SalesAmount, and you use the technique already learned in Chapter 2, "Getting Started with the Tabular Model," to create calculated columns. To do that, you must write the following DAX formula in a new calculated column, which you can call *GrossMargin*.

```
= FactInternetSales[SalesAmount] - FactInternetSales[TotalProductCost]
```

This new formula is repeated automatically for all the rows of the table, resulting in a new column in the table. In this example, you are using a DAX expression to define a calculated column. You can see the resulting column in Figure 4-2. (Later, you see that DAX is used also to define measures.)

FIGURE 4-2 The *GrossMargin* calculated column has been added to the table.

This DAX expression handles numeric values and returns a numeric value. DAX can work with data types other than numbers. In the next section, you learn the different data types available in DAX and how to work with them.

DAX Data Types

DAX can compute values for seven data types:

- *Integer*

- *Real*

- *Currency*

- *Date (datetime)*

- *TRUE/FALSE (Boolean)*

- *String*

- *BLOB* (binary large object)

DAX has a powerful type-handling system so that you do not have to worry much about data types. When you write a DAX expression, the resulting type is based on the type of the terms used in the expression and on the operator used. Type conversion happens automatically during the expression evaluation.

Be aware of this behavior in case the type returned from a DAX expression is not the expected one; in such a case, you must investigate the data type of the terms used in the expression. For example, if one of the terms of a sum is a date, the result is a date, too. However, if the data type is an integer, the result is an integer. This is known as operator overloading, and you can see an example of its behavior in Figure 4-3, in which the *OrderDatePlusOne* column is calculated by adding 1 to the value in the *OrderDate* column, by using the following formula.

```
= FactInternetSales[OrderDate] + 1
```

The result is a date because the *OrderDate* column is of the *date* data type.

TotalProductCost	SalesAmount	GrossMargin	TaxAmt	Freight	OrderDate	OrderDatePlusOne
$1.87	$4.99	$3.12	$0.40	$0.12	7/1/2003 12:00:00 AM	7/2/2003 12:00:00 AM
$1.87	$4.99	$3.12	$0.40	$0.12	7/1/2003 12:00:00 AM	7/2/2003 12:00:00 AM
$1.87	$4.99	$3.12	$0.40	$0.12	7/2/2003 12:00:00 AM	7/3/2003 12:00:00 AM
$1.87	$4.99	$3.12	$0.40	$0.12	7/2/2003 12:00:00 AM	7/3/2003 12:00:00 AM
$1.87	$4.99	$3.12	$0.40	$0.12	7/2/2003 12:00:00 AM	7/3/2003 12:00:00 AM
$1.87	$4.99	$3.12	$0.40	$0.12	7/2/2003 12:00:00 AM	7/3/2003 12:00:00 AM
$1.87	$4.99	$3.12	$0.40	$0.12	7/2/2003 12:00:00 AM	7/3/2003 12:00:00 AM
$1.87	$4.99	$3.12	$0.40	$0.12	7/3/2003 12:00:00 AM	7/4/2003 12:00:00 AM
$1.87	$4.99	$3.12	$0.40	$0.12	7/3/2003 12:00:00 AM	7/4/2003 12:00:00 AM
$1.87	$4.99	$3.12	$0.40	$0.12	7/3/2003 12:00:00 AM	7/4/2003 12:00:00 AM
$1.87	$4.99	$3.12	$0.40	$0.12	7/3/2003 12:00:00 AM	7/4/2003 12:00:00 AM

FIGURE 4-3 Adding an integer to a date results in a date increased by the corresponding number of days.

In addition to operator overloading, DAX automatically converts strings into numbers and numbers into strings whenever it is required by the operator. For example, if you use the & operator, which concatenates strings, DAX automatically converts its arguments into strings. If you look at the formula

```
= 5 & 4
```

it returns a "54" string result. However, the formula

```
= "5" + "4"
```

returns an integer result with the value of 9.

As you have seen, the resulting value depends on the operator and not on the source columns, which are converted following the requirements of the operator. Even if this behavior is convenient, later in this chapter you see the types of errors that might occur during these automatic conversions.

Date Data Type

PowerPivot stores dates in a *datetime* data type. This format uses a floating point number internally, wherein the integer corresponds to the number of days (starting from December 30, 1899), and the decimal identifies the fraction of the day. (Hours, minutes, and seconds are converted to decimal fractions of a day.) Thus, the expression

```
= NOW() + 1
```

increases a date by one day (exactly 24 hours), returning the date of tomorrow at the same hour/minute/second of the execution of the expression itself. If you must take only the date part of a *DATETIME*, always remember to use *TRUNC* to get rid of the decimal part.

DAX Operators

You have seen the importance of operators in determining the type of an expression; you can now see, in Table 4-1, a list of the operators available in DAX.

TABLE 4-1 Operators

Operator Type	Symbol	Use	Example
Parenthesis	( )	Precedence order and grouping of arguments	(5 + 2) * 3
Arithmetic	+ - * /	Addition Subtraction/negation Multiplication Division	4 + 2 5 − 3 4 * 2 4 / 2
Comparison	= <> > >= < <=	Equal to Not equal to Greater than Greater than or equal to Less than Less than or equal to	[Country] = "USA" [Country] <> "USA" [Quantity] > 0 [Quantity] >= 100 [Quantity] < 0 [Quantity] <= 100
Text concatenation	&	Concatenation of strings	"Value is " & [Amount]
Logical	&& || !	AND condition between two Boolean expressions OR condition between two Boolean expressions NOT operator on the Boolean expression that follows	[Country] = "USA" && [Quantity] > 0 [Country] = "USA" || [Quantity] > 0 ! ([Country] = "USA")

Moreover, the logical operators are available also as DAX functions, with syntax very similar to Excel syntax. For example, you can write these conditions

```
AND( [Country] = "USA", [Quantity] > 0 )
OR( [Country] = "USA", [Quantity] > 0 )
NOT( [Country] = "USA" )
```

that correspond, respectively, to

```
[Country] = "USA" && [Quantity] > 0
[Country] = "USA" || [Quantity] > 0
!( [Country] = "USA" )
```

DAX Values

You have already seen that you can use a value directly in a formula, for example, USA or 0, as previously mentioned. When such values are used directly in formulas, they are called literals and, although using literals is straightforward, the syntax for referencing a column needs some attention. Here is the basic syntax.

```
'Table Name'[Column Name]
```

The table name can be enclosed in single quote characters. Most of the time, quotes can be omitted if the name does not contain any special characters such as spaces. In the following formula, for example, the quotes can be omitted.

```
TableName[Column Name]
```

The column name, however, must always be enclosed in square brackets. Note that the table name is optional. If the table name is omitted, the column name is searched in the current table, which is the one to which the calculated column or measure belongs. However, we strongly suggest that you always specify the complete name (table and column) when you reference a column to avoid any confusion.

Understanding Calculated Columns and Measures

Now that you know the basics of DAX syntax, you must learn one of the most important concepts in DAX: the difference between calculated columns and measures. Even though they might appear similar at first sight because you can make some calculations both ways, you must use measures to implement the most flexible calculations. This is a key to unlock the true power of DAX.

Calculated Columns

If you want to create a calculated column, you can move to the last column of the table, which is named *Add Column*, and start writing the formula. The DAX expression must be inserted into the formula bar, and Microsoft IntelliSense helps you during the writing of the expression.

A calculated column is just like any other column in a Tabular table and can be used in rows, columns, filters, or values of a Microsoft PivotTable. The DAX expression defined for a calculated column operates in the context of the current row of the table to which it belongs. Any reference to a column returns the value of that column for the row it is in. You cannot access the values of other rows directly.

> **Note** As you see later, there are DAX functions that aggregate the value of a column for the whole table. The only way to get the value of a subset of rows is to use DAX functions that return a table and then operate on it. In this way, you aggregate column values for a range of rows and possibly operating on a different row by filtering a table made of only one row. More on this topic is in Chapter 5, "Understanding Evaluation Context."

One important concept that must be well understood about calculated columns is that they are computed during the Tabular database processing and then stored in the database, just as any other column. This might seem strange if you are accustomed to SQL-computed columns, which are computed at query time and do not waste space. In Tabular, however, all calculated columns occupy space in memory and are computed once during table processing.

This behavior is handy whenever you create very complex calculated columns. The time required to compute them is always process time and not query time, resulting in a better user experience. Nevertheless, you must always remember that a calculated column uses precious RAM. If, for example, you have a complex formula for a calculated column, you might be tempted to separate the steps of computation into different intermediate columns. Although this technique is useful during project development, it is a bad habit in production because each intermediate calculation is stored in RAM and wastes space.

Measures

You have already seen in Chapter 2 how to create a measure by using the measure grid; now you learn the difference between a calculated column and a measure to understand when to use which one.

Calculated columns are easy to create and use. You have already seen in Figure 4-2 how to define the *GrossMargin* column to compute the amount of the gross margin.

```
[GrossMargin] = FactInternetSales[SalesAmount] - FactInternetSales[TotalProductCost]
```

But what happens if you want to show the gross margin as a percentage of the sales amount? You could create a calculated column with the following formula.

```
[GrossMarginPerc] = FactInternetSales[GrossMargin] / FactInternetSales[SalesAmount]
```

This formula computes the right value at the row level, as you can see in Figure 4-4.

OrderQuantity	UnitPrice	ExtendedAmount	ProductStandardCost	TotalProductCost	SalesAmount	GrossMargin	GrossMarginPerc
1	$4.99	$4.99	$1.87	$1.87	$4.99	$3.12	62.60 %
1	$4.99	$4.99	$1.87	$1.87	$4.99	$3.12	62.60 %
1	$4.99	$4.99	$1.87	$1.87	$4.99	$3.12	62.60 %
1	$4.99	$4.99	$1.87	$1.87	$4.99	$3.12	62.60 %
1	$4.99	$4.99	$1.87	$1.87	$4.99	$3.12	62.60 %
1	$4.99	$4.99	$1.87	$1.87	$4.99	$3.12	62.60 %
1	$4.99	$4.99	$1.87	$1.87	$4.99	$3.12	62.60 %
1	$4.99	$4.99	$1.87	$1.87	$4.99	$3.12	62.60 %
1	$4.99	$4.99	$1.87	$1.87	$4.99	$3.12	62.60 %

FIGURE 4-4 The *GrossMarginPerc* column shows the Gross Margin as a percentage, calculated row by row.

Nevertheless, when you compute the aggregate value, you cannot rely on calculated columns. In fact, the aggregate value is computed as the sum of gross margin divided by the sum of sales amount. Thus, the ratio must be computed on the aggregates; you cannot use an aggregation of calculated columns. In other words, you compute the ratio of the sum, not the sum of the ratio.

The correct formula for the *GrossMarginPerc* is as follows.

```
= SUM( FactInternetSales[GrossMargin] ) / SUM( FactInternetSales[SalesAmount] )
```

But, as already stated, you cannot enter it into a calculated column. If you need to operate on aggregate values instead of on a row-by-row basis, you must create measures, which is the topic of the current section.

Measures and calculated columns both use DAX expressions; the difference is the context of evaluation. A measure is evaluated in the context of the cell of the pivot table or DAX query, whereas a calculated column is evaluated at the row level of the table to which it belongs. The context of the cell (later in the book, you learn that this is a filter context) depends on the user selections on the pivot table or on the shape of the DAX query. When you use *SUM([SalesAmount])* in a measure, you mean the sum of all the cells that are aggregated under this cell, whereas when you use *[SalesAmount]* in a calculated column, you mean the value of the *SalesAmount* column in this row.

When you create a measure, you can define a value that changes according to the filter that the user applies on a pivot table. In this way, you can solve the problem of calculating the gross margin percentage. To define a measure, you can click anywhere inside the measure grid and write the following measure formula by using the assignment operator :=:.

```
GrossMarginPct := SUM( FactInternetSales[Gross Margin] ) / SUM( FactInternetSales[SalesAmount] )
```

You can see the formula bar in Figure 4-5.

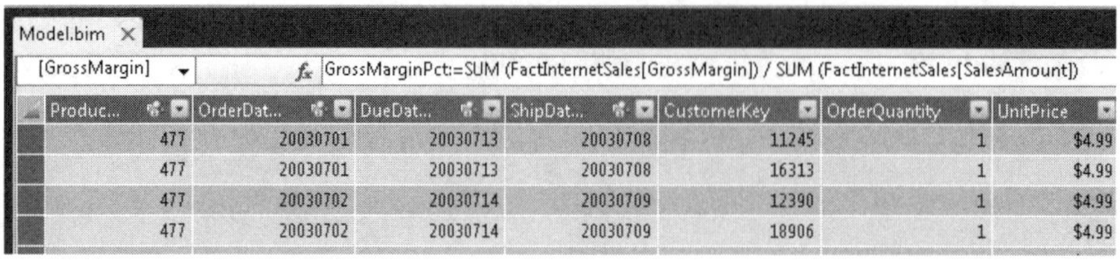

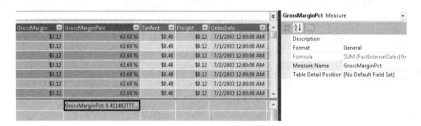

Model.bim
[GrossMargin]
GrossMarginPct:=SUM (FactInternetSales[GrossMargin]) / SUM (FactInternetSales[SalesAmount])
Produc... OrderDat... DueDat... ShipDat... CustomerKey OrderQuantity UnitPrice
477 20030701 20030713 20030708 11245 1 $4.99
477 20030701 20030713 20030708 16313 1 $4.99
477 20030702 20030714 20030709 12390 1 $4.99
477 20030702 20030714 20030709 18906 1 $4.99

FIGURE 4-5 You can create measures in the formula bar.

After the measure is created, it is visible in the measure grid, as you can see in Figure 4-6.

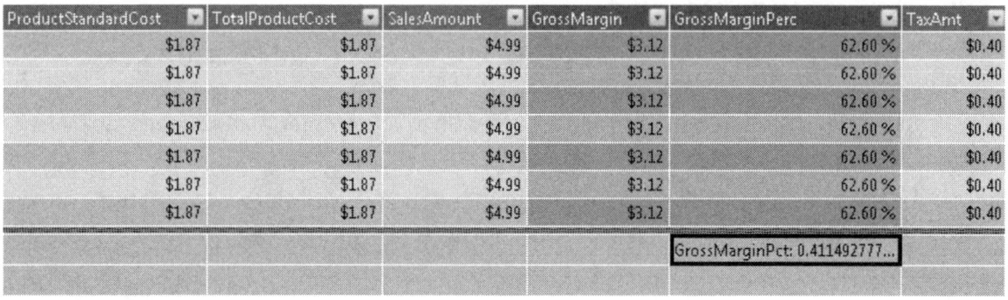

ProductStandardCost TotalProductCost SalesAmount GrossMargin GrossMarginPerc TaxAmt
$1.87 $1.87 $4.99 $3.12 62.60 % $0.40
$1.87 $1.87 $4.99 $3.12 62.60 % $0.40
$1.87 $1.87 $4.99 $3.12 62.60 % $0.40
$1.87 $1.87 $4.99 $3.12 62.60 % $0.40
$1.87 $1.87 $4.99 $3.12 62.60 % $0.40
$1.87 $1.87 $4.99 $3.12 62.60 % $0.40
$1.87 $1.87 $4.99 $3.12 62.60 % $0.40
GrossMarginPct: 0.411492777...

FIGURE 4-6 Measures are shown in the measure grid.

A few interesting things about measures are shown in the measure grid. First, the value shown is dynamically computed and takes filters into account. Thus, the value 0.41149... is the gross margin in percentage for all *AdventureWorks* sales. If you apply a filter to some columns, the value will be updated accordingly.

You can move the measure anywhere in the measure grid by using the technique of cut and paste. To move the measure, cut it and paste it somewhere else. Copy and paste also works if you want to make a copy of a formula and reuse the code.

Measures have more properties that cannot be set in the formula. They must be set in the Properties window. In Figure 4-7, you can see the Properties window for the example measure.

GrossMargin GrossMarginPerc TaxAmt Freight OrderDate
$3.12 62.60 % $0.40 $0.12 7/1/2003 12:00:00 AM
$3.12 62.60 % $0.40 $0.12 7/1/2003 12:00:00 AM
$3.12 62.60 % $0.40 $0.12 7/2/2003 12:00:00 AM
$3.12 62.60 % $0.40 $0.12 7/2/2003 12:00:00 AM
$3.12 62.60 % $0.40 $0.12 7/2/2003 12:00:00 AM
$3.12 62.60 % $0.40 $0.12 7/2/2003 12:00:00 AM
$3.12 62.60 % $0.40 $0.12 7/2/2003 12:00:00 AM
GrossMarginPct: 0.411492777...
GrossMarginPct Measure
Description
Format General
Formula SUM (FactInternetSales[Gr
Measure Name GrossMarginPct
Table Detail Position [No Default Field Set]

FIGURE 4-7 Measures properties are set in the Properties window.

The Properties window is dynamically updated based on the format of the measure. In Figure 4-7, you can see that the default format for a measure is General. The General format does not have any formatting property. Because you want to format the measure as a percentage (0.41149 really means

41.15%), change the format to Percentage. The updated Properties window (see Figure 4-8) now shows the number of decimal places among the properties of the measure.

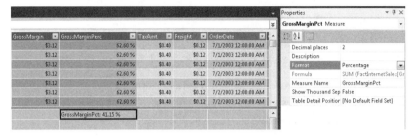

FIGURE 4-8 The properties of a measure are updated dynamically based on the format.

Editing Measures by Using DAX Editor

Simple measures can be easily authored by using the formula bar, but, as soon as the measures start to become more complex, using the formula bar is no longer a viable option. Unfortunately, SQL Server Data Tools (SSDT) does not have any advanced editor in its default configuration.

As luck would have it, a team of experts has developed DAX Editor, a Microsoft Visual Studio add-in that greatly helps in measure authoring. You can download the project from CodePlex at *http://daxeditor.codeplex.com*.

DAX Editor supports IntelliSense and automatic measure formatting and enables you to author all the measures in a project by using a single script view, which is convenient for developers. In addition, DAX Editor enables you to add comments to all your measures, resulting in a self-documented script that will make your life easier when maintaining the code.

In Figure 4-9, you can see the DAX Editor window with a couple of measures and some comments.

```
Model.dax X  Model.bim

-----------------------------------------------------------------
-- PowerPivot measures command (do not modify manually) --
-----------------------------------------------------------------


--
-- Gross Margin as a percentage of SalesAmount
--
CREATE MEASURE 'FactInternetSales'[GrossMarginPct] =
    SUM (FactInternetSales[GrossMargin]) / SUM (FactInternetSales[SalesAmount]);
--
-- Sum of SalesAmount
--
CREATE MEASURE 'FactInternetSales'[SumOfSalesAmount] =
    SUM (FactInternetSales[SalesAmount]);
```

FIGURE 4-9 DAX Editor has syntax highlighting and many useful functions to author DAX code.

We do not want to provide here a detailed description of this add-in, which, being on CodePlex, will be changed and maintained by independent coders, but we strongly suggest that you download and install the add-in. Regardless of whether your measures are simple or complex, your authoring experience will be a much better one.

Choosing Between Calculated Columns and Measures

Now that you have seen the difference between calculated columns and measures, you might be wondering when to use calculated columns and when to use measures. Sometimes either is an option, but in most situations, your computation needs determine your choice.

You must define a calculated column whenever you intend to do the following:

- Place the calculated results in an Excel slicer or see results in rows or columns in a pivot table (as opposed to the Values area).

- Define an expression that is strictly bound to the current row. (For example, *Price * Quantity* must be computed before other aggregations take place.)

- Categorize text or numbers (for example, a range of values for a measure, a range of ages of customers, such as 0–18, 18–25, and so on).

However, you must define a measure whenever you intend to display resulting calculation values that reflect pivot table selections made by the user and see them in the Values area of pivot tables, for example:

- When you calculate profit percentage of a pivot table selection

- When you calculate ratios of a product compared to all products but filter by both year and region

Some calculations can be achieved by using calculated columns or measures, even if different DAX expressions must be used in these cases. For example, you can define *GrossMargin* as a calculated column.

```
= FactInternetSales[SalesAmount] - FactInternetSales[TotalProductCost]
```

It can also be defined as a measure.

```
= SUM( FactInternetSales[SalesAmount] ) - SUM( FactInternetSales[TotalProductCost] )
```

The final result is the same. We suggest you favor the measure in this case because it does not consume memory and disk space, but this is important only in large datasets. When the size of the database is not an issue, you can use the method with which you are more comfortable.

Handling Errors in DAX Expressions

Now that you have seen some basic formulas, you learn how to handle invalid calculations gracefully if they happen. A DAX expression might contain invalid calculations because the data it references is not valid for the formula. For example, you might have a division by zero or a column value that is not a number but is used in an arithmetic operation, such as multiplication. You must learn how these errors are handled by default and how to intercept these conditions if you want some special handling.

Before you learn how to handle errors, the following list describes the different kinds of errors that might appear during a DAX formula evaluation. They are:

- Conversion errors

- Arithmetical operations errors

- Empty or missing values

The following sections explain them in more detail.

Conversion Errors

The first kind of error is the conversion error. As you have seen before in this chapter, DAX values are automatically converted between strings and numbers whenever the operator requires it. To review the concept with examples, all these are valid DAX expressions.

```
"10" + 32 = 42
"10" & 32 = "1032"
10 & 32 = "1032"
DATE(2010,3,25) = 3/25/2010
DATE(2010,3,25) + 14 = 4/8/2010
DATE(2010,3,25) & 14 = "3/25/201014"
```

These formulas are always correct because they operate with constant values. What about the following expression?

```
SalesOrders[VatCode] + 100
```

Because the first operator of this sum is obtained by a column (which, in this case, is a text column), you must be sure that all the values in that column are numbers to determine whether they will be converted and the expression will be evaluated correctly. If some of the content cannot be converted to suit the operator needs, you will incur a conversion error. Here are typical situations.

```
"1 + 1" + 0 = Cannot convert value '1+1' of type string to type real
```

```
DATEVALUE("25/14/2010")  = Type mismatch
```

To avoid these errors, you must write more complex DAX expressions that contain error detection logic to intercept error conditions and always return a meaningful result.

Arithmetical Operation Errors

The second category of errors is arithmetical operations, such as division by zero or the square root of a negative number. These kinds of errors are not related to conversion; they are raised whenever you try to call a function or use an operator with invalid values.

Division by zero, in DAX, requires special handling because it behaves in a way that is not very intuitive (except for mathematicians). When you divide a number by zero, DAX usually returns the special value Infinity. Moreover, in the very special cases of 0 divided by 0 or Infinity divided by Infinity, DAX returns the special *NaN* (not a number) value. These results are summarized in Table 4-2.

TABLE 4-2 Special Result Values for Division by Zero

Expression	Result
10 / 0	Infinity
-7 / 0	-Infinity
0 / 0	Infinity
(10 / 0) / (7 / 0)	NaN

Note that *Infinity* and *NaN* are not errors but special values in DAX. In fact, if you divide a number by Infinity, the expression does not generate an error but returns 0.

```
9954 / (7 / 0) = 0
```

Apart from this special situation, arithmetical errors might be returned when calling a DAX function with a wrong parameter, such as the square root of a negative number.

```
SQRT( -1 ) = An argument of function 'SQRT' has the wrong data type or the result is too large
or too small
```

If DAX detects errors like this, it blocks any further computation of the expression and raises an error. You can use the special *ISERROR* function to check whether an expression leads to an error, something that you use later in this chapter. Finally, even if special values such as *NaN* are displayed correctly in the SSDT window, they show as errors in an Excel PivotTable, and they will be detected as errors by the error detection functions.

Empty or Missing Values

The third category of errors is not a specific error condition but the presence of empty values, which might result in unexpected results or calculation errors.

DAX handles missing values, blank values, or empty cells by a special value called *BLANK*. *BLANK* is not a real value but a special way to identify these conditions. It is the equivalent of *NULL* in SSAS Multidimensional. The value *BLANK* can be obtained in a DAX expression by calling the *BLANK* function, which is different from an empty string. For example, the following expression always returns a blank value.

```
= BLANK()
```

On its own, this expression is useless, but the *BLANK* function itself becomes useful every time you want to return or check for an empty value. For example, you might want to display an empty cell instead of 0, as in the following expression, which calculates the total discount for a sale transaction, leaving the cell blank if the discount is 0.

```
= IF( Sales[DiscountPerc] = 0, BLANK(), Sales[DiscountPerc] * Sales[Amount] )
```

If a DAX expression contains a blank, it is not considered an error—it is considered an empty value. So an expression containing a blank might return a value or a blank, depending on the calculation required. For example, the following expression

```
= 10 * Sales[Amount]
```

returns *BLANK* whenever *Sales[Amount]* is *BLANK*. In other words, the result of an arithmetic product is *BLANK* whenever one or both terms are *BLANK*. This propagation of *BLANK* in a DAX expression happens in several other arithmetical and logical operations, as you can see in the following examples.

```
BLANK() + BLANK()      = BLANK()
10 * BLANK()           = BLANK()
BLANK() / 3            = BLANK()
BLANK() / BLANK()      = BLANK()
BLANK() || BLANK()     = BLANK()
BLANK() && BLANK()     = BLANK()
```

However, the propagation of *BLANK* in the result of an expression does not happen for all formulas. Some calculations do not propagate *BLANK* but return a value depending on the other terms of the formula. Examples of these are addition, subtraction, division by *BLANK*, and a logical operation between a blank and a valid value. In the following expressions, you can see some examples of these conditions along with their results.

```
BLANK() - 10           = -10
18 + BLANK()           = 18
4 / BLANK()            = Infinity
0 / BLANK()            = NaN
FALSE() || BLANK()     = FALSE
FALSE() && BLANK()     = FALSE
TRUE() || BLANK()      = TRUE
TRUE() && BLANK()      = FALSE
BLANK() = 0            = TRUE
```

Understanding the behavior of empty or missing values in a DAX expression and using *BLANK()* to return an empty cell in a calculated column or in a measure are important skills to control the results of a DAX expression. You can often use *BLANK()* as a result when you detect wrong values or other errors, as you learn in the next section.

Intercepting Errors

Now that you have seen the various kinds of errors that can occur, you can learn a technique to intercept errors and correct them or, at least, show an error message with some meaningful information. The presence of errors in a DAX expression frequently depends on the value contained in tables and columns referenced in the expression itself, so you might want to control the presence of these error conditions and return an error message. The standard technique is to check whether an expression returns an error and, if so, replace the error with a message or a default value. A few DAX functions have been designed for this.

The first of them is the *IFERROR* function, which is very similar to the *IF* function, but instead of evaluating a *TRUE/FALSE* condition, it checks whether an expression returns an error. You can see two typical uses of the *IFERROR* function here.

```
= IFERROR( Sales[Quantity] * Sales[Price], BLANK() )
= IFERROR( SQRT( Test[Omega] ), BLANK() )
```

In the first expression, if either *Sales[Quantity]* or *Sales[Price]* are strings that cannot be converted into a number, the returned expression is *BLANK*; otherwise the product of *Quantity* and *Price* is returned.

In the second expression, the result is *BLANK* every time the *Test[Omega]* column contains a negative number.

When you use *IFERROR* this way, you follow a more general pattern that requires the use of *ISERROR* and *IF*. The following expressions are functionally equivalent to the previous ones, but the usage of *IFERROR* in the previous ones makes them shorter and easier to understand.

```
= IF( ISERROR( Sales[Quantity] * Sales[Price] ), BLANK(), Sales[Quantity] * Sales[Price] )
= IF( ISERROR( SQRT( Test[Omega] ) ), BLANK(), SQRT( Test[Omega] ) )
```

You should use *IFERROR* whenever the expression that has to be returned is the same as that tested for an error; you do not have to duplicate the expression, and the resulting formula is more readable and safer in case of future changes. You should use *IF*, however, when you want to return the result of a different expression when there is an error.

For example, the *ISNUMBER* function can detect whether a string (the price in the first line) can be converted to a number and, if it can, calculate the total amount; otherwise, a *BLANK* can be returned.

```
= IF( ISNUMBER( Sales[Price] ), Sales[Quantity] * Sales[Price], BLANK() )
= IF( Test[Omega] >= 0, SQRT( Test[Omega] ), BLANK() )
```

The second example detects whether the argument for *SQRT* is valid, calculating the square root only for positive numbers and returning *BLANK* for negative ones.

A particular case is the test against an empty value, which is called *BLANK* in DAX. The *ISBLANK* function detects an empty value condition, returning *TRUE* if the argument is *BLANK*. This is especially important when a missing value has a meaning different from a value set to 0. In the following example, you calculate the cost of shipping for a sales transaction by using a default shipping cost for the product if the weight is not specified in the sales transaction itself.

```
= IF( ISBLANK( Sales[Weight] ),
      RELATED( Product[DefaultShippingCost] ),
      Sales[Weight] * Sales[ShippingPrice] )
```

If you had just multiplied product weight and shipping price, you would have an empty cost for all the sales transactions with missing weight data.

Common DAX Functions

Now that you have seen the fundamentals of DAX and how to handle error conditions, take a brief tour through the most commonly used functions and expressions of DAX. In this section, we show the syntax and the meaning of various functions. In the next section, we show how to create a useful report by using these basic functions.

Aggregate Functions

Almost every Tabular data model must operate on aggregated data. DAX offers a set of functions that aggregate the values of a column in a table and return a single value. We call this group of functions *aggregate functions*. For example, the expression

```
= SUM( Sales[Amount] )
```

calculates the sum of all the numbers in the *Amount* column of the Sales table. This expression aggregates all the rows of the Sales table if it is used in a calculated column, but it considers only the rows that are filtered by slicers, rows, columns, and filter conditions in a pivot table whenever it is used in a measure.

In Table A-1 of the Appendix, you can see the complete list of aggregated functions available in DAX. The four main aggregation functions (*SUM*, *AVERAGE*, *MIN*, and *MAX*) operate on only numeric values. These functions work only if the column passed as argument is of numeric or date type.

DAX offers an alternative syntax to these functions to make the calculation on columns that can contain both numeric and nonnumeric values such as a text column. That syntax adds the suffix A to the name of the function, just to get the same name and behavior as Excel. However, these functions are useful for only columns containing *TRUE/FALSE* values because *TRUE* is evaluated as 1 and *FALSE* as 0. Any value for a text column is always considered 0. Empty cells are never considered in the calculation, so even if these functions can be used on nonnumeric columns without returning an error, there is no automatic conversion to numbers for text columns. These functions are named *AVERAGEA*, *COUNTA*, *MINA*, and *MAXA*.

The only interesting function in the group of A-suffixed functions is *COUNTA*. It returns the number of cells that are not empty and works on any type of column. If you are interested in counting all the cells in a column containing an empty value, you can use the *COUNTBLANK* function. Finally, if you want to count all the cells of a column regardless of their content, you want to count the number of rows of the table, which can be obtained by calling the *COUNTROWS* function. (It gets a table as a parameter, not a column.) In other words, the sum of *COUNTA* and *COUNTBLANK* for the same column of a table is always equal to the number of rows of the same table.

You have four functions by which to count the number of elements in a column or table:

- *COUNT* operates only on numeric columns.

- *COUNTA* operates on any type of columns.

- *COUNTBLANK* returns the number of empty cells in a column.

- *COUNTROWS* returns the number of rows in a table.

Finally, the last set of aggregation functions performs calculations at the row level before they are aggregated. This is essentially the same as creating a column calculation and a measure calculation in one formula. This set of functions is quite useful, especially when you want to make calculations by using columns of different related tables. For example, if a Sales table contains all the sales transactions and a related Product table contains all the information about a product, including its cost, you might calculate the total internal cost of a sales transaction by defining a measure with this expression.

```
Cost := SUMX( Sales, Sales[Quantity] * RELATED( Product[StandardCost] ) )
```

This function calculates the product of *Quantity* (from the Sales table) and *StandardCost* of the sold product (from the related Product table) for each row in the Sales table, and it returns the sum of all these calculated values.

Generally speaking, all the aggregation functions ending with an X suffix behave this way: they calculate an expression (the second parameter) for each of the rows of a table (the first parameter) and return a result obtained by the corresponding aggregation function (*SUM*, *MIN*, *MAX*, or *COUNT*) applied to the result of those calculations. We explain this behavior further in Chapter 5. Evaluation context is important for understanding how this calculation works. The X-suffixed functions available are *SUMX*, *AVERAGEX*, *COUNTX*, *COUNTAX*, *MINX*, and *MAXX*.

Among the counting functions, one of the most used is *DISTINCTCOUNT*, which does exactly what its name suggests: counts the distinct values of a column, which it takes as its only parameter.

DISTINCTCOUNT deserves a special mention among the various counting functions because of its speed. If you have some knowledge of counting distinct values in previous versions of SSAS, which implemented Multidimensional only, you already know that counting the number of distinct values of a column was problematic. If your database was not small, you had to be very careful whenever you wanted to add distinct counts to the solution and, for medium and big databases, a careful and complex handling of partitioning was necessary to implement distinct counts efficiently. However, in Tabular, *DISTINCTCOUNT* is amazingly fast due to the nature of the columnar database and the way it stores data in memory. In addition, you can use *DISTINCTCOUNT* on any column in your data model without worrying about creating new structures, as in Multidimensional.

> **Note** *DISTINCTOUNT* is a function introduced in the 2012 version of both Microsoft SQL Server and PowerPivot. The earlier version of PowerPivot did not include the *DISTINCTCOUNT* function and, to compute the number of distinct values of a column, you had to use *COUNTROWS(DISTINCT(ColName))*. The two patterns return the same result even if *DISTINCTCOUNT* is somewhat easier to read, requiring only a single function call.

Following what you have already learned in Chapter 1, "Introducing the Tabular Model," if you have a previous SSAS cube that has many problematic *DISTINCTCOUNT* results, measuring performance of the same solution rewritten in Tabular is definitely worth a try; you might have very pleasant surprises and decide to perform the transition of the cube for the sole presence of *DISTINCTCOUNT*.

Logical Functions

Sometimes you might need to build a logical condition in an expression—for example, to implement different calculations depending on the value of a column or to intercept an error condition. In these cases, you can use one of the logical functions in DAX. You have already seen in the previous section, "Handling Errors in DAX Expressions," the two most important functions of this group, which are *IF* and *IFERROR*. In Table A-3 of the Appendix, you can see the list of all these functions (which are *AND*, *FALSE*, *IF*, *IFERROR*, *NOT*, *TRUE*, and *OR*) and their syntax. If, for example, you want to compute the *Amount* as *Quantity* multiplied by *Price* only when the *Price* column contains a correct numeric value, you can use the following pattern.

```
Amount := IFERROR( Sales[Quantity] * Sales[Price], BLANK() )
```

If you did not use the *IFERROR* and the *Price* column contains an invalid number, the result for the calculated column would be an error because if a single row generates a calculation error, the error is propagated to the whole column. The usage of *IFERROR*, however, intercepts the error and replaces it with a blank value.

Another function you might put inside this category is *SWITCH*, which is useful when you have a column containing a low number of distinct values, and you want to get different behaviors, depending on the value. For example, the column *Size* in the DimProduct table contains L, M, S, and XL, and you might want to decode this value in a more meaningful column. You can obtain the result by using nested *IF* calls.

```
SizeDesc :=
    IF (DimProduct[Size] = "S", "Small",
      IF (DimProduct[Size] = "M", "Medium",
        IF (DimProduct[Size] = "L", "Large",
          IF (DimProduct[Size] = "XL", "Extra Large", "Other"))))
```

The following is a more convenient way to express the same formula, by using *SWITCH*.

```
SizeDesc :=
    SWITCH (DimProduct[Size],
      "S", "Small",
      "M", "Medium",
      "L", "Large",
      "XL", "Extra Large",
      "Other"
    )
```

The code in this latter expression is more readable, even if it is not faster, because, internally, switch statements are translated into nested *IF* calls.

Information Functions

Whenever you must analyze the data type of an expression, you can use one of the information functions that are listed in Table A-4 of the Appendix. All these functions return a TRUE/FALSE value and can be used in any logical expression. They are: *ISBLANK, ISERROR, ISLOGICAL, ISNONTEXT, ISNUMBER,* and *ISTEXT.*

Note that when a table column is passed as a parameter, the *ISNUMBER, ISTEXT,* and *ISNONTEXT* functions always return *TRUE* or *FALSE*, depending on the data type of the column and on the empty condition of each cell.

You might be wondering whether *ISNUMBER* can be used with a text column just to check whether a conversion to a number is possible. Unfortunately, you cannot use this approach; if you want to test whether a text value can be converted to a number, you must try the conversion and handle the error if it fails.

For example, to test whether the column *Price* (which is of type *String*) contains a valid number, you must write the following.

```
IsPriceCorrect = ISERROR( Sales[Price] + 0 )
```

To get a *TRUE* result from the *ISERROR* function, for example, DAX tries to add a zero to the *Price* to force the conversion from a text value to a number. The conversion fails for the *N/A* price value, so you can see that *ISERROR* is *TRUE*.

If, however, you try to use *ISNUMBER*, as in the following expression

```
IsPriceCorrect = ISNUMBER( Sales[Price] )
```

you will always get *FALSE* as a result because, based on metadata, the *Price* column is not a number but a string.

Mathematical Functions

The set of mathematical functions available in DAX is very similar to those in Excel, with the same syntax and behavior. You can see the complete list of these functions and their syntax in Table A-5 of the Appendix. The mathematical functions commonly used are *ABS, EXP, FACT, LN, LOG, LOG10, MOD, PI, POWER, QUOTIENT, SIGN,* and *SQRT*. Random functions are *RAND* and *RANDBETWEEN*.

There are many rounding functions, summarized here.

```
FLOOR = FLOOR( Tests[Value], 0.01 )
TRUNC = TRUNC( Tests[Value], 2 )
ROUNDDOWN = ROUNDDOWN( Tests[Value], 2 )
MROUND = MROUND( Tests[Value], 0.01 )
ROUND = ROUND( Tests[Value], 2 )
CEILING = CEILING( Tests[Value], 0.01 )
ROUNDUP = ROUNDUP( Tests[Value], 2 )
INT = INT( Tests[Value] )
FIXED = FIXED(Tests[Value],2,TRUE)
```

In Figure 4-10, you can see the different results when applied to some test values.

Value	FLOOR	TRUNC	ROUNDDOWN	MROUND	ROUND	CEILING	ROUNDUP	INT	FIXED	ISO
1.12345	1.12	1.12	1.12	1.12	1.12	1.13	1.13	1	1.12	1.13
1.265	1.26	1.26	1.26	1.26	1.27	1.27	1.27	1	1.27	1.27
1.265001	1.26	1.26	1.26	1.27	1.27	1.27	1.27	1	1.27	1.27
1.499999	1.49	1.49	1.49	1.5	1.5	1.5	1.5	1	1.50	1.5
1.51111	1.51	1.51	1.51	1.51	1.51	1.52	1.52	1	1.51	1.52
1.000001	1	1	1	1	1	1.01	1.01	1	1.00	1.01
1.999999	1.99	1.99	1.99	2	2	2	2	1	2.00	2

FIGURE 4-10 Different rounding functions lead to different values.

As you can see, *FLOOR, TRUNC,* and *ROUNDDOWN* are very similar, except in the way you can specify the number of digits on which to round. In the opposite direction, *CEILING* and *ROUNDUP* are very similar in their results. You can see a few differences in the way the rounding is done (see row B, in which the 1.265 number is rounded in two ways on the second decimal digit) between the

MROUND and *ROUND* functions. Finally, note that *FLOOR* and *MROUND* functions do not operate on negative numbers, whereas other functions do.

Text Functions

Table A-6 of the Appendix contains a complete description of the text functions available in DAX: they are *CONCATENATE*, *EXACT*, *FIND*, *FIXED*, *FORMAT*, *LEFT*, *LEN*, *LOWER*, *MID*, *REPLACE*, *REPT*, *RIGHT*, *SEARCH*, *SUBSTITUTE*, *TRIM*, *UPPER*, and *VALUE*.

These functions are useful for manipulating text and extracting data from strings that contain multiple values, and are often used in calculated columns to format strings or find specific patterns.

Conversion Functions

You learned that DAX performs automatic conversion of data types to adjust them to the need of the operators. Even if it happens automatically, a set of functions can still perform explicit conversion of types.

CURRENCY can transform an expression into a currency type, whereas *INT* transforms an expression into an integer. *DATE* and *TIME* take the date and time parts as parameters and return a correct DATETIME. *VALUE* transforms a string into a numeric format, whereas *FORMAT* gets a numeric value as the first parameter and a string format as its second parameter, and can transform numeric values into strings.

Date and Time Functions

In almost every type of data analysis, handling time and date is an important part of the job. DAX has a large number of functions that operate on date and time. Some of them make simple transformations to and from a *datetime* data type, such as the ones described in Table A-7 of the Appendix. These are *DATE*, *DATEVALUE*, *DAY*, *EDATE*, *EOMONTH*, *HOUR*, *MINUTE*, *MONTH*, *NOW*, *SECOND*, *TIME*, *TIMEVALUE*, *TODAY*, *WEEKDAY*, *WEEKNUM*, *YEAR*, and *YEARFRAC*. To make more complex operations on dates, such as comparing aggregated values year over year or calculating the year-to-date value of a measure, there is another set of functions, called time intelligence functions, which is described in Chapter 8, "Understanding Time Intelligence in DAX."

As mentioned before in this chapter, a *datetime* data type internally uses a floating-point number by which the integer part corresponds to the number of days starting from December 30, 1899, and the decimal part indicates the fraction of the day in time. (Hours, minutes, and seconds are converted into decimal fractions of the day.) Thus, adding an integer number to a datetime value increments the value by a corresponding number of days. However, most of the time, the conversion functions are used to extract day, month, and year from a date.

Relational Functions

Two useful functions that enable you to navigate through relationships inside a DAX formula are *RELATED* and *RELATEDTABLE*. In Chapter 5, you learn all the details of how these functions work; because they are so useful, it is worth describing them here.

You already know that a calculated column can reference column values of the table in which it is defined. Thus, a calculated column defined in FactResellerSales can reference any column of the same table. But what can you do if you must refer to a column in another table? In general, you cannot use columns in other tables unless a relationship is defined in the model between the two tables. However, if the two tables are in relationship, then the *RELATED* function enables you to access columns in the related table.

For example, you might want to compute a calculated column in the FactResellerSales table that checks whether the product that has been sold is in the Bikes category and, if it is, apply a reduction factor to the standard cost. To compute such a column, you must write an *IF* that checks the value of the product category, which is not in the FactResellerSales table. Nevertheless, a chain of relationships starts from FactResellerSales, reaching DimProductCategory through DimProduct and DimProductSubcategory, as you can see in Figure 4-11.

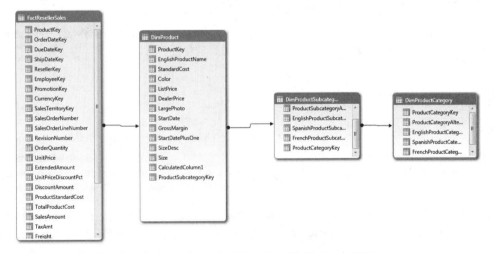

FIGURE 4-11 FactResellerSales has a chained relationship with DimProductCategory.

It does not matter how many steps are necessary to travel from the original table to the related one; DAX will follow the complete chain of relationship and return the related column value. Thus, the formula for the *AdjustedCost* column can be

```
=IF (
    RELATED (DimProductCategory[EnglishProductCategoryName]) = "Bikes",
    [ProductStandardCost] * 0.95,
    [ProductStandardCost]
)
```

In a one-to-many relationship, *RELATED* can access the one side from the many side because, in that case, only one row, if any, exists in the related table. If no row is related with the current one, *RELATED* returns *BLANK*.

If you are on the one side of the relationship and you want to access the many side, *RELATED* is not helpful because many rows from the other side are available for a single row in the current table. In that case, *RELATEDTABLE* will return a table containing all the related rows. For example, if you want to know how many products are in this category, you can create a column in DimProductCategory with this formula.

```
= COUNTROWS (RELATEDTABLE (DimProduct))
```

This calculated column will show, for each product category, the number of products related, as you can see in Figure 4-12.

ProductCategor...	EnglishProductCategoryName	NumOfProducts
1	Bikes	125
2	Components	189
3	Clothing	48
4	Accessories	35

FIGURE 4-12 Count the number of products by using *RELATEDTABLE*.

As is the case for *RELATED*, *RELATEDTABLE* can follow a chain of relationships, always starting from the one side and going in the direction of the many side.

Using Basic DAX Functions

Now that you have seen the basics of DAX, it is useful to check your knowledge of developing a sample reporting system. With the limited knowledge you have so far, you cannot develop a very complex solution. Nevertheless, even with your basic set of functions, you can already build something interesting.

Start loading some tables from *AdventureWorksDW* into a new Tabular project. You are interested in DimDate, DimProduct, DimProductCategory, DimProductSubcategory, and FactResellerSales. The resulting data model is shown in Figure 4-13.

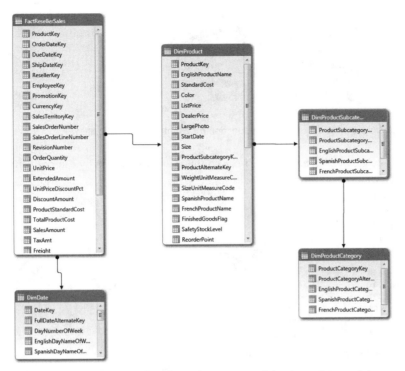

FIGURE 4-13 The Diagram View shows the structure of the demo data model.

To test your new knowledge of the DAX language, use this data model to solve some reporting problems.

First, count the number of products and enable the user to slice them with category and subcategory as long as it is with any of the DimProduct columns. It is clear that you cannot rely on calculated columns to perform this task; you need a measure that just counts the number of products, which we call *NumOfProducts*. The code is the following.

```
NumOfProducts := COUNTROWS (DimProduct)
```

Although this measure seems very easy to author, it has an issue. Because DimProduct is a slowly changing dimension of type 2 (that is, it can store different versions of the same product to track changes), the same product might appear several times in the table, and you should count it only once. This is a common scenario and can be easily solved by counting the number of distinct values of the natural key of the table. The natural key of DimProduct is the *ProductAlternateKey* column. Thus, the correct formula to count the number of products is as follows.

```
NumOfProducts := DISTINCTCOUNT (DimProduct[ProductAlternateKey])
```

You can see in Figure 4-14 that, although the number of rows in the table is 606, the number of products is 504. This number correctly takes into account different versions of the same product, counting them only once.

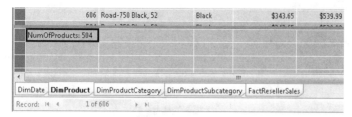

FIGURE 4-14 *DISTINCTCOUNT* is a useful and common function for counting.

This measure is already very useful and, when browsed through Excel, slicing by category and subcategory produces a report like the one shown in Figure 4-15.

Row Labels	NumOfProducts
⊞ **Accessories**	29
⊟ **Bikes**	97
Mountain Bikes	32
Road Bikes	43
Touring Bikes	22
⊞ **Clothing**	35
⊞ **Components**	134
⊟	209
	209
Grand Total	504

FIGURE 4-15 This is a sample report using *NumOfProducts*.

In this report, the last two rows are blank because there are products without a category and subcategory. After investigating the data, you discover that many of these uncategorized products are nuts, whereas other products are of no interest. Thus, you decide to override the category and subcategory columns with two new columns by following this pattern:

- If the category is not empty, then display the category.

- If the category is empty and the product name contains the word "nut," show "Nuts" for the category and "Nuts" for the subcategory.

- Otherwise, show "Other" in both category and subcategory.

Because you must use these values to slice data, this time you cannot use measures; you must author some calculated columns. Put these two calculated columns in the DimProduct table and call them *ProductCategory* and *ProductSubcategory*.

```
ProductSubcategory =
    IF(
        ISBLANK( DimProduct[ProductSubcategoryKey] ),
        IF(
            ISERROR( FIND( "Nut", DimProduct[EnglishProductName] ) ),
            "Other",
            "Nut"
        ),
        RELATED( DimProductSubcategory[EnglishProductSubcategoryName] )
    )
```

This formula is interesting because it uses several of the newly learned functions. The first *IF* checks whether the *ProductSubcategoryKey* is empty and, if so, it searches for the word "nut" inside the product name. *FIND*, in the case of no match, returns an error, and this is why you must surround it with the *ISERROR* function, which intercepts the error and enables you to take care of it as if it is a correct situation (which, in this specific scenario, is correct). If *FIND* returns an error, the result is "Other"; otherwise, the formula computes the subcategory name from the DimProductSubcategory by using the *RELATED* function.

> **Note** Note that the *ISERROR* function can be slow in such a scenario because it raises errors if it does not find a value. Raising thousands, if not millions, of errors can be a time-consuming operation. In such a case, it is often better to use the fourth parameter of the *FIND* function (which is the default return value in case of no match) to always get a value back, avoiding the error handling. In this formula, we are using *ISERROR* for educational purposes. In a production data model, it is always best to take care of performances.

With this calculated column, you have solved the issue with the *ProductSubcategory*. The same code, by replacing *ProductSubcategory* with *ProductCategory*, yields to the second calculated column, which makes the same operation with the category.

```
ProductCategory =
    IF(
        ISBLANK( DimProduct[ProductSubcategoryKey] ),
        IF(
            ISERROR( FIND( "Nut", DimProduct[EnglishProductName] ) ),
            "Other",
            "Nut"
        ),
        RELATED( DimProductCategory[EnglishProductCategoryName] )
    )
```

Note that you still must check for the emptiness of *ProductSubcategoryKey* because this is the only available column in DimProduct to test whether the product has a category.

If you now browse this new data model with Excel and use the newly created calculated column on the rows, you get the result shown in Figure 4-16.

Row Labels	NumOfProducts
⊞ Accessories	29
⊟ Bikes	97
Mountain Bikes	32
Road Bikes	43
Touring Bikes	22
⊞ Clothing	35
⊞ Components	134
⊟ Nut	79
Nut	79
⊟ Other	130
Other	130
Grand Total	**504**

FIGURE 4-16 You can build a report with the new product category and subcategory, taking care of nuts.

Summary

In this chapter, you explored the syntax of DAX, its data types, and the available operators and functions. The most important concept you have learned is the difference between a calculated column and a measure. Although both are authored in DAX, the difference between them is huge, and you will always have to choose whether a value should be computed by using a calculated column or a measure.

You also learned the following:

- How to handle errors and empty values in DAX expressions by using common patterns.

- The groups of functions available in DAX. These functions can be learned only by using them; we provided the syntax and a brief explanation. During the demo of the next chapters, you learn how to use them in practice.

- With the last exercise, you put into practice some of the key concepts you learned, creating a complete reporting system that, although simple, already shows some of the power of Tabular.

CHAPTER 5

Understanding Evaluation Context

To get the best from DAX, you need to understand the evaluation context. We introduced this terminology when we talked about calculated columns and measures in Chapter 4, "DAX Basics," mentioning that calculated columns and measures differ mainly in their evaluation context. Now we look at how the evaluation context is defined and, most importantly, how it works. In this chapter, we also introduce DAX functions to manipulate the evaluation context, functions such as *EARLIER* and *CALCULATE*.

> **Note** Understanding the content of this chapter is important if you want to use DAX in Tabular. Nevertheless, the topics described here are demanding, so do not be concerned if some concepts seem obscure during your first read. We suggest that you read this chapter again when you start creating your own DAX expressions; you are likely to discover that many concepts are clearer as soon as you implement your own DAX expressions and see the need to better understand evaluation context.

There are two kinds of evaluation context:

- **Filter context** The set of active rows in a calculation
- **Row context** The current row in a table iteration

We explain these in detail in the next topics.

Evaluation Context in a Single Table

This section introduces the evaluation context by working with a single table. The evaluation context in a model with a single table does not have to consider side effects of relationships. Even if this is not common in a model, it is the starting point to understand how the evaluation context works.

Filter Context in a Single Table

We start with the filter context. When a DAX expression is evaluated, imagine that there is a set of filters over the tables, which define the set of *active rows* that will be used for the calculation. We call this set of filters a *filter context*. The filter context corresponds to a subset of all the rows, including the special cases of the whole set of all the rows (no filters at all) and the empty set (filters exclude all the rows).

To better understand the filter context, consider the table shown in Figure 5-1, which is part of the sample Ch05\EvaluationContexts.bim model in the companion content.

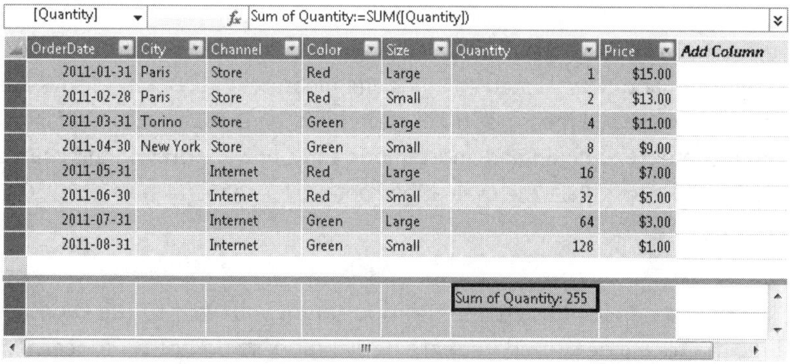

OrderDate	City	Channel	Color	Size	Quantity	Price	Add Column
2011-01-31	Paris	Store	Red	Large	1	$15.00	
2011-02-28	Paris	Store	Red	Small	2	$13.00	
2011-03-31	Torino	Store	Green	Large	4	$11.00	
2011-04-30	New York	Store	Green	Small	8	$9.00	
2011-05-31		Internet	Red	Large	16	$7.00	
2011-06-30		Internet	Red	Small	32	$5.00	
2011-07-31		Internet	Green	Large	64	$3.00	
2011-08-31		Internet	Green	Small	128	$1.00	

[Quantity] f_x Sum of Quantity:=SUM([Quantity])

Sum of Quantity: 255

FIGURE 5-1 This is a simple Orders table.

To explain the filter context, query the model by using a Microsoft PivotTable in Microsoft Excel. Each cell of the PivotTable defines a different filter context, which calculates the value of the measure in that cell. Roughly speaking, the filter context of a cell is determined by its coordinates in Excel as defined by the headers, rows, slicers, and filters in which it is currently evaluating and defines a corresponding set of filters on the underlying table.

Slicers in Excel

The following examples query the Tabular model by using an Excel 2010 PivotTable. You can add the slicers by clicking the Insert Slicer button in the PivotTable Tools Options ribbon you see in Figure 5-2.

FIGURE 5-2 This is the Insert Slicer button.

In the Insert Slicers window shown in Figure 5-3, you can select which attributes you want to use to create corresponding slicers in your workbook.

FIGURE 5-3 This is the Insert Slicers window.

Each slicer can be linked to more PivotTables. You can edit these links by using the PivotTable Connections button in the Slicer Tools Options ribbon shown in Figure 5-4.

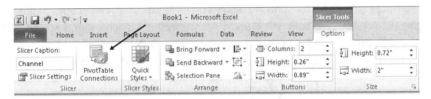

FIGURE 5-4 This is the PivotTable Connections button.

You can customize and name the slicer by using other buttons on the same ribbon.

In Figure 5-5, the E5 cell (which has the value of *64* for the Quantity measure) corresponds to a filter context that includes these conditions:

- Color Green (on the row axis)

- Size Large (on the column axis)

- Channel Internet (on the slicer)

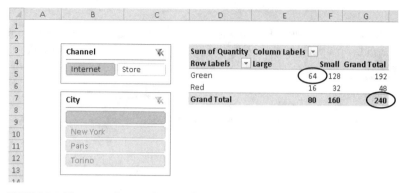

FIGURE 5-5 These are the coordinates of cells E5 and G7.

You can think of the filter context as a set of conditions in a *WHERE* clause of a *SQL SELECT* statement. For example, the equivalent SQL statement for cell E5 would be similar to the following.

```
SELECT ...
FROM ...
WHERE Color = "Green" AND Size = "Large" AND Channel = "Internet"
```

There is no filter on the *City* attribute. In this example, the filter context corresponds to a single row of the underlying table. The filter context can also be thought of as intersections in the data table that are determined by evaluating column values, which act as filters. Each column acts as a filter, and the combination of all the column filters determines the intersection of filter context, as you can see in the following table, in which filters are applied to *Channel*, *Color*, and *Size* columns.

OrderDate	City	Channel	Color	Size	Quantity	Price	(notes)
2011-01-31	Paris	Store	Red	Large	1	15	
2011-02-28	Paris	Store	Red	Small	2	13	
2011-03-31	Torino	Store	Green	Large	4	11	
2011-04-30	New York	Store	Green	Small	8	9	
2011-05-31		Internet	Red	Large	16	7	
2011-06-30		Internet	Red	Small	32	5	
2011-07-31		Internet	Green	Large	64	3	<<< Only this row meets all filter conditions
2011-08-31		Internet	Green	Small	128	1	

The G7 cell, however, is the sum of all the rows that have the Internet channel, regardless of their *Color*, *Size*, and *City* values. The sum of these rows has a value of *240*. Figure 5-6 shows the relationship between table rows and PivotTable cells.

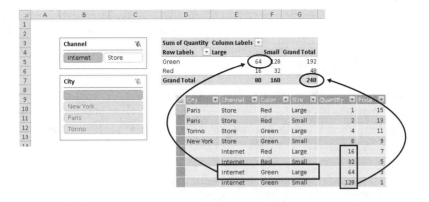

FIGURE 5-6 Here are the relationships between table rows and PivotTable cells.

Each selection you make in a PivotTable (on columns, rows, filters, and slicers) corresponds to a filter in the queried table. If a column of the table is not used in any part of the PivotTable, there is no filter on that column.

This first example considered only one table in the model. If you have more than one table, your work gets more complicated. Before examining this scenario, let us introduce the second kind of evaluation context: the row context.

Row Context in a Single Table

Row context is conceptually close to the idea of *current row*. When a calculation is applied to a single row in a table, we say that a row context is active for the calculation. If you reference a column in the table, you want to use the value of that column in the current row. As you see later, certain DAX expressions are valid only when there is an active row context (such as the simple reference of a column).

> **Tip** As an example, you can think of the DAX expression you put in a calculated column in a table. Or, if you have a SQL background, you can think of the expression you put in a column of a *SELECT* statement. The expression has to be evaluated for every row, and the row context corresponds to the current row used to evaluate the expression during the iteration over the table rows.

There are two cases in which there is an active row context:

- Evaluation of a calculated column
- Evaluation of a DAX function that iterates over a table

The first case is simpler because it is similar to how a computed column works with Microsoft SQL Server. The expression contained in a calculated column is evaluated once for each row of the table. When a row context is active over a table, any reference to a column of that table is valid and returns the value of the column for the current row.

In Figure 5-7, you can see that the formula for the calculated column Amount computes a product, and for each row, the computation is made by using the corresponding values of *Quantity* and *Price* in the same row. This is pretty much the same behavior as an Excel table or a SQL-computed column and is truly intuitive.

[Amount]	▼		f_x =Orders[Quantity] * Orders[Price]					▼
City	Channel	Color	Size	Quantity	Price	Amount	Add Column
Paris	Store	Red	Large	1	$15.00	15	
Paris	Store	Red	Small	2	$13.00	26	
Torino	Store	Green	Large	4	$11.00	44	
New York	Store	Green	Small	8	$9.00	72	
	Internet	Red	Large	16	$7.00	112	
	Internet	Red	Small	32	$5.00	160	
	Internet	Green	Large	64	$3.00	192	
	Internet	Green	Small	128	$1.00	128	
			Sum of Quantity: 255				

FIGURE 5-7 This is an example of a calculated column.

Let us clarify this process with an example: How is the formula evaluated for row 1 in Figure 5-7? Analysis Services creates a row context containing only row 1 and then evaluates the formula, which requires the evaluation of Orders[Quantity]. To get the value of the expression, it searches for the value of the Quantity column in the row context, and this yields a value of *1*. The same evaluation process is necessary for Orders[Price], which in the row context has the value of *15*. At the end, the two values are multiplied, and the final result is stored.

Note The expression defined in a calculated column is evaluated in a row context that is automatically defined for each row of the table.

The second case in which there is an active row context is when you want to perform the same calculation without adding a calculated column. If you do not have a calculated column for Amount and you want to create it by using a measure, you might be tempted to use the expression you used previously for the *Amount* calculated column for a CalcAmount measure. But this will not work, as you can see in Figure 5-8.

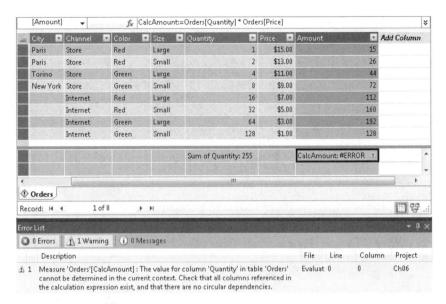

FIGURE 5-8 You get an error message when you define a measure by referencing a row value.

The error shown in Figure 5-8 indicates a problem related to the evaluation of a column in the current context. Unless you have a clear understanding of evaluation context, you are likely to find the error message cryptic. To make it meaningful, consider that when you are browsing a PivotTable, for each cell of the result you have a different filter context, but no row context is defined. The expression Orders[Quantity] requires a row context to be correctly evaluated, so the error message is about the lack of a context in which the formula can be understood.

If you try to use the *SUM* function to aggregate the expression, you get another error, although a different one (Figure 5-9).

As you can see in Figure 5-9, you cannot use an expression as an argument of the *SUM* function because the *SUM* function works only with a column as a parameter and does not accept a generic expression. However, you can obtain the result you want by using a different formula.

```
CalcAmount := SUMX( Orders, Orders[Quantity] * Orders[Price] )
```

The *SUMX* aggregation function iterates the table passed as the first parameter (Orders) and, for each row of the table, makes the calculation specified in the second parameter (Orders[Quantity] * Orders[Price]). The expression is evaluated in a row context corresponding to the current row of the iteration. The result of the expression for each row is summed up for all the rows, and the *SUMX* function returns the result of this aggregation, as shown in Figure 5-10.

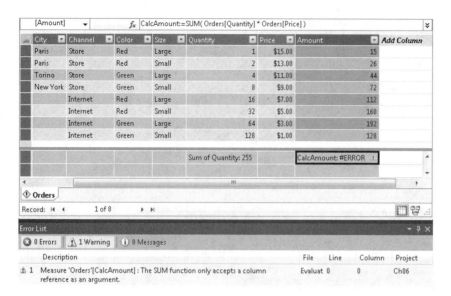

FIGURE 5-9 You get an error message when you use *SUM* passing an expression as parameter.

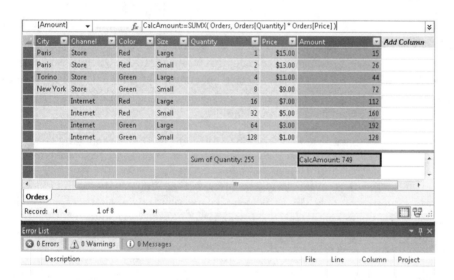

FIGURE 5-10 Here is the correct definition of measure, using *SUMX*.

In Figure 5-10, the *SUMX* function is used to apply the initial expression to each of the rows of the Orders table that are active in the current filter context. As you can see in Figure 5-11, the CalcAmount measure works.

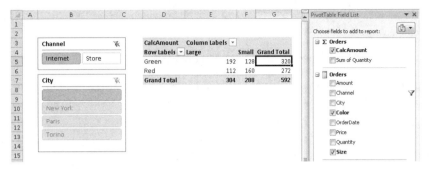

FIGURE 5-11 This is the resulting value of the CalcAmount measure.

It is important to understand that the filter context defined by the coordinates of each cell in the PivotTable is used, during the computation of the *SUMX* function, to filter the rows of the Orders table that is then iterated by *SUMX*. This is the crux of the matter: The expression in the *SUMX* function has been evaluated under both a filter context and a row context.

To better understand what happened, look at the exact sequence of operations performed to calculate the value in cell G5, which is highlighted in Figure 5-11.

- The filter context is defined by the coordinates of cell G5, which are <Green, Internet>.

- The value required is *CalcAmount*, which is the measure defined with the expression SUMX (Orders, Orders[Quantity] * Orders[Price]).

- The *SUMX* function iterates all the rows of the Orders table that are active in the filter context, so only the two rows highlighted in Figure 5-12 will be iterated.

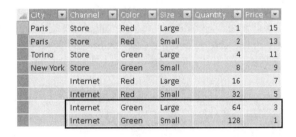

FIGURE 5-12 These are the rows iterated by *SUMX* to calculate cell G5 of the PivotTable.

- For each of these two rows, the Orders[Quantity] * Orders[Price] calculation is performed by using that row as the row context.

- The resulting values of these two rows (*192* and *128*, respectively) are aggregated, summing them, because you are using *SUMX*.

- The final result of *320* is returned by *SUMX* and fills the G5 cell.

A set of functions shows the same behavior as *SUMX* but uses a different aggregation criterion. These functions are named with the name of the aggregation operation and end with an X character.

- *AVERAGEX*

- *COUNTAX*

- *COUNTX*

- *MAXX*

- *MINX*

- *SUMX*

Remember that these functions create a row context from the existing filter context. They iterate over the rows visible under the current filter context and activate a row context for each of these rows.

Testing Evaluation Context in SQL Server Data Tools and SQL Server Management Studio

Up to now, you have used an Excel PivotTable to browse data and generate evaluation contexts in an intuitive way. You can also test DAX measures by using the table filters in SQL Server Data Tools (SSDT). SSDT enables you to filter a table to mimic the effect of a query filter and, hence, force a filter context. For example, in Figure 5-13, you can see that filters are applied to some columns (the *Channel* column filters only Internet, and the *Color* column filters only Green), so all the measures of the Orders table show the value computed by using the filter context defined by the applied filters.

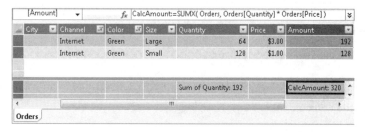

FIGURE 5-13 The filter context is defined by the filter on the *Channel* and *Color* columns.

The CalcAmount measure is evaluated by considering only the rows that match the filter, which correspond to the active filter context for all the measures in the measure grid. For this reason, *320* is the value computed for CalcAmount, which corresponds to the sum of the values matching the filter in the *Amount* column.

You can also use SQL Server Management Studio to run a DAX query that computes values by using a particular evaluation context. In Figure 5-14, you can see that by opening an MDX query window, you can also write a DAX query, run it, and see its results. In this case, the DAX query returns the total for each Green and Red color filtered by the Internet channel.

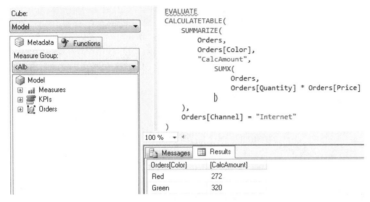

FIGURE 5-14 This is a DAX query using SQL Server Management Studio.

You will see the DAX query syntax in more detail in the following chapter. In this chapter, we will use the DAX query syntax to illustrate some concepts. You can use SQL Server Management Studio (SSMS) to test these DAX queries.

Working with Evaluation Context for a Single Table

The most powerful way to manipulate the evaluation is by using the *CALCULATE* function. However, for didactic purposes, we start with some examples by using *ALL* and *FILTER* functions, and only after that discussion will we discuss the more flexible and powerful *CALCULATE* function.

> **Important** Using *CALCULATE* is the best practice by which to manipulate filter context because it provides the best performance. Do not use *FILTER* as parameter for aggregate functions such as *SUMX*; use a *CALCULATE* alternative whenever possible.

The filter context can be modified while evaluating a DAX expression to compute the formula in a different context. For instance, you might want to sum a value over a subset of the rows of a table. In that case, you need a way to define the rows you want to include in that calculation.

All the *aggX* aggregation functions have two parameters. The first parameter is the table that is used to iterate rows (filtered by the current filter context); the second parameter is the expression computed during each of the iterations.

```
SUMX( <table>, <expression> )
```

Instead of a table, the first parameter can be a function returning a table. For example, you can use the *FILTER* function, which returns a table that has been filtered by using the Boolean expression, which is received as the second parameter.

```
FILTER( <table>, <filter expression> )
```

In other words, the expression passed to a *FILTER* function adds that filter to the current filter context for that table. For example, remembering this is only for didactic purposes, if you write the following

```
CalcAmountB := SUMX( FILTER( Orders, Orders[Quantity] > 1 ), Orders[Amount] )
```

instead of

```
CalcAmountB := SUMX( Orders, Orders[Amount] )
```

the *FILTER* function skips just the <Internet, Green, Small> row from the table you saw in Figure 5-12 (which has a price of 1 and is excluded by the filter condition). Using that formula for your CalcAmountB measure, you ignore that row in the PivotTable calculation.

As you can see in Figure 5-15, there is no value for the highlighted F4 cell in the PivotTable, and the total for rows and columns also ignores the filtered row. Therefore, the *FILTER* function can filter data by restricting the filter context used, for example, to calculate aggregations in a PivotTable.

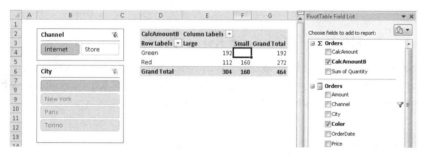

FIGURE 5-15 The F4 cell is empty because the CalcAmountB measure considers only rows with a price greater than 1.

Now that you have seen how to add a filter to the existing filter context, look at how to remove one of the existing filters. If you need to remove a filter from the filter context or if you want to remove the filter context on a table altogether, you need a slightly different approach. The first technique is to remove all the filters on a table. For example, if you want to get the value of all the orders, regardless of any selection made by the user in the PivotTable, you can use the *ALL* function, which returns a table containing all the rows of the specified table, regardless of the existing filter context, and then pass its result to the *SUMX* function. For example, you can create an AllAmount measure by using the following expression.

```
AllAmount := SUMX( ALL( Orders ), Orders[Amount] )
```

In Figure 5-16, you can see that for any cell of the PivotTable in which AllAmount is calculated, the value is always the same (it is always *749*) because the *ALL* function ignores the filter context.

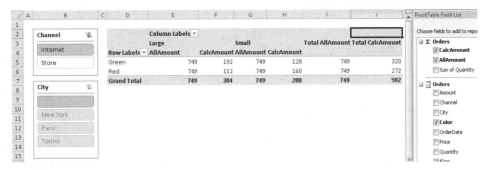

FIGURE 5-16 The AllAmount measure always considers all the rows in the Orders table.

Note From a certain point of view, the *ALL* function does not change the filter context, but creates a new one, at least when it is applied to a table. Shortly, you will see that *ALL* can be used also with a single column as parameter to eliminate any filter from the filter context for just one column.

If you need to filter all rows according to a specific restriction (regardless of any user filters applied, so ignoring the current filter context), you can combine *FILTER* and *ALL* to get, for example, all the rows in Orders for the Internet Channel. You can define an AllInternet measure by using the following DAX expression (the result of which you can see in Figure 5-17).

```
AllInternet := SUMX( FILTER( ALL( Orders ), Orders[Channel]="Internet" ), Orders[Amount] )
```

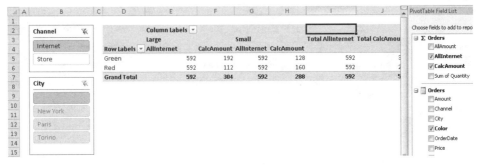

FIGURE 5-17 The AllInternet measure always considers all the rows in the Orders table.

In Figure 5-17, the AllInternet value is always *592*, which corresponds to the total of Amount for Internet Channel. However, you can see that this approach is limited because filters on other attributes (such as *Color, Size, Channel,* and so on) are not considered in the calculation, so you cannot use the existing selection of these attributes in your filter condition. In other words, you are replacing the filter context for a table with a new filter context, but you cannot change only part of the filter context by using this process. When you want to remove only one selection (for example, *Channel*) while keeping all the other filters, you need to use the *CALCULATE* function. We will describe the *CALCULATE* function more thoroughly later because it is powerful and flexible and deserves its own section; nevertheless, it is useful to start considering it now.

Imagine that you want to remove the filter on the *Channel* attribute from the filter context but want to keep all the other filters. By using *CALCULATE*, you can specify a filter on a column that overrides any existing filter for that column only. You can define an AllChannels measure by using the following expression.

```
AllChannels := CALCULATE( SUMX( Orders, Orders[Amount] ), ALL( Orders[Channel] ) )
```

The first parameter of *CALCULATE* is the expression you want to evaluate in a filter context that is modified by the other parameters.

> **Note** Any number of parameters could be in the *CALCULATE* function after the first parameter, and each of these parameters defines a set of values for a column or a table that clears the existing corresponding filter of the current filter context, replacing it with a new one.

In the example, the *ALL* function receives a column reference as a parameter (previously, a table reference was used as a parameter) and returns all the values from that column, regardless of the existing filter context. Using *CALCULATE* and *ALL* with one or more column parameters clears the existing filter context for those columns for the expression passed to and evaluated by the *CALCULATE* function.

The AllChannels measure defined in Figure 5-18 returns the total for all the channels, even if you have a different selection in the PivotTable.

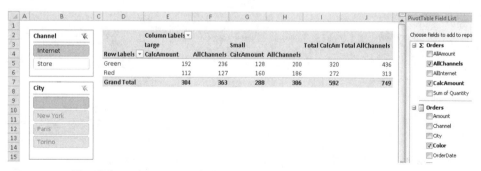

FIGURE 5-18 The AllChannels measure calculates amount by ignoring the *Channel* selection.

> **Important** When you use *CALCULATE*, you can use *SUM* instead of *SUMX* whenever the expression of *SUMX* is made of a single column. In other words, these two expressions are equivalent.
>
> ```
> CALCULATE( SUMX( Orders, Orders[Amount] ), ALL( Orders[Channel] ) )
> ```
>
> ```
> CALCULATE( SUM( Orders[Amount] ), ALL( Orders[Channel] ) )
> ```
>
> You still need *SUMX* whenever the expression that has to be aggregated contains more terms.
>
> ```
> CALCULATE(
>     SUMX( Orders, Orders[Quantity Orders[Price] ),
>     ALL( Orders[Channel] )
> )
> ```
>
> In that case, you do not have an alternative syntax based on *SUM* unless you move the expression in a calculated column, like the *Amount* column in the Orders table. However, because *SUMX* has the same performance as *SUM* for simple expressions involving columns of the same row, storing the result of such an expression in a calculated column is not recommended because it consumes additional memory. You will find more information about why *SUM* and *SUMX* performance might be equivalent or different in Chapter 9, "Understanding xVelocity and Direct Query," within the explanation of the xVelocity architecture.

CALCULATE is a fundamental function for operating on the filter context; it can calculate over rows that are not part of the current selection but are needed to make comparisons, ratios, and so on. It enables you to evaluate expressions in a filter context that is not dictated by the query and the cell that is currently being evaluated but, rather, a filter context you determine.

Finally, if you want to remove filters from all but a few columns in a table, you can use *ALLEXCEPT*. Using the Orders table as an example, the following statements are equivalent.

```
CALCULATE(
    SUM( Orders[Amount] ),
    ALL(
        Orders[Channel], Orders[Color], Orders[Size],
        Orders[Quantity], Orders[Price], Orders[Amount]
    )
)
```

```
CALCULATE( SUM( Orders[Amount] ), ALLEXCEPT( Orders, Orders[City] ) )
```

Understanding the *EARLIER* Function

You have seen that there are two distinct concepts in evaluation context: the row context and the filter context. The *CALCULATE* function can change the evaluation context, and functions such as *FILTER*, *SUMX*, and other aggregation functions ending with an X character define a new row context for each iterated value. It is interesting to note that a new row context might be generated while an external operation in the same expression is using another row context on the same table, so a row context might be nested within another row context while you use several DAX functions nested in each other. However, only the innermost row context remains active.

For example, consider the *OrderDate* and *Quantity* columns of the Order table you can see in Figure 5-19.

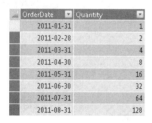

OrderDate	Quantity
2011-01-31	1
2011-02-28	2
2011-03-31	4
2011-04-30	8
2011-05-31	16
2011-06-30	32
2011-07-31	64
2011-08-31	128

FIGURE 5-19 Look at the *OrderDate* and *Quantity* columns in the Orders table.

Suppose that you want to create a running total that sums the *Quantity* value for all the rows with a date less than or equal to the current row. In SQL, you would solve the problem this way.

```
SELECT
    o1.OrderDate,
    o1.Quantity,
    ( SELECT SUM( o2.Quantity )
      FROM Orders o2
      WHERE o2.OrderDate <= o1.OrderDate
    ) AS RunningTotal
FROM Orders o1
```

In SQL, you can reference the same table multiple times and use a table alias to disambiguate the reference to *OrderDate* in the *WHERE* condition of the correlated subquery that calculates the *RunningTotal* value.

In DAX, you need to define a calculated column that filters only the rows that have to be computed. You should write something like this

```
Orders[RunningTotal] =
SUMX( FILTER( Orders, <condition> ), Orders[Quantity] )
```

where <condition> determines whether the row iterated in the *FILTER* condition is filtered, comparing its date with the date of the current row in the external loop (which is the iteration of the rows in the Orders table with which you calculate the value of *RunningTotal* for each row). However, in DAX, you do not have table alias syntax to disambiguate the reference to the *OrderDate* column.

It is important to remember what will happen. There will be a loop over all the rows of the Orders table. For each of these rows, the DAX expression of the *RunningTotal* calculated column is evaluated. The presence of a *FILTER* function creates another loop, and this means a new row context. At this point, every access to a column of this table operates in the new row context, but this is a problem if you want to get the value of the previous row context, the one that invoked the calculation of the *RunningTotal* column.

The *EARLIER* function in DAX provides exactly this behavior: getting data from the previous row context. Any column referenced in an *EARLIER* function call returns the value of that column in the previous row context. Thus, because you need the *OrderDate* value of the current row before the execution of the *FILTER* statement, you can use the *EARLIER* syntax.

```
EARLIER( Orders[OrderDate] )
```

The right DAX definition of the *RunningTotal* calculated column is the following.

```
Orders[RunningTotal] =
SUMX(
    FILTER( Orders, Orders[OrderDate] <= EARLIER( Orders[OrderDate] ) ),
    Orders[Quantity]
)
```

You can see in Figure 5-20 the result of the *RunningTotal* calculated column in the table on the left. On the right side, you can see the values that are computed for each row of the Orders table to evaluate the *RunningTotal* value for rows corresponding to 2011-03-31 and 2011-05-31. The highlighted rows are those that are returned by the *FILTER* function.

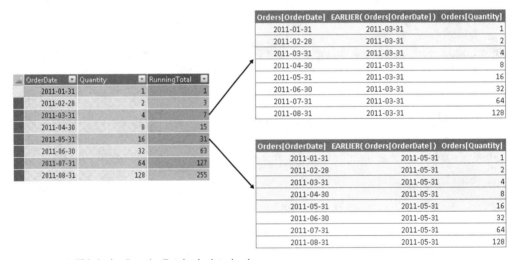

FIGURE 5-20 This is the *RunningTotal* calculated column.

The *EARLIER* function has a second, optional, parameter that specifies how many evaluation passes have to be discarded. This is useful when you have multiple, iterating, nested functions changing the row context multiple times. If the second parameter is omitted, it defaults to 1, which indicates the previous row context.

A similar function, named *EARLIEST*, has a single parameter, which is the column name. It returns the column value from the outer evaluation pass. (In other words, it is the first row context of the whole DAX expression.) You can get the same result of *EARLIEST* by passing -1 to the second parameter of *EARLIER*.

Finally, consider that each table might have its own row context, and *EARLIER* operates only on the table implicitly defined by the column passed as a parameter. If you have multiple tables involved in a DAX expression, each one has its own row context, and they can be accessed without requiring any other DAX instructions. *EARLIER* and *EARLIEST* have to be used only when a new iteration starts on a table in which a row context already exists. In the next section, you see how to interact with row contexts of multiple tables.

 Note You can recognize when to use *EARLIER* writing a calculated column, because a row context is always defined when the formula is evaluated, and any function that iterates a table defines a nested row context. When you write a measure, you do not have an initial row context, so *EARLIER* becomes useful whenever you have a second iterative function used in the expression evaluated for each row of an external iteration. You can find a more detailed description by reading the article at *http://javierguillen.wordpress.com/2012/02/06/can-earlier-be-used-in-dax-measures/*.

Understanding Evaluation Context in Multiple Tables

By introducing multiple tables and relationships in a model, evaluation contexts behave in a different way, and you must understand what happens when relationships are involved in calculation.

Row Context with Multiple Tables

You can take a step further by adding a new table to the data model—for example, the Channels table, which has a discount percentage for each channel type, as you can see in Figure 5-21.

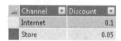

FIGURE 5-21 The Channels table is added to the Tabular model.

The Orders and Channels tables have a relationship based on the *Channel* column, as shown in Figure 5-22.

This is a one-to-many relationship between Channels and Orders. For each row in the Channels table, there could be zero, one, or more corresponding rows in the Orders table. For each row in the Orders table, there could be only zero or one corresponding rows in the Channels table. If at least one row in Orders does not have a corresponding row in Channels (zero corresponding rows), one virtual blank member is automatically created in the Channels lookup table to match any missing Channels value used in the Orders table. To make an analogy, this is similar to the behavior of an outer join between two tables in SQL. You can use the *ALLNOBLANKROW* function instead of *ALL* to return all the values from a table or a column except the virtual blank one if it exists.

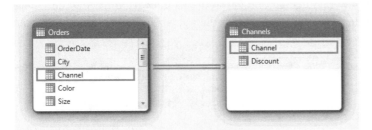

FIGURE 5-22 Look at the relationship between the Orders and Channels tables.

Note The table (in this case, Channels) on the one side of the one-to-many relationship is also called the *lookup table*. The lookup term is used in this chapter to identify that side of the relationship. If the lookup table does not contain any row corresponding to the value on the many side of the relationship, a single blank value is virtually added to the lookup table. This special member has the same purpose as an "unknown" member in a Multidimensional model, but it is not physically added to the table; it appears only in query results to group data with no related members.

You might want to calculate the discounted amount for each transaction by defining a calculated column in the Orders table. So the first idea is to define a formula this way.

```
Orders[DiscountedAmount] = Orders[Amount] * (1 - Channels[Discount])
```

However, this produces an error, as you can see in Figure 5-23.

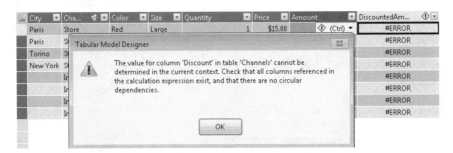

FIGURE 5-23 This is an error produced by using the *Discount* column from the Channels table in a calculated column in Orders.

This is what happens when you try to define this column: The *Discount* column is in the Channels table, which is not the table in which you are defining the new *DiscountedAmount* calculated column. Because the calculated column is defined in the Orders table, a row context exists only for such a table. For this reason, if you want to read the value from the Channels table (which does not have a row context and is on the one side of the one-to-many relationship between Orders and Channels), you must use the *RELATED* function.

From a conceptual point of view, the result of the relationship between the Orders and Channels tables is a logical monolithic table, similar to what you would obtain in SQL by joining the two tables, denormalizing them into a single table.

OrderDate	City	Channel	Color	Size	Quantity	Price	Discount
2011-01-31	Paris	Store	Red	Large	1	15	0.05
2011-02-28	Paris	Store	Red	Small	2	13	0.05
2011-03-31	Torino	Store	Green	Large	4	11	0.05
2011-04-30	New York	Store	Green	Small	8	9	0.05
2011-05-31		Internet	Red	Large	16	7	0.1
2011-06-30		Internet	Red	Small	32	5	0.1
2011-07-31		Internet	Green	Large	64	3	0.1
2011-08-31		Internet	Green	Small	128	1	0.1

Thus, the *RELATED* function is a syntax that enables you to reference a column in another table by traversing existing relationships. The *RELATED* function evaluates the column passed as the parameter by applying the appropriate row context following the existing relationship. The starting point is the many side of the relationship, and *RELATED* evaluates the corresponding row on the one side of such a relationship, which is also called the lookup table. You could say that the *RELATED* function propagates the row context to another table by following the existing relationship.

Note The row context is limited to a single row, and relationships between tables do not propagate the row context to other tables by default. The *RELATED* function propagates the effect of row context to a lookup table, provided that a valid relationship to a lookup table exists.

In Figure 5-24, you can see the *DiscountedAmount* calculated column correctly calculated by using the following formula.

```
Orders[DiscountedAmount] = Orders[Amount] * ( 1 - RELATED( Channels[Discount] ) )
```

City	Cha...	Color	Size	Quantity	Price	Amount	DiscountedAmount
Paris	Store	Red	Large	1	$15.00	15	14.25
Paris	Store	Red	Small	2	$13.00	26	24.7
Torino	Store	Green	Large	4	$11.00	44	41.8
New York	Store	Green	Small	8	$9.00	72	68.4
	Internet	Red	Large	16	$7.00	112	100.8
	Internet	Red	Small	32	$5.00	160	144
	Internet	Green	Large	64	$3.00	192	172.8
	Internet	Green	Small	128	$1.00	128	115.2

FIGURE 5-24 Here is a valid calculation for the *DiscountedAmount* calculated column.

On the opposite side of the relationship, you might want to calculate over the set of rows related to a channel selection in the Channels table. For example, you might want to calculate the total number of orders for each channel in a calculated column of the Channels table, as in the *OrdersCount* calculated column shown in Figure 5-25, which is defined by using the following formula.

```
Channels[OrdersCount] = COUNTROWS( RELATEDTABLE( Orders ) )
```

Channel	Discount	OrdersCount
Internet	0.1	4
Store	0.05	4

FIGURE 5-25 This is a calculated column in the Channels table that uses the *RELATEDTABLE* function.

The *RELATEDTABLE* function returns a table composed of only the rows that are related to the current row context. That table can be used as a parameter to any *aggX* function or to other DAX functions requiring a table, such as *FILTER* or *COUNTROWS* (which are used in the example).

> **Important** As you see later in this chapter, you can use *CALCULATE* instead of *RELATEDTABLE*, and usually *CALCULATE* gets better performance. Although this might not be important for calculated columns (it does not affect query performance because calculated columns are evaluated at process time), it is almost always possible for measures and when it is necessary to manipulate the filter context, as you see in the following sections.

Understanding Row Context and Chained Relationships

Both *RELATED* and *RELATEDTABLE* functions can traverse a list of chained relationships with a single call without making nested calls. However, the relationships must all run in the same direction. For example, consider the relationships existing among the Product, Product Subcategory, and Product Category tables in the Adventure Works DW tabular model, as in Figure 5-26.

FIGURE 5-26 These are product-related tables in the Adventure Works DW tabular model.

The Product table contains two calculated columns to denormalize subcategory and category names. The *Product Subcategory Name* calculated column is defined as follows.

```
Product[Product Subcategory Name] = RELATED( 'Product Subcategory'[Product Subcategory Name] )
```

The *Product Category Name* calculated column has a similar syntax, but references the Product Category table, which requires the traversal of two relationships, first from Product to Product Subcategory and then from Product Subcategory to Product Category.

```
Product[Product Category Name] = RELATED( 'Product Category'[Product Category Name] )
```

In Figure 5-27, you can see the resulting calculated columns in the Product table.

Product Name	Product Subcategory Name	Product Category Name
Fender Set - Mountain	Fenders	Accessories
All-Purpose Bike Stand	Bike Stands	Accessories
Hydration Pack - 70 oz.	Hydration Packs	Accessories
ML Mountain Seat/Saddle	Saddles	Components
HL Mountain Seat/Saddle	Saddles	Components
LL Road Seat/Saddle	Saddles	Components

FIGURE 5-27 Here are the *Product Subcategory* and *Product Category* calculated columns in the Product table.

RELATEDTABLE can traverse multiple relationships. You can define the *Products Count* calculated column in the Product Category table by using the following formula, which considers all the products related to all subcategories related to each category.

```
'Product Category'[Products Count] = COUNTROWS( RELATEDTABLE( Product ) )
```

Figure 5-28 shows the *Products Count* calculated column in the Product Category table.

Product Category Id	Product Category Name	Products Count
1	Bikes	125
2	Components	189
3	Clothing	48
4	Accessories	35

FIGURE 5-28 Look at the *Products Count* calculated column in the Product Category table.

Using Filter Context with Multiple Tables

Now that you have seen how to use row context with related tables, you might find it interesting to note that table relationships directly affect the filter context of involved tables regardless of the DAX expressions used. For example, you can add a Cities table to the model like the one in Figure 5-29, which has a one-to-many relationship with the Orders table through the *City* column (see Figure 5-30).

City	Country	Continent
Paris	France	Europe
New York	USA	North America
Torino	Italy	Europe
Madrid	Spain	Europe

FIGURE 5-29 The Cities table contains *Country* and *Continent* columns.

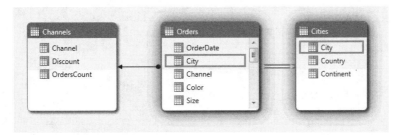

FIGURE 5-30 This is the relationship between the Orders and Cities tables.

When you browse the data by using a PivotTable, you can choose Continent (from the Cities table) and Channel (from the Channels table) as the slicers, Sum of DiscountedAmount as a measure, and *Color* and *Size* in Rows and Columns, respectively.

In Figure 5-31, you can see the data of all the rows in the Orders table partitioned by *Color* and *Size* attributes. Despite the presence of Continent and Channel as slicers, no filter is active on these slicers because all the members are selected. Keep in mind that the Continent slicer also contains an empty member that corresponds to all the sales made in the Internet channel that do not have a corresponding City. (See Figure 5-24 to look at raw data.)

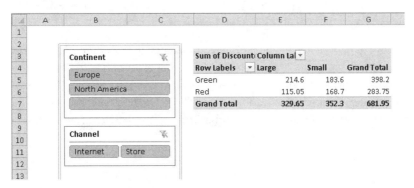

FIGURE 5-31 Browse data without a filter.

Whenever you make a selection on the Continent slicer, you also define a filter context on the Cities table that immediately propagates its effects on related tables. In fact, you are making a filter on a lookup table, and this implies that all the tables that have a relationship with that lookup table are also filtered. In this example, the Orders table has a relationship with the Cities table, which contains the *Continent* column. If you select the North America member, only the row with New York is filtered in the Cities table, and this propagates to the Orders table by filtering only the rows corresponding to New York.

You can imagine that all the columns of the lookup tables are denormalized into the destination table. For example, the model made by the Orders, Channels, and Cities tables can be seen as a single OrdersExtended table composed as follows. (Gray background is used for columns coming from lookup tables.)

OrderDate	City	Channel	Color	Size	Quantity	Price	Channel	Discount	Orders Count	City	Country	Continent
2011-01-31	Paris	Store	Red	Large	1	15	Store	0.05	4	Paris	France	Europe
2011-02-28	Paris	Store	Red	Small	2	13	Store	0.05	4	Paris	France	Europe
2011-03-31	Torino	Store	Green	Large	4	11	Store	0.05	4	Torino	Italy	Europe
2011-04-30	New York	Store	Green	Small	8	9	Store	0.05	4	New York	United States	North America
2011-05-31		Internet	Red	Large	16	7	Internet	0.1	4			
2011-06-30		Internet	Red	Small	32	5	Internet	0.1	4			
2011-07-31		Internet	Green	Large	64	3	Internet	0.1	4			
2011-08-31		Internet	Green	Small	128	1	Internet	0.1	4			

Every column used for the relationships between tables is present twice, and this is why you see that sometimes the filter applied to one of these columns does not override filters present on other columns. Also, calculated columns are denormalized in this extended table. If you come from a SQL background, you can understand this table as the result of an outer join between the base table (Orders) with all its lookup tables. If you have multiple related tables joined at different levels, like in a snowflake schema (for instance, Product, Product Subcategory, and Product Category), the join is propagated to all the reachable levels until any lookup table is reached.

Figure 5-32 illustrates the behavior of the filter context defined by the selection of the North America member in the Continent slicer. The rows in the tables that are included in the filter context are highlighted through a box. Notice that the Channel slicer is also affected by this filter context because even if there are two members visible and selected (Store and Internet), Store is colored and Internet appears dimmed; in fact, there are no rows in the Orders table that are active in the current filter context for Internet channel.

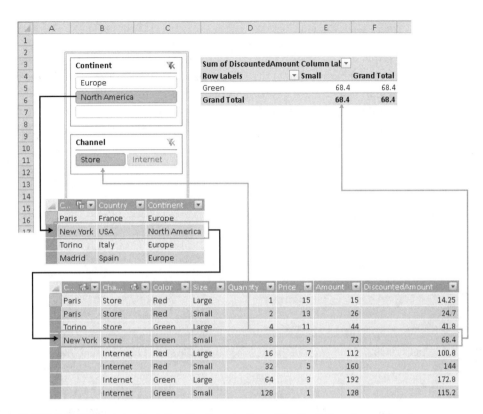

FIGURE 5-32 Filter context is defined by the selection of the North America continent.

Note An item that appears dimmed in a slicer indicates that the selection of that member does not have any effect on the result of the PivotTable because values for that item are already filtered out by selections of other attributes, that is, by the filter context. To make items appear dimmed in slicers, Excel has to send other queries to Analysis Services, which can have an impact on performance. You can disable this behavior by clearing the Visually Indicate Items With No Data check box in the Slice Setting dialog box (see Figure 5-33), which you can open for each slicer by choosing the Slicer Settings menu in the Slicer Tools Options ribbon (see Figure 5-4).

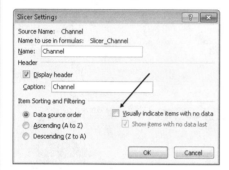

FIGURE 5-33 Visually Indicate Items With No Data can be disabled in Slicer Settings to improve performance.

If you change the selection of the Continent slicer by choosing Europe, the filter context activates three rows in the Cities table. Only rows corresponding to these cities are active in the Orders table, as you can see in Figure 5-34.

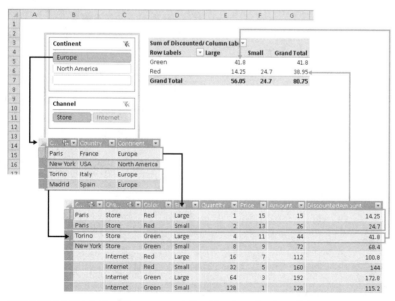

FIGURE 5-34 This is the filter context defined by the selection of Europe.

The filter context defined for the Orders table is further reduced when single cells of the PivotTable are evaluated. For example, cell E5 includes only the <Torino, Store, Green, Large> row because it is the only row that satisfies the <Europe, Green, Large> user filter that results from user selection. This type of user filter is <Europe, Red> for cell G6 and includes two rows from the Orders table.

At this point, you can still add filters to the evaluation context by using *FILTER* as a parameter of an aggregation function such as *SUMX* in the same way you can for a single table. However, you need to use a different approach if you need to remove filters from the filter context—for example, if you want to calculate a ratio between the amount for a color and the corresponding amount for an item regardless of the color.

> **Note** Usually you apply a filter in lookup tables; the filter is propagated to related tables, and you use only that for simple measures calculation. However, when you filter the whole base table (and not just a column) by using a *FILTER* statement, its effect propagates to lookup tables, even if this does not happen in the same way it happens when going the other direction (from the lookup to the base table) and may not be visible in a measure displayed in a PivotTable. Apparently, the filter is propagated only from the lookup table to the base table and not in the opposite direction. You can partially visualize this behavior when you look at items that appear dimmed in slicers of a PivotTable (even if this visualization is not obtained as a direct effect of filter propagation). It is important to consider the propagation of filters in the extended table made by all the lookup tables when you create DAX calculations in complex models involving many related tables. You can find a deeper explanation about cross table filtering at *http://mdxdax.blogspot.com/2011/03/logic-behind-magic-of-dax-cross-table.html*.

Understanding Row and Filter Context Interactions

Row and filter context are separate parts of the evaluation context that have a different behavior. DAX functions might use one or both of them, and a few DAX functions, such as *CALCULATE* and *CALCULATETABLE*, generate an interaction between them.

Using Row Context and *CALCULATE*

When you write *CALCULATE* in an expression that is evaluated in an active row context, that row context is transformed into a filter context made by all the equivalent rows. Usually, the filter context is made by a single row, but if the table does not have a key column and contains duplicated rows, the filter context includes all duplicated rows with the same value as the columns in the initial row context. This is a fundamental concept you must learn because it is used often in any DAX formula. To understand how this works, consider the following *Sum1* calculated column.

```
Orders[Sum1] = SUM( Orders[Quantity] )
```

This formula results in the same value for all the rows, which are the sum of all the rows of the Orders table if you embed this calculation in a *CALCULATE* statement, as in the following *Sum2* calculated column.

```
Orders[Sum2] = CALCULATE( SUM( Orders[Quantity] ) )
```

The result is the same value as the *Quantity* column for each row, as you can see in Figure 5-35.

City	Cha...	Color	Size	Quantity	Sum1	Sum2
Paris	Store	Red	Large	1	255	1
Paris	Store	Red	Small	2	255	2
Torino	Store	Green	Large	4	255	4
New York	Store	Green	Small	8	255	8
	Internet	Red	Large	16	255	16
	Internet	Red	Small	32	255	32
	Internet	Green	Large	64	255	64
	Internet	Green	Small	128	255	128

FIGURE 5-35 Use *CALCULATE* to transform row context into filter context.

As you have seen before in this chapter, the filter context is automatically propagated through relationships differently than it is by the row context. Thus, you can obtain the same result as *RELATED* and *RELATEDTABLE* by using *CALCULATE* and *CALCULATETABLE*. For example, the following two expressions used in the Orders table return the same value.

```
Orders[Discount] = RELATED( Channels[Discount] )
```

```
Orders[Discount] = CALCULATE( VALUES( Channels[Discount] ) )
```

Important The *VALUES* function (like *DISTINCT*) usually returns a list of values. However, when this list is made of a single row, *VALUES* and *DISTINCT* can be used as scalar functions. If the referenced table is a lookup table and your current row context is in the many table, these functions never return more than one row. If more than one row is returned, which might happen only if the relationship is missing or a wrong reference is specified, an error is raised and the expression fails. Consider that *RELATED* checks the existence of a relationship in the tabular model, whereas *CALCULATE* does not make any check in terms of metadata (so you do not get any warning if a relationship that you assume exists does not exist).

Likewise, you can write a *CALCULATETABLE* statement instead of using *RELATEDTABLE* for a calculated column in the Channels table.

```
Channels[Orders Count] = COUNTROWS( RELATEDTABLE( Orders ) )
```

```
Channels[Orders Count] = COUNTROWS( CALCULATETABLE( Orders ) )
```

In reality, *RELATEDTABLE* is a synonym for the *CALCULATETABLE* function. The former should be used to get the rows of a table following an active relationship; the latter should be used to manipulate the filter context in more complex ways. Both functions transform the row context of the Channels table in a filter context and propagate the filter to the Orders table. For example, you should use *CALCULATETABLE* you want to count only the orders of a Red color.

```
Channels[Red Orders Count] = COUNTROWS( CALCULATETABLE( Orders, Orders[Color] = "Red" ) )
```

However, you can also write a *CALCULATE* statement instead of using *RELATEDTABLE* or *CALCULATETABLE* for the same calculation, and this will be the more common way to write such expressions.

```
Channels[Orders Count] = CALCULATE( COUNTROWS( Orders ) )
```

```
Channels[Red Orders Count] = CALCULATE( COUNTROWS( Orders ), Orders[Color] = "Red" )
```

In this case, *CALCULATE* transforms the row context of the Channels table in a filter context and propagates the filter to the Orders table. In this way, *COUNTROWS* inside *CALCULATE* only accesses the Orders rows related to the corresponding channel of the current row. Even if the results are identical, conceptually *RELATEDTABLE* is like *FILTER* (it returns a table), whereas the *CALCULATE* statement alters the filter context in which the calculation is made. You see in the next section that syntax based on *CALCULATE* or *CALCULATETABLE* is necessary whenever you want to use inactive relationships in your calculation.

Understanding Row Context and Inactive Relationships

The automatic detection of relationships made by DAX functions you have seen up to now only follows active relationships. You have to use the *CALCULATE* syntax to apply an inactive relationship to your calculation. For example, consider the relationships between the Date and Internet Sales tables in the Adventure Works DW tabular model shown in Figure 5-36.

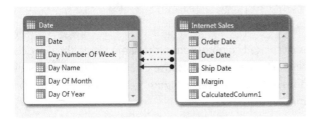

FIGURE 5-36 This figure shows the relationships between the Date and Internet Sales tables.

The active relationship uses the *Order Date* column of the Internet Sales table. For example, you can write an *Ordered Lines* calculated column in the Date table by using either of these formulas.

```
'Date'[Ordered Lines] = COUNTROWS( RELATEDTABLE( 'Internet Sales' ) )
```

```
'Date'[Ordered Lines] = CALCULATE( COUNTROWS( 'Internet Sales' ) )
```

Two other relationships are inactive, based on the *Due Date* and *Ship Date* columns in the Internet Sales table. By using *CALCULATETABLE*, you can obtain the value of *Shipped Lines* by specifying *USERELATIONSHIP* as a filter parameter. The *USERELATIONSHIP* function has the following syntax.

```
USERELATIONSHIP( <column1>, <column2> )
```

The presence of *USERELATIONSHIP* replaces the active relationship with the one specified in its parameters. An inactive relationship corresponding to these parameters has to be defined in the tabular model between the two columns passed as *USERELATIONSHIP* arguments; otherwise, you get an error. The following formula calculates the *Shipped Lines* calculated column in the Date table.

```
'Date'[Shipped Lines] =
COUNTROWS(
    CALCULATETABLE(
        'Internet Sales',
        USERELATIONSHIP( 'Internet Sales'[Ship Date], 'Date'[Date] )
    )
)
```

> **Note** The Date table must be referenced between single quotes, even if it is a single name, because Date is a reserved word in DAX.

You can obtain the same result by manipulating the filter context used by *COUNTROWS('Internet Sales')* through a *CALCULATE* statement by using the same *USERELATIONSHIP* function you have used in the previous example.

```
'Date'[Shipped Lines] =
CALCULATE(
    COUNTROWS( 'Internet Sales' ),
    USERELATIONSHIP( 'Internet Sales'[Ship Date], 'Date'[Date] )
)
```

Even if both versions of *Shipped Lines* calculated columns return the same result, the *CALCULATE* version is preferable because it has better performance and because *CALCULATETABLE* requires a temporary table, whereas *CALCULATE* does not. You can see in Figure 5-37 the results of the *Ordered Lines* and *Shipped Lines* calculated columns.

Date	Ordered Lines	Shipped Lines
6/30/2001		
7/1/2001	5	
7/2/2001	4	
7/3/2001	5	
7/4/2001	2	
7/5/2001	5	
7/6/2001	4	
7/7/2001	3	
7/8/2001	3	5
7/9/2001	6	4
7/10/2001	3	5

FIGURE 5-37 These are the *Ordered Lines* and *Shipped Lines* calculated columns in the Date table.

Important If you want to use inactive chained relationships, each relationship must be specified in a different *USERELATIONSHIP* call. Every *USERELATIONSHIP* must correspond to an existing relationship, whether the relationship is active or not.

Looking at the opposite direction, an *Order Day Name* column in the Internet Sales table can be written by using both *RELATED* or *CALCULATE*. The following formula returns the same value.

```
'Internet Sales'[Order Day Name] = RELATED( 'Date'[Day Of Week] )
```

```
'Internet Sales'[Order Day Name] = CALCULATE( VALUES( 'Date'[Day Of Week] ) )
```

Unfortunately, in SQL Server Analysis Services 2012, there is no support for *USERELATIONSHIP* for navigating toward the lookup table in the relationship. As a workaround, you can use this formula to create a calculated column in the Internet Sales table that denormalizes the Day Of Week of the Ship Date.

```
'Internet Sales'[Ship Day Name] =
CALCULATE(
    VALUES( 'Date'[Day Of Week] ),
    FILTER( 'Date', 'Date'[Date] = 'Internet Sales'[Ship Date] )
)
```

You read more about using *FILTER* as one of the *CALCULATE* parameters later in this chapter.

Modifying Filter Context for Multiple Tables

We previously introduced the *CALCULATE* function to remove filters from filter context for a single table and to convert a row context into a filter context. *CALCULATE* can do more than these tasks, and it is the most important function for manipulating the filter context.

The *CALCULATE* function accepts two forms of filter parameters. The first type is a Boolean expression, similar to a filter condition in a *FILTER* function. This type of filter for *CALCULATE* is also called a *table filter*. For example, this expression calculates the total amount for Europe regardless of the selection in the Continent slicer. (It is called EuropeSales in Figure 5-38.)

```
EuropeSales := CALCULATE( SUM( Orders[Amount] ), Cities[Continent] = "Europe" )
```

This expression is similar to the following.

```
EuropeSales :=
SUMX( FILTER( Orders, RELATED( Cities[Continent] ) = "Europe" ), Orders[Amount] )
```

In reality, the *CALCULATE* version replaces existing filters on the *Continent* column of the Cities table, whereas the *FILTER*-based version would return a blank if another continent was selected in the PivotTable. Thus, to replace a filter on a column without affecting filters on other columns, use the *CALCULATE* version.

Moreover, it is always better to write the *CALCULATE* version even if you do not have to worry about other existing filters because it is faster than the *FILTER*-based version. In general, whenever you can write an expression by using *CALCULATE* or *FILTER*, always use *CALCULATE* rather than *FILTER* for performance reasons. This is another reason learning *CALCULATE* is important.

> **Note** The reason the *CALCULATE* function is faster than the *FILTER* function lies in the way the filter is made in the Orders table.
>
> When you use *CALCULATE*, the filter is applied to the Cities table, and the real filter of the Orders table is made by using the City set that belongs to the Europe Continent data in the Cities table. This operation is fast because it uses internal indexes and does not require a complete iteration over all the rows of the Orders table.
>
> By using *SUMX*, the filter on the Orders table is made by the *FILTER* function, which could iterate the Orders table row by row, making an evaluation of the filter condition for each Orders row, without taking advantage of existing internal indexes defined by the relationship between the Cities and Orders tables.
>
> That said, be careful before creating a calculated column to convert a *SUMX* into a *SUM*. For simple calculation, there are no performance differences due to internal optimizations of the calculation engine. Moreover, the memory required to store the result of the calculated column might lower overall performance, making *SUMX* a faster option. Always run a test on a real amount of data before making a decision about which method to use.

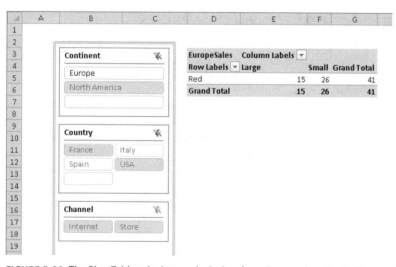

FIGURE 5-38 The PivotTable calculates only Orders from France, despite the filter on the North America Continent data.

In Figure 5-38, you can see that the filter made on Europe Continent by the EuropeSales measure returns data from France only; the filter made on the Continent slicer is ignored for that measure, but the filter on Country is still valid and removes the Italy rows of the Orders table from the filter context. Again, the *FILTER*-based version of EuropeSales would not work with the selection of North America as it is shown here because the two conflicting filters (Europe and North America) would result in an empty set. Only the *CALCULATE* version of EuropeSales produces the result of the PivotTable you have seen.

The second form of filter parameter for the *CALCULATE* function is a list of values for a column or a list of rows for a table. For example, you could get the total Amount for all the *Continent* columns by using this expression (called AllContinents in Figure 5-39).

```
AllContinents := CALCULATE( SUM( Orders[Amount] ), ALL( Cities[Continent] ) )
```

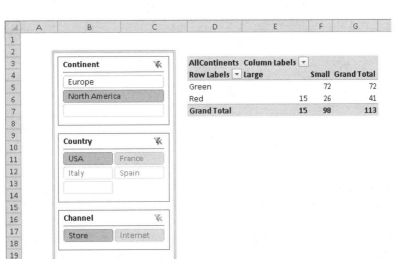

FIGURE 5-39 The PivotTable excludes Orders from Italy and Spain, despite ignoring the Continent selections.

In this case, the measure ignores any selections in the Continent slicer, but it makes use of the Country slicer selection in the filter context to calculate the sum of Amount, as you can see in Figure 5-39.

> **Important** Actually, the user has to select an existing combination of Continent and Country in the slicers. For example, if you select USA and Europe, there are no valid rows in the Cities table; this stops the calculation for Orders and shows no data at all. This limitation is valid for all the following examples. If you are accustomed to Multidimensional models, you would expect that different attributes belonging to the same dimension might have a hierarchical relationship. In a Tabular model, there are no relationships between columns of a table, and the hierarchies that you can define are there only for display purposes. The resulting behavior in Tabular is like the behavior in Multidimensional when all the attributes depend on the key attribute of a dimension, and user hierarchies are not natural hierarchies.

If you want to ignore any of the selections in the columns of the Cities table (which are *Continent*, *Country*, and *City*), you can write this expression.

```
AllCities := CALCULATE( SUM( Orders[Amount] ), ALL( Cities ) )
```

The *ALL(Cities)* function returns the original Cities table completely unfiltered. Because the whole Cities table is returned, any filter on any *City* column is overridden by this statement. As you can see in Figure 5-40, the new AllCities measure ignores any selections made by Country and Continent slicers.

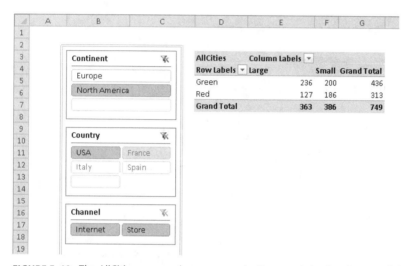

FIGURE 5-40 The AllCities measure ignores any selections made by Continent and Country slicers.

The *CALCULATE* function enables you to define a new filter context based on the existing one. However, you can completely overwrite the existing filter context if you specify a new filter for each of the columns of the tables. In fact, you can specify more filtering by passing multiple table filter parameters in the same *CALCULATE* function call. You could write an expression like the following, which ignores any selection of Continent, Country (both of these belong to the Cities table), and Channel slicers.

```
AllCitiesChannels := CALCULATE( SUM( Orders[Amount] ), ALL( Cities ), ALL( Channels ) )
```

Using *ALLEXCEPT* with Multiple Tables

When you use the *ALLEXCEPT* function in a model with multiple tables, *ALLEXCEPT* also affects related tables, removing possible filters implicitly included by those relationships. *ALLEXCEPT* propagates its effects following the relationships going from the target table to all the related lookup tables. For example, consider the following expression.

```
CALCULATE( SUM( Orders[Amount] ), ALLEXCEPT( Orders, Orders[Price] ) )
```

If you want to get the same result as *ALLEXCEPT*, you need to add the entire list of *ALL* calls—that is, you should include an *ALL* call for each table related to the one on which you are basing your calculation (Orders in this example). The following use of the *CALCULATE* function is equivalent to the previous usage of the *ALLEXCEPT* function.

```
CALCULATE( SUM( Orders[Amount] ),
        ALL( Channels ), ALL( Cities ),
        ALL( Orders[Channel], Orders[City], Orders[Size],
            Orders[Color], Orders[Quantity], Orders[Amount] ) )
```

For this reason, we recommend the use of *ALLEXCEPT* whenever you want to exclude almost all the filters from a table.

All the filter conditions that you specify in a *CALCULATE* function call have to be satisfied to make a row active in the filter context. In other words, all the filter conditions are in logical *AND*. However, the order of filter conditions is not relevant for result or performance. (There is no short-circuit evaluation of the *AND* condition.) Usually by mixing *ALL* on some columns and specifying Boolean conditions for others, you obtain the filter context that you want.

For example, if you wanted to filter Italy and France only and ignore the selection of the *City* attribute, you can use this expression.

```
AllCitiesItalyAndFrance :=
CALCULATE(
    SUM( Orders[Amount] ),
    Cities[Country] = "Italy" || Cities[Country] = "France",
    ALL( Cities[City] )
)
```

Sometimes, the *CALCULATE* function syntax cannot be used—for example, when you need to compare more columns at a row level in a table. Unfortunately, these kinds of filter conditions cannot be used directly in a *CALCULATE* filter. For example, the following measure definition

```
PriceQuantity := CALCULATE( SUM( Orders[Amount] ), Orders[Quantity] * 2 < Orders[Price] )
```

generates the following error:

```
Measure 'Orders'[PriceQuantity] : The expression contains multiple columns, but only a single
column can be used in a True/False expression that is used as a table filter expression.
```

In the next section, you see how to work around this. For now, pay attention to the first parameter passed to the *FILTER* function included in a *CALCULATE* call; the next paragraphs will explain further.

You have seen how to operate by using *CALCULATE* by replacing existing column filters on filter context with a new filter, unrelated to the existing filter. In fact, this measure definition

```
ItalyAndFrance :=
CALCULATE( SUM( Orders[Amount] ), Cities[Country] = "Italy" || Cities[Country] = "France" )
```

is equivalent to this one:

```
ItalyAndFrance :=
CALCULATE(
    SUM( Orders[Amount] ),
    FILTER( ALL( Cities[Country] ), Cities[Country] = "Italy" || Cities[Country] = "France" )
)
```

In other words, the condition that filters cities only in Italy or France operates on all the values of the *Country* column. In fact, it always returns a value, regardless of the user selection of Country. If you want to consider the current filter context and further restrict it by adding another condition without replacing the current selection, you need to use the *VALUES* function instead of *ALL*.

```
ItalyAndFrance :=
CALCULATE(
    SUM( Orders[Amount] ),
    FILTER( VALUES( Cities[Country] ), Cities[Country] = "Italy" || Cities[Country] = "France" )
)
```

VALUES returns a one-column table that contains the distinct values from the specified column (duplicates are eliminated) that are active in the current filter context. You can also write the same measure, putting the *VALUES* result in a different filter argument, even if the *Country* column is used twice in the same *CALCULATE* function. The final result is the intersection of the two parameters, as if they were put in a logical *AND* condition.

```
ItalyAndFrance :=
CALCULATE(
    SUM( Orders[Amount] ),
    VALUES( Cities[Country] ),
    Cities[Country] = "Italy" || Cities[Country] = "France"
)
```

 Note *VALUES* is similar to the *DISTINCT* function. The only difference is that *VALUES* might return a *BLANK* row if you are referencing a column in a lookup table and there are no corresponding rows for one or more values following the relationship.

Final Considerations for Evaluation Context

Filter context and row context are two important concepts that you need to understand to create advanced DAX expressions.

This is a short list of the more important concepts you have learned about evaluation context.

- *RELATED* always refers to the row context.
- Column references with the syntax Table[Column] always refer to the row context.
- *CALCULATE*, *CALCULATETABLE*, and *RELATEDTABLE* convert all row contexts to filter context.
- *VALUES* is bound to filter context.
- Base tables used as arguments for *aggX* and *FILTER* functions are filtered by filter context.
- Using *CALCULATE* instead of *FILTER* or *RELATEDTABLE* might get better performance.

You find other insights about evaluation contexts in Chapter 7, "DAX Advanced," after you have learned how to write DAX queries in Chapter 6, "Querying Tabular."

Summary

In this chapter, you have seen that evaluation context is formed by row context and filter context. Relationships in a Tabular model are automatically propagated in a filter context, whereas special DAX functions are required to use these relationships with row context.

The *CALCULATE* and *CALCULATETABLE* functions are important in DAX because they allow the manipulation of the filter context in a calculation. To write measures in a Tabular model that can be correctly used in any query sent from a client tool, it is important to understand how to manipulate filter context and row context properly. It is important to choose correctly between column and table filters in a *CALCULATE* or *CALCULATETABLE* function. You can practice these differences by writing DAX queries with local scoped measures defined in the queries themselves, as you will see in the next chapter.

Querying Tabular

As you have seen, a Tabular Business Intelligence Semantic Model (BISM) can be queried by using both MDX and DAX languages. These two languages use different abstraction concepts to represent the underlying data model and have different syntaxes. A client tool might generate queries in one of these languages. For example, a Microsoft Excel PivotTable generates queries in MDX, whereas Power View generates queries in DAX. If you are writing your own report, for example by using Reporting Services, you can choose between both languages.

A query written in DAX manipulates tables and returns a table. If you have a BISM Tabular model, you might prefer using DAX because DAX natively returns a table, whereas MDX natively returns a cellset.

The MDX language is used to query a Multidimensional model, and the Tabular model is exposed as a Multidimensional model for this purpose. There are simple rules to map Tabular concepts in a Multidimensional model. In this chapter, you learn how this mapping works; however, learning MDX is not a goal for this book. (There are very good books devoted to that topic.)

As a rule, you will probably prefer using DAX to query a BISM Tabular model. It is easier to learn, and it gives you a higher degree of control over the query (unless you prefer MDX because you already know it). For this reason, most of this chapter is dedicated to queries in DAX, covering its syntax, and only a few pages are dedicated to MDX to map the Tabular entities to the MDX concepts.

Tools for Querying Tabular

In this first section, you learn how to execute simple queries against a Tabular model. To query Tabular, you need a user interface that enables you to write the query in either DAX or MDX, run it, and see its results. SQL Server Management Studio (SSMS) can do that even if its user interface is optimized for MDX and does not offer the same help (such as Microsoft IntelliSense) when you are writing a DAX query. Regardless of the language you want to use, you can open a query editor window by using the File | New | Analysis Services MDX Query menu in SSMS. This opens the MDX editor window that you can see in Figure 6-1.

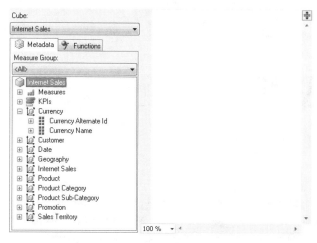

FIGURE 6-1 This is the MDX Query editor.

Even if you have connected to a Tabular model, the metadata in the left pane represents a Multidimensional model with dimensions, attributes, and measures instead of only a list of tables. You can use this pane as a help to edit a query in this way:

1. Click the *Currency Name* attribute of the Currency dimension.

2. Drag that attribute to the query editor window on the right and drop it there.

You will see the text [*Currency*].[*Currency Name*] inserted.

As a result of the drag-and-drop operation, you get the MDX syntax that represents the entity you selected. This syntax is different from the one used by DAX to represent tables and columns. (In DAX, you have to write **Currency[Currency Name]** to reference the same entity.) Thus, you can use the left pane as a reminder for available names, but you always need to write the correct DAX syntax manually. Whether the query is MDX or DAX, the result of the query is always shown as a table.

> **Tip** Because the editor is optimized for MDX, you might look for a better editor for DAX. Unfortunately, as of this writing, no add-ins are available for SSMS, but you can consider using the DAX editor for SQL Server extension in Visual Studio 2010 (*http://daxeditor .codeplex.com*), which was originally developed by a few members of the Analysis Services team (*http://blogs.msdn.com/b/cathyk/archive/2011/10/14/dax-editor-for-sql-server-going-to-codeplex.aspx*).

DAX Query Syntax

In this section, you learn how DAX can be used as a query language. Up to now, you have used DAX to author formulas, but you can also use DAX to query data models and get back results. A DAX query is just a DAX expression that returns a table. The *EVALUATE* keyword is required to retrieve data from such an expression. The complete DAX query syntax is the following.

```
[DEFINE { MEASURE <tableName>[<name>] = <expression> }]
EVALUATE <table>
[ORDER BY {<expression> [{ASC | DESC}]} [, …]
    [START AT {<value>|<parameter>} [, …]] ]
```

Before introducing more complex queries, start with a very simple query that returns all the rows and columns from an existing table. For example, type the following text in the query editor window connected to the Adventure Works DW database.

```
EVALUATE 'Sales Territory'
```

You can execute the query by pressing F5, and you obtain the following result in the Results pane below the query editor window.

Sales Territory Id	Sales Territory Alternate Id	Sales Territory Region	Sales Territory Country	Sales Territory Group
10	10	United Kingdom	United Kingdom	Europe
9	9	Australia	Australia	Pacific
7	7	France	France	Europe
5	5	Southeast	United States	North America
11	0	NA	NA	NA
2	2	Northeast	United States	North America
8	8	Germany	Germany	Europe
6	6	Canada	Canada	North America
4	4	Southwest	United States	North America
1	1	Northeast	United States	North America
3	3	Central	United States	North America

To control the sort order, you can use the *ORDER BY* clause.

```
EVALUATE 'Sales Territory'
ORDER BY
    'Sales Territory'[Sales Territory Group] ASC,
    'Sales Territory'[Sales Territory Country] ASC,
    'Sales Territory'[Sales Territory Region]
```

Note Please note that the Sort By Column property defined in a Tabular model does not have an effect in Tabular. You might see sorted data by querying a single column according to the Sort By Column property, but you do not have to rely on this behavior, just as you cannot rely on a clustered index in a SQL query. In both DAX and SQL, you must always use an explicit *ORDER BY* condition to get sorted data as a result.

The ASC and DESC keywords are optional; if they are not included, ASC is used by default.

Sales Territory Id	Sales Territory Alternate Id	Sales Territory Region	Sales Territory Country	Sales Territory Group
7	7	France	France	Europe
8	8	Germany	Germany	Europe
10	10	United Kingdom	United Kingdom	Europe
11	0	NA	NA	NA
6	6	Canada	Canada	North America
3	3	Central	United States	North America
2	2	Northeast	United States	North America

Sales Territory Id	Sales Territory Alternate Id	Sales Territory Region	Sales Territory Country	Sales Territory Group
1	1	Northwest	United States	North America
5	5	Southeast	United States	North America
4	4	Southwest	United States	North America
9	9	Australia	Australia	Pacific

The *START AT* condition is also optional and must be used in conjunction with an *ORDER BY* clause. You can specify the starting value for each column in the *ORDER BY* statement. The *START AT* condition is useful for pagination in stateless applications that read only a limited number of rows from a query and then send another query when the user asks for the next page of data. For example, look at the following query.

```
EVALUATE 'Sales Territory'
ORDER BY
    'Sales Territory'[Sales Territory Group] ASC,
    'Sales Territory'[Sales Territory Country] ASC,
    'Sales Territory'[Sales Territory Region]
    START AT "North America", "United States"
```

The query returns a table that contains only the rows starting from North America, United States.

Sales Territory Id	Sales Territory Alternate Id	Sales Territory Region	Sales Territory Country	Sales Territory Group
3	3	Central	United States	North America
2	2	Northeast	United States	North America
1	1	Northwest	United States	North America
5	5	Southeast	United States	North America
4	4	Southwest	United States	North America
9	9	Australia	Australia	Pacific

Please note that the notion of "starting from" is related to the order direction specified in the *ORDER BY* clause. If you specified *DESC*, Canada would have been included in the result.

To filter rows and change the columns returned by a DAX query, you must manipulate the table expression after the *EVALUATE* keyword by using specific DAX functions.

Using *CALCULATETABLE* and *FILTER*

In the previous section, you learned how to query a complete table. Now you learn how to filter the rows returned by the query you write. You have seen in the previous chapter how filter context can be manipulated by using *CALCULATE* and *CALCULATETABLE*. *CALCULATETABLE* can be used to filter rows in a table, and its syntax is as follows.

```
CALCULATETABLE( <expression> [,<filter1>] [,<filter2>] [, …] )
```

The expression in the first parameter must return a table, which is evaluated in a context that is modified by the filters passed in other parameters. In the following example, *CALCULATETABLE* is used to control the rows returned by the query.

```
EVALUATE
CALCULATETABLE(
    'Sales Territory',
    'Sales Territory'[Sales Territory Country] = "United States"
)
ORDER BY 'Sales Territory'[Sales Territory Alternate Id]
```

The result contains all the columns of the Sales Territory table filtered by Sales Territory Country equal to United States.

Sales Territory Id	Sales Territory Alternate Id	Sales Territory Region	Sales Territory Country	Sales Territory Group
1	1	Northeast	United States	North America
2	2	Northeast	United States	North America
3	3	Central	United States	North America
4	4	Southwest	United States	North America
5	5	Southeast	United States	North America

Another function used to filter rows is *FILTER*, which can apply a filter iterating every row of a table expression. In the following example, the predicate is executed in a row context and can reference more than one column of the same table and related tables.

```
EVALUATE
FILTER(
    'Internet Sales',
    'Internet Sales'[Ship Date] > 'Internet Sales'[Due Date]
)
```

In this case, the order of evaluation is the "natural" one, starting from the innermost function. For example, if you write

```
EVALUATE
FILTER(
    FILTER(
        'Internet Sales',
        'Internet Sales'[Ship Date] > 'Internet Sales'[Due Date]
    ),
    'Internet Sales'[Unit Price] > 2
)
```

for each row in the Internet Sales table, the "*Ship Date condition greater than Due Date*" will be evaluated first. Then, only for those rows that satisfy that condition, the following "*Unit Price greater than two*" condition will be tested. However, because only those rows that satisfy both conditions will be returned, a functionally equivalent query is as follows.

```
EVALUATE
FILTER(
    'Internet Sales',
    'Internet Sales'[Ship Date] > 'Internet Sales'[Due Date]
        && 'Internet Sales'[Unit Price] > 2
)
```

In other words, nested *FILTER* statements are functionally equivalent to a single *FILTER* that puts the filter conditions in a short circuit logical *AND* statement. So the expression

```
FILTER( FILTER( T, A ), B )
```

corresponds to

```
FILTER( T, A && B )
```

Please refer to the previous chapter to look at other examples and differences between *FILTER* and *CALCULATETABLE*. These are the two main DAX functions that enable filtering rows in a DAX Query.

Order of Evaluation in Nested *CALCULATETABLE*

You are probably accustomed to not caring about the order of evaluation of parameters in a function call. However, the order of evaluation of *CALCULATE* and *CALCULATETABLE* is important to understand, though somewhat counterintuitive, and nesting more than one *CALCULATETABLE* results in a complex pattern. For example, consider the following formula.

```
CALCULATETABLE ( 'Internet Sales', 'Internet Sales'[Unit Price] > 2 )
```

In this formula, because *CALCULATETABLE* is used, the condition is evaluated first, and the table expression 'Internet Sales' is evaluated only after the condition, in a filter context modified by that condition. Things become more difficult to follow with nested calls. For instance, consider this expression.

```
CALCULATETABLE( CALCULATETABLE( T, <innermost-condition> ), <outermost-condition> )
```

In this case, the filter context is evaluated starting from the outer *CALCULATETABLE* (by using outermost-condition), and then it is applied to the inner expressions. Thus, the innermost condition modifies the filter context defined by the outermost-condition. The order of evaluation of filter context starts from the outermost *CALCULATETABLE*, following a direction that is the opposite of the regular order of evaluation of nested functions. For example, consider the following query.

```
EVALUATE
CALCULATETABLE(
    CALCULATETABLE(
        'Sales Territory',
        'Sales Territory'[Sales Territory Country] = "United States"
```

```
    ),
    ALL( 'Sales Territory'[Sales Territory Country] )
)
```

You might think that the innermost *CALCULATETABLE* returns just five rows (those of United States), and the outermost *CALCULATETABLE* removes the filter over Country, returning all the rows of the Sales Territory table. But this is not the case. The filter context is first defined in the outermost table, and then the expression of the first parameter is evaluated in such a filter context. Thus, the innermost *CALCULATETABLE* receives a filter context from the outermost *CALCULATETABLE*, applies the changes to the filter context, and then evaluates the first parameter, which is the Sales Territory table. Thus, the preceding query returns only rows from United States.

To apply a filter context to Country and then remove it, you have to write the following query, which returns all the rows from the Sales Territory table.

```
EVALUATE
CALCULATETABLE(
    CALCULATETABLE(
        'Sales Territory',
        ALL( 'Sales Territory'[Sales Territory Country] )
    ),
    'Sales Territory'[Sales Territory Country] = "United States"
)
```

In this case, the filter to United States is defined first, and then it is removed in the innermost *CALCULATETABLE*. It is important to understand this concept because when you write more complex queries, you might need to obtain intermediate results in a different filter context than the one used to define the granularity of the rows returned as a result.

 Note *CALCULATETABLE* is a function that can apply filters to an existing table, just like a *WHERE* condition in a SQL statement. However, because a filter context can be changed by both adding and removing filters, you can pass a table expression to *CALCULATETABLE* that would return a certain set of rows, and by using other parameters, you can remove part or all of the existing filters.

Using *ADDCOLUMNS*

In the previous section, you saw how to control rows returned by a query; now you learn how to control columns. You can extend any DAX table expression, adding columns to it by using the *ADDCOLUMNS* function. The behavior is similar to what you obtain by adding a calculated column to a table. However, by using *ADDCOLUMNS*, the value for the new column is computed at query time, and it is not persisted in the xVelocity storage engine. The syntax of *ADDCOLUMNS* is as follows.

```
ADDCOLUMNS( <table>,
            <column1_name>, <column1_expression>
            [,<column2_name>, <column2_expression>]
            [, …] )
```

For each column you want to add, you must specify two parameters: the column name, which has to be a string, and the column expression, which is the DAX code that is evaluated in a row context for each row of the table passed as first parameter. For example, this query creates a column that adds a margin percentage column to Internet Sales.

```
EVALUATE
ADDCOLUMNS(
    'Internet Sales',
    "Margin%",
        ( 'Internet Sales'[Sales Amount] - 'Internet Sales'[Total Product Cost] )
            / 'Internet Sales'[Total Product Cost]
)
```

You can also write more complex DAX expressions that calculate values in related tables. For example, in the next formula, you compute the number of products for each product category.

```
EVALUATE
ADDCOLUMNS(
    'Product Category',
    "Products Count", COUNTROWS( RELATEDTABLE( 'Product' ) )
)
```

The result is the following table.

Product Category[Product Category Id]	Product Category[Product Category Alternative Id]	Product Category[Product Category Name]	[Products Count]
1	1	Bikes	125
2	2	Components	189
3	3	Clothing	48
4	4	Accessories	35

In the former DAX query, you used Products Count as column name without any table qualifier. By doing that, the resulting column has just that name, without a table qualifier. This is the most common use of *ADDCOLUMNS*, but, in case you want to return several columns with the same column name that differ only by the table name, you must include the table qualifier to disambiguate them. For this reason, you can use any name as table identifier, even one that does not represent any existing table.

For example, the following query returns the number of subcategories in a column by using a table name (TableX) that does not exist in the data source and by using Product Category (which is the name of an existing table) as table qualifier for the *Products* column containing the number of products.

```
EVALUATE
ADDCOLUMNS(
    'Product Category',
    "TableX[SubCategories Count]", COUNTROWS( RELATEDTABLE( 'Product Subcategory' ) ),
    "'Product Category'[Products Count]", COUNTROWS( RELATEDTABLE( 'Product' ) )
)
```

Product Category[Product Category Id]	Product Category[Product Category Alternative Id]	Product Category[Product Category Name]	TableX[SubCategories Count]	Product Category[Products Count]
1	1	Bikes	3	125
2	2	Components	14	189
3	3	Clothing	8	48
4	4	Accessories	12	35

Unfortunately, although you can add columns to a table by using *ADDCOLUMNS*, it is not possible to run a query that returns some but not all columns from a table. Thus, the concept of projection that you have in SQL by using the *SELECT* statement is not completely present in DAX, even if you have separate functions to add columns to (*ADDCOLUMNS*) and to remove columns from (the simplest one is by using *SUMMARIZE*) a table in the results of a query.

A column added by using *ADDCOLUMNS* can be used in a subsequent filter condition iterating its results, as in the following query that filters only those product categories that have more than 100 products and more than 10 subcategories.

```
EVALUATE
FILTER(
    ADDCOLUMNS(
        'Product Category',
        "TableX[SubCategories Count]", COUNTROWS( RELATEDTABLE( 'Product Subcategory' ) ),
        "Products Count", COUNTROWS( RELATEDTABLE( 'Product' ) ) ),
    [Products Count] > 100 && TableX[SubCategories Count] > 10
)
```

However, the columns added by *ADDCOLUMNS* are not part of the filter context and cannot be used in the filter parameter of a *CALCULATE* or *CALCULATETABLE* function. Moreover, these columns cannot be used as a group-by column in a *SUMMARIZE* function, an example of which you will see in the next section.

Using *SUMMARIZE*

In the previous section, you learned how to filter rows and how to add columns in a query. In this section, you see how to group rows of data in the query result. You can produce a summary table of data by using *SUMMARIZE*. This function groups data by one or more columns, and for each row, it adds new columns that evaluate the specified expressions. The syntax is as follows.

```
SUMMARIZE( <table>,
          <group_by_column1>
          [,<group_by_column2>]
          [, …]
          [,ROLLUP( <group_by_columnX> [,<group_by_columnY>] [, …] )]
          [,<column1_name>, { <column1_expression> | ISSUBTOTAL( <group_by_column> ) } ]
          [,<column2_name>, { <column2_expression> | ISSUBTOTAL( <group_by_column> ) } ]
          [, …] )
```

The behavior of *SUMMARIZE* is similar to the *GROUP BY* syntax of a *SELECT* statement in SQL. For example, consider the following query.

```
EVALUATE
SUMMARIZE(
    'Internet Sales',
    'Internet Sales'[Order Date],
    "Sales Amount", SUM( 'Internet Sales'[Sales Amount] )
)
```

This query calculates the total of Sales Amount for each date in which there is at least one order, producing this result.

Internet Sales[Order Date]	[Sales Amount]
07/01/2001 00:00:00	14477.3382
07/02/2001 00:00:00	13937.52
07/03/2001 00:00:00	15012.1782
…	…

DISTINCT and *ADDCOLUMNS* Equivalency

Instead of using *SUMMARIZE*, you can obtain the same result by generating a table with just the distinct dates you want to obtain as a result. Then, for each date, you can calculate the sum of Sales Amount in the related Internet Sales table. To do that, you can use this syntax.

```
EVALUATE
ADDCOLUMNS(
    DISTINCT( 'Internet Sales'[Order Date] ),
    "Sales Amount", CALCULATE( SUM( 'Internet Sales'[Sales Amount] ) ) )
)
```

However, the *SUMMARIZE* function might be a better choice because it displays data only for which there is at least one row with data in the grouped table, whereas the *DISTINCT*-based version returns every distinct date, even those with no sales. If you get data from a single table (as in the previous example), the result is identical, but the result can be different as soon as you query several tables related to each other.

You can also use *SUMMARIZE* to perform a query projection. If you include only <table> and <group_by_column> arguments, you obtain the same result you would obtain with a *SELECT DISTINCT* statement in SQL. For example, consider the following DAX query.

```
EVALUATE
SUMMARIZE(
    Product,
    Product[Product Id],
    Product[Product Name],
    Product[List Price]
)
```

It corresponds to the following SQL statement.

```
SELECT DISTINCT [Product Id], [Product Name], [List Price]
FROM [Product]
```

Just as in SQL, if you include in the projection the columns that uniquely identify a row in the table (just the *Product Id* column in this case), you obtain the same number of rows of the original table; otherwise, duplicate rows will be excluded from the output.

Note You can read more about query projection in DAX at *http://www.sqlbi.com/articles/ from-sql-to-dax-projection*.

You can include data from several tables in a *SUMMARIZE* statement; relationships are automatically considered in the calculation because the filter context automatically propagates the following relationships.

Note If more tables are involved in a *SUMMARIZE* statement, a relationship must exist between those tables; otherwise, you get an error if you try to summarize on a column that is not related to the original table.

For example, if you want to group data by year, you can use the *Calendar Year* column from the Date table.

```
EVALUATE
SUMMARIZE(
    'Internet Sales',
    'Date'[Calendar Year],
    "Sales Amount", SUM( 'Internet Sales'[Sales Amount] )
)
```

Date[Calendar Year]	[Sales Amount]
2001	3266373.6566
2002	6530343.5264
2003	9791060.2977
2004	9770899.74

It is important to note the role of the table passed as first parameter. In fact, if you use the Date table in the first parameter, you are saying that you want to group the Date table. For example, consider this query.

```
EVALUATE
SUMMARIZE(
    'Date',
    'Date'[Calendar Year],
    "Sales Amount", SUM( 'Internet Sales'[Sales Amount] )
)
```

It groups the *Calendar Year* column in the Date table and, for each existing year in that table, returns the corresponding Sales Amount in the related Internet Sales table.

Date[Calendar Year]	[Sales Amount]
2000	
2001	3266373.6566
2002	6530343.5264
2003	9791060.2977
2004	9770899.74
2005	
2006	

The result contains years (2000, 2005, and 2006) for which there are no corresponding sales. Thus, it is important to consider the table you pass as *SUMMARIZE* to be the first parameter to get the desired result.

Tip You can also use *SUMMARIZE* without adding columns. For example, the following query returns the list of Categories and Subcategories of Products, regardless of the existence of corresponding sales; the relevant filter is the existence of a Subcategory.

```
EVALUATE
SUMMARIZE(
    'Product Subcategory',
    'Product Category'[Product Category Name],
    'Product Subcategory'[Product Subcategory Name]
)
```

You can choose to include roll-up rows in the result of a *SUMMARIZE* function based on one or more of the groups you specified. The roll-up rows have a *BLANK* value for the column used to group results. For example, the following query adds a row with the total for all the years, which is identified by a *BLANK* value for Calendar Year.

```
EVALUATE
SUMMARIZE(
    'Internet Sales',
    ROLLUP( 'Date'[Calendar Year] ),
    "Sales Amount", SUM( 'Internet Sales'[Sales Amount] )
)
ORDER BY 'Date'[Calendar Year]
```

Date[Calendar Year]	[Sales Amount]
	29358677.2207
2001	3266373.6566
2002	6530343.5264
2003	9791060.2977
2004	9770899.74

Because the roll-up rows have a *BLANK* value for the grouping columns, if the result is sorted, you get the roll-up row before the detail rows that it represents. If you want to roll up more columns, you must specify all of them as parameters of a single *ROLLUP* call, whereas other grouping columns can be specified before or after the *ROLLUP* call. In other words, only one *ROLLUP* call can be used in a single *SUMMARIZE* statement. For example, the following query calculates roll-up for category and class of products without calculating a total for all the years. (Calendar Year is out of the *ROLLUP* function.)

```
EVALUATE
SUMMARIZE(
    'Internet Sales',
    'Date'[Calendar Year],
    ROLLUP( 'Product Category'[Product Category Name], Product[Class] ),
    "Sales Amount", SUM( 'Internet Sales'[Sales Amount] )
)
ORDER BY 'Date'[Calendar Year], 'Product Category'[Product Category Name], Product[Class]
```

Date[Calendar Year]	Product Category[Category Name]	Product[Class]	[Sales Amount]
2001			3266373.6566
2001	Bikes		3266373.6566
2001	Bikes	H	3187375.56
2001	Bikes	L	78998.0966
...	...	...	...

Date[Calendar Year]	Product Category[Category Name]	Product[Class]	[Sales Amount]
2003			9791060.2977
2003	**Accessories**		**217275.63**
2003	**Accessories**		**293709.71**
2003	Accessories	H	33177
2003	Accessories	L	18441.01
2003	Accessories	M	24816.07
...	...	...	...

As you can see from the previous result, just checking the *BLANK* value in a column is not a reliable way to identify roll-up rows. In fact, there are two rows for Accessories in 2003 that have a *BLANK* value in the *Class* column. One of these two rows corresponds to the total of Accessories that does not have a Class specified in the Product table, and the other row is the total of Accessories in 2003 for any Class of products. Moreover, the ordering does not guarantee the order of these two rows, and in this case the roll-up row (the one with the higher Sales Amount value) is after the row that represents only those products without a Class specified. For these reasons, do not assume that the *BLANK* value in a column corresponds to a roll-up row.

Tip Using a foreign key that contains only existing values in the lookup table is a best practice for a Tabular model. You can use the classic transformation used in a star schema, in which a surrogate key for "unknown" members is used in fact tables to map application keys not found in the corresponding dimension table. Relying on the built-in Tabular mechanism that displays data in blank rows should be a second choice.

To understand whether a row is the roll-up result for a grouping column, you can add columns to the result by using the *ISSUBTOTAL* function, which accepts a grouping column as a parameter and returns *True* if the row contains a subtotal value (which is the case in a roll-up row); otherwise, it returns *False*. The following query adds two columns that identify whether the row is a roll-up row for the specified grouping column.

```
EVALUATE
SUMMARIZE(
    'Internet Sales',
    'Date'[Calendar Year],
    ROLLUP( 'Product Category'[Product Category Name], Product[Class] ),
    "Sales Amount", SUM( 'Internet Sales'[Sales Amount] ),
    "Category SubTotal", ISSUBTOTAL( 'Product Category'[Product Category Name] ),
    "Class SubTotal", ISSUBTOTAL( Product[Class] )
)
ORDER BY 'Date'[Calendar Year], 'Product Category'[Product Category Name], Product[Class]
```

Date[Calendar Year]	Product Category[Category Name]	Product[Class]	[Sales Amount]	[Category SubTotal]	[Class SubTotal]
2001			3266373.6566	True	True
2001	Bikes		3266373.6566	False	True
2001	Bikes	H	3187375.56	False	False
2001	Bikes	L	78998.0966	False	False
...	...	...	...	...	...
2003			9791060.2977	True	True
2003	**Accessories**		**217275.63**	**False**	**False**
2003	**Accessories**		**293709.71**	**False**	**True**
2003	Accessories	H	33177	False	False
2003	Accessories	L	18441.01	False	False
2003	Accessories	M	24816.07	False	False
...	...	...	...	...	...

As you can see in the result, the *Class SubTotal* column contains *True* for the Accessories in 2003 row that is a sum of all the Classes of products and contains *False* for the row that represents Accessories in 2003 without a Class specified in the products table. The *ISSUBTOTAL* function is useful to obtain information for conditional formatting of the result in a report.

The order of rows in the result shows the Class subtotal before the details of the Class, and the same happens for the Category subtotal. If you want the subtotal row to be displayed after the rows it is summarizing, you can change the *ORDER BY* clause by using the *Category SubTotal* and *Class SubTotal* columns, as you can see in the following query.

```
EVALUATE
SUMMARIZE(
    'Internet Sales',
    'Date'[Calendar Year],
    ROLLUP( 'Product Category'[Product Category Name], Product[Class] ),
    "Sales Amount", SUM( 'Internet Sales'[Sales Amount] ),
    "Category SubTotal", ISSUBTOTAL( 'Product Category'[Product Category Name] ),
    "Class SubTotal", ISSUBTOTAL( Product[Class] )
)
ORDER BY
    'Date'[Calendar Year],
    [Category SubTotal] ASC,
    'Product Category'[Product Category Name],
    [Class SubTotal] ASC,
    Product[Class]
```

Date[Calendar Year]	Product Category[Category Name]	Product[Class]	[Sales Amount]	[Category SubTotal]	[Class SubTotal]
2001	Bikes	H	3187375.56	False	False
2001	Bikes	L	78998.0966	False	False
2001	Bikes		3266373.6566	False	True
2001			3266373.6566	True	True
...	...	...	...	...	...
2003	Accessories		217275.63	False	False
2003	Accessories	H	33177	False	False
2003	Accessories	L	18441.01	False	False
2003	Accessories	M	24816.07	False	False
2003	Accessories		293709.71	False	True
...	...	...	...	...	...

By using this changed *ORDER BY* clause, the subtotal rows are after the corresponding summarized rows. Please note that in DAX you cannot use expressions in the *ORDER BY* clause; you can only reference columns that are part of the produced result.

Use of Inactive Relationships in *SUMMARIZE*

Inactive relationships can be used in a *SUMMARIZE* statement by using the *USERELATIONSHIP* function. For instance, the Internet Sales table contains three dates columns (*Order Date Id*, *Due Date Id*, and *Ship Date Id*). In the examples you have seen for *SUMMARIZE*, the relationship with *Order Date Id* has been used because it is the active relationship in the data model. If you want to use another relationship, you have to execute *SUMMARIZE* inside a *CALCULATETABLE* function that calls *USERELATIONSHIP*. For example, the following query returns the Sales Amount grouped by *Due Date Id* in each order.

```
EVALUATE
CALCULATETABLE(
    SUMMARIZE(
        'Internet Sales',
        'Date'[Calendar Year],
        "Due Sales Amount",
        SUM( 'Internet Sales'[Sales Amount] )
    ),
    USERELATIONSHIP( 'Internet Sales'[Due Date Id], 'Date'[Date Id] )
)
```

Date[Calendar Year]	[Due Sales Amount]
2001	2986977.1218
2002	6602117.1591
2003	9346328.4398
2004	10423254.5

However, if you want to use different relationships in different column expressions, you must extend the result of *SUMMARIZE* by using the *ADDCOLUMNS* syntax, as in the following example, which shows the total of Sales Amount grouped by Order Date, Due Date, and Ship Date.

```
EVALUATE
ADDCOLUMNS(
    SUMMARIZE(
        'Internet Sales',
        'Date'[Calendar Year],
        "Order Sales Amount", SUM( 'Internet Sales'[Sales Amount] )
    ),
    "Due Sales Amount",
        CALCULATE(
            SUM( 'Internet Sales'[Sales Amount] ),
            USERELATIONSHIP( 'Internet Sales'[Due Date Id], 'Date'[Date Id] )
        ),
    "Ship Sales Amount",
        CALCULATE(
            SUM( 'Internet Sales'[Sales Amount] ),
            USERELATIONSHIP( 'Internet Sales'[Ship Date Id], 'Date'[Date Id] )
        )
)
```

Date[Calendar Year]	[Order Sales Amount]	[Due Sales Amount]	[Ship Sales Amount]
2001	3266373.6566	2986977.1218	3105587.3292
2002	6530343.5264	6602117.1591	6576978.9811
2003	9791060.2977	9346328.4398	9517548.5304
2004	9770899.74	10423254.5	10158562.38

In this case, you do not change the filter context of the *SUMMARIZE* function, which uses the active relationship on *Order Date Id*. For each row of the result, two *CALCULATE* statements perform a calculation by using a different relationship for each added column, *Due Date Id*–based and *Ship Date Id*–based relationships, respectively.

Using *CROSSJOIN*, *GENERATE*, and *GENERATEALL*

The use of *SUMMARIZE* is convenient whenever the columns involved in grouping belong to tables related each other. However, there are cases in which you might need to generate all the combinations between values of two or more columns, regardless of the existence of corresponding data in the underlying data model. This is usually required when you want to get a result that also contains rows for missing data. For example, consider the following query.

```
EVALUATE
SUMMARIZE(
    Product,
    'Product'[Color],
    'Product'[Size],
    "Products", COUNTROWS( Product ) )
ORDER BY 'Product'[Color], 'Product'[Size]
```

Product[Color]	Product[Size]	[Products]
...	...	...
Blue	L	1
Blue	M	1
Blue	S	1
Gray		1
Multi		3
Multi	L	4
Multi	M	4
Multi	S	4
Multi	XL	3
...	...	...

The result does not contain combinations of Color and Size that do not have any product in the table. To include these rows, you must write the query by using the *CROSSJOIN* syntax.

```
CROSSJOIN( <table>, <table> [, <table>] [, …]  )
```

The *CROSSJOIN* function returns the Cartesian product of the rows from the tables specified as parameters. If you apply *CROSSJOIN* to the *Color* and *Size* columns, you need to add a column that counts the number of rows of the Product table to get the number of rows corresponding to each combination of Color and Size.

```
EVALUATE
ADDCOLUMNS(
    CROSSJOIN(
        DISTINCT( 'Product'[Color] ),
        DISTINCT( 'Product'[Size] )
    ),
```

```
    "Products", COUNTROWS( RELATEDTABLE( Product ) ) )
)
ORDER BY 'Product'[Color], 'Product'[Size]
```

Product[Color]	Product[Size]	[Products]
...	...	...
Blue	L	1
Blue	M	1
Blue	S	1
Blue	XL	
Gray		1
Gray	L	
Gray	M	
Gray	S	
Gray	XL	
Multi		3
Multi	L	4
Multi	M	4
Multi	S	4
Multi	XL	3
...	...	...

You can think of the result of *CROSSJOIN* as a temporary table that is related to the underlying tables by using the columns you extracted. If you did not use the *RELATEDTABLE* function in the previous *COUNTROWS* call, you would have obtained the same number of products for every row in the result.

> **Tip** *RELATEDTABLE* is required because the filter context is not automatically propagated from the row context of the *CROSSJOIN* result to the Product table. In fact, an alternative syntax that returns the same result uses *CALCULATE* instead of *RELATEDTABLE*.
>
> ```
> EVALUATE
> ADDCOLUMNS(
>     CROSSJOIN(
>         DISTINCT( 'Product'[Color] ),
>         DISTINCT( 'Product'[Size] )
>     ),
>     "Products", CALCULATE( COUNTROWS(Product ) )
> )
> ORDER BY 'Product'[Color], 'Product'[Size]
> ```

The *CROSSJOIN* function in DAX is conceptually similar to the *CROSS JOIN* syntax in SQL Server because it performs the Cartesian product between two tables. However, you might want to perform other operations between tables, such as those offered by *CROSS APPLY* and *OUTER APPLY* in SQL. To do that, you can use *GENERATE* and *GENERATEALL*, respectively. These functions get two table expressions as parameters. The following is their syntax.

```
GENERATE( <table1>, <table2> )
```

```
GENERATEALL( <table1>, <table2> )
```

The *GENERATE* function performs a Cartesian product between each row in table1 and the corresponding rows in table2. In other words, the table expression defined for table2 is executed for each row of table1. For example, you can obtain a table that contains all the valid combinations of product categories and subcategories by writing the following query.

```
EVALUATE
GENERATE(
    'Product Category',
    RELATEDTABLE( 'Product Subcategory' )
)
ORDER BY
    'Product Category'[Product Category Id],
    'Product Subcategory'[Product Subcategory Id]
```

In this case, the result is similar to an *INNER JOIN* statement in SQL, even if the corresponding SQL operation is *CROSS APPLY*, because the expression for table2 is evaluated for each row of table1.

Product Category [Product Category Id]	Product Category [Category Name]	Product Subcategory [Product Subcategory Id]	Product Subcategory [Subcategory Name]	Product Subcategory [Category Id]
1	Bikes	1	Mountain Bikes	1
1	Bikes	2	Road Bikes	1
1	Bikes	3	Touring Bikes	1
2	Components	4	Handlebars	2
2	Components	5	Bottom Brackets	2
2	Components	6	Brakes	2
...	...	...	...	...

> **Note** If you omitted the *RELATEDTABLE* function in the second parameter, you would obtain the same result you obtained by using *CROSSJOIN* instead of *GENERATE* because you would lack the transformation of a row context into a filter context provided by *RELATEDTABLE*, which is an alias for *CALCULATEDTABLE*. In fact, the following queries are equivalent.
>
> ```
> EVALUATE
> GENERATE( 'Product Category', 'Product Subcategory' )
>
> EVALUATE
> CROSSJOIN( 'Product Category', 'Product Subcategory' )
> ```

Thus, the table2 parameter in a *GENERATE* call usually contains a *RELATEDTABLE* or *CALCULATETABLE* statement.

Because you used *RELATEDTABLE*, a relationship must exist between tables in the data model. By using *CALCULATETABLE* instead of *RELATEDTABLE*, you can specify different conditions to filter the data in the second table. For example, the following query returns, for each day, all the sales shipped in that particular day by using the relationship between Internet Sales and Date tables based on the *Ship Date* column.

```
EVALUATE
GENERATE(
    'Date',
    CALCULATETABLE(
        'Internet Sales',
        USERELATIONSHIP( 'Internet Sales'[Ship Date Id], 'Date'[Date Id] )
    )
)
ORDER BY 'Date'[Date]
```

Date[Date]	Date[Day Name]	Internet Sales[Sales Order Number]	...
7/8/2001	Sunday	SO43698	...
7/8/2001	Sunday	SO43701	...
...	...	...	...
7/9/2001	Monday	SO43705	...
7/9/2001	Monday	SO43704	...
...	...	...	...

The previous query returns just those dates on which a shipment has been made. If you want to also include dates without any corresponding sales shipped, you can use *GENERATEALL* instead of *GENERATE*.

```
EVALUATE
GENERATEALL(
    'Date',
```

```
CALCULATETABLE(
    'Internet Sales',
    USERELATIONSHIP( 'Internet Sales'[Ship Date Id], 'Date'[Date Id] )
    )
)
ORDER BY 'Date'[Date]
```

Date[Date]	Date[Day Name]	Internet Sales[Sales Order Number]	...
1/1/2000	Saturday		
1/2/2000	Sunday		
1/3/2000	Monday		
...	...		
7/7/2001	Saturday		
7/8/2001	Sunday	SO43698	...
7/8/2001	Sunday	SO43701	...
...	...	...	...
7/9/2001	Monday	SO43705	...
7/9/2001	Monday	SO43704	...
...	...	...	...

In this case, the result is similar to a *LEFT JOIN* statement in SQL Server even if the corresponding SQL operation is *OUTER APPLY,* because the expression for table2 is evaluated for each row of table1 instead of applying a join condition to the Cartesian product of the two tables as the *JOIN* operation does in SQL.

Table 6-1 summarizes the DAX functions corresponding to common SQL constructs. However, remember that there is no direct translation between SQL and DAX constructs because DAX can use existing relationships defined in the data model, whereas SQL always requires specifying relationships in the query syntax.

TABLE 6-1 SQL–DAX Correspondence

SQL	DAX
CROSS JOIN	*CROSSJOIN*
INNER JOIN *CROSS APPLY*	*GENERATE*
LEFT JOIN *OUTER APPLY*	*GENERATEALL*

Finally, it is important to note that the filter context can be propagated between columns of the same table. For educational purposes, you can consider this an alternative way to obtain existing combinations of column values inside a table. For example, if you want to reduce the columns of the Date table, returning just year and date columns, you can write the following query.

```
EVALUATE
GENERATE(
    VALUES( 'Date'[Calendar Year] ),
    CALCULATETABLE( VALUES( 'Date'[Date] ) )
)
ORDER BY 'Date'[Calendar Year], 'Date'[Date]
```

Date[Calendar Year]	Date[Date]
2000	1/1/2000
2000	1/2/2000
...	...
2000	12/31/2000
2001	1/1/2001
2001	1/2/2001
...	...

However, remember that the same result of the previous query can be obtained by using *SUMMARIZE*, which is faster and probably simpler to read, as in the following query.

```
EVALUATE
SUMMARIZE(
    'Date',
    'Date'[Calendar Year],
    'Date'[Date]
)
ORDER BY 'Date'[Calendar Year], 'Date'[Date]
```

Even if there is no syntax in DAX to perform the projection of a table by reducing the columns produced in the output of a query, you can use *SUMMARIZE*, *CROSSJOIN*, *GENERATE*, and *GENERATEALL* to perform the required data transformation.

Using *ROW*

The *EVALUATE* statement has to return a table. If you want to perform a computation of one or more scalar values and you do not have a corresponding table, you can use the *ROW* function, which returns a table with a single row containing the desired columns.

```
ROW( <column1_name>, <column1_expression>
    [,<column2_name>, <column2_expression>]
    [, ...] )
```

The column_name parameter is the name of the column, and the corresponding column_expression is evaluated to compute a scalar value for that column in the returned row. The rules for the column_name naming convention are the same as those for the *ADDCOLUMNS* function. You can add as many columns as you want.

Tip *ROW* performs an operation similar to a *SELECT* statement without any *FROM* clause in SQL.

You might consider using this function whenever you need to return more than one scalar value; instead of performing several DAX queries, you can execute just one. For example, the following statement returns a row with two columns containing Sales Amount computed for 2002 and 2003.

```
EVALUATE
ROW(
    "Sales 2002",
        CALCULATE( SUM('Internet Sales'[Sales Amount]), 'Date'[Calendar Year] = 2002),
    "Sales 2003",
        CALCULATE( SUM('Internet Sales'[Sales Amount]), 'Date'[Calendar Year] = 2003)
)
```

[Sales 2002]	[Sales 2003]
6530343.5264	9791060.2977

The *ROW* function can also be used in any DAX expression that requires a table. However, because there are no functions that perform a *UNION* of two or more tables in DAX, you cannot use a combination of *ROW* calls to return a table made by more rows arbitrarily defined.

Using *CONTAINS*

You can use *FILTER* and *CALCULATETABLE* functions to filter rows from a table. However, if you need to check whether at least one row exists in a table within certain conditions, you might calculate more rows than necessary by using these functions. The *CONTAINS* function just checks the existence, in the table passed as first parameter, of at least one row that contains all the column values specified in the following parameters. This is the syntax.

```
CONTAINS( <table>,
          <column1_name>, <column1_expression>
          [,<column2_name>, <column2_expression>]
          [, …] )
```

For example, you might want to check whether the Internet Sales table contains at least one sale with a unit price of 564.99. Because the result of *CONTAINS* is a scalar value, you can embed it in a *ROW* function to execute the query.

```
EVALUATE
ROW(
    "SalesExist",
    CONTAINS(
        'Internet Sales',
        'Internet Sales'[Unit Price], 564.99
    )
)
```

[SalesExist]
True

The preceding query corresponds to the following.

```
EVALUATE
ROW(
    "SalesExist",
    COUNTROWS(
        CALCULATETABLE( 'Internet Sales', 'Internet Sales'[Unit Price] = 564.99 )
    ) > 0
)
```

Usually, the *CONTAINS* syntax has better performance for simple filter conditions, whereas *CALCULATETABLE* is preferable for more complex expressions. The *CONTAINS* function just checks for an exact match, and you must use *CALCULATETABLE*, *FILTER*, or both if you need more complex filtering conditions. However, you can combine more column conditions, and the columns can also belong to related tables. (As usual, you have to specify *USERELATIONSHIP*, embedding the *CONTAINS* call in a *CALCULATE* statement if you want to use an inactive relationship.) For example, the following query returns *True* when at least one sale has been made in Australia with a unit price of 564.99.

```
EVALUATE
ROW(
    "SalesAustralia",
    CONTAINS(
        'Internet Sales',
        'Internet Sales'[Unit Price], 564.99,
        'Sales Territory'[Sales Territory Country], "Australia"
    )
)
```

[SalesAustralia]
True

In this case, the preceding query corresponds to the following.

```
EVALUATE
ROW(
    "SalesExist",
    COUNTROWS(
        CALCULATETABLE(
            'Internet Sales',
            'Internet Sales'[Unit Price] = 564.99,
            'Sales Territory'[Sales Territory Country] = "Australia"
        )
    ) > 0
)
```

A practical use of *CONTAINS* is as a filter condition when you want to obtain a list of elements that have at least one corresponding row in another table. For example, the following query returns the list of dates in which there has been at least one sale in the city of Columbus.

```
EVALUATE
FILTER(
    VALUES( 'Date'[Date] ),
    CONTAINS(
        RELATEDTABLE( 'Internet Sales' ),
        Geography[City], "Columbus"
    )
)
ORDER BY 'Date'[Date]
```

Date[Date]
8/2/2002
4/14/2004
5/29/2004

As you can see, the *CONTAINS* function is executed within a different row context for each date. The row context for each date is transformed into a filter context by the *RELATEDTABLE* function so that *CONTAINS* considers only the sales for these rows and returns True when at least one row exists for the city of Columbus on that particular date.

> **Tip** The *CONTAINS* function is used in a way similar to the *EXISTS* keyword in SQL. For example, the previous query could have been written in this way in SQL.
>
> ```
> SELECT d.[Date]
> FROM [Date] d
> WHERE EXISTS ( SELECT NULL
>                FROM FactInternetSales s
>                INNER JOIN Geography g
>                      ON s.SalesTerritoryKey = g.SalesTerritoryKey
>                WHERE g.City = 'Columbus'
>                  AND s.OrderDateKey = d.DateKey )
> ```

Using *LOOKUPVALUE*

In the previous section, you saw how to check whether at least one row exists in a table. However, you will often need to decode a value in a lookup table. To do this, the *LOOKUPVALUE* function in DAX has the following syntax.

```
LOOKUPVALUE( <result_column_name>,
             <search_column1_name>, <search_column1_expression>
             [,<search_column2_name>, <search_column2_expression>]
             [, ...] )
```

The first argument is the column that contains the value to return. The following parameters are pairs of column name and value (as scalar expression) to perform the lookup operation in the table containing the column specified in the first argument. For example, the following query transforms the CA country code into the corresponding country name.

```
EVALUATE
ROW(
    "Country",
    LOOKUPVALUE(
        Geography[Country Region Name],
        Geography[Country Region Code], "CA"
    )
)
```

[Country]
Canada

You can specify more columns to perform the matching operation, and you can refer to columns of related tables. For example, the following query returns the name of the product that has a Silver color and belongs to the Accessories category.

```
EVALUATE
ROW(
    "Product",
    LOOKUPVALUE(
        'Product'[Product Name],
        'Product'[Color], "Silver",
        'Product Category'[Product Category Name], "Accessories"
    )
)
```

[Product]
Hydration Pack - 70 oz.

If there are multiple rows matching the search values, an error is returned if different values are returned in result_column_name, whereas a BLANK value is returned if there are no matching rows. However, if there is a single distinct value for result_column_name, even if multiple rows in the underlying table match the search values, the LOOKUPVALUE function returns only that unique value. For example, the following query returns the name of a month containing all the days of week 7 in quarter 1 of year 2000.

```
EVALUATE
ROW(
    "MonthName",
    LOOKUPVALUE(
        'Date'[Month Name],
        'Date'[Calendar Year], 2000,
        'Date'[Week Number Of Year], 7
    )
)
```

[MonthName]
February

If week 7 was overlapping two months in year 2000, *LOOKUPVALUE* would have returned an error.

Tip Most of the time, a *RELATED* function performs the required lookup operation when you have a row context and you need to get the value of a column in a related table. However, if you do not have a relationship between two tables in an underlying data model, or if you have to implement a particular logic for a lookup operation, you can use *LOOKUPVALUE* instead of *RELATED*. You might also rewrite the *LOOKUPVALUE* call by using the *CALCULATE* function, even if it is not a best practice. For example, the previous query can be rewritten as follows.

```
EVALUATE
ROW(
    "MonthName",
    CALCULATE(
        VALUES('Date'[Month Name]),
        'Date'[Calendar Year] = 2000,
        'Date'[Week Number Of Year] = 7
    )
)
```

Using *LOOKUPVALUE* instead of *CALCULATE* makes the intent more explicit. Thus, using *LOOKUPVALUE* is the preferred way to implement a lookup operation if *RELATED* cannot be used. Use *CALCULATE* only if the matching condition cannot be expressed through *LOOKUPVALUE* arguments.

Defining Measures Inside a Query

Now that you have learned the building blocks of a DAX query, you can improve your productivity by learning how to define measures inside a query. When you write a DAX query, often you have computations that can be used in several parts of the query, or you might want to split a long and complex calculation into simpler parts. Doing that by creating measures in a Tabular model might pollute the model with many intermediate measures that are not useful outside your query, and you experience some latency every time you make a modification to a measure definition. A better approach is to split a complex calculation into simpler parts by defining measures that are local to a DAX query. This technique can also be used to improve speed development and testing of new measures in a Tabular model.

At the beginning of this chapter, you were introduced to the DAX query syntax. The first part of the syntax enables the definition of one or more measures.

```
[DEFINE { MEASURE <tableName>[<name>] = <expression> }]
EVALUATE <table>
```

Each measure must be related to one table that exists in the data model. You can refer to these local measures in any part of the DAX query, including other definitions of local measures. For example, consider this query, which you have already seen in this chapter.

```
EVALUATE
ADDCOLUMNS(
    'Product Category',
    "'Product Category'[Subcategories Count]",
        COUNTROWS( RELATEDTABLE( 'Product Subcategory' ) ),
    "Products Count", COUNTROWS( RELATEDTABLE( 'Product' ) )
)
```

By using *DEFINE MEASURE*, you can define two local measures to calculate the number of products and subcategories related to a product category.

```
DEFINE
    MEASURE 'Product Category'[Subcategories Count] =
        COUNTROWS( RELATEDTABLE( 'Product Subcategory' ) )
    MEASURE 'Product Category'[Products Count] =
        COUNTROWS( RELATEDTABLE( 'Product' ) )
EVALUATE
ADDCOLUMNS(
    'Product Category',
    "'Product Category'[SubCategories]", [Subcategories Count],
    "Products Count", 'Product Category'[Products Count]
)
```

As you can see, the syntax to reference these local measures in your query is identical to the syntax you use to reference a measure defined in the Tabular model. You can include or omit the name of the table when you reference a measure and when it is local to a query. For example, the previous query contains 'Product Category'[Products Count] to reference the corresponding local measure, whereas [Subcategories Count] does not use the table identifier. However, it is always better to use the table identifier to reference a column and to omit the table identifier to reference a measure. Therefore, hereafter, we will never use the table identifier when referencing a measure, regardless of whether it is defined in the model or local to the query.

Note In DAX, a measure that is defined locally to a query has the same performance as a measure that is defined in the Tabular model. If you are accustomed to MDX, you might think that the cache might offer better performance for a measure defined in the model than for a measure local to a query, due to different scopes of the caches used, but this is not the case for DAX measures. DAX implements a completely different cache system than MDX that is limited to the storage engine and does not work at the formula engine level. You can find a further discussion of the internal architecture in Chapter 9, "Understanding xVelocity and DirectQuery."

Defining a local measure is useful whenever you must repeat the same DAX expression in several parts of the query. For example, if you want to show only those categories that have at least 10 subcategories, you can write the following query.

```
DEFINE
    MEASURE 'Product Category'[SubCategories Count] =
        COUNTROWS( RELATEDTABLE( 'Product Subcategory' ) )
    MEASURE 'Product Category'[Products Count] =
        COUNTROWS( RELATEDTABLE( 'Product' ) )
EVALUATE
ADDCOLUMNS(
    FILTER( 'Product Category', [SubCategories Count] > 10 ),
    "'Product Category'[SubCategories Count]", [SubCategories Count],
    "Products Count", [Products Count]
)
```

Product Category[Product Category Id]	Product Category[Product Category Alternative Id]	Product Category[Product Category Name]	Product Category[SubCategories Count]	[Products Count]
2	2	Components	14	189
4	4	Accessories	12	35

The SubCategories Count measure centralizes the calculation and is referenced twice in the query to avoid code duplication.

> **Tip** The previous query could have been written by moving the *FILTER* after
> *ADDCOLUMNS* to reference the *SubCategories* column introduced by *ADDCOLUMNS*.
>
> ```
> EVALUATE
> FILTER(
>     ADDCOLUMNS(
>         'Product Category',
>         "'Product Category'[SubCategories Count]",
>             COUNTROWS( RELATEDTABLE( 'Product Subcategory' ) ),
>         "Products Count", COUNTROWS( RELATEDTABLE( 'Product' ) )
>     ),
>     [SubCategories Count] > 10
> )
> ```
>
> However, filtering first is better, because you can avoid the evaluation of other added
> columns (such as *Products*) for those rows that will be filtered. Thus, the definition of mea-
> sures that are local to a query can improve readability and performance of a DAX query.

Test Your Measures with a Query

When you define the measures in a Tabular model, you can test them by using the measure grid in
SQL Server Data Tools (SSDT). However, the process of creating and testing a new measure in SSDT is
not ideal, especially if you want to run a more complex DAX query to test the correctness of a measure by looking at some query results. A latency is involved in publishing a measure and switching
between different windows to define and then test the measure.

You can define and test the measures for your Tabular model by creating a test DAX query that
contains the definition of all the measures you want as local measures to the DAX query itself. If a
local measure overrides an existing measure in the Tabular model, the local expression is used, and
it replaces the formula defined in the Tabular model for the query execution. You can rely on this
behavior to use SSMS and the MDX query editor as a single environment to write and test the DAX
measures for your Tabular model. For example, the following query defines and tests a few measures
on the Internet Sales table.

```
DEFINE
    MEASURE 'Internet Sales'[Internet Total Sales] = SUM([Sales Amount])
    MEASURE 'Internet Sales'[Internet Total Product Cost] = SUM([Total Product Cost])
    MEASURE 'Internet Sales'[Internet Total Margin] =
        [Internet Total Sales] - [Internet Total Product Cost]
EVALUATE
SUMMARIZE(
    'Internet Sales',
    'Date'[Calendar Year],
    "Sales", 'Internet Sales'[Internet Total Sales],
    "Cost", 'Internet Sales'[Internet Total Product Cost],
    "Margin", 'Internet Sales'[Internet Total Margin]
)
```

The same measures defined here also exist in the Tabular model, but the definitions in this query override those in the Tabular model for the scope of this query. Thus, you can change and test DAX expressions in the query without any deployment of the model. After the results satisfy you, the DAX expressions of the local measures can be copied and pasted in the Tabular model by using the measure grid in SSDT.

 Important If a measure defined locally to a query has the same name as an existing column name of the same table, the column is used, and the measure definition is ignored. In other words, a measure that overrides an existing column cannot be referenced in the DAX query. If you try to do this within a Tabular model, you get an error whenever you have duplicate names between measures and column definitions. However, you do not get any error when this conflict happens for measures that are local to the query. The worst-case scenario is when you deploy a report containing local measure definitions in DAX queries. If, after this deployment, someone adds a column with the same name of a measure defined in DAX queries of your report, subsequent executions of the report will use the column rather than the DAX expression to evaluate that name in the query. We hope that this behavior will change in the future, raising an error when a local measure overrides an existing column name, protecting your reports from unwanted results in case of similar conflicts. You can check the state of this request by looking at this feedback on Microsoft Connect at *https://connect.microsoft.com/SQLServer/feedback/details/726596/local-measure-definition-in-dax-query-are-ignored-it-there-is-a-table-column-with-the-same-name.*

 Tip Even if it is not useful for testing new measures, you can create a measure local to a session that can be reused in different queries by following instructions provided at *http://sqlblog.com/blogs/marco_russo/archive/2012/02/28/create-a-dax-measure-in-a-session-in-bism-tabular.aspx.*

Parameters in DAX Query

In the previous sections of this chapter, you saw several examples of DAX queries sent to a Tabular model. When you write DAX queries in reports and custom applications, most of the time you must parameterize the query. In this section, you see how to do that and what limitations might exist.

The DAX query can support named parameters prefixed by the @ symbol. For example, the following query returns the list of product subcategories for the Bikes product category.

```
EVALUATE
CALCULATETABLE(
    'Product Subcategory',
    'Product Category'[Product Category Name] = "Bikes"
)
```

Instead of the constant Bikes string, you can use the @Category name to define a named parameter called Category, the values of which have to be passed in the parameter list for every execution of the same query.

```
EVALUATE
CALCULATETABLE(
    'Product Subcategory',
    'Product Category'[Product Category Name] = @Category
)
```

This syntax is supported by sending the DAX query to Analysis Services in an XMLA *Execute* method. For example, the following is an XMLA command that requests the list of subcategories for the Bikes product category by passing Bikes as a parameter in the *Parameters* element.

```
<Execute xmlns="urn:schemas-microsoft-com:xml-analysis">
    <Command>
        <Statement>
EVALUATE
CALCULATETABLE(
    'Product Subcategory',
    'Product Category'[Product Category Name] = @Category )
        </Statement>
    </Command>
    <Properties>
        <PropertyList>
            <Catalog>AdventureWorks Tabular Model SQL 2012</Catalog>
        </PropertyList>
    </Properties>
    <Parameters>
        <Parameter>
            <Name>Category</Name>
            <Value>Bikes</Value>
        </Parameter>
    </Parameters>
</Execute>
```

> **Note** XMLA is the XML for Analysis open standard that supports data access to data sources. You can find more information at *http://msdn.microsoft.com/en-us/library/ms187190(v=SQL.110).aspx*.

If you write your own code in Microsoft C# or Microsoft Visual Basic .NET (VB.NET), you should use the ADOMD.NET connection to pass parameters to the DAX query. You cannot use a regular OLE DB connection because of an issue in the .NET library. You can find more information and a few examples in C# at *http://www.sqlbi.com/articles/execute-dax-queries-through-ole-db-and-adomd-net*.

Unfortunately, you cannot use parameterization of the query in this way when you use an OLE DB connection in Report Builder, but you can use the DMX query editor if you use SSDT to design reports for Reporting Services.

Using DAX Query in SQL Server Reporting Services

It is very useful to write a DAX query in a report for SQL Server Reporting Services. If you are using the Report Designer included in SQL Server Developer Tools, you can parameterize a DAX query by using the DMX Command Type button. To do so, after you create a data source with a SQL Server Analysis Services (SSAS) connection type, click the Command Type DMX button in the Query Designer dialog box shown in Figure 6-2.

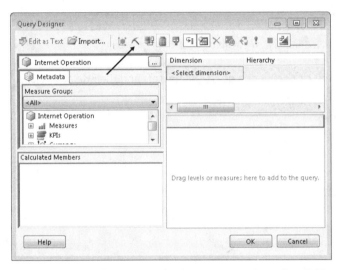

FIGURE 6-2 This is the Query Designer in Report Designer for a DAX query to a Tabular model.

The Query Designer starts in design mode by default, and you must disable it by clicking the Design Mode icon indicated in Figure 6-3, which shows the DAX query manually inserted because it is a DMX query.

Note DMX stands for Data Mining Extension. You do not write this type of query for Tabular, but you can use the same editor tool to write a parameterized DAX query.

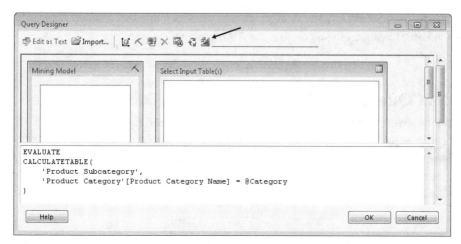

FIGURE 6-3 This is the Query Designer in Command Type DMX mode.

Finally, by clicking Parameter, you can define the query parameters and their default value.

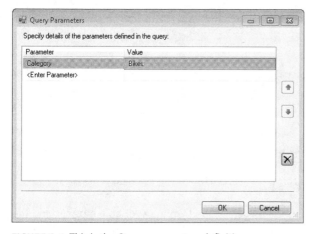

FIGURE 6-4 This is the Query parameters definition.

However, you cannot rely on the standard Analysis Services Data Source by using Report Builder, which supports MDX as only a query language and does not include the DMX editor. You must create your query by replacing parameter names with actual parameter values in a string format by using the following instructions.

You must define a data source by using the OLE DB connection type, specifying in the connection string MSOLAP as Provider, and passing the Analysis Services instance name to Data Source and the database name to Catalog, as you can see in Figure 6-5.

After you define the data source, you can create the dataset by choosing the data source you just created and inserting the query directly in Text mode, as you can see in Figure 6-6.

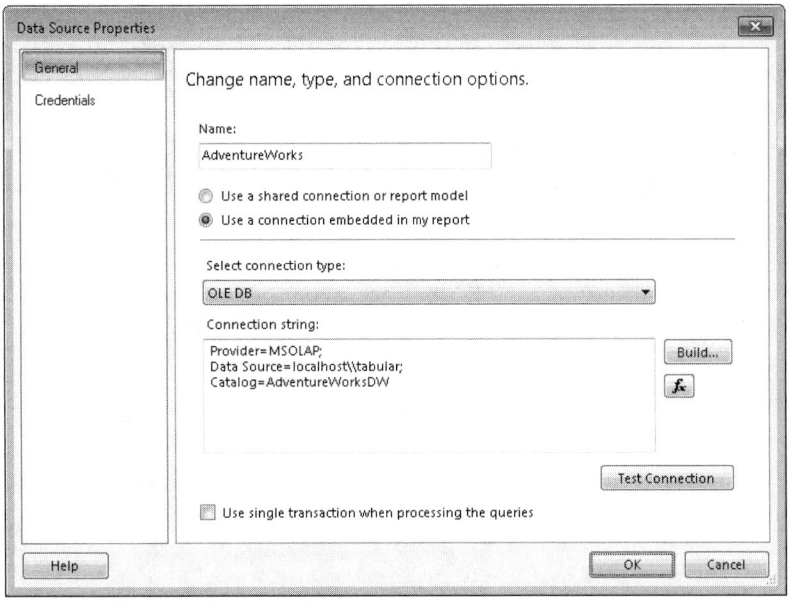

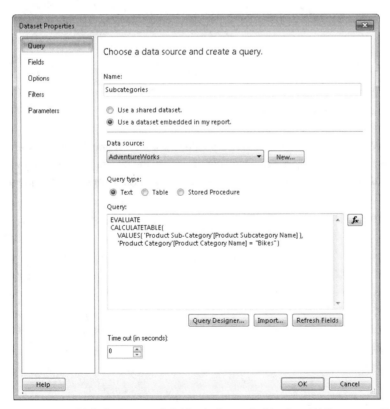

FIGURE 6-5 This is the Data Source definition in Report Builder for a DAX query to a Tabular model.

FIGURE 6-6 This is the Dataset definition in Report Builder for a DAX query to a Tabular model.

You can open Query Designer and test the query, as you can see in Figure 6-7, even if you do not have any tool that shows you table and column names available in the Tabular model to which you have connected.

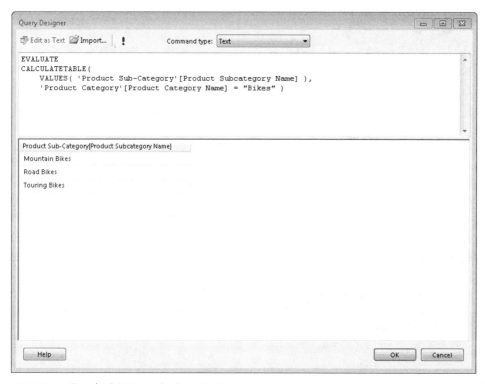

FIGURE 6-7 Test the DAX query in Query Designer.

To parameterize the query, you must rely on string concatenation after manually defining a parameter for your report. In Figure 6-8, you can see how to replace the constant Bikes string with the Category parameter defined in the same Report by using the Expression editor for the query text you saw in Figure 6-6.

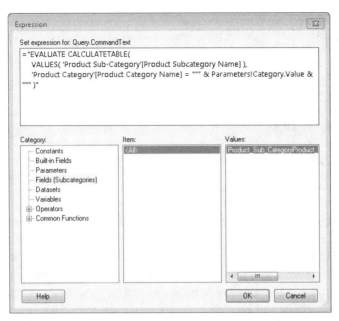

FIGURE 6-8 Parameterize a DAX query by using a Reporting Services expression.

Thus, to use DAX queries in Report Builder, you must use the OLE DB connection type. You do not have a direct support for query parameterization, but you obtain a typed result that can be easily manipulated, for example, to customize number formatting. Otherwise, you must use the Command Type DMX mode in Query Designer if you want to use the Analysis Services connection type in Report Designer within SSDT.

Querying by Using MDX

A Tabular model is a semantic model that can be natively queried by using DAX queries, and you have seen in this chapter how to build a DAX query. However, to maintain compatibility with existing clients, a Tabular model can be also queried by using MDX, the language on which a Multidimensional model is based. In this section, you learn how to use MDX to query a Tabular model and how its entities are translated in an equivalent model queryable with MDX.

When you query a Tabular model with MDX, you access a multidimensional representation of the Tabular model. The founding concepts of a Tabular model are tables, columns, measures, and relationships. A Multidimensional model contains dimensions, attributes, measure groups, and measures. Any Tabular model is automatically converted into a Multidimensional model by using the conversion schema in Table 6-2.

TABLE 6-2 Tabular-to-Multidimensional Conversion

Tabular	Multidimensional
Table	Dimension, plus a measure group for each Tabular table containing at least one measure
Column	Attribute
Sort By Column	Attribute OrderBy
Measure	Measure, plus a measure group for each Tabular table containing at least one measure
Table Relationship	Dimension Relationship
KPI	KPI
Hierarchy	User Hierarchy

Every column of a table in a Tabular model becomes an attribute of a corresponding dimension in Multidimensional. Relationships between tables of a Tabular model do not appear in the Multidimensional view, but they are used to perform calculation of measures. Measures defined in Tabular also appear as measures in Multidimensional. The measure group to which each measure belongs in Multidimensional has the same name as the table to which the measure belongs in Tabular. Thus, every table in Tabular becomes a dimension and a measure group if it contains at least one measure. Otherwise, a corresponding measure group does not appear in Multidimensional for a Tabular table. In Figure 6-9, you can see an example of a Multidimensional model represented in SSMS. In the left pane is the list of dimensions that corresponds to the list of tables defined in the Adventure Works Tabular model. Only those tables that also contain measures are displayed as folders under the Measures nodes, and each folder includes all the visible measures belonging to the corresponding table.

FIGURE 6-9 The Tabular table corresponds to dimensions and measures folders in Multidimensional metadata.

Moreover, a Tabular model contains metadata definitions that are used implicitly only in MDX, which expects such a metadata from the corresponding Multidimensional model. However, DAX does not use this metadata information. For example, you can define a hierarchy in Tabular that corresponds to a user hierarchy in Multidimensional; MDX has specific functions to navigate user hierarchies, but there are no corresponding constructs in DAX. For example, the Sort By Column property in Tabular corresponds to the OrderBy Attribute setting in Multidimensional, which automatically defines the attribute sorting used by MDX. In contrast, DAX always requires an explicit *ORDER BY* condition to define the requested sort order and ignores the Sort By Column metadata information.

> **Note** Any Tabular model can be seen as a Multidimensional model to be queried with MDX. Unfortunately, a Multidimensional model cannot be seen as a Tabular model. However, this feature will be introduced after the initial release of SQL Server Analysis Services 2012. You can find more details on this in the "Analysis Services 2012 Architecture" section in Chapter 1, "Introducing the Tabular Model."

Some features in Multidimensional do not have a corresponding feature in Tabular. The following is a list of the most relevant features that affect MDX and DAX usage.

- **Attribute Key/Name/Value** A column in Tabular becomes an attribute key in Multidimensional without any different definition for attribute name and attribute value. Thus, visible names are the same names saved in a query.

- **Attribute Relationships** There are no relationships between columns in Tabular and, for this reason, no attribute relationships are defined. As a consequence, there are no side effects in MDX calculation caused by attribute relationships. For further details, read the article written by Jeffrey Wang at *http://mdxdax.blogspot.com/2011/02/mdx-overwrite-semantics-and-complex.html*.

- **MDX Script** This is not supported in Tabular; you do not have a custom MDX script as the corresponding Multidimensional model does.

> **Note** An MDX script exists in the Tabular model, but it is used internally to store DAX measure definitions. Modifying it is not supported, and we do not suggest altering it. You can find more information about it by reading *http://blogs.msdn.com/b/cathyk/archive/2011/11/29/powerpivot-measures-command-no-really-don-t-modify-it-manually.aspx* and *http://javierguillen.wordpress.com/2011/10/14/observations-on-interoperability-between-bism-tabular-and-olap-clients*.

Now that you know the limitations of MDX, it is useful to know that querying a Tabular model with MDX is powerful because you can use the extensive set of MDX functions that are available, and you can mix DAX and MDX calculations in the same query.

> **Note** From a performance point of view, DAX could be faster than MDX. A query written in MDX is not translated in an equivalent DAX query, and some constructs might be more efficient if written in a native DAX query. If you have a performance issue for an MDX query, consider rewriting it in DAX if possible and do a comparison between them.

For example, to query the total sales for each category product, you can write the following MDX code.

```
SELECT [Measures].[Internet Total Sales] ON COLUMNS,
       NON EMPTY [Product Category].[Product Category Name].[Product Category Name] ON ROWS
FROM [Model]
```

	Internet Total Sales
Accessories	$700,759.96
Bikes	$28,318,144.65
Clothing	$339,772.61

To obtain the same result in DAX, you can use the following DAX query.

```
EVALUATE
SUMMARIZE(
    'Internet Sales',
    'Product Category'[Product Category Name],
    "Internet Total Sales", 'Internet Sales'[Internet Total Sales]
)
ORDER BY 'Product Category'[Product Category Name]
```

As you can see, MDX makes an implicit assumption about the grouping of data and the sort order, which depend on the underlying data model and are not required to be an explicit part of the query, like they are in DAX.

When compared to DAX, MDX makes it shorter to define a different context in which a measure has to be calculated. For example, consider the following MDX query, which shows Internet Sales in United States compared between years 2003 and 2004 in different columns of the result.

```
WITH
    MEMBER Measures.[Sales 2003]
        AS ([Measures].[Internet Total Sales], [Date].[Calendar Year].&[2003] )
    MEMBER Measures.[Sales 2004]
        AS ([Measures].[Internet Total Sales], [Date].[Calendar Year].&[2004] )
    MEMBER Measures.[Difference]
        AS Measures.[Sales 2004] - Measures.[Sales 2003]
SELECT
    { Measures.[Sales 2003], Measures.[Sales 2004], Measures.[Difference] } ON COLUMNS,
    NON EMPTY [Product Category].[Product Category Name].[Product Category Name] ON ROWS
FROM [Model]
WHERE ( [Geography].[Country Region Name].&[United States] )
```

	Sales 2003	Sales 2004	Difference
Accessories	$108,251.16	$148,170.91	$39,919.75
Bikes	$2,677,338.35	$3,095,275.19	$417,936.85
Clothing	$52,922.85	$80,585.06	$27,662.21

The *WHERE* condition of the MDX query defines a filter that applies to all the measures. By using calculated measure definitions local to the query, you can define particular calculations not only for columns but also for rows (which would not be easy in DAX). The previous MDX query would have required the following equivalent query in DAX.

```
DEFINE
    MEASURE 'Internet Sales'[Sales 2003] =
        CALCULATE( 'Internet Sales'[Internet Total Sales], 'Date'[Calendar Year] = 2003 )
    MEASURE 'Internet Sales'[Sales 2004] =
        CALCULATE( 'Internet Sales'[Internet Total Sales], 'Date'[Calendar Year] = 2004 )
    MEASURE 'Internet Sales'[Difference] =
        'Internet Sales'[Sales 2004] - 'Internet Sales'[Sales 2003]
EVALUATE
SUMMARIZE(
    CALCULATETABLE(
        'Internet Sales',
        Geography[Country Region Name] = "United States"
    ),
    'Product Category'[Product Category Name],
    "Sales 2003", 'Internet Sales'[Sales 2003],
    "Sales 2004", 'Internet Sales'[Sales 2004],
    "Difference", 'Internet Sales'[Difference]
)
ORDER BY 'Product Category'[Product Category Name]
```

Another scenario in which MDX offers features that are not available in DAX is when you need to navigate into a hierarchy defined in the data model. For example, consider the following MDX query that returns sales data at the semester level but also grouped by year and with the grand total.

```
SELECT
    [Measures].[Internet Total Sales] ON COLUMNS,
    NON EMPTY DESCENDANTS( [Date].[Calendar].[All],
                           [Date].[Calendar].[Semester], SELF_AND_BEFORE ) ON ROWS
FROM [Model]
```

The result contains member descriptions coming from different columns in the underlying data model.

	Internet Total Sales
All	$29,358,677.22
2001	$3,266,373.66
2	$3,266,373.66
2002	$6,530,343.53
1	$3,805,710.59
2	$2,724,632.94
2003	$9,791,060.30
1	$3,037,501.36
2	$6,753,558.94
2004	$9,770,899.74

	Internet Total Sales
1	$9,720,059.11
2	$50,840.63

You cannot obtain exactly the same result in DAX because DAX does not understand hierarchies. The nearest corresponding query you can write is the following one.

```
EVALUATE
ADDCOLUMNS(
    SUMMARIZE(
        'Internet Sales',
        ROLLUP( 'Date'[Calendar Year], 'Date'[Calendar Semester] ),
        "Internet Total Sales", [Internet Total Sales],
        "IsAllYear", ISSUBTOTAL( 'Date'[Calendar Year] ),
        "IsYear", ISSUBTOTAL( 'Date'[Calendar Semester] )
    ),
    "Period",
        IF(
            [IsAllYear],
            "All",
            IF(
                [IsYear],
                FORMAT( 'Date'[Calendar Year], "" ),
                FORMAT( 'Date'[Calendar Semester], "" )
            )
        )
)
ORDER BY 'Date'[Calendar Year], 'Date'[Calendar Semester]
```

The result contains a few columns that have been used to build the last *Period* column, which contains the same label used in the first column of the result produced by the MDX query.

Date[*Calendar Year*]	Date[*Calendar Semester*]	[*Internet Total Sales*]	[*IsAllYear*]	[*IsYear*]	[*Period*]
		$29,358,677.22	True	True	All
2001		$3,266,373.66	False	True	2001
2001	2	$3,266,373.66	False	False	2
2002		$6,530,343.53	False	True	2002
2002	1	$3,805,710.59	False	False	1
2002	2	$2,724,632.94	False	False	2
2003		$9,791,060.30	False	True	2003
2003	1	$3,037,501.36	False	False	1
2003	2	$6,753,558.94	False	False	2
2004		$9,770,899.74	False	True	2004
2004	1	$9,720,059.11	False	False	1
2004	2	$50,840.63	False	False	2

It is beyond the scope of this book to discuss MDX further. The main reason to support MDX for Tabular is its compatibility with existing client tools. However, it is important to note that MDX as a language can be more concise and has a higher level of abstraction than DAX, especially for defining calculations that implicitly apply to a subset of the data of your model.

Using DAX Local Measures in MDX Queries

An important feature that is available in a Tabular model when you query it with MDX is the ability to define a measure not only by using MDX but also by using DAX. Consider the formal syntax of an MDX *SELECT* statement.

```
[ WITH <SELECT WITH clause> [ , <SELECT WITH clause>...n ] ]
SELECT
    [ * | ( <SELECT query axis clause> [ , <SELECT query axis clause>,...n ] ) ]
FROM
    <SELECT subcube clause> [ <SELECT slicer axis clause> ] [ <SELECT cell property list clause>
]
```

The *SELECT WITH* clause syntax is as follows.

```
<SELECT WITH clause> ::=
    ( CELL CALCULATION <CREATE CELL CALCULATION body clause> )
    | ( [ CALCULATED ] MEMBER <CREATE MEMBER body clause>)
    | ( SET <CREATE SET body clause>)
    | ( MEASURE = <measure body clause> )
```

The *MEASURE* syntax is the same that you saw in the previous section, which described how to define measures that are local to DAX queries. Thus, you can define DAX measures in an MDX query, and you can mix DAX and MDX measures in an MDX query.

For example, assume you need to get the total of sales in United Sales shipped by year and product category. Because the Ship Date of Internet Sales is not used by the active relationship in the Tabular model, you have to rely on a DAX expression to invoke the *USERELATIONSHIP* function. You can define this part of the calculation in DAX, and you can reference this measure in other MDX expressions within the same MDX query, such as in the following example.

```
WITH
    MEASURE 'Internet Sales'[Ship Sales Amount] =
        CALCULATE(
            'Internet Sales'[Internet Total Sales],
            USERELATIONSHIP( 'Internet Sales'[Ship Date Id], 'Date'[Date Id] )
        )
    MEMBER Measures.[Ship Sales 2003]
        AS ([Measures].[Ship Sales Amount], [Date].[Calendar Year].&[2003] )
    MEMBER Measures.[Ship Sales 2004]
        AS ([Measures].[Ship Sales Amount], [Date].[Calendar Year].&[2004] )
    MEMBER Measures.[Difference]
        AS Measures.[Ship Sales 2003] - Measures.[Ship Sales 2004]
SELECT
    { Measures.[Ship Sales 2003], Measures.[Ship Sales 2004], Measures.[Difference] } ON
COLUMNS,
```

```
     NON EMPTY [Product Category].[Product Category Name].[Product Category Name] ON ROWS
FROM [Model]
WHERE ( [Geography].[Country Region Name].&[United States] )
```

	Ship Sales 2003	Ship Sales 2004	Difference
Accessories	101917.44	154504.63	-52587.19
Bikes	2569266.7192	3220417.22	-651150.5008
Clothing	50798.95	82708.96	-31910.01

> **Tip** Be careful of the differences in syntax between MDX and DAX local measures in an
> MDX query. An MDX measure is defined by using
>
> ```
> MEMBER Measures.<name> AS <MDX expression>
> ```
>
> whereas a DAX measure is defined by using
>
> ```
> MEASURE <tableName>[<name>] = <DAX expression>
> ```
>
> It can be easy to confuse these syntaxes, getting a syntax error as a result. Also be aware
> that MDX calculated measures can see DAX calculated measures, but DAX calculated mea-
> sures cannot reference MDX calculated measures.

Drillthrough in MDX Queries

An important feature MDX offers is drillthrough, which can be useful when a user wants to drill down
from aggregated sales figures directly to individual invoice lines. A client tool might implement
drillthrough in several ways. For example, Microsoft PivotTable in Excel enables drillthrough by inter-
cepting the double click on a particular cell containing data. In the background, a *DRILLTHROUGH*
MDX query is sent to the server. For example, the following query returns the list of sales made in
Santa Monica with a reseller promotion in 2003.

```
DRILLTHROUGH
SELECT
    { Measures.[Internet Total Sales] } ON COLUMNS
FROM [Model]
WHERE ( [Geography].[Country Region Name].&[United States],
        [Date].[Calendar Year].&[2003],
        [Geography].[City].[Santa Monica],
        [Promotion].[Promotion Category].[Reseller],
        [Product Category].[Product Category Name].&[Bikes] )
RETURN
    [$Internet Sales].[Sales Order Number],
    [$Internet Sales].[Order Date],
    [$Internet Sales].[Ship Date],
    [$Geography].[City],
    [$Promotion].[Promotion Category]
```

Sales Order Number	Order Date	Ship Date	Product Name
SO56106	10/14/2003	10/21/2003	Mountain-200 Silver, 46
SO60825	12/26/2003	1/2/2004	Road-750 Black, 52
SO50970	6/20/2003	6/27/2003	Mountain-200 Black, 46

This method of querying data can be seen as a way to project the result of a DAX query into a smaller set of rows than the initial source table. In DAX, a specific syntax for drillthrough does not exist because it is not required; you can always query a table in a Tabular model at the native granularity. What is missing in DAX that can be obtained with an MDX drillthrough is a way to project a table into a smaller number of columns. For example, a similar DAX query that returns the same rows as the previous example is the following query; however, it will return all the *Internet Sales* columns and not only those selected in the *RETURN* clause of the preceding MDX *DRILLTHROUGH* query.

```
EVALUATE
ADDCOLUMNS(
    CALCULATETABLE(
        'Internet Sales',
        'Date'[Calendar Year] = 2003,
        'Geography'[City] = "Santa Monica",
        'Geography'[Country Region Name] = "United States",
        'Promotion'[Promotion Category] = "Reseller",
        'Product Category'[Product Category Name] = "Bikes"
    ),
    "Product Name", RELATED( Product[Product Name] )
)
```

The *DRILLTHROUGH* statement in MDX must operate on a cell defined by a tuple that identifies a physical member and not a calculated one. If you try to perform a drillthrough on a calculated measure defined in MDX, you get an error as a result. For example, the following MDX query should perform a drillthrough over all the sales made in 2004.

```
DRILLTHROUGH
WITH MEMBER Measures.[Sales 2004]
        AS ([Measures].[Internet Total Sales], [Date].[Calendar Year].&[2004] )
SELECT {Measures.[Sales 2004]} ON COLUMNS
FROM [Model]
WHERE ( [Geography].[Country Region Name].&[United States] )
```

However, the result of the execution of this query is an error.

```
You cannot drillthrough if the cell in a select clause is a calculated cell.
```

Analysis Services identifies this issue because the Sales 2004 measure is calculated in MDX. If it is defined in DAX, it seems to work, even if its result is not what you might expect.

```
DRILLTHROUGH
WITH MEASURE 'Internet Sales'[Sales 2004] =
        CALCULATE( SUM( 'Internet Sales'[Sales Amount] ), 'Date'[Calendar Year] = 2004 )
```

```
SELECT { Measures.[Sales 2004] } ON COLUMNS
FROM [Model]
WHERE ( [Geography].[Country Region Name].&[United States] )
```

The result shows all the sales made in the United States, regardless of the date of the order. In other words, the DAX expression calculates the Sales 2004 measure in the right way, but it does not have any effect on filtering data for the *DRILLTHROUGH* operation in MDX.

> **Note** A client tool such as Excel PivotTable makes it possible to ask for drillthrough on any visible cell of the result. Only when the query is sent to the server is an error raised if the cell in the PivotTable is obtained as a result of a calculated member in MDX; it works if the cell is obtained as the result of a DAX measure. In such a case, you cannot change the MDX drillthrough query that is automatically generated by the client.

In such a case, if you can modify the MDX query, it is sufficient to move the 2004 filter in the *WHERE* condition.

```
DRILLTHROUGH
SELECT { Measures.[Internet Total Sales] } ON COLUMNS
FROM [Model]
WHERE ( [Geography].[Country Region Name].&[United States],
        [Date].[Calendar Year].&[2004] )
```

However, if that part of the filter logic cannot be expressed in MDX, you have a more difficult problem to solve. For example, consider the *DRILLTHROUGH* of Sales made in Santa Monica with a reseller promotion sent in 2003.

```
DRILLTHROUGH
WITH
    MEASURE 'Internet Sales'[Ship Sales Amount] =
        CALCULATE(
            'Internet Sales'[Internet Total Sales],
            USERELATIONSHIP( 'Internet Sales'[Ship Date Id], 'Date'[Date Id] )
        )
SELECT {Measures.[Ship Sales Amount]} ON COLUMNS
FROM [Model]
WHERE ( [Geography].[Country Region Name].&[United States],
        [Date].[Calendar Year].&[2003],
        [Geography].[City].[Santa Monica],
        [Promotion].[Promotion Category].[Reseller],
        [Product Category].[Product Category Name].&[Bikes] )
RETURN
    [$Internet Sales].[Sales Order Number],
    [$Internet Sales].[Order Date],
    [$Internet Sales].[Ship Date],
    [$Product].[Product Name]
```

Sales Order Number	Order Date	Ship Date	Product Name
SO56106	10/14/2003	10/21/2003	Mountain-200 Silver, 46
SO60825	**12/26/2003**	**1/2/2004**	**Road-750 Black, 52**
SO50970	6/20/2003	6/27/2003	Mountain-200 Black, 46

The result includes the order SO60825 that was shipped in 2004. Thus, even if you do not get an error and you have a correct Ship Sales Amount calculation, the drillthrough includes a wrong line, according to the requirements. In this case, you can use a DAX query to apply the correct filter instead of using *DRILLTHROUGH* in MDX.

```
EVALUATE
ADDCOLUMNS(
    CALCULATETABLE(
        'Internet Sales',
        'Date'[Calendar Year] = 2003,
        'Geography'[City] = "Santa Monica",
        'Geography'[Country Region Name] = "United States",
        'Promotion'[Promotion Category] = "Reseller",
        'Product Category'[Product Category Name] = "Bikes",
        USERELATIONSHIP( 'Internet Sales'[Ship Date Id], 'Date'[Date Id] )
    ),
    "Product Name", RELATED( Product[Product Name] )
)
```

By adding *USERELATIONSHIP*, you get the right result because the filter made on year 2003 uses the Ship Date relationship instead of the Order Date relationship used by default.

> **Tip** Pay attention to calculated measures defined in DAX used in a *DRILLTHROUGH* statement in MDX. Even if they do not generate an error as an MDX calculated member would, the result you obtain from the *DRILLTHROUGH* statement does not consider any change to filter context made by such a measure to determine the rows returned by the query.

Choosing Between DAX and MDX

After you have seen that you can query a Tabular model by using two query languages, MDX and DAX, you might wonder which language to choose. In this section, you see a few considerations that will help you in making this choice.

Sometimes you do not have a choice. If you are using a client tool that automatically connects to a Tabular model, reads its metadata, and automatically generates queries based on user interaction, then the language to use in the query has already been chosen by the client tool, and you cannot change it. For example, PivotTable in Excel generates queries in MDX, whereas Power View generates queries in DAX only. In general, this is related to the type of model (Tabular or Multidimensional) that has been used as a reference in the client tool design. All existing client tools designed for Analysis Services versions previous to 2012 support only Multidimensional and therefore support only MDX. Hereafter, we concentrate our attention on those cases in which you can make a choice.

A common scenario in which a choice can be made is Reporting Services. When you design a report that queries a Tabular model by using either Report Builder or SSDT, you always get a rowset as a result of a query, regardless of the language used (MDX or DAX). In this case, you can choose the language that fits your needs better. The main advantage of using DAX in this scenario is that you can include in a query a relationship between two tables without having defined that relationship in the underlying model. This is not possible in MDX. However, MDX offers a much more abstracted way to interact with data and has specific functions by which to use existing hierarchies in the model, something that is not available in Tabular. In this scenario, you might prefer to use DAX unless you want to use specific MDX functions that are not available and would require a more complex statement construction in DAX.

Another scenario is a custom application that integrates the result of a query made to a Tabular model into an application, such as customer relationship management (CRM) or line of business (LOB). In such cases, another difference is related to the application programming interface (API) used to send the queries and get results back. If you use a standard OLE DB ADO.NET or ADOMD. NET connection, you can receive the result in a rowset that can be easily bound to a user interface component. You can use either MDX or DAX as the query language, even if DAX seems more natural for such a choice because it returns typed data, whereas MDX returns everything as a variant, making it more difficult to convert. If you prefer to use MDX and get the result as a cellset, which is the correct conceptual representation of the result of an MDX query that can project results on multiple axes, you must use ADOMD.NET or OLE DB for OLAP instead. With a cellset, all the results are loaded in client memory before you can start using them, and you need special user interface components to bind them automatically to this type of result. In contrast, with a rowset, you can stop reading the result any time, even if you received only part of the result, just as you can when reading the result of any SQL query.

Finally, if you are designing a general-purpose client tool that connects to a Tabular model, you should interpret metadata coming from Analysis Services in a different way than you can with a Multidimensional model. In fact, the low-level API used by Tabular uses the same XMLA commands used by Multidimensional, although you have to handle different metadata returned by a Tabular model. At the time of writing (February 2012), you do not have a simpler .NET API like ADOMD.NET to browse metadata that is available for a Multidimensional model. You can use ADOMD.NET to access a Tabular model as if it were a Multidimensional model, but you see every table as a dimension, and you do not have access to specific properties of a Tabular model. Therefore, you have to consider the greater effort required to access metadata information in a Tabular model.

Summary

In this chapter, you have seen how to query a Tabular model by using the DAX query syntax. The DAX query language offers a set of functions that enables you to filter, group, and join data. Many functions perform operations that are similar to those available in SQL to manipulate sets of rows. However, DAX does not offer syntax to project the result of a queried table in a different set of columns (you can only add new columns with *ADDCOLUMNS*) and does not have the equivalent of a *UNION* operation in SQL to merge two tables with an identical set of columns into a single result.

A DAX query can define measures that are scoped locally to the query, and this is useful to develop and test the measures that you put in a Tabular model. DAX measures can also be defined locally to an MDX query. To enable the use of existing client tools, a Tabular model is also exposed as a Multidimensional model, presenting a set of dimensions and measures of the model to be queried by using MDX. If you already know MDX, you can use your existing skills to write the query for your reports.

DAX Advanced

In the previous chapter, you learned how to query a Tabular model in both DAX and MDX. When you write a measure in a Tabular model, the measure can be executed in different contexts, and it is important to understand how to interact with them in your calculation. This is a significant skill to learn, regardless of whether the measure is defined in the model or defined locally to a query.

In this chapter, you gain more insight into manipulating filter context with *CALCULATE* and *CALCULATETABLE*, you see how to control filters and selection, and you learn how the row and filter contexts are used when an MDX query is evaluated. Finally, you learn other DAX functions to control ranking-based filtering of elements and to perform common statistical calculations.

Understanding *CALCULATE* and *CALCULATETABLE* Functions

In Chapter 5, "Understanding Evaluation Context," you learned how evaluation context works and examined some examples based on queries generated by using a Microsoft Excel PivotTable. The queries generated by Excel PivotTable are written in MDX, but internally to Analysis Services, the evaluation of measures in a Tabular model is based on DAX functions. This does not mean that MDX is translated into DAX, but any calculation in a Tabular model has to compute a DAX formula, even if the context in which it is evaluated could be defined by an MDX query. To explain in more detail the inner workings of *CALCULATE* and *CALCULATETABLE*, in this section you see examples of using DAX queries, which are compared to equivalent SQL queries, showing more complex iterations.

In the queries of this section, you use a model made with a single table called Orders, containing the following data. (This is the same Single Table sample you used in Chapter 5.)

OrderDate	City	Channel	Color	Size	Quantity	Price
2011-01-31	Paris	Store	Red	Large	1	15
2011-02-28	Paris	Store	Red	Small	2	13
2011-03-31	Torino	Store	Green	Large	4	11
2011-04-30	New York	Store	Green	Small	8	9
2011-05-31		Internet	Red	Large	16	7
2011-06-30		Internet	Red	Small	32	5

OrderDate	City	Channel	Color	Size	Quantity	Price
2011-07-31		Internet	Green	Large	64	3
2011-08-31		Internet	Green	Small	128	1

Evaluation Context in DAX Queries

Consider the Microsoft PivotTable in Figure 7-1, in which you ask for the Sum of Quantity measure grouped by channel.

FIGURE 7-1 The quantity of orders is grouped by channel.

You might obtain such a result by writing a *SQL SELECT* statement with a *GROUP BY* condition such as the following.

```
SELECT
    Channel,
    SUM( Quantity ) AS [Sum of Quantity]
FROM        Orders
GROUP BY  Channel
ORDER BY  Channel
```

The corresponding DAX query you can use as follows.

```
DEFINE
    MEASURE Orders[Sum of Quantity] = SUM( Orders[Quantity] )
EVALUATE
ADDCOLUMNS(
    ALL( Orders[Channel] ),
    "Sum of Quantity", Orders[Sum of Quantity]
)
ORDER BY Orders[Channel]
```

Note The *ORDER BY* clause is required in both SQL and DAX queries to get the result in the desired order. Only MDX can use the Sort by Column property you can define in a Tabular model.

You have seen in Chapter 6, "Querying Tabular," that the first parameter of *ADDCOLUMNS* is the table to return; then follows a list of pairs (name, expression) that has to be computed for each row, adding columns to the results. Each row of the table in the first parameter defines a row context in which every column expression is evaluated.

Important When you specify a measure in an expression (such as the Orders[Sum of Quantity] in this query), an implicit *CALCULATE* surrounds the measure. As a result, the row context defined on Orders is transformed into a filter context that is propagated to Orders, applying the *SUM* of Orders[Quantity] to only related orders.

This particular DAX query does not return a Grand Total row, but this is not relevant for this discussion. (This can be accomplished by using *ROLLUP* and *SUMMARIZE*.) The following is the result of the previous DAX query.

Orders[Channel]	[Sum of Quantity]
Internet	240
Store	15

You can add a measure definition that is local to the scope of the query by using the *DEFINE MEASURE* syntax, like the TotalAmount measure defined in the following DAX query:

```
DEFINE
    MEASURE Orders[Sum of Quantity] = SUM( Orders[Quantity] )
    MEASURE Orders[TotalAmount] = SUMX( Orders, Orders[Quantity] * Orders[Price] )
EVALUATE
ADDCOLUMNS(
    ALL( Orders[Channel] ),
    "Sum of Quantity", Orders[Sum of Quantity],
    "TotalAmount", Orders[TotalAmount]
)
ORDER BY Orders[Channel]
```

Important The definition of a measure before the *EVALUATE* statement improves readability and reuse of the same measure in the query. Moreover, every time you define a measure in a Tabular model, you are writing an expression that will operate in an evaluation context that you cannot control. (It will be part of a larger query that you do not know before defining the measure.) For this reason, it is important to realize that measures can operate in any filter context. However, the same query might be defined by placing the measure formula inline, including it in a *CALCULATE* function (which is implicit when you define an expression in a measure) to transform the row context (in this case, the Channel value) into a filter context, as in the following example.

```
DEFINE
    MEASURE Orders[Sum of Quantity] = SUM( Orders[Quantity] )
EVALUATE
ADDCOLUMNS(
    ALL( Orders[Channel] ),
    "Sum of Quantity", Orders[Sum of Quantity],
    "TotalAmount", CALCULATE( SUMX( Orders, Orders[Quantity] * Orders[Price] ) )
)
ORDER BY Orders[Channel]
```

The result of a DAX query is always a table. Defining a measure in the Tabular model or in a DAX query produces the same result and has the same behavior in terms of performance. (As mentioned in the prior chapter, if you are used to MDX in Multidimensional, you might expect different perfor- mance, but this is not the case in DAX.) The *ADDCOLUMNS* function produces a row context for each row that has to be returned. Because the TotalAmount measure is executed in an implicit *CALCULATE* statement, such a row context becomes a filter context to evaluate TotalAmount. The previous query returns the following result.

Orders[Channel]	[Sum of Quantity]	[TotalAmount]
Internet	240	592
Store	15	157

A corresponding SQL query for obtaining the same result would be similar to the following.

```
SELECT
    Channel,
    SUM( Quantity ) AS [Sum of Quantity],
    SUM( Quantity * Price ) AS TotalAmount
FROM       Orders
GROUP BY   Channel
```

Note The DAX query used the *ADDCOLUMNS* function, which adds some calculations as columns to a table of the channels. Conceptually, this is not equivalent to a *GROUP BY* in SQL (like the *SUMMARIZE DAX* function, which we discussed in Chapter 6, "Querying Tabular"). A more precise SQL query equivalent of the *ADDCOLUMNS DAX* query would be the following.

```
SELECT DISTINCT
    Channel,
    ( SELECT SUM( Quantity )
      FROM Orders o2
      WHERE o2.Channel = o1.Channel
    ) AS [Sum of Quantity],
    ( SELECT SUM( Quantity * Price )
      FROM Orders o3
      WHERE o3.Channel = o1.Channel
    ) AS TotalAmount
FROM       Orders o1
GROUP BY   Channel
```

Modifying Filter Context by Using *CALCULATETABLE*

A filter on a column made through a slicer of a filter condition in a PivotTable affects all the cells of the PivotTable. For example, consider the PivotTable in Figure 7-2, in which a slicer on the *Size* column filters only Large.

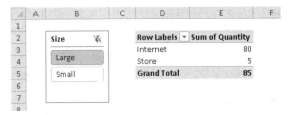

FIGURE 7-2 The Size slicer filters all the measures in the PivotTable.

To apply the same change to the initial filter context used by *ADDCOLUMNS*, you can write the following DAX query.

```
DEFINE
    MEASURE Orders[Sum of Quantity] = SUM( Orders[Quantity] )
EVALUATE
CALCULATETABLE(
    ADDCOLUMNS(
        ALL( Orders[Channel] ),
        "Sum of Quantity", Orders[Sum of Quantity]
    ),
    Orders[Size] = "Large" )
ORDER BY Orders[Channel]
```

The *CALCULATETABLE* function defines a filter context for the table expression passed as the first parameter, affecting any calculation performed in such an expression. The corresponding SQL statement would add a *WHERE* condition with the corresponding filter.

```
SELECT
    Channel,
    SUM( Quantity ) AS [Sum of Quantity]
WHERE     Size = 'Large'
FROM      Orders
GROUP BY  Channel
```

The *CALCULATE* and *CALCULATETABLE* functions are the keys to many DAX calculations. However, they are not very intuitive, and for this reason, they deserve a section dedicated to them so that you can take the time you need to discover the intricacies of these functions.

First, review the syntax.

```
CALCULATE( <expression>, <filter1>, <filter2>… )
```

```
CALCULATETABLE( <expression>, <filter1>, <filter2>… )
```

- The result is the evaluation of the expression represented by the first parameter.

- *CALCULATE* returns a value, so its expression parameter must be a function that returns a value.

- *CALCULATETABLE* returns a table, so its expression parameter must be a function that returns a table.

- The expression is evaluated in a context that is modified by the subsequent filters passed as parameters. A key point is that these filters can both enlarge and restrict the filter context.

Because the result of *CALCULATE* must be a value and not a table, the expression provided to *CALCULATE* is usually an aggregation function such as *SUM, MIN, MAX, COUNTROWS*, and so on.

The *CALCULATETABLE* function must return a table. If you want to control the layout of this result instead of just filtering an existing table, you will probably use functions such as *ADDCOLUMNS* and *SUMMARIZE*.

You can start to explore the *CALCULATE* behavior by defining a measure, such as AllChannels, that computes the quantity, ignoring any filter made on the *Channel* column. .

```
DEFINE
    MEASURE Orders[Sum of Quantity] = SUM( Orders[Quantity] )
    MEASURE Orders[AllChannels] =
        CALCULATE( SUM( Orders[Quantity] ), ALL( Orders[Channel] ) )
EVALUATE
ADDCOLUMNS(
    ALL( Orders[Channel] ),
    "Sum of Quantity", Orders[Sum of Quantity],
    "AllChannels", Orders[AllChannels]
)
ORDER BY Orders[Channel]
```

The previous query returns the following result.

Orders[Channel]	[Sum of Quantity]	[AllChannels]
Internet	240	255
Store	15	255

The *CALCULATE* statement in the AllChannels measure removes the filter on Channel implicitly defined by the row context coming from *ADDCOLUMNS*, which is transformed into a filter context by the *CALCULATE* function itself. For this reason, you always see the same number in the *AllChannels* column, regardless of the Channel in the first row, which defines the corresponding filter for the Sum of Quantity measure. Note that this behavior is very different from what you would need to do to get the same result in SQL.

```
SELECT
    Channel,
    SUM( Quantity ) AS [Sum of Quantity],
    ( SELECT SUM( Quantity ) FROM Orders ) AS AllChannels
FROM    Orders
GROUP BY Channel
```

In SQL, the only way to remove some filter or grouping condition defined by the *WHERE* or *GROUP BY* clause in a *SELECT* statement is to create a subquery, referencing the same table more than once. In contrast, a DAX query can have a different filter context for each value returned. The filter context is built by combining the initial filter context (the whole table) with other filters applied by DAX functions, which can be nested together. For example, the Sum of Quantity measure uses the *Channel* column, which comes from the row context defined by the surrounding *ADDCOLUMNS* function in the previous DAX query. The AllChannels measure defines a change in the filter context (by using the *CALCULATE* function) that removes any existing filter defined on the *Channel* column (the column used by Sum of Quantity).

To see how the filter context can be manipulated with a column granularity, look at the following DAX query, which groups results by Color and Channel.

```
DEFINE
    MEASURE Orders[Sum of Quantity] = SUM( Orders[Quantity] )
    MEASURE Orders[QtyAllChannels] =
        CALCULATE( SUM( Orders[Quantity] ), ALL( Orders[Channel] ) )
EVALUATE
ADDCOLUMNS(
    CROSSJOIN( ALL( Orders[Color] ), ALL( Orders[Channel] ) ),
    "Sum of Quantity", Orders[Sum of Quantity],
    "QtyAllChannels", Orders[QtyAllChannels]
)
ORDER BY Orders[Color], Orders[Channel]
```

The QtyAllChannels measure removes only the selection of Channel from the filter context and does not affect other parts of the filter context. For this reason, in the results produced by the query, you can see that the *QtyAllChannels* column has the same value for each row belonging to the same Color, whereas *Sum of Quantity* has the value filtered by Color and Channel.

Orders[Color]	Orders[Channel]	[Sum of Quantity]	[QtyAllChannels]
Green	Internet	192	204
Green	Store	12	204
Red	Internet	48	51
Red	Store	3	51

To put this in perspective, look at the filter context (defined by the list of items within angle brackets) existing for each measure in the result.

Orders[Color]	Orders[Channel]	[Sum of Quantity]	[QtyAllChannels]
Green	Internet	<Green, Internet>	<Green>
Green	Store	<Green, Store>	<Green>
Red	Internet	<Red, Internet>	<Red>
Red	Store	<Red, Store>	<Red>

To create the same result in SQL, you would need to use a correlated subquery that transfers part of the filter to the nested subquery, as in the following example.

```
SELECT
    Color,
    Channel,
    SUM( Quantity ) AS [Sum of Quantity],
```

```
   ( SELECT SUM( Quantity )
     FROM [Demo01].[Orders] o2
     WHERE o1.Color = o2.Color
   ) AS QtyAllChannels
FROM      [Demo01].[Orders] o1
GROUP BY Color, Channel
```

Using *FILTER* in *CALCULATE* and *CALCULATETABLE* Arguments

You have seen two examples of how *CALCULATE* can enlarge the filter context. The filter context can be defined by a DAX or an MDX query; the latter is used by the Excel PivotTable. Regardless of the query source, the filter context evaluation is identical.

If the filter context has a filter on a column of a table, *any reference* for that column in one or more filter parameters of the *CALCULATE* function replaces the existing filter context for that column. In other words, any argument of *CALCULATE* or *CALCULATETABLE* overrides existing filters over the same columns in the filter context existing before the *CALCULATE* or *CALCULATETABLE* call. The filters specified in the *CALCULATE* or *CALCULATETABLE* parameters are then combined with the rest of the outside filter context by using a logical *AND* condition among them. In other words, only rows that satisfy all the filter conditions in the filter context are considered.

For instance, consider a filter on the color Green, using a Boolean expression in the *CALCULATE* function for the QtyGreen measure.

```
DEFINE
    MEASURE Orders[Sum of Quantity] = SUM( Orders[Quantity] )
    MEASURE Orders[QtyGreen] = CALCULATE( SUM( Orders[Quantity] ), Orders[Color] = "Green" )
EVALUATE
ADDCOLUMNS(
    CROSSJOIN( ALL( Orders[Color] ), ALL( Orders[Channel] ) ),
    "Sum of Quantity", Orders[Sum of Quantity],
    "QtyGreen", Orders[QtyGreen]
)
ORDER BY Orders[Color], Orders[Channel]
```

The QtyGreen calculation will override the filter context on the *Color* column but will preserve the remaining filter context (on the *Channel* column).

Remember that a Boolean expression used as a filter parameter in a *CALCULATE* function corresponds to an equivalent *FILTER* expression that operates on all the values of a column. Thus, the measure in the previous query is equivalent to the following measure.

```
    MEASURE Orders[QtyGreen] =
        CALCULATE(
            SUM( Orders[Quantity] ),
            FILTER( ALL( Orders[Color] ), Orders[Color] = "Green" )
        )
```

For this reason, only a single column can be specified in a Boolean expression that is used as a table filter expression in a *CALCULATE* call.

Now the QtyGreen measure always filters by color Green, and the rows for Red display the value for Green in that measure, as you can see from the results of the previous query.

Orders[Color]	Orders[Channel]	[Sum of Quantity]	[QtyGreen]
Green	Internet	192	192
Green	Store	12	12
Red	Internet	48	192
Red	Store	3	12

Looking at the filter context used to compute each cell of the result, it is clear that the filter of Green replaces any selection made on the *Color* column.

Orders[Color]	Orders[Channel]	[Sum of Quantity]	[QtyGreen]
Green	Internet	<Green, Internet>	<Green, Internet>
Green	Store	<Green, Store>	<Green, Store>
Red	Internet	<Red, Internet>	<Green, Internet>
Red	Store	<Red, Store>	<Green, Store>

Any filter expression in a *CALCULATE* statement overrides the existing filter context for the columns it contains. Previously, we highlighted the reference definition because the *FILTER* that is used internally in place of the Boolean expression uses a *FILTER* expression that returns a set of values for the *Color* column. Therefore, the existing selection for the color (*Color* is used as a group column) is overridden by your filter, and only Green rows in the source table are considered for calculating the value of the QtyGreen measure. You lose the current selection on the color attribute because the ALL(Orders[Color]) expression used in the *FILTER* statement returns a set of all the color values and ignores the existing filter in the resulting row.

If you do not want to lose the existing filter context for a column, you can use a function that takes the existing selection into account. Instead of using the ALL(Orders[Color]) expression, you can use VALUES(Orders[Color]), which keeps the existing filter and returns only the Color values active in that filter.

For example, consider the QtyGreenFiltered measure in the following DAX query.

```
DEFINE
    MEASURE Orders[Sum of Quantity] = SUM( Orders[Quantity] )
    MEASURE Orders[QtyGreenFiltered] =
        CALCULATE(
            SUM( Orders[Quantity] ),
            FILTER( VALUES( Orders[Color] ), Orders[Color] = "Green" )
        )
EVALUATE
ADDCOLUMNS(
    CROSSJOIN( ALL( Orders[Color] ), ALL( Orders[Channel] ) ),
    "Sum of Quantity", Orders[Sum of Quantity],
    "QtyGreenFiltered", Orders[QtyGreenFiltered]
)
```

```
ORDER BY Orders[Color], Orders[Channel]
```

The Color filter of the resulting row is still active, and the *QtyGreenFiltered* column now correctly computes no value for the Red rows, as you can see in the results of the query.

Orders[Color]	Orders[Channel]	[Sum of Quantity]	[QtyGreenFiltered]
Green	Internet	192	192
Green	Store	12	12
Red	Internet	48	
Red	Store	3	

The reason you do not see any value for QtyGreenFiltered is that no rows are both Green and Red, as would be required by the filter context for the corresponding cells in the result.

Orders[Color]	Orders[Channel]	[Sum of Quantity]	[QtyGreenFiltered]
Green	Internet	<Green, Internet>	<Green, Internet>
Green	Store	<Green, Store>	<Green, Store>
Red	Internet	<Red, Internet>	<Green && Red, Internet>
Red	Store	<Red, Store>	<Green && Red, Store>

The *FILTER* expression in a *CALCULATE* function always replaces the previous context for the referenced columns. However, you can save the existing context by using an expression that uses the existing context and further restricts the members you want to consider for one or more columns. This is what you did when you used the *VALUES* function instead of *ALL* as the first parameter of the *FILTER* call.

At this point, you can summarize the effect of the various combinations of *FILTER*, *ALL*, and *VALUES* in a *CALCULATE* statement. The following syntaxes for QtyGreen are equivalent, and both clear the existing Color filter and then set a filter on the Green color.

```
MEASURE Orders[QtyGreen] =
    CALCULATE(
        SUM( Orders[Quantity] ),
        Orders[Color] = "Green"
    )

MEASURE Orders[QtyGreen] =
    CALCULATE(
        SUM( Orders[Quantity] ),
        FILTER( ALL( Orders[Color] ), Orders[Color] = "Green" )
    )
```

The following syntax for QtyGreenFiltered keeps the existing Color filters by adding a further filter on Green.

```
MEASURE Orders[QtyGreenFiltered] =
    CALCULATE(
        SUM( Orders[Quantity] ),
        FILTER( VALUES( Orders[Color] ), Orders[Color] = "Green" )
    )
```

The syntax for QtyGreen2 returns the same result as QtyGreenFiltered and keeps existing Color filters by adding a further filter on Green.

```
MEASURE Orders[QtyGreen2] =
    CALCULATE(
        SUM( Orders[Quantity] ),
        FILTER( ALL( Orders[Color] ), Orders[Color] = "Green" ),
        VALUES( Orders[Color] )
    )
```

Note that the first filter (FILTER(ALL ...)) would consider all the colors, but the second expression (*VALUES*) considers only the current selection of colors. The two filters work by using an *AND* condition, and the result is the same as if you used *VALUES* instead of *ALL* in the first parameter of the *FILTER* call, as in the QtyGreenFiltered definition.

The following syntax for QtyGreen3 clears existing filters on all the columns of the Orders table and then sets a filter on *all* the columns (*City*, *Channel*, *Size*, and so on, not just *Color*) by using the rows of the Orders table that meet the filter condition (in this case, the rows that are Green).

```
MEASURE Orders[QtyGreen3] =
    CALCULATE(
        SUM( Orders[Quantity] ),
        FILTER( ALL( Orders ), Orders[Color] = "Green" )
    )
```

Important Notice that a filter parameter for *CALCULATE* has a slightly different behavior if it represents a set of members of a single column or a set of rows from a table. In this latter case, as in QtyGreen3 definition, any column filter in the same table existing in the filter context before the *CALCULATE* call is cleared by the presence of this set of rows. However, there could be other filter parameters that specify other conditions for rows, columns, or both rows and columns of the same table. If the same column or the same table is filtered in more parameters of the same *CALCULATE* call, the resulting filter context contains only rows that satisfy all the filter conditions.

The result of the query by using QtyGreen3 measure is the following.

Orders[Color]	Orders[Channel]	[Sum of Quantity]	[QtyGreen3]
Green	Internet	192	204
Green	Store	12	204
Red	Internet	48	204
Red	Store	3	204

The filter context defined in the QtyGreen3 definition removes any filter from all the columns except *Color*. The following table summarizes the filter contexts used by the calculation defined in each of the measures we have considered. The QtyGreenFiltered and QtyGreen2 measures define the same evaluation context by using two syntaxes.

Orders[Color]	Orders[Channel]	[QtyGreen]	[QtyGreenFiltered] [QtyGreen2]	[QtyGreen3]
Green	Internet	<Green, Internet>	<Green, Internet>	<Green >
Green	Store	<Green, Store>	<Green, Store>	<Green >
Red	Internet	<Green, Internet>	<Green && Red, Internet>	<Green >
Red	Store	<Green, Store>	<Green && Red, Store>	<Green >

Finally, we caution you about the first parameter you pass to the *FILTER* function. In this possible definition of a measure

```
MEASURE Orders[QtyGreenFiltered3] =
    CALCULATE(
        SUM( Orders[Quantity] ),
        FILTER( Orders, Orders[Color] = "Green" )
    )
```

you pass the whole Orders table to the *FILTER* condition without saying ALL(Orders), which results in a filter of the filter context with *all the columns of the Orders table*! The result of QtyGreenFiltered3 is the same as QtyGreen2 and QtyGreenFiltered.

Orders[Color]	Orders[Channel]	[QtyGreenFiltered3]	[QtyGreenFilতerd3] – filter context
Green	Internet	192	<Green, Internet>
Green	Store	12	<Green, Store>
Red	Internet		<Green && Red, Internet>
Red	Store		<Green && Red, Store>

> **Note** The FILTER(Orders) in the previous query is refining the current filter context further, unlike FILTER(ALL(ORDERS)), which replaces the current filter context. In fact, the expression
>
> ```
> CALCULATE( SUM( Order[Quantity] ) )
> ```
>
> is equivalent to
>
> ```
> CALCULATE( SUM( Order[Quantity] ), FILTER( Orders, 1 = 1 ) )
> ```

Accordingly, you apply a restriction on the color Green, and you get the same result as before (no rows for any color but green; the selection of Color of the outer query is still applied, so that row for the color Red returns an empty cell for QtyGreenFiltered3), but remember, the *FILTER* function is returning *all* the columns. What does this mean?

Consider an existing filter context wherein the *Size* attribute is filtered by Large. You can obtain this by surrounding the *ADDCOLUMNS* statement with a *CALCULATETABLE* function.

```
DEFINE
    MEASURE Orders[Sum of Quantity] = SUM( Orders[Quantity] )
    MEASURE Orders[QtyGreenFiltered3] =
        CALCULATE(
            SUM( Orders[Quantity] ),
            FILTER( Orders, Orders[Color] = "Green" )
        )
EVALUATE
CALCULATETABLE(
    ADDCOLUMNS(
        CROSSJOIN( ALL( Orders[Color] ), ALL( Orders[Channel] ) ),
        "Sum of Quantity", Orders[Sum of Quantity],
        "QtyGreenFiltered3", Orders[QtyGreenFiltered3]
    ),
    Orders[Size] = "Large"
)
ORDER BY Orders[Color], Orders[Channel]
```

The result appears similar to the one you previously saw for the QtyGreenFiltered measure; the only difference is that you are filtering the *Size* column also.

Orders[Color]	Orders[Channel]	[Sum of Quantity]	[QtyGreenFiltered]
Green	Internet	64	64
Green	Store	4	4
Red	Internet	16	
Red	Store	1	

Now add another filter to the *CALCULATE* function so that you also filter the rows with Size equal to Small, defining a QtyGreenSmall measure.

```
MEASURE Orders[QtyGreenSmall] =
    CALCULATE(
        SUM( Orders[Quantity] ),
        FILTER( Orders, Orders[Color] = "Green" ),
        Orders[Size] = "Small"
    )
```

As you saw before, that definition corresponds to the following.

```
MEASURE Orders[QtyGreenSmall] =
    CALCULATE(
        SUM( Orders[Quantity] ),
        FILTER( Orders, Orders[Color] = "Green" ),
        FILTER( ALL( Orders[Size] ), Orders[Size] = "Small" )
    )
```

The result is that the filter for Large defined in the *CALCULATETABLE* function of the DAX query, plus the filter for Small defined in the QtyGreenSmall measure, returns no rows in the measure result, as you can see in the following results. This behavior is not very intuitive.

Orders[Color]	Orders[Channel]	[Sum of Quantity]	[QtyGreenFiltered]	[QtyGreenSmall]
Green	Internet	64	64	
Green	Store	4	4	
Red	Internet	16		
Red	Store	1		

This is due to the conflicting filter condition on the *Size* column.

Orders[Color]	Orders[Channel]	[QtyGreenFiltered]	[QtyGreenSmall] – filter context
Green	Internet	<Green, Internet>	<Green, Internet, Large && Small>
Green	Store	<Green, Store>	<Green, Store, Large && Small>
Red	Internet	<Green && Red, Internet>	<Green && Red, Internet, Large && Small>
Red	Store	<Green && Red, Store>	<Green && Red, Store, Large && Small>

The filter of the *Size* column in the *CALCULATE* expression of the QtyGreenSmall measure is restricting the current selection (because you used the Orders table as the first parameter in the *FILTER* function) and is not replacing it. Nevertheless, if you apply the filter only on *Size*, without the filter on *Color*, you have this QtySmall measure definition.

```
MEASURE Orders[QtySmall] =
    CALCULATE(
        SUM( Orders[Quantity] ),
        Orders[Size] = "Small"
    )
```

In the result produced, you are looking at values for Size Large in the *Sum of Quantity* column and at values for Size Small in the *QtySmall* column. Remember to look at the table at the beginning of the chapter for the original values in the Orders table.

Orders[Color]	Orders[Channel]	[Sum of Quantity]	[QtySmall]
Green	Internet	64	128
Green	Store	4	8
Red	Internet	16	32
Red	Store	1	2

This last calculation (QtySmall) exhibits the same behavior you saw previously with the first QtyGreen measure, wherein the filter of the color Green replaced any existing color selection in the PivotTable. The difference in the QtyGreenSmall calculation is the other *FILTER* parameter, which returns all the columns from the Orders table. Because all columns are returned, all the rows from the Orders table that satisfy the current filter context come back. Therefore, rows with a *Size* value of either *Large* or *Small* are returned as long as the Green color condition is satisfied. Consider the boldface filter in the QtyGreenSmall definition.

```
MEASURE Orders[QtyGreenSmall] =
    CALCULATE(
        SUM( Orders[Quantity] ),
        FILTER( Orders, Orders[Color] = "Green" ),
        FILTER( ALL( Orders[Size] ), Orders[Size] = "Small" )
    )
```

The filter on the color Green returns all the columns of the Orders table in the current filter context. If you consider the corresponding rows for the first row in the query result (<Green, Internet, Large>), this is just one row (the one with *64* as Quantity), and this row has the *Large* value for the *Size* column. (Look at the table at the beginning of this chapter for the original values in the Orders table.) When you apply the second filter, you have a single value for the *Size* attribute, which is *Small*. At this point, the intersection between those two sets of *Size* (one is only Large, the other is only Small) is an empty set. So the result for the QtyGreenSmall measure is empty because there are no corresponding rows for your filters. The following table resumes the filter context you have in QtyGreenSmall and QtySmall cases.

Orders[Color]	Orders[Channel]	[QtyGreenSmall]	[QtySmall]
Green	Internet	<Green, Internet, Large && Small>	<Green, Internet, Small>
Green	Store	<Green, Store, Large && Small>	<Green, Store, Small>
Red	Internet	<Green && Red, Internet, Large && Small>	<Red, Internet, Small>
Red	Store	<Green && Red, Store, Large && Small>	<Red, Store, Small>

Recap of *CALCULATE* and *CALCULATETABLE* Behavior

To summarize, *CALCULATE* exhibits the following behavior. (The same consideration applies to *CALCULATETABLE*, which returns a table instead of a scalar value.)

- The *CALCULATE* function executes the calculation passed in the first parameter, considering the resulting filter context obtained by selectively replacing the filters currently in place with the table or column filter constraints passed as parameters (the second and following arguments of the *CALCULATE* function).

- Each filter constraint in a *CALCULATE* function can be either a table filter constraint or a column filter constraint.

- A column filter constraint has values for only one column and is defined by using a Boolean filter constraint or a function returning a single column table.

- A table filter constraint can have values for one or more columns and is defined by using a function returning a table with more than one column. (A table made by a single column behaves like a column filter.)

- Each filter constraint is computed individually in the filter expressions of the *CALCULATE* function.

- If a column value is specified in at least one filter, it replaces the preexisting selection of the filter context for that column.

- If a filter expression returns more than one column, it is a table filter constraint. The *CALCULATE* function considers only table rows that have at least one matching row in the table filter constraint. (Only columns that are part of the table filter are considered in the match operation.)

- If a column is specified in many filter constraints, the resulting values are the intersection of these sets of values (for that column).

- After all the filters have been evaluated, the intersection of all the filter constraints determines the filter context for the expression passed as the first parameter to the *CALCULATE* function.

Despite its complexity, this calculation is fast. The key point is to understand all the side effects when a filter returns more columns than those you explicitly specified in the filter condition itself, which is something you have to consider carefully each time you use one or more *FILTER* functions in a *CALCULATE* or *CALCULATETABLE* expression.

Control Filters and Selections

Any measure is evaluated in a filter context that is defined as the result of a complex process produced by the interactions of many DAX functions such as *CALCULATETABLE*, *CALCULATE*, *FILTER*, and so on. In this section, you learn how to interact with this filter, which can be the representation of a filter or selection made by the end user on a client tool such as the PivotTable in Excel.

Using *ALLSELECTED* for Visual Totals

A common scenario in which you need additional DAX function is that of visual totals. The reason is that in DAX, it is not easy to obtain the total corresponding to the items selected in a query. For example, consider the PivotTable in Figure 7-3.

English Country Region Name	United States	
Calendar	2003	

Row Labels	Internet Total Sales
Accessories	$108,251.16
Clothing	$52,922.85
Grand Total	**$161,174.01**

FIGURE 7-3 The PivotTable shows visual totals.

The result in Grand Total is a visual total because, instead of the total of all the accessories in the database, it represents the sum of Accessories and Clothing product categories only, which are the only members selected for the rows, as you can see in Figure 7-4.

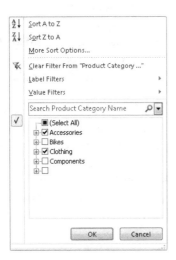

FIGURE 7-4 The selection of Product Category is Accessories and Clothing.

If you want to obtain the same result in MDX, you can use the *VISUALTOTAL* function that calculates the All member by considering only the members selected in the query. For example, consider the following MDX query.

```
WITH
    MEMBER Measures.[Sales Percentage]
        AS Measures.[Internet Total Sales]
            / ([Product Category].[Product Category Name].[All],
                Measures.[Internet Total Sales]),
            FORMAT_STRING = "Percent"
SELECT
    { Measures.[Internet Total Sales], Measures.[Sales Percentage] } ON COLUMNS,
    NON EMPTY VisualTotals( { [Product Category].[Product Category Name].[All],
                              [Product Category].[Product Category Name].&[Accessories],
```

```
                    [Product Category].[Product Category Name].&[Clothing] } ) ON ROWS
FROM [Model]
WHERE ( [Date].[Calendar Year].&[2003],
        [Geography].[Country Region Name].&[United States] )
```

> **Note** You can use subselects in MDX instead of the *VISUALTOTALS* function.

The result of the preceding query also contains the weight percentage of each category compared to the visual total.

	Internet Total Sales	Sales Percentage
All	$161,174.01	100.00%
Accessories	$108,251.16	67.16%
Clothing	$52,922.85	32.84%

To write the preceding query in DAX, you must move in the filter context all the filter conditions defined in the *WHERE* clause of the MDX query and then define a DAX expression that calculates the visual total. As you saw in Chapter 6, every cell produced by an MDX query usually corresponds to a row in the result of a DAX query. In this case, because you have only measures on columns in MDX, you can obtain the same result's shape in DAX. If you use the *SUMMARIZE* DAX function that makes the aggregation over the Internet Sales table, you can get the same Internet Total Sales results. However, to calculate the ratio, you need an expression that results in the visual total for all the selected categories. If you use the *ALL* function to get the total result for all the products, this would replace the filter over product categories, resulting in the nonvisual total instead of the visual total. Unfortunately, in DAX you do not have a syntax that corresponds to the tuple syntax of MDX to get the visual total (even if some workaround is possible, as shown in *http://javierguillen.wordpress .com/2011/09/13/using-slicer-values-in-dax-calculations*). Instead, you must use a special DAX function called *ALLSELECTED*. Consider the following DAX query.

```
DEFINE
    MEASURE 'Internet Sales'[Visual Total] =
        CALCULATE( [Internet Total Sales], ALLSELECTED('Product Category') )
    MEASURE 'Internet Sales'[Non Visual Total] =
        CALCULATE( [Internet Total Sales], ALL('Product') )
    MEASURE 'Internet Sales'[Sales Percentage] =
        [Internet Total Sales] / 'Internet Sales'[Visual Total]
EVALUATE
CALCULATETABLE(
    SUMMARIZE(
        'Internet Sales',
        ROLLUP( 'Product Category'[Product Category Name] ),
        "Sales", [Internet Total Sales],
        "Sales Percentage", [Sales Percentage],
        "Visual Total", [Visual Total],
```

```
        "Non Visual Total", [Non Visual Total]
    ),
    'Date'[Calendar Year] = 2003,
    Geography[Country Region Name] = "United States",
    FILTER(
        'Product Category'[Product Category Name],
        'Product Category'[Product Category Name] = "Accessories"
            || 'Product Category'[Product Category Name] = "Clothing"
    )
)
)
ORDER BY 'Product Category'[Product Category Name]
```

The result contains the same Sales Percentage measure as the MDX result (without percentage formatting). This measure is calculated by dividing the Internet Total Sales computed for a category (the current row in the result) by the Visual Total measure, which is computed in a *CALCULATE* call that alters the current filter context by using the *ALLSELECTED* function, removing the filter context derived from a row context and considering only the row context defined by direct filters.

Product Category[Product Category Name]	[Internet Total Sales]	[Sales Percentage]	[Visual Total]	[Non Visual Total]
	161,174.01	1	161174.01	2838512.355
Accessories	108,251.16	0.6716	161174.01	2838512.355
Clothing	52,922.85	0.3284	161174.01	2838512.355

The *ALLSELECTED* function can be called with just one parameter, which must a table or a column. Without such a call, the current row context (corresponding to the category in the first column) would be transformed in a filter context and propagated to other tables. Because of this row context, the calculation of Internet Total Sales is correct. However, in the Visual Total calculation, you want to consider all the categories that are included in the filter context *before* the *SUMMARIZE* call. The parameter passed to *ALLSELECTED* must be a table or a column. All the filter contexts on such a table that are derived from a row context are ignored, and only direct filters (such as those defined in the *CALCULATETABLE* parameter) are considered to produce the resulting table. Because you have the product categories on the rows and you want to remove only this derived filter, you must pass the Product Category table as parameter.

In the last column of the result, you can also view the Non Visual Total measure, which performs the aggregation over all the product categories.

Note The table passed to *ALL*, defining the Non Visual Total measure, is Product instead of Product Category. The reason is that by calling *ALL* with the Product Category table as parameter, you would not eliminate the filters produced by the intermediate tables Product Subcategory and Product on the Internet Sales table that is the target of the *SUMMARIZE* function. This would produce a result similar to the result obtained with *ALLSELECTED* applied to the same Product Category table. To remove the selection on Product Category from the Non Visual Total result of the query, you must apply *ALL* to the Product table, which is directly referenced by the summarized table (Internet Sales). This behavior is caused by the nature of the *SUMMARIZE* function, which propagates the initial grouping condition (on the *Product Category Name* column from the Product Category table) to the other columns and tables through cross-filtering behavior. Such a propagated filter on tables related to Product Category are not automatically removed by the *ALL* function, which has to operate on the Product table that is directly related to Internet Sales to clear the Categories selection for the Non Visual Totals calculation. You learn more about cross filtering later in this chapter. This is another reason for using a star schema instead of a snowflake schema.

You can also obtain the desired result by specifying Product as parameter to both *ALLSELECTED* and *ALL* calls.

```
DEFINE
    MEASURE 'Internet Sales'[Visual Total] =
        CALCULATE( [Internet Total Sales], ALLSELECTED('Product') )
    MEASURE 'Internet Sales'[Non Visual Total] =
        CALCULATE( [Internet Total Sales], ALL('Product') )
...
```

If you want to consider the visual totals regardless of the filter, you can use the Internet Sales table as parameter to *ALLSELECTED*. Remember that the query filters data by Country, Year, and Product Category, showing only United States, 2003, and Accessories or Clothing, respectively. However, such a parameter passed to *ALL* would return a Non Visual Total that ignores any filter passed to *CALCULATETABLE*, including any country and any year, instead of filtering by United States and year 2003.

```
DEFINE
    MEASURE 'Internet Sales'[Visual Total] =
        CALCULATE( [Internet Total Sales], ALLSELECTED('Internet Sales') )
    MEASURE 'Internet Sales'[Non Visual Total] =
        CALCULATE( [Internet Total Sales], ALL('Internet Sales') )
...
```

Product Category[Product Category Name]	[Internet Total Sales]	[Sales Percentage]	[Visual Total]	[Non Visual Total]
	161,174.01	1	161174.01	29358677.2207
Accessories	108,251.16	0.6716	161174.01	29358677.2207
Clothing	52,922.85	0.3284	161174.01	29358677.2207

Important You can also call *ALLSELECTED* without parameters to remove any filter context produced by row contexts from any table. However, the initial release of Analysis Services 2012 contains a bug that might produce bad results if no parameters are passed to *ALLSELECTED*. In most cases, you can obtain the desired result by passing to *ALLSELECTED* the table containing the columns that are computed by the measure (Internet Sales table in the previous example). This bug is discussed at *https://connect.microsoft.com/SQLServer/ feedback/details/714581/allselected-produces-wrong-results-if-called-without-parameters* and will be fixed in an update or service pack of Analysis Services 2012 after its initial release to manufacturing version (RTM).

Thus, *ALLSELECTED* is an important DAX function that enables you to write visual total calculations in your queries. Internally, row context and filter context have different roles, and it is important to understand these roles to use *ALLSELECTED* properly.

Filters and Cross Filters

In the previous section, you saw that *ALLSELECTED* manipulates the filter context to obtain a result that depends on selections made in the outer filter context and in the row context. The filter context for a table is obtained as a result of combining direct filters on columns of the table and indirect filters obtained as a side effect of the filters on other referenced tables. You might want to discriminate between direct and indirect filters in the filter context and, in this section, you learn how to do it.

Using *ISFILTERED* and *ISCROSSFILTERED*

A column can be filtered for two reasons.

- It is directly filtered by a condition on that column in *CALCULATE* or *CALCULATETABLE*, in the axes, or in the slicer of an MDX query.

- It is indirectly filtered by the propagation of the filter context over relationships or over columns of the same table.

To determine if a column is filtered, you can use the *ISFILTERED* and *ISCROSSFILTERED* functions, both of which get a single column name as a parameter and return a Boolean value that indicates whether that column is directly or indirectly filtered, respectively.

For example, a filter in the *Product Category Name* column produces, as a side effect, a corresponding filter over all the other columns of the same table (*Product Category* and *Product Category ID*) and over all the columns of all the tables that are on the many side of a relationship with the Product Category table. The indirect filter that is produced on related columns and tables is called a *cross filter*. For example, in Figure 7-5, you can see that all the columns other than *Product Category Name* are highlighted because all are cross filtered.

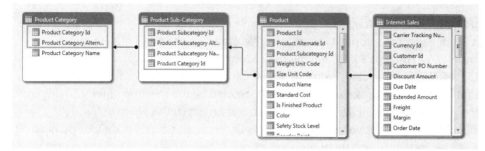

FIGURE 7-5 This is how the cross filter propagates because of a filter on Product Category Name.

The cross filter does not propagate to the one side of a relationship. In Figure 7-6, you can see that by filtering over Product Subcategory Name, the cross filter is not propagated to the Product Category table.

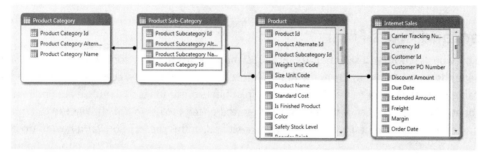

FIGURE 7-6 This is how the cross filter propagates because of a filter on Product Subcategory Name.

The *ISFILTERED* function returns *TRUE* if a column is part of a direct filter. The *ISCROSSFILTERED* function returns *TRUE* if a column is part of a cross filter, regardless of the source of the cross filter. Thus, to perform a calculation in DAX, only those rows that are included in all the filters and cross filters are computed.

Note You have to remember that you can check whether a column is cross filtered, but you do not know the source filter that originates the cross filter. Every filter produces side effects, and all the cross filters are applied in a logical *AND* condition.

To consider this behavior from a DAX perspective, consider the following query that shows the *ISFILTERED* value for several columns.

```
EVALUATE
CALCULATETABLE(
    ADDCOLUMNS(
        SUMMARIZE(
            'Internet Sales',
            'Date'[Calendar Year],
            'Product Category'[Product Category Name],
```

```
            "Sales", SUM( 'Internet Sales'[Sales Amount] )
        ),
        "F-Year", ISFILTERED( 'Date'[Calendar Year] ),
        "F-CatName", ISFILTERED( 'Product Category'[Product Category Name] ),
        "F-CatAltId", ISFILTERED( 'Product Category'[Product Category Alternate Id] ),
        "F-SubCatName", ISFILTERED( 'Product Subcategory'[Product Subcategory Name] )
    ),
    'Product Category'[Product Category Name] = "Bikes"
)
```

Date[Calendar Year]	Product Category[Product Category Name]	[Sales]	[F-Year]	[F-CatName]	[F-CatAltId]	[F-SubCatName]
2001	Bikes	3266373.6566	False	True	False	False
2002	Bikes	6530343.5264	False	True	False	False
...	...	...	...	...	...	...

The external *CALCULATETABLE* applies a filter context to the *ADDCOLUMNS* function. The *SUMMARIZE* produces a list of all the years and a single product category (Bikes) that is the only category available in such a filter context. For every row produced by *SUMMARIZE*, you obtain the same result for all the *ISFILTERED* columns; for this reason, we included only the first two. Only the *Product Category Name* column returns *TRUE* for the *ISFILTERED* function because there is an external filter context, set by *CALCULATETABLE*, which is filtering values on the column. No other columns, including *Calendar Year*, are directly filtered.

Now, consider a similar query that returns the *ISCROSSFILTERED* result for the same columns.

```
EVALUATE
CALCULATETABLE(
    ADDCOLUMNS(
        SUMMARIZE(
            'Internet Sales',
            'Date'[Calendar Year],
            'Product Category'[Product Category Name],
            "Sales", SUM( 'Internet Sales'[Sales Amount] )
        ),
        "CF-Year", ISCROSSFILTERED( 'Date'[Calendar Year] ),
        "CF-CatName", ISCROSSFILTERED( 'Product Category'[Product Category Name] ),
        "CF-CatAltId", ISCROSSFILTERED( 'Product Category'[Product Category Alternate Id] ),
        "CF-SubCatName", ISCROSSFILTERED( 'Product Subcategory'[Product Subcategory Name] )
    ),
    'Product Category'[Product Category Name] = "Bikes"
)
```

Date[Calendar Year]	Product Category[Product Category Name]	[Sales]	[CF-Year]	[CF-CatName]	[CF-CatAltId]	[CF-SubCatName]
2001	Bikes	3266373.6566	False	True	True	True
2002	Bikes	6530343.5264	False	True	True	True
...	...	...	...	...	...	...

In this case, all the columns of the Products Category table are cross filtered, just like all the columns of the related Product Subcategory table. At this point, you might be wondering why the *Calendar Year* column is neither filtered nor cross filtered. The reason is that the *ADDCOLUMNS* call defines a row context for each combination of *Calendar Year* and *Product Category Name* produced by the *SUMMARIZE* function. Such a row context does not produce a filter context unless a *CALCULATE* function is called. Therefore, the filter is defined by *CALCULATETABLE* that filters on *Product Category Name* and related columns (*Product Category Alternate Id* and *Product Subcategory Name*) but not on *Calendar Year*, which is not cross filtered as a result.

> **Note** The *Sales* column does not require *CALCULATE* before *SUM* because it is inside *SUMMARIZE*. However, if you want to perform the same calculation outside the *SUMMARIZE* call, you would have to surround the *SUM* call with a *CALCULATE* call, as you will see in the next example.

The transformation of a row context into a filter context also transforms the row context selection into a filter that is detected by *ISFILTERED* and *ISCROSSFILTERED*. In the following query, you can observe the difference obtained by surrounding these functions with a *CALCULATE* function.

```
EVALUATE
CALCULATETABLE(
    ADDCOLUMNS(
        SUMMARIZE(
            'Internet Sales',
            'Date'[Calendar Year],
            'Product Category'[Product Category Name],
            "Sales", SUM( 'Internet Sales'[Sales Amount] )
        ),
        "All Bikes Sales", SUM( 'Internet Sales'[Sales Amount] ),
        "Row Sales", CALCULATE( SUM( 'Internet Sales'[Sales Amount] ) ),
        "F-Year", ISFILTERED( 'Date'[Calendar Year] ),
        "CF-Month", ISCROSSFILTERED( 'Date'[Month] ),
        "Calc-F-Year", CALCULATE( ISFILTERED( 'Date'[Calendar Year] ) ) ,
        "Calc-CF-Month", CALCULATE( ISCROSSFILTERED( 'Date'[Month] ) )
    ),
    'Product Category'[Product Category Name] = "Bikes"
)
```

Date[Calendar Year]	Product Category[Product Category Name]	[Sales]	[All Bikes Sales]	[Row Sales]	[F-Year]	[CF-Month]	[Calc-F-Year]	[Calc-CF-Month]
2001	Bikes	3266373.6566	28318144.6507	3266373.6566	False	False	True	True
2002	Bikes	6530343.5264	28318144.6507	6530343.5264	False	False	True	True
...	...		...		...	...	...	...

As you can see in the *ADDCOLUMNS* parameters after the *SUMMARIZE* call, if you do not specify *CALCULATE*, the filter context does not filter the *Calendar Year*, and the *All Bikes Sales* column contains the same value for all the rows, which corresponds to the sum of all the sales of any product belonging to the Bikes category. The *Row Sales* column does contain a *CALCULATE* statement, which converts the row context into a filter context to compute only the sales of the corresponding calendar year in the same row of the result. (In this way, you obtain the same result of the *Sales* column computed inside the *SUMMARIZE* call.) By applying *CALCULATE* also to the *ISFILTERED* expression, you obtain True as a result because, at that point, Calendar Year is part of the filter context. You can observe the same effect of *CALCULATE* on the cross-filtered *Month* column of the Date table.

> **Note** In this example, *ADDCOLUMNS* has been used to show filters and cross filters. Inside the *SUMMARIZE* function, you have a different semantic that makes it more difficult to show the filters applied from external *CALCULATETABLE* functions because the row context for each group is automatically transformed into a filter context to perform the correct calculation.

Using *FILTERS* and *VALUES*

You saw in the previous chapters that *VALUES* can be used to get a list of values that are active in the filter context. Now that you know the difference between filter and cross filter, you can understand that *VALUES* operates at the cross-filter level. If you want to obtain a list of only those values that are directly filtered, without considering cross filters, you can use the *FILTERS* function.

FILTERS and *VALUES* functions have a similar syntax, requiring a single parameter that has to be a single column. In the following example, you can see that, by filtering the Product Category name on Bikes, *FILTERS* and *VALUES* return the same number of items for Product Category.

```
EVALUATE
CALCULATETABLE(
    ROW(
        "Values Cat", COUNTROWS( VALUES( 'Product Category'[Product Category Name] ) ),
        "Filters Cat", COUNTROWS( FILTERS( 'Product Category'[Product Category Name] ) ),
        "All Cat", COUNTROWS( ALL( 'Product Category'[Product Category Name] ) )
    ),
    'Product Category'[Product Category Name] = "Bikes"
)
```

[Values Cat]	[Filters Cat]	[All Cat]
1	1	5

As you can see, only one category is returned by both *FILTERS* and *VALUES* (see Values Cat and Filters Cat in the result), whereas there are five categories in the *Product Category Name* column without any filter active (see All Cat in the result).

The results are different if you consider the *Product Subcategory* column.

```
EVALUATE
CALCULATETABLE(
    ROW(
```

```
    "Values Subcat", COUNTROWS( VALUES( 'Product Subcategory'[Product Subcategory Name] ) ),
    "Filters Subcat",
        COUNTROWS( FILTERS( 'Product Subcategory'[Product Subcategory Name] ) ),
    "All Subcat", COUNTROWS( ALL( 'Product Subcategory'[Product Subcategory Name] ) )
    ),
    'Product Category'[Product Category Name] = "Bikes"
)
```

[Values Subcat]	[Filters Subcat]	[All Subcat]
3	38	38

The *VALUES* function returns for Product Subcategory only the subcategories belonging to the Bikes product category (Values Subcat returns 3), whereas *FILTERS* returns the number of all subcategories, regardless of the category to which they belong. (Filters Subcat returns 38, which is the same number returned by All Subcat.) In other words, *FILTERS* ignores any existing cross filter and restricts the result to direct filters made to the column passed as argument, whereas *VALUES* returns only values that are cross filtered.

FILTERS and *ALLSELECTED*

It is interesting to note that *FILTERS* considers any selection made on a filter context to be a meaningful filter that has to be used for its results. Therefore, an *ALLSELECTED* call can transform a cross filter into a direct filter. For example, consider the following query.

```
EVALUATE
CALCULATETABLE(
    ADDCOLUMNS(
        VALUES('Product Subcategory'[Product Subcategory Name]),
        "Values Subcat",
            COUNTROWS( VALUES( 'Product Subcategory'[Product Subcategory Name] ) ),
        "Filters Subcat",
            COUNTROWS( FILTERS( 'Product Subcategory'[Product Subcategory Name] ) ),
        "AllSelected Subcat",
            COUNTROWS( ALLSELECTED( 'Product Subcategory'[Product Subcategory Name] ) )
    ),
    'Product Category'[Product Category Name] = "Bikes"
)
```

Product Subcategory[Product Subcategory Name]	[Values Subcat]	[Filters Subcat]	[AllSelected Subcat]
Mountain Bikes	3	38	3
Road Bikes	3	38	3
Touring Bikes	3	38	3

The *CALCULATETABLE* function contains a filter over the Bikes category. This filter determines the number of rows in the output, which is the list of subcategories belonging to the Bikes category. In this condition, the *FILTERS* function returns the list of all the unfiltered 38 subcategories (*Filter Subcat* column), whereas *VALUES* returns just the subcategories belonging to the Bikes category that is filtered by the *CALCULATETABLE* function, and *ALLSELECTED* returns the same result as *VALUES* in this case.

In the following query, the *VALUES*, *FILTERS*, and *ALLSELECTED* functions are wrapped in a *CALCULATE* call.

```
EVALUATE
CALCULATETABLE(
    ADDCOLUMNS(
        VALUES('Product Subcategory'[Product Subcategory Name]),
        "Calc Values Subcat",
            CALCULATE( COUNTROWS( VALUES( 'Product Subcategory'[Product Subcategory Name] ) ) ),
        "Calc Filters Subcat",
            CALCULATE( COUNTROWS( FILTERS( 'Product Subcategory'[Product Subcategory Name] ) ) ),
        "Calc AllSelected Subcat",
            CALCULATE(
                COUNTROWS( ALLSELECTED( 'Product Subcategory'[Product Subcategory Name] ) ) )
            ),
        'Product Category'[Product Category Name] = "Bikes"
)
```

Product Subcategory[Product Subcategory Name]	[Calc Values Subcat]	[Calc Filters Subcat]	[Calc AllSelected Subcat]
Mountain Bikes	1	1	3
Road Bikes	1	1	3
Touring Bikes	1	1	3

For each column in the result, another *CALCULATE* transforms the row context (determined by the Product Subcategory Name displayed on the resulting row) into a filter context, performing a calculation that is filtered by a single subcategory. In this case, both *FILTERS* and *VALUES* return just one Subcategory (see the *Calc Filters Subcat* and *Calc Values Subcat* columns, respectively), whereas *ALLSELECTED* always returns three subcategories because it is not affected by the filter context. (See the *Calc AllSelected Subcat* column.)

At this point, you can look at the difference obtained by applying *ALLSELECTED* to the calculation of each column.

```
EVALUATE
CALCULATETABLE(
    ADDCOLUMNS(
        VALUES( 'Product Subcategory'[Product Subcategory Name] ),
        "AllSel Values Subcat",
            CALCULATE(
                COUNTROWS( VALUES( 'Product Subcategory'[Product Subcategory Name] ) ),
                ALLSELECTED( 'Product Subcategory' )
            ),
        "AllSel Filters Subcat",
            CALCULATE(
                COUNTROWS( FILTERS( 'Product Subcategory'[Product Subcategory Name] ) ),
                ALLSELECTED( 'Product Subcategory' )
            )
```

```
        ),
        'Product Category'[Product Category Name] = "Bikes"
)
```

Product Subcategory[Product Subcategory Name]	[AllSel Values Subcat]	[AllSel Filters Subcat]
Mountain Bikes	3	3
Road Bikes	3	3
Touring Bikes	3	3

By applying *ALLSELECTED*, the filter context obtained from the row context is ignored, and only the filter context obtained by the external *CALCULATETABLE* is considered. Thus, all the subcategories that are part of the cross filter are used to define a new filter context in which both *FILTERS* and *VALUES* are then evaluated. For this reason, the results of *VALUES* and *FILTERS* are identical in this case (see the *AllSel Values Subcat* and *AllSel Filters Subcat* columns in the result).

Using *HASONEVALUE* and *HASONEFILTER*

By using the *FILTERS* and *VALUES* functions you saw in the previous section, you might use *COUNTROWS* to check the number of elements selected. In this section, you see how you can simplify such a pattern when you want to check whether just one element has been selected by using *HASONEVALUE* and *HASONEFILTER*.

Consider the following query, which returns the list of Subcategories for a selection of product categories.

```
EVALUATE
CALCULATETABLE(
    SUMMARIZE(
        'Product Subcategory',
        'Product Subcategory'[Product Subcategory Name],
        "Values Subcategories",
            COUNTROWS( VALUES( 'Product Subcategory'[Product Subcategory Id] ) ),
        "Filters Subcategories",
            COUNTROWS( FILTERS( 'Product Subcategory'[Product Subcategory Id] ) )
    ),
    'Product Category'[Product Category Name] = "Bikes"
        || 'Product Category'[Product Category Name] = "Clothing"
)
```

Product Subcategory[Product Subcategory Name]	[Values Subcategories]	[Filters Subcategories]
Mountain Bikes	1	11
Road Bikes	1	11
Touring Bikes	1	11
Bib-Shorts	1	11
...	...	...

For each row, the number of categories in the filter context (always 1 because the subcategory in the row context becomes part of the filter context because it is in a *SUMMARIZE* call) and the number of subcategories are filtered. (In this case, the value *11* is the total of subcategories belonging to Bikes and Clothing categories filtered outside of the *SUMMARIZE* call.)

By using *HASONEVALUE* and *HASONEFILTER*, you get *TRUE* if the corresponding *COUNTROWS* returns 1; otherwise, you get *FALSE*, as you can see in the following example.

```
EVALUATE
CALCULATETABLE(
    SUMMARIZE(
        'Product Subcategory',
        'Product Subcategory'[Product Subcategory Name],
        "Single Value", HASONEVALUE( 'Product Subcategory'[Product Subcategory Id] ),
        "Single Filter", HASONEFILTER( 'Product Subcategory'[Product Subcategory Id] )
    ),
    'Product Category'[Product Category Name] = "Bikes"
        || 'Product Category'[Product Category Name] = "Clothing"
)
```

Product Subcategory[Product Subcategory Name]	[Single Value]	[Single Filter]
Mountain Bikes	True	False
Road Bikes	True	False
Touring Bikes	True	False
Bib-Shorts	True	False
...	...	...

The biggest advantage of using *HASONEVALUE* and *HASONEFILTER* is readability of the DAX query.

When to Use *HASONEFILTER*

It is interesting to note that *HASONEFILTER* might be useful if you want to test the filter outside *SUMMARIZE* and if the same filtered column is included in the result. For example, consider the following query.

```
EVALUATE
CALCULATETABLE(
    SUMMARIZE(
        'Product Subcategory',
        'Product Subcategory'[Product Subcategory Name],
        "Single Category Values", HASONEVALUE( 'Product Category'[Product Category Id] ),
        "Single Category Filter", HASONEFILTER( 'Product Category'[Product Category Id] )
    ),
    'Product Category'[Product Category Name] = "Bikes"
        || 'Product Category'[Product Category Name] = "Clothing"
)
```

Product Subcategory[Product Subcategory Name]	[Single Category Value]	[Single Category Filter]
Mountain Bikes	False	False
Road Bikes	False	False
Touring Bikes	False	False
Bib-Shorts	False	False
…	…	…

In this case, *HASONEVALUE* and *HASONEFILTER* seem to be returning the same value because both *FILTERS* and *VALUES* return the list of Bikes and Clothing categories filtered by the outermost *CALCULATETABLE*. However, as soon as you include Product Category Name in a column of the result, the filter context becomes restricted to the category displayed in the row, whereas *FILTERS* would still return the list of the two values. In the following query, you can see that *HASONEFILTER* becomes the only way to check whether a single Product Category has been selected outside the *SUMMARIZE* call.

```
EVALUATE
CALCULATETABLE(
    SUMMARIZE(
        'Product Subcategory',
        'Product Category'[Product Category Name],
        'Product Subcategory'[Product Subcategory Name],
        "Single Category Values",
            HASONEVALUE( 'Product Category'[Product Category Id] ),
        "Single Category Filter",
            HASONEFILTER( 'Product Category'[Product Category Id] )
    ),
    'Product Category'[Product Category Name] = "Bikes"
        || 'Product Category'[Product Category Name] = "Clothing"
)
```

Product Category[Product Category Name]	Product Subcategory[Product Subcategory Name]	[Single Category Value]	[Single Category Filter]
Bikes	Mountain Bikes	True	False
Bikes	Road Bikes	True	False
Bikes	Touring Bikes	True	False
Clothing	Bib-Shorts	True	False
	…	…	…

Thus, even if *HASONEFILTER* and *HASONEVALUE* might return similar values, it is important to recognize the scenarios in which their values can be different and to determine which value you want to check.

Maintaining Complex Filters by Using *KEEPFILTERS*

Up to now, you have seen how to control filters in your calculation and how to modify them according to your needs. However, there are scenarios in which the manipulation of filter context might lose important filter information. In this section, you see how to handle these special cases by using the *KEEPFILTER* function.

You saw at the beginning of this chapter a few examples of how to obtain visual totals in DAX without having a specific function for it as you have in MDX. For example, consider the following MDX query.

```
SELECT
    [Measures].[Internet Total Sales] ON COLUMNS,
    VISUALTOTALS(
        { [Date].[Calendar].[Year].&[2002],
          [Date].[Calendar].[Year].&[2002].&[2].&[3],
          [Date].[Calendar].[Year].&[2002].&[2].&[4],
          [Date].[Calendar].[Year].&[2003],
          [Date].[Calendar].[Year].&[2003].&[1].&[1],
          [Date].[Calendar].[Year].&[2003].&[1].&[2]
        } ) ON ROWS
FROM [Model]
```

The result contains visual totals for 2002 and 2003, which include only quarters that have been selected (quarters 3 and 4 of 2002 and quarters 1 and 2 of 2003).

	Internet Total Sales
2002	$2,724,632.94
3	$1,396,833.62
4	$1,327,799.32
2003	$3,037,501.36
1	$1,413,530.30
2	$1,623,971.06

An equivalent query in DAX can be written by using *SUMMARIZE*.

```
EVALUATE
CALCULATETABLE(
    SUMMARIZE(
        'Internet Sales',
        'Date'[Calendar Year],
        ROLLUP( 'Date'[Calendar Quarter] ),
        "Sales", [Internet Total Sales]
    ),
    FILTER(
        CROSSJOIN( VALUES( 'Date'[Calendar Year] ), VALUES( 'Date'[Calendar Quarter] ) ),
        ('Date'[Calendar Year] = 2002 && 'Date'[Calendar Quarter] = 3)
            || ('Date'[Calendar Year] = 2002 && 'Date'[Calendar Quarter] = 4)
            || ('Date'[Calendar Year] = 2003 && 'Date'[Calendar Quarter] = 1)
```

```
            || ('Date'[Calendar Year] = 2003 && 'Date'[Calendar Quarter] = 2)
        )
    )
ORDER BY 'Date'[Calendar Year], 'Date'[Calendar Quarter]
```

Date[Calendar Year]	Date[Calendar Quarter]	[Sales]
2002		2724632.9392
2002	3	1396833.617
2002	4	1327799.3222
2003		3037501.3577
2003	1	1413530.2997
2003	2	1623971.058

The result is correct because *SUMMARIZE* starts considering the rows in Internet Sales that have been filtered and returns only years and quarters that have data associated with rows that have been filtered in Internet Sales. In other words, the selection that has been made in filtering the sales will be represented in the same selection of years and quarters in the query result.

However, if you try to query the *Calendar Year* and *Calendar Quarter* columns of the Date table directly, you might find that the original selection, which has been defined by filtering the result of a *CROSSJOIN*, has been lost. For example, consider the following query that uses *SUMMARIZE* over the result of the same *CROSSJOIN* instead of over Internet Sales.

```
EVALUATE
CALCULATETABLE(
    SUMMARIZE(
        CROSSJOIN( VALUES( 'Date'[Calendar Year] ), VALUES( 'Date'[Calendar Quarter] ) ),
        'Date'[Calendar Year],
        ROLLUP( 'Date'[Calendar Quarter] ),
        "Sales", [Internet Total Sales]
    ),
    FILTER(
        CROSSJOIN( VALUES( 'Date'[Calendar Year] ), VALUES( 'Date'[Calendar Quarter] ) ),
        ('Date'[Calendar Year] = 2002 && 'Date'[Calendar Quarter] = 3)
            || ('Date'[Calendar Year] = 2002 && 'Date'[Calendar Quarter] = 4)
            || ('Date'[Calendar Year] = 2003 && 'Date'[Calendar Quarter] = 1)
            || ('Date'[Calendar Year] = 2003 && 'Date'[Calendar Quarter] = 2)
    )
)
ORDER BY 'Date'[Calendar Year], 'Date'[Calendar Quarter]
```

The result of such a query can appear strange at first. It contains all four quarters for both 2002 and 2003 because the *CROSSJOIN* inside *SUMMARIZE* loses the combined filters returned by the *FILTER* statement that operates an independent *CROSSJOIN*.

Date[Calendar Year]	Date[Calendar Quarter]	[Sales]
2002		6530343.5264
2002	1	1791698.453
2002	2	2014012.1342
2002	3	1396833.617
2002	4	1327799.3222
2003		9791060.2977
2003	1	1413530.2997
2003	2	1623971.058
2003	3	2744340.48
2003	4	4009218.46

The reason for this result is that *CROSSJOIN* inside *SUMMARIZE* produces a new Cartesian product of all the years and all the quarters that are active in the current filter context, which has been previously modified by the *CALCULATETABLE* function. Thus, because each column is evaluated independently from the others, you get as a result the product between years (2002 and 2003) and quarters (1, 2, 3, and 4) that appear at least once in the result. As a consequence, the combination of year and quarter filters is lost. To keep the filters on other columns when you consider a column in a new filter operation (like the one performed by *SUMMARIZE*), you can use *KEEPFILTER*, which receives a table as a parameter and transfers existing filters on other columns to the new filter context.

For example, the following query can be rewritten by surrounding *CROSSJOIN* in the *SUMMARIZE* function with a *KEEPFILTERS* call.

```
EVALUATE
CALCULATETABLE(
    SUMMARIZE(
        KEEPFILTERS(
            CROSSJOIN( VALUES( 'Date'[Calendar Year] ), VALUES( 'Date'[Calendar Quarter] ) )
        ),
        'Date'[Calendar Year],
        ROLLUP( 'Date'[Calendar Quarter] ),
        "Sales", [Internet Total Sales]
    ),
    FILTER(
        CROSSJOIN( VALUES( 'Date'[Calendar Year] ), VALUES( 'Date'[Calendar Quarter] ) ),
        ('Date'[Calendar Year] = 2002 && 'Date'[Calendar Quarter] = 3)
            || ('Date'[Calendar Year] = 2002 && 'Date'[Calendar Quarter] = 4)
            || ('Date'[Calendar Year] = 2003 && 'Date'[Calendar Quarter] = 1)
            || ('Date'[Calendar Year] = 2003 && 'Date'[Calendar Quarter] = 2)
    )
)
ORDER BY 'Date'[Calendar Year], 'Date'[Calendar Quarter]
```

This query produces the following result.

Date[Calendar Year]	Date[Calendar Quarter]	[Sales]
2002		2724632.9392
2002	1	
2002	2	
2002	3	1396833.617
2002	4	1327799.3222
2003		3037501.3577
2003	1	1413530.2997
2003	2	1623971.058
2003	3	
2003	4	

However, even if in this case the Sales result is correct (and it represents a visual total when you group by year), it still contains rows for quarters that have been excluded by the filter in *CALCULATETABLE*. The reason is that the *SUMMARIZE* function is operating on a virtual table that is the Cartesian product between the Internet Sales table (which is used by the Internet Total Sales measure) and all the related tables. The first argument of *SUMMARIZE* is used as a filter context to calculate the *Sales* column, but the effect of *KEEPFILTERS* is applied to only Internet Sales and not on *CROSSJOIN*, which returns the Cartesian product of all existing combinations between Calendar Year and Calendar Quarter, regardless of the existence of data in the Orders table. You can remove the unwanted rows by using *FILTER*.

```
EVALUATE
CALCULATETABLE(
    SUMMARIZE(
        FILTER(
            KEEPFILTERS(
                CROSSJOIN( VALUES( 'Date'[Calendar Year] ), VALUES( 'Date'[Calendar Quarter] ) )
            ),
            [Internet Total Sales] <> 0
        ),
        'Date'[Calendar Year],
...
```

Note In this case, *KEEPFILTERS* is applied to the Internet Total Sales evaluated in the *FILTER* statement and does not apply to the external *SUMMARIZE* statement. If you want to keep the filters on *SUMMARIZE*, for example, to aggregate also other measures, you should include the entire *FILTER* in another *KEEPFILTER* call.

From the previous examples, it might be clear that *KEEPFILTERS* also operates on columns that are not part of the query result. For example, consider the following query that should display only the total of years 2002 and 2003, considering only the same quarters that were selected in the previous examples.

```
EVALUATE
CALCULATETABLE(
    ADDCOLUMNS(
        VALUES( 'Date'[Calendar Year] ),
        "Sales", [Internet Total Sales]
    ),
    FILTER(
        CROSSJOIN( VALUES( 'Date'[Calendar Year] ), VALUES( 'Date'[Calendar Quarter] ) ),
        ('Date'[Calendar Year] = 2002 && 'Date'[Calendar Quarter] = 3)
            || ('Date'[Calendar Year] = 2002 && 'Date'[Calendar Quarter] = 4)
            || ('Date'[Calendar Year] = 2003 && 'Date'[Calendar Quarter] = 1)
            || ('Date'[Calendar Year] = 2003 && 'Date'[Calendar Quarter] = 2)
    )
)
ORDER BY 'Date'[Calendar Year]
```

In this case, the *Sales* column contains the total of sales in years 2002 and 2003, ignoring any filters on Calendar Quarter.

Date[Calendar Year]	[Sales]
2002	6530343.5264
2003	9791060.2977

This is because the *ADDCOLUMNS* syntax transforms the row context (one year) into a filter context (all the dates of that year), replacing any filter context existing on the columns of that table (Date). If you do not want to lose the existing filter context on combinations of Calendar Year and Calendar Quarter values, you can apply *KEEPFILTERS* to the table passed to *ADDCOLUMNS* to include in the filter context other related columns as defined in the external filter context because the *CALCULATETABLE* filters are applied first, replacing the external filter context, and the *ADDCOLUMNS* call is subsequently evaluated. In this way, the *VALUES* function will return not only the values from the selected column but also the values from other columns (such as *Calendar Quarter* in this case), even if they are not explicitly mentioned in the result.

```
EVALUATE
CALCULATETABLE(
    ADDCOLUMNS(
        KEEPFILTERS( VALUES( 'Date'[Calendar Year] ) ),
        "Filtered Sales", [Internet Total Sales],
        "Year Sales", CALCULATE( [Internet Total Sales], ALL( 'Date'[Calendar Quarter] ) )
    ),
    FILTER(
        CROSSJOIN( VALUES( 'Date'[Calendar Year] ), VALUES( 'Date'[Calendar Quarter] ) ),
        ('Date'[Calendar Year] = 2002 && 'Date'[Calendar Quarter] = 3)
            || ('Date'[Calendar Year] = 2002 && 'Date'[Calendar Quarter] = 4)
            || ('Date'[Calendar Year] = 2003 && 'Date'[Calendar Quarter] = 1)
```

```
        || ('Date'[Calendar Year] = 2003 && 'Date'[Calendar Quarter] = 2)
    )
)
ORDER BY 'Date'[Calendar Year]
```

The previous query returns only the total of selected quarters for each year in the *Filtered Sales* column and returns the total of all the quarters of each year in the *Year Sales* column.

Date[Calendar Year]	[Filtered Sales]	[Year Sales]
2002	2724632.9392	6530343.5264
2003	3037501.3577	9791060.2977

In these educational examples, you could have used *SUMMARIZE* to avoid the use of *KEEPFILTERS*. However, it is important to understand how *KEEPFILTERS* works in these examples because you might need it in scenarios that are more complex. For example, a DAX measure that has to be used over an arbitrarily shaped set defined in MDX could require such a function. A longer and more complete example of *KEEPFILTERS* usage is available at *http://sqlblog.com/blogs/alberto_ferrari/ archive/2011/09/09/keepfilters-a-new-dax-feature-to-correctly-compute-over-arbitrary-shaped-sets.aspx.*

Sorting Functions

In the previous chapter, you saw how to order the results produced by a DAX query by using the *ORDER BY* clause. In this section, you see how to use the sort order inside a DAX formula to produce rank value and to filter data based on rank position.

Using *TOPN*

When you write a DAX query, you might limit the number of rows you read by controlling the number of rows that are extracted from the client. However, this is possible only if you write the code of the client and stop the reading loop after a certain number of rows. Writing a query for a report, you might prefer to limit the number of rows returned by stating it directly into the DAX query. For example, consider the following query that returns the product sold through the Internet in the United States, sorted by sales amount.

```
EVALUATE
CALCULATETABLE(
    SUMMARIZE(
        'Internet Sales',
        Product[Product Name],
        "Sales", 'Internet Sales'[Internet Total Sales]
    ),
    Geography[Country Region Name] = "United States"
)
ORDER BY [Sales] DESC
```

The result is sorted according to the *Sales* column, which has been calculated for sales made to customers in the United States.

Product[Product Name]	[Sales]
Mountain-200 Black, 46	525060.9256
Mountain-200 Silver, 42	485872.1892
Road-150 Red, 48	483066.45
Mountain-200 Silver, 46	473277.9576
...	...

Note If you had specified the *Internet Total Sales* column in the *ORDER BY* clause, you would have seen a sort order according to sales made to all countries, ignoring the filter on United States.

The preceding query returns 130 products when executed on the *AdventureWorksDW* database. If you are interested in returning just the top 10 products for the United States, you can limit the number of rows returned to the first 10 by using the same order used for the previous query. To do that, you can use the *TOPN* function that has the following syntax.

```
TOPN( <n_value>, <table>, <orderBy_expression> [, <order>
      [,<orderBy_expression> [, <order>]]…] )
```

The <n_value> parameter specifies the maximum number of rows that should be returned from <table> according to the sort order specified by <orderBy_expression> and <order> parameters. You can have multiple <orderBy_expression>; if multiple rows have the same value for the first <orderBy_expression>, the second one will be evaluated and so on. The <order> parameter is 0 or False (default) to rank in descending order and 1 or True to rank in ascending order.

Important In case of a tie, all the tied rows are returned, and the total number of rows returned can be greater than <n_value> if the *n*th row is a tie.

Note By default, the *ORDER BY* clause of a DAX query sorts data in ascending order, whereas *TOPN* sorts data in descending order.

For example, the previous query can be written in this way to return the top 10 products for United States.

```
EVALUATE
CALCULATETABLE(
    TOPN(
```

```
        10,
        SUMMARIZE(
            'Internet Sales',
            Product[Product Name],
            "Sales", 'Internet Sales'[Internet Total Sales]
        ),
        [Sales]
    ),
    Geography[Country Region Name] = "United States"
)
ORDER BY [Sales] DESC
```

As you can see, the <orderBy_expression> repeats the same expression used in the *ORDER BY* clause. Moreover, *ORDER BY* is still required to obtain a result sorted by Sales in descending order; otherwise, the top 10 products would not be sorted in a particular way because *TOPN* does not guarantee any sort order for the results.

If you are interested in the bottom five products in United States, you can add the <order> parameter with value *1*.

```
EVALUATE
CALCULATETABLE(
    TOPN(
        5,
        SUMMARIZE(
            'Internet Sales',
            Product[Product Name],
            "Sales", 'Internet Sales'[Internet Total Sales]
        ),
        [Sales],
        1
    ),
    Geography[Country Region Name] = "United States"
)
ORDER BY [Sales] ASC
```

Product[Product Name]	[Sales]
Racing Socks, L	961.93
Racing Socks, M	1168.7
Touring Tire Tube	1806.38
Road Tire Tube	2657.34
Patch Kit/8 Patches	2667.85

The result includes only products that have been sold in the United States at least once. This is caused by the *SUMMARIZE* function, which operates on the Internet Sales table, filtering sales made to customers in the United States. If you use Product instead of Internet Sales as the table to summarize, you would obtain the same result produced by the following query, which uses *ADDCOLUMNS*.

```
EVALUATE
CALCULATETABLE(
    TOPN(
```

```
        5,
        ADDCOLUMNS(
            VALUES(Product[Product Name]),
            "Sales", 'Internet Sales'[Internet Total Sales]
        ),
        [Sales],
        1
    ),
    Geography[Country Region Name] = "United States"
)
ORDER BY [Sales] DESC
```

Product[Product Name]	[Sales]
ML Mountain Seat Assembly	
Bearing Ball	
BB Ball Bearing	
Headset Ball Bearings	
Blade	
LL Crankarm	
...	

In this case, the result would contain all the products with no sales in the United States, which have a corresponding sales value of *0*. Because tied products are part of the same ranking, you can see more than five products in the result. (The actual number is 374 in the *AdventureWorksDW* sample.)

Up to now, you have seen how to apply *TOPN* only once in each query because there was always a filter over the United States country. If you want to apply *TOPN* multiple times in the same query, you must use the *GENERATE* function. For example, the following query returns the top three products for every country.

```
EVALUATE
GENERATE(
    ALL( Geography[Country Region Name] ),
    TOPN(
        3,
        SUMMARIZE(
            'Internet Sales',
            Product[Product Name],
            "Sales", 'Internet Sales'[Internet Total Sales]
        ),
        [Sales]
    )
)
ORDER BY Geography[Country Region Name], [Sales] DESC
```

Geography[Country Region Name]	Product[Product Name]	[Sales]
Australia	Road-150 Red, 62	397187.97
Australia	Road-150 Red, 48	390031.43
Australia	Road-150 Red, 56	382874.89
Canada	Mountain-200 Black, 42	131716033
Canada	Road-150 Red, 52	114504.64
Canada	Road-150 Red, 48	110926.37
France	Mountain-200 Black, 46	138601003
...	...	...

As you can see, *TOPN* is executed for every country passed as first argument to the *GENERATE* function.

Using *RANKX*

In the previous section, you saw how to filter data based on ranking. If you want to show the actual ranking value, you can use the *RANKX* function that is described in this section. Its syntax is the following.

```
RANKX( <table>, <expression> [, <value>[, <order>[, <ties>]]]
          [, <expression> [, <value>[, <order>[, <ties>]]]] … )
```

The <value> argument is ranked over the values returned by <expression> for every row of the <table>. If <value> is omitted, <expression> is used to compute the value for ranking in the evaluation context that calls the *RANKX* function.

> **Note** Both <expression> and <value> are evaluated in a row context. The <expression> argument is evaluated in a row context defined for each row of <table>. The <value> argument is evaluated in the row context defined by the caller of the *RANKX* function. In both cases, you can use *CALCULATE* to convert the row context into a filter context. Remember that a measure implicitly performs a *CALCULATE* operation.

The <order> parameter is 0 or False (default) to rank in descending order and 1 or True to rank in ascending order. The <ties> argument is a string that can be *DENSE* or *SKIP* to control the rank value after a tie. *DENSE* always returns the next rank value after a tie, whereas *SKIP* returns a value that skips as many values as tied values. For example, if four values are tied with a rank of 5, the next value will receive a rank of 9 for *SKIP* and a rank of 6 for *DENSE*.

For example, the next query returns the Rank value for each product sold to United States customers.

```
EVALUATE
CALCULATETABLE(
```

```
    SUMMARIZE(
        'Internet Sales',
        Product[Product Name],
        "Sales", 'Internet Sales'[Internet Total Sales],
        "Rank", RANKX( ALL( Product[Product Name] ), 'Internet Sales'[Internet Total Sales] )
    ),
    Geography[Country Region Name] = "United States"
)
ORDER BY [Sales] DESC
```

Product[Product Name]	[Sales]	[Rank]
Mountain-200 Black, 46	525060.9256	1
Mountain-200 Silver, 42	485872.1892	2
Road-150 Red, 48	483066.45	3
Mountain-200 Silver, 46	473277.9576	4
...	...	...

It is important to consider which <table> parameter to pass to the *RANKX* function to obtain the desired result. In the previous query, it was necessary to specify ALL(Product[Product Name]) because you want to obtain the ranking of each product. The following example shows the result if ALL(Product) was used.

```
EVALUATE
CALCULATETABLE(
    SUMMARIZE(
        'Internet Sales',
        Product[Product Name],
        "Sales", 'Internet Sales'[Internet Total Sales],
        "Rank", RANKX( ALL( Product ), 'Internet Sales'[Internet Total Sales] )
    ),
    Geography[Country Region Name] = "United States"
)
ORDER BY [Sales] DESC
```

In this case, the result would contain strange values for the *Rank* column.

Product[Product Name]	[Sales]	[Rank]
Mountain-200 Black, 46	525060.9256	1
Mountain-200 Silver, 42	485872.1892	1
Road-150 Red, 48	483066.45	1
Mountain-200 Silver, 46	473277.9576	2
Mountain-200 Silver, 38	453889.47	2
Mountain-200 Black, 38	452031.0654	2
Road-150 Red, 62	447283.75	2
Mountain-200 Black, 42	443096.9972	3
...	...	...

The reason for this is that instead of comparing the Sales value of each Product Name with the ranking of all Product Name values, you compare it with the ranking of all the products, and the Product table contains several rows for each Product Name. Look at the result of the following query that returns a row for every product, including the *Product Id* column, which is a unique identifier for every row in the Product table.

```
EVALUATE
CALCULATETABLE(
    SUMMARIZE(
        'Internet Sales',
        Product[Product Id],
        Product[Product Name],
        "Sales", 'Internet Sales'[Internet Total Sales]
    ),
    Geography[Country Region Name] = "United States"
)
ORDER BY [Sales] DESC
```

Product[Product Id]	Product[Product Name]	[Sales]
312	Road-150 Red, 48	483066.45
310	Road-150 Red, 62	447283.75
363	Road-150 Red, 48	406213.23
313	Mountain-200 Black, 46	400766.24
	...	...

As you can see, all the Product Name rows that have a Sales value greater than or equal to 483066.45 got a rank value of *1* in the *Rank* column of the previous example, and all the Sales values between 447283.75 and 483066.45 got a rank value of *2*.

At this point, you might be wondering where the values of the other two products that had a ranking of 1 came from. The explanation is that there are several Product rows with the same names, as you can see from the results of the following query.

```
EVALUATE
CALCULATETABLE(
    SUMMARIZE(
        'Internet Sales',
        Product[Product Id],
        Product[Product Name],
        "Sales", 'Internet Sales'[Internet Total Sales]
    ),
    Geography[Country Region Name] = "United States",
    Product[Product Name] = "Mountain-200 Black, 46"
        || Product[Product Name] = "Mountain-200 Silver, 42"
)
ORDER BY Product[Product Name], Product[Product Id]
```

Product[Product Id]	Product[Product Name]	[Sales]
362	Mountain-200 Black, 46	118847.6956
363	Mountain-200 Black, 46	406213.23
354	Mountain-200 Silver, 42	107713.8192
355	Mountain-200 Silver, 42	378158.37

The third parameter of *RANKX* specifies a value if it has to be calculated in a way different from the expression applied to each row of the table passed to *RANKX*. For example, if you want to calculate the global product ranking of the first three products for each category sold in the United States, you must write a query like the following one.

```
EVALUATE
CALCULATETABLE(
    GENERATE(
        FILTER(
            DISTINCT( 'Product Category'[Product Category Name] ),
            'Internet Sales'[Internet Total Sales] > 0
        ),
        TOPN(
            3,
            SUMMARIZE(
                'Internet Sales',
                Product[Product Name],
                "Sales", 'Internet Sales'[Internet Total Sales],
                "Rank in Category",
                    RANKX(
                        ALL( Product[Product Name] ),
                        'Internet Sales'[Internet Total Sales]
                    ),
                "Rank in All Products",
                    RANKX(
                        ALL( Product[Product Name] ),
                        CALCULATE(
                            'Internet Sales'[Internet Total Sales],
                            ALLEXCEPT( Product, Product[Product Name] )
                        )
                    )
            ),
            [Sales]
        )
    ),
    Geography[Country Region Name] = "United States"
)
ORDER BY 'Product Category'[Product Category Name], [Sales] DESC
```

Product Category[Product Category Name]	Product[Product Name]	[Sales]	[Rank in Category]	[Rank in All Products]
Accessories	Sport-100 Helmet, Blue	25787.63	1	58
Accessories	Sport-100 Helmet, Black	25682.66	2	60

Product Category[Product Category Name]	Product[Product Name]	[Sales]	[Rank in Category]	[Rank in All Products]
Accessories	Sport-100 Helmet, Red	25297.77	3	61
Bikes	Mountain-200 Black, 46	525060.9256	1	1
Bikes	Mountain-200 Silver, 42	485872.1892	2	2
Bikes	Road-150 Red, 48	483066.45	3	3
Clothing	Women's Mountain Shorts, M	12948.15	1	83
Clothing	Women's Mountain Shorts, S	11758.32	2	85
Clothing	Women's Mountain Shorts, L	11758.32	2	85

The *GENERATE* function generates the list of the first three products for each product category by using the *TOPN* function. The interesting parts are the two columns that calculate the ranking.

The *Rank in Category* column calculates the product ranking locally to each category by using the *RANKX* function with two parameters. The ALL(Product[Product Name]) table passed as the first parameter returns the list of all the products, regardless of their category, but the following Internet Total Sales measure is evaluated in a filter context that contains the Product Category selection in the same row. Thus, the result will be blank for any product that does not belong to the "current" category and, therefore, the ranking will consider only the products of the corresponding category.

The *Rank in All Products* column has to calculate the ranking over all the products, regardless of the category. To do this, you must change the filter context in which the expression has to be evaluated for each product, removing any filter other than Product Name. For this reason, the filter context has been modified by using the *ALLEXCEPT* function in a *CALCULATE* call.

Up to now, you have used only the first two arguments of the *RANKX* function. The third argument is, by default, the same expression passed as the second parameter to *RANKX*. For example, consider the following query that returns the ranking of the current silver products.

```
EVALUATE
CALCULATETABLE(
    SUMMARIZE(
        Product,
        Product[Product Name],
        Product[List Price],
        "Rank Price", RANKX( ALLSELECTED( Product ), Product[List Price] )
    ),
    Product[Product Status] = "Current",
    Product[Color] = "Silver"
)
ORDER BY [Rank Price]
```

Product[Product Name]	Product[List Price]	[Rank Price]
Mountain-200 Silver, 46	2319.99	1
Mountain-200 Silver, 42	2319.99	1

Product[Product Name]	Product[List Price]	[Rank Price]
Mountain-200 Silver, 38	2319.99	1
HL Mountain Frame - Silver, 42	1364.5	4
HL Mountain Frame - Silver, 46	1364.5	4
HL Mountain Frame - Silver, 38	1364.5	4
Mountain-400-W Silver, 46	769.49	7
Mountain-400-W Silver, 38	769.49	7

The Product[List Price] argument is evaluated for each product to perform the ranking and then is evaluated for each row of the *SUMMARIZE* output to calculate the <value> parameter. In other words, the two following expressions are equivalent.

```
RANKX( ALLSELECTED( Product ), Product[List Price] )
RANKX( ALLSELECTED( Product ), Product[List Price], Product[List Price] )
```

There are two scenarios in which you might want to specify the <value> parameter in an explicit way. The first is when you do not have a valid row context to evaluate the same expression passed as second argument. For example, if you remove the *Product[List Price]* column from the group by columns specified in the *SUMMARIZE* argument of the previous query, you would get the following error.

The value for column 'List Price' in table 'Product' cannot be determined in the current context. Check that all columns referenced in the calculation expression exist, and that there are no circular dependencies.

To execute a valid query, you must specify the <value> parameter by using a *CALCULATE* statement that transforms the row context into a filter context, which is automatically propagated to the other columns of the same table, making the reference to List Price valid. If you do not do that, the <value> expression is evaluated in a row context of a table that has *Product[Product Name]* as a single column. For this reason, after removing *Product[List Price]* from the group by columns, any direct reference to *Product[List Price]* is no longer valid. Inside *CALCULATE*, the filter context should correspond to only one row, making any aggregation return the same value for List Price.

```
EVALUATE
CALCULATETABLE(
    SUMMARIZE(
        Product,
        Product[Product Name],
        "Rank List Price",
            RANKX(
                ALLSELECTED( Product ),
                Product[List Price],
                CALCULATE( VALUES( Product[List Price] ) )
            )
    ),
    Product[Product Status] = "Current",
    Product[Color] = "Silver"
)
ORDER BY [Rank List Price]
```

The use of *VALUES* instead of *MIN* or *MAX* inside *CALCULATE* in this example is intentional. If there are more rows as a result, it would mean that there are more prices for a given product, and this should not happen, considering the Current on Product Status filter. Only one row for each product name should be selected in this case, considering that the Product table is a slowly changing dimension of type 2. Using *MIN* or *MAX*, the error in data would not be propagated to an error in the query, whereas using *VALUES* will propagate data errors to a query error, which is preferable because the data shown as a result are more reliable.

The second scenario in which you might want to specify the <value> parameter in the *RANKX* function is when you want to perform the ranking of a value that is obtained with a different calculation from the one used to make the comparison. For example, the following query calculates, for each product subcategory, the average price list and the average sale price of products, performing the ranking SQL of both against the price list. In other words, the Rank Price is calculated by using the Avg Price as a term of comparison.

```
EVALUATE
SUMMARIZE(
    'Internet Sales',
    'Product Subcategory'[Product Subcategory Name],
    "Avg Price", AVERAGE( Product[List Price] ),
    "Rank Sales",
        RANKX(
            ALL( 'Product Subcategory'[Product Subcategory Name] ),
            CALCULATE( AVERAGE( Product[List Price] ) )
        ),
    "Avg Sales", AVERAGE( 'Internet Sales'[Sales Amount] ),
    "Rank Price",
        RANKX(
            ALL( 'Product Subcategory'[Product Subcategory Name] ),
            CALCULATE( AVERAGE( Product[List Price] ) ),
            AVERAGE( 'Internet Sales'[Sales Amount] )
        )
)
ORDER BY [Rank Price]
```

Product Subcategory[Product Subcategory Name]	[Avg Price]	[Rank Sales]	[Avg Sales]	[Rank Price]
Mountain Bikes	1820.861	1	2002.5673	1
Road Bikes	1428.3263	2	1799.7749	2
Touring Bikes	**1425.2482**	**3**	**1774.2506**	**2**
Bike Stands	159	4	159	4
Bike Racks	120	5	120	5
...	...	...	...	...

The row for Touring Bikes has a different value for Rank Sales and Rank Price because Rank Price compares the Avg Sales value with the Avg Price value. Because both Road Bikes and Touring Bikes have an Avg Sales value that is between Avg Price of the first and second subcategories, they both get 2 as a result from *RANKX*. When there is no exact match, the nearest lowest value in ranking is considered for matching.

 Note In this case, the <ties> parameter would not have any effect on the Rank Price result, which would always return 4 for Bike Stands regardless of whether *DENSE* or *SKIP* was used.

The <ties> argument controls the value used for ranking after a tie. By default, it is *SKIP*, so this is the behavior you have observed up to now. Look at the following example in which *DENSE* is used.

```
EVALUATE
CALCULATETABLE(
    SUMMARIZE(
        Product,
        Product[Product Name],
        Product[List Price],
        "Rank Price", RANKX( ALLSELECTED( Product ), Product[List Price],,, DENSE )
    ),
    Product[Product Status] = "Current",
    Product[Color] = "Silver"
)
ORDER BY [Rank Price]
```

Product[Product Name]	Product[List Price]	[Rank Price]
Mountain-200 Silver, 46	2319.99	1
Mountain-200 Silver, 42	2319.99	1
Mountain-200 Silver, 38	2319.99	1
HL Mountain Frame - Silver, 42	1364.5	2
HL Mountain Frame - Silver, 46	1364.5	2
HL Mountain Frame - Silver, 38	1364.5	2
Mountain-400-W Silver, 46	769.49	3
Mountain-400-W Silver, 38	769.49	3

The *Rank Price* column does not contain any gaps, even after ties. The *DENSE* parameter is positional, and you can omit <value> and <order> arguments by specifying only commas, as in the previous example.

Finally, the <order> argument is 0 by default, which means that rank is in descending order. By specifying 1, you can obtain the rank in ascending order, as in the following example.

```
EVALUATE
CALCULATETABLE(
    SUMMARIZE(
        Product,
        Product[Product Name],
        Product[List Price],
```

```
        "Rank Price", RANKX( ALLSELECTED( Product ), Product[List Price],, 1, SKIP )
    ),
    Product[Product Status] = "Current",
    Product[Color] = "Silver"
)
ORDER BY [Rank Price]
```

Product[Product Name]	Product[List Price]	[Rank Price]
Chainring Bolts		1
Freewheel		1
Lock Ring		1
Front Derailleur Cage		1
Chainring Nut		1
Front Derailleur Linkage		1
Rear Derailleur Cage		1
Chain	20.24	8
Hydration Pack - 70 oz.	54.99	9
Front Derailleur	91.49	10

Using *RANK.EQ*

The *RANK.EQ* function in DAX is similar to the same function in Excel and returns the ranking of a number in a list of numbers, offering a subset of the features available with the *RANKX* functions. You rarely use it in DAX unless you are migrating an Excel formula. It has the following syntax.

```
RANK.EQ( <value>, <column> [, <order>] )
```

The value can be a DAX expression that has to be evaluated, and the column is the name of an existing column against which rank will be determined. The order is optional and can be 0 for descending order and 1 for ascending order. In Excel, the same function can accept a range of cells for column argument, whereas in DAX it is often the same column used for value expression, meaning that you want to calculate the ranking of a column over itself. One scenario in which you might want to use a different column is when you have two tables, one with elements that you want to rank (for example, a specific group of product) and another with the entire set of elements to use for ranking (for example, the list of all the products). However, because of the limitations applied to the column parameter (it cannot be an expression or a column created by using *ADDCOLUMNS*, *ROW*, or *SUMMARIZE*), *RANK.EQ* is commonly used by passing the same column for value and column parameters in a calculated column expression, referring columns of the same table as in the following example.

```
Product[Price Rank] := RANK.EQ( Product[List Price], Product[List Price] )
```

If you need a more flexible or dynamic ranking, you can use *RANKX* instead of *RANK.EQ*, which is provided mainly for Excel compatibility.

Statistical Functions

In this section, you see a few advanced statistical functions available in DAX. Common calculations in many statistical and distribution analyses include variance and standard deviation. These indicators measure how much variation there is from the average of a population. In other words, they are an indicator of how far the values are from their mean.

Standard Deviation and Variance by Using *STDEV* and *VAR*

The variance of a variable is the squared deviation of that variable from its mean and is calculated by using the following formula.

$$\sigma^2 = \frac{1}{N} \sum_{i=1}^{N} \left(x_i - \overline{x} \right)^2$$

The $\overline{x}$ indicates the average of the values and the σ indicates the resulting value of the standard deviation, which is the square root of the variance. Thus, the standard deviation is defined as follows.

$$\sigma = \sqrt{\frac{1}{N} \sum_{i=1}^{N} \left(x_i - \overline{x} \right)^2}$$

The standard deviation is expressed in the same units as the data, so it is simpler to use. You can read more details about its usage at *http://en.wikipedia.org/wiki/Standard_deviation*.

In DAX, several aggregation functions are available to calculate variance and standard deviation of a population, beginning with *STDEV* and *VAR*, respectively. Here is the syntax of the available functions.

```
VAR.S( <column> )
VAR.P( <column> )
VARX.S( <table>, <expression> )
VARX.P( <table>, <expression> )
STDEV.S( <column> )
STDEV.P( <column> )
STDEVX.S( <table>, <expression> )
STDEVX.P( <table>, <expression> )
```

The difference between the .P and .S suffixes (which stand for Population and Sample) is in the formula used to perform the calculation. Functions ending with .P use the formulas previously described, assuming that the data in the filter context represent the entire population. Functions ending with .S have to be used when available data represents a sample of the entire population, which requires the following, slightly different, formula.

$$\sigma = \sqrt{\frac{1}{N-1} \sum_{i=1}^{N} \left(x_i - \overline{x} \right)^2}$$

Just as with other *aggX* functions, you should use *VARX* and *STDEVX* whenever the expression is more complex than a single column, but you can use *VAR* and *STDEV* when your calculation requires the value of only one column.

For example, the following query calculates the standard deviation of Order Quantity for each product category and shows the range of values that includes 95 percent of the orders received.

```
EVALUATE
ADDCOLUMNS(
    SUMMARIZE(
        'Reseller Sales',
        'Product Category'[Product Category Name],
        "Avg Quantity", AVERAGE( 'Reseller Sales'[Order Quantity] ),
        "StDev.P Quantity", STDEV.P( 'Reseller Sales'[Order Quantity] ),
        "StDev.S Quantity", STDEV.S( 'Reseller Sales'[Order Quantity] ),
        "Min", MIN( 'Reseller Sales'[Order Quantity] ),
        "Max", MAX( 'Reseller Sales'[Order Quantity] )
    ),
    "Distribution", "95% between 1 and " & ROUND( [Avg Quantity] + 2 * [StDev.P Quantity], 0 )
)
```

Product Category[Product Category Name]	[Avg Quantity]	[StDev.P Quantity]	[StDev.S Quantity]	[Min]	[Max]	[Distribution]
Bikes	3.02479	2.29837	2.29841	1	30	95% between 1 and 8
Components	2.62359	1.82105	1.82110	1	23	95% between 1 and 6
Clothing	5.25776	4.32324	4.32341	1	44	95% between 1 and 14
Accessories	5.06548	3.63412	3.63448	1	29	95% between 1 and 12

There is a small difference between the *STDEV.P* and *STDEV.S* results. The text in the distribution comment shows a range starting from 1 because it would not make sense to show a negative number as a lower boundary of the range.

The next query shows a similar example, calculating distribution of freight cost by product category by using *STDEVX* functions.

```
EVALUATE
ADDCOLUMNS(
    SUMMARIZE(
        'Reseller Sales',
        'Product Category'[Product Category Name],
        "Avg Freight",
            AVERAGEX(
                'Reseller Sales',
                'Reseller Sales'[Freight] / 'Reseller Sales'[Order Quantity]
            ),
        "StDevX.P Freight",
            STDEVX.P(
                'Reseller Sales',
                'Reseller Sales'[Freight] / 'Reseller Sales'[Order Quantity]
            ),
```

```
            "StDevX.S Freight",
                STDEVX.S(
                    'Reseller Sales',
                    'Reseller Sales'[Freight] / 'Reseller Sales'[Order Quantity]
                ),
            "Min",
                MINX(
                    'Reseller Sales',
                    'Reseller Sales'[Freight] / 'Reseller Sales'[Order Quantity]
                ),
            "Max",
                MAXX(
                    'Reseller Sales',
                    'Reseller Sales'[Freight] / 'Reseller Sales'[Order Quantity]
                )
        ),
        "Distribution", "95% between 0 and " & ROUND( [Avg Freight] + 2 * [StDevX.P Freight], 2 )
)
```

Product Category[Product Category Name]	[Avg Freight]	[StDevX.P Freight]	[StDevX.S Freight]	[Min]	[Max]	[Distribution]
Bikes	21.9382	13.1351	13.1354	1.6949	53.6741	95% between 0 and 48.21
Components	6.2845	6.2558	6.2560	0.2876	21.4725	95% between 0 and 18.8
Clothing	0.7028	0.3507	0.3507	0.0972	1.3499	95% between 0 and 1.4
Accessories	0.5385	0.4407	0.4408	0.0325	1.8	95% between 0 and 1.42

In this case, the standard deviation is calculated assuming that a sample of the population (*STDEVX.S*) has a slightly higher value than the calculation over the entire population. This extends the estimated distribution range of values obtained as a result, even if you do not see any difference in the Distribution comment because of the rounding chosen for display.

Sampling by Using the *SAMPLE* Function

If you must query a sample of data from a table, you can use the *SAMPLE* function, which has the following syntax.

```
SAMPLE( <number_of_rows>, <table>,
        <columnName_0> [, <order_0>]
        [, <columnName_1> [, <order_1>]] […] )
```

The *SAMPLE* function returns the rows defined by the <number_of_rows> parameter from <table> specified in the second argument, which can be either a physical table or the result of a function returning a table.

The remaining arguments specify one or more columns that will be used to order data before choosing the row that will be returned as the sample. The algorithm logically sorts data according to these parameters and then divides it in <number_of_rows> blocks, returning one row from each block. The <column_name> usually corresponds to a column name but can be any DAX expression evaluated in a row context of <table>. The <order> parameter is 0 to return data sorted by <column> in descendant order, 1 for ascendant order; if missing, it defaults to 0 (descendant).

For example, the following query returns only one row for every month.

```
EVALUATE SAMPLE( 12, 'Date', 'Date'[Month] )
```

Date[Date]	Date[Month]	...
12/17/2004 12:00:00 AM	12	...
11/16/2003 12:00:00 AM	11	...
10/25/2004 12:00:00 AM	10	...
9/13/2005 12:00:00 AM	9	...
8/26/2001 12:00:00 AM	8	...
07/04/2005 00:00	7	...
06/10/2001 00:00	6	...
5/22/2004 12:00:00 AM	5	...
4/24/2005 12:00:00 AM	4	...
03/04/2001 00:00	3	...
2/28/2003 12:00:00 AM	2	...
01/03/2006 00:00	1	...

The *Date* column seems randomly distributed, whereas the *Month* column (other columns have been omitted for readability) is sorted in a descendant order because by omitting the <order> column, the default value of 0 is considered.

You can repeat <column> and <order>, and you can omit <order> to specify two columns, as in the following.

```
EVALUATE
SAMPLE(
    100,
    SUMMARIZE(
        'Date',
        'Date'[Date],
        'Date'[Month],
        'Date'[Calendar Year]
    ),
    'Date'[Month],
    ,
    'Date'[Calendar Year]
)
```

Date[Date]	Date[Month]	Date[Year]
12/17/2006 12:00:00 AM	12	2006
12/26/2006 12:00:00 AM	12	2006
12/05/2005 12:00:00 AM	12	2005
12/26/2004 12:00:00 AM	12	2004
12/09/2003 12:00:00 AM	12	2003
12/20/2002 12:00:00 AM	12	2002
12/14/2001 12:00:00 AM	12	2001
12/02/2001 12:00:00 AM	12	2001
12/03/2000 12:00:00 AM	12	2000
11/14/2006 12:00:00 AM	11	2006
11/17/2005 12:00:00 AM	11	2005
...	...	...

If the column you specify is not regularly distributed, you should see the same distribution of data in the sample extracted. For example, consider the following query that extracts six rows from the Geography table considering the Country Region Name for distribution.

```
EVALUATE
SAMPLE(
    6,
    SUMMARIZE(
        Geography,
        Geography[City],
        Geography[Country Region Name]
    ),
    Geography[Country Region Name]
)
```

Geography[City]	Geography[Country Region Name]
Irving	United States
Nashville	United States
Chula Vista	United States
Columbus	United States
Roncq	France
Lavender Bay	Australia

A few countries are missing (for example, Germany), whereas United States is present several times. This is because there are many more cities in the United States than in Germany, so it occurs more frequently than other countries. The *SAMPLE* function is used by client tools such as Power View to evaluate distribution of data without having to query the entire data set and define the axis scale accordingly.

Summary

In this chapter, you saw how to control filter context to adapt your measures to the selection made by the user browsing data, because these selections are translated in filter context and row context according to the query generated by the application used. Then you learned how to control the sort order of a result, how to filter data according to ranking, and how to calculate absolute ranking and ranking local to a subset of data. You also saw statistical functions for standard deviation and variance and how to get a sample of data from a table.

Understanding Time Intelligence in DAX

Almost all data analyses have to deal with dates. DAX offers a number of functions that simplify many calculations on dates, but using the right function in the right way requires some explanation, starting from the requirements in data modeling.

In this chapter, you see how to correctly define a Date table in a Tabular model and how to handle more dates related to the same entity. Then, you learn how to implement common date-related calculations such as year-to-date, year-over-year, comparisons over years, and so on, including non-additive measures.

Tabular Modeling with Date Table

As you have seen in examples in previous chapters, it is common to aggregate data by year and month by using columns of a particular table containing one row for each day instead of by extracting the date part from a single column of type date or datetime. There are a few reasons for this choice. You obtain a model wherein all attributes about dates are included in a separate table and are easy to access when you browse data by using a Microsoft PivotTable, and you can use special DAX functions that perform Time Intelligence calculations but require a separate Date table to work correctly. In this section, you see how to correctly create a Tabular model with a Date table.

Defining a separate Date table is a common practice in any star schema, and the Adventure Works sample is no exception. This technique is suggested for any Tabular model and for when you do not have a star schema as a starting point. Thus, whenever you have a date column you want to analyze, you should create a relationship with a Date table. If you have multiple date columns in a table, you can create multiple inactive relationships to the Date table in addition to a single active one, as shown in the Internet Sales table in Figure 8-1.

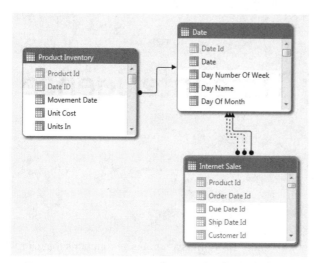

FIGURE 8-1 The Date table has multiple relationships with Internet Sales in Adventure Works.

You can also choose to create a different Date table for each date column you have in a table. Later, you see the pros and cons of these two alternatives. In any case, you will always need to create at least one Date table in your Tabular model whenever you have one or more dates in your data.

Creating a Date Table

The first step for handling date calculation in a Tabular model is to create a Date table. A date table simplifies any date-related calculation. Because of its importance, you should be careful when you create a Date table. In this section, you learn the best practices regarding the creation of a Date table.

First, you need a data source that contains at least one column with all days included in the period of time you want to analyze. For example, if the minimum and maximum dates contained in Sales data are July 3, 2001, and July 27, 2004, respectively, the range of dates you should consider is between January 1, 2001, and December 31, 2004. In this way, you have all the days for all the years containing sales data.

> **Important** Every year in a Date table must contain all the days for that year; otherwise, many business intelligence (BI) functions in DAX will not work properly because they assume that the Date table includes all days in one year.

After you have a list of dates, you can choose to create other columns, such as Day, Month, and Year, and calculated columns by using DAX expressions. However, it is best to move these simple calculations in the data source so that you use calculated columns only when the external data source does not support a particular column you need. In this way, you obtain a better memory usage for the imported column because a calculated column results in less optimal storage compression.

If you are building a Tabular model by using a star schema as a data source, as is the case in Adventure Works, you will probably find an existing Date table and use it. For example, the Date table in Adventure Works corresponds to a direct binding to the DimDate table in the *AdventureWorksDW* database. If you do not have such a table in your data source and you cannot create one there, you have at least three other options.

- Generate dates in a SQL query or view.

- Create a Date table in Microsoft Excel and import it in the Tabular model.

- Import a Date table from DateStream on Windows Azure Marketplace.

You see these options in more detail in the following sections.

 Note Because the Date name is a reserved keyword in DAX, you must embed the Date name in quotes when referring to the table name, even if there are no spaces or special characters in that name. You might prefer using *Dates* instead of *Date* as the name of the table to avoid this requirement. However, because the sample Adventure Works Tabular model uses Date as the name of the table, we use Date in this chapter. Moreover, it is better to be consistent in table names, so if you use the singular form for all the other table names, it is better to keep it singular for the Date table, too.

Generating Dates in a SQL Query or View

If you are using a data source that supports SQL language (for example, Microsoft SQL Server), you can write a SQL query that generates all the dates included in a range and returns the data required for your Date table without persisting them in a physical table in your data source. For example, the following SQL query generates all the dates for years between 2000 and 2006 and creates a few basic columns such as day, year, and month.

```
DateTableQuery.sql

DECLARE @StartYear AS INT = 2000 ;
DECLARE @EndYear AS INT = 2006 ;

WITH    Years
          AS ( SELECT    YYYY = @StartYear
               UNION ALL
               SELECT    YYYY + 1
               FROM      Years
               WHERE     YYYY < @EndYear
             ),
        Months
          AS ( SELECT    MM = 1
               UNION ALL
```

```
              SELECT    MM + 1
              FROM      Months
              WHERE     MM < 12
         ),
      Days
       AS ( SELECT    DD = 1
            UNION ALL
            SELECT    DD + 1
            FROM      Days
            WHERE     DD < 31
         ),
      DatesRaw
       AS ( SELECT    YYYY = YYYY,
                      MM = MM,
                      DD = DD,
                      ID_Date = YYYY * 10000 + MM * 100 + DD,
                      Date = CASE WHEN ISDATE(YYYY * 10000 + MM * 100 + DD) = 1
                                  THEN CAST(CAST(YYYY * 10000 + MM * 100
                                       + DD AS VARCHAR) AS DATE)
                                  ELSE NULL
                             END
            FROM      Years
            CROSS JOIN Months
            CROSS JOIN Days
            WHERE     ISDATE(YYYY * 10000 + MM * 100 + DD) = 1
         )
      SELECT  d.ID_Date,
              d.Date,
              [Year] = YEAR(d.Date),
              MonthNumber = MONTH(d.Date),
              [Month] = DATENAME(MONTH, d.Date),
              DayOfMonth = DAY(d.Date),
              DayOfWeekNumber = DATEPART(dw, d.Date),
              [DayOfWeek] = DATENAME(dw, d.Date),
              WorkingDay = CAST(CASE DATEPART(dw, d.Date)
                                WHEN 1 THEN 0 -- Sunday
                                WHEN 7 THEN 0 -- Saturday
                                ELSE 1 -- Might lookup for a holidays table here
                           END AS BIT)
      FROM    DatesRaw d
      ORDER BY d.Date
```

The generated table has two candidate keys: an *ID_Date* column that is of *int* data type and a *Date* column that is of *date* data type. In this way, it is possible to create a relationship between this table and other tables containing dates expressed in any format. (Usually, star schemas use the integer format, whereas the *date* data type is more common in other data sources.) The *WorkingDay* column also contains a *0* or *1* value that allows a calculation of working days by summing the column.

ID_Date	Date	Year	Month Number	Month	DayOfMonth	DayOfWeek Number	DayOfWeek	WorkingDay
20000101	2000-01-01	2000	1	January	1	7	Saturday	0
20000102	2000-01-02	2000	1	January	2	1	Sunday	0
20000103	2000-01-03	2000	1	January	3	2	Monday	1
...	...	...	...	...	...	...	...	

The query you see has two variables (*StartYear* and *EndYear*) that have been initialized with constant values. However, you might assign a value in a more dynamic way, for example, by querying the minimum and maximum year in which data is included in your data source.

Creating a Date Table in Excel and Importing It in the Tabular Model

If you are creating a prototype or you are importing data from data sources other than relational databases, you can create a Date table manually in Excel and import it in your Tabular model. We do not suggest doing this, however, because refreshing your data model will depend on an external file, and this might create other issues on the deployment side. If your solution is based on Microsoft SharePoint and you save the Excel file in a SharePoint folder, you depend on only the right permission. If your Excel file is saved in the file system, you have to consider that Analysis Services will require accessing the file to refresh the table.

Another option is to copy and paste a table from Excel into the Tabular model. By doing this, you obtain a table by which data will be deployed to the server without requiring any refresh. You can consider this option for prototypes that require a fast deployment on a server that cannot access external data other than the tables with data you have to analyze.

To create a Date table in Excel, you can create a column in a table containing all the dates you need and then add other columns to the table by using Excel formulas that produce the desired result, as you can see in Figure 8-2.

Date	Year	MonthNumber	MonthName	Day	WeekDay	Quarter	FiscalYear	FiscalQuarter
1/1/2001	2001	1	01 - January	1	2	Q1	FY-2001	FQ2
1/2/2001	2001	1	01 - January	2	3	Q1	FY-2001	FQ2
1/3/2001	2001	1	01 - January	3	4	Q1	FY-2001	FQ2
1/4/2001	2001	1	01 - January	4	5	Q1	FY-2001	FQ2
1/5/2001	2001	1	01 - January	5	6	Q1	FY-2001	FQ2
1/6/2001	2001	1	01 - January	6	7	Q1	FY-2001	FQ2

FIGURE 8-2 The Date table can be created in Excel.

Importing a Date Table from DateStream on DataMarket

Because a Date table usually requires columns that are defined following common patterns, you can use existing data sources on the web that provide the required data. For example, DateStream is a free data source available on Windows Azure Marketplace (*https://datamarket.azure.com/dataset/1542c52d-d466-4094-a801-9ef8fd7c6485*) whose source code and documentation are available on *http://datestream.codeplex.com*.

You can find a step-by-step example of how to import a table from Windows Azure Marketplace in the "Loading from the Azure DataMarket" section in Chapter 3, "Loading Data Inside Tabular," and an explanation of how to set range parameters (for example, to limit import for a set of years) at *http://www.bp-msbi.com/2011/10/range-queries-with-azure-datamarket-feeds*.

Handling Wrong or Missing Dates

To handle wrong or missing dates, you have two choices. By default, a date in the fact table that is missing in the Date table is displayed as BLANK when you query the Tabular model. If your process of extract, transform, and load (ETL) intercepts missing dates and wants to assign them to a special date (which is the best practice in a star schema and in a Multidimensional model), you can add a special date in the Date table that corresponds to this special value (for example, ID_Date might be equal to 0) by using NULL for the Date column, 0 for numeric values, and a special name (such as <unknown>) for string values, as in the following example.

ID_Date	Date	Year	Month Number	Month	DayOfMonth	DayOfWeek Number	DayOfWeek	WorkingDay
0		0	0	<unknown>	0	0	<unknown>	0
20000101	2000-01-01	2000	1	January	1	7	Saturday	0
20000102	2000-01-02	2000	1	January	2	1	Sunday	0
20000103	2000-01-03	2000	1	January	3	2	Monday	1
...	...	...	...	...	...	...	...	

You can add this special row in the SQL query that generates data or in the Excel table used as a data source. However, if you import dates from DateStream on DataMarket, adding a row to the imported table is not possible.

Defining Relationship with Date Tables

After you have created a Date table, you have to define a relationship with tables containing one or more date columns. In this section, you see how to accomplish this step in the Tabular model.

The Date table should have two candidate keys, one based on an integer key and the other based on a *date* data type. These are the *Date Id* and *Date* columns in the *AdventureWorksDW* database, respectively.

Date Id	Date	...
20050101	1/1/2005 12:00:00 AM	...
20050102	1/2/2005 12:00:00 AM	...
...	...	...

In Adventure Works, you always use the integer *Date Id* column to define relationships because the star schema data model uses surrogate keys to relate dimensions and facts tables. However, if you need to create relationship or DAX formulas based on data that was not designed to be related to the date dimension, you can do that by using the *Date* column. For example, the Product table has two columns, *Start Date* and *End Date*, containing a *date* data type value.

Product Id	Product Alternate Id	Start Date	End Date	...
322	BK-R50R-60	7/1/2001 12:00:00 AM	6/30/2002 12:00:00 AM	...
323	BK-R50R-60	7/1/2002 12:00:00 AM	6/30/2003 12:00:00 AM	...
...		...	...	...

You see later in the book how to handle a slowly changing dimension, such as the one illustrated here, in a DAX formula. In this case, you do not use relationship in the data model.

You often need to define a relationship between a table containing the date for an event and the Date table. For example, the Product Inventory table uses the *Date ID* column to define the relationship with the Date table, which is used as the lookup table.

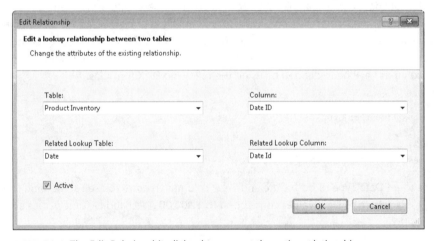

FIGURE 8-3 The Edit Relationship dialog box can set the active relationship.

As you can see in Figure 8-3, the *Active* flag is selected in this relationship. This is also the only relationship between these two tables. However, you might have other fact tables in which every event has many dates associated with it. For example, the Internet Sales table has three dates: Order Date, Due Date, and Ship Date. These dates are stored by using the *integer* data type format.

Sales Order Number	Order Date Id	Due Date Id	Ship Date Id	...
SO43697	20010701	20010713	20010708	...
SO43703	20010702	20010714	20010709	...
...		...	...	...

You can define three relationships between the Internet Sales and Date tables, but only one of them can have the *Active* flag selected; in the others, it will be cleared, and you will call them inactive relationships. In AdventureWorks, the relationship based on Order Date Id is the active one. You should choose as active the relationship that identifies the most important date. If you are analyzing, the date in which the order was generated is usually the most common to use in further analysis. However, you can also use inactive relationships in DAX formulas by using the *USERELATIONSHIP* function, as you saw in Chapter 5, "Understanding Evaluation Context." However, remember that handling other dates by using inactive relationships is only one of the options you have; sometimes you might need a different design. For example, if one of the requirements you must fulfill is the ability to browse data by shipping date, you might prefer to duplicate the Date table, as you see in the next section.

Separating Time from Date

Using the *integer* data type to create the relationship with a Date table is the preferred way not only because it corresponds to the design choice of a star schema but also because it avoids possible mistakes and missing values. The reason is the presence of time information in a *Date* column.

What is called a *date* data type in Tabular is in reality a *datetime* data type, which can store both date and time. As you saw in Chapter 4, "DAX Basics," it is internally represented as a floating point number, and you can get the date part by using the *TRUNC* function. For example, the following Transactions table contains the date and time of each transaction in the *Timestamp* column. *Date* and *Time* calculated columns have been defined by using the following DAX formulas.

```
Transactions[Date] =
TRUNC( Transactions[Timestamp], 0 )

Transactions[Time] =
Transactions[Timestamp] - Transactions[Date]
```

It is important to set Data Type of both *Date* and *Time* columns to *date*. You see something similar to the following table, where all Date values correspond to 12:00:00 A.M., and all Time values are assigned to 12/30/1899.

Transaction	Timestamp	Date	Time	...
4546126	6/20/2008 2:00:01 AM	6/20/2008 12:00:00 AM	12/30/1899 2:00:01 AM	...
4546127	7/22/2008 3:04:45 AM	7/22/2008 12:00:00 AM	12/30/1899 3:04:45 AM	...
...		...	...	...

To improve the display, you can set the Data Format of the *Date* column to Short Date and the Data Format of *Time* column to h:mm:ss tt, as you can see in Figure 8-4.

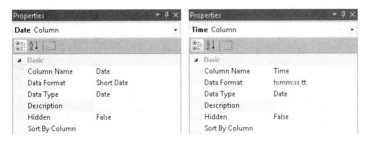

FIGURE 8-4 The Data Type and Data Format properties are different for *Date* and *Time* columns.

You obtain the following visualization.

Transaction	Timestamp	Date	Time	...
4546126	6/20/2008 2:00:01 AM	6/20/2008	2:00:01 AM	...
4546127	7/22/2008 3:04:45 AM	7/22/2008	3:04:45 AM	...
...		...	...	...

However, the most important thing is that the *Date* column is now usable to define a relationship with the Date table by using the *Date* column. As an alternative, you can use a calculated column that defines the Date Id in an integer format, for example, by using the following DAX formula for a *Date Id* calculated column.

```
Transactions[Date Id] =
YEAR( Transactions[Time] ) * 10000 + MONTH( Transactions[Time] ) * 100
+ DAY( Transactions[Time] )
```

Transaction	Timestamp	Date	Time	Date Id	...
4546126	6/20/2008 2:00:01 AM	6/20/2008	2:00:01 AM	20080620	...
4546127	7/22/2008 3:04:45 AM	7/22/2008	3:04:45 AM	20080722	...
...		...	...		...

At this point, you could use either *Date* or *Date Id* to define the relationship with the Date table. In a very large dataset, you should use the integer *Date Id* column for performance reasons. However, with a large dataset, we suggest creating only one column, either *Date* and *Date Id*, to save memory. In any case, it is always a best practice to hide these columns from the end user, forcing him or her to use the columns of the Date table to browse data, avoiding possible mistakes in your DAX formula that will always assume that the Date table has been used for selecting periods of time.

Important The division between Date and Time in the transaction table should be done before importing data into the Tabular model. As you see in Chapter 9, "Understanding xVelocity and DirectQuery," a single column with a high number of distinct values can be expensive. Because a *Timestamp* column is useless in aggregated analysis and can be split in two columns (*Date* and *Time*) with a smaller number of distinct values, doing this split in the query that imports data in Tabular saves memory and reduces processing time.

 Note If you want to browse time by using hierarchies such as hour/minute, hour/quarter/minute, hour band, and so on, create a Time table containing one row for every minute or second, depending on the granularity you want. To create the relationship, your *Time* calculated column should round the time down to minute or second according to the granularity you chose in the Time table; otherwise, you might have a Time value that contains a fraction of a second and does not match any row in the Time table.

Managing Date Granularity

Up to now, it was assumed that the information related to dates has a day granularity. In other words, every event or fact can be related to a specific day. However, you might have data that are related to a year, a quarter, or a month but cannot be mapped to a specific day. For example, sales might be recorded at the day level, but budget might be stored by month. If you want to compare sales and budget by using the same Date table, these tables must be joined. This section shows the options you have in similar scenarios.

Consider that you have a budget table defined as follows.

Year	Month	Product Id	Budget
2008	1	624	775
2008	1	541	620
2008	2	624	725
2008	2	624	580
...		...	...

If you can prepare data by using some ETL, you can generate a table that divides the monthly budget into daily values, loading this Daily Budget table in the Tabular model and defining the relationship by using the *Date Id* column.

Year	Month	Date Id	Product Id	Budget
2008	1	20080101	624	25
2008	1	20080101	541	20

2008	1	20080102	624	25
2008	1	20080102	541	20
...	...	...	...	...

This might not always be possible, and can produce meaningless numbers. (For example, you might wrongly assign a budget to nonworking days.) However, the data would still be meaningful at the month granularity level. If you hide the day columns on the Date table, the user cannot explore data deeply at a granularity level that is not visible. Another option is to intercept the selection of days/weeks in measures to display *BLANK* if the user is not looking at budget-related data at the proper granularity level.

A similar technique is to assign each row of the budget table to an arbitrary day in the month. For example, you can create calculated columns to generate the first and last day of every month, choosing which one to use for the relationship with the Date table.

```
Date[StartMonthDate] =
DATE( Budget[Year], Budget[Month], 1 )
```

```
Date[EndMonthDate] =
EOMONTH( Budget[StartMonthDate], 0 )
```

Year	Month	StartMonthDate	EndMonthDate	Product Id	Budget
2008	1	1/1/2008	1/31/2008	624	775
2008	1	1/1/2008	1/31/2008	541	620
2008	2	2/1/2008	2/29/2008	624	725
2008	2	2/1/2008	2/29/2008	624	580
...				...	...

Also, in this case, the navigation of data would be meaningful at only the month level, so you should hide budget data to navigation at a more granular level.

Finally, another scenario is to leave the budget table untouched and not define any relationship with the Date table. In this case, you must create measures by using DAX expressions that mimic the missing relationships operating at a month level. For example, you can look at this article for an example of a budget table handled in PowerPivot: *http://www.sqlbi.com/articles/budget-and-other-data-at-different-granularities-in-powerpivot*. You can apply the same technique to a Tabular model.

Note We did not mention the creation of a second Date table containing only years and months as a possible alternative because it would make the model less clear and more difficult (if not impossible) to use. You would end up writing complex DAX measures to hide the model complexity, and we think it is better to write the business logic directly in DAX formula in these cases, keeping the Tabular model simple.

Duplicating the Date Table

You have seen that when there are multiple date columns in a table, you can create multiple relationships with a single Date table. In this section, you learn when and how to handle this scenario by creating a different Date table for each date column you have in a table.

To understand the differences between the two techniques, consider the Internet Sales table in Adventure Works. Every order has three dates: Order Date, Due Date, and Ship Date. By using an active relationship for Order Date and inactive relationships for the other two dates, every measure related to *Internet Sales* columns you create will refer to Order Date unless you write a specific DAX expression that uses an inactive relationship. In other words, for every calculation related to Due Date or Ship Date, you must create a separate measure. For example, if you want to compute the total of Sales Amount grouped by any of the three dates, you must define three measures, repeating the same duplication of measure for every possible calculation you want to be available for any date column.

In a Tabular model, there is an alternative approach, which is the only approach available in a Multidimensional model. Instead of duplicating every measure, you can show to the user different Date tables, one for each date you have, so that every measure is grouped according to the date selected by the end user (or used in a query to the Tabular model). From a maintenance point of view, this might seem a better solution because it lowers the number of measures that have to be created in the model, and it allows selecting orders that intersect two months. (For example, you can easily see the total number of orders received in January and delivered in February of the same year.) This approach is also known as the role-playing dimension in a Multidimensional model; the Date table is a dimension that is duplicated (logically or physically) as many times as the number of relationships existing between a facts table (for example, the Internet Sales table) and a dimension. In reality, these two options (using inactive relationships and duplicating the Date table) are complementary to each other, as you see after an example of how to create duplicated Date tables in the model.

To create a Ship Date table and a Due Date table for Adventure Works, you must add the same source table twice more by using the Model / Existing Connections menu item in SQL Server Data Tools (SSDT) and opening a table from the same connection used to get other tables. (In Tabular, you must physically duplicate the Date table, whereas in Multidimensional, you can read it once from the data source.) In every import, you must rename the friendly name to Ship Date or Due Date, as you can see in Figure 8-5, and then select only the required columns by using the Preview & Filter button.

After you import the Date table in the Tabular model, you must define an active relationship between it and the corresponding *Date* column in the fact table (Internet Sales in this case), and you can rename columns to make their names easier to use. However, using the same column names you used for the existing Date table in the model is not a good idea because the user browsing the model might obtain a report that is difficult to read. For example, in Figure 8-6, you can see a PivotTable in which the Calendar Year from Order Date has been put in rows and in the first slicer, and the Calendar Year from Ship Date has been put in columns and in the second slicer. The problem is that there is no way to determine which date table is put into slicers, filters, rows, or columns of the user interface.

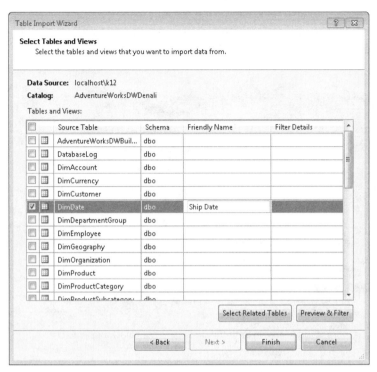

FIGURE 8-5 Import the DimDate table as the Ship Date table in the Tabular model.

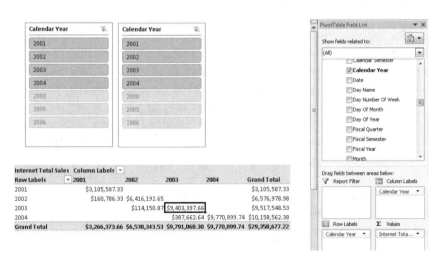

FIGURE 8-6 Columns with the same name from different tables are not recognizable.

Thus, if you create a model with multiple copies of the same tables, you should differentiate the names of the columns so that they are immediately recognizable in a report. You can edit the column names in SSDT by adding a prefix to each column. For example, in Figure 8-7, you can see that the previous report after each column in the Order Date and Ship Date tables has been prefixed with the word Order and Ship, respectively.

Tip You can rename the slicer regardless of the underlying table and column names. This is a fast workaround if you cannot change the Tabular model.

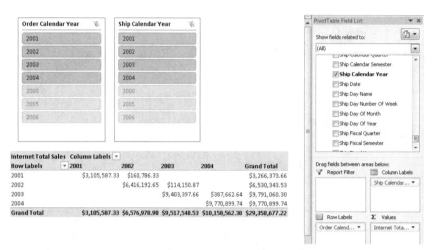

FIGURE 8-7 Column prefixes are more recognizable in both the slicers and the PivotTable Field List.

Using Views as a Decoupling Layer

Because of the work required to rename columns in SSDT, it is better to consider creating views in your data source, importing them instead of binding the relational tables directly in your Tabular model. You can use views as a decoupling layer between the Tabular model and the underlying physical database, so that a change in the database structure does not break the existing Tabular model as soon as you provide a view that has the same name and type for all the columns. Editing column names inside the view makes importing duplicate copies of the same table easier and simplifies debugging issues in data because you have an easy way to query the data source by using the same column names you see in the Tabular model.

You can import the Ship Date table in the same way you imported the Due Date table. A final result for your data model might be the one shown in Figure 8-8, in which all three Date tables are related to Internet Sales, and the Date table still has inactive relationships for Due Date and Ship Date columns and an active relationship for Order Date.

It would be wrong to choose a single method, either duplicating tables or using multiple relationships, in handling multiple date tables. They are both useful for different needs, and your choice should correspond to existing requirements.

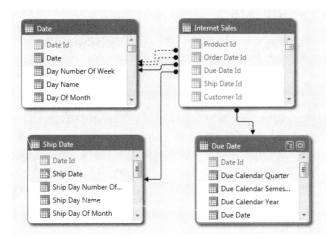

FIGURE 8-8 Multiple dates in Adventure Works can be related to three Date tables.

You should use duplicate Date tables if the end user would like to browse all the measures across all the dates or wants to cross two dates, as you saw in Figure 8-6. However, this approach might confuse the end user and, often, the larger choice of dimensions you have available does not make the model simpler to use. Moreover, you might have some issue when defining time-related calculations, such as year-to-date, because it might not be obvious to which date such a calculation applies. For example, imagine a year-over-year difference of sales measure in the PivotTable you saw in Figure 8-6. Would it be related to Ship Year or Calendar Year? It would be difficult to answer this question by just looking at data! You should also consider adding a prefix to the columns' content if you duplicate Date tables. For example, it would be better to read SY 2011 for Ship Year 2011 and OY 2011 for Order Year 2011 than to read an ambiguous 2011 for both.

Using multiple relationships allows greater control over possible calculations because every measure using an inactive relationship (such as Due Date and Ship Date in the example) should be explicitly defined in the Tabular model. The side effect is that end users are not able to ask for a calculation over an alternative date if it has not been provided in the Tabular model up front. Moreover, if you want to provide the same calculation for several dates, you end up having many duplicating measures that differ only by the date selection. In this case, this could be a very long list of measures.

Based on our experience, we suggest carefully considering adding duplicate Date tables in your data model to avoid duplicating any measure for any Date table that has inactive relationships. The best practice is exposing in the Tabular model only those tables, columns, and measures that are meaningful for the end user, avoiding any possible ambiguity between similar names. Using perspectives in the data model might help you expose a subset of tables, columns, and measures that are useful for a particular type of analysis. This is particularly important whenever you cannot avoid duplicating Date tables or creating multiple measures with similar names because of the need to satisfy different requirements. Usually, every user needs only a subset of data you create, and showing him or her the model through perspectives can offer a better user experience.

Setting Metadata for a Date Table

After you import a Date table in a Tabular model, it is important to set the right metadata so that the engine can take advantage of them and enable you to use all the Time Intelligence functions, which you see later in this chapter. In this section, you see how to set these metadata correctly in the Tabular model.

Many DAX functions that operate over dates (such as *TOTALYTD*, *SAMEPERIODLASTYEAR*, and many others) require a Date table to exist and assume that a column of *date* data type exists. To specify the column to use for date calculations in date tables, you must select the *Date* column by using the Mark As Date Table dialog box that you can open by choosing the Table / Date / Mark As Date Table menu command in SSDT. You can see this dialog box in Figure 8-9, in which the *Date* column from the Date table in Adventure Works has been selected.

FIGURE 8-9 The Mark As Date Table dialog box requires the selection of a Date column.

After you mark a table as a Date table, you can change the *Date* column by opening the dialog box again by choosing the Table / Date / Date Table Settings menu command.

Another important action you must perform in a Date table is setting the correct sort order for month and day names. Because each column is sorted in alphabetical order by default, you must specify that day and month names have to be sorted by the corresponding day and month numbers (which are columns that must be created earlier, when you generate the Date table). For example, in Figure 8-10, you can see the Sort By Column property of the *Day Name* column that has been set to Day Number Of Week.

You set the Sort By Column property of the *Month Name* column to Month, which contains the month number in Adventure Works. You must adapt these names to those used for the column in the Date table of your own Tabular model.

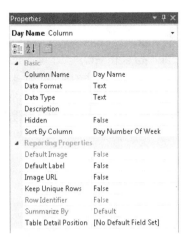

FIGURE 8-10 The Sort By Column property must be set to sort day and month names correctly.

 Important The Sort By Column property has an effect on MDX queries, but it does not affect the result of a DAX query in a direct way. Instead, it is a property that has to be read by client tools to create a proper DAX query. Thus, you must specify the Day Number Of Week column in an *ORDER BY* clause of a DAX query instead of specifying the Day Name.

Time Intelligence Functions in DAX

In the first part of this chapter, you saw how to correctly create a Date table in your Tabular model. This is an important prerequisite to perform date-based calculation such as aggregation and comparison over time. From now on, you see how to implement these calculations by using both general-purpose and dedicated DAX functions.

Aggregating and Comparing over Time

The first set of DAX functions and patterns you see is related to aggregation and comparison of data over time. For example, you might want to calculate the aggregated value of a measure from the beginning of the year up to the period you are selecting. (This is commonly called year-to-date aggregation.) You might also want to compare the sales of this year with the sales of the previous year. In the next sections, you see the tools available to implement measures for these and other scenarios.

Year-to-Date, Quarter-to-Date, and Month-to-Date

The calculations of year-to-date (YTD), quarter-to-date (QTD), and month-to-date (MTD) are all very similar. Month-to-date is meaningful only when you are looking at data at the day level, whereas year-to-date and quarter-to-date calculations are often used to look at data at the month level. In the following examples, measures (and columns) are added to the following DAX query. For example, in Figure 8-11, you can see the Internet Total Sales measure aggregated by year, quarter, and month.

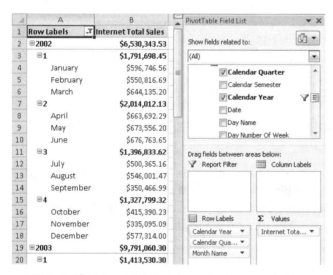

FIGURE 8-11 The Internet Sales Total measure is aggregated by the corresponding period in row.

Remember that the Internet Total Sales measure is defined as the sum of the *Sales Amount* column of the Internet Sales table.

```
[Internet Total Sales] := SUM( 'Internet Sales'[Sales Amount] )
```

You can calculate the year-to-date value of Sales for each month by using a measure that operates on the filter context, modifying the filter context on dates for a range that starts on January 1 and ends on the month corresponding to the calculated cell. You can define a YTD Sales measure by using the following DAX formula.

```
[YTD Sales] := CALCULATE( [Internet Total Sales], DATESYTD( 'Date'[Date] ) )
```

DATESYTD is a built-in Time Intelligence DAX function that returns a list of all the dates from the beginning of the year until the last date included in the current filter context. This list is passed as an argument to the *CALCULATE* function to set the filter for the Internet Total Sales calculation. You can see the new measure in action in Figure 8-12.

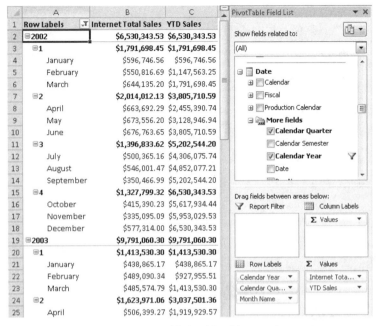

	A	B	C
1	Row Labels	Internet Total Sales	YTD Sales
2	⊟2002	$6,530,343.53	$6,530,343.53
3	⊟1	$1,791,698.45	$1,791,698.45
4	January	$596,746.56	$596,746.56
5	February	$550,816.69	$1,147,563.25
6	March	$644,135.20	$1,791,698.45
7	⊟2	$2,014,012.13	$3,805,710.59
8	April	$663,692.29	$2,455,390.74
9	May	$673,556.20	$3,128,946.94
10	June	$676,763.65	$3,805,710.59
11	⊟3	$1,396,833.62	$5,202,544.20
12	July	$500,365.16	$4,306,075.74
13	August	$546,001.47	$4,852,077.21
14	September	$350,466.99	$5,202,544.20
15	⊟4	$1,327,799.32	$6,530,343.53
16	October	$415,390.23	$5,617,934.44
17	November	$335,095.09	$5,953,029.53
18	December	$577,314.00	$6,530,343.53
19	⊟2003	$9,791,060.30	$9,791,060.30
20	⊟1	$1,413,530.30	$1,413,530.30
21	January	$438,865.17	$438,865.17
22	February	$489,090.34	$927,955.51
23	March	$485,574.79	$1,413,530.30
24	⊟2	$1,623,971.06	$3,037,501.36
25	April	$506,399.27	$1,919,929.57

FIGURE 8-12 The YTD measure is side by side with a regular measure.

This approach requires you to use the *CALCULATE* function, but because this pattern (using a *CALCULATE* and a *DATESYTD* function) is very common, DAX offers a dedicated function that simplifies (and makes more readable) the syntax of the YTD calculation, *TOTALYTD*.

```
[YTD Sales] := TOTALYTD( [Internet Total Sales] , 'Date'[Date] )
```

The syntax requires the hoped-for aggregation as the first parameter and the date column as the second parameter. The behavior is identical to the original measure, but the name of the *TOTALYTD* function immediately communicates the intention of the formula. However, you must know the behavior of the original *CALCULATE* syntax because it enables a more complex calculation that you will see later in this chapter.

What Date Column to Use

Keep in mind that the date column you must use when calling *TOTALYTD* (and other similar functions) is the date column of the Date table and not the date column of the table that is the object of analysis. In this case, the *Date[Date]* column was used instead of the *'Internet Sales'[Order Date]* column. If the latter had been used, the calculation would have been wrong. You can see in Figure 8-13 the result that would have been produced by using the following formula for the YTD measure.

```
[YTD Sales] := TOTALYTD( [Internet Total Sales], 'Internet Sales'[Order Date] )
```

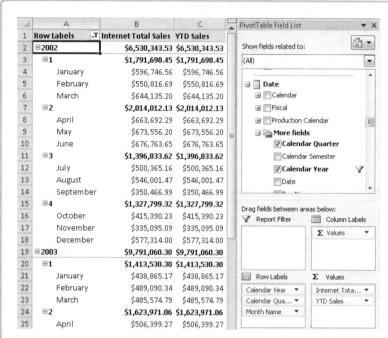

FIGURE 8-13 The wrong year-to-date calculation returns the same value as the Internet Total Sales measure.

The problem is that the existing filter on year and month would still be applied. There are possible workarounds that you can use, but our suggestion is to always define and use a Date table. Further details on the issue and possible workarounds are available in this blog post written by Kasper de Jonge: *http://www.powerpivotpro.com/2010/06/powerpivot-time-intelligent-functions-why-use-all-and-how-to-work-around-it.*

As you define the year-to-date calculation, you can also define quarter-to-date and month-to-date calculations with built-in functions, as in these measures.

```
[QTD Sales] := TOTALQTD( [Internet Total Sales] , 'Date'[Date] )
```

```
[MTD Sales] := TOTALMTD( [Internet Total Sales] , 'Date'[Date] )
```

In Figure 8-14, you can see the year-to-date and quarter-to-date measures used in a PivotTable. Note that the quarter-to-date measure makes the year total equal to the last quarter of the year.

To calculate a year-to-date measure over the fiscal year when it does not end on December 31, you must use an optional parameter that specifies the end day of the fiscal year. For example, you can calculate the fiscal year-to-date for Sales by using the following measure.

```
[Fiscal YTD Sales] := TOTALYTD( [Internet Total Sales] , 'Date'[Date], "06-30" )
```

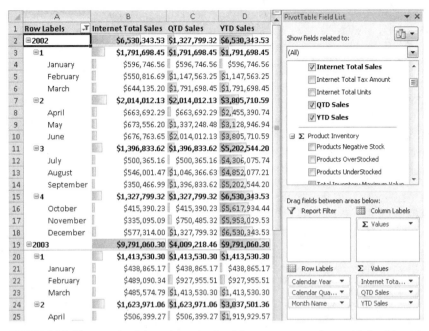

FIGURE 8-14 The year-to-date and quarter-to-date measures are shown side by side with a regular measure.

The last parameter corresponds to June 30, which in our Date table corresponds to the end of the fiscal year. You can find several Time Intelligence functions that have a last, optional YE_Date parameter for this purpose: *STARTOFYEAR, ENDOFYEAR, PREVIOUSYEAR, NEXTYEAR, DATESYTD, TOTALYTD, OPENINGBALANCEYEAR*, and *CLOSINGBALANCEYEAR*.

Periods from the Prior Year

Users commonly need to get a value from a period of the prior year (PY). This can be useful for making comparisons of trends during a period last year to the same period this year. This is the DAX expression you must calculate for that value.

```
[PY Sales] := CALCULATE( [Internet Total Sales], SAMEPERIODLASTYEAR( 'Date'[Date] ) )
```

SAMEPERIODLASTYEAR returns a set of dates shifted one year back in time. The *SAMEPERIODLASTYEAR* function is a specialized version of the more generic *DATEADD* function, which can be used by specifying the number and type of periods to shift. For example, the same PY Sales measure can be defined by this equivalent expression.

```
[PY Sales] := CALCULATE( [Internet Total Sales], DATEADD( 'Date'[Date], -1, YEAR ) )
```

Sometimes, you must look at the total amount of a measure for the previous year, usually to compare it with the year-to-date total. To do that, you can use the *PARALLELPERIOD* function, which is similar to *DATEADD* but returns the full period specified in the third parameter instead of the partial period returned by *DATEADD*. The PY Sales measure that calculates the total of sales for the previous year can be defined this way.

```
[PY Total Sales] :=
    CALCULATE( [Internet Total Sales], PARALLELPERIOD( 'Date'[Date], -1, YEAR ) )
```

In Figure 8-15, you can see the result of the PY Sales and PY Total Sales measures. The quarters data in 2002 for the Internet Total Sales column has been copied into the respective quarters of year 2003 in the PY Sales column. The PY Total Sales reports for every period the total amount of the *Internet Total Sales* column for the previous year.

Row Labels	Internet Total Sales	PY Sales	PY Total Sales
⊟2002	$6,530,343.53	$3,266,373.66	$3,266,373.66
1	$1,791,698.45		$3,266,373.66
2	$2,014,012.13		$3,266,373.66
3	$1,396,833.62	$1,453,522.89	$3,266,373.66
4	$1,327,799.32	$1,812,850.77	$3,266,373.66
⊟2003	$9,791,060.30	$6,530,343.53	$6,530,343.53
1	$1,413,530.30	$1,791,698.45	$6,530,343.53
2	$1,623,971.06	$2,014,012.13	$6,530,343.53
3	$2,744,340.48	$1,396,833.62	$6,530,343.53
4	$4,009,218.46	$1,327,799.32	$6,530,343.53
Grand Total	$16,321,403.82	$9,796,717.18	$9,796,717.18

FIGURE 8-15 The prior year calculations show the data shifted by one year.

When you want to calculate the year-to-date of the prior year because, typically, you want to compare it with the current year-to-date measure, you must mix the two techniques. Instead of passing the Date[Date] parameter to *SAMEPERIODLASTYEAR*, which corresponds to the list of dates that are active in the current filter context, you can use the *DATESYTD* function to make a transformation of these dates, defining the year-to-date group first. However, you can also invert the order of these calls without affecting the result. The two following definitions of PY YTD Sales are equivalent.

```
[PY YTD Sales] :=
    CALCULATE(
        [Internet Total Sales],
        SAMEPERIODLASTYEAR( DATESYTD( 'Date'[Date] ) )
    )

[PY YTD Sales] :=
    CALCULATE(
        [Internet Total Sales],
        DATESYTD( SAMEPERIODLASTYEAR( 'Date'[Date] ) )
    )
```

You can see the results of the PY YTD Sales in Figure 8-16. The values of YTD Sales are reported for PY YTD Sales shifted by one year. In the same result, you can also see the Fiscal YTD Sales measure that you saw at the end of the previous section; the horizontal lines between Q2 and Q3 in that column highlight the points at which the year-to-date calculation restarts.

Row Labels	Internet Total Sales	YTD Sales	PY YTD Sales	Fiscal YTD Sales
⊟ 2002	$6,530,343.53	$6,530,343.53	$3,266,373.66	$2,724,632.94
1	$1,791,698.45	$1,791,698.45		$5,058,072.11
2	$2,014,012.13	$3,805,710.59		$7,072,084.24
3	$1,396,833.62	$5,202,544.20	$1,453,522.89	$1,396,833.62
4	$1,327,799.32	$6,530,343.53	$3,266,373.66	$2,724,632.94
⊟ 2003	$9,791,060.30	$9,791,060.30	$6,530,343.53	$6,753,558.94
1	$1,413,530.30	$1,413,530.30	$1,791,698.45	$4,138,163.24
2	$1,623,971.06	$3,037,501.36	$3,805,710.59	$5,762,134.30
3	$2,744,340.48	$5,781,841.84	$5,202,544.20	$2,744,340.48
4	$4,009,218.46	$9,791,060.30	$6,530,343.53	$6,753,558.94
Grand Total	$16,321,403.82	$9,791,060.30	$6,530,343.53	$6,753,558.94

FIGURE 8-16 The year-to-date calculation for prior year and fiscal year can appear in the same PivotTable.

Another commonly requested calculation that eliminates seasonal changes in sales is the moving annual total (MAT), which always considers the past 12 months. For example, the value of MAT Sales for March 2002 is calculated by summing the range of dates from April 2001 to March 2002. Consider the following MAT Sales measure definition, which calculates the moving annual total for Sales.

```
[MAT Sales] :=
    CALCULATE(
        [Internet Total Sales],
        DATESBETWEEN(
            'Date'[Date],
            NEXTDAY( SAMEPERIODLASTYEAR( LASTDATE( 'Date'[Date] ) ) ),
            LASTDATE( 'Date'[Date] )
        )
    )
```

The implementation of this measure requires some attention. You must use the *DATESBETWEEN* function, which returns the dates from a column included between two specified dates. Because this calculation is always made at the day level, even if you are querying data at the month level, you must calculate the first day and the last day of the interval you want. The last day can be obtained by calling the *LASTDATE* function, which returns the last date of a given column (always considering the current filter context). Starting from this date, you can get the first day of the interval by requesting the following day (by calling *NEXTDAY*) of the corresponding last date one year before. (You can do this by using *SAMEPERIODLASTYEAR*.)

In Figure 8-17, you can see a PivotTable using the moving annual total calculation. For example, the 2003 Q2 data has been calculated by summing Q3 and Q4 of 2002, plus Q1 and Q2 of 2003. In the middle, you see the classic year-to-date calculation, which has the same value of moving annual total only for the last period of each year (in this case, Q4).

Row Labels	Internet Total Sales	YTD Sales	MAT Sales
⊟2002	$6,530,343.53	$6,530,343.53	$6,530,343.53
1	$1,791,698.45	$1,791,698.45	$5,058,072.11
2	$2,014,012.13	$3,805,710.59	$7,072,084.24
3	$1,396,833.62	$5,202,544.20	$7,015,394.98
4	$1,327,799.32	$6,530,343.53	$6,530,343.53
⊟2003	$9,791,060.30	$9,791,060.30	$9,791,060.30
1	$1,413,530.30	$1,413,530.30	$6,152,175.37
2	$1,623,971.06	$3,037,501.36	$5,762,134.30
3	$2,744,340.48	$5,781,841.84	$7,109,641.16
4	$4,009,218.46	$9,791,060.30	$9,791,060.30
Grand Total	$16,321,403.82	$9,791,060.30	$9,791,060.30

FIGURE 8-17 The moving annual total is compared to the year-to-date calculation.

Difference over Previous Year

A common operation that compares a measure with its value in the prior year is calculating the difference between these values. That difference can be expressed as an absolute value or by using a percentage. You have already seen how to obtain the value for the prior year with the PY Sales measure.

```
[PY Sales] := CALCULATE( [Internet Total Sales], SAMEPERIODLASTYEAR( 'Date'[Date] ) )
```

The absolute difference of Internet Total Sales over previous year (year-over-year, YOY) is a simple subtraction. You can define a YOY Sales measure with the following expression.

```
[YOY Sales] := [Internet Total Sales] - [PY Sales]
```

The analogous calculation for comparing the year-to-date measure with a corresponding value in the prior year is a simple subtraction of two measures, YTD Sales and PY YTD Sales, which you saw in the previous section; we report it here as a reminder.

```
[YTD Sales] := TOTALYTD( [Internet Total Sales], 'Date'[Order Date] )

[PY YTD Sales] :=
    CALCULATE( [Internet Total Sales], SAMEPERIODLASTYEAR( DATESYTD( 'Date'[Date] ) ) )

[YOY YTD Sales] := [YTD Sales] - [PY YTD Sales]
```

Most of the time, the year-over-year difference is better expressed as a percentage in a report. You can define this calculation by dividing YOY Sales by the PY Sales; in this way, the difference uses the prior read value as a reference for the percentage difference (100 percent corresponds to a value that is doubled in one year). In the following expressions that define the YOY Sales% measure, the *IF* statement avoids a divide-by-zero error if there is no corresponding data in the prior year. (The second version uses the default *BLANK()* value for the third parameter.)

```
[YOY Sales%] := IF( [PY Sales] = 0, BLANK(), [YOY Sales] / [PY Sales] )

[YOY Sales%] := IF( [PY Sales] <> 0, [YOY Sales] / [PY Sales] )
```

A similar calculation can be made to display the percentage difference of a year-over-year comparison for the year-to-date aggregation. You can define YOY YTD Sales% by using one of the following formulas.

```
[YOY YTD Sales%] := IF( [PY YTD Sales] = 0, BLANK(), [YOY YTD Sales] / [PY YTD Sales] )
```

```
[YOY YTD Sales%] := IF( [PY YTD Sales] <> 0, [YOY YTD Sales] / [PY YTD Sales] )
```

In Figure 8-18, you can see the results of these measures in a PivotTable.

Row Labels	Internet Total Sales	PY Sales	YOY Sales	YOY YTD Sales	YOY Sales%	YOY YTD Sales%	PY YTD Sales	YTD Sales
⊟2002	$6,530,343.53	$3,266,373.66	$3,263,969.87	$3,263,969.87	99.93%	99.93%	$3,266,373.66	$6,530,343.53
1	$1,791,698.45		$1,791,698.45	$1,791,698.45				$1,791,698.45
2	$2,014,012.13		$2,014,012.13	$3,805,710.59				$3,805,710.59
3	$1,396,833.62	$1,453,522.89	($56,689.27)	$3,749,021.32	-3.90%	257.93%	$1,453,522.89	$5,202,544.20
4	$1,327,799.32	$1,812,850.77	($485,051.45)	$3,263,969.87	-26.76%	99.93%	$3,266,373.66	$6,530,343.53
⊟2003	$9,791,060.30	$6,530,343.53	$3,260,716.77	$3,260,716.77	49.93%	49.93%	$6,530,343.53	$9,791,060.30
1	$1,413,530.30	$1,791,698.45	($378,168.15)	($378,168.15)	-21.11%	-21.11%	$1,791,698.45	$1,413,530.30
2	$1,623,971.06	$2,014,012.13	($390,041.08)	($768,209.23)	-19.37%	-20.19%	$3,805,710.59	$3,037,501.36
3	$2,744,340.48	$1,396,833.62	$1,347,506.86	$579,297.63	96.47%	11.13%	$5,202,544.20	$5,781,841.84
4	$4,009,218.46	$1,327,799.32	$2,681,419.14	$3,260,716.77	201.94%	49.93%	$6,530,343.53	$9,791,060.30
Grand Total	$16,321,403.82	$9,796,717.18	$6,524,686.64	$3,260,716.77	66.60%	49.93%	$6,530,343.53	$9,791,060.30

FIGURE 8-18 All the year-over-year (YOY) measures can be used in the same PivotTable.

Browsing Data by Using a Period Table

In the previous sections, you saw how to create single measures with special calculations over time such as year-to-date, year-over-year, and so on. One drawback of this approach is that you have to define one measure for each of these calculations, and the list of the measures in your model might grow too long.

A possible solution to this issue, which is also an interesting generic modeling solution, is to create a special table containing one line for each of the calculations you may want to apply to a measure. In this way, the end user has a shorter list of measures and possible operations on them instead of having the Cartesian product of these two sets. However, you can see that this solution has its own drawbacks, and maybe it is better to create just the measures you really want to use in your model and try to expose only the combinations of measures and calculations that are meaningful for the expected analysis of your data.

Note In a Multidimensional model, this approach is known as adding a Tool dimension and is described at *http://www.sqlbi.com/tools/datetool-dimension/*. The same approach is not possible in Tabular because you cannot rely on a feature similar to MDX Script, which allows you to apply a calculation over existing measures.

First, add a Period table in the Tabular model that the list of possible calculations should be applied to a measure, as you can see in Figure 8-19.

FIGURE 8-19 A Period table can be defined in the Tabular model.

Such a table can be defined by creating a new table (named Period) from an existing connection to SQL Server and writing a query that specifies the data to import, like the following.

```
          SELECT 1 AS Position, 'Current' AS Period
UNION ALL SELECT 2, 'MTD'
UNION ALL SELECT 3, 'QTD'
UNION ALL SELECT 4, 'YTD'
UNION ALL SELECT 5, 'PY Current'
UNION ALL SELECT 6, 'PY MTD'
UNION ALL SELECT 7, 'PY QTD'
UNION ALL SELECT 8, 'PY YTD'
UNION ALL SELECT 9, 'YOY'
UNION ALL SELECT 10, 'YOY%'
UNION ALL SELECT 11, 'YOY YTD'
UNION ALL SELECT 12, 'YOY% YTD'
```

The Period table will have the *Position* column hidden and the *Period* column with the *Sort By* column set to Position. You do not have to define any relationships between this table and other tables in your model because you use the selected member of the Period table to change the behavior of a measure through its DAX definition.

At this point, you can define a single measure that checks the selected value of the Period table and uses a DAX expression to return the corresponding calculation. Because there are no relationships with the Period table, the selected value in the Period table is always the one chosen by the user whenever that table is used as a filter, or the selected value is the corresponding value in a row or a column whenever Period is used in Row or Column labels. In general, follow this generic pattern.

```
IF( HASONEVALUE( Period[Period] ),
    SWITCH(
        VALUES( Period[Period] ),
        "Current", <expression>,
        "MTD", <expression>,
        ...
```

The first condition checks that no multiple values are active in the filter context. In this case, you should avoid any calculation because of the ambiguity of having multiple active values; otherwise, you should generate an error in the calculation instead of returning a wrong value without warning the user. Then in the next step, each value is checked by a *SWITCH* statement, which evaluates the correct expression corresponding to the Period value. Assuming you have all the measures previously defined in this chapter, you must replace the expression tag with the corresponding specific measure. For example, you can define a generic Sales measure, which is used to apply one or more of the operations described in the Period table to the Internet Total Sales measure.

```
Sales :=
    IF( HASONEVALUE( Period[Period] ),
        SWITCH(
            VALUES( Period[Period] ),
            "Current", [Internet Total Sales],
            "MTD", [MTD Sales],
            "QTD", [QTD Sales],
            "YTD", [YTD Sales],
            "PY Current", [PY Sales],
            "PY MTD", [PY MTD Sales],
            "PY QTD", [PY QTD Sales],
            "PY YTD", [PY YTD Sales],
            "YOY", [YOY Sales],
            "YOY%", [YOY Sales%],
            "YOY YTD", [YOY YTD Sales],
            "YOY% YTD", [YOY YTD Sales%],
            BLANK()
        ),
        BLANK()
    )
```

 Important The RTM version of Analysis Services 2012 has an issue in *SWITCH* implementation, which is internally rewritten as a series of nested *IF* calls. Because of this performance issue, if there are too many nested *IF* statements (or too many values to check in a *SWITCH* statement), there could be a slow response and an abnormal memory consumption. You can look at *https://connect.microsoft.com/SQLServer/feedback/details/716986/dax-measure-fails-mdx-queries* to see whether the issue has been fixed.

You have to repeat this definition for each of the measures to which you want to apply the Period calculations. You can avoid defining all the internal measures by replacing each reference to a measure with its corresponding DAX definition. This would make the Sales definition longer and more difficult to maintain, and it would make your reports perform worse, but it is a design choice you can follow.

 Tip Remember that you can hide a measure by using the Hide From Client Tool command. If you do not want to expose internal calculations, you should hide all the measures previously defined and make only the Sales measure visible.

At this point, you can browse data by using the Period values crossed with the Sales measure. In Figure 8-20, only the Sales measure has been selected; the Period values are in the columns, and a selection of years and quarters is in the rows.

Sales	Column Labels											
Row Label	Current	MTD	QTD	YTD	PY Current	PY MTD	PY QTD	PY YTD	YOY	YOY%	YOY YTD	YOY% YTD
⊟2002	6,530,343.53	577,314.00	1,327,799.32	6,530,343.53	3,266,373.66	755,527.89	1,812,850.77	3,266,373.66	3,263,969.87	1.00	3,263,969.87	1.00
1	1,791,698.45	644,135.20	1,791,698.45	1,791,698.45					1,791,698.45		1,791,698.45	
2	2,014,012.13	676,763.65	2,014,012.13	3,805,710.59					2,014,012.13		3,805,710.59	
3	1,396,833.62	350,466.99	1,396,833.62	5,202,544.20	1,453,522.89	473,943.03	1,453,522.89	1,453,522.89	-56,689.27	-0.04	3,749,021.32	2.58
4	1,327,799.32	577,314.00	1,327,799.32	6,530,343.53	1,812,850.77	755,527.89	1,812,850.77	3,266,373.66	-485,051.45	-0.27	3,263,969.87	1.00
⊟2003	9,791,060.30	1,731,787.77	4,009,218.46	9,791,060.30	6,530,343.53	577,314.00	1,327,799.32	6,530,343.53	3,260,716.77	0.50	3,260,716.77	0.50
1	1,413,530.30	485,574.79	1,413,530.30	1,413,530.30	1,791,698.45	644,135.20	1,791,698.45	1,791,698.45	-378,168.15	-0.21	-378,168.15	-0.21
2	1,623,971.06	554,799.23	1,623,971.06	3,037,501.36	2,014,012.13	676,763.65	2,014,012.13	3,805,710.59	-390,041.08	-0.19	-768,209.23	-0.20
3	2,744,340.48	1,010,258.13	2,744,340.48	5,781,841.84	1,396,833.62	350,466.99	1,396,833.62	5,202,544.20	1,347,506.86	0.96	579,297.63	0.11
4	4,009,218.46	1,731,787.77	4,009,218.46	9,791,060.30	1,327,799.32	577,314.00	1,327,799.32	6,530,343.53	2,681,419.14	2.02	3,260,716.77	0.50

FIGURE 8-20 The Period calculations can be applied to the Sales measure.

As anticipated, this solution has several drawbacks.

- After you put Period in rows or columns, you cannot change the order of its members. Although you can do this by using some Excel features, it is not as immediate and intuitive as changing the Position value in the Period view used to populate the Period table.

- The number format of the measure cannot change for particular calculations requested through some Period values. For example, in Figure 8-20, you can see that the YOY% and YOY% YTD calculations do not display the Sales value as a percentage because you can define a single number format for a measure in Tabular, and it cannot be dynamically changed by using an expression (as it can Multidimensional with MDX). A possible workaround is to change the number format directly in the client tool (Excel cells in this case), but this change might be lost as soon as you navigate into the PivotTable.

- If you use more than one measure in the PivotTable, you must create a set by using the Manage Sets command in Excel based on column items, choosing only the combination of measures and Period values that you want to see in the PivotTable.

- You must create a specific DAX expression for each combination of Period calculations and measures that you want to support. This is not as flexible and scalable as a more generic solution might be.

You have to evaluate case by case whether these drawbacks make the implementation of a Period table a good option.

Calculation Parameters by Using an Unrelated Table

In the previous section, you saw a technique that depends on a table in the Tabular model that does not have any relationships with other tables in the model. In general, this technique can be useful as a way to pass information to a measure as if it were a parameter. For example, imagine that you define a table that contains all the integers from 1 to 10, calling it SimulationParameter. At this point, you might use the value selected in this table in the DAX expressions of your measures, using that number as if it were a parameter passed to your formula. Moving that table into a slicer would be a convenient way for an end user to look at results by changing the selected value. You can find an example of this technique at *http://www.powerpivotpro.com/2012/01/comparing-scientific-and-other-data-across-trials*.

Querying Time Intelligence–Based Measures

In the previous sections, you saw how to query measures that aggregate and compare data over time by using the PivotTable in Excel. The queries sent to a Tabular model from Excel are always MDX queries. If you want to write DAX queries, you have to be careful about some pitfalls, as you see in this section.

By writing a DAX query, you might expect that *SUMMARIZE* over the fact table, for example, Internet Sales, should produce the correct result. In fact, the following query works as expected.

```
EVALUATE
SUMMARIZE(
    'Internet Sales',
    'Date'[Calendar Year],
    'Date'[Month],
    'Date'[Month Name],
    "Sales", [Internet Total Sales]
)
ORDER BY 'Date'[Calendar Year], 'Date'[Month]
```

Date[Calendar Year]	Date[Month]	Date[Month Name]	[Sales]
...			
2001	11	November	543993
2001	12	December	755528
2002	1	January	596747
2002	2	February	550817
2002	3	March	644135
2002	4	April	663692
...			

However, as soon as you introduce a measure that contains a *SAMEPERIODSLASTYEAR* or *DATEADD* function, you might incur an error.

```
DEFINE
    MEASURE 'Internet Sales'[PY Sales] =
        CALCULATE( [Internet Total Sales], SAMEPERIODLASTYEAR( 'Date'[Date] ) )
EVALUATE
SUMMARIZE(
    'Internet Sales',
    'Date'[Calendar Year],
    'Date'[Month],
    'Date'[Month Name],
    "Sales", [Internet Total Sales],
    "PY Sales", [PY Sales]
)
ORDER BY 'Date'[Calendar Year], 'Date'[Month]
```

The preceding query returns the following error.

> *Query (2, 77) Calculation error in measure 'Internet Sales'[PY Sales]: Function 'SAMEPERIODLASTYEAR' only works with contiguous date selections.*

The reason for the error is that by using *SUMMARIZE*, the Date table is filtered according to the dates for which there are corresponding rows in Internet Sales. Thus, because there are days in which there are no sales, the *SAMEPERIODLASTYEAR* fails in performing its operation because it requires a contiguous date selection to work.

> **Important** This type of calculation error cannot be intercepted by using *IFERROR*. *SAMEPERIODLASTYEAR* requires a contiguous date selection. You can look for possible updates about this behavior in future releases at *https://connect.microsoft.com/SQLServer/ feedback/details/726607/sameperiodlastyear-error-in-non-contiguous-date-selection- cannot-be-intercepted-by-iferror.*

The solution is to avoid the *SUMMARIZE* that starts on Internet Sales. In this case, you can obtain the desired result by writing the following formula.

```
DEFINE
    MEASURE 'Internet Sales'[PY Sales] =
        CALCULATE( [Internet Total Sales], SAMEPERIODLASTYEAR( 'Date'[Date] ) )
EVALUATE
ADDCOLUMNS(
    FILTER(
        SUMMARIZE(
            'Date',
            'Date'[Calendar Year],
            'Date'[Month],
            'Date'[Month Name],
            "Sales", [Internet Total Sales]
        ),
        [Sales] <> 0
    ),
    "PY Sales", [PY Sales]
)
ORDER BY 'Date'[Calendar Year], 'Date'[Month]
```

Date[Calendar Year]	Date[Month]	Date[Month Name]	[Sales]	[PY Sales]
...				
2002	11	November	335095	543993
2002	12	December	577314	755528
2003	1	January	438865	596747
2003	2	February	489090	550817
2003	3	March	485575	644135
2003	4	April	506399	663692
...				

SUMMARIZE provides the *Sales* column that contains the Internet Total Sales measure. Only rows with Sales other than zero are returned by *FILTER*, and the PY Sales measure is added to these rows. In this way, the Date table is not filtered by existing rows in Internet Sales, and *SAMEPERIODLASTYEAR* (like any other DAX function based on *DATEADD*) works as expected.

Thus, you have to be careful writing DAX queries that access measures containing functions based on *DATEADD*, such as *SAMEPERIODLASTYEAR*, because these functions require a contiguous date selection that can be lost by summarizing data on a fact table, and the error produced cannot be intercepted by using *IFERROR*.

Semiadditive Measures

In the previous section, you saw how to aggregate values over time. However, some measures cannot be aggregated over time. For example, measures such as balance account and product inventory units can be aggregated over any attribute but time. These measures are called semiadditive, and in this section, you see how to define them in a Tabular model.

Whenever a measure is defined by using either the *SUM* or *COUNT* aggregation function, the measure is called an additive measure because *SUM/COUNT* is applied over all dimensions. Whenever another function is applied, such as *AVERAGE*, *MIN*, or *MAX*, the measure is called a nonadditive measure because an aggregation function other than *SUM* is applied over all dimensions. However, it is important to note that for both additive and nonadditive measures, the same aggregation function is always applied over all dimensions without exception.

Some measures should behave in a different way. For example, think about the product inventory. If you consider several products, you can calculate the Units Balance for a product category by summing all the balances of products belonging to that category. However, you cannot sum the same product twice, and you probably have several product inventory lines of the same product that measure the balance over time. For example, in the following table, you can see an excerpt of the Product Inventory table in Adventure Works; the same product has a Units Balance value for each date. This type of measure is called a semiadditive measure because it can be aggregated by using *SUM* over some dimensions but requires a different aggregation algorithm over other dimensions.

Product[Product Name]	Product Inventory[Date ID]	Product Inventory[Units In]	Product Inventory[Units Out]	Product Inventory[Units Balance]
...	...	...	...	...
Road-650 Red, 44	20010630	0	0	88
Road-650 Red, 44	20010701	0	44	44
Road-650 Red, 44	20010702	34	0	78
Road-650 Red, 62	20010630	0	0	88
Road-650 Red, 62	20010701	0	19	69
Road-650 Red, 62	20010702	12	0	81
...	...	...	...	...

In the case of Product Inventory [Units Balance], the only dimension that cannot be summed is the Date. With the term dimension Date, all the attributes of a Date table related to the table containing the real measures (Product Inventory in this case) are included. For the Date attributes, you must consider only the values belonging to the last date in the evaluated period. In other words, you must implement a logic that can produce the results that you see in Figure 8-21, in which the aggregate value is the same as the last period. (For example, the value for quarter 1 is the same as March, the value for quarter 2 is the same as June, and so on.)

Total Units	Column Labels		
Row Labels	Road-650 Red, 44	Road-650 Red, 62	Grand Total
1	164	180	344
January	163	185	348
February	172	170	342
March	164	180	344
2	185	170	355
April	170	173	343
May	184	165	349
June	185	170	355
3	175	176	351
July	179	165	344
August	183	158	341
September	175	176	351
4	179	166	345
October	173	175	348
November	187	173	360
December	179	166	345
Grand Total	179	166	345

FIGURE 8-21 The semiadditive Total Units measure is not aggregated on quarter and year.

The Total Units used in Figure 8-21 calculates the total of a quarter by using the last date available in that period. For each month, only the last date for that month is considered, so the total of a quarter is calculated by using only the last day of that quarter. The Total Units measure is defined as follows.

```
Total Units :=
    CALCULATE( SUM( [Units Balance] ), LASTDATE( 'Product Inventory'[Movement Date] ) )
```

The definition of the Total Units measure uses the *LASTDATE* function to keep just the last date that is active in the current filter context. Therefore, only the last date for which there is available data in the selected period is considered in the *CALCULATE* call.

> **Important** Remember that a drillthrough operation on a measure does not consider the changes in the filter context defined by the measure itself. Thus, the drillthrough on a month returns all the rows for all the days of the month, even if *LASTDATE* filters just one day to compute the result.

It is interesting to note that, in this case, the Movement Date is a date column in the Product Inventory table, which is related to the Date table for navigation on other Date attributes. By using a date column in the Movement Date table, only filtered rows in Product Inventory are considered. This can have an interesting side effect. For every cell, only the last date available for the product selected and the period selected is considered. If, for example, the "Road-650 Red, 44" product did not have a line for May 31 but had one for May 30, then May 30 would be considered for that product. The other product, "Road-650 Red, 62," would consider May 31 as the last day of May, but the problem would be the Grand Total. Instead of considering the sum of May 30 for one product and May 31 for the other, Grand Total would show just the value for May 31 of the second product because May 31 would be the last date available in the selection (May transactions for two products). This is not the result you want to obtain, and to avoid this situation, you must be sure that data is stored for every product and for every date in the Product Inventory table.

An alternative approach is using the *Date* column in the Date table as the parameter passed to the *LASTDATE* function.

```
Total Units := CALCULATE( SUM( [Units Balance] ), LASTDATE( 'Date'[Date] ) )
```

In this case, the last date in a period is the last date available in the Date table (mentioned in the preceding formula) and not the last date for which there is raw data. Thus, for May, it will always be May 31, even if there are no rows in the Product Inventory table. However, this might have unwanted consequences. If your data does not have values for the last day of a month, and the Date table contains all the days for that month (as it should), the Total Units formula defined with *LASTDATE* returns no data (a *BLANK* value) for that month.

For example, if the Product Inventory table contains transactions until only December 15, the *LASTDATE* function based on the Date table would filter Product Inventory data for December 31, which is not available, resulting in a PivotTable that would return data until only November. A solution is to use the *LASTNONBLANK* function, which returns the last date for which a particular expression is not blank. The use of this function is not very intuitive when the *Date* column and the expression you want to evaluate manage different tables. This is a formula for a Total Units measure that uses the *LASTNONBLANK* function.

```
Total Units :=
    CALCULATE(
        SUM( [Units Balance] ),
        LASTNONBLANK(
            'Date'[Date],
            COUNTROWS( RELATEDTABLE( 'Product Inventory' ) )
        )
    )
```

The preceding formula produces exactly the result you saw in Figure 8-21 even when there are data up to December 15 and you reference the *Date[Date]* column instead of *'Product Inventory'[Movement Date]*. This might be helpful when you do not have a date column in the fact table (*LASTDATE* works with a column of *date* data type only); otherwise, you can obtain the same result by using the original definition of Total Units that uses a date column in the fact table.

Using *FIRSTNONBLANK* and *LASTNONBLANK* Functions

The *LASTNONBLANK* function you have just seen has a particular behavior, shared by *FIRSTNONBLANK*. The syntax of these functions is the following.

```
FIRSTNONBLANK( <column>, <expression> )
```

```
LASTNONBLANK( <column>, <expression> )
```

These functions return the first or last value in <column>, filtered by the current context, wherein <expression> is not blank, so these functions behave like *SUMX* or similar functions in this regard. They set a row context for a value of <column> and then evaluate <expression> by using that row context. If <expression> and <column> manage data of the same table, everything works. However, whenever <expression> uses columns of tables other than the one to which <column> belongs, you must transform a row context into a filter context by using *RELATEDTABLE* or *CALCULATE*. This is a very common situation every time you have a separate Date table, which is the best practice for every date-related calculation.

It is important to note that <column> is sorted numerically or alphabetically according to its data type, regardless of the Sort By Column property you have defined in the Tabular model. Thus, you can use these functions on a date column, but if you want to use them on the month name column, the first considered month will be April instead of January even if the Sort By Column property is set to Month Number. You have to build a name that concatenates the month number and the month name, such as 01 January, 02 February, and so on.

To get the right value for the last nonblank date for a given measure/table, you must use something like this.

```
LASTNONBLANK( Date[Date], CALCULATE( COUNT( Inventory[Balance] ) ) )
```

It returns the last date (in the current filter context) for which there are values for the Balance column in the Inventory table. You can also use an equivalent formula.

```
LASTNONBLANK( Dates[Date], COUNTROWS( RELATEDTABLE( Inventory ) ) )
```

This formula returns the last date (in the current filter context) for which there is a related row in the Inventory table.

```
LASTNONBLANK( Date[Date], CALCULATE( COUNT( Inventory[Balance] ) ) )
```

ClosingBalance and OpenBalance

DAX provides several functions to get the first and last dates of a period (year, quarter, or month) that are useful whenever you must get that value of a selection that is smaller than the whole period considered. For example, looking at the month level (which might be displayed in rows), you might want to also display the value of the end of the quarter and the end of the year in the same row, as you can see in Figure 8-22.

Category	Clothing ⊤

Row Labels ⊤	Total Units	ClosingMonth	ClosingQuarter	ClosingYear
⊟2004	182	182	182	182
⊟1	164	164	164	182
January	157	157	164	182
February	158	158	164	182
March	164	164	164	182
⊟2	162	162	162	182
April	159	159	162	182
May	154	154	162	182
June	162	162	162	182
⊟3	182	182	182	182
July	163	163	182	182
August	182	182	182	182
September	182	182	182	182
⊟4	182	182	182	182
October	182	182	182	182
November	182	182	182	182
December	182	182	182	182
Grand Total	**182**	**182**	**182**	**182**

FIGURE 8-22 The Total Units at end of month, quarter, and year for each month is always the corresponding closing balance.

The formulas used to calculate ClosingMonth, ClosingQuarter, and ClosingYear measures are the following.

```
ClosingMonth := CLOSINGBALANCEMONTH( SUM( 'Product Inventory'[Units Balance] ), 'Date'[Date] )

ClosingQuarter :
   = CLOSINGBALANCEQUARTER( SUM( 'Product Inventory'[Units Balance] ), 'Date'[Date] )

ClosingYear := CLOSINGBALANCEYEAR( SUM( 'Product Inventory'[Units Balance] ), 'Date'[Date] )
```

These formulas use the *LASTDATE* function internally, but they operate on a set of dates that can extend the current selection in the PivotTable. For example, the *CLOSINGBALANCEYEAR* function considers the LASTDATE of Date[Date], which is applied to the last year period of the dates included in the filter context. Therefore, for February 2004 (and for any month or quarter of 2004), this date is December 31, 2004. The *CLOSINGBALANCEYEAR* function behaves like a *CALCULATE* expression, using the *ENDOFYEAR* function as a filter. As usual, the use of *CALCULATE* is more generic and flexible, but specific DAX functions such as *CLOSINGBALANCEYEAR* better express the intention of the designer better. The following are measures equivalent to the ones previously shown, using *CALCULATE* syntax.

```
ClosingEOM := CALCULATE( SUM( 'Product Inventory'[Units Balance] ), ENDOFMONTH( 'Date'[Date] ) )

ClosingEOQ :
   = CALCULATE( SUM( 'Product Inventory'[Units Balance] ), ENDOFQUARTER( 'Date'[Date] ) )

ClosingEOY := CALCULATE( SUM( 'Product Inventory'[Units Balance] ), ENDOFYEAR( 'Date'[Date] ) )
```

Tip The DAX functions *OPENINGBALANCEMONTH*, *OPENINGBALANCEQUARTER*, and *OPENINGBALANCEYEAR* use *FIRSTDATE* internally instead of the *LASTDATE* of the considered period. They correspond to the *CALCULATE* formula, which uses *STARTOFMONTH*, *STARTOFQUARTER*, and *STARTOFYEAR* internally as its filters.

Updating Balances by Using Transactions

If you do not have a Product Inventory table, you can obtain the Units Balance measure by summing all the movements recorded in your history. This might seem an expensive operation, but with xVelocity it is affordable and might be useful when you already have a Units Balance calculated in an Inventory and you want to verify its correctness with respect to recorded movements. In this section, you see how to perform similar calculations.

Note The Adventure Works Tabular model already has a Total Units measure that provides the Units Balance value for the last date of the selected period. For educational purposes, we are repeating the same calculation in a different way. You use the initial balance stored in the first date as the initial value in the calculation, assuming you cannot obtain the right balance by summing all the movements because they lack the initial balance.

The Adventure Works sample does not have a table with all the movements of the products, but you can simulate the situation by using the Total Units Movement measure that is defined on the Product Inventory table and based on the *Units In* and *Units Out* columns, which contain the total of input and output movements for each day and each product. Using this information, you can create a measure that calculates the Units Balance measure by summing the Total Units Movement to the initial historical Units Balance of products.

To get the initial balance of products, you must get the Units Balance for the first day stored in the Product Inventory table by using the following expression.

```
CALCULATE(
    SUM( [Units Balance] ),
    ALL( 'Date' ),
    FIRSTDATE( ALL( 'Product Inventory'[Movement Date] ) )
)
```

The *FIRSTDATE* function returns the first date on which there are rows in the Product Inventory table. The *ALL* function on the Date table is required to eliminate any other filter on other Date attributes (such as Year, Month, and so on) that would interfere with getting just the first date in the whole table. After you get this number, you must sum the Total Units Movement measure calculated over a period that starts from the first date available to the last date of the observed period. You can do this with the following expression.

```
CALCULATE(
    [Total Units Movement],
    DATESBETWEEN( 'Date'[Date], BLANK(), LASTDATE( 'Date'[Date] ) )
)
```

In practice, instead of filtering just *LASTDATE*, you filter all the dates from the beginning of available dates to the *LASTDATE* of the period selected. Finally, you can display the balance only when there are movements to avoid displaying dates when no movements are available. This is the definition of the Total Units Calculated measure.

```
Total Units Calculated :=
    IF( [Total Units Movement] = 0,
        BLANK(),
        CALCULATE(
            SUM( [Units Balance] ),
            ALL( 'Date' ),
            FIRSTDATE( ALL( 'Product Inventory'[Movement Date] ) )
        )
        + CALCULATE(
            [Total Units Movement],
            DATESBETWEEN( 'Date'[Date], BLANK(), LASTDATE( 'Date'[Date] ) )
        )
    )
```

By using this measure, you can obtain the result shown in Figure 8-23.

Total Units Calculated	Column Labels		
Row Labels	Road-650 Red, 44	Road-650 Red, 62	Grand Total
⊟2002	179	166	345
January	163	185	348
February	172	170	342
March	164	180	344
April	170	173	343
May	184	165	349
June	185	170	355
July	179	165	344
August	183	158	341
September	175	176	351
October	173	175	348
November	187	173	360
December	179	166	345
⊟2003	184	159	343
January	183	159	342
February	191	174	365
March	190		364
April	186	171	357
May	173	168	341
June	184	159	343
Grand Total	184	159	343

FIGURE 8-23 Total Units Calculated is displayed only when there are movements in the period for at least one of the products selected.

You can use the same technique used in Total Units Calculated also when the transactions are stored in a different table from initial balance, so you may apply the difference calculated with the transactions to an initial balance obtained from an Inventory table. You can also create a measure with the difference between Total Units Calculated and the Total Units measure that uses the pre-calculated Units Balance value to investigate the differences (which would indicate an error either in data or in DAX calculation).

Finally, by using the initial *IF* statement in the Total Units Calculated definition, you observe a value only for periods that had at least one movement. This is particularly useful if you navigate down to the day level, as you can see in Figure 8-24. Thanks to the automatic removal of empty rows by the PivotTable, you see only dates in which at least one movement has been made for selected products.

Total Units Calculated	Column Labels		
Row Labels	Road-650 Red, 44	Road-650 Red, 62	Grand Total
⊟2002	179	166	345
⊞January	163	185	348
⊞February	172	170	342
⊞March	164	180	344
⊟April	170	173	343
4/1/2002	107	136	243
4/2/2002	173	177	350
4/10/2002	172		349
4/19/2002	171		348
4/20/2002		176	347
4/24/2002	170		346
4/25/2002		174	344
4/28/2002		173	343
⊞May	184	165	349
⊞June	185	170	355
⊞July	179	165	344
⊞August	183	158	341
⊞September	175	176	351
⊞October	173	175	348
⊞November	187	173	360
⊞December	179	166	345
Grand Total	179	166	345

FIGURE 8-24 Only dates with at least one movement are present in the PivotTable.

These techniques can be useful when you want to offer the ability to explore data deeply, focusing only on relevant events. In terms of performance, you will be surprised at the speed xVelocity provides in performing such calculations. The design choice of calculating balance value on the fly based on underlying transactions is much more affordable in Tabular than it would be in Multidimensional. You should consider this solution, which can also save you the time required to create the Product Inventory table.

Summary

In this chapter, you saw how to create a Date table in Tabular model by using the right metadata, and how to handle multiple dates by using both inactive relationships and duplicated Date tables. You also learned how to write DAX formula to perform typical date-related calculations such as year-to-date, year-over-year, comparisons over years, and so on. Finally, you discovered how to handle semi-additive measures and how to perform balance calculation by using underlying transactions.

Understanding xVelocity and DirectQuery

n the first chapters of this book, you learned what a Tabular model is, how to build and query a Tabular model, and how to use DAX to implement more advanced calculations. Now you take a look at the internal engine of a Tabular model. This knowledge can affect the way you model your data to optimize memory consumption and overall performance.

In this chapter, you discover the internal architecture of Analysis Services 2012 for Tabular models. You can deploy a Tabular model by choosing between the In-Memory mode (xVelocity in-memory analytics engine, also known as VertiPaq) and the Microsoft SQL Server–based mode (DirectQuery). (Because the xVelocity name has been introduced late in the development cycle, many internal counters and references still use the VertiPaq name.) You see how xVelocity processes and queries data and how it stores data in memory and on disk. You also learn how a Tabular model can query data by using either the xVelocity in-memory analytics engine (VertiPaq) or DirectQuery, and what the differences between using these two techniques are. The goal of this chapter is to provide a basic understanding of the main concepts behind xVelocity and DirectQuery to improve your ability to make data-modeling choices and to troubleshoot.

You might decide to skip this chapter now to finish learning about the Tabular model, but we suggest that you come back later if you decide to skip it now, because you might make wrong data-modeling choices if you just follow the best practices you learned in the past for relational databases and previous versions of Analysis Services. In-memory columnar databases require a different approach and offer great benefits if you are able to adapt to their characteristics.

Tabular Model Architecture in Analysis Services 2012

In this first section, you see the internal architecture of Analysis Services 2012 for Tabular models and understand the main differences between xVelocity and DirectQuery.

When you define a Tabular model, you can choose between two modes to deploy it: In-Memory and DirectQuery. The In-Memory mode is also called xVelocity in-memory analytics engine (VertiPaq), which is the internal storage engine used in that mode. DirectQuery relies on the external data source and converts the query sent to Analysis Services into a SQL query sent to the external data source.

In Figure 9-1, you can see what happens when a query is sent to an Analysis Services 2012 Tabular model. The query is handled in one of two ways, depending on the deployment mode. With In-Memory mode, data is retrieved by accessing to the xVelocity engine, whereas with DirectQuery mode, the query is converted into a SQL query sent to the external data source, without using any storage, cache, or both in Analysis Services.

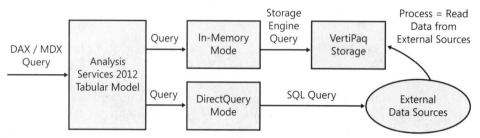

FIGURE 9-1 This is how a query is executed in an Analysis Services 2012 Tabular model.

The *In-Memory mode* is the default for deploying a Tabular model; it is the same engine used by Microsoft PowerPivot for Microsoft Excel. The In-Memory mode uses a storage engine called xVelocity in-memory analytics engine, which is an in-memory columnar-oriented storage engine that provides the best query performance, requiring data to be processed and stored in Analysis Services memory.

In-Memory mode is the favorite choice for Tabular models, but *DirectQuery mode* is also available, and it uses the external data source as a single repository and query engine without duplicating data in Analysis Services. By using DirectQuery, the Tabular model becomes just a semantic layer on top of a SQL Server database, and every DAX query to the Tabular model is converted into a SQL query. (MDX queries are not supported in DirectQuery mode.) This includes DAX calculations, which are translated into equivalent SQL expressions. DirectQuery allows real-time queries and does not require a copy of data to be stored in Analysis Services, but it has several limitations and drawbacks.

Note A similar deployment choice in a Multidimensional model is between MOLAP and ROLAP. However, Multidimensional allows a partition-level choice, whereas in Tabular, you have to make a decision for the whole model at the connection level. (Hybrid mode enables you to choose the model to use for each connection, but you cannot define mixed modes within the same query.)

In-Memory Mode and xVelocity

The In-Memory mode requires the longer description because it is based on the xVelocity in-memory analytics engine (VertiPaq), which is a columnar-oriented database. In this section, you learn how a query is executed by using the In-Memory mode, what the role of xVelocity is, how it works, and what the main differences between row-oriented and column-oriented are.

Query Execution in In-Memory Mode

By using the In-Memory mode, you store a copy of data in the xVelocity (VertiPaq) storage engine. This copy is created during process operations, which are described later in this chapter. The xVelocity storage engine is queried at the lower level of the query execution plan, when data has to be computed. In Figure 9-2, you can see how a query is handled when In-Memory mode is active.

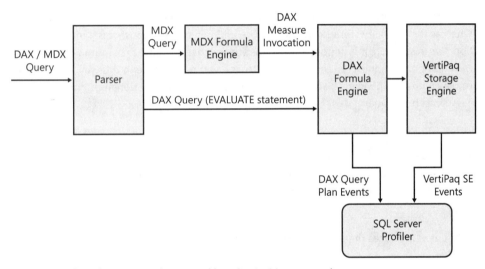

FIGURE 9-2 This is how a query is executed by using In-Memory mode.

DAX and MDX queries sent to a Tabular model are handled in a different way. A DAX query is evaluated by the DAX formula engine, which generates a DAX query plan that is then transformed into commands sent to the xVelocity (VertiPaq) storage engine. An MDX query is analyzed by the MDX formula engine, which calls the DAX formula engine to solve DAX measures and generates a query plan, which performs requests, to the xVelocity storage engine. Thus, an MDX query is not converted into an equivalent DAX syntax; it directly generates one or more commands to the DAX formula engine and then to the xVelocity storage engine to retrieve values and evaluate the DAX measures it requires. (At the lower level, any query to a Tabular model has to evaluate DAX expressions that might be used by MDX for further computations.) For this reason, when we show equivalent DAX and MDX syntaxes in this book, we are referring to expressions that return the same result but that internally might perform different operations and might have different performance.

Note You can find a more detailed description about how DAX query plans are generated by reading *http://mdxdax.blogspot.com/2011/12/dax-query-plan-part-1-introduction.html* and *http://mdxdax.blogspot.com/2012/01/dax-query-plan-part-2-operator.html.*

The MDX formula engine and DAX storage engine might cache results to improve performance of similar queries. If you want to clear the cache to analyze performance, you can use the same XMLA *ClearCache* command that you can use for MDX queries. (You can find some examples at *http://www .ssas-info.com/analysis-services-faq/27-mdx/133-mdx-how-do-i-clear-analysis-services-ssas-database-cache.*) By using SQL Profiler, you can intercept two classes of trace events: DAX Query Plan events are generated by the DAX formula engine, whereas VertiPaq SE events (Storage Engine events) events are generated by the xVelocity (VertiPaq) storage engine. (The VertiPaq name is still used in Profiler events.)

It is important to know that both MDX and DAX formula engines perform single-threaded operations, whereas the xVelocity storage engine can use multiple cores because it is a multithread-enabled operation. For this reason, it is important to write queries that push the maximum workload by using the fewest number of requests to the xVelocity storage engine, because in this way, the workload for the formula engine will be low. The next section provides more information about how the storage engine is involved in a query.

Analyzing In-Memory Mode Events by Using SQL Profiler

The queries sent to the xVelocity (VertiPaq) storage engine are represented in a SQL-like format in the VertiPaq SE Query events. For example, consider the following DAX query.

```
EVALUATE Products
```

This query produces the following request to the xVelocity storage engine.

```
SELECT
    [Products_dd961ff2-be69-4a31-8f59-63f885a3e060].[RowNumber],
    [Products_dd961ff2-be69-4a31-8f59-63f885a3e060].[ID_Product],
    [Products_dd961ff2-be69-4a31-8f59-63f885a3e060].[Product],
    COUNT()
FROM [Products_dd961ff2-be69-4a31-8f59-63f885a3e060];
```

The table name includes a unique identifier to identify the object uniquely. You do not have any control over this part of the name, and that part is removed from the following queries to make them more readable. Moreover, the internal *RowNumber* column is also queried, even if it is never shown to the user.

Now, consider the following query that involves at least two tables, Product Category and Internet Sales.

```
EVALUATE
SUMMARIZE(
    'Internet Sales',
    'Product Category'[Product Category Name],
```

```
        "Sales", [Internet Total Sales]
)
```

This query produces the following single request to the xVelocity storage engine. (Please note that table names have been cleaned, removing the unique identifier.)

```
SELECT
    [Product Category].[EnglishProductCategoryName],
    SUM([Internet Sales].[SalesAmount]), COUNT()
FROM [Internet Sales]
    LEFT OUTER JOIN [Product]
        ON [Internet Sales].[ProductKey]=[Product].[ProductKey]
    LEFT OUTER JOIN [Product Subcategory]
        ON [Product].[ProductSubcategoryKey]=[Product Subcategory].[ProductSubcategoryKey]
    LEFT OUTER JOIN [Product Category]
        ON [Product Subcategory].[ProductCategoryKey]=[Product Category].
[ProductCategoryKey];
```

As you can see, several tables are involved, following the relationship existing between the Internet Sales and Product Category tables.

> **Note** The SQL-like format used to express the queries sent to the xVelocity storage engine does not represent a language that actually exists and that can be used directly by querying Analysis Services. It is just a readable format of an internal request.

The same xVelocity storage engine is used to solve the following MDX query.

```
SELECT
    [Internet Total Sales] ON COLUMNS,
    NON EMPTY [Product Category].[Product Category Name].[Product Category Name].MEMBERS
ON ROWS
FROM [Model]
```

Thus, MDX and DAX queries might use similar xVelocity engine operations even if their execution plans have been built in different ways. You can understand how the storage engine is used by looking at the complexity and number of queries it receives. For example, consider the following DAX query.

```
EVALUATE
SUMMARIZE(
    'Internet Sales',
    'Product Category'[Product Category Name],
    "Sales",
        SUMX(
            'Internet Sales',
            RELATED( Product[List Price] ) * 'Internet Sales'[Order Quantity]
        )
)
```

The DAX query produces a single request to the xVelocity storage engine.

```
FROM [Internet Sales]
  LEFT OUTER JOIN [Product]
    ON [Internet Sales].[ProductKey]=[Product].[ProductKey]
  LEFT OUTER JOIN [Product Subcategory]
    ON [Product].[ProductSubcategoryKey]=[Product Subcategory].[ProductSubcategoryKey]
  LEFT OUTER JOIN [Product Category]
    ON [Product Subcategory].[ProductCategoryKey]=[Product Category].[ProductCategoryKey];
```

In this case, the *SUMX* operation is fast because it can be executed in a single query sent to the xVelocity storage engine. Because the product between List Price and Order Quantity is computed by xVelocity, you obtain the same performance as having a calculated column contain the result of this operation.

If you have a single DAX or MDX query that generates many requests to the xVelocity storage engine, you have a clear indication that a large effort is performed by the formula engine, which is single-threaded, whereas the storage engine can scale on multiple cores. This is one of the reasons you may observe worse performance when the query requires more work from the formula engine.

> **Tip** If you are interested in different execution plans for equivalent queries, you can try to replace the *RELATED* function with a *LOOKUPVALUE* call to get the List Price for each product. The result is a higher number of requests to the xVelocity storage engine.

Different versions of the same query might affect the execution plan and the resources required to produce the results. It is beyond the scope of this chapter to explain execution plans in more detail, but you will find more information in Chapter 18, "Optimizations and Monitoring."

Row-Oriented vs. Column-Oriented Databases

Most of the relational databases, including SQL Server, are row-oriented databases, so every table of the database stores data row by row. For example, consider the following table of data.

ID_Author	FirstName	LastName	Blog	Posts
1	Alberto	Ferrari	*http://sqlblog.com/blogs/alberto_ferrari*	27
2	Chris	Webb	*http://cwebbbi.wordpress.com/*	43
3	Marco	Russo	*http://sqlblog.com/blogs/marco_russo*	38

A row-oriented database physically stores data row by row, so you might have an index pointing to all the columns of a certain row. For example, the second item in the list contains all the columns of the row describing Chris's data.

Row ID	Row Data
1	1, Alberto, Ferrari, *http://sqlblog.com/blogs/alberto_ferrari*, 27
2	2, Chris, Webb, *http://cwebbbi.wordpress.com/*, 43
3	3, Marco, Russo, *http://sqlblog.com/blogs/marco_russo*, 38

The physical implementation depends on the database product. For example, SQL Server divides the storage space in pages (8 KB each), and every page stores one or more rows. The longer the row, the smaller the number of rows in a page. To retrieve a row, the database must retrieve the page in which the row is contained. To improve performance, SQL Server usually uses indexes, which are implemented by storing a higher number of smaller rows in a lower number of pages by using a sorted order that further reduces the number of pages required to perform a query. In general, a row-oriented database requires a full scan of all the rows of a table if you want to query all the values of a single column of a table (for example, for an aggregation). The cost of a complete table scan is the same regardless of the number of columns requested in a query, unless a specific index has been built in advance.

A column-oriented database uses a different approach. Instead of considering the row of a table as the main unit of storage, it considers every column as a separate entity and stores data for every column in a separate way. For example, you can imagine that data in the initial table is logically stored in this way.

Column Name	Column Data
ID_Author	1, 2, 3
FirstName	Alberto, Chris, Marco
LastName	Ferrari, Webb, Russo
Blog	*http://sqlblog.com/blogs/alberto_ferrari*, *http://cwebbbi.wordpress.com/*, *http://sqlblog.com/blogs/marco_russo*
Posts	27, 43, 38

This makes it very fast to query data for a single column but requires a higher computational effort to retrieve data for several columns of a single row. The worst-case scenario is the request for all the columns from a row, which requires access to the storage of all the rows. For example, to retrieve Chris's data, the query is required to identify Chris in the *FirstName* column. Because it is the second element in the column, getting the second element from every other column will retrieve all of Chris's data. Moreover, to calculate the total of posts by all the authors, it will be necessary to access only the *Posts* column data.

From the point of view of data retrieval, a column-oriented database might be faster because data access is optimized for many query scenarios. In fact, the most frequent requests in an analytical system require data from only a few columns, usually to aggregate data from a column by grouping results according to the value of other columns. However, as soon as you need to add or delete a single row of the original table, it is necessary to add or delete an item in every column. This is usually much more expensive than in a row-oriented database. Moreover, adding, deleting, or changing a row is not possible by using the xVelocity engine. As you see later, you can process only a whole partition.

 Important Other column-oriented database products support insert, delete, and update operations on single rows. The limitation is specific to the xVelocity engine, at least in its current implementation.

In Figure 9-3, you can see a comparison between row-oriented and column-oriented storages.

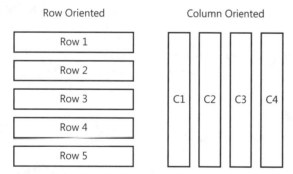

FIGURE 9-3 Look at the row-oriented vs. column-oriented databases.

 Note SQL Server 2012 offers xVelocity memory-optimized columnstore indexes, which store data for every column in separate pages and internally use an algorithm derived by the xVelocity in-memory analytics engine (VertiPaq) used by Analysis Services. The algorithm used by Analysis Services is faster but requires data to be stored in memory. This is not required in SQL Server columnstore indexes, even if the memory demand is still high while processing the index.

xVelocity (VertiPaq) Storage

In the previous section, you were introduced to column-oriented databases. The xVelocity in-memory analytics engine (VertiPaq) belongs to this category of engines. In this section, you learn the main characteristics of the xVelocity-specific implementation in Analysis Services 2012.

As you have probably seen by using it, xVelocity is very fast and stores data in a highly compressed way. This is possible because of its particular storage architecture. Every table you process is divided into columns, and every column has its own storage. For every column, a dictionary of all the distinct values is created, so the real storage for that column is a bitmap index that references the dictionary. Both dictionary and bitmap index are then highly compressed and stored in a compressed way on both RAM and disk. The disk is a backup of data to provide persistent storage so that the database will not require reprocessing if the service is restarted. All the queries are made by loading all the column data in memory. For example, consider the following table.

ID	Category	Product	Color
546	Accessories	Lock	Silver
235	Accessories	Brakes	Silver
987	Bikes	Mountain Bike	Red
988	Bikes	Mountain Bike	Silver
742	Bikes	Touring Bike	Red
744	Bikes	Touring Bike	Silver

xVelocity stores this table in a way that is similar to the following schema: For every column, a sorted dictionary of all the distinct values and a bitmap index references the actual values of each item in the column by using a zero-based index to the dictionary.

Column	Dictionary	Values
ID	235,546,742,744,987,988	1,0,4,5,2,3
Category	Accessories, Bikes	0,0,1,1,1,1
Product	Brakes, Lock, Mountain Bike, Touring Bike	1,0,2,2,3,3
Color	Red, Silver	1,1,0,1,0,1

You can see that the storage space required for the dictionary can be the most expensive part, especially for columns that have many distinct values. Columns that have a low number of distinct values require a smaller dictionary, and this makes the values bitmap index more efficient. xVelocity has several optimizations by which to build and scan these structures quickly, but the general principle behind the scene is the one just described. Thus, you can now understand two implications of this design choice:

- To compress data and obtain high efficiency, the entire table (or at least a partition of it) has to be processed as a whole. Building the dictionary with all the distinct values is critical.

- The insert, update, and delete operations in the Values bitmap index require a lot of computational work, and they are not supported in Analysis Services 2012.

xVelocity is also an in-memory database. This means that it has been designed and optimized assuming that the whole database is loaded in memory. To store more data and improve performance, data is also kept compressed in memory and dynamically uncompressed during each query. This is why it requires fast CPUs with a high memory bandwidth. Analysis Services can handle paging of data to disk, but this should be limited to scenarios in which the paging activity is temporary.

Note Paging can be disabled by setting the Memory\VertiPaqPagingPolicy advanced property to 0. (It defaults to 1, enabling this a behavior.) You can find a more detailed discussion about xVelocity (VertiPaq) memory settings at *http://www.sqlbi.com/ articles/memory-settings-in-tabular-instances-of-analysis-services.*

For example, the full process of a database requires building a new copy of the database in memory, keeping the older one available to continue answering queries during the processing of the new version. In practice, you might need double the memory required to store one database in memory to process it again. By using paging, Analysis Services can process the database without raising memory errors if there is not enough memory to store two copies of the same database. However, paging operations can severely degrade query performance, and you should consider this scenario an exception, limiting it to off-peak hours for a server in production.

After you understand the general principles of the xVelocity in-memory storage engine, it is useful to know some details of its internal structures.

xVelocity stores its data in structures that are persisted on files that you can find in the data folder of Analysis Services. (It is defined by the DataDir property of the Analysis Services instance.) Every database contains a folder in which you can find a directory structure that is based on the Multidimensional semantic, which in turn is based on dimensions and cubes. In Tabular, every table is a dimension, and cubes contain only metadata defining measures. (You will see more details on this in Chapter 16, "Interfacing with Tabular.") Every table in Tabular corresponds to a dimension folder, which contains several files for each column of the table, each one recognizable by the names of table and column included in the file name. Every table has a virtual column named *RowNumber* that identifies the rows in the table; this column does not require any physical storage. All XML files in the folder contain metadata used by xVelocity, whereas other files have different roles, depending on their file name. Every column has the following components:

- **Dictionary** The dictionary file has a .DICTIONARY extension and defines the mapping of a DataID to each value in the column and vice versa. The DataID is an internal unique identifier of every distinct value in the column. It is always a hash for strings. For non-string columns, this mapping can be virtual and, in that case, the .DICTIONARY file is not created because the DataID is based on the value itself.

- **Data** The data file has a simple .IDF extension that contains compressed column storage. (There are other .IDF files that are indexes and can be recognized by other parts of the file name.) In this chapter, this file has also been identified like the bitmap index that stores column data.

- **Indexes** The .IDF files that contain POS_TO_ID and ID_TO_POS in their file name map the position of the DataID in the hierarchy built from the column (technically, the attribute hierarchy level in a Multidimensional view of the Tabular model) and vice versa, according to the Sort By Column property of the column in the Tabular model. The .HIDX is an auxiliary index data structure for performance. The concept of attribute hierarchy comes from Multidimensional models and is used internally as part of the xVelocity storage system.

You might have these additional components for each table:

- **Relationships** The .HIDX file containing a globally unique identifier (GUID) name that corresponds to the internal name of the relationship. (You can find more information about GUIDs at *http://en.wikipedia.org/wiki/Globally_Unique_Identifier.*)

- **Hierarchies** The .IDF files that contain CHILD_COUNT, FIRST_CHILD_POS, MULTI_LEVEL_ID and PARENT_POS in their file name after the name of the hierarchy. These files are created only if hierarchies are defined in a table. A hierarchy structure is also marked as natural or unnatural according to its content. If each member value in a level has only one parent in all possible paths of the hierarchy, the structure is natural; otherwise, it is unnatural. This information is evaluated every time these files are refreshed, and it is especially useful for MDX queries because the MDX Formula Engine yields better performance handling natural hierarchies.

If a table is partitioned, only data files are duplicated for each partition, whereas the files of all other components are updated for the whole column. (Table partitioning is discussed in Chapter 17, "Tabular Deployment.")

These files represent the compressed data that xVelocity stores also in memory. Even if the numbers cannot be completely accurate, a safe estimation is that the memory cost of a table in xVelocity is double the size of the files belonging to the table itself. (In other words, the RAM required for a table is double the size to store it on disk. Do not confuse this with the double-the-size memory requirement for processing a table.) More detailed information about memory usage is available by querying Dynamic Management Views (DMVs), as you will see in Chapter 18.

> **Tip** You can find an Excel workbook you can use to browse memory used by Analysis Services at *http://www.powerpivotblog.nl/what-is-using-all-that-memory-on-my-analysis-server-instance.*

Memory Usage in xVelocity (VertiPaq)

Up to now, you have seen the differences between xVelocity and DirectQuery and how xVelocity stores its data internally. In this section, you learn how xVelocity uses the memory.

All the columns of a database are stored in memory, and this is the most relevant factor of memory consumption. xVelocity needs other memory during table refresh (we will call this the processing phase) and when querying the tables.

Data Memory Usage

A common question you might need to answer while designing a database-based solution is a forecast about database size from which to derive disk and memory sizing. Knowing the database size is important to assess the amount of memory required to run Analysis Services, which stores the database in memory by using xVelocity. However, you will see that answering this question is not easy with this engine.

Estimation of database size is an exercise that can be relatively easy to do for a relational database in SQL Server because 90 percent of data is probably consumed by a small number of tables, and the size of each table can be estimated by calculating the product of the number of rows by the size of each row. The number of rows is usually estimated (for example, number of customers, number of transactions in five years, and so on), whereas the size of the row depends on the number of columns and their types. Having a sample set of data is often sufficient to make a good estimation of the average row size (you might have variable-length columns), including indexes. Detailed techniques for making such estimations are well known and documented. A good starting point is *http://msdn .microsoft.com/en-us/library/ms187445.aspx*.

When it comes to xVelocity, database size estimation is a much more difficult exercise because it is very difficult to know in advance the most important drivers that will affect database size. In fact, the number of rows is no longer the most important factor for determining the size of a table!

The table size in xVelocity is determined by a combination of factors:

- The number of columns

- The cardinality of each column

- The data type of each column (for strings, the average size is relevant)

- The number of rows

Not only do you have many variables to consider, but there is also no linear formula that produces a number by starting from these values. Assuming that you are interested in only the size of bigger tables in a database, you can approximate. A starting point can be the following approximating formula.

$$RowCount * \left(RowIterationCost + \sum_{c=0}^{columns} AverageDictionaryCost(c) \right)$$

This formula is not easy to apply; the average column cost can be quite different among columns and largely depends on the size of the dictionary, which is based on the number of distinct values in the column. You can see that adding rows to a table does not necessarily mean that you have a linear growth of table size. In fact, if you add rows that use existing values in column dictionaries, you use only the first part of the multiplication (RowCount). If you add values that also increase the dictionary size, the AverageDictionaryCost for affected columns will increase, resulting in a product that grows faster. Finally, the effect of adding a column depends on the size of the dictionary, so adding a column with a low cardinality costs less than adding a column with high cardinality.

This is a general principle that helps you estimate. However, it is much harder to translate these general concepts into concrete numbers because the dictionary cost depends on many factors (different data types, dictionary strategies, string length, and so on). There are different types of dictionaries that xVelocity automatically uses, depending on the type and data distribution of each column.

For these reasons, we suggest basing any estimation on a heuristic approach. Use a significant amount of real data and measure the size of a processed table. Then double the number of rows and measure the increment in size. Double again and measure again. You will obtain a more accurate estimate in this way than by using a theoretical approach that is difficult to apply if you do not know data distribution.

Processing Memory Usage

During processing, every table is read from the data source and loaded in memory to create the dictionary of unique values and the related index for each column. If you already have the table in memory and you do not first unprocess the table (which means that you remove the data of the table from xVelocity database), you will have two copies of the table until the process transaction commits. As you saw previously in this chapter, because of the paging of Analysis Services, the process might not break if you do not have enough memory to store two copies of the same tables that are part of the processing batch, assuming you have enough virtual memory available. If Analysis Services starts paging, query and processing performance might suffer. You should measure memory consumption during processing to avoid paging if possible.

If more tables are processed in the same processing batch, they can be processed in parallel if the batch command requests it. However, every table is read serially even if it has multiple partitions. (This is different from Multidimensional, which can parallelize partition processing for measure groups.)

Every partition that is processed is divided into segments, each with eight million rows. After a segment is read, every column is processed and compressed. This part of the processing can scale on multiple cores and requires more memory, depending on the number of distinct values that are present in the segment. For this reason, as you saw in Chapter 3, "Loading Data Inside Tabular," sorting a table might reduce the memory pressure during processing and during queries, requiring less memory to store data. The reason is that reading sorted data implies reading a smaller number of distinct values per segment, improving compression rates and memory used. Ideally, you would obtain the best results by sorting the table, starting by the column with the smaller number of distinct values, then including other columns until you arrive at the column with the maximum granularity. However, this sorting might be too expensive for the data source, and you should find the right tradeoff for tables that require more segments to be processed, making this consideration less important for partitions smaller than eight million rows.

Important You can optimize compression of tables with more than eight million rows by providing sorted data to Analysis Services. In Tabular, you can specify for each partition a SQL statement that contains an *ORDER BY* condition. How to optimize such a query in the relational database is not discussed here, but it is something you should think about to keep the processing time at a reasonable level.

Querying Memory Usage

Every query performs one or more scans of the columns involved in the query. Some query constructs cause memory pressure because they must store temporary and intermediate results. When running very complex queries on large tables, you might observe very high memory pressure caused by internal materialization of data when expressions cannot be managed by keeping data in compressed form. This could be critical if you do not have enough memory available. You should monitor memory pressure during queries to correctly size the memory available to Analysis Services. Concurrent users can increase the memory pressure if complex queries run simultaneously.

Note High memory pressure is caused by particularly complex DAX queries. Many queries do not require much memory even when they operate on very large tables. This warning is intended to apply to possible critical conditions that might be raised by a single query that exhausts server resources. You see more details on this in Chapter 18.

Optimizing Performance by Reducing Memory Usage

As you saw in the previous sections, the memory used to store a table depends primarily on the dictionary cost of each column, and memory cost is directly related to performance in xVelocity. Now you learn how to choose the data type and the content to be stored in a column to reduce the memory footprint and improve performance in xVelocity.

The cardinality of a column directly affects its size in xVelocity. Its actual cost also depends on the data type of the column. The combination of these two factors (cardinality and data type) determines the actual cost of memory, and you should control both to achieve optimization.

Reducing Dictionary Size

You can obtain a reduction of dictionary cost by reducing its size, and this can be achieved mainly by reducing the cardinality of a column.

The first suggestion is to remove columns that contain data that are not relevant for analysis. This is something you probably already do when you design a relational data warehouse or data mart. However, the goal in a relational database is to minimize the size of each column without worrying too much about its cardinality, provided that the chosen data size can represent the value, whereas in xVelocity, the cardinality of a column is much more important than its data type.

For example, adding an INT column in SQL Server might seem better than adding eight columns of type TINYINT; you should save half the space, and this is the reason for creating junk dimensions in a star schema. (You can read more at *http://en.wikipedia.org/wiki/Dimension_(data_warehouse)*.) Because, in xVelocity, the cardinality of a column is more important than the data type for its storage cost, you might find that you do not save space by using the junk dimension approach. Note that this is not a general rule, and you should test on a case-by-case basis, but the point is that when using xVelocity, you should not make the same assumptions you make when working with a relational database.

A column with a unique value for every row is most likely the most expensive column of your table. You cannot remove keys from tables that are used as lookup tables, such as dimension tables of a star schema. However, if you have a star schema and an identity column on the fact table (usually used as a primary key), by removing the identity column from the fact table imported in xVelocity, you can save a lot of space and, more importantly, reduce the percentage of increase when adding more rows to the table.

From a performance point of view, a calculated column might be expensive when it creates a large dictionary. This might be unnecessary if you have a simple expression involving only columns from the same table in which the calculated column is defined. For example, consider this calculated column.

```
Table[C] = Table[A] * Table[B]
```

The number of distinct values for the C column is a number between MinDistinctC and MaxDistinctC, calculated as follows.

```
MinDistinctC :=
IF(
    COUNTROWS( DISTINCT( A ) ) > COUNTROWS( DISTINCT( B ) ),
    COUNTROWS( DISTINCT( A ) ),
    COUNTROWS( DISTINCT( B ) )
)

MaxDistinctC := COUNTROWS( DISTINCT( A ) ) * COUNTROWS( DISTINCT( B ) )
```

Thus, in the worst-case scenario, you have a dictionary with a size that is orders of magnitude larger than the dictionaries of the separate columns. In fact, one of the possible optimizations is removing such a column and splitting the content into separate columns with a smaller number of distinct values.

The next step in this optimization is reducing the number of values of a column without reducing its informative content. For example, if you have a *DATETIME* column that contains a timestamp of an event (for example, both date and time), it is more efficient to split the single *DATETIME* column into two columns, one for the date and one for the time (as you saw in Chapter 8, "Understanding Time Intelligence in DAX"). You might use *DATE* and *TIME* data types in SQL Server, but in xVelocity, you always use the same *date* data type. The date column always has the same time, and the time column always has the same date. In this way, you have a maximum number of rows for date, which is 365, multiplied by the number of years stored, and a maximum number of rows for time that depends on time granularity (for example, you have 86,400 seconds per day). This approach makes it easier to group data by date and time even if it becomes harder to calculate the difference in hours/minutes/seconds between two dates. However, you probably want to store the difference between two date-time columns in a new xVelocity column when you read from your data source instead of having to perform this calculation at query time.

> **Note** Transforming a *DATETIME* column into separate columns, one for date and one for time, has to be done by using a transformation on the data source, like a SQL query. This is another reason you should use views as a decoupling layer, putting these transformations there. If you obtain them by using a calculated column in Tabular, you still store the *DATETIME* column in xVelocity, losing the memory optimization you are looking for.

A similar approach might be possible when you have a column that identifies a transaction or a document and has a very high cardinality, such as an *Order ID* or *Transaction ID*. In a large fact table, such a column might be a value with millions if not billions of distinct values, and its cost is typically the highest of the table. A best practice is to remove such a column from the Tabular model, but if you need it to identify each single transaction, you might try to lower its memory cost by optimizing the model schema. Because the cost is largely due to the column dictionary, you can split the column value into two or more columns with a smaller number of distinct values that can be combined to get the original one. For example, if you have an ID column with numbers ranging from 1 to 100 million, you would pay a cost nearly 3 GB just to store it on disk. By splitting the value into two numbers ranging from 1 to 10,000, you would drop the cost below 200 MB, saving more than 90 percent of memory. This requires executing a simple arithmetical operation to split the value writing data to the table and to compose the original value by reading data from the table, as in the following formulas.

$$LowID = ID - 10,000 \left\lfloor \frac{ID}{10,000} \right\rfloor$$

$$HighID = \frac{ID}{10,000}$$

$$ID = HighID * 10,000 + LowID$$

These formulas can be translated into the following DAX expressions.

```
HighID = INT( [ID] / 10000 )
```

```
LowID = MOD( [ID], 10000 )
```

You can find a further discussion of this optimization technique at *http://www.sqlbi.com/articles/optimizing-high-cardinality-columns-in-vertipaq*.

Important Splitting a column into multiple columns to lower its cardinality is an optimization that you should consider only for measures or attributes that are not related to other tables, because relationships can be defined by using a single column and implicitly defining a unique constraint for that column in the lookup table.

A similar optimization is possible when you have other values in a fact table that represents measures of a fact. For example, you might be accustomed to storing the sales amount for each row or order. This is what happens in the Internet Sales table of Adventure Works.

Order Quantity	Unit Price	Sales Amount
1	100	100
2	100	200
1	60	60
3	60	180
2	60	120
...	...	...

The *Sales Amount* column is obtained by the product of *Order Quantity* by *Unit Price*. However, if you have 100 possible values in *Order Quantity* and 100 possible values in *Unit Price*, you would have up to 10,000 unique values in the *Sales Amount* column. You can optimize the memory footprint by storing only *Order Quantity* and *Unit Price* in xVelocity, obtaining *Sales Amount* by using the following measure.

```
Sales Amount :=
    SUMX( 'Internet Sales', 'Internet Sales'[Order Quantity] * 'Internet Sales'[Unit Price] )
```

You will not have any performance penalty at query time by using this approach because the multiplication is a simple arithmetical operation that is pushed down to the xVelocity storage engine and is not in charge of the formula engine. The benefit of this approach is that you pay the cost of two columns of 100 values each instead of the cost of a single column with a cost that is two orders of magnitude larger (10,000 instead of 200).

Important In a Multidimensional model, you have to use a different approach, and you store only measures that can be aggregated. Thus, in Multidimensional, you must choose Order Quantity and Sales Amount to get better performance. If you are accustomed to building cubes by using Analysis Services, you should be careful when using the different design pattern you have in Tabular.

Note The first version of PowerPivot for Excel had a performance penalty by using *SUMX* instead of *SUM*. For this reason, if you find documents that suggest storing a column such as *Sales Amount* in Tabular by using *SUM* instead of *SUMX*, this suggestion is no longer valid in Tabular and in the new version of PowerPivot released with SQL Server 2012. If you want to be sure that the expression is resolved by the xVelocity (VertiPaq) storage engine, you must verify that it is included in the VertiPaq *SE Query* event that you can capture with SQL Server Profiler, as you will see in Chapter 18.

A further optimization is reducing the precision of a number. This is not related to the data type but to the actual values stored in a column. For example, a *Date* column in xVelocity uses a floating point as internal storage in which the decimal part represents the fraction of a day. In this way, it is possible to also represent milliseconds. If you are importing a *DATETIME* column from SQL Server that includes milliseconds, you have many rows displaying the same hour/minute/second value (which is the common display format) because they are different values internally. Thus, you can round the number to the nearest second to obtain a maximum of 86,400 distinct values (seconds per day). By rounding the number to the nearest minute, you would obtain a maximum of 1,440 distinct values (minutes per day). Thus, reducing the precision of a column in terms of actual value (without changing the data type) can save a lot of memory.

You might use a similar approach for other numeric values, although it might be difficult to use for numbers related to financial transactions. You don't want to lose some decimals of a measure that represents the value of an order, but you might accept losing some precision in a number that, by its nature, can have an approximation or an error in the measure or a precision that is not relevant to you. For example, you might save the temperature of the day for every sale transaction of an ice cream shop. You know that there should be a correlation between temperature and sales, and actual data might represent that in great detail, helping you plan ice cream production based on the weather forecast. You might have a very good digital thermometer connected to your cash system that stores the temperature with two decimals for every transaction. However, storing such a value would result in a very high number of values, whereas you might consider the integer part, or just one decimal, to be enough. Rounding a number helps you save a lot of space in a column, especially for a decimal number that is stored as a floating point in your data source.

Choosing Data Type

In a relational database such as SQL Server, every data type might have a different size because of the range of values it can represent, not because of the actual data stored. In xVelocity, the differences in size are less relevant, and the choice of a data type has to be based only on the range of values that the column has to represent.

From the point of view of internal storage, there are two categories of data types. The first includes all the numeric data types:

- Whole number, which stores 64-bit integer values

- Decimal number, which stores 64-bit real numbers limited to 17 decimal digits

- Currency, which stores numbers with four-decimal digits of fixed precision by using an underlying 64-bit integer value

- Date, which stores dates and times by using an underlying real number

- Binary, which stores images or similar large chunks of binary data (also called BLOBs, binary large objects)

All the numeric data types have an overall dictionary-related storage cost in the range of 20 to 30 bytes, which includes the value and indexes cost. Thus, memory required to store one million numbers is approximately 20 to 30 MB. The actual value might vary because different dictionary storage types can be used for numeric data types, depending on data distribution.

The second category of data types includes strings. Every string is compressed, and the memory required for dictionary-related storage can be estimated by considering a typical overhead cost of 16 bytes for every string, which has to be summed to the size of the compressed string value. The final dictionary cost for string columns depends on the length of the strings and the compression ratio that can be reached. You can safely assume that it is unlikely a string will have a dictionary-related cost lower than 20 bytes, whereas its actual cost depends on average string length and compression rate. As a rule, you can estimate the cost of a string as 16 bytes plus half of the string length. Thus, if you have one million strings with an average length of 50 characters, you might expect an average dictionary cost of 40 to 42 bytes per string, resulting in a 40 MB dictionary.

Important Remember that the memory cost of a column is calculated by dictionary and values index. The latter depends on number of rows and number of values in dictionary and data distribution. It is much harder to estimate the size of the values index of a column in xVelocity.

Even if a numeric column sometimes has a larger dictionary-related storage size than a corresponding string column (you can always convert a number to a string), from a performance point of view, the numeric column is faster. The reason for a larger memory footprint is related to indexes that are not always included in the table scan operations xVelocity makes. Thus, you should always favor a numeric data type if the semantic of the value is numeric because using strings would produce a performance penalty.

Tip You can use a string data type instead of a numeric one if the semantic of the column does not include an arithmetical operation. For example, the order number might be expressed as a string even if it is always an integer because you will never sum two order numbers. However, if you do not really need the order number in your Tabular model, the best optimization is removing the column.

There is no reason to choose between numeric data types based on their memory footprint. The choice has to be made by considering only the range of values the numeric column has to represent (including significant digits, decimal digits, and precision). To represent a null value, xVelocity uses the boundary values of the range that can be expressed by a numeric type. Importing these values might raise a Value Not Supported error, as described at *http://msdn.microsoft.com/en-us/library/gg492146(v=SQL.110).aspx*.

Understanding Processing Options

After you've learned how the xVelocity engine uses memory, in this section you see the actions performed during table processing and what resources are required during this operation. You also learn the differences between processing options.

Every table in a Tabular model is copied in an internal structure for the xVelocity engine unless DirectQuery is being used. This operation is called data processing, and it can occur at different levels of granularities: database, table, and partition. You do not have any constraint on the process order, and you can process lookup tables after tables referencing them. Remember that the storage is by column, and every column has its own data. The real dependencies are calculated columns, which have to be refreshed after processing any table that is directly or indirectly referenced by the DAX expression defining the calculated column.

> **Note** In a Multidimensional model, you must process dimensions before measure groups, and you might have to process a measure group after you process a dimension, depending on the type of processing. In a Tabular model, this is not required, and processing a table does not have any side effect on other tables already processed. It is your responsibility to invalidate a table if it contains data that are no longer valid. Integrity issues are the responsibility of the source system, and these errors will not be picked up by processing a Tabular model (as they would be in a Multidimensional model).

In this chapter, the processing options are discussed at a functional level. Many, but not all, of these operations can be performed through the SQL Server Management Studio (SSMS) user interface. You see in Chapter 16 how to control process operations in a programmatic way, accessing all the available features. In Chapter 17, you learn how to use these features correctly, depending on the requirements of specific Tabular models.

What Happens During Processing

When you execute a full process on a Tabular database, every partition of every table is processed, and all calculated columns are refreshed. However, you might want to control this operation to optimize the processing time and memory required, especially for large models. For example, you can process only those tables that have been updated on the data source, and by using partitioning, you can limit the table refresh operation to only the part of the table that contains changed data. Because every table is processed independently from every other table, you can examine the process operation at a table level. The same operation is repeated for every table involved in a process batch.

A table or partition process operation is divided into two steps:

- **Process Data** The rows are sequentially read from the source table. If the process is on a table, a single dictionary is created for each column, and data files are created for each partition and each column. If the process is on a partition and a dictionary already exists, only new values are added to the dictionary, and existing values are kept in the dictionary, even if they no longer exist in any rows of the source table. This update of the dictionary can create fragmentation, which can be eliminated with a specific operation that you will see in the "Available Processing Options" section later in this chapter. The data files of the processed partition are always rebuilt.

- **Process Other Structures** A number of objects can be created or refreshed only after the Process Data operation has completed. Some of these structures can belong to tables other than those that have been processed. These structures are:

  - **Calculated columns** All calculated columns of a table that have been processed must be refreshed. Moreover, any calculated column containing an expression that directly or indirectly depends on a processed table must be refreshed. The calculated columns might need to be calculated for all the partitions of a table, regardless of the partitions that have been processed.

  - **Indexes** All the indexes that are used internally by the xVelocity engine have to be rebuilt because they depend on the column dictionary, which might have changed. Only indexes of the refreshed table are affected. The cost of rebuilding indexes is related to the dictionary size.

  - **Relationships** If the table contains references to other lookup tables, the internal structures have to be rebuilt; either that table or the lookup table is processed. However, the cost of rebuilding relationship structures depends on the size of the dictionary of the involved column and not on the size of the tables or the number of partitions.

  - **Hierarchies** If hierarchies exist in a table, their structures have to be rebuilt after the data have been processed.

There are specific processing instructions to control these two steps of a process operation. In fact, the process of other structures is usually done after all the data processing operations have been completed. Processing operations are memory-intensive and processor-intensive operations. During the Process Data operation, partitions are loaded serially, but other parts of the processing can use more cores if available. Moreover, different tables can be processed in parallel, and this might raise memory requirements. To avoid peak level, you can control the process operation to avoid a high peak level of memory usage.

Because of this condition, during processing Analysis Services might use paging to access the physical memory available to complete the operation. However, if during a process operation Analysis

Services receives a query on the existing Tabular model that has been paged, you might observe a severe degradation in query performance that also affects processing time. You have to measure the peak level of memory usage and the paging activity during the processing operation, and you must adopt countermeasures if the processing operation exhausts server memory resources.

Available Processing Options

You have several processing options; each of them can be applied to one or more objects granularly. You will find a more detailed discussion in Chapter 17 and in the blog post at *http://blogs.msdn .com/b/cathyk/archive/2011/09/26/processing-tabular-models-101.aspx*.

In general terms, for each table, you can perform one of the following operations:

- **Process Data**   Reads from the data source and populates a partition or a table. After that, related structures of the table involved (even if you loaded only a single partition) are no longer valid and require a Process Recalc operation.

- **Process Recalc**   Refreshes all table-related structures (calculated columns, indexes, relationships, and hierarchies) that must be refreshed because underlying data in the partition or tables is changed. This operation can be directly executed only at database level, affecting all the structures of *all* the tables that require refreshing. If you want to limit the process to only affected objects after a single table has been changed, without refreshing structures that have been invalidated and that you want to update later, you must use the Process Full or Process Default processing options, which internally perform a recalc action of only those objects that have been invalidated by other operations.

- **Process Full**   Performs a Process Data and then a Process Recalc of the related structures. When it is requested at a database level, it rebuilds all the tables. When it is executed on a table or on a partition, it performs a Process Data on the requested object followed by a Process Recalc limited to structures that are related to the table involved in the first operation. Process Add is a special case of Process Full because it runs in an incremental process that only adds rows to an existing partition. Executing Process Full or Process Add operations on two or more tables in separate transactions might require several Process Recalc steps of the same structures in other tables; for example, when you have a calculated column in another table that depends on data of the table that is being processed by one of these commands.

- **Process Defrag**   Optimizes the table dictionary and rebuilds table data for all partitions. If you process data at a partition level, you might end up having a fragmented dictionary containing entries that are no longer used in the table. For example, you might remove a partition from a table, and all values that were used only in that partition will still be part of the dictionary, even though they are no longer referenced by the column's data structures. This does not affect the correctness of query results, but it consumes more memory and might indirectly affect performance. Process Defrag might be an expensive operation for a large table. This operation can be executed at table or database level. (The latter is not exposed in the SSMS user interface.)

As a rule, to minimize the processing time when you do not have to full process the whole database, you should use Process Data for tables or partitions that have to be refreshed. After all data have been loaded, you can perform a single Process Recalc at database level, processing the affected structures just once. In this way, if a calculated column depends on two or more tables that have been modified, it will be refreshed just once. The side effect of this approach is that some structures (indexes and calculated columns of processed and related tables) will not be available from the first Process Data operation until the Process Default at database level completes unless they are executed in a single transaction (which requires more memory because two copies of data will be stored in memory during processing). Choosing other strategies, such as performing Process Full on single partitions or tables in separate batches, might require a longer time (because related structures will be processed more than once), but will reduce or eliminate the unavailability window of the Tabular model.

Note Compared to a Multidimensional model, the processing options in Tabular are simpler and easier to manage. You do not have the strong dependencies between dimensions and measure groups, even if the relationships between tables and the formulas in calculated columns define dependencies between tables, affecting structures that require refreshing. However, because these operations have a column granularity, the actual cost is limited to the parts of the table that require refreshing. Moreover, the unavailability of data in a Tabular model can be limited to calculated columns requiring refreshing rather than affecting the whole table, as you might expect coming from a Multidimensional background.

Using DirectQuery and Hybrid Modes

As you saw at the beginning of this chapter, a Tabular model can use either the xVelocity or the DirectQuery engine. In this section, you learn how to configure DirectQuery and how to obtain a model that supports both engines, giving the client the choice of which to use.

By default, a Tabular model is set to use the xVelocity in-memory database. If the tables of the Tabular model are defined according to the DirectQuery limitations you see in the following section, you can choose to switch to DirectQuery mode, or you can enable a hybrid mode that supports both xVelocity and DirectQuery. Choosing a hybrid mode enables you to create a single model that can be queried by using DirectQuery by client tools that generate queries in DAX (such as Power View), whereas xVelocity is still used by clients that generate queries in MDX (such as Excel).

Note An xVelocity-based model can always be queried in both DAX and MDX. The hybrid mode is useful if you want to use MDX queries on a model that uses DirectQuery for DAX queries because MDX is not supported in DirectQuery mode.

DirectQuery Mode

The In-Memory mode based on the xVelocity storage engine is the default choice for any Tabular model you create. However, you also have the option to use an alternative approach that converts a query to a Tabular model into a SQL query to the data source without using the xVelocity engine. This option is called DirectQuery mode, and in this section, you learn its purpose. You learn how to use it in your Tabular model later in this chapter.

As you know, a Tabular model is a description of a BI semantic model (BISM) that is table-oriented, whereas a Multidimensional model is dimension-oriented. Both models in Analysis Services have an internal engine to store data, but there is also the option to keep the data in the data source by using the model as a semantic layer that translates a native query (DAX for Tabular and MDX for Multidimensional) into a SQL query sent to the data source. This option is called DirectQuery mode for a Tabular model, and it has a corresponding ROLAP mode for the Multidimensional model, although there are large differences between these two modes. Tabular converts any DAX query into a SQL query, whereas Multidimensional uses an internal cache and a formula engine, generating a SQL query for only data that are not available in Analysis Services.

> **Note** You can find more information about ROLAP on MSDN at *http://msdn.microsoft.com/en-us/library/ms174915.aspx*.

With DirectQuery mode enabled, DAX queries are not sent to the xVelocity engine but are converted into equivalent SQL queries that are sent to the data source.

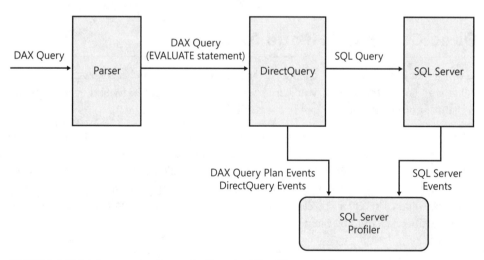

FIGURE 9-4 This is how a query is executed by using DirectQuery mode.

As you can see in Figure 9-4, in DirectQuery, no formula engine is involved in Analysis Services. Moreover, DirectQuery does not cache any data, and every DAX query is converted to a SQL query even if it was the same query that was just executed. In other words, DirectQuery relies on the cache of the external database server to improve performance. By using SQL Profiler, you can intercept two classes of trace events from Analysis Services, DAX Query Plan and DirectQuery events, both generated by the DirectQuery engine. You can also intercept queries sent to the relational database by connecting to SQL Server, which is important if you want to analyze performance and resources used. If you just want to look at the SQL query generated by DirectQuery, you can look at the *DirectQuery* event generated by Analysis Services.

In the current implementation of DirectQuery in Analysis Services 2012, there are a few limitations:

- Only DAX queries can use DirectQuery mode. An MDX query cannot use DirectQuery.

- Not all DAX functions are supported in DirectQuery mode. You can find a complete list of limitations and semantic differences at *http://msdn.microsoft.com/library/hh213006.aspx*.

- Calculated columns are not supported in DirectQuery. You can only define measures in DAX within the existing limitations on DAX functions that were mentioned earlier in this chapter.

- Only SQL Server is supported as a data source; no other database providers are supported.

Thus, you can use DirectQuery only when you have a client that generates native DAX queries (such as Power View or your own report with DAX-embedded queries) and when all the tables in the model have been extracted from SQL Server 2005 or later versions (SQL Server 2008 R2 or later versions are preferred for performance reasons). If you want to support both DAX and MDX queries for the same model, you can choose a hybrid mode that uses DirectQuery for DAX queries and xVelocity for MDX queries. (You can also deploy two identical databases, one in DirectQuery and one in xVelocity). You find more detail about possible DirectQuery configurations in the "DirectQuery Settings" section later in this chapter.

Despite its limitations, here is a list of reasons to choose DirectQuery for your data model:

- **Real-time reporting**   With DirectQuery, no latency on data is caused by processing time.

- **No processing window**   If the time required to process data and refresh tables in xVelocity is too long or not affordable, DirectQuery completely eliminates this time.

- **Not enough memory to store data in memory**   If your database is so large that it is not possible to store in memory with xVelocity, despite its compression capabilities, you can keep data on SQL Server.

- **Defines a semantic layer on top of a SQL Server database**   If you just want to query a SQL Server database with a semantic layer, a Tabular model offers this capability, although it is limited to DAX queries in this version.

We think that the main reasons to use DirectQuery are real-time reporting and very large databases that do not fit in memory. In the first case, you will probably have a relatively small database with data that changes continuously, and the need of real-time reporting by using tools such as Power View requires a DAX-enabled data source (whereas for custom reporting, you might use SQL as a query language). For a very large database, you should have a powerful SQL Server machine to get answers with decent performance. By using SQL Server 2012, you might use columnstore indexes to improve speed, even if you have to consider the cost required to build the columnstore index, which could be similar to processing an equivalent table in Tabular. However, with the same dataset, the query performance of DAX using xVelocity (VertiPaq) will probably be better than the corresponding performance of the same model in DirectQuery mode that accesses a SQL Server database optimized with columnstore indexes, because xVelocity in Analysis Services uses a higher compression and requires data to be stored in memory.

We hope that in future versions of Analysis Services, DirectQuery will support MDX queries and relational databases other than SQL Server and also support existing clients and use existing data warehouses stored in database products of other vendors. For example, Teradata is a common choice for large data warehouses, and being able to query it directly from DAX would be helpful.

Analyzing DirectQuery Mode Events by Using SQL Profiler

You can see the queries sent to SQL Server by DirectQuery in the SQL Profiler by monitoring the *DirectQuery Begin* and *DirectQuery End* event classes. They both report the SQL-generated query in the TextData column, and *DirectQuery End* also provides the duration in milliseconds. For example, consider the following DAX query.

```
EVALUATE Products
```

Such a query produces the following request to SQL Server.

```
SELECT
    [t1].[ID_Product] AS [c1_Products_ID_Product],
    [t1].[Product] AS [c2_Products_Product]
FROM (
    (SELECT [dbo].[Products].* FROM [dbo].[Products])
) AS [t1]
```

As you can see, the query composition contains unnecessary duplicated code, but this is not relevant because the SQL query plan optimizes that, resulting in an optimal query. Now, consider the following query that involves at least two tables, Product Category and Internet Sales.

```
EVALUATE
ADDCOLUMNS(
    Products,
    "Quantity", CALCULATE( SUM( Orders[Quantity] ) )
)
```

This query produces the following request to SQL Server.

```
SELECT [c1_Products_ID_Product], [c2_Products_Product], [c3] AS [c4__Quantity]
FROM (
    SELECT [t2].[c1_Products_ID_Product], [c2_Products_Product], [c3]
    FROM ( (
        SELECT
            [t4].[ID_Product] AS [c1_Products_ID_Product],
```

```
        [t4].[Product] AS [c2_Products_Product]
    FROM ( (
        SELECT [dbo].[Products].*
        FROM [dbo].[Products] ) ) AS [t4] ) AS [t2]
        LEFT OUTER JOIN (
            SELECT [c1_Products_ID_Product], SUM([c5_Orders_Quantity]) AS [c3]
            FROM (
                SELECT
                    [t7].[ID_Product] AS [c1_Products_ID_Product],
                    [t6].[Quantity] AS [c5_Orders_Quantity]
                FROM ( (
                    SELECT [dbo].[Orders].*
                    FROM [dbo].[Orders] ) AS [t6]
                LEFT OUTER JOIN (
                    SELECT [dbo].[Products].*
                    FROM [dbo].[Products] ) AS [t7]
                ON ( [t6].[ID_Product] = [t7].[ID_Product] ) ) ) AS [t5]
            GROUP BY [c1_Products_ID_Product] ) AS [t3]
        ON ( [t2].[c1_Products_ID_Product] ) = ( [t3].[c1_Products_ID_Product] )
    )
) AS [t1]
```

This SQL query is more complex than a SQL query you might have written manually, but the resulting query plan is fine. The complexity of the SQL code generated is caused by the internal algorithm that has to handle other DAX constructs and thus results in a greater number of nested queries.

Different DAX queries returning the same result can generate very different SQL queries by using DirectQuery mode. When you want to optimize DirectQuery, look at the query plan in SQL Server executed for the SQL query sent by DirectQuery. If you cannot add indexes and statistics in SQL Server to improve query performance, you must change the DAX query to generate a more efficient SQL query. It is beyond the scope of this book to discuss DirectQuery optimizations in more detail.

DirectQuery Settings

The DirectQuery settings are present in two parts of a Tabular model: the deployment properties of the project and the file properties of the BIM file (usually named Model.bim). These settings have different roles, as you will see in the following paragraphs.

The first setting to change is the setting in the BIM file properties. When you select the Model .bim file in the Solution Explorer pane, you can edit the DirectQuery Mode property in the Properties pane, as shown in Figure 9-5.

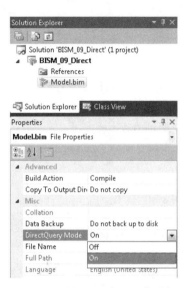

FIGURE 9-5 You can change the DirectQuery Mode property in Model.bim File Properties in SQL Server Data Tools (SSDT).

By changing DirectQuery Mode to On, the SQL Server Data Tools (SSDT) designer enforces all DirectQuery mode restrictions. For example, you can no longer create a calculated column after you set this property to On. If the model already uses features that are not supported by DirectQuery, you get an error when trying to set this property to On, and the Error List pane contains a list of errors that prevent DirectQuery from working. You can solve all these issues (for example, by removing existing calculated columns) until DirectQuery Mode can successfully be set to On.

Tip The DirectQuery Mode setting should be set to On early in development to avoid using features that are not supported by DirectQuery.

After you set DirectQuery Mode to On, you can change the Query Mode property in the Deployment Options of your Tabular project. You can open the project Properties window you see in Figure 9-6 by selecting the Project / Properties menu item.

By default, the Query Mode property is set to In-Memory, which means that only xVelocity will be used for the deployment of the Tabular model. This is the only possible setting if DirectQuery Mode is set to Off. Whichever setting you choose, you can change the setting after the model has been deployed by changing the DirectQueryMode property in SSMS. If you right-click a Tabular database in SSMS and select the Properties menu item, you get the Database Properties window shown in Figure 9-7.

FIGURE 9-6 You can set the Query Mode property in the project Properties window in SSDT.

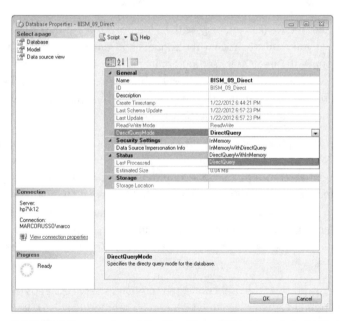

FIGURE 9-7 You can also set the DirectQueryMode property in the Database Properties window in SSMS.

Also in SSMS, changing DirectQueryMode is allowed only if the Tabular model does not use features that are not supported by DirectQuery.

The possible DirectQuery Mode settings are the following:

- **In-Memory** Every table in the deployed model will be processed and stored in xVelocity. At query time, only xVelocity will be used.

- **DirectQuery**   Every table in the deployed model is not loaded in memory during processing, and any DAX query will be converted into a SQL query. Queries in MDX are not supported by this mode.

- **DirectQuery With In-Memory**   Every table in the deployed model will be processed and stored in xVelocity. At query time, by default, any DAX query will be converted into a SQL query. The client can select the query mode by using the DirectQueryMode setting in the connection string. A client tool can choose to use xVelocity by placing DirectQueryMode=InMemory in the connection string. This is mandatory for a client tool (for example, Excel) that sends queries by using MDX. By default, DirectQuery will be chosen if this setting is missing in the connection string.

- **In-Memory With DirectQuery**   Every table in the deployed model will be processed and stored in xVelocity. At query time, by default, any query will be sent to xVelocity. The client can select the query mode by using the DirectQueryMode setting in the connection string. A client tool can choose to use DirectQuery by placing DirectQueryMode=DirectQuery in the connection string. By default, xVelocity will be chosen if this setting is missing in the connection string.

The choice between the two hybrid modes (DirectQuery With In-Memory and In-Memory With DirectQuery) depends on the default you want to obtain when connecting from a client tool to a Tabular model. Using the In-Memory With DirectQuery setting grants that any client will always work, and DirectQuery will be used only when explicitly requested in the connection string, whereas the DirectQuery With In-Memory setting will make DirectQuery the default choice, forcing any MDX client to choose the In-Memory setting explicitly in the connection string.

There is another area in Deployment options that is specific to DirectQuery Options, and it contains the impersonation settings. When you process a Tabular model, Analysis Services connects to data sources by using security credentials according to connection settings. However, when you query a Tabular model in DirectQuery mode, Analysis Services can connect to SQL Server by using either the same setting that would be used to process tables (if xVelocity is enabled, as in any hybrid mode) or the current user who is querying Tabular model from a client tool. To impersonate the current user, you must change the DirectQuery Impersonation Settings in the Deployment Options of your Tabular project, as you see in Figure 9-8.

When you choose ImpersonateCurrentUser, the user connected to Analysis Services needs permission for SQL Server tables that are queried as a result of the DAX queries sent to Analysis Services. Note that row-level security defined in a Tabular model is not supported by DirectQuery. You can define permission in SQL Server with a column granularity, something that is not possible in Analysis Services. Nevertheless, consider that current users can be impersonated only in DirectQuery mode; if you have a hybrid model, there are two security models in place, depending on the connection made by the client tool. You can find a longer discussion about DirectQuery impersonation at *http://blogs .msdn.com/b/cathyk/archive/2011/12/13/directquery-impersonation-options-explained.aspx.*

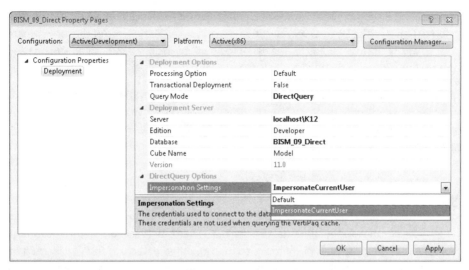

FIGURE 9-8 You can change DirectQuery Impersonation Settings in the Project Properties window in SSDT.

Development by Using DirectQuery

When you are developing a Tabular model, you always use xVelocity during development even if you enabled the DirectQuery mode. In this section, you see how to control the data that are loaded in xVelocity during development to avoid loading all the database content in memory.

By default, a table has a single partition, which is entirely loaded in memory even when you are developing your model. As you will see in Chapter 17, you can define multiple partitions for every table, and this is the key to controlling what data are processed by xVelocity during a Tabular model development and in a hybrid model. Only one of these partitions corresponds to the partition used in DirectQuery mode; all other partitions are used only for xVelocity processing. Every partition has a Processing Options setting that can have one of the following two values:

- **Allow partition to be processed**   This is the default and processes the partition in xVelocity. Data in this partition is used every time the query is resolved by xVelocity.

- **Never process this partition**   With this setting, the partition is never loaded in xVelocity. This setting is useful to identify the single DirectQuery partition, which has to map to the whole table, and which you do not want to process in xVelocity because it would overlap other partitions.

If you are developing a DirectQuery-only model, you probably want to load just a subset of data during the development. To do that, define a DirectQuery partition that will be never processed and another partition that loads only a subset of data by using a view that limits the number of rows loaded from the table.

If you are creating a hybrid model with multiple partitions for xVelocity data, you need overlapping partition definitions; the DirectQuery partition must include all the rows of the table, whereas other partitions will be used by xVelocity. The same rows will be included in both an xVelocity and the DirectQuery partition because they will never be used together.

You will find some examples and a more complete discussion of partitions in Chapter 17. You can also read more about configuring multiple partitions, when DirectQuery is involved, at *http://blogs.msdn.com/b/cathyk/archive/2011/09/15/configuring-multiple-partitions-in-a-directquery-with-vertipaq-model-step-by-step.aspx.*

Summary

In this chapter, you saw that a Tabular model can use both xVelocity (VertiPaq) and DirectQuery engines. You saw that xVelocity is an in-memory, column-oriented database, and you learned the internal structures used to store data and how data can be processed. You also saw how DirectQuery can be used to convert DAX queries into SQL queries, obtaining real-time answers and eliminating the need to process and store data in memory. DirectQuery has several limitations. You can also use hybrid modes that offer both xVelocity and DirectQuery engines to the client, which can choose the engine to use through a setting in the connection string.

Because the xVelocity engine stores data in memory, it is critical to understand how data are compressed and which columns cause more memory pressure, usually because of their data dictionary size. Finally, you learned how xVelocity processes data and how to control process phases to minimize latency and optimize data structures.

Building Hierarchies

Hierarchies are a much more important part of a Tabular model than you might think. Even though a Tabular model can be built without any hierarchies, hierarchies add a lot to the usability of a model, and usability issues often determine the success or failure of a business intelligence (BI) project. The basic process of building a hierarchy was covered in Chapter 2, "Getting Started with the Tabular Model," but in this chapter, we look at the process in more detail and discuss some of the more advanced aspects of creating hierarchies: when you should build them, what the benefits and disadvantages of using them are, how you can build ragged hierarchies, and how you can model parent/child relationships.

Basic Hierarchies

First, we look at what a hierarchy actually is and how to build basic hierarchies.

What Are Hierarchies?

By now, you are very familiar with the way a Tabular model appears to a user in a front-end tool, such as Microsoft Excel, and the way the distinct values in each column in your model can be displayed on the rows or columns of a Microsoft PivotTable. This provides a very flexible way of building queries, but it has the disadvantage that every new level of nesting that you add to the row or column axis requires a certain amount of effort for the user. First, the user must find what he or she wants to add and then click and drag it to where it should appear. More importantly, it requires the user to have a basic level of understanding of the data he or she is using. To build meaningful reports, the user must know information—such as the fact that a Fiscal Semester contains many Fiscal Quarters, but a Fiscal Quarter can be in only one Fiscal Semester—so that he or she can order these items appropriately on an axis.

Hierarchies provide a solution to these problems. They can be thought of as predefined pathways through your data that help your users explore down from one level of granularity to another in a meaningful way. A typical example of a hierarchy would be on a Date table, in which users very often start to view data at the Year level and then navigate down to Quarter, Month, and Date level. A hierarchy enables you to define this type of navigation path. Figure 10-1 shows what a hierarchy looks like when used in an Excel PivotTable.

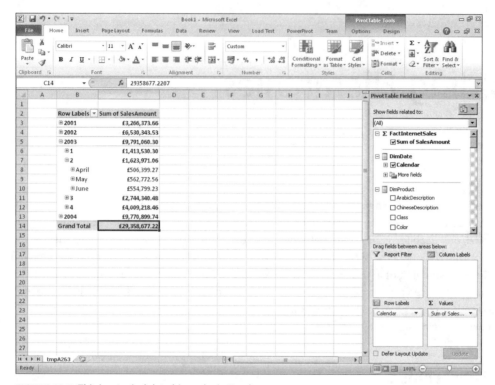

FIGURE 10-1 This is a typical date hierarchy in Excel.

A hierarchy like this can save time for your users by helping them find what they are looking for quickly. With a hierarchy, there is only one thing to drag and drop into a PivotTable, after which users just double-click an item to drill down until they get to the level of detail they require.

Hierarchies can also prevent users from running queries that return more data than they want and which may perform badly. For example, instead of dragging every date in the Date table onto the rows of a PivotTable and then filtering those rows to show just the ones in which the user is interested (which would be slow because displaying every date could result in a query that returns hundreds of rows), a hierarchy encourages the user to choose a year, navigate to display just the quarters in that year, and then navigate until he or she reaches the date level, which results in much smaller, faster queries at each step.

Note The release to manufacturing (RTM) version of Power View does not recognize or display hierarchies built in the Tabular model, so Power View users cannot take advantage of this feature; you should design your model with this limitation in mind.

When to Build Hierarchies

There are several advantages to building hierarchies, but that does not mean you should build hundreds of them on every table. Here are a few guidelines on when to build hierarchies and when not to:

- Hierarchies should be built when one-to-many relationships exist between the columns in a single table because this usually indicates the existence of an underlying pattern in the data itself—and, very often, these patterns represent a natural way for users to explore the data. A hierarchy going from Year to Quarter to Month to Date has already been described; other common examples include hierarchies going from Country to State to City to ZIP Code to Customer, or going from Product Category to Product Subcategory to Product. You might also consider building a hierarchy when using calculated columns to create your own bandings on a table, as described in Chapter 12, "Using Advanced Tabular Relationships."

- Hierarchies can also be built when one-to-many relationships do not exist between columns but when certain columns are frequently grouped together in reports. For example, a retailer might want to drill down from Product Category to Brand to Style to Color to Product even if there is a many-to-many relationship among Brand, Style, and Color.

- Hierarchies tend to be more useful the more levels they have. There is no point in building a hierarchy with just one level in it, and hierarchies with two levels might not provide much benefit.

- Hierarchies can be made visible to perspectives, and you can choose whether attributes that are used in hierarchies are visible for each perspective. You can force users to use only a hierarchy instead of its underlying columns by hiding those columns, as you see in the "Hierarchy Design Best Practices" section later in this chapter.

- With the ease of use that hierarchies bring comes rigidity. If you have defined a hierarchy that goes from Product Category to Brand, and if the underlying columns are hidden, users will not be able to define a report that places Brand before Product Category, nor will they be able to place Product Category and Brand on opposing axes in a report.

Building Hierarchies

There are essentially two steps involved in building a hierarchy. First, prepare your data appropriately; next, build the hierarchy on your table. The initial data-preparation step can be performed inside the Tabular model itself, and in this chapter a number of techniques are demonstrated to do this. The main advantages of doing your data preparation inside the Tabular model are that, as a developer, you do not need to switch between several tools when building a hierarchy, and you have the power of DAX at your disposal. This might make it easier and faster to write the logic involved. As an alternative, the data preparation may be performed inside your extract, transform, and load (ETL) process in a view or in the SQL code used to load data into the tables in your Tabular model. The advantage of this approach are that it keeps relational logic in the relational database, which is better for maintainability and reuse. It also reduces the number of columns in your model so that your model has a smaller memory footprint. Additionally, if you are more comfortable writing SQL than DAX, it might be easier from an implementation point of view.

Hierarchies are designed in SQL Server Data Tools (SSDT) in the Diagram View. To create a hierarchy on a table (it is not possible to build a hierarchy that spans more than one table), you can either click the Create Hierarchy button in the top-right corner of the table or select one or more columns in the table. Right-click and select Create Hierarchy to use those columns as the levels in a new hierarchy. To add a new level to an existing hierarchy, you can drag and drop a column into it at the appropriate position, or you can right-click the column, select Add To Hierarchy, and then click the name of the hierarchy to which you wish to add it. After a hierarchy has been created, the levels in it can be moved up or down or deleted by right-clicking them; it can also be renamed by right-clicking its name. Figure 10-2 shows what a hierarchy created in SSDT looks like.

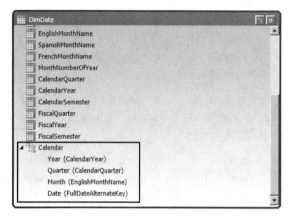

FIGURE 10-2 This is a hierarchy in the Diagram View of SSDT.

Hierarchy Design Best Practices

Here are a few tips to consider when designing hierarchies:

- After a column from a table has been included as a level in a hierarchy, the column itself can be hidden by right-clicking it and selecting Hide From Client Tools. It is then visible only to your users as a level in a hierarchy. This is usually a good idea because it stops users from becoming confused about whether they should use the original column or the hierarchy in their reports or whether there is any difference between the column and the hierarchy. Users then also have a shorter list of items to search when building their reports, making finding what they want easier. However, in some client tools, it can make filtering on values that make up lower levels of the hierarchy (such as Month in the hierarchy shown in Figure 10-2) much harder; and, if you are using Power View, which does not support hierarchies, hiding columns in this way stops users from using these columns completely.

- Levels in different hierarchies should not have the same name if they represent different things. For example, if you have Fiscal and Calendar hierarchies on your Date dimension, the top levels should be Fiscal Year and Calendar Year, respectively, and both should not be named Year. This removes a possible cause of confusion for your users.

- It can be a good idea to follow a standard naming convention for hierarchies to help your users understand what they contain. For example, you might have a hierarchy that goes from Year to Quarter to Month to Date and another that goes from Year to Week to Date; calling the first hierarchy Year-Month-Date and the second Year-Week-Date would make it easy for your users to find the one they need in their front-end tool.

Hierarchies Spanning Multiple Tables

Even if it is not possible to create hierarchies that span multiple tables, you might find yourself needing to do this if you have snowflaked dimension tables. One solution is to denormalize the dimension tables in the relational data source, for example in a view; the same effect can also be achieved relatively easily by using calculated columns.

The Product dimension in the Adventure Works database is a good example of a snowflaked dimension. It is made up of three tables: DimProductCategory, DimProductSubcategory, and DimProduct, as shown in Figure 10-3.

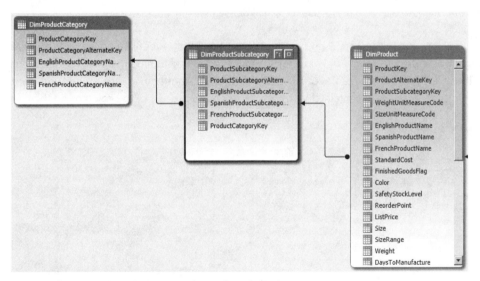

FIGURE 10-3 This is the Adventure Works Product dimension.

It is possible that, given a dimension like this, users would want to drill down from Product Category to Product Subcategory to Product. To enable this, you must first bring the names of the Subcategory and Category for each Product down to the DimProduct table by creating two calculated columns there. The DAX required to do this is fairly simple.

```
DimProduct[SubCategory] =
RELATED( DimProductSubcategory[EnglishProductSubcategoryName] )
```

```
DimProduct[Category] =
RELATED( DimProductCategory[EnglishProductCategoryName] )
```

Figure 10-4 shows what these two new calculated columns look like on the DimProduct table.

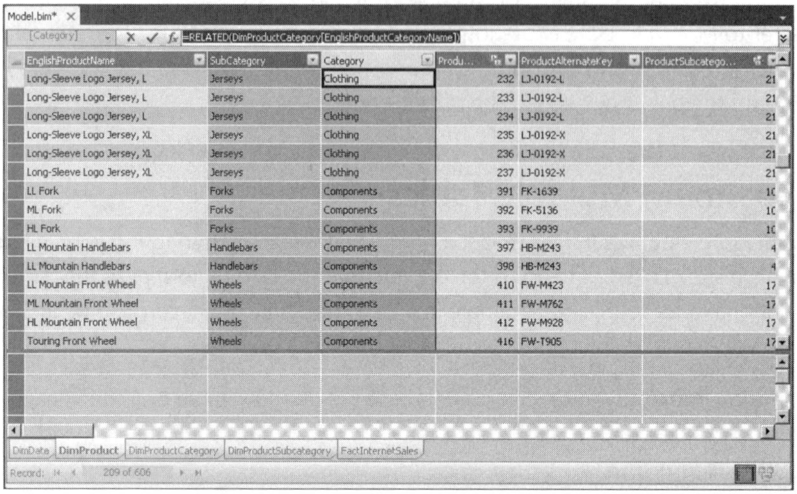

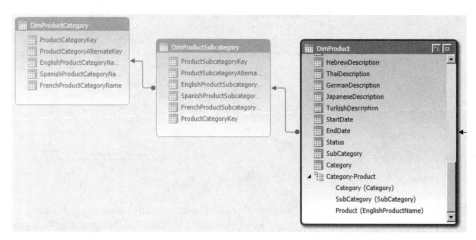

FIGURE 10-4 Here are the two new calculated columns on the DimProduct table.

You can then create a hierarchy on the DimProduct table that goes from Category to Subcategory to Product, as shown in Figure 10-5. As a final step, it is advisable to hide the DimProductCategory and DimProductSubcategory tables completely (by right-clicking them and selecting Hide From Client Tools) because the new hierarchy removes the need to use any of the columns on them.

FIGURE 10-5 This is the Product hierarchy.

Note Readers familiar with Multidimensional models might know that it is possible to create ragged hierarchies in them, in which the user skips a level in a hierarchy in certain circumstances. One example of when this is useful is in a Geography hierarchy that goes from Country to State to City, but in which the user can drill down from Country directly to City for countries that are not subdivided into states. Another example is when leaf members exist on different levels of a hierarchy. It is unfortunate that the Tabular model does not support this functionality, and it is not possible to create ragged hierarchies in SSDT, although at the time of writing it looks as though BIDS Helper may, in the future, enable you to create ragged hierarchies by exposing unsupported functionality in the Analysis Services Tabular engine.

Parent/Child Hierarchies

Now that you have seen how to create a basic hierarchy, let's take a look at a more complex example: parent/child hierarchies.

What Are Parent/Child Hierarchies?

A parent/child hierarchy in dimensional modeling is a hierarchy in which the structure is defined by a self-join on a dimension table rather than by modeling each level as a separate column, as in a regular dimension. Typical scenarios in which you might use a parent/child hierarchy include the organizational structure of a company or a chart of accounts. The main advantage of this way of modeling a dimension is that you do not need to know the maximum depth of the hierarchy at design time, so if, for example, your company undergoes a reorganization and there are suddenly twenty steps in the chain of command—from the lowliest employee up to the CEO—when previously there were only ten, you do not need to change your dimension table. Figure 10-6 shows the DimEmployee table in the Adventure Works database that contains such a parent/child hierarchy.

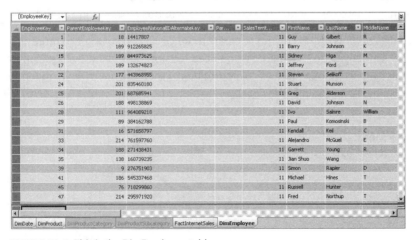

FIGURE 10-6 This is the DimEmployee table.

In Figure 10-6, the primary key of the table is the *EmployeeKey* column, and each row represents an individual employee of the Adventure Works corporation. The employees' names are held in the *FirstName* and *LastName* columns. The *ParentEmployeeKey* column holds the value of the *EmployeeKey* column for the employee's manager.

Configuring Parent/Child Hierarchies

After all this explanation, it might come as something of a letdown to discover that, unlike the Multidimensional model, Tabular does not support true parent/child hierarchies. However, it does have some very useful DAX functionality for flattening parent/child hierarchies into regular, column-based hierarchies. This is good enough for most scenarios, although it means that you have to make an educated guess at design time about what the maximum depth of your hierarchy will be. In this section, you learn how to configure a simple parent/child hierarchy by using the DimEmployee table as an example; you also find out how to handle more complex design problems.

Building a Basic Parent/Child Hierarchy

Before you start to build a hierarchy on the DimEmployee table, it is a good idea to create a calculated column to concatenate the first and last names of all the employees in the table, because it is these names you want to see in your hierarchy. This can be achieved by creating a new calculated column called *FullName* with the following definition.

```
DimEmployee[FullName] =
DimEmployee[FirstName] & " " & DimEmployee[LastName]
```

The next step is to create another calculated column that contains the list of values for *EmployeeKey* from the top of the hierarchy down to the current employee. To do this, create a calculated column called *EmployeePath* and use the following DAX expression.

```
DimEmployee[EmployeePath] =
PATH( DimEmployee[EmployeeKey], DimEmployee[ParentEmployeeKey] )
```

The output of the *PATH()* function is a pipe-delimited list of values (so if your key column contains pipe characters, you might have some extra data cleaning work to do), as shown in Figure 10-7.

You can then use the contents of this column to create more calculated columns to represent each level in your hierarchy. Before you do that, though, you need to know how many levels you must create. You can do this by creating one more calculated column, called *HierarchyDepth*, that returns the number of items in the list returned in the *EmployeePath* column by using the *PATHLENGTH()* function.

```
DimEmployee[HierarchyDepth] =
PATHLENGTH( DimEmployee[EmployeePath] )
```

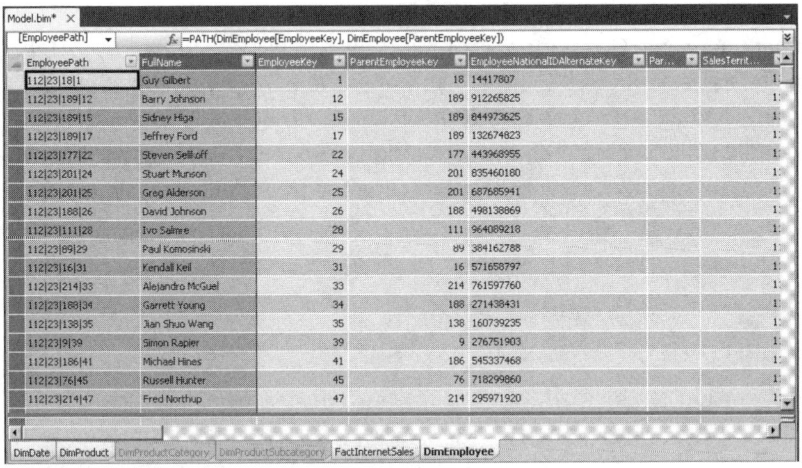

FIGURE 10-7 This is the output of the *PATH()* function.

You can then build a measure to return the maximum value in this column by using the following definition.

```
[Max Depth] :=
MAX( DimEmployee[HierarchyDepth] )
```

In the case of the DimEmployee table, the maximum depth of the hierarchy is five levels, so you must create at least five new calculated columns for the levels of your new hierarchy, but, as mentioned previously, it might be wise to build some extra levels in case the hierarchy grows deeper over time.

To populate these new calculated columns, you must find the employee name associated with each key value in the path returned in the *EmployeePath* calculated column. To find the key value at each position in the path contained in the *EmployeePath* column, you can use the *PATHITEM()* function as follows.

```
PATHITEM( DimEmployee[EmployeePath], 1, INTEGER )
```

There are three parameters to the *PATHITEM()* function. The first takes the name of the column that contains the path; the second contains the 1-based position in the path for which you want to return the value; and the third, optional parameter can be either *TEXT*, which means the value will be returned as text, or *INTEGER*, which means the value will be returned as an integer. You can also use 0 for *TEXT* and 1 for *INTEGER*, although we recommend using the enumeration name to make the formula easier to read.

Note The third parameter can be important for matching the value returned by *PATHITEM* with the value in the key column of the table. If you omit the third parameter, it will be returned as *TEXT* by default, but in this case, if the value has to be compared with an integer (as in the example shown here), then the conversion from text to integer will be made implicitly at the moment of the comparison. In any case, the three following syntaxes are equivalent.

```
PATHITEM( DimEmployee[EmployeePath], 1, INTEGER )

INT( PATHITEM( DimEmployee[EmployeePath], 1, TEXT ) )

INT( PATHITEM( DimEmployee[EmployeePath], 1 ) )
```

Because the conversion can be made automatically when you make a comparison of this value with another value, as when using *LOOKUPVALUE*, it is important to specify the third parameter only when you want to store the result of *PATHITEM* in a calculated column, which will be created with the data type according to the value of the third parameter. That said, using the third parameter is good practice because it shows other developers who might see your code what type of values you are expecting to return.

Key values on their own are not very useful, however; you must find the name of the employee associated with each key, and you can do that by using the *LOOKUPVALUE()* function. Here is the complete expression that can be used to return the name of the employee for the first level in the hierarchy.

```
DimEmployee[EmployeeLevel1] =
LOOKUPVALUE(
    DimEmployee[FullName],
    DimEmployee[EmployeeKey],
    PATHITEM( DimEmployee[EmployeePath], 1, INTEGER )
)
```

Here is the expression for the second level in the hierarchy.

```
DimEmployee[EmployeeLevel2] =
LOOKUPVALUE(
    DimEmployee[FullName],
    DimEmployee[EmployeeKey],
    PATHITEM( DimEmployee[EmployeePath], 2, INTEGER )
)
```

With all five calculated columns created for the five levels of the hierarchy, the table will look like the screenshot in Figure 10-8.

FIGURE 10-8 These are the calculated columns created for the Employee hierarchy.

The final step is to create a hierarchy from these columns in the way you saw earlier in this chapter. In Excel, the result looks like the hierarchy shown in Figure 10-9.

FIGURE 10-9 This is an example of a basic parent/child hierarchy.

Handling Empty Items

The approach described in the previous section is sufficient for many parent/child hierarchies, but as you can see from Figure 10-9, the hierarchy built from the DimEmployee table contains some items that have no name. This is because not all branches of the hierarchy reach the maximum depth of five levels. Rather than show these empty values, it might be better to repeat the name of the member that is immediately above in the hierarchy, and this can be achieved by using the *IF()* function. Here is an example of what the calculated column expression for the lowest level in the hierarchy looks like with this change.

```
DimEmployee[EmployeeLevel5] =
IF(
    ISBLANK( PATHITEM(DimEmployee[EmployeePath], 5, 1 ) ),
    DimEmployee[EmployeeLevel4],
    LOOKUPVALUE(
        DimEmployee[FullName], DimEmployee[EmployeeKey],
        PATHITEM( DimEmployee[EmployeePath], 5, 1 )
    )
)
```

This makes the hierarchy a bit tidier, but it is still not an ideal situation. Instead of empty items, you now have repeating items at the bottom of the hierarchy on which the user can drill down. You can work around this by using the default behavior of tools such as Excel to filter out rows in PivotTables in which all measures return blank values. If the user has drilled down beyond the bottom of the original hierarchy, all measures should display a *BLANK* value.

To find the level in the hierarchy to which the user has drilled down, you can create a measure that uses the *ISFILTERED* function.

```
[Current Hierarchy Depth] :=
IF(
    ISFILTERED( DimEmployee[EmployeeLevel5] ), 5,
    IF(
        ISFILTERED( DimEmployee[EmployeeLevel4] ), 4,
        IF(
            ISFILTERED( DimEmployee[EmployeeLevel3] ), 3,
            IF(
                ISFILTERED( DimEmployee[EmployeeLevel2] ), 2, 1
            )
        )
    )
)
```

As you saw in Chapter 7, "DAX Advanced," the *ISFILTERED()* function returns *True* if the column it references is used as part of a direct filter. Thus, in this case, a series of nested *IF()* functions test each level of the hierarchy from the bottom up to determine whether each level is part of a direct filter; if it is, the item that is being displayed must be at least at that level. The final step is to test whether the currently displayed item is beyond the bottom of the original hierarchy. To do this, you can compare the value returned by the Current Hierarchy Depth measure with the value returned by the Max Depth measure created earlier in this chapter, as follows. (In this case, the measure returns *1*, but in a real model, it would return some other measure value.)

```
[DemoMeasure] :=
IF( [Current Hierarchy Depth] > [Max Depth], BLANK(), 1 )
```

The result is a hierarchy that looks like the one displayed in Figure 10-10.

FIGURE 10-10 This is the finished parent/child hierarchy.

Unary Operators

In the Multidimensional model, parent/child hierarchies are often used in conjunction with unary operators and custom rollup formulas when building financial applications. Although the Tabular model does not include built-in support for unary operators it is possible to reproduce the functionality to a certain extent in DAX, and in this section you find out how. It is not possible to re-create custom rollup formulas, unfortunately, and the only option is to write extremely long and complicated DAX expressions in measures.

How Unary Operators Work

Full details about how unary operators work in the Multidimensional model can be found in Books Online at *http://technet.microsoft.com/en-us/library/ms175417.aspx*, but here is a quick summary. Each item in the hierarchy can be associated with an operator that controls how the total for that member aggregates up to its parent. Operators can be one of the following values:

- ■ +   The plus sign means that the value for the current item is added to the aggregate of its siblings (that is, all the items that have the same parent) that occur before the current item on the same level of the hierarchy.

- ■ **–** The minus sign means that the value for the current item is subtracted from the value of its siblings that occur before the current item on the same level of the hierarchy.

- ■ ***** The asterisk means that the value for the current item is multiplied by the aggregate of all the siblings that occur before the current item on the same level of the hierarchy.

- ■ **/** The forward slash means that the value for the current item is divided by the aggregate of all the siblings that occur before the current item on the same level of the hierarchy.

- ■ **~** The tilde means that the value for the current item is ignored when calculating the value of the parent.

- ■ **A value between 0 and 1** This means that the value of the current item is multiplied by this value when aggregation takes place, and the result is added to the aggregate of its siblings.

The DAX for implementing unary operators gets more complex the more of these operators are used in a hierarchy, so for the sake of clarity and simplicity, in this section only, the three most common operators are used: the plus sign (+), the minus sign (–), and the tilde (~). Calculations that use the forward slash and asterisk unary operators, / and *, return different results, depending on the order in which they are executed, so any DAX implementation will be even more complicated. Table 10-1 shows a simple example of how these three operators behave when used in a hierarchy.

TABLE 10-1 How Unary Operators Are Calculated

Item Name	Unary Operator	Measure Value
Profit		150
- Sales	+	100
- Other Income	+	75
- Costs	–	25
- Headcount	~	493

In this example, the Sales, Other Income, Costs, and Headcount items appear as children of the Profit item in the hierarchy. The value of Profit is calculated as

+ [Sales Amount] + [Other Income] - [Costs]

with the value of Headcount ignored, to give the total of 150.

Implementing Unary Operators by Using DAX

The key to implementing unary operator functionality in DAX is to recalculate the value of your measure at each level of the hierarchy rather than to calculate it at a low level and aggregate it up. This means that the DAX needed can be very complicated, and it is a good idea to split the calculation into multiple steps so that it can be debugged more easily.

To illustrate how to implement unary operators, you need a dimension with some unary operators on it. The DimEmployee table in Adventure Works unfortunately does not include unary operators, but for the purposes of this section, the following expression can be used in a calculated column called *UnaryOperator* to add some.

```
DimEmployee[UnaryOperator] =
IF(
    LEFT( DimEmployee[MiddleName], 1 ) < "J",
    "+",
    IF( LEFT(DimEmployee[MiddleName], 1 ) < "S", "-", "~" )
)
```

The value returned can then be added to the *FullName* calculated column created earlier in this chapter to make the calculations easier to debug.

```
DimEmployee[FullName] =
DimEmployee[FirstName] & " " & DimEmployee[LastName] & " (" & DimEmployee[UnaryOperator] & ")"
```

Figure 10-11 shows the part of a parent/child hierarchy that this section will show you how to build.

⊟Roberto Tamburello (+)	154.577
⊟Dylan Miller (+)	-39.25
Diane Margheim (-)	40.8654
Gigi Matthew (-)	40.8654
Michael Raheem (+)	42.4808
Gail Erickson (+)	32.6923
Jossef Goldberg (+)	32.6923
Michael Sullivan (+)	36.0577
⊟Ovidiu Cracium (~)	0
Janice Galvin (-)	25
Thierry D'Hers (+)	25
Rob Walters (+)	59.6924
Sharon Salavaria (+)	32.6923

FIGURE 10-11 This shows the parent/child hierarchy with unary operators.

The example shown in Figure 10-11 uses a measure that is based on the value of the *BaseRate* column on DimEmployee; making it aggregate correctly is the toughest part of the problem, and that is the topic of the rest of this section. As you would expect, it aggregates according to the unary operators shown for each Employee, so, for example, the value for Dylan Miller is calculated as follows.

$-40.8654 - 40.8654 + 42.4808 = -39.25$

The first point to note when approaching this problem is that the measure value for each item in the hierarchy can be calculated from the values of the leaf items underneath it; that is, the items that have no other items underneath them. So the value for Dylan Miller is calculated from the values for Diane Margheim, Gigi Matthew, and Michael Raheem; the value for Roberto Tamburello is derived from the values for Diane Margheim, Gigi Matthew, Michael Raheem, Gail Erickson, Jossef Goldberg, Michael Sullivan, Janice Galvin, Thierry D'Hers, Rob Walters, and Sharon Salavaria. These leaf items can be identified in the hierarchy by creating a calculated column called *IsLeaf* with the following definition, which returns *True* for all leaf items.

```
DimEmployee[IsLeaf] =
COUNTROWS(
    FILTER(
        ALL( DimEmployee ),
        PATHCONTAINS( DimEmployee[EmployeePath], EARLIER( DimEmployee[EmployeeKey] ) ) )
    )
) = 1
```

A further complication in DimEmployee is that it is a type 2 slowly changing dimension, so it is also necessary to identify items that look like leaf items but that are actually older instances of non-leaf items. In addition, some of the data in the Employee table is dirty: For example, a type 2 change has taken place for the employee named Laura Norman, but other rows in the table still refer to the non-current record. To ensure that this example aggregates properly the dirty data must be ignored, and you cannot rely on the contents of the *Status* column alone. A second calculated column, called *IsSCDLeaf*, is needed to do this.

```
DimEmployee[IsSCDLeaf] =
COUNTROWS(
    FILTER( ALL( DimEmployee ),
        DimEmployee[EmployeeNationalIDAlternateKey]
            = EARLIER( DimEmployee[EmployeeNationalIDAlternateKey] )
        && DimEmployee[IsLeaf] = FALSE
    )
) = 0
```

The second key point to note is that although each item's value can be derived from its leaves' values, the question of whether a leaf value is added or subtracted when aggregating is determined not only by its own unary operator but also by that of all the items in the hierarchy between it and the item whose value is to be calculated. To go back to the example of Roberto Tamburello and his leaves, although Janice Galvin has the unary operator—associated with her because Ovidiu Cracium has a tilde (~)—Janice's effective unary operator when aggregating up to Roberto's level is also a tilde (~). The effective unary operator for each leaf member can be pre-calculated in three more calculated columns. (The lowest level, level five, does not need to be aggregated up, and level four uses the unary operator column that already exists.). Here is an example of the expression used for the calculated column *SignToUseL3* for level three—the level Roberto Tamburello is on—to calculate the effective unary operators for each leaf.

```
DimEmployee[SignToUseL3] =
IF(
    [HierarchyDepth] = 4,
    [UnaryOperator],
    SWITCH(
        LOOKUPVALUE(
            DimEmployee[UnaryOperator],
            DimEmployee[EmployeeKey],
            PATHITEM( DimEmployee[EmployeePath], 4, 1 )
        ),
        "~", "~",
        "+", SWITCH( DimEmployee[UnaryOperator], "+", "+", "-", "-", "~", "~" ),
```

```
        "-", SWITCH( DimEmployee[UnaryOperator], "+", "-", "-", "+", "~", "~" )
    )
)
```

For the level above, level two, the expression for the calculated column *SignToUseL2* is

```
DimEmployee[SignToUseL2] =
IF(
    [HierarchyDepth] = 3,
    [UnaryOperator],
    SWITCH(
        LOOKUPVALUE(
            DimEmployee[UnaryOperator],
            DimEmployee[EmployeeKey],
            PATHITEM( DimEmployee[EmployeePath], 3, 1 )
        ),
        "~", "~",
        "+", SWITCH( DimEmployee[SignToUseL3], "+", "+", "-", "-", "~", "~" ),
        "-", SWITCH( DimEmployee[SignToUseL3], "+", "-", "-", "+", "~", "~" )
    )
)
```

And for level one, the expression for the calculated column *SignToUseL1* is

```
DimEmployee[SignToUseL1] =
IF(
    [HierarchyDepth] = 2,
    [UnaryOperator],
    SWITCH(
        LOOKUPVALUE(
            DimEmployee[UnaryOperator],
            DimEmployee[EmployeeKey],
            PATHITEM( DimEmployee[EmployeePath], 2, 1 )
        ),
        "~", "~",
        "+", SWITCH( DimEmployee[SignToUseL2], "+", "+", "-", "-", "~", "~" ),
        "-", SWITCH( DimEmployee[SignToUseL2], "+", "-", "-", "+", "~", "~" )
    )
)
```

The logic is as follows. Taking level one as an example for each of the leaves, if the leaf is at level two (immediately below level one), use the unary operator. If it is lower, take the effective unary operator that was calculated for the level below and combine it with the unary operator of the parent of the leaf at level two to get the new effective unary operator.

The effective unary operators are shown in Figure 10-12.

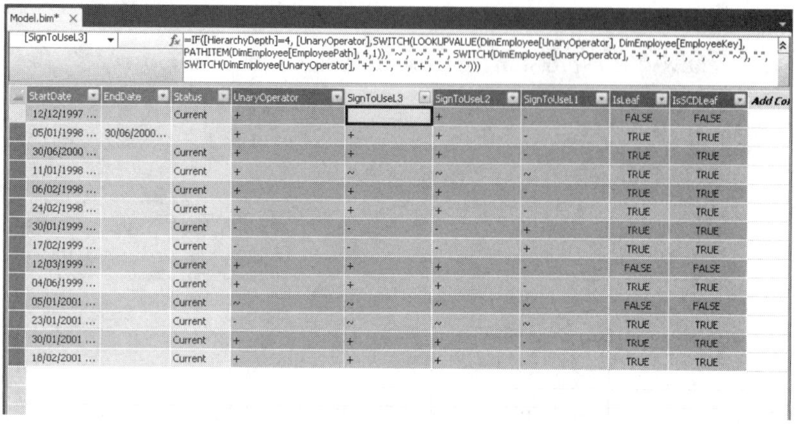

StartDate	EndDate	Status	UnaryOperator	SignToUseL3	SignToUseL2	SignToUseL1	IsLeaf	IsSCDLeaf
12/12/1997 ...		Current	+		+	-	FALSE	FALSE
05/01/1998 ...	30/06/2000...		+	+	+	-	TRUE	TRUE
30/06/2000 ...		Current	+	+	+	-	TRUE	TRUE
11/01/1998 ...		Current	+	~	~	~	TRUE	TRUE
06/02/1998 ...		Current	+	+	+	-	TRUE	TRUE
24/02/1998 ...		Current	+	+	+	-	TRUE	TRUE
30/01/1999 ...		Current	-	-	-	+	TRUE	TRUE
17/02/1999 ...		Current	-	-	-	+	TRUE	TRUE
12/03/1999 ...		Current	+	+	+	-	FALSE	FALSE
04/06/1999 ...		Current	+	+	+	-	TRUE	TRUE
05/01/2001 ...		Current	~	~	~	~	FALSE	FALSE
23/01/2001 ...		Current	-	~	~	~	TRUE	TRUE
30/01/2001 ...		Current	+	+	+	-	TRUE	TRUE
18/02/2001 ...		Current	+	+	+	-	TRUE	TRUE

FIGURE 10-12 This shows the effective unary operators used at each level in the hierarchy.

The final step is to create a measure that aggregates values by using the correct set of effective unary operators for each level. Here is the definition for that measure.

```
Base Rate With Unary Operators :=
IF(
    [Current Hierarchy Depth] > [Max Depth], BLANK(),
    IF(
        [Current Hierarchy Depth] =[Max Depth],
        SUM( DimEmployee[BaseRate] ),
        SWITCH(
            [Current Hierarchy Depth],
            4,
                CALCULATE(
                    SUM( DimEmployee[BaseRate] ),
                    DimEmployee[UnaryOperator] = "+",
                    DimEmployee[IsSCDLeaf] = TRUE
                )
                -
                CALCULATE(
                    SUM( DimEmployee[BaseRate] ),
                    DimEmployee[UnaryOperator] = "-",
                    DimEmployee[IsSCDLeaf] = TRUE
                ),
            3,
                CALCULATE(
                    SUM( DimEmployee[BaseRate] ),
                    DimEmployee[SignToUseL3] = "+",
                    DimEmployee[IsSCDLeaf] = TRUE
                )
                -
                CALCULATE(
                    SUM( DimEmployee[BaseRate] ),
                    DimEmployee[SignToUseL3] = "-",
                    DimEmployee[IsSCDLeaf] = TRUE
                ),
```

```
        2,
            CALCULATE(
                SUM( DimEmployee[BaseRate] ),
                DimEmployee[SignToUseL2] = "+",
                DimEmployee[IsSCDLeaf] = TRUE
            )
            -
            CALCULATE(
                SUM( DimEmployee[BaseRate] ),
                DimEmployee[SignToUseL2] = "-",
                DimEmployee[IsSCDLeaf] = TRUE
            ),
        1,
            CALCULATE(
                SUM( DimEmployee[BaseRate] ),
                DimEmployee[SignToUseL1] = "+",
                DimEmployee[IsSCDLeaf] = TRUE
            )
            -
            CALCULATE(
                SUM( DimEmployee[BaseRate] ),
                DimEmployee[SignToUseL1] = "-",
                DimEmployee[IsSCDLeaf]=TRUE
            )
        )
    )
)
```

The logic for this calculation is as follows:

- If the item on the hierarchy is below the maximum depth that you want to display, return a *BLANK()* value. This is the same technique described in the "Handling Empty Items" section earlier in this chapter.

- If the item is at the bottom of the hierarchy, return the sum of the *BaseRate* column.

- For all other levels:

  - Find the sum of all leaves underneath the current item that have the effective unary operator +.

  - Subtract the sum of all leaves underneath the current item that have the effective unary operator −.

Notice that in the code relating to the last bullet, the *CALCULATE()* statement sums all the items that have effective unary operators of + or −; this is more efficient than using *SUMX()* and iterating over each individual leaf, even if that approach might be more readable.

Summary

This chapter demonstrated how many types of hierarchy can be implemented in the Tabular model. Regular hierarchies are important for the usability of your model and can be built very easily. Parent/ child hierarchies, when they are needed, present more of a problem, but this can be solved with clever use of DAX in calculated columns and measures.

Data Modeling in Tabular

Data modeling plays a very important role in Tabular development. Choosing the right data model can dramatically change the performance and usability of the overall solution. Even if we cannot cover all the many data modeling techniques available to analytical database designers, we believe that it is important to dedicate a full chapter to data modeling to give you some information about which techniques work best with Tabular.

In the data warehouse world, there are two main approaches to the database design: the school of William Inmon and the school of Ralph Kimball. Additionally, if data comes from online transaction processing (OLTP) databases, there is always the possibility that an analytical solution can be built directly on top of the OLTP system. In this chapter, you learn how to work with these different systems from the Tabular point of view, which one is best, and what approach to take with each data model.

Finally, because we believe many readers of this book already have a solid understanding of data modeling for Multidimensional, in this chapter you learn the main differences between data modeling for Multidimensional and data modeling for Tabular. Because they are different systems, the two types of BI semantic modeling (BISM) require a different approach when designing the underlying database.

Understanding Different Data Modeling Techniques

Before we discuss the details of how to use Tabular over different data models, it is worth learning the different kinds of data modeling techniques with which you are likely to work when developing a Tabular solution.

Data sources for analytics usually conform to three broad categories of data modeling:

- The OLTP databases are normally composed of one or many sources of data holding all the company information. This type of database is not specifically designed for analytical needs, but it is always present, and it is often the original source for any kind of analysis.

- William Inmon's theory is to build a slightly denormalized version of a database that is capable of holding all the company information along with its historical changes (the Corporate Information Factory). This database should be independent from any OLTP system already in place and be designed to answer most of, if not all, the analytical requirements of the company. The data warehouse, after it is built by using Inmon's techniques, then feeds separate data marts containing the analytical databases exposed in a dimensional model.

- Ralph Kimball's theory is different from Inmon's because it does not require building an initial relational data warehouse. However, following Kimball's bus technique, you build single data marts that, following the conformed dimension model, merge in a single data warehouse composed of the sum of all data marts.

It is beyond the scope of this book to describe in detail the different techniques adopted by followers of the Inmon and Kimball schools or any of their variations. The goal of this chapter is to point out the major differences between the two.

In Inmon's view, the different OLTP systems need to be loaded inside a physical database that models all the corporate information. From there, one or more data marts are created to enable users to generate reports. In Figure 11-1, you see the diagram for an Inmon solution.

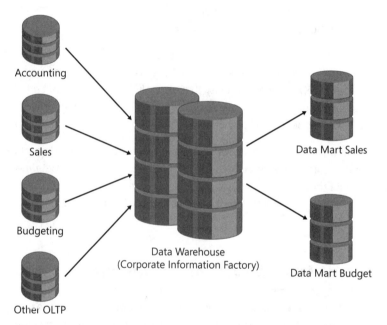

FIGURE 11-1 In the Inmon vision of a BI solution, the relational data warehouse plays a central role.

Kimball's vision is different because, in Kimball's methodology, the data warehouse is nothing but the sum of all the data marts. Kimball's model is somewhat simpler in concept because there is no need to build a corporate information factory. However, Kimball's methodology is based heavily on dimensional modeling because the dimensional model is the only model for the corporate information; there is no space for a relational data model. Figure 11-2 shows a diagram of a Kimball solution.

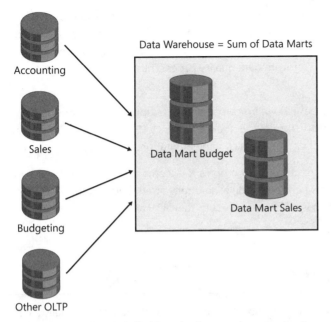

FIGURE 11-2 In the Kimball vision of a data warehouse you only use dimensional modeling

Note that both Inmon and Kimball expose, at the end, a dimensional model. Inmon has an additional step with a relational data model, whereas Kimball goes directly to dimensional modeling. The OLTP database, however, is very different from a data warehouse. Thus, it requires some special considerations, which you learn about in the next section.

Using the OLTP Database

The OLTP database can be a sales system, customer relationship management (CRM), accounting manager, or—in general—any kind of database users adopt to manage their business.

Sometimes the source is not a real database; it might consist of files generated by processes running on a host, Microsoft Excel workbooks, or other media. In this case, you can still import it into a simple Microsoft SQL Server database, which is usually your best option. Therefore, regardless of the specific media used to read the source, we refer to it as a database.

The OLTP database is not built to quickly answer massive queries such as the one that Tabular issues when processing the database; its main task is to answer daily queries that often touch a reduced set of information. Nevertheless, you might ask yourself whether you really need to build a data warehouse to create an analytical system. The answer is yes. You need a data warehouse.

There are very rare situations in which data can flow directly from the OLTP to the analytical data model, but these are so specific that their description is outside the scope of this book.

Building an analytical solution is complex work that starts with the correct design for the data marts. If you have a dimensional data mart, you have a database that holds dimensions and fact tables in which you can perform cleansing and computations. We, the authors, have personally never seen an OLTP database that did not suffer from data quality issues. Thus, you need a place to cleanse the data.

If you rely solely on the OLTP database, building complex queries upon it, you might finish your first data model in less time, but the structure of the queries to the OLTP database will be so complex that you will lose all the time you saved at the first new implementation.

Moreover, you will not be able to create complex models to accommodate user needs and make your solution fit the tool requirements perfectly. Tabular solutions often require a specific approach when developing a data model, which is different from both the OLTP and the dimensional data modeling techniques.

Working with Dimensional Models

Whether you follow Kimball or Inmon methodology, the final analytical database is usually a data mart. A *data mart* is a database that is modeled according to the rules of Kimball's dimensional modeling methodology and is composed of fact and dimension tables. In this section, we review the basics of dimensional modeling to ensure you have a good background on the topic.

The core of a data mart dimensional structure is that of separating the database into only two types of entity:

- **Dimension**   A dimension is an analytical object used to separate numbers. A dimension can be made of products, customers, time, or any other entity used to analyze your numbers. Some facts about dimensions are:

    - Dimensions have attributes. An attribute of a product can be its color, its manufacturer, or its weight. An attribute of a date might be its weekday or its month. Each dimension has a unique and specific set of attributes.

    - Dimensions normally have both natural and surrogate keys. The natural key is the original product code, customer ID, or real date. The surrogate key is usually a new, meaningless integer number used in the data marts to join facts to dimensions.

    - Dimensions change over time, and the term *slowly changing dimension* refers to a dimension that is updated over time.

    - A dimension has relationships with facts. A dimension exists to qualify numeric information contained in facts and, to perform this, it must have a relationship with facts.

    - A dimension might reference other dimensions, correlate to other dimensions, or both, even if its main purpose is to join to facts. Data models in which dimensions are related to one another are more complex to use and analyze, but these relationships are often needed.

- **Fact**   A fact is something that has happened or has been measured. A fact can be the sale of a product to a customer, the total number of sales of a specific item during a month, the number of working hours of an employee, or any other fact expressed as a number. From the analytical point of view, a fact is a number that you want to aggregate in several forms to generate reports and get insights into your data.

  - A fact is related to several dimensions, but facts are not related to other facts in any way.

  - Facts are normally related to dimensions through the surrogate key.

  - Facts are interesting when they are aggregated at a higher level. You are not normally interested in the details of a single sale; you want to analyze sales of one month against sales of another month at a higher level of abstraction.

Both facts and dimensions are stored in tables. Fact tables contain numeric data that is to be aggregated, whereas dimension tables contain numeric and nonnumeric values that are used to slice facts. Several categories of dimensions listed here might need some special handling in Tabular:

- Type 1 slowly changing dimensions are dimensions in which you are interested in only the last value of any attribute. Whenever the source changes, you update your dimension accordingly, losing the previous value of attributes.

- Type 2 slowly changing dimensions are dimensions in which the business key might be duplicated because these dimensions contain several versions of the same item to track their updates.

- Degenerate dimensions are attributes that are stored directly in the fact table, and are normally used for dimensions that have a granularity of the same order of magnitude as the fact table.

- Junk dimensions are dimensions created by merging several attributes that do not belong to any other dimension, which you don't want to keep as separate dimensions to avoid dimensional explosion.

There are other data structures, such as factless fact tables used to mimic many-to-many relationships, about which you learn in Chapter 12, "Using Advanced Tabular Relationships."

Generally speaking, dimensional models are a perfect data source for a Tabular solution. It is important to note that, although in Multidimensional the usage of dimensional modeling as a source is fairly mandatory, in Tabular this requirement is very relaxed. There is no real need to divide the complete data model into facts and dimensions because these entities, after they are loaded in Tabular, become simple tables. This has both advantages and disadvantages, which we cover in the next sections of this chapter.

Working with Slowly Changing Dimensions

Using slowly changing dimensions (SCD) in Tabular is straightforward. You see in the DimProduct table that the table identifier is *ProductKey*, which is the surrogate key, whereas the business key is stored in *ProductAlternateKey*. A new row is added to this table whenever a column changes a value. In Figure 11-3, you see an example with two products selected, each of which has three rows.

Produc...	ProductAlternatekey	EnglishProductName	StandardCost	ListPrice	StartDate	EndDate	Status
296	FR-M94B-42	HL Mountain Frame - Black, 42	$617.03	$1,191.17	7/1/2001 12:00:00 AM	6/30/2002 12:00:00 AM	
297	FR-M94B-42	HL Mountain Frame - Black, 42	$653.70	$1,226.91	7/1/2002 12:00:00 AM	6/30/2003 12:00:00 AM	
298	FR-M94B-42	HL Mountain Frame - Black, 42	$739.04	$1,349.60	7/1/2003 12:00:00 AM		Current
304	FR-M94B-38	HL Mountain Frame - Black, 38	$617.03	$1,191.17	7/1/2001 12:00:00 AM	6/30/2002 12:00:00 AM	
305	FR-M94B-38	HL Mountain Frame - Black, 38	$653.70	$1,226.91	7/1/2002 12:00:00 AM	6/30/2003 12:00:00 AM	
306	FR-M94B-38	HL Mountain Frame - Black, 38	$739.04	$1,349.60	7/1/2003 12:00:00 AM		Current

FIGURE 11-3 With SCD, each product might have more than one version.

In Figure 11-3, the price and the standard cost of the product change over time, and the table dimension keeps track of those changes, creating new rows and using the three canonical SCD handling columns: *StartDate*, *EndDate*, and *Status*.

The current price of the product is the one stored in the row with Status equal to Current; other rows represent old versions of the same product. If you browse this data model by using Excel, you can produce a report that shows sales made at different prices, as you see in Figure 11-4.

ProductAlternateKey	(Multiple Items)				

SumOfSalesAmount	Column Labels				
Row Labels	2001	2002	2003	2004	Grand Total
☐ HL Mountain Frame - Black, 38	50,029.30	148,172.51	208,034.71	95,551.68	501,788.20
1191.1739	50,029.30	42,167.55			92,196.85
1226.9091		106,004.95	89,809.75		195,814.70
1349.6			118,224.96	95,551.68	213,776.64
☐ HL Mountain Frame - Black, 42	62,179.27	291,056.20	387,212.52	161,142.24	901,590.23
1191.1739	62,179.27	64,323.39			126,502.66
1226.9091		226,732.81	152,382.12		379,114.93
1349.6			234,830.40	161,142.24	395,972.64
Grand Total	112,208.58	439,228.71	595,247.23	256,693.92	1,403,378.43

FIGURE 11-4 By using SCD, you can analyze sales made at different prices over time.

This behavior of SCD is normal and expected because the *ListPrice* column holds the historical price. Nevertheless, a very frequent request is to slice data by using both the current and the historical value of an attribute (the price in our example) to make comparisons. The problem is that the table does not contain the current price of the product for all the rows.

This scenario is often solved at the relational level by creating two tables: one with historical values and one with the current values, maintaining two keys in the fact table for the two dimensions. The drawback of this solution is that two tables are needed to hold a few columns that might be both historical and current and, at the end, the data model exposed to the user is more complex both to use and to understand.

In Tabular, there is an interesting alternative to the creation of two tables. You can create some calculated columns in the dimension table that compute the current value of the attribute inside the Tabular data model without the need to modify the relational data model.

Using the Adventure Works example, the CurrentListPrice can be computed by using the *Status* column and the following formula.

```
CurrentListPrice =
CALCULATE(
    VALUES( DimProduct[ListPrice] ),
    ALLEXCEPT( DimProduct, DimProduct[ProductAlternateKey] ),
    DimProduct[Status] = "Current"
)
```

Inside *CALCULATE, ALLEXCEPT* filters all the products with the same *ProductAlternateKey*, whereas the further condition on the status filters only the row with the current status. *VALUES* computes the distinct values of ListPrice, but because of the content of the table, you know that a single row will be found with these characteristics. Thus, *VALUES* is converted to a scalar value (a table with one row and one column, which is converted into a single value when needed), and the formula returns the current price of the product.

In Figure 11-5, you see the result of this calculated column.

Produc...	ProductAlternateKey	EnglishProductName	StandardCost	ListPrice	StartDate	EndDate	Status	CurrentListPrice
296	FR-M94B-42	HL Mountain Frame - Black, 42	$617.03	$1,191.17	7/1/2001 12:00:00 AM	6/30/2002 12:00:00 AM		1349.6
297	FR-M94B-42	HL Mountain Frame - Black, 42	$653.70	$1,226.91	7/1/2002 12:00:00 AM	6/30/2003 12:00:00 AM		1349.6
298	FR-M94B-42	HL Mountain Frame - Black, 42	$739.04	$1,349.60	7/1/2003 12:00:00 AM		Current	1349.6
304	FR-M94B-38	HL Mountain Frame - Black, 38	$617.03	$1,191.17	7/1/2001 12:00:00 AM	6/30/2002 12:00:00 AM		1349.6
305	FR-M94B-38	HL Mountain Frame - Black, 38	$653.70	$1,226.91	7/1/2002 12:00:00 AM	6/30/2003 12:00:00 AM		1349.6
306	FR-M94B-38	HL Mountain Frame - Black, 38	$739.04	$1,349.60	7/1/2003 12:00:00 AM		Current	1349.6

FIGURE 11-5 The *CurrentListPrice* calculated column always contains the last price of a product.

In Figure 11-6, you see a Microsoft PivotTable containing both the CurrentListPrice and the historical ListPrice.

ProductAlternateKey (Multiple Items)

SumOfSalesAmount Row Labels	Column Labels 2001	2002	2003	2004	Grand Total
HL Mountain Frame - Black, 38	50,029.30	148,172.51	208,034.71	95,551.68	501,788.20
1349.6	50,029.30	148,172.51	208,034.71	95,551.68	501,788.20
1191.1739	50,029.30	42,167.55			92,196.85
1226.9091		106,004.95	89,809.75		195,814.70
1349.6			118,224.96	95,551.68	213,776.64
HL Mountain Frame - Black, 42	62,179.27	291,056.20	387,212.52	161,142.24	901,590.23
1349.6	62,179.27	291,056.20	387,212.52	161,142.24	901,590.23
1191.1739	62,179.27	64,323.39			126,502.66
1226.9091		226,732.81	152,382.12		379,114.93
1349.6			234,830.40	161,142.24	395,972.64
Grand Total	112,208.58	439,228.71	595,247.23	256,693.92	1,403,378.43

FIGURE 11-6 It is easier to perform comparisons by using CurrentListPrice and ListPrice.

The interesting aspect of this solution is that the calculated column is computed during the Tabular database processing, when all data is in memory, and without persisting it on disk with all the inevitable locking and deadlock issues.

Data Stored in the Tabular Data Model

In scenarios such as the one of slowly changing dimensions, some columns are computed in the Tabular data model only. That is, they are not stored in SQL Server tables. If the Tabular solution is the only reporting system, this solution works fine. If, however, other systems are querying the relational data model directly to provide some kind of reporting, it is better to persist this information on the database so that all of the reporting system sees at a coherent view of data.

Before leaving this topic, note that the formula for CurrentListPrice uses the presence of a column that clearly identifies the current version of the product. If you face a database in which no such column exists, you can still compute the CurrentListPrice by using only the *StartDate* and *EndDate* columns.

If you have a data model that contains an EndDate with *BLANK* to indicate the current version of the product, you can update the formula so that it searches for the only row containing *BLANK* in the *EndDate* column.

```
CurrentListPrice =
CALCULATE(
    VALUES( DimProduct[ListPrice] ),
    ALLEXCEPT( DimProduct, DimProduct[ProductAlternateKey] ),
    ISBLANK( DimProduct[EndDate] )
)
```

Another version of the formula is needed in the uncommon case when you have only StartDate available. The formula is slightly more complicated because it must search for the row that has the maximum date among all the dates of the product.

```
CurrentListPrice =
CALCULATE(
    VALUES( DimProduct[ListPrice] ),
    FILTER (
        ALLEXCEPT( DimProduct, DimProduct[ProductAlternateKey] ),
        DimProduct[StartDate] = CALCULATE(
            MAX( DimProduct[StartDate] ),
            ALLEXCEPT( DimProduct, DimProduct[ProductAlternateKey] )
        )
    )
)
```

You can use a similar pattern to compute the current value by using a minimum of information (the start of validity of a row).

Working with Degenerate Dimensions

Another common, nonstandard dimensional modeling technique is degenerate dimensions, and in this section, you learn how to handle this technique. Degenerate dimensions are commonly used in Multidimensional when an attribute has a granularity that is very similar to that of the fact table and is used to expose the metadata values that are, in effect, stored inside the fact table.

In the Adventure Works data warehouse, you see in Figure 11-7 the *FactResellerSales* attribute in the *SalesOrderNumber* column, which is a string stored in the fact table that represents the order number.

Produc...	OrderDat...	DueDateKey	ShipDateKey	SalesOrderNumber	ResellerKey
317	20010801	20010813	20010808	SO43912	403
322	20010801	20010813	20010808	SO43912	403
316	20010801	20010813	20010808	SO43912	403
270	20010801	20010813	20010808	SO43912	403
314	20010801	20010813	20010808	SO43912	403
215	20010801	20010813	20010808	SO43912	403
285	20010801	20010813	20010808	SO43912	403
272	20011101	20011113	20011108	SO44564	403
326	20011101	20011113	20011108	SO44564	403

FIGURE 11-7 The *SalesOrderNumber* column is stored inside the fact table.

Because *SalesOrderNumber* is an attribute that has many values, the data modeler decided not to create a separate dimension to hold the attribute but to store it directly inside the fact table, following the best practices for dimensional modeling.

When facing such a scenario in Multidimensional, you are forced to create a dimension to hold SalesOrderNumber, and this dimension is based on the fact table. This kind of modeling often leads to long processing times due to the way SQL Server Analysis Services (SSAS) queries dimensions to get the list of distinct values of each attribute.

 Important In Tabular, there is no need to create a separate dimension to hold this attribute, because the very concept of dimension is missing; each table in Tabular is a table and can be used as both a dimension and a fact table, depending on the need.

Using Snapshot Fact Tables

There are several scenarios in which a big fact table is aggregated into a smaller one, called a snapshot fact table, which contains periodic aggregated snapshots of the bigger fact table. A good example of this is warehouse stocking. You might have a table holding all sales and transactions of goods, but to speed up querying, you often store a monthly snapshot of the product stock so that monthly reports do not need to traverse the complete fact table to compute the periodic stock. In this section, you learn how to handle scenarios such as this.

Figure 11-8 shows a classic example of a snapshot table: the FactProductInventory table, which, in the Adventure Works data warehouse, holds the daily inventory of products.

FIGURE 11-8 FactProductInventory is a classic snapshot table.

This snapshot table contains, for each day, the number of products that entered and exited the warehouse and, to query it, you must implement a semi-additive pattern (which you learned to manage in Chapter 8, "Understanding Time Intelligence in DAX"). Note that snapshot fact tables are computed during an additional extract, transform, and load (ETL) step, aggregating the fact table that holds all the transactions and that stores the original values.

Snapshot fact tables reduce the computational effort needed to retrieve the aggregated value. There is no reason to use this modeling technique except to get better performance, and in that respect, they are similar to the creation of other aggregate tables. However, Snapshot fact tables have the unwelcome characteristic of reduced flexibility. In fact, FactProductInventory holds some values: the unit cost and the in/out numbers. If, for example, you wanted to hold the minimum and maximum number of items sold in a single transaction, or the weighted average cost, you would still need to scan the transaction fact table to compute these values.

In other words, whenever you create a snapshot fact table, you are fixing, during ETL time, the kind of analysis that can be performed by using the snapshot because you are storing data at a predefined granularity and already aggregated by using a predefined aggregation function. Any other kind of analysis requires much greater effort, either from scanning the original fact table or updating the snapshot table and adding the new columns.

In Tabular, you can use the tremendous speed of the xVelocity in-memory engine to get rid of snapshots. Scanning a fact table is usually so fast that snapshots are not needed. Based on our experience, there is no visible gain in taking a snapshot of a fact table with less than a hundred million rows. When you have greater sizes—that is, in the billions range—snapshots might be useful. Nevertheless, the bar is so high that in many data warehouses, you can avoid taking any snapshots, greatly reducing the ETL effort and gaining data model flexibility. In some cases, a snapshot table could be many times larger than the transaction table on which it is based if you have a large number of products, you have relatively few transactions, and you take snapshots daily.

Finally, it is worth describing a common scenario when snapshots are not only useless, they also become harmful. If you have a big fact table, say one billion rows, containing transactions, you want to create a snapshot to get monthly aggregated values. This is fine; the size of the fact table justifies the creation of a snapshot. But then you might be tempted to use this snapshot to speed up other measures at the daily level, and this can cause trouble. The following scenario is an example. In Figure 11-9, you see that a MonthlySnapshot table is added to the Adventure Works data warehouse, which contains the monthly sold quantity for each product.

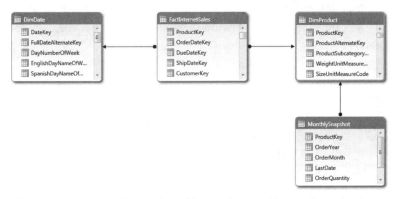

FIGURE 11-9 The MonthlySnapshot table contains monthly snapshots of order quantity.

You can create a YTD order quantity column by using the following formula.

```
QtyYTD :=
CALCULATE(
    SUM( MonthlySnapshot[OrderQuantity] ),
    FILTER (
        MonthlySnapshot,
        MonthlySnapshot[LastDate] <= MAX( DimDate[FullDateAlternateKey] ) &&
        MonthlySnapshot[OrderYear] = MAX( DimDate[CalendarYear] )
    )
)
```

Clearly, this formula, by working on the snapshot table, can be computed at the month level only. It will provide wrong values at the daily level, as you can check in Figure 11-10, which shows an Excel PivotTable with the QtyYTD measure and a simple *SUM* of FactInternetSales[OrderQuantity].

CalendarYear   2003 🔽

Row Labels 🔽	QtyYTD	SumOfQty
⊞ January	244	244
⊟ February	516	272
2/1/2003	244	10
2/2/2003	244	10
2/3/2003	244	9
2/4/2003	244	17
2/5/2003	244	8
2/6/2003	244	14
2/7/2003	244	8
2/8/2003	244	11
2/9/2003	244	11
2/10/2003	244	7
2/11/2003	244	4
2/12/2003	244	10
2/13/2003	244	11
2/14/2003	244	11

FIGURE 11-10 The YTD computed over the snapshot does not work at the daily level.

You might be tempted to compute the QtyYTD by working with both tables: the snapshot to reach the beginning of the current month and the original fact table to compensate for the transactions that occurred during the current month. At the end, the number of rows Tabular needs to compute is much lower, and the algorithm should be faster. The formula, however, is not very easy to author, but it can be done with the following code.

```
QtyYTDMixed :=
    CALCULATE(
        SUM( MonthlySnapshot[OrderQuantity] ),
        FILTER(
            MonthlySnapshot,
            MonthlySnapshot[LastDate] < MAX( DimDate[FullDateAlternateKey] )
                && MonthlySnapshot[OrderYear] = MAX( DimDate[CalendarYear] )
        )
    )
    +
    CALCULATE(
        SUM( FactInternetSales[OrderQuantity] ),
        FILTER(
            ALLEXCEPT( DimDate, DimDate[EnglishMonthName], DimDate[CalendarYear] ),
            DimDate[FullDateAlternateKey] <= MAX ( DimDate[FullDateAlternateKey] )
        )
    );
```

This code works well, as Figure 11-11 illustrates, and accomplishes your goal of using the fewest number of rows to compute the correct result.

CalendarYear 2003 ⊤

Row Labels ⊤	QtyYTD	SumOfQty	QtyYTDMixed
⊞ January	244	244	244
⊟ February	516	272	516
2/1/2003	244	10	254
2/2/2003	244	10	264
2/3/2003	244	9	273
2/4/2003	244	17	290
2/5/2003	244	8	298
2/6/2003	244	14	312
2/7/2003	244	8	320
2/8/2003	244	11	331
2/9/2003	244	11	342
2/10/2003	244	7	349
2/11/2003	244	4	353
2/12/2003	244	10	363
2/13/2003	244	11	374
2/14/2003	244	11	385

FIGURE 11-11 The YTD can be computed on both the snapshot and the fact table.

Spend some time to consider whether computing YTD this way is a good idea. As you recall from Chapter 9, "Understanding xVelocity and DirectQuery," the query time of the xVelocity engine is not very sensitive to the amount of data that must be retrieved, but is sensitive to the size of the columns in the complete table. Thus, computing the *SUM* of FactInternetSales[OrderQuantity] for one month is not much faster than computing the same *SUM* over a complete year.

It turns out that the QtyYTDMixed measure is in fact slower to evaluate than a simple YTD that scans the complete fact table because the mixed measure must scan two tables, whereas a simpler YTD on the fact table scans only one of them.

Thus, the usage of snapshots in Tabular is very seldom a convenient choice. It is much better to keep simpler formulas that scan big tables than to make complex formulas that try to speed up the algorithm. Even if this behavior is sometimes counterintuitive, we strongly suggest double-checking performance on sample data before designing a complex data model with snapshot tables; you might save time and money by using a simpler data model and getting better performance.

Computing Weighted Aggregations

A very common scenario, especially in financial applications, is the need to compute weighted aggregations. This scenario needs different handling in Tabular and in Multidimensional due to the difference between the two flavors of SSAS. In this section, you learn these differences and, most importantly, the reason Tabular needs a specific data model.

We use, as an example, the computation of the average sell price of products sold by Adventure Works. In Figure 11-12, you see the FactResellerSales table, in which the last two columns are *OrderQuantity* and *UnitPrice*.

Produc...			OrderDat...			DueDateKey		ShipDateKey		SalesOrderNumber		OrderQuantity		UnitPrice	
436			20040501			20040513		20040508		SO69496		1		$356.90	
390			20040501			20040513		20040508		SO69502		1		$672.29	
384			20040501			20040513		20040508		SO69519		1		$672.29	
600			20040501			20040513		20040508		SO69533		1		$323.99	
559			20040501			20040513		20040508		SO69565		1		$12.14	
586			20040601			20040613		20040608		SO71850		1		$445.41	
498			20040601			20040613		20040608		SO71883		1		$602.35	
543			20040601			20040613		20040608		SO71927		1		$37.25	
315			20010701			20010713		20010708		SO43684		2		$874.79	
347			20010701			20010713		20010708		SO43695		2		$2,039.99	
346			20010901			20010913		20010908		SO44098		2		$2,039.99	

FIGURE 11-12 *OrderQuantity* and *UnitPrice* are useful to compute the WeightedAveragePrice.

The weighted average sell price is not to be computed as a simple average of the price because you want to weight the sell price by the quantity so that most-sold products count more against the average. It is easy to note the difference between the two values by using this SQL query.

```
SELECT
    WeightedAveragePrice = SUM( OrderQuantity * UnitPrice ) / SUM( OrderQuantity ),
    AveragePrice = AVG( UnitPrice )
FROM
    FactResellerSales
```

The results are different: The weighted average is 337.74, whereas the average price is 444.31.

Now, when you compute this value in Tabular, there are two distinct options:

- You can use an iterator such as *AVGX*, making it iterate over the fact table and compute the weight expression for each row. This solution looks naïve because it requires an iteration over the complete fact table. In this simple scenario, the formula for WeightedAveragePrice is the following.

```
= SUMX(
        FactResellerSales,
        FactResellerSales[OrderQuantity] * FactResellerSales[UnitPrice]
  )
  /
  SUM( FactResellerSales[OrderQuantity] )
```

- You can store the value of OrderQuantity * UnitPrice in a calculated column and then use *SUM* instead of *SUMX*. This solution is usually preferred because it does not require an iteration but uses internal optimizations of *SUM* in Tabular. Finally, if you are accustomed to Multidimensional projects, using this technique enables you to use aggregations and, thus, to compute *SUM* in a quick way. After you define the calculated column *WeightedPrice*, the formula for the WeightedAveragePrice is as follows.

```
= SUM( FactResellerSales[WeightedPrice] ) / SUM( FactResellerSales[OrderQuantity] )
```

For small datasets, smaller than 10 million rows, the difference between the two solutions is negligible because xVelocity is so fast, but in big datasets, some interesting considerations are worth learning. It turns out that *SUMX* outperforms *SUM* on larger datasets for the following reasons.

Suppose that you chose to use a calculated column to hold the value of OrderQuantity * UnitPrice. In Figure 11-13, you see the FactResellerSales table with the new calculated column, *WeightedPrice*.

Produc...	OrderDat...	DueDateKey	ShipDateKey	SalesOrderNumber	OrderQuantity	UnitPrice	WeightedPrice
436	20040501	20040513	20040508	SO69496	1	$356.90	356.898
390	20040501	20040513	20040508	SO69502	1	$672.29	672.294
384	20040501	20040513	20040508	SO69519	1	$672.29	672.294
600	20040501	20040513	20040508	SO69533	1	$323.99	323.994
559	20040501	20040513	20040508	SO69565	1	$12.14	12.144
586	20040601	20040613	20040608	SO71050	1	$445.41	445.41
498	20040601	20040613	20040608	SO71883	1	$602.35	602.346
543	20040601	20040613	20040608	SO71927	1	$37.25	37.254
315	20010701	20010713	20010708	SO43684	2	$874.79	1749.588
347	20010701	20010713	20010708	SO43695	2	$2,039.99	4079.988
346	20010901	20010913	20010908	SO44098	2	$2,039.99	4079.988

FIGURE 11-13 The *WeightedPrice* calculated column is stored at the fact table level.

You already know that calculated columns are stored in the xVelocity database; that is, they consume memory. How much memory will the *WeightedPrice* column consume? You learned that the size in memory of a column in xVelocity depends on the number of distinct values of that column. Thus, the question is: "How many distinct values are in *WeightedPrice*?"

The answer, in general, is not easy and requires some advanced statistics, but you can answer the question in this specific case by using some measures. You can create the following three measures, which will perform the computation for the FactResellerSales table.

```
NumOfQuantities      := DISTINCTCOUNT( FactResellerSales[OrderQuantity] )
NumOfPrices          := DISTINCTCOUNT( FactResellerSales[UnitPrice] )
NumOfWeightedPrices  := DISTINCTCOUNT( FactResellerSales[WeightedPrice] )
```

The results are interesting. There are 41 quantities, 233 prices (remember that the price changes with the product and will be the same for many sales), and 1,406 weighted prices. In other words, the calculated column has an order of magnitude more distinct values than the source columns used to compute it. Thus, it uses a lot of memory, and scanning it to compute the sum requires time.

Note Please note that this is not only a theoretical discussion about the number of distinct values. On a real-world production database, with four billion rows in the fact table, the weighted column was using 9 GB or RAM out of 25 GB of total size of the fact table. Removing that row saves a lot of useful space in memory.

Another important factor in the evaluation of this scenario is that iterators over simple expressions (such as the simple multiplication in this scenario) are not computed in the formula engine. The expression is pushed down to the xVelocity engine and computed during the column scanning. See Chapter 18, "Optimizations and Monitoring," to learn more about the difference between the xVelocity Storage Engine and the formula engine.

It turns out that scanning the *WeightedPrice* column takes more time than the separate scan of the two source columns, and, because the computation is performed directly during scanning, Tabular performs much better by using the *SUMX* formula than by using *SUM*.

Understanding Circular Dependencies

When you design a data model for Tabular, pay attention to circular dependencies in formulas. In this section, you learn what circular dependencies are and how to avoid them in your data model.

Before speaking about circular dependencies, it is worth discussing simple, linear dependencies. Look at an example with the following calculated column.

```
DimProduct[Profit] := DimProduct[ListPrice] - DimProduct[StandardCost]
```

The new calculated column depends on two columns that are present in the table. In such a case, we say that the *Profit* column depends on *ListPrice* and *StandardCost*. You can then create a new column, such as *ProfitPct*, with the following formula.

```
DimProduct[ProfitPct] := DimProduct[Profit] / DimProduct[ListPrice]
```

It is clear that *ProfitPct* depends on *Profit* and *ListPrice*. Thus, when Analysis Services must compute the calculated columns in the table, it knows that *ProfitPct* must be computed only after *Profit* has been calculated and stored. Otherwise, it cannot recover a valid value for the formula.

Linear dependency is not something you should normally worry about. It is used internally by the SSAS engine to detect the correct order of computation of calculated columns during the processing of the database. On a normal Tabular data model with many calculated columns, the dependency of calculations turns into a complex graph, which SSAS handles gracefully.

Circular dependency is a situation that happens when a loop appears in this graph. For example, circular dependency appears if you try to modify the definition of Profit in this formula.

```
DimProduct[Profit] := DimProduct[ProfitPct] * DimProduct[StandardCost]
```

Because *ProfitPct* depends on *Profit* and, in this new formula, *Profit* depends on *ProfitPct*, SQL Server Data Tools (SSDT) refuses to modify the formula and displays the error shown in Figure 11-14.

FIGURE 11-14 When circular dependencies are found, SSDT shows an error message.

Up to now, you have learned what circular dependencies are from the point of view of columns; that is, you have detected the existence of a dependency by looking at the expression without looking at the table content. There is a more subtle and complex type of dependency, which is introduced by the usage of *CALCULATE*, filters, or both inside any expression. Here is an example, starting from a subset of columns of DimProduct, as shown in Figure 11-15.

ProductKey	ProductAlternateKey	StandardCost	ListPrice
458	TG-W091-L	$30.93	$74.99
459	SB-M891-S	$37.12	$89.99
460	SB-M891-M	$37.12	$89.99
461	SB-M891-L	$37.12	$89.99
462	GL-H102-S	$9.71	$23.55
463	GL-H102-S	$9.16	$24.49
464	GL-H102-M	$9.71	$23.55
465	GL-H102-M	$9.16	$24.49
466	GL-H102-L	$9.71	$23.55

FIGURE 11-15 A subset of columns of DimProduct is useful to explain circular dependencies.

We are interested in describing the dependency list for a new calculated column that uses the *CALCULATE* function, such as the following.

```
SumOfListPrice := CALCULATE( SUM( DimProduct[ListPrice] ) )
```

At first glance, it might seem that the column depends on *ListPrice* only because this is the only column used in the formula. Nevertheless, we used *CALCULATE* to transform the current row context into a filter context. Thus, if we expand the meaning of the *CALCULATE* call, the formula really says:

Sum the value of ListPrice for the entire row in the DimProduct table, which has the same value for ProductKey, ProductAlternateKey, StandardCost, and ListPrice.

When you read the formula in this way, it is now clear that the formula depends on all the columns of DimProduct because the newly introduced filter context filters all the columns of the table. Figure 11-16 shows the resulting table.

ProductKey	ProductAlternateKey	StandardCost	ListPrice	SumOfListPrice
458	TG-W091-L	$30.93	$74.99	$74.99
459	SB-M891-S	$37.12	$89.99	$89.99
460	SB-M891-M	$37.12	$89.99	$89.99
461	SB-M891-L	$37.12	$89.99	$89.99
462	GL-H102-S	$9.71	$23.55	$23.55
463	GL-H102-S	$9.16	$24.49	$24.49
464	GL-H102-M	$9.71	$23.55	$23.55

FIGURE 11-16 You can create the *SumOfListPrice* calculated column in the DimProduct table.

Now, you might try to define a new calculated column, using the same formula, in the same table. You can try to add *NewSumOfListPrice* by using the following formula, which is identical to the previous one.

```
NewSumOfListPrice := CALCULATE( SUM( DimProduct[ListPrice] ) )
```

Surprisingly, SSDT refuses to create this new formula and returns the error shown in Figure 11-17.

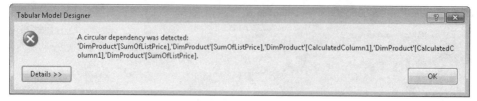

FIGURE 11-17 Adding a new *CALCULATE* on the same table raises an error.

Analysis Services has detected a circular dependency in the formula, which was not detected before. And, because nothing was changed in the formula, the error seems very strange. Something has changed, and it is the number of columns in the table. If you were able to add the *NewSumOfListPrice* to the table, you would reach a situation in which the two formulas have these meanings:

- **SumOfListPrice**   Sum the value of *ListPrice* for the entire row in the DimProduct table, which has the same value for *ProductKey*, *ProductAlternateKey*, *StandardCost*, *ListPrice*, and *NewSumOfListPrice*.

- **NewSumOfListPrice**   Sum the value of *ListPrice* for the entire row in the DimProduct table, which has the same value for *ProductKey*, *ProductAlternateKey*, *StandardCost*, *ListPrice*, and *SumOfListPrice*.

Having added the calculated column, these columns become part of the filter context introduced by *CALCULATE* and, therefore, they are part of the dependency list. It is clear from the previous definition that there is a circular dependency between the two formulas, and this is why Analysis Services refuses to create the *NewSumOfListPrice* column.

Understanding this error is not easy. However, finding a solution is straightforward even if it is not very intuitive. The problem is that any calculated column containing *CALCULATE* (or a call to any measure, which adds an automatic *CALCULATE*) creates a dependency on all the columns of the table. The scenario would be different if the table had a row identifier (a primary key, in SQL terms). If the table has a column that acts as a row identifier, all columns containing *CALCULATE* could depend on the row identifier, thus reducing their dependency list to a single column.

In the DimProduct table, there is such a column: *ProductKey*. To mark *ProductKey* as a row identifier, there are two options:

- You can create a relationship from any table into DimProduct by using *ProductKey* as the destination column. Performing this operation ensures that *ProductKey* is a unique value for DimProduct.

- You can set the property of Row Identifier for *ProductKey* manually to *TRUE* by using the Properties window inside SSDT, as shown in Figure 11-18.

FIGURE 11-18 You can update the Row Identifier property in the Properties window.

One of these operations teaches SSAS that the table has a row identifier and, in such a scenario, you can define the *NewSumOfListPrice* column, avoiding circular dependency.

In conclusion, it is always a good idea to set the Row Identifier property of a table, if such a column exists in the data model, because the xVelocity engine uses this information to optimize all calculations. Nevertheless, row identifiers occupy space in the data model, and their memory usage is high because they have the maximum number of distinct values (a different value for each row). Thus, if a row identifier is not needed inside a table (for example, for fact tables), it is always a good idea to avoid loading it inside the Tabular data model. Then, if you face the circular dependency issue, it might be necessary to add the row identifier column to the table to solve the problem.

There are other techniques to avoid circular dependencies. For example, using *ALLEXCEPT* to remove the calculated columns from the set of columns that become part of the dependency list is a viable option, but it makes all formulas more complicated. Using *ALLEXCEPT*, however, might be useful for very big tables, in which the addition of a row identifier would cause the memory footprint to grow too much.

Understanding the Power of Calculated Columns: ABC Analysis

Calculated columns are stored inside the database. This is a fact that you learned during the first chapters of this book, and at this point, it should no longer surprise you. That said, this opens new ways of modeling data, and in this section, you look at some scenarios that you can solve efficiently with calculated columns.

We believe that calculated columns are the most relevant improvement in the modeling options of Tabular versus Multidimensional. Calculated columns are present in SQL and in Multidimensional, but both can compute only row-level values easily. In Tabular, however, a calculated column can refer to any table in the data model and, by using DAX, can store intermediate computations that greatly speed up the queries.

As an example of the usage of calculated columns, you now learn how to solve the scenario of ABC analysis by using Tabular. ABC analysis is similar to the Pareto principle. The goal of ABC analysis is to assign to each product a category (A, B, or C) by which:

- Products in class *A* account for 70 percent of the revenues.

- Products in class *B* account for 20 percent of the revenues.

- Products in class *C* account for the remaining 10 percent of the revenues.

The goal of ABC analysis is to identify which products have a significant impact on the overall business so that managers can focus their effort on these products. You can find more information on ABC analysis at *http://en.wikipedia.org/wiki/ABC_analysis*. The goal is to find a solution to compute ABC analysis in Tabular.

To compute the *ABC* class of a product, you must compute the total sales of that product and compare it with the grand total. This gives you the percentage of the overall sales for which that single product accounts. Then, you sort products based on that percentage and perform a rolling sum. As soon as the rolling sum reaches 70 percent, you have identified products in class *A*. Remaining products will be in class *B* until you reach 90 percent (70+20), and further products will be in class *C*.

Computing ABC analysis can be done in SQL, but this requires complex queries and often the need to store temporary tables with the total sold per product, with the creation of suitable indexes to speed up further queries. If the volume of data grows, you must inevitably build summary tables to reduce the I/O needed to compute the classes.

The data model for this scenario is shown in Figure 11-19.

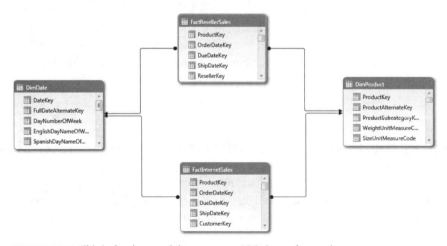

FIGURE 11-19 This is the data model to compute *ABC* classes for products.

Sales information is stored in two fact tables: FactResellerSales and FactInternetSales. First, you must compute the total sales for each product, which you can accomplish by using a calculated column.

```
TotalSales =
CALCULATE( SUM( FactInternetSales[SalesAmount] ) + SUM( FactResellerSales[SalesAmount] ) )
```

In Figure 11-20, you see the DimProduct table with this new calculated column in which data has been sorted in descending order by *TotalSales*.

ProductKey	ProductAlternateKey	EnglishProductName	TotalSales
359	BK-M68B-38	Mountain-200 Black, 38	$2,589,363.78
361	BK-M68B-42	Mountain-200 Black, 42	$2,265,485.38
353	BK-M68S-38	Mountain-200 Silver, 38	$2,160,981.60
363	BK-M68B-46	Mountain-200 Black, 46	$1,957,528.24
355	BK-M68S-42	Mountain-200 Silver, 42	$1,914,547.85
357	BK-M68S-46	Mountain-200 Silver, 46	$1,906,248.55
314	BK-R93R-56	Road-150 Red, 56	$1,847,818.63
358	BK-M68B-38	Mountain-200 Black, 38	$1,811,229.02
583	BK-R79Y-48	Road-350-W Yellow, 48	$1,774,883.56
310	BK-R93R-62	Road-150 Red, 62	$1,769,096.69

FIGURE 11-20 *TotalSales* is computed as a calculated column in the DimProduct table.

Now, compute a running total of TotalSales over the DimProduct table ordered by *TotalSales*. Because in DAX there is no way to sort a table and iterate over it, you need a different approach, which has to be set-based. If you think in terms of sets, the running total of each product is the sum of all the products that have a value for *TotalSales* greater than or equal to the current value. Clearly, this definition is not iterative and, thus, is harder to imagine. Nevertheless, this is the DAX way to produce running totals. You can define a new calculated column, *RunningTotalSales*, with the following formula.

```
RunningTotalSales =
CALCULATE(
    SUM( DimProduct[TotalSales] ),
    ALL( DimProduct ),
    DimProduct[TotalSales] >= EARLIER( DimProduct[TotalSales] )
)
```

Note the *ALL* (DimProduct) used inside *CALCULATE* because you must extend the filter context created by *CALCULATE* to include all products so that the only effective filter is the subsequent one on DimProduct[TotalSales]. In Figure 11-21, you see the DimProduct table with this new column.

ProductKey	ProductAlternateKey	EnglishProductName	TotalSales	RunningTotalSales
359	BK-M68B-38	Mountain-200 Black, 38	$2,589,363.78	$2,589,363.78
361	BK-M68B-42	Mountain-200 Black, 42	$2,265,485.38	$4,854,849.16
353	BK-M68S-38	Mountain-200 Silver, 38	$2,160,981.60	$7,015,830.75
363	BK-M68B-46	Mountain-200 Black, 46	$1,957,528.24	$8,973,359.00
355	BK-M68S-42	Mountain-200 Silver, 42	$1,914,547.85	$10,887,906.85
357	BK-M68S-46	Mountain-200 Silver, 46	$1,906,248.55	$12,794,155.40
314	BK-R93R-56	Road-150 Red, 56	$1,847,818.63	$14,641,974.03
358	BK-M68B-38	Mountain-200 Black, 38	$1,811,229.02	$16,453,203.05
583	BK-R79Y-48	Road-350-W Yellow, 48	$1,774,883.56	$18,228,086.61
310	BK-R93R-62	Road-150 Red, 62	$1,769,096.69	$19,997,183.30

FIGURE 11-21 *RunningTotalSales* computes a running total over rows sorted by *TotalSales*.

The final step is to compute the running total sales as a percentage over the grand total of sales. A new calculated column solves the problem. You can add a *RunningTotalSalesPct* column by using this formula.

```
RunningTotalSalesPct =
    DimProduct[RunningTotalSales] /
    ( SUM( FactInternetSales[SalesAmount] ) + SUM( FactResellerSales[SalesAmount] ) )
```

Because *SUM* computed at the denominator is outside any *CALCULATE*, that sum is the grand total of sales of both fact tables, whereas *RunningTotalSales* is the running total of the row inside which the formula is evaluated. In Figure 11-22, you see the new calculated column.

ProductKey	ProductAlternateKey	EnglishProductName	TotalSales	RunningTotalSales	RunningTotalSalesPct
355	BK-M68S-42	Mountain-200 Silver, 42	$1,914,547.85	$10,887,906.85	9.92 %
357	BK-M68S-46	Mountain-200 Silver, 46	$1,906,248.55	$12,794,155.40	11.65 %
314	BK-R93R-56	Road-150 Red, 56	$1,847,818.63	$14,641,974.03	13.33 %
358	BK-M68B-38	Mountain-200 Black, 38	$1,811,229.02	$16,453,203.05	14.98 %
583	BK-R79Y-48	Road-350-W Yellow, 48	$1,774,883.56	$18,228,086.61	16.60 %
310	BK-R93R-62	Road-150 Red, 62	$1,769,096.69	$19,997,183.30	18.21 %
360	BK-M68B-42	Mountain-200 Black, 42	$1,744,009.38	$21,741,192.68	19.80 %
576	BK-T79U-60	Touring-1000 Blue, 60	$1,721,242.51	$23,462,435.19	21.37 %
580	BK-R79Y-40	Road-350-W Yellow, 40	$1,657,198.18	$25,119,633.38	22.88 %
573	BK-T79U-46	Touring-1000 Blue, 46	$1,586,953.57	$26,706,586.95	24.32 %
312	BK-R93R-48	Road-150 Red, 48	$1,540,803.06	$28,247,390.01	25.72 %

FIGURE 11-22 *RunningTotalSalesPct* computes the percentage of running total over the grand total.

The work is almost complete. The final touch is to transform the percentage into the class. If you use the values of *70*, *20*, and *10*, the formula for the *ABC* class is straightforward, as you see in the following formula.

```
ABC Class =
IF (
    DimProduct[RunningTotalSalesPct] <= 0.7,
    "A",
    IF (
        DimProduct[RunningTotalSalesPct] <= 0.9,
        "B",
        "C"
    )
)
```

You can see the result in Figure 11-23.

ProductKey	ProductAlternateKey	EnglishProductName	TotalSales	RunningTotalSales	RunningTotalSalesPct	ABC Class
359	BK-M68B-38	Mountain-200 Black, 38	$2,589,363.78	$2,589,363.78	2.36 %	A
361	BK-M68B-42	Mountain-200 Black, 42	$2,265,485.38	$4,854,849.16	4.42 %	A
353	BK-M68S-38	Mountain-200 Silver, 38	$2,160,981.60	$7,015,830.75	6.39 %	A
363	BK-M68B-46	Mountain-200 Black, 46	$1,957,528.24	$8,973,359.00	8.17 %	A
355	BK-M68S-42	Mountain-200 Silver, 42	$1,914,547.85	$10,887,906.85	9.92 %	A
357	BK-M68S-46	Mountain-200 Silver, 46	$1,906,248.55	$12,794,155.40	11.65 %	A
314	BK-R93R-56	Road-150 Red, 56	$1,847,818.63	$14,641,974.03	13.33 %	A
358	BK-M68B-38	Mountain-200 Black, 38	$1,811,229.02	$16,453,203.05	14.98 %	A
583	BK-R79Y-48	Road-350-W Yellow, 48	$1,774,883.56	$18,228,086.61	16.60 %	A
310	BK-R93R-62	Road-150 Red, 62	$1,769,096.69	$19,997,183.30	18.21 %	A

FIGURE 11-23 The result of the *ABC* class is the calculated column, *ABC Class*.

Because the *ABC* class is a calculated column, it is stored inside the database, and you can use it on slicers, filters, rows, or columns to produce reports. In Figure 11-24, for example, you can see the number of products in each class along with the total sales for each class.

Row Labels ▼	NumOfProducts	InternetSalesAmount	ResellerSalesAmount
A	62	24,957,237.32	51,884,758.17
B	72	2,993,433.21	18,909,512.27
C	472	1,408,006.69	9,656,326.55
Grand Total	606	29,358,677.22	80,450,596.98

FIGURE 11-24 Analysis of the *ABC* class is straightforward because it is a calculated column.

It is easy, for example, to see that sales on the web behave in a different way than reseller sales because the ratio of the amount over the grand total is very different. Moreover, it is immediately noticeable that only 62 products are in class *A* and 472 are in class *C*. It is clearly more interesting to focus efforts on these few products than to spend time on other, less interesting ones.

These considerations might lead to a definition of *ABC* classes over Internet and reseller sales as different classes or to changing the way the classes are computed, for example, taking into account sales of the past year only, so that the class changes each year, by using more recent data. All of these are interesting exercises you can perform. Note that the whole process of defining classes is very easy and can be completed in a matter of minutes, leading to a very short time to market. The comparison with the development of the same solution by using SQL or any other ETL tool makes Tabular a clear winner in these scenarios and shows the power of calculated columns.

Note We have shown the definition of *ABC* classes, by using many calculated columns to store intermediate values, for educational purposes. Because each calculated column uses precious RAM, it might be useful, when in production, to merge some formulas to reduce the number of columns. This is not usually an issue with dimensions such as DimProduct, which is small. Nevertheless, always pay attention to intermediate values stored in RAM; if you can afford to remove them by making the formulas slightly more complicated, it is usually worth the effort.

Modeling with DirectQuery Enabled

You already know that Tabular data models store the information in memory and provide you with a very fast query engine. The only drawback of this architecture is that, before you start querying the model, you must process it; that is, create the in-memory data structure that represents the xVelocity database. If your scenario requires real-time BI or if your data model does not fit in memory, you can use DirectQuery, which you learned in Chapter 9. However, DirectQuery comes with several limitations that might seriously reduce the available data modeling options. In this section, you learn about these limitations.

These are the main differences to keep in mind while developing a solution by using DirectQuery:

- The model can use only a single data source connected to Microsoft SQL Server.

- Calculated columns are not supported.

- Security is enforced in SQL Server only and cannot be set in the Tabular model.

- Some DAX functions are not available or have a slightly different behavior.

- The data model can be queried by using DAX only; MDX is not available.

Let us review all of these in more detail. First, if a data model uses DirectQuery, all of its data must come from a single connection to SQL Server. This is not usually an issue because, in a corporate environment, it is very likely that all the data comes from a single data warehouse. Nevertheless, it is something to keep in mind while designing a solution. Moreover, the connection must be to SQL Server. The DirectQuery engine generates queries that are specific to SQL Server and, at present, it is not compatible with any other relational engine.

The fact that calculated columns are not available is a huge limitation, and it strongly affects the modeling options because calculated columns are probably the most powerful feature of Tabular. If your data model uses row-level calculated columns (that is, formulas in which the result depends solely on columns in the same row), you can use SQL calculated columns by using views or calculated columns directly on tables. Note that, in this case, the columns will be computed by SQL Server on demand, behaving differently than Tabular calculated columns. Thus, many of the modeling options described in this book that make extensive usage of calculated columns cannot be used if the Tabular model is in DirectQuery mode.

Security is another major issue. If the model is in DirectQuery mode, the security model of SSAS cannot be used. Although you can still provide read and process permissions to roles, if the data model is in DirectQuery mode, you cannot apply DAX filters to tables. The only security tool you can use is the security at the SQL Server level. If you run a report and configure Tabular to impersonate the current user, when the query is run against the server, it obeys SQL Server security. Nevertheless, because there is no easy way to provide row-level filtering on SQL Server (unless you use views with complex *WHERE* clauses to manage security), it is not wrong to say that security in DirectQuery models is missing.

Thus, for security concerns, DirectQuery can be used only if security is not an issue (which is almost never the case) or when your data model will be queried in a controlled way. If, for example, the Tabular data model is used only by reports, custom software, or both, you can implement security outside the model.

Another big limitation concerns client tools. DirectQuery-enabled models cannot be queried by using MDX; they support only DAX. At the time of writing, the only client able to use DAX to query a Tabular model is Power View. All other clients (Excel included) use MDX. Thus, if you plan to release a Tabular solution that will be queried by using Excel, DirectQuery is not a viable option.

Finally, some DAX functions cannot be used in the DirectQuery Tabular model. You can find the official reference at *http://msdn.microsoft.com/en-us/library/hh213006(v=sql.110).aspx*. Surprisingly, we think that the limitation on DAX function is the least important. If you cannot author a measure by using a function, it is likely that you can author it in a different way, provided that the vast majority of DAX functions are correctly translated in SQL by the engine.

Note Among the various functions, one that is missing is the *PATH* function, which handles parent/child relationships. The fact that the function is missing does not mean that you cannot handle parent/child hierarchies; it just means that you must compute the path column (and all other columns needed to handle parent/child hierarchies) before loading data into Tabular.

Therefore, you can use DirectQuery if:

- Security is not an issue (or you have full control over who queries your data model).

- The model is queried by DAX clients only.

- Your data model does not require DAX-calculated columns.

- You have a single SQL Server database as the source for your data model.

This list is very restrictive. It leads to the conclusion that, apart from very rare and specific cases, DirectQuery can be enabled only for Tabular models that are used to feed reports built by using Reporting Services (or any reporting system that enables you to issue DAX queries) or Power View, provided that these reports do not include any kind of security or that the security can be handled differently by limiting access to restricted sets of information by using other means.

Warning If you must use DirectQuery, spend some time looking at the SQL code that is generated to resolve your DAX queries so that you can create the necessary indexes to make SQL answer as fast as possible the various kinds of queries that are generated by your system. Because DirectQuery does not seem designed to be queried directly by users, your result should be a limited set of queries that can be optimized.

Before considering DirectQuery as a viable solution for your data model, we strongly suggest double-checking all these requirements. Even with all these limitations, DirectQuery is still a good candidate when you need to work with real-time BI or when your data does not fit in memory. In such a scenario, DirectQuery is the only solution with which you can obtain zero-time processing.

Using Views to Decouple from the Database

When loading from SQL Server, one question that always arises is, "Should I load data in Tabular from tables, or should I write a SQL query instead, loading information from a SQL statement?" The answer is neither of these, and, in this final section, you learn why.

If you load data directly from a table, you are creating a very strong dependency between the table structure in the database and your Tabular solution. This is never a good idea. Databases tend to change over time due to requirements, and you don't want your solution to depend so strongly on any metadata update that might happen on the database. You may to prefer to load data from SQL statements so that the dependency is weakened and, if the metadata of the table changes, you can always update your SQL statements to prevent changes that might break your solution.

However, loading from a SQL statement hides the important information about which columns you are reading and what relationships you are following from the database administrator. Moreover, if you must make any change, you must update the table metadata and deploy a new solution, which, in a big database, might lead to some wasted processing time.

The best option, as is the case in Multidimensional, is always to create SQL views in the database that clearly show the database administrator the data you are interested in loading, and then load data inside Tabular from these views as if they were tables. (You should have already noticed that views are shown as tables when you load data inside PowerPivot from tables.)

In this way, you get several important benefits:

- If the data structure changes, you can update the views without changing in any way the SSAS solution. From the SSAS point of view, it is always loading data from the same media even if, by changing the view definition, you can make the loading process follow a completely different path. Moreover, you can spend time optimizing the query plan in SQL Server Management Studio (SSMS) without having to open SSDT to update the SQL code.

- If you later develop a new solution that needs to load the same set of data, you can use the same view without creating a new SQL statement to load the same entity.

- The database administrator is completely aware of your queries and can optimize them by adding necessary indexes to the database.

Finally, by using views, you can have different view definitions in development or production. During development, you know that you should not work on the complete dataset to obtain a responsive development environment. You can obtain this solution by creating a set of views in the development database that expose only a subset of data. The same set of views loads all the information so that when the database is put in production, all information is visible.

Summary

In this chapter, you learned some techniques related to data modeling in Tabular. You have seen that Tabular data modeling requires some special attention. Examples such as snapshot fact tables and weighted aggregations show that a data model shaped to be optimal in Tabular has to follow rules that are somewhat counterintuitive. Finally, using Tabular features enables you to discover new ways to solve common problems, as you saw in the ABC analysis example.

Using Advanced Tabular Relationships

Tabular is capable of handling only basic forms of relationship between tables, that is, a simple relationship based on a single column, which has to be a key in the target table. However, in the real world there are more complex kinds of relationships. You might need to use more than one column to relate two tables, you might need to define a many-to-many relationship between two entities, or you might want to handle more complex scenarios such as banding.

In this chapter, you learn how to use the DAX programming language to model all these scenarios through a set of examples of increasing complexity, which guide you through the most commonly used kinds of complex relationships.

Even if you do not need all these data models now, it is advisable to read the whole chapter to learn some of the most advanced techniques in Tabular data modeling. Later, when you need a specific scenario, you might return to this chapter to go deeper and learn more details about the model you intend to build.

Using Multicolumn Relationships

In Tabular, a relationship can be set with one column only, but sometimes you must use more than one column as the keys for a relationship. In this section, you learn how to handle such a scenario.

Imagine that you have a table containing the maximum discount allowed for each reseller and product. Such a table contains *ProductKey*, *ResellerKey*, and values that indicate which of the various discounts can be applied to that product for the reseller. You end up with a data diagram like the one shown in Figure 12-1.

FIGURE 12-1 In this data diagram, the missing relationship is based on two keys.

It is impossible to set the relationship between FactResellerSales and Discounts because neither *ProductKey* nor *ResellerKey* is a valid row identifier for the Discounts table. If you were to solve this in SQL or in Multidimensional, you could create a foreign key by using multiple columns, but in Tabular, this option is not available.

If you want to bring the *AvgDiscount* column into FactResellerSales to create a calculated column that indicates whether a single sale has been executed outside the discount range, you have several options.

As a first option, you can create a calculated column by using *LOOKUPVALUE* to perform the search for the correct MaxDiscount value in the Discounts table, denormalizing the relationship in this way. The calculated column would have the following formula.

```
=LOOKUPVALUE(
    Discounts[MaxDiscount],
    Discounts[ProductKey], FactResellerSales[ProductKey],
    Discounts[ResellerKey], FactResellerSales[ResellerKey]
)
```

This technique works if you must push a single column (or a few columns) from the Discounts table to the fact table. If, however, the Discount table contains a lot of columns, denormalizing all of them would make the data model complex.

You can create a composite key by merging *ProductKey* and *ResellerKey* into two calculated columns: one in FactResellerSales and one in Discounts. After these columns exist in both tables, you can use them to create the relationship between the two tables. You can merge the two columns in many ways, for example, by using string concatenation or some math.

For instance, you can use the following formula to define the *ProductAndReseller* column (and an analogous column in related tables).

```
ProductAndReseller = Discounts[ProductKey] & "-" & Discounts[ResellerKey]
```

In Figure 12-2, you see the *ProductAndReseller* calculated column that holds the combination of *ProductKey* and *ResellerKey* created by using simple string concatenation.

ProductKey	ResellerKey	MinDiscount	MaxDiscount	AvgDiscount	ProductAndReseller
470	2	0.02	0.02	0.02	470-2
214	3	0.02	0.02	0.02	214-3
224	3	0.02	0.02	0.02	224-3
231	3	0.02	0.02	0.02	231-3
233	3	0.02	0.02	0.02	233-3
236	3	0.02	0.02	0.02	236-3
327	3	0.02	0.02	0.02	327-3
333	3	0.02	0.02	0.02	333-3

FIGURE 12-2 Merging two columns into a single column is useful for multiple-column relationships.

Note that this data model uses more memory than the original because it must hold three columns, two of which are probably now useless (the original *ProductKey* and *ResellerKey* columns). If memory usage is an issue, you can safely perform the concatenation in the source view that feeds the Tabular table and avoid storing the original keys.

At the end, you see how the new data model looks in Figure 12-3.

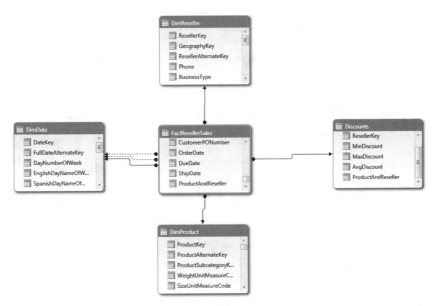

FIGURE 12-3 In this data model, you can use the new calculated column to create the relationship.

Banding in Tabular

Banding is a common technique used in data analysis that consists of grouping several values to reduce the fragmentation of an attribute and to give insights into data. A common scenario is banding prices. In the FactInternetSales table is the *UnitPrice* column, which contains the real price at which a product has been sold. Clearly, putting *UnitPrice* in rows or a slicer is not an option to get any insight into data because the number of distinct values for the discounted price is too high. Thus, it is useful to group prices in ranges such as Low Price, High Price, and so on and let the user browse data by using these ranges instead of the actual price. In this section, you learn how to efficiently handle banding in Tabular.

Because you want your users to be able to modify ranges, you must have a configuration table containing the price bands. As an example, we use a simple *SELECT* statement that returns fixed values because the Adventure Works data warehouse does not contain such a table. Figure 12-4 shows the resulting table.

Id	BandName	MinPrice	MaxPrice
1	Low Price	0	100
2	Medium Price	100	500
3	High Price	500	1500
4	Very High Price	1500	999999

FIGURE 12-4 A configuration table is holding the band names and parameters.

After you load this table in a data model, along with the FactInternetSales table and some dimensions, you get the data model shown in Figure 12-5.

FIGURE 12-5 In this data model, no relationship can be created with the PriceBands table.

Note that in this data model, no relationship starts from FactInternetSales and goes to the PriceBands table. The reason is that such a relationship cannot be created because it would be based on a *BETWEEN* clause, which is not available in Tabular. Moreover, you cannot use the *LOOKUPVALUE* DAX function because *LOOKUPVALUE* must find an exact match between two columns.

The key to solving this scenario is to create a calculated column that denormalizes the value of BandName from PriceBand directly into the FactInternetSales table, creating a suitable filter context that filters the correct band for each row in the fact table.

```
PriceBand =
CALCULATE(
    VALUES( PriceBands[BandName] ),
    PriceBands[MaxPrice] >= EARLIER( FactInternetSales[UnitPrice] ),
    PriceBands[MinPrice] < EARLIER( FactInternetSales[UnitPrice] )
)
```

By using the fact that *VALUES* automatically converts a table made of one row and one column into a scalar value, you create a filter context in which the only row representing the correct price band is visible in the PriceBands table, and you get its BandName.

This formula works if the configuration table is correct; that is, there is always at most one price band for each sale. If you want to protect the solution from possible error, a better solution would be to surround *VALUES* with *IFERROR* so that you always get a result instead of an error, as in the following formula.

```
PriceBand =
CALCULATE(
    IFERROR( VALUES( PriceBands[BandName] ), "Wrong Configuration" ),
    PriceBands[MaxPrice] >= EARLIER( FactInternetSales[UnitPrice] ),
    PriceBands[MinPrice] < EARLIER( FactInternetSales[UnitPrice] )
)
```

If you now browse the data model by using Microsoft Excel, you can create a report like the one shown in Figure 12-6.

Sum of SalesAmount	Column Labels				
Row Labels	2001	2002	2003	2004	Grand Total
High Price	$78,998.10	$447,794.66	$1,892,175.58	$2,055,195.57	$4,474,163.91
Low Price			$396,596.68	$564,984.89	$961,581.57
Medium Price			$35,361.00	$43,590.00	$78,951.00
Very High Price	$3,187,375.56	$6,082,548.86	$7,466,927.04	$7,107,129.28	$23,843,980.74
Grand Total	$3,266,373.66	$6,530,343.53	$9,791,060.30	$9,770,899.74	$29,358,677.22

FIGURE 12-6 Browsing the sales by using the price band gives you insights.

The issue that is still not solved is sorting the price band. Band names are mixed up because—by default—Tabular uses alphabetic sorting. If you try to sort the band name by using UnitPrice, you get the error shown in Figure 12-7 because there are many values of UnitPrice for the same PriceBand.

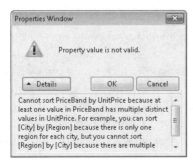

FIGURE 12-7 You cannot use UnitPrice to sort the *PriceBand* column.

The solution is to denormalize the *Id* column from the PriceBand table in the FactInternetSales table, using the same pattern used for PriceBand.

```
PriceBandSort =
CALCULATE(
    IFERROR( VALUES( PriceBands[Id] ), -1 ),
```

```
    PriceBands[MaxPrice] >= EARLIER( FactInternetSales[UnitPrice] ),
    PriceBands[MinPrice] < EARLIER( FactInternetSales[UnitPrice] )
)
```

Setting the Sort by Column property of PriceBand to the *PriceBandSort* column, you get the desired result, as shown in Figure 12-8.

Sum of SalesAmount	Column Labels				
Row Labels	2001	2002	2003	2004	Grand Total
Low Price			$396,596.68	$564,984.89	$961,581.57
Medium Price			$35,361.00	$43,590.00	$78,951.00
High Price	$78,998.10	$447,794.66	$1,892,175.58	$2,055,195.57	$4,474,163.91
Very High Price	$3,187,375.56	$6,082,548.86	$7,466,927.04	$7,107,129.28	$23,843,980.74
Grand Total	$3,266,373.66	$6,530,343.53	$9,791,060.30	$9,770,899.74	$29,358,677.22

FIGURE 12-8 Bands can be sorted by using the *PriceBandSort* calculated column.

The most interesting characteristic of banding in Tabular is the fact that, by using calculated columns and some basic DAX, you can create a fully configurable banding system that does not require any kind of extract, transform, and load (ETL) operation or any change in the data model. Moreover, to change the banding, you need only to update the configuration table and reprocess it, making it a very easy-to-use model.

Using Many-to-Many Relationships

Using many-to-many relationships is a useful data modeling technique because it enables the analyst to create complex models and produce interesting reports. Many business scenarios must be modeled by using many-to-many relationships due to the nature of data. Although you can model many-to-many relationships in Multidimensional, Tabular does not support many-to-many relationships natively. In this section, you learn how to develop DAX formulas that enable you to handle many-to-many relationships in your Tabular data model.

Because the Adventure Works database does not contain an interesting many-to-many relationship, we created a new scenario that is common in real-world sales analysis by adding some tables to Adventure Works. The sales manager of Adventure Works advertises products by using leaflets and TV spots during some periods in the year. Each advertisement contains references to some products and lasts for a definite period of time. Each advertisement campaign is assigned to designers (they work in teams of two or more), and the managers of Adventure Works want to perform analysis of all the campaigns in which a single designer was involved. To model this scenario, there are four new tables in Adventure Works.

- **DimAdvertisements** Contains the description of advertisements, each of which has a start and end date, and some descriptions such as of the media used to deliver them.

- **DimDesigners** Contains the list of all designers who work with Adventure Works.

- **BridgeAdvertisementProduct** Contains the list of all products included in the various advertisements. Each product can be shown in the advertisement in different time periods.

- **BridgeAdvertisementDesigners** Describes which team of designers was involved in each campaign.

If you want to reproduce the examples, you can find the script that adds the required tables here.

Figure 12-9 shows the complete data model.

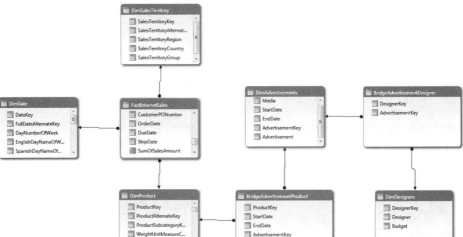

FIGURE 12-9 This example data model is useful for studying many-to-many relationships.

In this scenario, two many-to-many relationships are involved. Each product can belong to many advertisements, and each advertisement has been created by a team of many designers. The complete scenario is a cascading many-to-many relationship. Now you learn how to model the complete scenario by using DAX.

If you analyze this simple data model by using Excel after having defined a SumOfSalesAmount measure, which is the *SUM* of FactInternetSales[SalesAmount], you get the result shown in Figure 12-10.

SumOfSalesAmount	Column Labels				
Row Labels	Christmas Leaflet	Christmas TV Spot	Easter Leaflet	Easter TV Spot	Grand Total
Alberto Ferrari	29,358,677.22	29,358,677.22	29,358,677.22	29,358,677.22	29,358,677.22
Chris Webb	29,358,677.22	29,358,677.22	29,358,677.22	29,358,677.22	29,358,677.22
Katie Jordan	29,358,677.22	29,358,677.22	29,358,677.22	29,358,677.22	29,358,677.22
Louis Bonifaz	29,358,677.22	29,358,677.22	29,358,677.22	29,358,677.22	29,358,677.22
Marco Russo	29,358,677.22	29,358,677.22	29,358,677.22	29,358,677.22	29,358,677.22
Maurizio Macagno	29,358,677.22	29,358,677.22	29,358,677.22	29,358,677.22	29,358,677.22
Grand Total	**29,358,677.22**	**29,358,677.22**	**29,358,677.22**	**29,358,677.22**	**29,358,677.22**

FIGURE 12-10 Many-to-many relationships do not work with default settings.

Creating a simple *SUM* over the fact table and slicing data by using the designers (rows) and advertisements (columns) produces the same number for all cells. In other words, many-to-many relationships are not working, and you always get the grand total as the result for all the cells.

Using the knowledge you've gained up to now, the reason is easy to understand. The filter context propagates from the one side of the relationship through the many side one, but not vice versa. Thus, the filter imposed by the columns on DimDesigner is applied to filter BridgeAdvertisementDesigner but does not proceed further. In the same way, the filter applied on the columns on the DimAdvertisement table propagates through the relationship and filters BridgeAdvertisementProduct, but it cannot reach the fact table because of the direction of the next relationship.

Focus on the DimAdvertisement dimension, which is nearer the fact table and, thus, easier to handle. What you want is to:

- Use the automatic propagation of the filter from DimAdvertisement to BridgeAdvertisementProduct so that the bridge table is filtered.

- Gather the list of products in the bridge table that are still visible after the first filter has been applied.

- Use this latter list of products to filter the fact table, following the relationship from the fact table to the products.

With this algorithm in mind, you can author a formula that pushes the filter from DimAdvertisement to the fact table:

```
FactInternetSales[SalesAmountM2M] :=
CALCULATE(
    SUM( FactInternetSales[SalesAmount] ),
    FILTER(
        DimProduct,
        CALCULATE( COUNTROWS( BridgeAdvertisementProduct ) ) > 0
    )
)
```

Don't memorize this pattern because you will learn a better-performing pattern. But do understand it. The key of the formula is the inner *FILTER*, which filters the DimProduct table, returning only the products for which there is at least one row in the BridgeAdvertisementProduct table. Because the BridgeAdvertisementProduct table detects the filter coming from DimAdvertisement, only rows in the bridge table that belong to a selected advertisement are visible. Thus, at the end of its work, *FILTER* returns only the products that are associated with the specific advertisement filtered by the context.

The outermost *CALCULATE* applies the filter on DimProduct to the fact table and, at the end, the sum of SalesAmount is computed for only the selected products. You see the formula in action by browsing the data model by using Excel, as shown in Figure 12-11.

Row Labels	SalesAmountM2M
Christmas Leaflet	17,564,541.01
Christmas TV Spot	17,943,016.34
Easter Leaflet	17,687,870.53
Easter TV Spot	12,735,441.14
Grand Total	**27,894,615.99**

FIGURE 12-11 The SalesAmountM2M measure is correctly following the many-to-many relationship.

Whenever you face a many-to-many relationship, you must always follow this pattern, that is, to push the relationship from the farther table to the nearest one (to the fact table) by using a combination of *CALCULATE* and *FILTER* by which *FILTER* iterates on the nearest table, verifying the existence of a row in the bridge table.

> **Note** Because you cannot create a many-to-many relationship in the data model, whenever you have many-to-many relationships, you must create measures that compute the final value, taking into account the nature of the relationships. These measures are harder to write than the same versions without the many-to-many relationship, but, if carefully designed, they create a good user experience because the user does not have to worry about the presence of the many-to-many relationships. In fact, the SalesAmountM2M measure works both when DimDesigner is used to slice data and when it is not.

Now that you have learned how the measure works, spend some time searching for an optimized version of the formula. The major drawback of the formula is the usage of the *FILTER* iterator, which is not always an optimal choice. A slightly different approach is to make the selection of valid values of *ProductKey* by using a single function call, using the *SUMMARIZE* function.

If you want to get all the valid values of *ProductKey*, you can use *DISTINCT(BridgeAdvertisement Product[ProductKey])*, which returns the values of *ProductKey* visible under the current filter context. Now, even if the values returned are the right ones, they are values for BridgeAdvertisement Product[ProductKey], whereas to filter the DimProduct table, you need the same values tied to DimProduct[ProductKey]. You need a way to get the same set of distinct values with a reference to DimProduct. *SUMMARIZE* is the key to obtaining this set. By using *SUMMARIZE*, you can issue a *GROUP BY* on a table by using, as the key for grouping, a column of any table related with the source. The optimized version of the many-to-many pattern is the following one.

```
FactInternetSales[SalesAmountM2MOptimized] :=
CALCULATE(
    SUM( FactInternetSales[SalesAmount] ),
    SUMMARIZE( BridgeAdvertisementProduct, DimProduct[ProductKey] )
)
```

You see that the *FILTER* function has been replaced with *SUMMARIZE*, and the grouping column for *SUMMARIZE* is a column of DimProduct. The resulting table is then used to filter the DimProduct table by *CALCULATE*, and this, in turn, filters the fact table following the relationships.

Now that you have solved the easiest scenario, with the first many-to-many relationship, consider the more complex one, involving both many-to-many relationships. As you see in Figure 12-12, the DimAdvertisement table is correctly filtering the fact table, but the DimDesigner table is not.

SalesAmountM2M	Column Labels				
Row Labels	Christmas Leaflet	Christmas TV Spot	Easter Leaflet	Easter TV Spot	Grand Total
Alberto Ferrari	17,564,541.01	17,943,016.34	17,687,870.53	12,735,441.14	27,894,615.99
Chris Webb	17,564,541.01	17,943,016.34	17,687,870.53	12,735,441.14	27,894,615.99
Katie Jordan	17,564,541.01	17,943,016.34	17,687,870.53	12,735,441.14	27,894,615.99
Louis Bonifaz	17,564,541.01	17,943,016.34	17,687,870.53	12,735,441.14	27,894,615.99
Marco Russo	17,564,541.01	17,943,016.34	17,687,870.53	12,735,441.14	27,894,615.99
Maurizio Macagno	17,564,541.01	17,943,016.34	17,687,870.53	12,735,441.14	27,894,615.99
Grand Total	**17,564,541.01**	**17,943,016.34**	**17,687,870.53**	**12,735,441.14**	**27,894,615.99**

FIGURE 12-12 The SalesAmountM2M is not yet working with DimDesigner.

This is the issue you encountered before. The filter context does not propagate from the many side of the BridgeAdvertisementDesigner table through the one side of DimAdvertisement. Thus, the DimAdvertisement table is not filtered to show only the advertisement that a designer worked on.

This scenario is known as a *cascading many-to-many relationship*; that is, to reach the fact table, DimDesigner has to traverse two (or more) many-to-many relationships. The solution is fairly easy, even if it is difficult to read at first glance.

```
FactInternetSales[SalesAmountM2MCascading] :=
CALCULATE(
    SUM( FactInternetSales[SalesAmount] ),
    CALCULATETABLE(
        SUMMARIZE( BridgeAdvertisementProduct, DimProduct[ProductKey] ),
        SUMMARIZE( BridgeAdvertisementDesigner, DimAdvertisements[AdvertisementKey] )
    )
)
```

The key to understanding this formula is to follow the evaluation flow. The first function that is evaluated is the last *SUMMARIZE* over BridgeAdvertisementDesigner. This *SUMMARIZE* filters the DimAdvertisements table, and its result is used to evaluate the first *SUMMARIZE*, which filters the DimProduct table. At the end, *CALCULATETABLE* returns the filter on DimProduct to the outermost *CALCULATE*, which scans the filtered fact table to gather the final result.

In Figure 12-13, you see this new formula in action, correctly filtering the fact table by using both many-to-many relationships.

SalesAmountM2MCascading	Column Labels				
Row Labels	Christmas Leaflet	Christmas TV Spot	Easter Leaflet	Easter TV Spot	Grand Total
Alberto Ferrari	17,564,541.01	6,775,382.15		7,969,150.99	24,678,609.88
Chris Webb	13,463,757.01	17,943,016.34		7,969,150.99	24,975,605.97
Katie Jordan	7,757,805.58	7,804,796.23	14,858,595.24		19,967,434.58
Louis Bonifaz	13,452,995.36	8,783,201.09	12,566,681.80	6,729,565.75	26,107,120.70
Marco Russo	7,740,934.37	14,128,890.53	17,687,870.53	6,729,565.75	23,600,450.42
Maurizio Macagno		6,775,382.15	12,523,052.17	12,735,441.14	21,075,194.41
Grand Total	**17,564,541.01**	**17,943,016.34**	**17,687,870.53**	**12,735,441.14**	**27,894,615.99**

FIGURE 12-13 The SalesAmountM2MCascading formula is filtering both many-to-many relationships.

Using many-to-many relationships is a powerful data-modeling tool that, although not natively present in Tabular, can be implemented quite easily after you know the basic technique. The formula pattern is always the same, and you need to learn how to adapt it to the specifics of your data model. One major drawback of many-to-many implementation in Tabular, when compared to Multidimensional, is that the formula pattern has to be repeated for all the measures that must traverse the many-to-many chain, resulting in complex formulas. However, this drawback might be an advantage when the relationship, although based on a many-to-many pattern, has some peculiarities.

To understand this better, perform a deeper analysis of the data model. The DimAdvertisement table contains two dates: start and end. These are the dates when the advertisement was delivered. The same information is stored for each single product inside the bridge table, indicating the start and end date of advertisement for each product.

You might be interested in filtering the fact table by using these two sets of dates. The resulting formulas are harder to write, but at the end, you have created a new kind of relationship that, although based on many-to-many relationships, is more complex. The same scenario in Multidimensional would be a nightmare because the standard many-to-many handling does not cover such a complex relationship.

> ### The Many-to-Many Revolution
>
> If you are interested in more examples of handling many-to-many relationships, you can check the white paper, "The Many-To-Many Revolution 2.0," which can be downloaded from *http://www.sqlbi.com/articles/many2many* and is constantly updated with new information about many-to-many relationships in Analysis Services, both Tabular and Multidimensional.

Implementing Basket Analysis

Now that you have learned the basics of many-to-many relationships, you can apply this knowledge to a common scenario in which many-to-many relationships are hidden. In this section, you learn how to perform basket analysis by using the many-to-many pattern.

Consider the following scenario. A data analyst at Adventure Works is interested in answering a simple question: "Of all the customers who bought a mountain bike, how many have never bought a mountain bike tire tube?" This scenario is interesting for a few reasons:

- You will use the DimCustomer and DimProduct tables to perform this analysis. This time, the fact table will be a bridge table to create a many-to-many relationship between these two tables, demonstrating a creative way of using many-to-many relationships.

- You want to search for missing values, that is, customers who did not buy a mountain bike tire tube. This kind of computation is not easy to perform in Multidimensional, but it will yield straightforward results by using Tabular, due to the nature of the DAX programming language.

- Even if DimCustomer is a dimension, you will use it to count values as if it were a fact table. Again, the power of the Tabular data model becomes apparent because, in Tabular, there is no distinction between facts and dimensions.

Take a look at the data model, which is very simple and is shown in Figure 12-14.

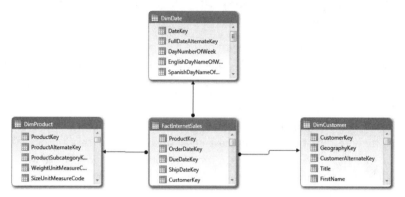

FIGURE 12-14 This is the data model you use to perform Basket Analysis by using many-to-many relationships.

The data model in Figure 12-14 is a classic star schema, but for the needs of our analysis, it is not sufficient. With an instance of DimProduct, you can select one product by using a slicer or a filter. If you look carefully at what the analysis needs, you must select two products: one is the mountain bike—that is, the product sold; the other is the mountain bike tire tube—that is, the product you want to analyze. Therefore, the data model must include a new instance of the DimProduct table. Figure 12-15 shows the resulting diagram.

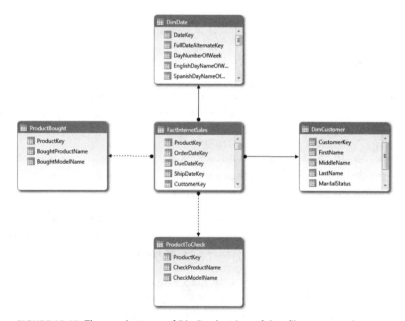

FIGURE 12-15 The new instance of DimProduct is useful to filter two products.

There are a few considerations about this new data model. First, because you now have two product tables, which act as roleplaying dimensions, the names of both have changed to reflect their roles: ProductBought will be the product customers have bought, and ProductToCheck will be the product (or family of products) the user wants to analyze. Moreover, you see that both the relationship from FactInternetSales to ProductBought and to ProductToCheck have been marked as inactive. If both relationships were active, choosing two products from the two tables would always result in an empty selection. However, you define the relationships in the data model but mark it as inactive so that they are used only when requested through *USERELATIONSHIP*.

 Important Always pay attention when there are many relationships starting from a single key in the fact table and pointing to different tables. SQL Server Data Tools (SSDT), by default, leaves them active, but there are very few cases in which you want two relationships active on the same key. We personally find it better to disable them and activate only the ones we need inside the formulas. Otherwise, there is always the risk of incurring complex side effects due to the interactions between the relationships. An interesting exercise would be to leave one of these two relationships (for example, the one with DimProduct) active and try to make the formula work. We suggest the brave reader take some time to do it.

Before learning the solution, it is worth looking at the final result you want to reach. Recall the original question: *"Of all the customers who bought a mountain bike, how many have never bought a mountain bike tire tube?"* In Figure 12-16, you see a report using this data model.

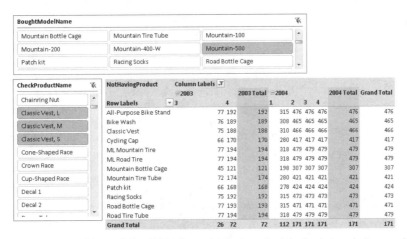

FIGURE 12-16 This Excel PivotTable shows the final result of the basket analysis scenario.

Note that the user has selected Mountain-500 as the bought product model name and, by using the slicer for CheckProductName, selected several products. What he or she wants to see is which customers have bought a Mountain-500 bike and have not bought any of the selected CheckProductNames.

There is a little issue with the calendar table. When a time period has been selected, will you detect the customer who bought the mountain bike during that time period or before it? The correct solution (or, at least, the one described here) is "before it." After all, if a customer bought a mountain bike in 2003, you still want to count it in 2004 to check whether the user is buying mountain bike tire tubes at any time after he or she bought the bike.

The problem can be divided into two steps:

1. Detect all the customers who bought a Mountain-500.

2. Check whether they have bought one of the products selected in CheckProductName.

Look at the following formula.

```
CALCULATE(
    CALCULATE(
        COUNTROWS( DimCustomer ),
        CALCULATETABLE(
            SUMMARIZE( FactInternetSales, DimCustomer[CustomerKey] ),
            USERELATIONSHIP( FactInternetSales[ProductKey], ProductBought[ProductKey] )
        ),
        FILTER(
            DimCustomer,
            CALCULATE(
                COUNTROWS( FactInternetSales ),
                USERELATIONSHIP( FactInternetSales[ProductKey], ProductToCheck[ProductKey] )
            ) = 0
        )
    ),
    FILTER(
        ALL( DimDate ),
        DimDate[DateKey] <= MAX( DimDate[DateKey] )
    )
)
```

Any formula with three nested *CALCULATE* functions is not an easy one, so take the necessary time to learn it.

- The outermost *CALCULATE* sets a filter on the DimDate table so that all computations are carried on in a filter context that uses a Time To Date pattern.

- The second *CALCULATE* uses two filters:

  - The first is the classic many-to-many pattern to filter the DimCustomer table, displaying only the customers who bought one of the ProductBought products. It is interesting to note that the role of the bridge table in this example is taken by the fact table, which acts as a bridge between the two dimensions (products and customers).

  - The second filter is a variation of the many-to-many pattern. It does not use *SUMMARIZE*; it uses the basic many-to-many formula instead. The reason is that *SUMMARIZE* is useful to find positive matches because it provides the distinct values of *CustomerKey*, which are present in the table. Because you are interested in finding missing values, you cannot use *SUMMARIZE*, so you must revert to the more basic version of the formula, which, by changing the condition from greater than zero to equal to zero, enables you to find missing values reflecting the customers who did not purchase the product.

Even if this formula is not an easy one, it clearly shows the power of Tabular as a data-modeling tool. Complex scenarios can be solved easily with some advanced DAX code, making it possible to create analytical models that follow very complex relationships with minimal effort.

Querying Data Models with Advanced Relationships

After you enter the world of advanced relationship handling in Tabular, you discover endless opportunities to use DAX to mimic complex scenarios. Nevertheless, remember that handling relationships in DAX comes at a price and, in this section, you learn some of the issues you might encounter when using advanced relationships in DAX and how to solve these issues.

The most important thing to remember when working with advanced relationships is that the data model is not aware of their existence and, for this reason, some of the automatic behaviors of the language will not work as expected. If you decide to handle some relationships by hand, you must always handle them. The following example clarifies this point.

Recall the many-to-many data model you learned in this chapter. In Figure 12-17, you see the cascading many-to-many data structure.

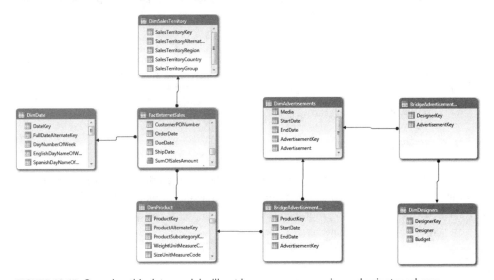

FIGURE 12-17 Querying this data model will not be as easy as querying a classic star schema.

If you query this data model by using Excel, you will have no problems, but if you want to use DAX to author a query, things are not straightforward. You can start with a simple DAX query, which returns the sales amount divided by year.

```
EVALUATE
SUMMARIZE(
    FactInternetSales,
    ROLLUP( DimDate[CalendarYear] ),
    "SalesAmount", [SalesAmountM2MCascading]
)
```

This query returns a correct dataset that, for each year, shows the total sales amount. You are not using any of the many-to-many relationships here, but, because the formula is working even when there are no filters over these tables, it works fine. You might be tempted to extend the pattern, adding the detail for the Advertisement, changing the query this way.

```
EVALUATE
SUMMARIZE (
    FactInternetSales,
    ROLLUP( DimDate[CalendarYear], DimAdvertisements[Advertisement] ),
    "SalesAmount", [SalesAmountM2MCascading]
)
```

Running this query results in an error.

> Query (2, 5) The column 'Advertisement' specified in the 'SUMMARIZE' function was not found in the input table.

The problem is that, because there are no relationships between the FactInternetSales and the DimAdvertisement tables, *SUMMARIZE* cannot build a path between the two tables. Thus, you cannot use *ROLLUP* on any column from the DimAdvertisement table when using *SUMMARIZE*.

To run this query, you must add the DimAdvertisement table manually to the context under which the *SUMMARIZE* function is called. One possible solution is the following.

```
EVALUATE
GENERATE(
    VALUES( DimAdvertisements[Advertisement] ),
    SUMMARIZE(
        FactInternetSales,
        ROLLUP( DimDate[CalendarYear] ),
        "SalesAmount", [SalesAmountM2MCascading]
    )
)
```

By using *GENERATE*, you are iterating over the DimAdvertisement table, and for each possible value of the *Advertisement* column, you run the inner *SUMMARIZE*, which works fine using only columns that can be reached by using modeled relationships. Look at the query, filtered for two years (to reduce the number of rows to analyze).

```
EVALUATE
CALCULATETABLE(
    GENERATE(
        VALUES( DimAdvertisements[Advertisement] ),
        SUMMARIZE(
            FactInternetSales,
            ROLLUP( DimDate[CalendarYear] ),
            "SalesAmount", [SalesAmountM2MCascading]
        )
    ),
    DimDate[CalendarYear] = 2001 || DimDate[CalendarYear] = 2002
)
ORDER BY DimDate[CalendarYear], DimAdvertisements[Advertisement]
```

This query returns the following dataset.

DimAdvertisements[Advertisement]	DimDate[CalendarYear]	[SalesAmount]
Christmas Leaflet		7318250.8131
Christmas TV Spot		6114854.2221
Easter Leaflet		4919467.1750
Easter TV Spot		5151033.4935
Christmas Leaflet	2001	2964011.4404
Christmas TV Spot	2001	1912535.6904
Easter Leaflet	2001	1429743.4792
Easter TV Spot	2001	1562409.2678
Christmas Leaflet	2002	4354239.3727
Christmas TV Spot	2002	4202318.5317
Easter Leaflet	2002	3489723.6958
Easter TV Spot	2002	3588624.2257

As you can see from the result, you get all the values for 2001, 2002, and their total, but you are missing the grand total. This is expected because the *GENERATE* function did not create a row for the grand total because it iterated over the values of Advertisement without generating the total row.

To get the desired result, you must change the way you query the data model. Instead of summarizing the fact table, create the *CROSSJOIN* of the values you want to query and then use *SUMMARIZE* on this temporary table, as you see in the following query.

```
EVALUATE
CALCULATETABLE(
    SUMMARIZE(
        CROSSJOIN(
            VALUES( DimAdvertisements[Advertisement] ),
            VALUES( DimDate[CalendarYear] )
        ),
        ROLLUP( DimAdvertisements[Advertisement], DimDate[CalendarYear] ),
        "SalesAmount", [SalesAmountM2MCascading]
    ),
    DimDate[CalendarYear] = 2001 || DimDate[CalendarYear] = 2002
)
ORDER BY DimDate[CalendarYear], DimAdvertisements[Advertisement]
```

The previous DAX query returns a better dataset, containing the desired subtotals, as shown in the following table.

DimAdvertisements[Advertisement]	DimDate[CalendarYear]	[SalesAmount]
		9776359.4430
Christmas Leaflet		7318250.8131
Christmas TV Spot		6114854.2221

DimAdvertisements[Advertisement]	DimDate[CalendarYear]	[SalesAmount]
Easter Leaflet		4919467.1750
Easter TV Spot		5151033.4935
Christmas Leaflet	2001	2964011.4404
Christmas TV Spot	2001	1912535.6904
Easter Leaflet	2001	1429743.4792
Easter TV Spot	2001	1562409.2678
Christmas Leaflet	2002	4354239.3727
Christmas TV Spot	2002	4202318.5317
Easter Leaflet	2002	3489723.6958
Easter TV Spot	2002	3588624.2257

The same pattern can also be used to query DimDesigner. In general, whenever you must query a data model in which some columns are not related to the main table used to compute the values required, you must use either *GENERATE* or *CROSSJOIN* to manually build the main dataset that fires the queries.

Complex Relationships and Power View

Power View is the new reporting tool available in the Microsoft business intelligence (BI) stack. One of the biggest issues with Power View is that, to present the user with a very simple user interface, it queries the Tabular data model and uses the metadata stored inside it to determine whether a table can be added to the report.

As a result, data models with chains of complex relationships cannot be easily queried by using Power View. For example, if you try to browse the many-to-many data model you used in this section, you will not be able to add any column from DimAdvertisement or DimDesigner to your data model because Power View cannot detect that these tables provide any filter to the measure.

Excel, however, does not have this limitation because it does not completely rely on the model metadata to filter the tables that the user can put on rows and columns. Because it is not as smart, Excel works better as a client for models with complex relationships.

It is hoped that this limitation will be removed in future versions of the tool, but at the time of writing this book, this severe limitation still applies and should be taken into account when designing the data model. If Power View is one of the most important user requirements, then advanced relationships cannot be defined by using DAX code, and you should use only standard relationships.

Implementing Currency Conversion

As a final example of how to handle complex relationships, you now learn a technique to handle currency conversion in DAX. Many techniques can be used to implement currency conversion in a Tabular solution, none of which is definitive because user requirements are very different in currency conversion. Nevertheless, because it is a good exercise, the following solution is based on the techniques you have learned so far for complex relationships.

There are three possible scenarios in which currency conversion comes into play:

- Data has been collected in a single currency, and you want to show in a report results in different currencies.

- Data has been collected in the original currency (for example, many different currencies), and you want to display results in a single currency to make comparisons.

- Data has been collected in the original currency (for example, many currencies), and you want to display results in many currencies.

This list is just the beginning of the complications that come when currency conversion comes into play. Because all three scenarios require currency conversion, the first question is which date to use to perform the conversion. Here, the business rules become complex. If the order was placed in euros at the first of December, you might be tempted to use the currency exchange of the first of December to perform the conversion. But if the customer paid in euros on the twelfth of December, and money has been left in a euro account until the end of the month, and only on the thirty-first of December it is converted to U.S. dollars (USD), which rate is the right one, the first, the twelfth, or the thirty-first of December? Only end users can advise you and decide a business rule. Nevertheless, because you must define a scenario and you want to use the Adventure Works database, use the following rules:

- Amounts stored in the fact table are always in USD. Conversion happened at some point during the population of the fact table, and you know it used the currency exchange of the date of the order.

- You want to report information about sales in original currencies, using two currency exchange rates:

  - The rate at the date of the order; thus, a different exchange for each order

  - The last available exchange rate (which, when in production, should be the current exchange rate)

As we said, this is an educational example; in the real world, business rules might be different, and in that case, you must change the formulas and the techniques to fit your specific needs.

You start loading DimDate, DimCurrency, FactInternetSales, and FactCurrencyRate in a new Tabular project, and you end up with a data model like the one shown in Figure 12-18.

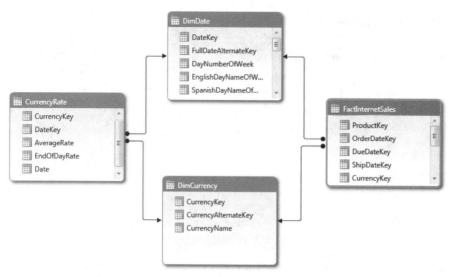

FIGURE 12-18 This is the data model you will use for currency conversion.

The data model is a star schema in which the fact table is related to two dimensions (DimDate and DimCurrency). The two dimensions are related through a many-to-many relationship through the FactCurrencyRate table, which states the exchange rate for each currency on that specific date. Note that, in reality, there is no relationship between the two dimensions. This information is more interesting and correct at the database level than at the analytical one. From the analytical point of view, dates and currencies are not related. The actual relationship is between the FactInternetSales and the FactCurrencyRate tables through the *OrderDateKey* and *CurrencyKey* keys.

This is a clear example of how the separation of your data model in facts and dimensions, which works fine for Multidimensional, is somehow a wrong representation for Tabular. In Tabular, there is no need to think of the FactCurrencyRate table as a fact table; it is a lookup table that you should use to gather the correct currency exchange for a specific date. For this reason, the Fact prefix is removed from the table name.

With this data model, it is easy to define a formula that computes the sales amount by using the original currency at the date of the order. You could create a multiple-column relationship from FactInternetSales to CurrencyRate, but because you want to be able to change the date of the exchange, you prefer to handle the relationship in DAX. Thus, the formula for OriginalAmount is the following.

```
[OriginalCurrencyAmount] :=
SUMX (
    FactInternetSales,
    FactInternetSales[SalesAmount] *
        LOOKUPVALUE(
            CurrencyRate[EndOfDayRate],
            CurrencyRate[DateKey], FactInternetSales[OrderDateKey],
            CurrencyRate[CurrencyKey], FactInternetSales[CurrencyKey]
        )
)
```

The formula iterates over all the orders, and for each order, it searches the correct currency rate in the CurrencyRate table to multiply the SalesAmount by the correct exchange rate.

On small data volumes, this formula is easy and works well, but if you care about performance, it is not an optimal one. The reason is that *LOOKUPVALUE* is a complex formula that must be resolved in the formula engine for each single order. If you have a hundred million orders, you start noticing that the formula is not as fast as it could be.

A better solution is to reduce the number of iterations. If you divide the FactInternetSales table into segments, each of which has a fixed exchange rate, you can compute the sum of the sales amount massively and multiply it by the single exchange rate. Looking at the formula should make the algorithm clearer. The following is a preliminary shape for the formula.

```
[OriginalCurrencyAmount] :=
SUMX(
    DimCurrency,
    SUMX(
        DimDate,
        CALCULATE( VALUES( CurrencyRate[AverageRate] ) * SUM( FactInternetSales[SalesAmount] ) )
    )
)
```

The number of iterations is now much lower because it is equivalent to the number of dates and currencies. For each combination of <Date, Currency>, there is a massive computation over the fact table that, this time, can be computed by the xVelocity in-memory engine in a highly parallelized way (due to the invariance of *VALUES(CurrencyRate[AverageRate])*, which is a constant in the expression and does not require multiple evaluations when scanning SalesAmount).

A more compact representation of the same formula is the following.

```
[OriginalCurrencyAmount] :=
SUMX(
    CROSSJOIN( DimCurrency, DimDate ),
    CALCULATE( VALUES( CurrencyRate[AverageRate] ) * SUM( FactInternetSales[SalesAmount] ) )
)
```

The behavior of the formula is the same, but by using *CROSSJOIN*, it becomes more compact and somewhat clearer. In Chapter 18, "Optimizations and Monitoring," you see a deeper analysis of the performances of the two formulas, and there you discover that the latter performs better, but it is too early now to describe performance analysis.

What should you change in the formula to take into account the fact that you might want to use a different exchange rate? One of the requirements is to be able to compute the value by using the last available exchange rate. The formula, thanks to the power of DAX, is easy to author. In this case, you do not need to iterate over DimDate because the value of the date is invariant. You just have to iterate DimCurrency because the value of the exchange rate is different for each currency.

```
[OriginalCurrencyAmountLastDate] :=
CALCULATE(
    SUMX(
        DimCurrency,
```

```
    CALCULATE(
        VALUES( CurrencyRate[AverageRate] ) * SUM( FactInternetsales[SalesAmount] )
    )
),
FILTER(
    VALUES( CurrencyRate[DateKey] ),
    CurrencyRate[DateKey] = MAX( CurrencyRate[DateKey] )
)
)
```

The last *FILTER* displays the exchange rate of only the last available date. Inside *SUMX*, which iterates over the currencies, the inner *CALCULATE* further restricts the filter on CurrencyRate so that only one row is visible, the row containing the exchange rate of the current currency for the last available date. It is clear that this formula outperforms the previous one in terms of speed because the number of iterations is reduced because there is no need to iterate over DimDate.

In this example, you learned how to use DAX to implement basic currency conversion. Your scenario might be different, but currency conversion in Tabular is just a complex relationship that can be handled by using the techniques you learned in this chapter.

Summary

Even though Tabular has a very simple relationship structure because it understands only one-column one-to-many relationships, by using DAX, you can build complex measures that perform computations by using much more complex kinds of relationships.

In this chapter, you learned how to handle:

- Multicolumn relationships.

- Banding; that is, *BETWEEN* relationships.

- Many-to-many relationships, both classic and cascading.

In addition, in the example of basket analysis, you saw the complete implementation of a system that, by using many-to-many relationships, can quite easily answer complex questions involving the detection of missing information.

Complex relationships come with a cost: They are harder both to author and to query, but the possibilities they open in data modeling are limitless. However, some client tools, such as Power View, have some limitations, at least in their current version, with complex relationships because these kinds of relationships are modeled in formulas and are not visible by analyzing the data-model metadata.

The Tabular Presentation Layer

One important consideration that is often ignored when designing Tabular models is usability. A Tabular model should be thought of as a user interface for the data it contains, and the success or failure of your project, to a large degree, depends on whether your end users find that interface intuitive and easy to use. This section covers a number of features the Tabular model provides to improve usability, such as the ability to sort data in a column and to control how measure values are formatted. It also covers perspectives, key performance indicators (KPIs), and actions. Although these features might seem less important than the ability to query vast amounts of data and perform complex calculations, they should not be dismissed or regarded as having only secondary importance; the functionality they provide is vital to helping your users make the most effective use of your Tabular model.

Naming, Sorting, and Formatting

The first aspect of the Tabular presentation layer to be considered—and probably the most important—is the naming, sorting, and formatting of objects.

Naming Objects

The naming of tables, columns, measures, and hierarchies is one area in which business intelligence (BI) professionals (especially if they come from a traditional database background) often make serious mistakes in usability. It's easy when developing a Tabular model to import data from various data sources and start building a model without thinking about naming, and as the development process continues, it becomes more difficult to change the names of objects because doing so breaks existing calculations and queries (including Microsoft Excel PivotTables and Power View reports). However, from an end user's point of view, naming objects is extremely important: It not only helps them understand what each object represents, but it also helps them produce professional-looking reports that are easy for their colleagues to understand.

As an example, consider the section of a Microsoft PivotTable field list shown in Figure 13-1.

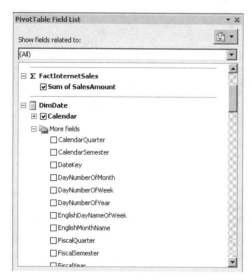

FIGURE 13-1 This shows an example of poor object naming.

Now ask yourself the following questions:

- Do your users know what a fact table is? The answer is likely to be no, in which case, will they understand what the Fact prefix in the FactInternetSales table name means? Wouldn't it be clearer to call the table Internet Sales?

- In a similar case, even if your users know what a dimension is, will they want all their dimension table names to be prefixed with Dim, as in DimDate and DimProduct? Wouldn't Date and Product look better?

- Technical naming conventions often remove spaces from names, but what purpose does this achieve in a Tabular model? Again, wouldn't putting spaces in names look more professional and help readability?

- Even if the Sum of SalesAmount measure does return the sum of values in the *SalesAmount* column, will your users want to build reports with Sum of Sales Amount as a column header and then show that report to their colleagues? Wouldn't using Sales Amount as a measure name be a better option?

Note Measures and table columns share the same namespace, and that can present a dilemma when you want to build a measure from a column such as *SalesAmount* and expose the column so it can be used on the rows or columns of a query. In this case, calling the measure Sales Amount and the underlying column *Sales Amount Values* might be appropriate, but in cases like this, you should always let your end users make the final decision.

Figure 13-2 shows what the same PivotTable field list looks like after these issues have been fixed.

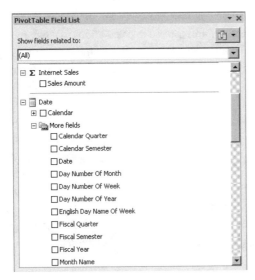

FIGURE 13-2 This shows an example of user-friendly object naming.

It is important to discuss the names of tables, columns, measures, and hierarchies with your users at a very early stage in the project life cycle because, as mentioned, this saves you many hours of tedious work fixing calculations and queries at the end of your project if users decide they can't work with the names you have given them. A strict naming convention is usually not necessary (and, indeed, can be counterproductive) so long as you follow these two rules:

- Always use names that help users understand what the data means in business terms. For example, if users always talk about "volume" rather than "units sold," use the term "volume" in your measure names.

- Always use names that a user would not be ashamed to put, unaltered, on a report that could be shown to the CEO; think about what looks good from a business standpoint rather than what is acceptable from an IT standpoint.

 Note Having told you to modify the names of your objects, we will ignore this good advice throughout this book and leave the object names from Adventure Works as they are when created. This makes it easier to follow our examples, but remember: Do as we say, not as we do!

Hiding Columns

One important point that has been made several times so far in this book is that if a column in your data warehouse will not be useful to your end users, you should not import it into your model because it will use up memory and increase processing time. Furthermore, useless columns also hurt usability because the more columns there are to choose from, the harder it is for your end users to find the columns they want to use in their reports. Some columns, however, are necessary for properties such as Row Identifier (described later in this chapter) and for use in calculations, so they must be present even if the user does not want to use them in a report. In these cases, the Hidden property of the column should be set to *True*, because the smaller the number of columns displayed to the end user, the easier the model is to use.

Organizing Measures

One useful piece of functionality from the Multidimensional model that is not yet supported in the Tabular model is the ability to group multiple measures into display folders so that users can find the measure for which they are looking more easily. Although it is likely that BIDS Helper will provide this functionality at some point (again, this is functionality that exists in the engine but is not exposed in SQL Server Data Tools [SSDT]), an alternative approach involving pasted tables is described by Cathy Dumas at *http://cathydumas.com/2012/02/09/pasted-tablesa-poor-womans-display-folder.*

Sorting Column Data

In many cases, the order in which values appear in a column is irrelevant; by default, Tabular does not apply any sorting to data in columns, and this usually causes no problems. The most common situations when alphabetical ordering for data is not suitable occur on Date dimension tables: Days of the week and months of the year have their own inherent order that must be used in any reports built on your model.

Sorting data in columns can be achieved by using the Sort By Column property of a column, as shown in Figure 13-3.

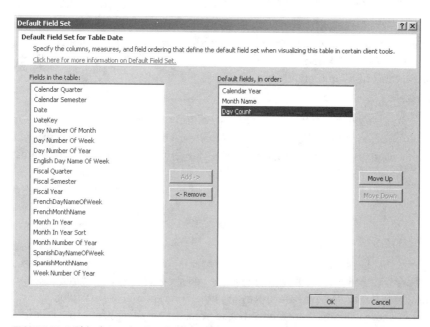

FIGURE 13-3 This shows the Sort By Column property.

The Sort By Column property appears fairly straightforward. For any column in a table, it enables you to specify another column in the same table to control the sort order. There are three important things to realize about this property, however:

- It is possible to sort in only ascending order according to the data in the Sort By Column.

- The data in the column to be sorted and the data in Sort By Column must be of the same granularity, so for each distinct value in the column, there must be a single, equivalent value in Sort By Column.

- For MDX client tools, this property affects how members are ordered on a hierarchy, but it does not directly affect DAX queries. Client tools such as Power View have to read this property value from the model metadata and then generate an appropriate *Order By* clause in the queries they generate.

For the *EnglishDayNameOfWeek* column shown in Figure 13-3, another column is already in the Date table that can be used for sorting: *DayNumberofWeek*, which contains day numbers from 1 to 7, in which 1 is Sunday and 7 is Saturday. Setting the Sort By Column property for *EnglishDayNameOfWeek* to *DayNumberOfWeek* means that the *EnglishDayNameOfWeek* column will be displayed in PivotTables, as shown in Figure 13-4.

Row Labels	Sales Amount
Sunday	4231641.557
Monday	4154919.587
Tuesday	4153092.89
Wednesday	4127214.747
Thursday	4113748.62
Friday	4235385.791
Saturday	4342674.03
Grand Total	29358677.22

FIGURE 13-4 This shows an example of sorted day names.

What happens if there isn't an obvious candidate for a column to use for sorting? Consider the *Month In Year* calculated column shown in Figure 13-5, which contains the month name concatenated with the year; for example, returning values such as January 2002 or March 2006.

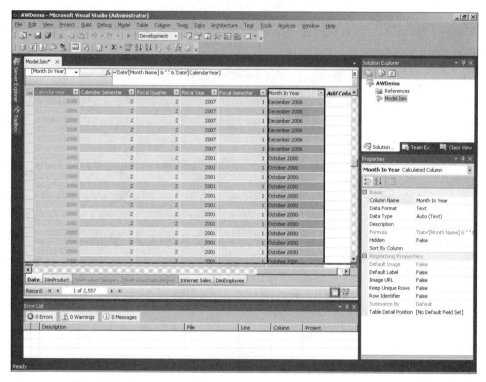

FIGURE 13-5 This shows the *Month In Year* column.

If there is no column with the same granularity (which means you need a column with one distinct value for each distinct value in *Month In Year*) by which to sort, you could try to sort by using a column with a different granularity. However, if you choose a column with a larger number of distinct values, such as the *DateKey* column, you get the error shown in Figure 13-6.

> *Cannot sort Month In Year by DateKey because at least one value in Month In Year has multiple distinct values in DateKey. For example, you can sort [City] by [Region] because there is only one region for each city, but you cannot sort [Region] by [City] because there are multiple cities for each region.*

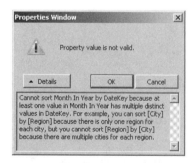

FIGURE 13-6 This is the Sort By Column error message.

If you sort by a column that has a smaller number of distinct values, such as *CalendarYear*, you will not get an error, but you won't get your values within sorted correctly either; you'll see each month sorted by year, but you can't guarantee the order within the year, as shown in Figure 13-7.

Row Labels	Sales Amount
July 2001	473388.163
September 2001	473943.0312
October 2001	513329.474
December 2001	755527.8914
November 2001	543993.4058
August 2001	506191.6912
April 2002	663692.2868
May 2002	673556.1978
June 2002	676763.6496
January 2002	596746.5568
August 2002	546001.4708
March 2002	644135.2022
December 2002	577314.0002
July 2002	500365.155
October 2002	415390.2333
September 2002	350466.9912
February 2002	550816.694
November 2002	335095.0887
June 2003	554799.2281
March 2003	485574.7923

FIGURE 13-7 This shows an example of incorrect sorting by year.

One solution is to create a new calculated column with the correct granularity specifically to sort the *Month In Year* column (the alternative is to create the column in your relational data source). This can be achieved with the following calculated column definition.

```
[Month In Year Sort] := ( DimDate[CalendarYear] * 100 ) + DimDate[MonthNumberOfYear]
```

This expression, for example, returns the value *200107* for the month of July 2007, as shown in Figure 13-8, and this means that the contents of the *Month In Year* column are sorted properly when the *Month In Year Sort* column is used in the Sort By Column property, as shown in Figure 13-9.

Month In Year	Month In Year Sort
July 2000	200007
July 2000	200007
July 2000	200007
July 2001	200107
July 2001	200107
July 2001	200107
July 2001	200107
July 2001	200107
July 2001	200107
July 2001	200107
July 2001	200107
July 2001	200107
July 2001	200107
July 2001	200107
July 2001	200107
July 2001	200107
July 2001	200107

FIGURE 13-8 This shows the *Month In Year Sort* column.

Row Labels	Sales Amount
July 2001	£473,388.16
August 2001	£506,191.69
September 2001	£473,943.03
October 2001	£513,329.47
November 2001	£543,993.41
December 2001	£755,527.89
January 2002	£596,746.56
February 2002	£550,816.69
March 2002	£644,135.20
April 2002	£663,692.29
May 2002	£673,556.20
June 2002	£676,763.65
July 2002	£500,365.16
August 2002	£546,001.47
September 2002	£350,466.99
October 2002	£415,390.23
November 2002	£335,095.09
December 2002	£577,314.00
January 2003	£438,865.17
February 2003	£489,090.34
March 2003	£485,574.79
April 2003	£506,399.27
May 2003	£562,772.56
June 2003	£554,799.23
July 2003	£886,668.84

FIGURE 13-9 This shows the *Month In Year* column sorted correctly.

Note Analysis Services checks that a column of appropriate granularity is used for Sort By Column only when that property is first set. As a result, new data can be loaded into the table that breaks the sorting, with no errors raised. You must be careful that this does not happen, and including a check for this in your extract, transform, and load (ETL) process might be a good idea.

Formatting

Numeric values in columns and measures can have formatting applied to them, and it is important to do this because unformatted or "raw" values can be extremely difficult to read and interpret.

Formatting Columns

Number formats for numeric data in both normal columns and calculated columns can be set with the Data Format property. The values available for this property are determined by the value of the Data Type property, which was discussed in Chapter 3, "Loading Data Inside Tabular," and sets the type for the values held in the column. Depending on the value selected for Data Format, other properties might become enabled that further control formatting. As with the Sort By Column property, number formatting is applied automatically only when connecting through an MDX client tool. DAX queries do not display formatted values, only the raw data, so if you are running DAX queries, you must read the metadata to determine the appropriate format and apply it to your results yourself.

The available Data Format property values for each data type (excluding *Text*) are listed here:

- For the *Date* type, a General format shows the date and time in the default format for the locale of the client querying the model. (See the following for more details about how language affects formatting.) There is also a long list of built-in formats for showing dates, times and dates, and times together in different formats, and you can also enter your own formats.

- For the *Whole Number* and *Decimal Number* types, the following formats are available:

  - General, which shows the number in the default format for the client tool.

  - Decimal Number, which shows the value formatted as a decimal number. When this format is selected, two further properties are enabled:

    - Decimal Places, to set the number of decimal places displayed

    - Show Thousand Separator, to set whether the thousand separator appropriate for the language of the client is displayed

  - Whole Number, which formats the value as a whole number. The Show Thousand Separator property is enabled when this format is selected.

  - Currency, which formats the value as a monetary value. When this format is selected, two further properties are enabled:

    - Decimal Places, which by default is set to *2*.

    - Currency Symbol, which sets the currency symbol used in the format. The default symbol used is the symbol associated with the language of the model.

  - Percentage, which formats the value as a percentage. Note that the formatted value appears to be multiplied by 100, so a raw value of 0.96 will be displayed as 96%. The Decimal Places and Show Thousand Separator properties are enabled when this format is selected.

  - Scientific, which formats the value in scientific form using exponential (e) notation. For more details on scientific form, see *http://en.wikipedia.org/wiki/Scientific_notation*. The Decimal Places property is enabled when this format is selected.

- For the *True/False* type, values can be formatted as *TRUE* or *FALSE* only.

 Note Number formats in the Tabular model are designed to be consistent with PowerPivot, which is designed to be consistent with Excel.

Formatting Measures

Measures can be formatted in much the same way as columns, although in the case of measures the property to use is called Format. The property values available for Format are the same as the values available for the Data Format property of a column.

Language and Collation

A Tabular model has both a Language property and a Collation property (visible in the Property pane when the .bim file of your model is selected in Solution Explorer in SSDT), which are both fixed when the model is created and which cannot subsequently be changed. The Collation of a model controls how sorting and comparison of values behaves. The Language of a model influences how formatting takes place for the General formats for dates and numeric values (for example, it controls the default currency symbol used), but these defaults can and should be overridden when configuring the Data Format and Format properties. The locale of the machine that is querying the Tabular model also plays an important role. For example, the date of the 4th of August, 2012, when formatted using the General format, will be displayed as 8/4/2012 00:00:00 on a machine using the English (US) locale, whereas it will be displayed as 04/08/2012 00:00:00 on a machine using the English (UK) locale. In a similar case, the thousands and decimal separators vary by locale. A value that is displayed as 123,456.789 in the English (US) locale will be displayed as 123.456,789 in the Italian locale.

The following links describe in more detail how languages and collations work and how they are set when a model is created:

- *http://msdn.microsoft.com/en-us/library/ms174872(v=SQL.110).aspx*

- *http://blogs.msdn.com/b/cathyk/archive/2011/10/21/collation-and-language-settings-in-tabular-models.aspx*

Perspectives

Most Tabular models that work on large and complex data sources contain many tables, each with many columns in it. Although hiding tables and columns that should never be used in queries or reports will go a long way to improving the usability of a model, it still may be the case that some groups of users will never want to see or use some parts of the model. For example, if a single model contains data from the HR, Marketing, and Finance departments, even if some users want to see and use all this data, it is equally possible that some users in the HR department want to use only the HR data; some users in Marketing will want to use only the Marketing data; and so on. Perspectives enable you to meet this requirement by creating something similar to a view in a relational database. You can create what looks like a new model for specific groups of users who want to see only part of the underlying mode by hiding the parts of the underlying model that these users don't want to see.

To create a new perspective, click Perspectives in the Model menu in SSDT. This displays all perspectives in the model. To create a new perspective, click the New Perspective button, enter a name for the perspective at the top of the new column that appears, and then check all the fields and measures in the dialog box under the new perspective's name to add them to the perspective, as shown in Figure 13-10. Click OK.

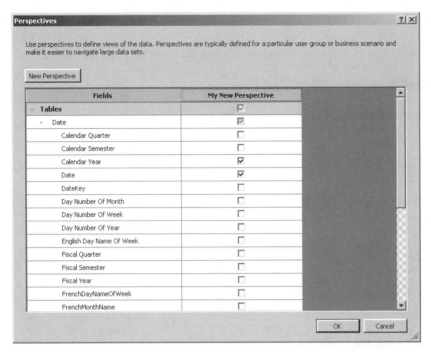

FIGURE 13-10 This is the Perspectives dialog box.

To test a perspective, click the Analyze In Excel button on the toolbar in SSDT and then, in the Perspective drop-down menu, choose the name of the perspective, as shown in Figure 13-11.

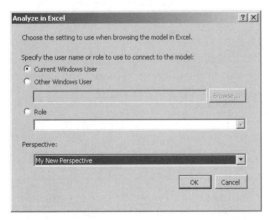

FIGURE 13-11 This shows how to choose a perspective to test.

This opens Excel with a new PivotTable connected to the perspective. As an alternative, if you want to create a new connection yourself in Excel in the way that end users will, select the perspective name from the list of cubes in the Data Connection Wizard, as shown in Figure 13-12.

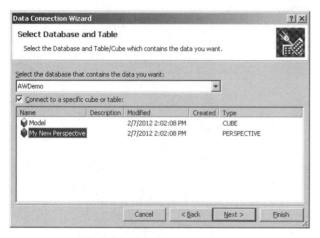

FIGURE 13-12 This shows how to connect to a perspective by using Excel.

You see that in the PivotTable field list, you can see only the tables, measures, and columns that you added to the perspective, but in all other respects, the experience is the same as querying the whole model.

It is extremely important to understand that perspectives are not a substitute for security and cannot be secured as objects. Even if a user cannot see an object in a perspective, he or she can still write DAX or MDX queries that return data from those objects if the user knows the object's name.

Note At the time of release to manufacturing (RTM) of SQL Server 2012, Power View is not able to "see" perspectives; it can only connect to the underlying model and therefore always displays all the visible tables, columns, and measures in the model.

Power View–Related Properties

A number of properties in the Tabular model act as metadata for Power View (or any other client tools that want to read them; Excel does not) to influence how the model is displayed in a client tool.

Default Field Set

The Default Field Set for a table is a set of columns and measures that is displayed automatically in a Power View canvas when a user double-clicks that table in the field list. Setting up a Default Field Set makes it faster for Power View users to create a report because it reduces the amount of dragging and dropping that is necessary.

To set up a Default Field Set, either select the Table in SSDT and click the Default Field Set property or select a measure or column in a table and click the Table Detail Position property. This opens the Default Field Set dialog box, as shown in Figure 13-13.

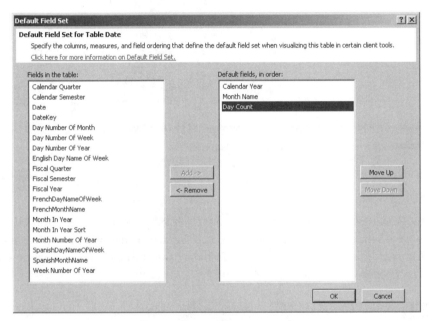

FIGURE 13-13 This shows the Default Field Set dialog box.

In this dialog box, you can choose which columns and measures are to be displayed and the order in which they are displayed. (The position is then subsequently stored as a 1-based index in the Table Detail Position property for a column or measure.)

After the model has been saved and deployed, in Power View, you can double-click the name of the table in the field list to create a table on the canvas with the selected columns and measures in it, as shown in Figure 13-14.

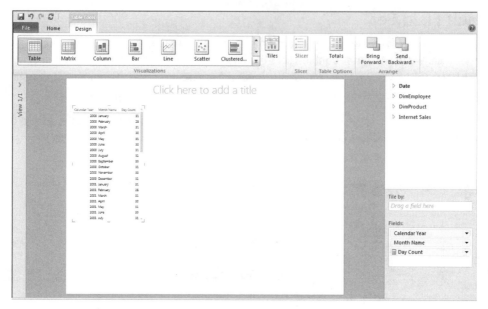

FIGURE 13-14 This shows a Power View report using the Default Field Set.

Table Behavior Properties

The Table Behavior Properties can be found by clicking a table in SSDT and then, in the Properties pane, clicking the Table Behavior property group to bring up the Table Behavior dialog box, as shown in Figure 13-15. (Don't try to expand the property group in the pane and edit the properties outside the dialog box; it isn't possible to do this.)

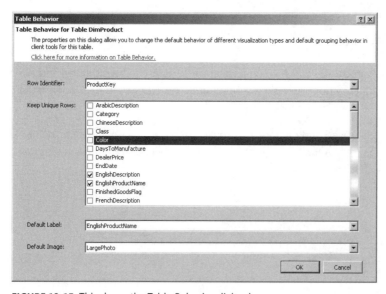

FIGURE 13-15 This shows the Table Behavior dialog box.

The properties that can be set in this dialog box are as follows:

- Row Identifier, which was discussed in Chapter 11, "Data Modeling in Tabular." This property enables you to specify a single column to act like the primary key of the table; it must have a unique value for each row. Setting a Row Identifier enables the Keep Unique Rows, Default Label, and Default Image properties; it also affects where subtotals are displayed in *Matrix* controls in reports. The process of marking a table as a Date table, which you saw in Chapter 8, "Understanding Time Intelligence in DAX," involves setting the Row Identifier, and after this is done, the Row Identifier property cannot be changed manually.

- Keep Unique Rows, which enables you to select columns which, when used in a Power View report, have their uniqueness determined by the column specified in the Row Identifier property. For example, this would be important on a Customer dimension table in which some customers might have the same name. Assuming there were a *Customer Key* column with a numeric key that identified individual customers, and a *Customer Name* column, you could set the Row Identifier property of the table to *Customer Key* and select *Customer Name* in Keep Unique Rows. This means that when you use the *Customer Name* column alone in a table in a Power View report, there is one row for each unique customer, not for each unique name. If there were two customers with the name John Smith, there would be two rows with that name. Again, this property does not have any automatic effect on DAX queries; it just informs Power View (and any other clients that look at this property in the metadata) that it should include the column specified in Row Identifier in any queries that use any of the columns selected in the Keep Unique Rows property.

- Default Label, which sets the column that contains the name or label that should be used for each unique row in the table. In the example of the Customer dimension, used in the previous bullet, if each row in the table represents a customer, the *Customer Name* column should be used as the Default Label. This property is used as the default label for a card or a chart in a Power View report.

- Default Image, which sets the column that contains either binary data containing an image or text data that can be interpreted as the URL of an image. (For a text column to be selectable in this case, it must have its Image URL property set to *True*.) This image is then used by Power View either in the navigation pane of a tile report or on the front of a card.

To illustrate how these properties work, first create a basic Power View report from a model that includes the DimProduct table with none of these properties set. If you drag the *EnglishProductName* column onto the canvas, you see that only the distinct product names are displayed; so, for example, the Mountain 200 – Black, 42 product name appears only once. Go back to the model and set the Table Behavior properties as shown in Figure 13-15: Set the Row Identifier to *ProductKey*, select EnglishDescription and EnglishProductName in Keep Unique Rows, set Default Label to EnglishProductName, and set Default Image to LargePhoto.

Go back to Power View and create a tile report layout in a new report by using the DimProduct table. Notice that the Mountain 200 – Black, 42 product name now appears three times. Because DimProduct is a type 2 slowly changing dimension, there are three distinct *ProductKey* values with this name. Notice also that some (although not all) products have images associated with them on the tiles, as shown in Figure 13-16.

FIGURE 13-16 This shows a Power View tile report with images.

 Note Power View reads metadata from a Tabular model by querying the DISCOVER_CSDL_ METADATA schema rowset, as documented at *http://msdn.microsoft.com/en-us/library/ gg471582(v=sql.110).aspx*.

Drillthrough

Drillthrough functionality enables an end user to double-click a cell of data in a client tool and display a table containing all the rows from the underlying table in the Tabular model. This can be useful if, for example, a user sees a strange sales figure in a report and wants to see all the invoice lines with values that contributed to that figure.

Unlike Drillthrough in the Multidimensional model, SSDT does not support the creation of new drillthrough actions for Tabular models. Only one default action is created per table, which returns every column in that table, and it's unlikely that users will want to see every column when they perform a drillthrough. It is, however, possible to add actions to an existing model by executing an XMLA

Alter command against it, as detailed in the blog post by Marco Russo at *http://sqlblog.com/blogs/ marco_russo/archive/2011/08/18/drillthrough-for-bism-tabular-and-attribute-keys-in-ssas-denali.aspx*. BIDS Helper also includes functionality for defining actions inside SSDT; find more information about that at *http://bidshelper.codeplex.com/wikipage?title=Tabular%20Actions%20Editor*.

> **Note** It should be stressed that although drillthrough actions are supported by Analysis Services 2012 in Tabular, issuing *Alter* commands in XMLA against a Tabular model is not supported. Use this technique at your own risk.

Drillthrough MDX commands can also be executed against a Tabular model. For more details about the syntax, see *http://technet.microsoft.com/en-us/library/ms145964.aspx*.

KPIs

A KPI, or key performance indicator, is a way of comparing the value of one measure to another. For example, you might want to analyze profitability by comparing the cost of goods used to make a product with the value at which the product is sold, or to see whether the time taken to deal with support calls on a helpdesk is within acceptable thresholds.

To create a KPI in a Tabular model, you must start with an existing measure. Using the FactInternetSales table in Adventure Works as an example, create two measures that sum the values of the *TotalProductCost* and *SalesAmount* columns, as shown in Figure 13-17.

	ProductStandardCost	TotalProductCost	SalesAmount	TaxAmt	
0.00 %	1.87E+000	£1.87	£4.99	£0.40	
0.00 %	1.87E+000	£1.87	£4.99	£0.40	
0.00 %	1.87E+000	£1.87	£4.99	£0.40	
0.00 %	1.87E+000	£1.87	£4.99	£0.40	
0.00 %	1.87E+000	£1.87	£4.99	£0.40	
0.00 %	1.87E+000	£1.87	£4.99	£0.40	
0.00 %	1.87E+000	£1.87	£4.99	£0.40	
0.00 %	1.87E+000	£1.87	£4.99	£0.40	
0.00 %	1.87E+000	£1.87	£4.99	£0.40	
0.00 %	1.87E+000	£1.87	£4.99	£0.40	
0.00 %	1.87E+000	£1.87	£4.99	£0.40	
0.00 %	1.87E+000	£1.87	£4.99	£0.40	
0.00 %	1.87E+000	£1.87	£4.99	£0.40	

Sum of TotalProductCost: £17,277,793.58   Sum of SalesAmount: £29,358,677.22   Sum of TaxAmt: …

FIGURE 13-17 This shows the measures used in the KPI example.

Next, select the measure that sums the *TotalProductCost* column and either click the Create KPI button in the toolbar or select Create KPI from the right-click menu. This displays the Key Performance Indicator dialog box shown in Figure 13-18.

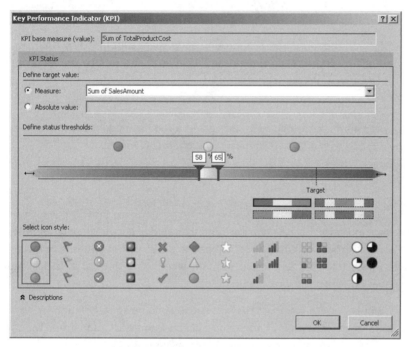

FIGURE 13-18 This shows the Key Performance Indicator dialog box.

The KPI Base Measure text box displays the name of the measure you have just selected. The next step is to define a target value, and this can be either another measure in the model or an absolute value that must be entered. In this case, choose the measure that returns the sum of *SalesAmount*. The ratio of the base measure to the target is compared to a set of thresholds that determine the status: good, intermediate, or bad.

You must then choose a threshold type by clicking one of the four rectangular boxes in the middle-right side of the dialog box. For example, the top-right threshold type defines a low ratio value as bad (red), a middling ratio value as intermediate (yellow), and a high ratio value as good (green), but the bottom-left threshold type inverts this and defines a low ratio value as good, and so on. Using the default threshold type, you must set the threshold values as percentages in the boxes above the slider in the center of the screen. In this example, use the value of 58% for the lower threshold and the value of 61% for the higher threshold. After that, you can select an icon style for your client tools to use. (The client tool will not necessarily use the icons shown in the dialog box; this is just a guide to the *style* of icon to use.) Finally, clicking the Descriptions arrow in the bottom-left corner of the dialog box displays a series of text boxes in which you can enter descriptions for the KPI, the value, the status, and the target. After clicking OK, the KPI appears in the measure grid in SSDT in the same place as the base measure, as shown in Figure 13-19, and can be edited by right-clicking that cell.

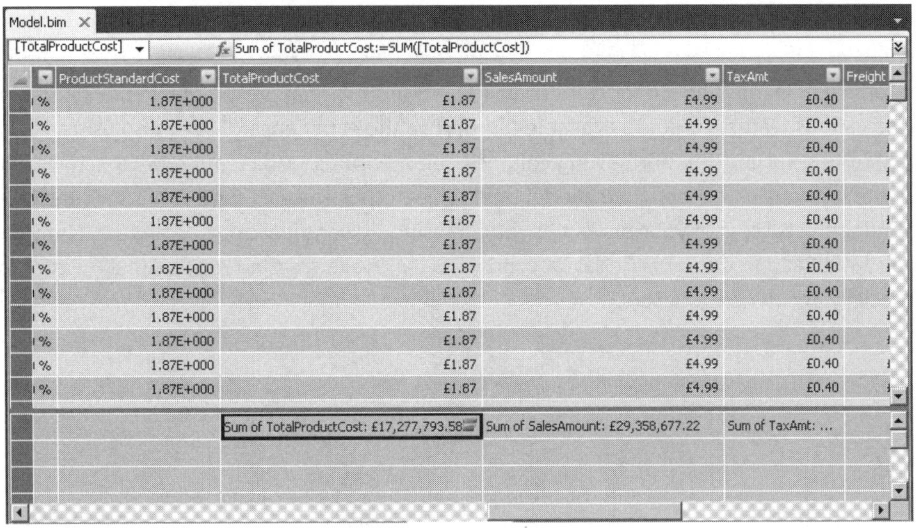

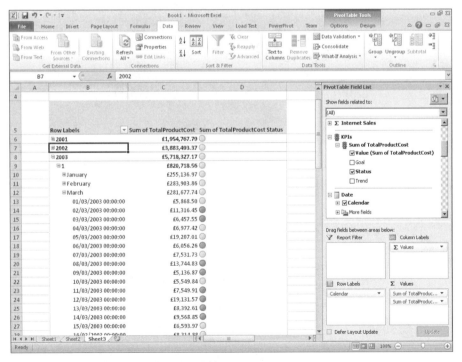

FIGURE 13-19 This shows a KPI in the measure grid.

After the KPI has been created, it can be used in an Excel PivotTable, as shown in Figure 13-20. It appears in the KPI section of the field list and behaves like a measure. Note that although a Trend value is available for selection in Excel, there is no way of configuring the Trend value for a KPI in SSDT for a Tabular model (although there is for a Multidimensional model).

FIGURE 13-20 This shows a KPI in a PivotTable.

Summary

In this chapter, you learned how important usability and professional presentation is to Tabular models, and the various features that are available to improve the experience of your end users. Naming, hiding or showing, sorting, and formatting columns and measures, and creating perspectives and KPIs can make the difference between your model being rejected or embraced by your users and therefore determine the success of your project. If you are using Power View on your project, configuring the Default Field Set and the Table Behavior properties can make creating reports much easier for users, especially inexperienced users.

Tabular and PowerPivot

At this point in the book, you have learned many interesting features of Tabular and the DAX language. The xVelocity in-memory analytics engine powers two other noteworthy Microsoft tools in the business intelligence (BI) world, PowerPivot for Microsoft Excel and PowerPivot for Microsoft SharePoint. PowerPivot is actually just another name for the xVelocity engine running over Tabular projects. Nevertheless, there are some differences among the products, even if what you learn about the DAX language and the modeling techniques applies to all of them, because they all share the same core.

In this chapter, you learn the differences between the versions of the engine and how to choose the right tool for your scenarios.

PowerPivot for Microsoft Excel 2010

In this section, you learn the basics of PowerPivot for Microsoft Excel, which is probably the best tool to prototype Tabular data models side by side with your customer, producing the first draft of the reports that will eventually be integrated in a corporate Tabular solution. We will not provide a complete description of how PowerPivot for Excel works or how to create measures and calculated columns in the tool; the focus of this section is on understanding the differences between Tabular and PowerPivot for Excel from a higher perspective.

PowerPivot for Excel is a free add-in that can be downloaded from www.powerpivot.com and contains the SQL Server Analysis Services (SSAS) engine configured to run in-process inside Excel, providing access to the tremendous power of the xVelocity engine. It requires Excel 2010 and is available in both 32-bit and 64-bit versions, depending on the Office installation. There are two versions of PowerPivot for Excel. Version 1.0 was released in June 2010, and version 2.0 is released with SQL Server 2012. In this chapter, we always refer to the latter version.

Because it's based on the xVelocity engine, PowerPivot for Excel makes available most of the interesting features of Tabular data models. The focus of PowerPivot for Excel is self-service BI, the capability to place useful BI data models in the hands of individuals. For this reason, none of the features of PowerPivot for Excel require you to open SQL Server Data Tools (SSDT); they are integrated in Excel.

After you install PowerPivot for Excel, you have a new tab in the Excel ribbon from which you can perform some basic operations (see Figure 14-1).

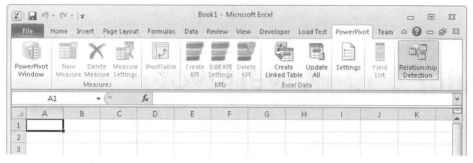

FIGURE 14-1 PowerPivot installs a new tab in the Excel 2010 ribbon.

Among the features available on the new PowerPivot tab, the most important is the ability to open the PowerPivot window, a new window that contains all the features of PowerPivot, as shown in Figure 14-2.

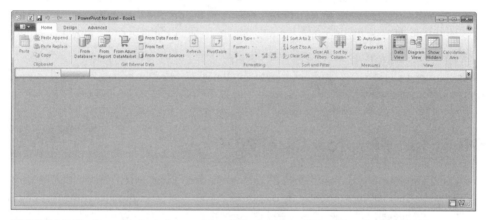

FIGURE 14-2 The PowerPivot window contains all the features of PowerPivot for Excel 2010.

As you can see, the user interface is very different from SSDT. The buttons are much larger to make the detection of features easier, and there is no menu; the complete user interface is contained in three tabs of a classic Office ribbon. The expected user of this interface is an Excel user, not a professional programmer. Among the tabs, the Advanced tab is activated only when PowerPivot runs in advanced mode, which is a feature available by using the small black button in the top-left corner of the window.

As mentioned, we will not show you how to complete all the basic operations by using PowerPivot for Excel; it is enough to say that, even though the user interface is completely different, most of the features of Tabular are available in PowerPivot for Excel. The main differences are:

- No security is available. PowerPivot for Excel is intended for a single user; thus, there is no option to create roles and set up security expressions on tables. After you have the Excel workbook available, all its content is visible. If you share the workbook with someone, you must be aware that all its data is available and visible.

- Partitioning is not present. Partitioning is a feature required to handle big datasets and to make it easier to add segments of data during periodic processing of the database. In PowerPivot, you have the option to refresh one table or the complete dataset, but every time you process the database, a full process of the tables is issued.

- Security and impersonation behave differently. Whenever PowerPivot for Excel processes a table, it impersonates the current user (the user working on the worksheet). For this reason, whenever you load data by using one of the data sources of PowerPivot for Excel, you cannot change the impersonation options because they are not used when refreshing data. However, you can still use Microsoft SQL Server authentication for storing username and password in the connection parameters so that a user will have the same credentials when refreshing data.

- PowerPivot for Excel has a 4-GB limit. The complete dataset, loaded in memory, must fit in 4 GB if you are using the 64-bit version of PowerPivot. For the 32-bit version, the limit is much smaller because PowerPivot for Excel can address only 2 GB and because around 800 MB must be used for various overhead functions, so there is no more than 1 GB of space that can be used for the data. This is not usually a strong limitation because working on a bigger dataset on a personal PC is not often a good choice. In Tabular, the only limitation on the size of a database is the available RAM, whereas in PowerPivot, no matter how much RAM is installed, you cannot create data models bigger than 4 GB.

- No application processing interface (API) is available. There is no supported way to interact programmatically with the xVelocity engine inside Excel or to create objects or query the database. Even if someone on the web has found a way to interact with the internal engine, this feature is not supported in PowerPivot for Excel; thus, it can be used only at your own risk. However, SSAS is designed to accept and work with XMLA commands and with Analysis Management Objects (AMOs), as you learn in Chapter 16, "Interfacing with Tabular."

Apart from these limitations, which are usually not an issue for self-service BI users, the full power of xVelocity and DAX is available in PowerPivot for Excel.

Where Does PowerPivot for Excel Store Data?

From a technical point of view, the Excel file contains a full backup of a Tabular data model, which is restored by the private instance of SSAS running inside Excel when the workbook is opened and then managed by the xVelocity engine.

If you want a more detailed explanation of how to open the backup, you can find information at *http://powerpivot-info.com/post/92-how-can-i-see-analysis-services-database-structure-that-is-stored-within-powerpivot*.

Using the PowerPivot Field List

When you browse a PowerPivot for Excel data model inside Excel, you do not use the classic field list; you use an optimized field list called the PowerPivot field list. In this section, you learn the main differences between the two flavors of field lists.

In Figure 14-3, you see a typical Excel report with the PowerPivot Field List menu on the left.

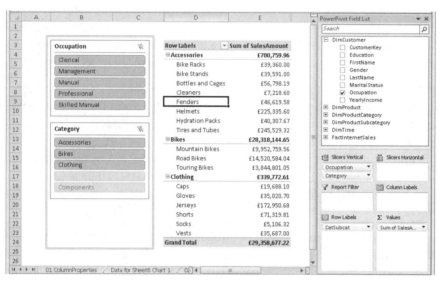

FIGURE 14-3 The PowerPivot Field List menu is open in a typical Excel report with PowerPivot for Excel.

There are several notable differences between the classic field list and the PowerPivot field list:

■ The data model shows tables, not dimensions and measure groups. Whenever Excel queries a Tabular data model, it shows the user the classic dimensional model built with dimensions and measure groups. However, the PowerPivot field list shows the Tabular model under the dimensional surface. There are no measure groups and no dimensions, just plain tables, each column of which can be used as either a slicing column or a measure.

■ The PowerPivot field list has implicit measure creation. Whenever you bring a column from a table and put it in the Values area, an implicit aggregation measure is created by the field list. Thus, if you want to see the sum of SalesAmount, you don't need to create a measure containing the formula because one is automatically created by the field list as required. Moreover, you can change the aggregation formula by using the user interface, as you learn in the next section of this chapter.

■ The PowerPivot field list has automatic slicer handling. If you want to add a slicer to the report, just drop one column into one of the two Slicer areas (Vertical and Horizontal), and the slicer is automatically added and sized to provide a good user experience. PowerPivot slicers are much easier to use than classic PivotTable slicers, even if, from the point of view of functionalities, they behave much the same.

Using Implicit Measures

When you use PowerPivot for Excel, you can change the aggregation function of columns by using the PowerPivot field list. In fact, whenever you drag a column into the Values area, an implicit measure is created automatically by the engine by using the *SUM* aggregation function. This behavior is different from Tabular data models, in which any measure must be explicitly created in the solution. Because PowerPivot for Excel is targeted to end users, the creation of automatic measures has been greatly simplified to provide a better user experience.

In Figure 14-3, the Sum of SalesAmount measure has been automatically created by the PowerPivot field list by using the *SUM* aggregation. If you want to change the aggregation function of an implicit measure, you can do this by using the menu on the implicit measure inside the Values box, as you see in Figure 14-4.

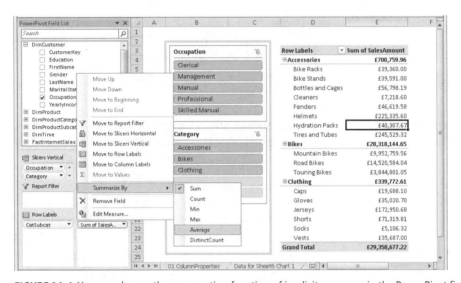

FIGURE 14-4 You can change the aggregation function of implicit measures in the PowerPivot field list.

Because this feature modifies the underlying database by adding or updating a measure, it is not available in Tabular databases.

Creating Measures

Another interesting feature available in PowerPivot for Excel is the ability to create measures directly from the PowerPivot field list. When you right-click a table and select Add New Measure, PowerPivot opens the Measure Settings window from which you can define all the parameters of the new measure. In Figure 14-5, you can see the Measure Settings dialog box.

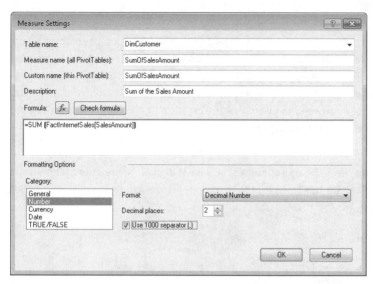

FIGURE 14-5 The Measure Settings dialog box enables you to create new measures easily.

This dialog box is simple to use and enables you to modify all the properties of a measure in a single window without the need to use the measure grid in the PowerPivot window. Moreover, PowerPivot for Excel has the unique ability to assign a local name to the measure. In fact, the same measure can have different names in different PivotTables by using the Custom Name box.

As you have seen, PowerPivot for Excel contains nearly all the features you need to start building a good prototype of a complete BI solution. The most interesting characteristic of PowerPivot for Excel, from the BI professional point of view, is that you can work on the data model side by side with an end user, immediately showing the result of any update to the model and building the formulas for calculated columns and measures, all while validating the results. When the prototype is complete, users can freely browse it and test all the features—and you will have time to transform the prototype in a fully functional Tabular data model.

The Classic PivotTable Field List on PowerPivot for Excel

If you are using PowerPivot for Excel to build a prototype that will eventually be transformed into a Tabular data model, don't forget to explain to your end users that they will browse the data model by using the classic field list and *not* the PowerPivot field list. You can activate the classic field list by disabling the PowerPivot field list and activating the classic field list; both of these operations can be completed by using the Excel ribbon.

Although you can use either the PowerPivot or the classic field list on a PowerPivot data model, you cannot use the PowerPivot field list over a Tabular data model, at least not in the current version of Excel. Thus, it is important to teach users to use the classic field list because they cannot use the PowerPivot field list after the model is in Tabular; therefore, the features you have seen in this section will not be available.

Understanding Linked Tables

Now that you've seen what's missing in PowerPivot for Excel, look at a feature that is available only in PowerPivot for Excel and is missing in Tabular. You already know that to load data inside Tabular, you must rely on a data source choosing the right one from among the many that are available in SSAS. In PowerPivot for Excel, the scenario is the same, and you have the same set of data sources. However, another loading option is unique to PowerPivot for Excel: linked tables. In this section, you learn what they are and how to use them to build data models or prototypes.

You can convert any Excel table of the current workbook into a PowerPivot table by using Create Linked Table in the PowerPivot ribbon. You cannot link tables stored in other workbooks (to load them, you must use the Excel Data Source); you are limited to tables stored in the currently open workbook. Even with this small limitation, linked tables provide tremendous power to the end user because by using them, he or she can enrich the current data model with any set of data just by typing them inside Excel.

When prototyping a new solution, linked tables are particularly useful. Suppose that, during the analysis, you recognize the need to have a new configuration table or a summary table containing information that is not currently available in your data warehouse. Instead of spending time creating the table on SQL Server and populating it by using the tools available in SQL Server Management Studio (SSMS) (which you might not have available at that point), you can type the content of the table inside any Excel workbook, format it as a table, and link it inside the PowerPivot data model.

After data is stored inside xVelocity, it is a table like any other, and you can use it to build your formulas and complete the prototype. Then, when the prototype is converted into a Tabular solution, you must load the content of the table from the correct data source, which is probably a view on top of a SQL Server table. Having the ability to create tables on the fly makes the process of building a prototype much smoother, avoiding the need to leave formulas incomplete while waiting for the data model to be finished.

PowerPivot for Microsoft SharePoint

Now that you have learned about PowerPivot for Excel 2010, look at its big brother: PowerPivot for Microsoft SharePoint. PowerPivot for SharePoint is a bridge between PowerPivot for Excel and a full-fledged Tabular data model.

PowerPivot for SharePoint is the engine of SSAS, running in SharePoint integration mode. Its name should be SQL Server Analysis Services for SharePoint because it is much more similar to Business Intelligence semantic model (BISM) Tabular than to PowerPivot for Excel. To install it, run SQL Server Setup and choose the SharePoint integration. The setup experience is not easy, but it is beyond the scope of this book; if you need this information, you can check *http://msdn.microsoft.com/en-us/library/ee210616.aspx*. Be sure to provide is to follow the guidelines. If you do something wrong, debugging and solving the issue might be very difficult. Thus, it is better to follow the instructions carefully and change any parameter only after you have a running system. If you want to install

PowerPivot for SharePoint, you need at least SharePoint 2010 Enterprise edition; previous and lower versions are not supported.

After PowerPivot for SharePoint is installed, you can upload any workbook created by using PowerPivot for Excel to SharePoint and then use Excel Services in SharePoint to surface the workbook as a web report, which can be browsed without having PowerPivot for Excel installed on the client. This feature makes authoring reports very convenient by using Excel (something that end users can do with a basic knowledge of PowerPivot for Excel) and sharing them in the company by SharePoint.

SharePoint has a dedicated gallery for PowerPivot workbooks. Figure 14-6 shows the PowerPivot Gallery.

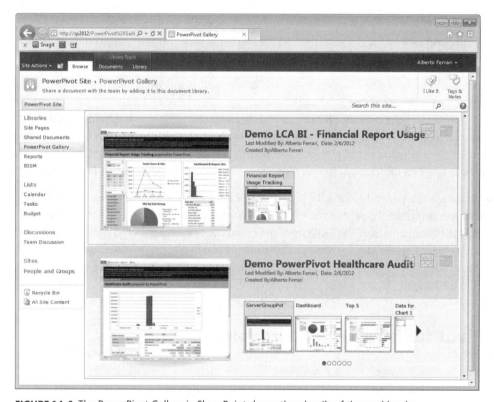

FIGURE 14-6 The PowerPivot Gallery in SharePoint shows thumbnails of the workbooks.

The gallery can be browsed by a user running a normal browser without the need to have either Excel or PowerPivot installed.

Whenever a user opens a report made by using PowerPivot for SharePoint, the SSAS engine activates and loads in memory the backup of the Tabular data model stored inside the workbook. Then, after the backup is restored, it performs all the necessary calculations to surface the report. If no one uses a report for a while, the engine frees memory by unloading it. If, for example, you click a report such as the Financial Report Usage tracking shown in Figure 14-6, SharePoint surfaces it inside the browser, as shown in Figure 14-7.

FIGURE 14-7 An example workbook is surfaced inside Explorer.

Most of the features of Excel browsing are available when the report is surfaced by Excel Services, making Excel and PowerPivot for SharePoint great tools to produce reports.

After the workbook is saved in SharePoint, you can use the Manage Data Refresh button to set automatic refreshing of data and then schedule it. Note that the minimum refresh interval is one day; you cannot automatically refresh a PowerPivot workbook more than once a day.

What limitations exist in PowerPivot for SharePoint? It has the same set of limitations as PowerPivot for Excel when compared with Tabular. There is no security, apart from the all-or-nothing provided by SharePoint; no partitioning; and the size of the database has the same limitations as PowerPivot for Excel. The database cannot be processed on the fly as it can in PowerPivot for Excel. Processing is scheduled at specified intervals and, when the engine queries data sources, it impersonates a user configured in SharePoint. (It does not use the current user, as in PowerPivot for Excel, because there is no current user.)

Thus, PowerPivot for SharePoint is essentially the Analysis Services engine, working side by side with SharePoint and with data models loaded and unloaded on the fly, deployed by using SharePoint as the deployment media and PowerPivot for Excel as the development tool.

PowerPivot for SharePoint bridges the gap between Tabular and PowerPivot for Excel, and it inherits the query feature from Tabular. In fact, although there is no way to query a PowerPivot for Excel workbook because the engine in that case is living in-process with Excel, you can query the PowerPivot engine in SharePoint as if it were an Analysis Services server. (It might be better to say "*because* it is an Analysis Services server," which PowerPivot for SharePoint is.)

Using the Right Tool for the Job

As you have learned, there are three tools you can use to create Tabular data models: PowerPivot for Excel, PowerPivot for SharePoint, and SQL Server Analysis Services. In this section, you learn some guidelines that might prove helpful in deciding which one is right for you.

- PowerPivot for Excel is intended for Excel power users who are interested in producing self-service BI. The data model is stored inside the workbook, and the final result can be easily shared with anyone who has installed PowerPivot for SharePoint. The ability to use linked tables makes the creation of a personal BI solution easy and convenient. However, lack of security is the major limitation of this tool; if there is a need to share results you must share the complete workbook along with all the information stored in it.

- PowerPivot for SharePoint is a great tool for collaborative BI. Data models created with PowerPivot for Excel can be uploaded to SharePoint and surfaced by Excel Services, making it very easy to share the reports with colleagues without sharing the complete data model. Moreover, the ability to connect to workbooks stored in SharePoint to query them and further process data makes it easy to create collaborative databases that can be used by many users and stored inside a global repository.

  Security in PowerPivot for SharePoint can be set only at the SharePoint level, which means an all-or-nothing policy: Either you grant access to the workbook, making all the information in it available, or you deny access, sharing no results. This level of security is limited, but for small companies or for scenarios in which this kind of security is good enough, PowerPivot for SharePoint is a great solution.

- SQL Server Analysis Services is for corporate BI. In the Tabular world, SSAS is the only tool that requires a BI professional to develop a solution. In fact, to develop an SSAS database, you must run SSDT, which is not intended as an end-user tool. The benefits of using SSDT are the many features that enable you to create a real corporate solution: partitioning, security, the ability to script database operations, many processing options, and DirectQuery function-alities. None of these features are needed for self-service and collaborative BI, but they are essential for any kind of corporate BI.

There is a clear upgrade path in the adoption of Tabular. Users can start with the free add-in for Excel, creating simple solutions and reports. After they feel the need to go collaborative, the adoption of PowerPivot for SharePoint opens new and amazing scenarios, making it possible to share reports with the community and creating a repository for BI information. When the solution becomes too complex or when you need to create a big solution that you can no longer handle with the tools available in Excel, it is time to start using SSAS and getting a BI professional to contribute to handling the more complex features available in SSAS.

Any data model created by using PowerPivot for Excel can be deployed on SharePoint, and any SharePoint data model can be turned into a full-fledged SSAS Tabular data model, even if, at each step, you observe some limitations.

It is worth observing that, with Tabular, you have many more options than you have with Multidimensional. Before the release of PowerPivot and Tabular, a customer who wanted to introduce BI in his or her company had to create a team of experts to start a complex project. Now, with the availability of PowerPivot for Excel and PowerPivot for SharePoint, the path is much easier, and you can create good BI reporting without the intervention of a BI professional. This does not mean that BI professionals are useless; the point is that the path to a complete BI solution is much smoother than before.

Because we think that many readers of this book are BI professionals, our advice is to learn all three tools and provide hints to your customers, helping them choose the right tool for the job. In several scenarios, the full power of SSAS is not necessary, and in these situations, implementing a BI infrastructure based on PowerPivot for Excel and PowerPivot for SharePoint is a good solution. SSAS should be considered only for corporate BI or to solve scenarios in which neither PowerPivot for Excel nor PowerPivot for SharePoint provides enough horsepower.

> ## BISM Normalizer
>
> If a user starts creating his or her own data models by using PowerPivot for Excel and PowerPivot for SharePoint, he or she will reach a point at which the same information is stored inside several workbooks. Moving these workbooks into a single SSAS Tabular database might be complex work because many workbooks must be updated to access a single repository of data.
>
> In this scenario, you might want to use a third-party tool such as BISM Normalizer (*http://visualstudiogallery.msdn.microsoft.com/5be8704f-3412-4048-bfb9-01a78f475c64*), which will help you merge several workbooks into a single SSAS Tabular solution and make the transition from self-service or collaborative BI to corporate BI much smoother.

Prototyping in PowerPivot, Deploying with Tabular

You learned in the previous sections of this chapter that PowerPivot for Excel is a wonderful proto-typing tool to start designing Tabular data models, which can then be deployed as Tabular solutions in SSAS. This is true not only because they both share the same engine so that any measure built in PowerPivot will also work in Tabular, but also because Microsoft has developed a specific feature in SQL Server Data Tools to make this transition easy to perform. In this section, you learn how to use this feature.

When you create a new Analysis Services project by using SSDT, among the various options, you can find Import From PowerPivot, as you see in Figure 14-8.

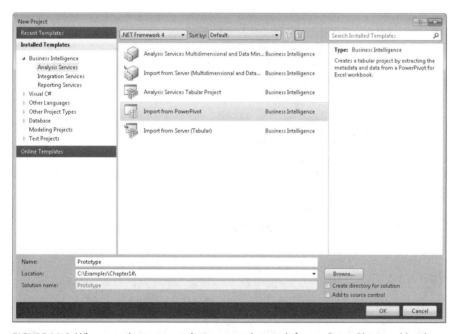

FIGURE 14-8 When creating a new project, you can import it from a PowerPivot workbook.

When you click OK, SSDT prompts you for an Excel workbook containing a PowerPivot for Excel data model. It will open it and load all the information in the workbook into a new Tabular data model.

All the data source connections, table data and metadata, calculated columns, measures, and key performance indicators (KPIs) are created in the Tabular data model, which is ready to be deployed on SSAS as soon as the project has been opened.

The only peculiar behavior is the handling of linked tables, which—because they are not available as a data source in Tabular—are loaded as copied data. (See Chapter 3, "Loading Data Inside Tabular," for more information on how copied data is stored inside the Tabular model.)

After the model is ready, you must:

- Update impersonation options for all the existing connections. By default, SSDT uses the account credentials for all imported connections, and this might not be the optimal choice for your enterprise solution.

- Add security to the solution. Because PowerPivot for Excel does not enable you to define roles and security, you must add roles and define DAX expressions to implement security correctly in the solution. You learn about Tabular security in Chapter 15, "Security."

- Verify the measures that have been implicitly created in the PowerPivot for Excel workbook. If the workbook has been used to generate demo reports, you have probably used many implicit measures in the PivotTable. These measures become explicit measures in the Tabular data model, so you should check their names and properties to verify that they fit your needs.

After you follow these steps, the solution will be ready to be deployed. You might need to add partitioning, define a process window, schedule it, and handle all the necessary steps to deploy a complete solution, but the time required to move from a prototype to a full-fledged solution is negligible.

Summary

In this chapter, you saw an overview of the three tools available to create Tabular models. Even if this book covers mainly SQL Server Analysis Services, it is worth learning both PowerPivot for Excel and PowerPivot for SharePoint.

PowerPivot for Excel is a great prototyping tool for Tabular data models, and it fits perfectly in scenarios in which self-service BI is needed. PowerPivot for SharePoint is the next step on the BI path, granting users the ability to share report results with colleagues and friends and, by using Excel Services, to surface PowerPivot reports on a browser.

SQL Server Analysis Services is the big brother, and it is intended for corporate BI. The added capabilities in terms of security, partitioning, and more complex processing options make it the perfect tool to solve complex BI scenarios. Among the three, SSAS is the only tool that requires a good technical knowledge to use because it can be programmed by using only SSDT, whereas both PowerPivot for Excel and PowerPivot for SharePoint can be programmed by using Excel.

Security

On many business intelligence (BI) projects, you'll find yourself working with some of the most valuable and sensitive data your organization possesses, so it's no surprise that implementing some form of security is almost always a top priority when working with Analysis Services. Making sure that only certain people have access to the model is one thing; very often, you'll need to make sure that certain people can see only some of the data and that different groups of users can see different slices of data. It's fortunate that the Tabular model has some comprehensive features for securing the data in your tables, as you will see in this chapter.

Roles

The Analysis Services Tabular model, like the Multidimensional model, uses the concept of roles to manage security. A role is a grouping of users who all perform the same tasks and therefore share the same permissions. When you grant a role the permission to do something, you are granting that permission to all users who are members of that role.

"Users" are either Microsoft Windows domain user accounts or local user accounts from the machine on which Analysis Services is installed. All Analysis Services security relies on Windows integrated security, and there is no way to set up your own user accounts with passwords in the way that you can in the Microsoft SQL Server relational engine by using SQL Server authentication. Instead of adding individual user accounts to a role, it is possible to add Windows user groups (either domain user groups or local user groups, preferably the former; also note that only security groups work, distribution groups do not) to a role instead, and this is usually the best option. If you create a domain user group for each role, when an individual user's permissions change, you need only to remove the user from the domain user group rather than edit the Analysis Services role.

There are two types of roles in the Tabular model:

- The Server Administrator role, which controls administrative permissions at the server level. This role is built into Analysis Services and cannot be deleted; it can be managed only by using SQL Server Management Studio (SSMS).

- Database roles, which control both administrative and data permissions at the database level. Database roles can be created and deleted by using SQL Server Data Tools (SSDT) and SSMS.

Creating Database Roles

Database roles can grant permissions only at the database level. They are created and edited in SSDT by selecting Roles from the Model menu; this opens the Role Manager dialog box, as shown in Figure 15-1.

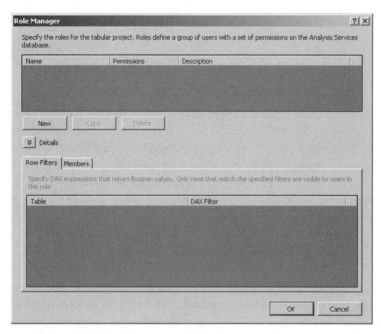

FIGURE 15-1 This is the Role Manager dialog box.

To create a new role, click the New button, which creates a new role with a default name in the list box at the top of the dialog box. You can then rename the role, enter a description, and set its permissions, as shown in Figure 15-2. On the Members tab in the bottom half of the dialog box, you can add Windows users and groups to this role.

Database roles can also be created in SSMS by connecting to the Analysis Services instance in Object Explorer, expanding a database, right-clicking the *Roles* node, and selecting New Role. This opens the Create Role dialog box, as shown in Figure 15-3, and enables you to do the same things you can do in SSDT, although some of the names are slightly different, as you see in the next section.

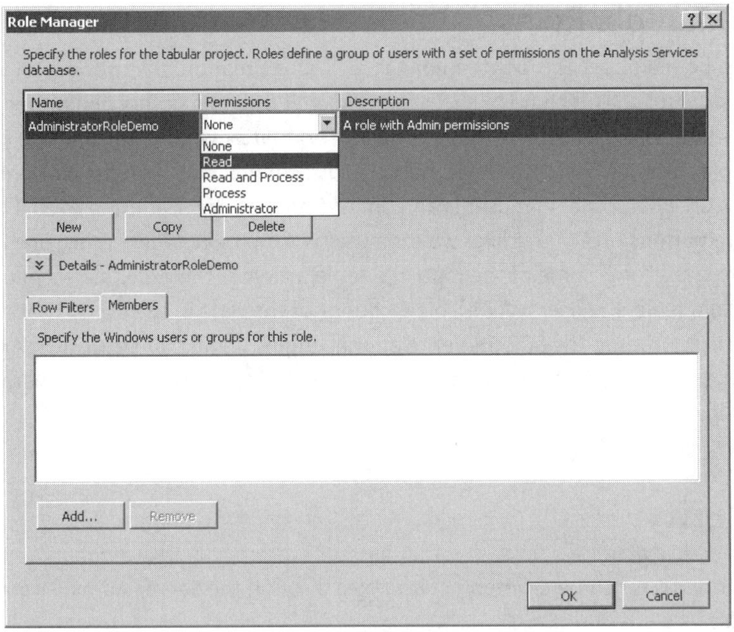

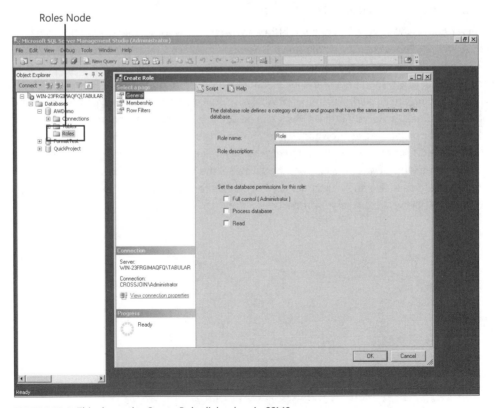

FIGURE 15-2 This shows a new role in the Role Manager dialog box.

Roles Node

FIGURE 15-3 This shows the Create Role dialog box in SSMS.

Membership of Multiple Roles

In some cases, users might be members of more than one role. In this situation, the user has all the permissions of each individual role of which he or she is a member. If one role grants him or her permission to do or see something, the user retains that permission no matter what other roles he or she is a member of. For example, if a user is a member of multiple roles, one of which grants him or her administrative permissions on a database, that user is an administrator on that database even if other roles grant more restrictive permissions. In a similar way, if a user is a member of two roles, one of which grants permission to query only some of the data in a table, whereas the other allows permission to query all the data in a table, the user will be able to query all the data in the table. There is no concept of "deny wins over grant" as in the SQL Server relational engine; in fact, all security in Analysis Services is concerned with granting permissions, and there is no way of specifically denying permission to do or see something.

Administrative Security

Administrative security permissions can be granted in two ways: through the Server Administrator role and through database roles.

The Server Administrator Role

The Server Administrator role is very straightforward: Any user who is a member of this role has administrator privileges over the whole Analysis Services instance. This means that server administrators can see all the data in all the tables in all the databases and create, delete, and process any objects. By default, any members of the local administrator group on the server on which Analysis Services is running are also administrators of Analysis Services. An Analysis Services server property called BuiltinAdminsAreServerAdmins (which can be set in SQL Server Management Studio in the advanced server properties, as shown in Figure 15-4, or in the msmdsrv.ini file) controls this behavior. By default, it is set to *True*; setting it to *False* means that only users or groups you add to the role have administrator privileges on your instance. Likewise, the Windows account the Analysis Services service is running as is also an Analysis Services administrator. This can be turned off by setting the ServiceAccountIsServerAdmin server property to *False*.

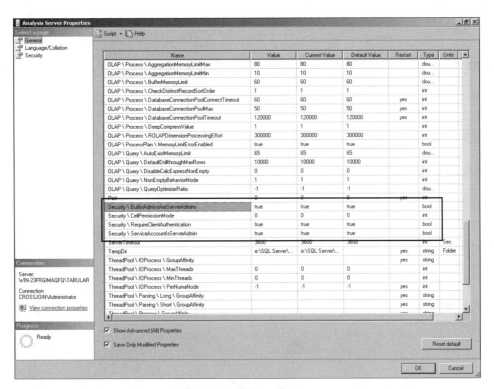

FIGURE 15-4 This is the server security properties dialog box.

At least one user must be added to the Server Administrator role during installation, on the Analysis Services Configuration step of the Installation Wizard (as shown in Chapter 3, "Loading Data Inside Tabular"). After that, users and groups can be added in SSMS by right-clicking the instance name, selecting Properties to display the Server Properties dialog box, and selecting the Security tab, as shown in Figure 15-5.

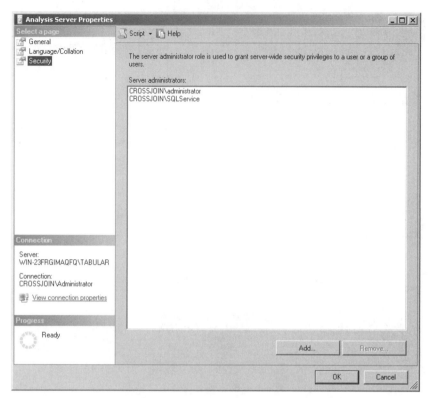

FIGURE 15-5 This shows how to add users to the Server Administrator role.

In a development environment, all developers are usually members of the Server Administrator role. In a production environment, however, production database administrators (DBAs) are members of this role.

Database Roles and Administrative Permissions

At the database level, only a very limited set of administrative permissions can be granted, and these are listed in the Permissions drop-down list in the Role Manager dialog box in SSDT that is shown in Figure 15-2:

- **None** This is the default setting; members of this role have no permissions on this database. Because a Windows user who is not a member of any role and is not an administrator has no permissions anyway, this option might seem unnecessary, but it forces you to explicitly grant permissions to a role for it to be useful, rather than blindly accept any defaults.

- **Read** This setting grants members of the role permission to read the data from tables, which means that they can query the model. The data that can be queried can be further controlled by applying row filters to tables, as discussed in the "Data Security" section later in this chapter.

- **Process** This setting grants members of the role permission to process any object within the database, but not to query it. This permission would be appropriate for applications, such as SQL Server Integration Services (SSIS), that automate processing tasks. Note that a user with Process permissions would not be able to process an object from SSMS because he or she would not have sufficient permissions to connect to Analysis Services in the Object Explorer pane.

- **Read and Process** This setting grants members of the role permission both to query the model and to process objects.

- **Administrator** This setting grants members of the role permission to query, process, create, alter, and delete any object. Developers and DBAs must be administrators of a database to do their jobs properly.

A slightly different set of options is presented when creating a role in SSMS. As Figure 15-3 shows, three check boxes control administrative permissions:

- **Full Control (Administrator)** Equivalent to the Administrator permission in SSDT

- **Process Database** Equivalent to the Process permission in SSDT

- **Read** Equivalent to the Read permission in SSDT

Selecting both the Process Database and Read check boxes is equivalent to the Read and Process permission shown in SSDT; checking any combination of boxes that includes Full Control (Administrator) is equivalent to the Administrator permission.

Data Security

It is an extremely common requirement on an Analysis Services project to make sure that some users can only see some of the data in a table. For example, in a multinational company, you might want to allow users at the head office to see sales data for the entire company, but allow staff in each of the local offices in each country see the sales for just that country. This can be achieved by the use of DAX expressions in roles that act as filters on tables, and is referred to as data security as opposed to administrative security.

Basic Data Security

Data security can be set up on a role in SSDT in the Role Manager dialog box by entering DAX filter expressions for one or more tables on the Row Filters tab, as shown in Figure 15-6. Data security can also be set up in roles in SSMS after the Read check box has been selected on the Row Filters page in the Create Role or Role Properties dialog boxes. The user interface is almost identical to the one described here for SSDT.

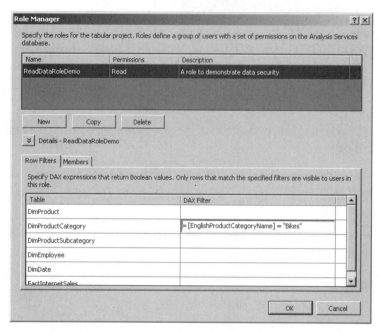

FIGURE 15-6 This shows how to configure Row Filters in the Role Manager dialog box.

The DAX expression used to filter a table must return a Boolean value. So, for example, the following expression would result in the user being able to access only data for rows in the DimProductCategory table where the *EnglishProductCategoryName* column is equal to the value *"Bikes."*

```
= [EnglishProductCategoryName] = "Bikes"
```

It is important to understand that data security can only be applied to the rows of tables. It is not possible to secure entire tables, columns on a table, or perspectives. Thus, it is not possible to secure individual measures in a model; a user can see all measures in a model if he or she has Read permissions on a database. (In contrast, in the Multidimensional model, it is possible to secure individual measures, although security on calculated measures is problematic.) However, it is possible, as you will see later, to apply a row filter that prevents the user from accessing any rows in a table, so this gives a result similar to denying access to an entire table.

After row filters have been applied to a table, a user can see only subtotals and grand totals in his or her queries based on the rows he or she is allowed to see. Additionally, DAX calculations are based on the rows for which the user has permission, not all the rows in a table. This is in contrast to the Multidimensional model in which, when using dimension security, the Visual Totals property controls whether subtotals and grand totals are based on all the members on an attribute or just the members on the attribute that the user has permission to see.

Note This does not mean that the *VisualTotals()* MDX function does not work when used in a query on Tabular model—it does. The *VisualTotals()* function has nothing to do with Visual Totals for roles.

If the data security permissions are granted to a role change, those changes come into force immediately, and there is no need to wait for a user to close and reopen a connection before they take effect.

Testing Data Security

When writing row filter expressions for data security, it is important that you can test whether they work properly. However, as a developer, you have administrative rights over the database on which you are working, so you can see all the data in all the tables. Therefore, before any further discussion of data security, it is necessary to examine how to test the roles you develop.

Testing Roles by Using Excel

The easiest way to test whether the row filters you have created work properly is to use Microsoft Excel. After you have created a role and clicked OK to close the Role Manager dialog box, from the Model menu, click Analyze In Excel to browse your model as you normally would. However, in the Analyze In Excel dialog box, you can choose to test security by browsing your model in one of two ways, as shown in Figure 15-7:

- As if you had logged in as a specific Windows user, by entering a username in the Other Windows User text box.

- As if you were a member of one or more roles by selecting the role names in the Roles drop-down list.

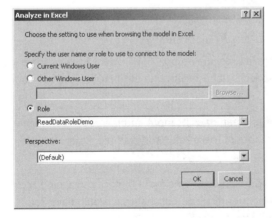

FIGURE 15-7 This shows how to test roles through the Analyze In Excel dialog box.

Clicking OK opens Excel with the permissions of that user or those role(s) applied, and you can browse the model as you normally would.

To illustrate what querying a model through a role looks like, Figure 15-8 shows a Microsoft PivotTable with a query on an Adventure Works model run by a user with Administrative permissions.

Row Labels	Sum of SalesAmount
⊞ Accessories	£700,759.96
⊟ Bikes	£28,318,144.65
⊞ Mountain Bikes	£9,952,759.56
⊞ Road Bikes	£14,520,584.04
⊞ Touring Bikes	£3,844,801.05
⊟ Clothing	£339,772.61
⊞ Caps	£19,688.10
⊞ Gloves	£35,020.70
⊞ Jerseys	£172,950.68
⊞ Shorts	£71,319.81
⊞ Socks	£5,106.32
⊞ Vests	£35,687.00
Grand Total	£29,358,677.22

FIGURE 15-8 This shows data in a model when browsing as an administrator.

Figure 15-9 shows the same PivotTable with the row filter on Bikes applied to the DimProduct table that was shown in the preceding section, "Basic Data Security."

Row Labels	Sum of SalesAmount
⊟ Bikes	£28,318,144.65
⊞ Mountain Bikes	£9,952,759.56
⊞ Road Bikes	£14,520,584.04
⊞ Touring Bikes	£3,844,801.05
Grand Total	£28,318,144.65

FIGURE 15-9 This shows data in the same model when browsing by using a role with data security.

Notice how the PivotTable shows data only for Bikes and how the Grand Total row at the bottom of the PivotTable is the same as the subtotal shown for Bikes.

Testing Roles by Using Connection String Properties

When you choose a user or a role in the Analyze In Excel dialog box, SSDT opens Excel in the background and creates a connection to the Workspace Database with one of the following two connection string properties set:

- **Roles** Takes a comma-delimited list of role names as its input and forces the connection to behave as if the user connecting is a member of these roles, for example: Roles=RoleName1, RoleName2

- **EffectiveUserName** Takes a Windows domain username (note that local machine accounts are not supported) and applies the security permissions that that user would have, for example: EffectiveUserName=MyDomain\MyUserName

The EffectiveUserName connection string property can be used by Analysis Services administrators only. Both properties can be applied directly in Excel by editing the connection string properties of a connection in a Workbook. You can do this by clicking the Connections button on the Data tab in the ribbon to edit an existing connection in the Workbook Connections dialog box, selecting the connection you wish to edit, clicking the Properties button to open the Connection Properties dialog box, and editing the connection string on the Definition tab, as shown in Figure 15-10.

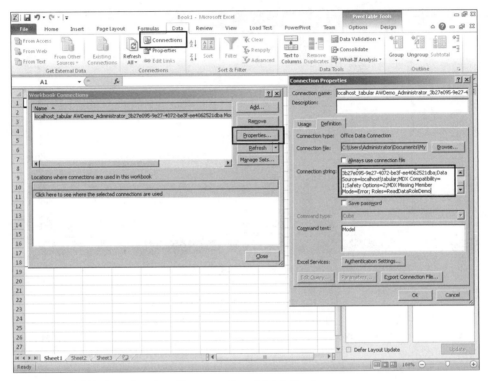

FIGURE 15-10 This shows how to edit a connection string in Excel.

These connection string properties can also be used in SQL Server Management Studio if you want to see how a DAX query is affected by security. You can do this by entering the connection string properties in the Connect To Analysis Services dialog box that appears when you open a new MDX query window. You must click the Options button at the bottom-right corner of the dialog box to display the advanced options, and then choose the Additional Connection Parameters tab, as shown in Figure 15-11.

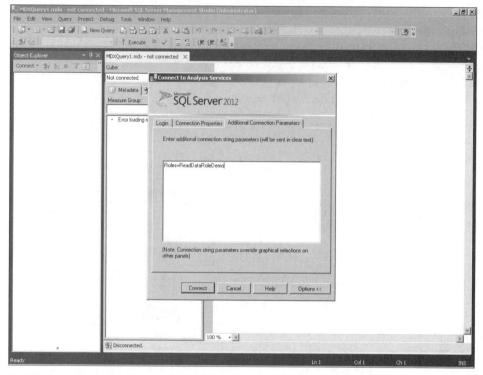

FIGURE 15-11 This shows how to edit connection string properties in SSMS.

After you do this, the appropriate roles are applied to the connection used to run queries from the MDX pane. These connection string properties are not, however, applied to the connection used to populate the metadata pane to the left of the query window, so you see all the MDX dimensions and hierarchies listed there.

Testing Roles by Impersonating Users

The third and final way of testing a role is to log on to a machine or run an application by using a specific user's credentials to see how security behaves. Although logging off and logging on as someone else can be time-consuming, it's relatively easy to run an application as another user. All you have to do is press the Shift key while right-clicking the .exe file or shortcut, select the Run As Different User option, and enter the username and password of the user whose security you wish to test.

Advanced Row Filter Expressions

In many cases some complex DAX is necessary to implement your security requirements. It is fortunate that the (initially very limited) amount of space available for entering row filter expressions in the Role Manager dialog box can be expanded by clicking the edge of the text box and dragging it out! In this section, you see some examples of row filters that address commonly encountered requirements. For all these examples, the Adventure Works Product dimension, consisting of the DimProduct, the DimProductSubcategory and DimProductCategory tables, and the DimDate table and the FactInternetSales table, is used. The relationships among these tables are shown in Figure 15-12.

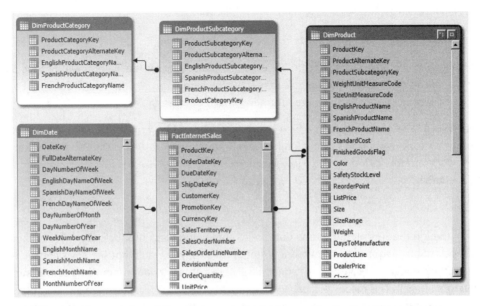

FIGURE 15-12 These are the relationships among the tables used for the Row Filter examples.

Filtering on Multiple Columns

When applying filters to multiple columns in a table, you usually use a mixture of And and Or logic. For example, if you want to filter DimProduct to show only the Products whose Color is Black and ListPrice is greater than 3,000, you can use the following expression.

```
= [Color] = "Black" && [ListPrice] > 3000
```

If you want to change the logic so that you show the Products whose Color is Black or ListPrice is greater than 3,000, you can use this expression.

```
= [Color] = "Black" || [ListPrice] > 3000
```

To get all the Products whose Color is anything other than Black, you can use this expression.

```
= [Color] <> "Black"
```

Finally, to deny access to every row in the DimProduct table, you can use the following expression.

```
= FALSE()
```

In this last example, although the table and all its columns remain visible in client tools, no data is returned when querying this table.

Filtering and Table Relationships

Filters applied on one table can also have an indirect impact on other tables in the model. For example, a filter such as this one on the DimProductCategory level

```
= [EnglishProductCategoryName] = "Bikes"
```

indirectly filters all the tables with which it has a one-to-many relationship, namely DimProductSubcategory, DimProduct, and FactInternetSales. Only the Subcategories, Products, and Sales that are related to the Product Category Bikes are returned in each of these tables.

Filtering on a table never results in a filter being applied to tables with which it has a many-to-one relationship, so, for example, applying a filter on DimProduct never results in DimProductSubcategory or DimProductCategory being filtered. However, if you apply a filter like the following one to the DimProduct table

```
= [Color] = "Black"
```

then, even though the Subcategories and Categories containing Black products are still present in the DimProductSubcategory and DimProductCategory tables, you would not see any sales values for them in FactInternetSales because DimProduct has a one-to-many relationship with FactInternetSales, and therefore filters it. This means you cannot create a role by which users can see all Categories and Subcategories but no Products and still see sales values for the Categories and Subcategories.

In some cases, you might need to filter on specific combinations of keys in your fact table. Imagine that you want to display only sales values for Black products in the year 2002 and for Silver products in the year 2003. If you apply a filter on DimProduct to return only rows in which the Color is Black or Silver and another filter on DimDate to return only rows in which the year is 2002 or 2003, you see sales for all combinations of those years and colors—and you do not want to allow access to the sales values for Black products in 2003 or for Silver products in 2002.

The solution here is to apply the filter to the FactInternetSales table itself and not to filter DimProduct or DimDate at all. Here is the row filter expression to use on FactInternetSales.

```
= ( RELATED( DimDate[CalendarYear] ) = 2002 && RELATED( DimProduct[Color] ) = "Black")
  ||
  ( RELATED( DimDate[CalendarYear] ) = 2003 && RELATED( DimProduct[Color] ) = "Silver" )
```

Figure 15-13 shows a PivotTable containing data for the years 2002 and 2003 and the colors Black and Silver with no security applied; Figure 15-14 shows the same PivotTable when used with a role that applies the preceding filter to FactInternetSales.

Sum of SalesAmount	Column Labels		
Row Labels	Black	Silver	Grand Total
2002	£1,728,251.55	£720,397.36	£2,448,648.91
2003	£3,851,090.66	£2,044,406.89	£5,895,497.56
Grand Total	£5,579,342.21	£2,764,804.25	£8,344,146.47

FIGURE 15-13 This is a PivotTable with no security applied.

Sum of SalesAmount	Column Labels		
Row Labels	Black	Silver	Grand Total
2002	£1,728,251.55		£1,728,251.55
2003		£2,044,406.89	£2,044,406.89
Grand Total	£1,728,251.55	£2,044,406.89	£3,772,658.45

FIGURE 15-14 This is a PivotTable with security on FactInternetSales applied.

> **Note** This last technique enables you to implement something similar to cell security in the Multidimensional model. However, by using cell security, it is also possible to secure by measures, and, as has been mentioned this is not possible in the Tabular model. That said, cell security in the Multidimensional model often results in very poor query performance and is usually best avoided, so the Tabular model is not at a disadvantage to the Multidimensional model because it does not have cell security.

Filtering and Calculated Columns

Because the values in calculated columns are evaluated at processing time, before any security is applied, this can be a factor to consider when you decide where to apply row filters and where to create calculated columns.

For example, if you create a calculated column on the DimProductCategory table that returns the sum of Internet Sales Amount for each category, like the following

```
[TotalCategorySales] = SUMX(RELATEDTABLE(FactInternetSales), FactInternetSales[SalesAmount])
```

and then denied access to every row in the DimProduct table by using this filter:

```
= FALSE()
```

you would find that, because you can still see all the rows in the DimProductCategory table after the filter has been applied, you can still see the total sales for each category. This could represent a security hole if, for instance, a user knows that there is only one Product in a particular category.

In the DimProduct table, if you use calculated columns to denormalize the Category and Subcategory names and then create a hierarchy (as described in the section "Hierarchies Spanning Multiple Tables" in Chapter 10, "Building Hierarchies"), you need to be aware that applying a row filter to DimProduct also affects that hierarchy. If, say, you applied a row filter to the *Color* column that resulted in all the rows for a particular subcategory being filtered out, that subcategory would no longer appear in the hierarchy. This filter would not affect the DimProductSubcategory table, though, so all subcategories would be present there. If you hide the DimProductSubcategory table and expect end users to use only the hierarchy, you must explain that they will not see the filtered subcategory as a result of security. If you do not hide DimProductSubcategory, you must explain that one subcategory will appear in the *EnglishProductSubcategoryName* column that will not appear in the hierarchy.

Using a Permissions Table

As your row filters become more complicated, you might find that it becomes more and more difficult to write and maintain the DAX expressions needed for them. Additionally, security permissions might become difficult for a developer to maintain because they change frequently, and because each change requires a deployment to production, this is a time-consuming task. You can use a data-driven approach instead, by which security permissions are stored in a new table in your model and your row filter expression queries this table.

In the example at the end of the "Filtering and Table Relationships" section earlier in this chapter, imagine that instead of hard-coding the combinations of 2002 and Black and 2003 and Silver in your DAX, you instead created a new table in your relational data source, like the one shown in the table below, and imported it into your model.

RoleName	CalendarYear	Color
MyRole	2002	Black
MyRole	2003	Silver

A permissions table like this enables you to store the unique combinations of CalendarYear and Color that you must secure, and the *RoleName* column enables you to store permissions for multiple roles in the same table. Inside your role definition, your row filter expression on FactInternetSales can then use an expression like the following one to check whether a row exists in the Permissions table for the current role, the current Year, and the current Color.

```
= CONTAINS( Permissions,
    Permissions[RoleName], "MyRole",
    Permissions[CalendarYear], RELATED( DimDate[CalendarYear] ),
    Permissions[Color], RELATED( DimProduct[Color] )
)
```

Adding new permissions or updating existing permissions for the role can then be done by adding, updating, or deleting rows in the Permissions table and then reprocessing that table. No alterations to the role itself are necessary.

As a final step, you should not only hide the Permissions table from end users by setting its Hide From Client Tools property to *True*, you should also make sure that end users cannot query it by using a row filter of

```
= FALSE()
```

for it in your role. Securing the Permissions table won't prevent the data in it from being queried when the role is evaluated; the row filter on the preceding FactInternetSales is evaluated before the row filter on Permissions is applied.

Dynamic Security

Dynamic security is a technique that enables a single role to apply different permissions for different users. It's useful when you would otherwise be forced to create and maintain a large number of individual roles. For example, if you had a sales force of a thousand people, and you wanted to grant each salesperson access to only sales in which he or she had been involved, a non-dynamic approach would force you to create a thousand individual roles.

DAX Functions for Dynamic Security

There are two DAX functions that can be used to implement dynamic security:

- **USERNAME**   Returns the Windows username of the user currently connected

- **CUSTOMDATA**   Returns the string value that has been passed to the CustomData connection string property

The following query shows how these functions can be used, and Figure 15-15 shows the results of the query when the connection string property

```
CustomData = "Hello World"
```

has been set. (See the earlier section, "Testing Roles by Using Connection String Properties," for details on how to do this in SSMS.)

```
EVALUATE
ROW(
    "Results from Username", USERNAME(),
    "Results from CustomData", CUSTOMDATA()
)
```

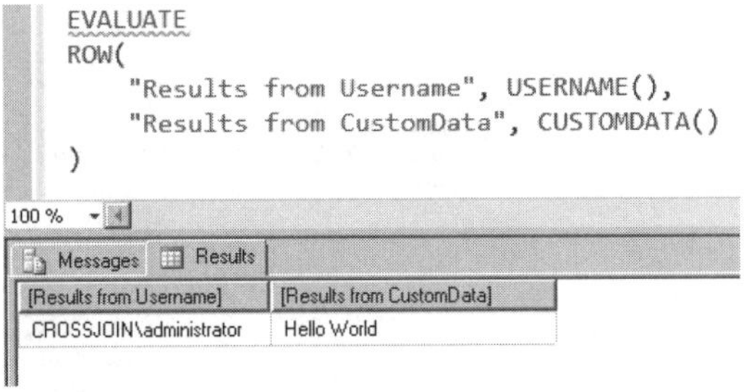

FIGURE 15-15   This shows the output from the *Username()* and *CustomData()* functions.

The key point is that these functions are useful because they can return different values for different users, so the same DAX expression used for a row filter in a role can return different rows for different users.

Note In the Multidimensional model, it is also possible to implement dynamic security by creating a custom MDX function (also known as an Analysis Services stored procedure) in a .NET dynamic link library (DLL), uploading the DLL to Analysis Services, and then calling the new function from inside the role definition. This approach is not possible in the Tabular model because Tabular does not support the creation of custom DAX functions.

Implementing Dynamic Security by Using *CUSTOMDATA*

The *CUSTOMDATA* function is used for dynamic security when a front-end application handles authentication of users itself but must push the job of applying data security back to Analysis Services. For instance, an Internet-facing reporting tool might not want to rely on Windows authentication and instead have its own system for authenticating end users. It would then open a connection to Analysis Services (as a single Windows user) for each query that was run, but each time it opened a connection, it would pass a different value through the CustomData connection string property to indicate the end user for whom the query was being run. Analysis Services would then use the value passed through the CustomData property as part of a row filter expression.

CUSTOMDATA is not suitable for dynamic security when end users connect to the Tabular model directly because, in those situations, an end user might be able to edit the connection string property in whatever client tool he or she is using and therefore see data he or she is not meant to see.

The use of *CUSTOMDATA* in a dynamic role can be demonstrated by creating a new role called CustomDataRole with Read permissions and adding the following row filter expression to the DimProductCategory table.

```
= IF(
    CUSTOMDATA() = "",
    FALSE(),
    DimProductCategory[EnglishProductCategoryName] = CUSTOMDATA()
)
```

If you then connect to the model in SSMS by using the following connection string properties

```
Roles=CustomDataRole; CustomData=Bikes
```

and then running the following DAX query

```
EVALUATE DimProductCategory
```

you see that only one row is returned from DimProductCategory—the row for the Bikes category, as shown in Figure 15-16.

```
EVALUATE DimProductCategory
```

DimProductCate...	DimProductCate...	DimProductCate...	DimProductCate...	DimProductCate...
1	1	Bikes	Bicicleta	Vélo

FIGURE 15-16 This shows the output of a query demonstrating the use of *CustomData()* in a role.

Implementing Dynamic Security by Using *USERNAME*

The *USERNAME* function is used to implement dynamic security when end users connect to a Tabular model directly, which means that they will be opening connections to the model by using their own Windows identities. Because one user is likely to need access to many rows on the same table, and one row on a table is likely to be accessible by more than one user, a variation on the Permissions table approach previously described is usually necessary when this flavor of dynamic security is used. To illustrate this, use the following Permissions table as a starting point. (Please note that Crossjoin is the domain name in this example; to make this work on your own machine, you must use the names of users that exist in your own domain.)

User	ProductCategory
Crossjoin\Chris	Bikes
Crossjoin\Chris	Accessories
Crossjoin\Marco	Accessories
Crossjoin\Marco	Clothing

Next, create a new role called UserNameDataRole, give it Read permissions, add the users Crossjoin\Chris and Crossjoin\Marco to it, and use the following row filter expression on the DimProductCategory table.

```
=CONTAINS(
    UserPermissions,
    UserPermissions[User], USERNAME(),
    UserPermissions[ProductCategory], DimProductCategory[EnglishProductCategoryName]
)
```

Then, in SQL Server Management Studio, open a new MDX query window with the following connection string properties set.

```
Roles=UserNameDataRole; EffectiveUserName=Crossjoin\Chris
```

Run the following DAX query again.

```
EVALUATE DimProductCategory
```

You see that the two rows associated with the Crossjoin\Chris user are returned from DimProductCategory—the rows for the Bikes and Accessories categories, as shown in Figure 15-17.

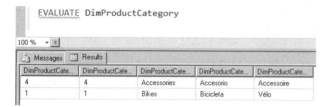

FIGURE 15-17 This shows the output of a query demonstrating the use of *UserName()* in a role.

Advanced Authentication Scenarios

Authenticating a connection is not always straightforward, and two common scenarios that cause problems are when users need to connect to Analysis Services from outside a domain, and when users are authenticated by a reporting tool that then needs to connect to an Analysis Services instance on another server.

Connecting to Analysis Services from Outside a Domain

Given that Analysis Services relies on Windows authentication, allowing users from outside a domain to access Analysis Services can represent a challenge. Additionally, it can be a problem for users to connect to Analysis Services when a firewall blocks the ports on which it listens for client connections. The solution is to configure Analysis Services to use HTTP access through Internet Information Server (IIS), as shown in Figure 15-18.

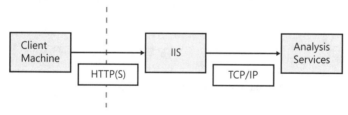

FIGURE 15-18 This is how HTTP connectivity works.

In this scenario, a DLL called msmdpump.dll inside IIS acts as a bridge between the client machine and Analysis Services, so when the client connects to IIS, IIS handles the authentication, and msmdpump.dll then opens a connection to Analysis Services by using the end user's credentials. You should use integrated Windows authentication with IIS whenever possible, but if you cannot do that (for example, because users are accessing from outside a trusted Windows domain), use anonymous access or basic authentication with IIS. If you are using basic authentication, you should always use HTTPS connections because, otherwise, user credentials would be transmitted without encryption over the wire, making the system more vulnerable to unauthorized access.

Describing how to configure HTTP connectivity for Analysis Services is outside the scope of this book, but plenty of resources are available on the Internet that cover how to do this for Analysis Services Multidimensional, and the steps are the same for the Tabular model. You can find a detailed description of how to configure HTTP access to Analysis Services on MSDN at *http://msdn.microsoft .com/en-us/library/gg492140(v=sql.110).aspx*.

Kerberos and the Double-Hop Problem

Figure 15-19 shows another common problem you might need to overcome when designing an Analysis Services solution: the scenario in which a client connects to a web-based reporting tool, and the web-based reporting tool must then connect to a separate Analysis Services server by using the end user's credentials to run a query.

FIGURE 15-19 This is a representation of the double-hop problem.

By default, this situation (known as the double-hop problem) is not possible with standard Windows authentication, but it can be solved in one of three ways:

- By using dynamic security and the *CUSTOMDATA* function, as described earlier in this chapter. This requires you to configure your web application to open a connection by using the CustomData connection string property and pass an appropriate value through it. This technique won't be possible in many cases, but SQL Server Reporting Services expression-based connection strings can be used to do this (see *http://msdn.microsoft.com/en-us/library/ ms156450.aspx* for more details).

- By using the EffectiveUserName connection string property. Because the user connecting to Analysis Services must be an Analysis Services administrator to use this connection string property, this technique represents a significant security concern. Nevertheless, this is the approach Microsoft uses inside the new BISM Connection file (described at *http://www .powerpivotblog.nl/power-view-tabular-mode-databases-sharepoint-and-kerberos*) to make it easier for Power View to connect to an instance of Analysis Services outside the Microsoft SharePoint farm. It is also used when you select the Impersonate Or Set Execution Context check box in a Reporting Services data source.

- By setting up constrained delegation and Kerberos. This is probably the best option, although setting up Kerberos is notoriously difficult, and many consultants and their customers would like to avoid it. A good starting point on enabling Kerberos for Analysis Services is the article from the Microsoft knowledge base at *http://support.microsoft.com/kb/917409*.

Monitoring Security

One final subject that must be addressed regarding security is monitoring. When you are trying to debug a security implementation, it is useful to see all the connections open on a server and find out which permissions they have. This is possible by running a trace in SQL Server Profiler traces and looking for the events shown in Figure 15-20.

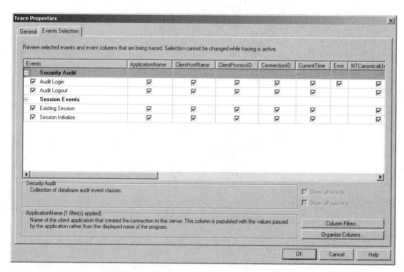

FIGURE 15-20 This shows the security-related Profiler events.

- **Audit Login/Logout**   These events are fired every time a user logs on and logs out of Analysis Services.

- **Existing Session**   This event lists all sessions that are currently active when the trace starts.

- **Session Initialize**   These events are fired every time a new session is created, which usually happens every time a user connects to Analysis Services.

The last two of these events contain much useful information, such as the user who is connecting to the model, the database to which he or she is connecting, all the properties from the connection string, and, crucially, the security roles applied to this session. It also shows the application from which he or she is connecting if the Application Name connection string property has been set. Some of the Microsoft client tools do this, and you might want to set it in your own applications to make debugging easier. When an administrator opens a session, you see a comma-delimited list of all the roles in the Analysis Services database, plus an asterisk at the beginning to show administrator rights, in the TextData pane in Profiler, as shown in Figure 15-21.

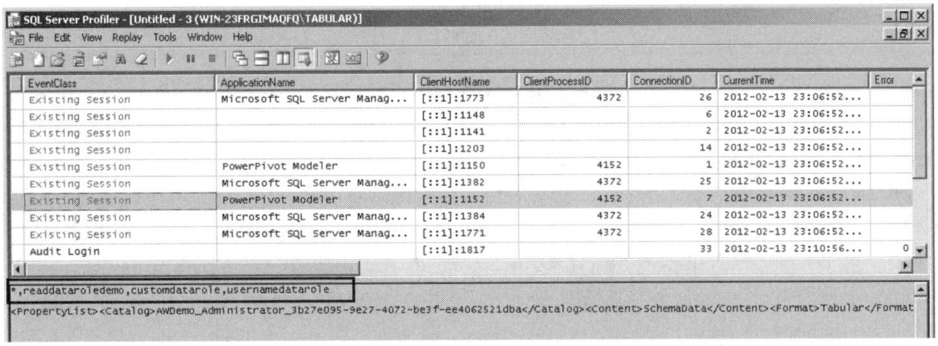

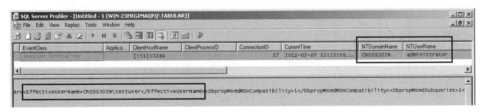

FIGURE 15-21 This shows the *Existing Session* event and roles used for an administrator.

When a user who is not an administrator connects, you see a list of the roles of which that user is a member instead, as shown in Figure 15-22.

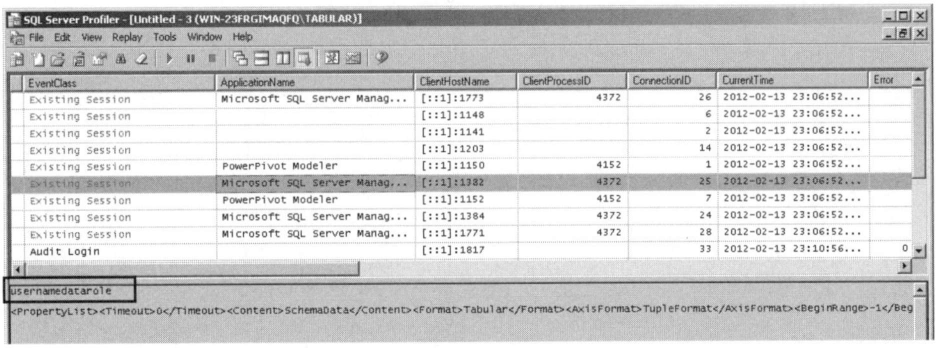

FIGURE 15-22 This shows the *Existing Session* event and roles used for a non-administrator.

The name of the user who is connecting is always shown in the *NTUserName* column; when the EffectiveUserName property is used, the value passed to that property is shown in the TextData pane along with the other connection string properties used, as shown in Figure 15-23.

FIGURE 15-23 This shows the actual username and the effective username.

Summary

In this chapter, you saw how to implement security in the Tabular model. Administrative security can be configured at the instance level through the Server Administrator role and at the database level by creating database roles with the Administrator permission. Data security can also be implemented through database roles by applying DAX row filters to tables to filter the data in each table to which a role allows access. Dynamic security can be used to make a single role apply different filters for different users. Finally, this chapter described more advanced security configurations, such as HTTP authentication and Kerberos, and how SQL Server Profiler can be used to monitor which roles are applied when a user connects to Analysis Services.

Interfacing with Tabular

One of the interesting features of SQL Server Analysis Services (SSAS) is that it is possible to interact programmatically with the server, using dedicated libraries and specific commands. By using this feature, you can handle complex scenarios in which you can control a database and a server through code. For example, you can handle the creation of new partitions and the processing of them as soon as new data is available without the need to handle them manually.

There are two ways to manage an SSAS instance:

- AMO (Analysis Management Object) is a .NET library containing several classes that can be used to manage an instance of SSAS.

- XMLA (XML for Analysis) is a SOAP (Simple Object Access Protocol)-based XML protocol designed to manage Multidimensional data sources.

The AMO library gives you full control over an SSAS instance. A complete reference of the libraries and commands needed to interact with the server would require too many pages, and it is beyond the scope of this chapter. However, here you learn the basics of Tabular interfaces and see some examples of how to use them.

Moreover, as awkward as it might seem, you must have a very good background in Multidimensional modeling to use AMO on a Tabular instance. Even if the Tabular data model is simple because it is based on tables and relations, the actual implementation of the storage is still based on the concepts of dimensions and measure groups. If you want to manage the server programmatically, you must understand these concepts and how the Tabular data model is translated in a Multidimensional model.

The interested reader can study the topics further by exploring the AMO2Tabular demonstration project on CodePlex *with the Adventure Works samples*. In the companion data of this book, you can find a project that implements all the examples you learn in this chapter, but to read a complete reference about AMO capabilities, the official Microsoft demo is worth studying.

Understanding Different Tabular Interfaces

Whenever you want to interact with a Tabular server, you always have to remember that, in reality, you are interacting with an SSAS server, and Tabular is just one of the two flavors of data modeling tool available in SSAS. Thus, the libraries and the commands need to work with both Tabular and Multidimensional. Finally, because the interface library is an extension of the one in SQL Server Analysis Services 2008 R2, which handles Multidimensional only, and no library is yet available to work easily with Tabular, all the interfaces and library objects are suited to handle Multidimensional more easily than Tabular.

When you want to create a table, for example, you must create both a dimension and a measure group, even if no dimension or measure group exists in the Tabular world. This aspect of the Tabular interface is somewhat cumbersome, and we hope that, in the future, a set of libraries dedicated to Tabular will be made available. As of the time of writing this book, however, no such library exists.

In this chapter, the focus is on the usage of AMO. Even if you intend to learn how to create and use basic XMLA commands, we think that using AMO leads to a cleaner programming model. AMO is an object library that produces XMLA commands, but it also makes it easier to interact with the server by providing classes that will hide the complexity of XMLA from the programmer.

One of the most interesting features of AMO is that it can be used by .NET code, for instance, in a Windows application written in Microsoft C#, but it can also be used in Microsoft Windows PowerShell scripts, which are much easier to code and handle to manage the everyday work on a business intelligence (BI) solution.

Understanding Tabular vs. Multidimensional Conversion

Before examining the complexity of the creation of a Tabular database by using AMO, you must learn how a Tabular project is translated into Multidimensional concepts. In this section, we briefly review the architecture of a Multidimensional solution. If you do not feel confident with the content of this section, you will probably find it hard to follow the remainder of the chapter, and we suggest that you study the Multidimensional architecture before further studying AMO on Tabular.

In Figure 16-1, you can see the Adventure Works Multidimensional database, browsed from inside SQL Server Management Studio (SSMS).

In Multidimensional, you start creating data sources, which are the connections with the data. A data source does not contain tables or data; it just defines the connection parameters. Then, you create data source views, that is, data models based on data sources (usually a 1:1 mapping between data source views and data sources) in which you define tables, relationships, and calculated columns. Note that the relationships and the data structures that you define in data source views are not part of the Multidimensional model; they are just a way of filtering the tables in the data source so you see only the ones with which you want to work in your model.

FIGURE 16-1 The Adventure Works Multidimensional database structure can be analyzed by using SSMS.

The core of a Multidimensional data model is made of cubes, measure groups, and dimensions. Dimensions belong to the database and can be used inside one or many cubes, whereas measure groups belong to a cube. A dimension in the database is a logical entity, but to define the relationships of the dimension with the measure groups, you must use the dimension inside a cube.

Dimensions and measure groups are linked by relationships, and two types of relationships are available:

- **Relationships between measure groups and dimensions** These are the standard relationships present in any star schema.

- **Relationships between dimensions** These relationships are normally used to relate measure groups with farther dimensions, that is, reference dimensions.

Note that there are three distinct places where you define properties of a dimension:

- In the data source view, you define the physical representation of data.

- In the database dimension, you define the business logic of the dimension, its hierarchies, and all its attributes. Here, the relationships are between columns and attributes within the same dimension table.

- When the dimension is used inside a cube, you define its relationships with the rest of the database (in terms of measure groups and other dimensions) by using the dimension usage tab.

Thus, in Multidimensional, complex objects such as dimensions have different properties set in different places, leading to a very clean yet complex data structure. In Tabular, everything is simpler. You do not have data sources and data source views; you have only connections, which are similar to data sources: They define the connection information with a source of data, but they do not contain data. Data is loaded from the connections inside tables that are already part of the Tabular data model, and you define calculated columns, measures, and relationships there.

With these concepts in mind, study how the Tabular model is mapped on a Multidimensional data structure. Start with some key points:

- Tabular connections are just Multidimensional data sources. Both structures contain connection information to a source of data, and they behave in the same way.

- Tabular tables cannot be stored in data source views; they need a physical storage, whereas data source views contain only metadata. Moreover, because a table acts as both a dimension and a measure group, you must create both a dimension and a measure group for each Tabular table.

- Data source views are still needed because, in Multidimensional, dimensions and measure groups are based on data source views.

- Calculated columns must be stored as physical members in both the dimension and the measure group created for the table.

- Tabular measures are calculated members, and they must be stored in the MDX script. The MDX script is a set of commands defined in the cube and globally available to all queries. Although it is normally used to store several kinds of calculations in Multidimensional, in Tabular it is used to store only the measure definitions.

- Relationships cannot be stored in the data source view; they must be stored inside the cube, between measure groups and dimensions. As you might imagine at this point, relationships will not be easy to design because, in Tabular, there is no distinction between a dimension and a measure group, whereas Multidimensional makes a big distinction between the two types of entities and provides you with different tools to set relationships.

Now you are ready to see the big picture of the translation between the two models:

- Each connection in Tabular becomes a DataSource.

- You must create a single DataSourceView, which will host all the metadata for the tables coming from different DataSources. By doing this, you break the 1:1 mapping between DataSource and DataSourceView that is usually present in Multidimensional.

- You create a single cube in the database, which hosts dimensions and measure groups and is linked to the single DataSourceView.

- For each table, you create both a dimension and a measure group in the cube.

- Each calculated column results in a new attribute in the dimension and a new member in the measure group.

- Each measure is added to the MDX script.

- Relationships are created inside the cube. Relationship handling is a complex topic because you must translate table relationships in dimension and measure groups, leading to a complex design.

For example, in Figure 16-2, you can see a sample database containing products, categories, and subcategories in both Tabular and Multidimensional, so you can visually appreciate the difference between the two data models and how Tabular is translated in Multidimensional.

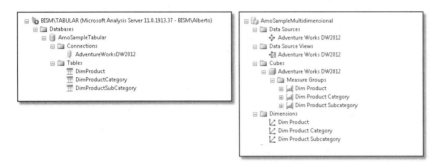

FIGURE 16-2 In this figure, you can see the differences between Tabular and Multidimensional on a simple model.

These guidelines are very important to learn and digest because, in the remaining sections of this chapter, you learn how to use AMO to perform these steps. Without a good understanding of how the conversion happens, it is very difficult to understand why some operations are needed. Again, keep in mind that using AMO is more like a BI semantic model (BISM) competency than a Tabular competency. A BISM expert knows both Multidimensional and Tabular and should be able to switch from one model to the other easily to follow the complexity of AMO programming.

Using AMO from .NET

Now that you have a solid background on the conversion procedures, you can start having fun with some code. In this section, you learn how to use the AMO library from inside a simple C# console application. The example will:

- Connect to a Tabular instance.

- List all the databases stored in that instance.

- Create a new, empty Tabular database.

- Create a SQL data source connection with a relational database.

This example will acquaint you with the usage of AMO. The next sections, describe more complex operations and describe the whole process of creating a database. We have chosen these steps as the first ones because they are easy, and they are similar to the operations you normally perform with Tabular even if, in this case, you are working with Multidimensional.

The first step is to create a new Microsoft Visual Studio project for a C# console application. After you have done that, to use the AMO library, you must add a reference to the correct .NET library, which is the Analysis Management Objects (version 11.0 for Microsoft SQL Server 2012), as you see in Figure 16-3.

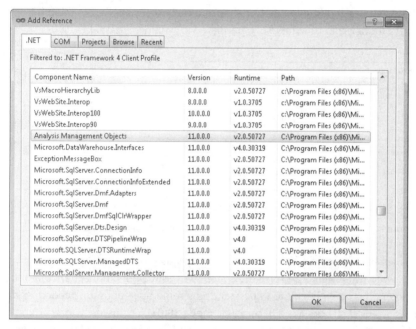

FIGURE 16-3 The Analysis Management Objects library must be referenced from your project.

When you have the project ready, with the library referenced, you can test your first connection with the server by using this sample code, which lists all the available databases on the server.

```csharp
using System;
using Microsoft.AnalysisServices;

namespace AmoSample {
    class Program {
        static void Main(string[] args) {
            Server server = new Server();
            server.Connect ("BISM\\Tabular");
            foreach (Database database in server.Databases) {
                Console.WriteLine (database.Name);
            }
            server.Disconnect();
        }
    }
}
```

As you can see from the code, you must create a *Server* object and connect it to the instance. (This is BISM\Tabular in the example—note the double backslash to escape the backslash and use your instance name when testing the code on your local PC.) Then you can access the content of the server by using the properties of the object. In this first code, you just iterate over all the databases in the server and output their names on the console.

The next step is to create a new Tabular database. To perform this, you must create an object of type *Database*, set its minimal properties (just the StorageEngineUsed property), and then add it to the server, as you can see from the following code.

```
Database newDatabase = new Database("AmoTest");
newDatabase.StorageEngineUsed = StorageEngineUsed.InMemory;
server.Databases.Add(newDatabase);
newDatabase.Update();
```

Note, at this point, that all modifications to AMO objects are performed in memory only, and to persist them on the server, you must always call the *Update* method of the object you have created or updated. Many AMO objects have the *Update* method with different parameters, depending on the kind of updates available. You can check that the database has been properly created by using SSMS. You should see the new database under the Databases tree of the server.

The next step in creating a database is to add a data source to it (a connection, in Tabular language). As you already know, a data source has both a connection string and impersonation information. To create your new data source, you must provide both, as you can see in the following code.

```
StringBuilder connString = new StringBuilder();
connString.AppendLine("Data Source=BISM;");
connString.AppendLine("Initial Catalog=AdventureWorksDW2012;");
connString.AppendLine("Persist Security Info=false;");
connString.AppendLine("Integrated Security=SSPI;");
connString.AppendLine("Provider=SQLNCLI11;");
DataSource newDataSource = newDatabase.DataSources.AddNew("TestDataSource");
newDataSource.ConnectionString = connString.ToString ();
newDataSource.ImpersonationInfo = new ImpersonationInfo(ImpersonationMode.
ImpersonateServiceAccount);
newDataSource.Update();
```

In this example, the data source is using the Service Account impersonation mode. Using a domain user is as easy as creating a different *ImpersonationInfo* object with the account credentials stored in it. Again, to persist information, the *Update* method is needed, this time on the DataSource.

Writing a Complete AMO Application

Now that you have learned the basics of AMO, it is time to write a complete application that enables you to create and populate a Tabular database. It is not the goal of this book to show you tons of code; this section highlights only the most relevant part of the code and might be useful to understand the overall flow of the program. If you want to learn the details, you should study the code of the project that is included with this book's companion code.

The project is basically a class (*TabularProject*) that implements these functionalities:

- Create a database.

- Add a SQL Server connection to the database.

- Add a SQL Server table to the database.

- Create a measure.

- Create a calculated column.

- Create a relationship between two tables.

You have already seen how to perform the first two operations; you learn the next steps in the following parts of this section.

Creating Data Source Views

Before you can proceed with the loading of a table, you must create both a cube to host the related measure group and a data source view to host the table metadata. In this section, you learn how to create a suitable data source view.

Although in Multidimensional you can have many data source views, in Tabular, you can have only one, due to internal constraints of the engine. A DataSourceView is linked to a DataSource, and you might be accustomed to having a DataSourceView hosting table coming from a single DataSource. In Tabular, because you have a single DataSourceView and many DataSources, the DataSourceView must host metadata from tables coming from different data sources. For this reason, the data source to which the data source view is linked is not important because every table will reference its data source, ignoring the data source of the data source view.

In the sample project, the data source view is created immediately after the creation of the first data source by using the following code.

```
DataSourceView newDataSourceView = Database.DataSourceViews.AddNew ("Sandbox");
newDataSourceView.DataSourceID = newDataSource.ID;
newDataSourceView.Schema = new DataSet ();
newDataSourceView.Update ();
```

The name of the data source view is set to Sandbox, following the SQL Server Data Tools (SSDT) standard. Because you have not loaded a table, the data source view starts as an empty dataset; the table metadata will be loaded as soon as you load the first table.

Creating a Cube

After you have created the data source view, you can create a cube that hosts the measure groups for the tables. When you create the cube, you must set some properties and add an empty MDX script that will host the measures later.

The code is straightforward; the following is the block of code that creates the empty cube.

```
Cube newModelCube = Database.Cubes.Add (cubeName);
newModelCube.Source = new DataSourceViewBinding (newDataSourceView.ID);
newModelCube.StorageMode = StorageMode.InMemory;
newModelCube.Language = Database.Language;
newModelCube.Collation = Database.Collation;
```

Immediately after, you should create the MDX script with a dummy measure that acts as the default member of the measures dimension. This dummy measure is needed due to the internals of Tabular.

```
MdxScript mdxScript = newModelCube.MdxScripts.Add ("MdxScript", "MdxScript");
StringBuilder initialCmd = new StringBuilder ();
initialCmd.AppendLine ("CALCULATE;");
initialCmd.AppendLine (
    "CREATE MEMBER CURRENTCUBE.Measures.[__No measures defined] AS 1;");
initialCmd.AppendLine (
    "ALTER CUBE CURRENTCUBE UPDATE DIMENSION Measures, " +
    "Default_Member = [__No measures defined];");
mdxScript.Commands.Add (new Command (initialCmd.ToString ()));
```

Loading a SQL Server Table

Now that you have performed the initial steps required to prepare the database, it is time to load the first table in the model. For educational purposes, we show how to load a table from SQL Server because, by using a SQL Server connection, it is much easier to grab the table metadata and define the list of columns of the table. If you plan to load from other sources, you must define the table columns and their data types by using your own table metadata.

The first step is to load the table metadata in the data source view, and this can be accomplished with the following code.

```
DataTable dataTable = new DataTable (tableName);
string metaDataConnString =
    dataSource.ConnectionString.Replace("Provider=SQLNCLI11;", "");
using (SqlConnection conn = new SqlConnection (metaDataConnString)) {
    SqlDataAdapter dataAdapter = new SqlDataAdapter (tableQuery, conn);
    dataAdapter.FillSchema (dataTable, SchemaType.Source);
}
dataTable.ExtendedProperties.Add ("DataSourceID", dataSource.ID);
dataSourceView.Schema.Tables.Add (dataTable);
```

In the first lines, you use a SqlDataAdapter to get the table schema (which depends on a SQL Server connection), but the most interesting line of this code is at the bottom. Because the table will be added to a data source view but might be linked to a different data source, you must store in the table schema the information about the data source from which this table originates. This has to be performed by using the ExtendedProperties of the data table where, in the property DataSourceID, you need to store the ID of the DataSource of the table. If you forget this step, the program will raise errors as soon as you try to process the cube because SSAS will try to load the table from the data source of the data source view which, in this case, does not know how to handle that table.

After the metadata is correctly stored in the data source view, you must create a dimension in the database and add it to the cube. After the dimension is set up, you create the measure group for the table. The creation of the dimension is straightforward, as you can see from the following code.

```
Dimension newDimension = Database.Dimensions.AddNew (tableName);
newDimension.Source = new DataSourceViewBinding (dataSourceView.ID);
newDimension.StorageMode = DimensionStorageMode.InMemory;
```

In the sample application, you see many other properties that must be set to complete the dimension definition, but they are not very interesting to show here in this book. The most important properties are the dimension source, which is set to the DataSourceView, and the storage mode, which must be In-Memory for Tabular.

A peculiarity of Tabular dimensions is the need for a special column, which is called *RowNumber*. This column can have any name, but it has a special attribute usage of *RowNumber*, meaning that this column will be the row identifier for the table. This column is required even if the table already has a primary key. In the code, you find more details, but the basic properties of the *RowNumber* column are shown in the next piece of code.

```
DimensionAttribute rowNumber = newDimension.Attributes.Add ("RowNumber");
rowNumber.Type = AttributeType.RowNumber;
rowNumber.KeyUniquenessGuarantee = true;
rowNumber.Usage = AttributeUsage.Key;
```

After you have created this special column, you must add all the other columns of the table to your new dimension, setting their attribute relationship directly with the *RowNumber* column. This is accomplished by looping over the columns defined in the metadata of the table in the data source view. The final step is to add the dimension to the cube. Remember that dimensions are defined in the database and can be used in the cube, so the final operation of adding the dimension to the cube is required to make it a cube dimension.

```
modelCube.Dimensions.Add (tableName);
```

When you have finished the dimension settings, you still need to create a measure group inside the cube for the same table. At this point, you might wonder whether the two items (dimension and measure group) will use twice the space needed for a table. Luckily, this is not the case because you will create a special measure group, called DegenerateMeasureGroupDimension, which is a measure group that can share the storage with the dimension, because they are based on the same source and data structure, if the ShareDimensionStorage property is set to StorageSharingMode.Shared.

```
MeasureGroup newMeasureGroup =
    modelCube.MeasureGroups.Add (tableName, tableName);
newMeasureGroup.StorageMode = StorageMode.InMemory;
newMeasureGroup.ProcessingMode = ProcessingMode.Regular;
DegenerateMeasureGroupDimension newMeasureGroupDimension =
    new DegenerateMeasureGroupDimension (tableName);
newMeasureGroup.Dimensions.Add (newMeasureGroupDimension);
newMeasureGroupDimension.ShareDimensionStorage = StorageSharingMode.Shared;
newMeasureGroupDimension.CubeDimensionID = newDimension.ID;
```

After you have created the measure group, you only need to iterate over all the dimension attributes and add all the attributes of the dimension to the measure group by using the proper data type. This operation is easy, and we will not show the code here; you can find the relevant code on the demo project.

There are still a couple of operations that must be completed before the measure group is set. You must add a default measure (in the example, we are using *COUNT*) and a default partition that will contain the data, as you can see in the following code.

```
String defaultMeasureID = string.Concat ("Count Of ", tableName);
Measure currentMeasure =
    newMeasureGroup.Measures.Add (defaultMeasureID, defaultMeasureID);
currentMeasure.AggregateFunction = AggregationFunction.Count;
currentMeasure.DataType = MeasureDataType.BigInt;
DataItem currentMeasureSource = new DataItem (new RowBinding (tableName));
currentMeasureSource.DataType = System.Data.OleDb.OleDbType.BigInt;
currentMeasure.Source = currentMeasureSource;
```

```
Partition currentPartition = new Partition (tableName, tableName);
currentPartition.StorageMode = StorageMode.InMemory;
currentPartition.ProcessingMode = ProcessingMode.Regular;
currentPartition.Source =
    new QueryBinding (dataSourceView.DataSource.ID, tableQuery);
newMeasureGroup.Partitions.Add (currentPartition);
```

After you have finished all these steps, the measure group is correctly defined, and you can process the database. At this point, the database is ready to be queried, and you can test whether it works properly by using SSMS.

Clearly, a database with only tables is not very useful; you will probably want to create calculated columns, measures, and relationships between tables to make this database useful.

Using Tabular as an ETL Tool

Even if a cube with only one table might not seem very useful for reporting, a scenario in which it might be useful is when you want to use a Tabular database as part of a more complex extract, transform, and load (ETL) process. If you must perform complex computations over a table and find that having the table inside the xVelocity in-memory analytics engine and querying it by using DAX can be helpful, you can use AMO to create a temporary database, load the table in xVelocity in-memory analytics, query it with the amazing speed of DAX, and, at the end of your process, delete the database. Having the ability to create databases programmatically opens new and interesting scenarios for any complex ETL process.

Creating a Measure

Now that you have learned how to load data, add some calculations to the data model. You have already learned that measures are stored inside the MDX script of the data model, and in this section, you learn how to create a measure.

In Tabular, the MDX script can contain only measure definitions written in DAX, and to maintain compatibility with SSDT, you must strictly follow some cumbersome standards in the way you express your formulas. The limitations are the following:

- All the measure definitions must be stored inside a single command of the MDX script.

- The MDX script should start with a string, which must be identical to the following one. Do not add a single space, a new line, or anything else; it has to be identical to this one. You can see further information at *http://blogs.msdn.com/b/cathyk/archive/2011/11/29/powerpivot-measures-command-no-really-don-t-modify-it-manually.aspx.*

```
------------------------------------------------------------
-- Tabular Model measures command (do not modify manually) --
------------------------------------------------------------
```

If you use a different standard, the engine will still work, but you will not be able to modify your project by using SSDT later because of the way SSDT reads the XML script of a Tabular model. This scenario might change in the future, but at the time of writing, this limitation still exists. Moreover, the syntax of measure definition does not have a command to define the format string. Thus, you must use calculation properties to inform SSAS of the format string that has to be linked to your measure.

```
Cube modelCube = Database.Cubes[0];
MdxScript mdxScript = modelCube.MdxScripts["MdxScript"];
StringBuilder measuresCommand = new StringBuilder ();
if (mdxScript.Commands.Count == 1) {
    measuresCommand.AppendLine (
        "------------------------------------------------------------");
    measuresCommand.AppendLine (
        "-- Tabular Model measures command (do not modify manually) --");
    measuresCommand.AppendLine (
        "------------------------------------------------------------");
    measuresCommand.AppendLine ();
    measuresCommand.AppendLine ();
    mdxScript.Commands.Add (new Command (measuresCommand.ToString ()));
} else {
    measuresCommand.Append (mdxScript.Commands[1].Text);
}
measuresCommand.AppendLine (String.Format (
    "CREATE MEASURE '{0}'[{1}]={2};", tableName, measureName,
measureExpression));
mdxScript.Commands[1].Text = measuresCommand.ToString ();
CalculationProperty newCalculationProperty =
    new CalculationProperty(measureName, CalculationType.Member);
newCalculationProperty.FormatString = measureFormatString;
newCalculationProperty.Visible = true;
mdxScript.CalculationProperties.Add (newCalculationProperty);
modelCube.Update (UpdateOptions.ExpandFull, UpdateMode.CreateOrReplace);
```

As you can see from the code, if the MDX script contains a single command (a first command was inserted during cube creation to host the default measure and the *CALCULATE* statement), you add a new command, following the standard format. Otherwise, you add the measure to the already existing command by appending the measure definition.

After the MDX script has been updated, you just need to update the cube so that the new MDX script is executed and measures are compiled.

Creating a Calculated Column

To add calculations to the cube, you now learn how to define new calculated columns. Calculated columns are slightly more complex to define than measures because they must be stored in memory. Remember that a table in Tabular is stored inside a dimension and in the degenerate measure group linked to that dimension. Thus, to create a calculated column, you must add an attribute to the dimension and then update the measure group by adding the same attribute to it.

The first step—adding an attribute to the dimension—is easy. The only difference between adding a table column and adding a calculated column is the *Source* attribute of the column, which must be an expression and not a physical column. In the following code, you can see the details.

```
Dimension dim = Database.Dimensions[tableName];
Dimensionttribute newDimAttribute = dim.Attributes.Add (calcColumnName);
newDimAttribute.Usage = AttributeUsage.Regular;
newDimAttribute.KeyUniquenessGuarantee = false;
newDimAttribute.KeyColumns.Add (
    new DataItem (tableName, calcColumnName, OleDbType.Empty));
newDimAttribute.KeyColumns[0].Source =
    new ExpressionBinding (calcColumnExpression);
newDimAttribute.KeyColumns[0].NullProcessing = NullProcessing.Preserve;
newDimAttribute.NameColumn =
    new DataItem (tableName, calcColumnName, OleDbType.WChar);
newDimAttribute.NameColumn.Source = new ExpressionBinding (calcColumnExpression);
newDimAttribute.NameColumn.NullProcessing = NullProcessing.ZeroOrBlank;
newDimAttribute.OrderBy = OrderBy.Key;
```

After the column has been added to the dimension, you must add an attribute relationship with the key of the table.

```
AttributeRelationship newAttributeRelationship =
    dim.KeyAttribute.AttributeRelationships.Add (newDimAttribute.ID);
newAttributeRelationship.Cardinality = Cardinality.Many;
newAttributeRelationship.OverrideBehavior = OverrideBehavior.None;
```

Note that, at this point, you have a single column that acts as the key of the table. That is, the *RowNumber* column has been added to the table during its definition. However, in Tabular, you might have more than one column behaving as the key of the table, and this can create slightly more complex scenarios that you learn about in the section about relationships later in this chapter.

After the attribute is set inside the dimension, you must add the same attribute to the measure group dimension by using the same pattern, as you see in the following code.

```
Cube modelCube = Database.Cubes[0];
MeasureGroup measureGroup = modelCube.MeasureGroups[tableName];
DegenerateMeasureGroupDimension measureGroupDimension =
    (DegenerateMeasureGroupDimension) measureGroup.Dimensions[tableName];
MeasureGroupAttribute measureGroupAttribute =
    new MeasureGroupAttribute (calcColumnName);
measureGroupAttribute.KeyColumns.Add (
    new DataItem (tableName, calcColumnName, OleDbType.Empty));
measureGroupAttribute.KeyColumns[0].Source =
    new ExpressionBinding (calcColumnExpression);
measureGroupDimension.Attributes.Add (measureGroupAttribute);
```

As you can see in this example, any operation that in Tabular involves a single table needs to be duplicated on both the dimension and the measure group derived from that table.

Creating Relationships

Now that you have learned the easier part of AMO programming, you are ready to learn something more complicated. In this section of the chapter, you learn how to handle relationships.

Understanding how relationships work is difficult because each Tabular table is both a dimension and a measure group. In Multidimensional, you can create relationships between dimensions, and then you must set the correct dimension usage properties to complete the work. To make things more complicated, you must correctly handle attribute relationships. Before speaking about relationships, we will introduce some terminology. Look at Figure 16-4.

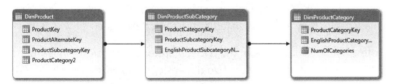

FIGURE 16-4 *AdventureWorksDW* uses a chain of relationships to link products with categories.

There are a few terms on which to agree. In the diagram, there is a relationship between DimProduct and DimProductSubcategory based on *ProductSubcategoryKey*.

- DimProduct is the source table, and *ProductSubcategoryKey* is the source column.

- DimProductSubCategory is the target table, and *ProductSubcategoryKey* is the target column.

- You can refer to the target column as the key column because it must be a key in the target table.

- The source table is sometimes referred to as the many side of the relationship, whereas the target table is the one side.

- The relationship can be thought of as starting from DimProduct and going to DimProductSubCategory. Thus, the source is also called the *from table*, and the target is called the *to table*.

It is important to understand attribute relationships. During table creation of DimProductSub Category, you added a dummy column called *RowNumber*, which is required in any table, and you set attribute relationships of all the attributes with that column. If you want to create a relationship in which DimProductSubCategory is the target, the target attribute (*ProductSubcategroyKey*) must be a key for the table, and, as you know, only one attribute in a dimension can be used as a key. Although this scenario works in Multidimensional, in Tabular you might have more than one column in a single table as the target of a relationship, which is like having more than one key in a dimension. To set up the relationship correctly, you must leave all the attribute relationships with the *RowNumber* column and change the cardinality of the relationship between *ProductSubcategoryKey* and *RowNumber* as one. (There is an identity relationship between the two attributes.)

```
DimensionAttribute targetAttribute =
    Database.Dimensions[targetTable].Attributes[targetColumn];
DimensionAttribute rowNumberAttribute =
    Database.Dimensions[targetTable].Attributes[rowNumberColumnName];
rowNumberAttribute.AttributeRelationships[targetAttribute.ID].Cardinality =
    Cardinality.One;
targetAttribute.KeyColumns[0].NullProcessing = NullProcessing.Error;
```

Note that by doing this, you are not really setting the target attribute as a key, but by setting a 1:1 relationship with the key and preventing *NULL* values from the column, you are instructing SSAS to use the target column as if it were a key. All attributes are still related to the *RowNumber* column, but because of the identity relationship, they are also related to the target attribute.

The next step is to create a relationship between the two dimensions. A relationship is stored in a *Relationship* object in AMO, which is useful to relate two dimensions. AMO uses the from-and-to terminology.

```
string relName = String.Format (
    "Rel from {0}_{1} to {2}_{3}",
    sourceTable, sourceColumn,
    targetTable, targetColumn);
Relationship newRelationship = sourceDimension.Relationships.Add (relName);
newRelationship.FromRelationshipEnd.DimensionID = sourceDimension.ID;
newRelationship.FromRelationshipEnd.Attributes.Add (sourceAttribute.ID);
newRelationship.FromRelationshipEnd.Multiplicity = Multiplicity.Many;
newRelationship.FromRelationshipEnd.Role = String.Empty;
newRelationship.ToRelationshipEnd.DimensionID = targetDimension.ID;
newRelationship.ToRelationshipEnd.Attributes.Add (targetAttribute.ID);
newRelationship.ToRelationshipEnd.Multiplicity = Multiplicity.One;
newRelationship.ToRelationshipEnd.Role = String.Empty;
```

After the relationship has been set, you must update the database and process the dimensions so that all changes are correctly detected by the engine.

Here is the most difficult part of this section. The two dimensions share a relationship, but to make the relationship work, you must store, in the measure group of the source table, the attributes of the target dimension, instructing SSAS to retrieve those attributes through a reference dimension relationship. Some figures can clarify this.

In Figure 16-5, you see a Multidimensional solution using a canonical relationship structure among the three tables on which you are working.

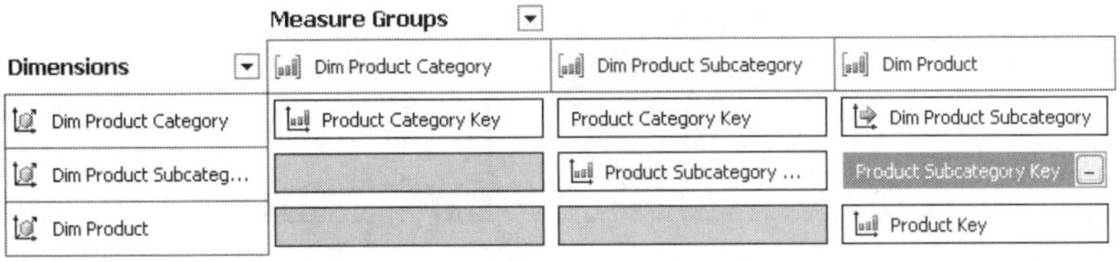

FIGURE 16-5 This is an example of attribute relationships in Multidimensional.

The DimProduct measure group has three relationships:

- A Fact relationship with the DimProduct dimension

- A regular relationship with DimProductSubcategory because the measure group contains *SubCategoryKey*

- A referenced dimension relationship with DimProductCategory because it must walk through the DimProductSubcategory dimension to retrieve the values of DimProductCategory

Although this is the usual reference relationship handling of Multidimensional solutions, Tabular uses a different way to create relationships. The following example focuses on the relationship between the DimProduct measure group and the DimProductSubcategory dimension. Knowing that a relationship exists between the DimProduct table and the DimProductSubcategory table, you can create the same relationship between the measure group and the DimProductSubcategory dimension by using a reference dimension relationship; use the DimProductSubcategory dimension as the intermediate dimension, as you see in Figure 16-6.

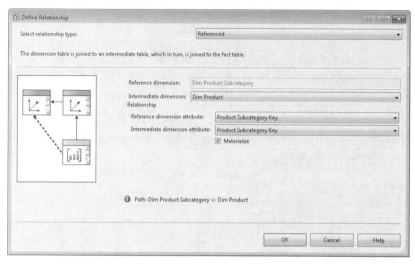

FIGURE 16-6 Tabular uses a reference dimension relationship.

From a data modeling point of view, the final result is the same because the measure group will be related to the dimension even if the path to follow is more complicated. The same pattern can be applied to the relationship between the DimProduct measure group and the DimProductCategory dimension.

In other words, in a Tabular data model, you have only two types of relationships:

- Fact relationships between the dimension and the measure group that represent the same Tabular table

- Reference relationships between a measure group and all the dimensions that can be reached following relationships between dimensions, where the path always starts from the dimension of the table and follows as many steps as needed

This relationship structure is simpler to handle from a programmatic point of view, but it is less intuitive because of the experience you might already have with Multidimensional data modeling. Nevertheless, this is the model you must author to represent a Tabular data model in AMO.

Finally, note that these relationships are stored in the measure group. Thus, you must create the chain of relationships inside all the measure groups whenever a dimension can be reached through any chain of relationships from that measure group. In Figure 16-7, you see how the Tabular data model should look.

You can see that all relationships are either fact or reference relationships. In such a scenario, whenever you add a relationship to a table, you should always check all the dimensions that can be reached from all the measure groups because adding a relationship can change the way all other measure groups are related with dimensions. For educational purposes, the following is a simpler version of the code, which does not traverse all the measure groups but covers only the one that is the source of the newly added relationship.

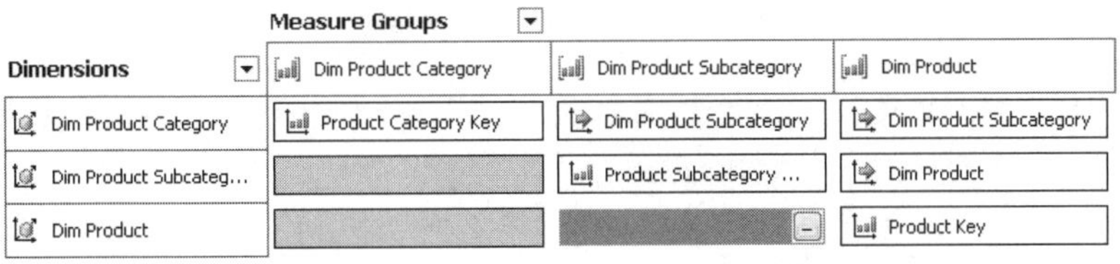

FIGURE 16-7 The Multidimensional representation of Tabular relationships is less intuitive, but it reaches the same result.

Now that you understand relationships, look at the code. First, you must add the attributes of the target dimension as measure group attributes of the source measure group, setting the granularity to the one that is the target key.

```
ReferenceMeasureGroupDimension newReferenceMGDim = new
ReferenceMeasureGroupDimension ();
foreach (DimensionAttribute da in targetDimension.Attributes) {
    MeasureGroupAttribute mgAttribute = new MeasureGroupAttribute (da.Name);
    if (targetAttribute.Name == da.Name) {
        mgAttribute.Type = MeasureGroupAttributeType.Granularity;
    }
    newReferenceMGDim.Attributes.Add (mgAttribute);
}
```

After all attributes have been correctly set, update the reference dimension properties before adding it to the measure group, as you see in the following code.

```
newReferenceMGDim.CubeDimensionID = targetDimension.ID;
newReferenceMGDim.IntermediateCubeDimensionID = sourceDimension.ID;
newReferenceMGDim.IntermediateGranularityAttributeID = sourceAttribute.ID;
newReferenceMGDim.Materialization = ReferenceDimensionMaterialization.Regular;
newReferenceMGDim.RelationshipID = relName;
sourceMeasureGroup.Dimensions.Add (newReferenceMGDim);
```

Now, imagine you are creating the relationship between DimProduct and DimProductSubcategory. At this point, you can reach all the attributes of DimProductSubcategory from the DimProduct measure group, but you cannot use any attribute of DimProductCategory because, to get those attributes, you must traverse a chain of two relationships. For this reason, you should check whether other dimensions can be reached, starting from the newly added relationship and following further dimension relationships. The next piece of code starts from the current target dimension and traverses dimension relationships, adding all the relationships that should be added to the measure group inside a list. Later, you will use this list to add these relationships to the current measure group.

```
List<Relationship> relationshipsToAdd = new List<Relationship> ();
List<Dimension> dimensionsToSearch = new List<Dimension> ();
dimensionsToSearch.Add (Database.Dimensions[targetTable]);
while (dimensionsToSearch.Count () > 0) {
    foreach (Relationship r in dimensionsToSearch[0].Relationships) {
        if (!sourceMeasureGroup.Dimensions.Contains (
            r.ToRelationshipEnd.DimensionID)) {
            relationshipsToAdd.Add (r);
            dimensionsToSearch.Add (
                Database.Dimensions[r.ToRelationshipEnd.DimensionID]
            );
        }
    }
    dimensionsToSearch.RemoveAt (0);
}
```

The final step is to add all the relationships that have been stored inside the list to the current measure group so that all dimensions that can be reached are now correctly configured.

```
foreach (Relationship r in relationshipsToAdd) {
    ReferenceMeasureGroupDimension rr = new ReferenceMeasureGroupDimension ();
    foreach (DimensionAttribute da
        in Database.Dimensions[r.ToRelationshipEnd.DimensionID].Attributes) {
        MeasureGroupAttribute mgAttribute = new MeasureGroupAttribute (da.Name);
        if (r.ToRelationshipEnd.Attributes[0].AttributeID == da.Name) {
            mgAttribute.Type = MeasureGroupAttributeType.Granularity;
        }
        rr.Attributes.Add (mgAttribute);
    }
    rr.CubeDimensionID = r.ToRelationshipEnd.DimensionID;
    rr.IntermediateCubeDimensionID = r.FromRelationshipEnd.DimensionID;
    rr.IntermediateGranularityAttributeID =
        r.ToRelationshipEnd.Attributes[0].AttributeID;
    rr.Materialization = ReferenceDimensionMaterialization.Indirect;
    rr.RelationshipID = r.ID;
    sourceMeasureGroup.Dimensions.Add (rr);
}
```

Remember, this code is for educational purposes. In a real-world application, you should check all the measure group relationships and verify that everything is correctly set. Processing the measure group is the final step to make the relationship work.

Drawing Some Conclusions

As you have learned, using AMO to create Tabular data models is not an easy task. It requires you to dive deeply into the Multidimensional representation of the Tabular data model and then follow the steps to reproduce it by using AMO. In this section, we show the most important topics of this process and give you some hints about how to work with AMO. There are other topics and other details that are beyond the scope of this chapter because they would make the chapter too difficult and complex. More examples are provided in the sample application, which you can study to glean more information, and in the Amo2Tabular project provided by Microsoft as documentation about how to work on Tabular by using AMO.

The best way to understand how a Tabular data model is stored as a Multidimensional database is by following this procedure:

- Create the database by using Tabular. Keep it as simple as possible—reduce the number of columns in each table to the minimum and use only the tables needed to understand the specific topic you are studying.

- Deploy the model on the server.

- From inside SSMS, script the database as a *CREATE* script into a new window. This shows you the XMLA command needed to build the database.

- Inside the XMLA command, you will find all the necessary information about the data model. This information is not easy to read and understand, but it is there. Take your time and study the topic; it is worth learning if you are serious about understanding the internals of Tabular representation in Multidimensional.

Performing Common Operations in AMO with .NET

In the previous section, you learned how to create a database from scratch and how to complete some basic (yet complex) operations by using AMO. That section is useful to understand the underlying Multidimensional data structure that represents Tabular in Multidimensional. However, we do not expect that every reader of this book will need to use AMO to create a Tabular database. After all, SSDT makes it simple to create Tabular solutions. That said, AMO can be useful to automate some daily operations that can be performed easily, such as the process of a database, the process of a measure group, or the creation of a new partition into an existing measure group. In this section, you learn how to handle these useful operations by using AMO from a .NET program. Later in this chapter, you see how to perform the same operations by using PowerShell.

Processing an Object

Processing a database or a measure group is easy. All the objects in AMO that can be processed implement a *Process* method, and processing them is as easy as calling that method.

For example, to run a full process of the whole database, you can use the following code.

```
using System;
using Microsoft.AnalysisServices;

namespace AmoSample {
    class Program {
        static void Main(string[] args) {
            Server server = new Server();
            server.Connect ("BISM\\Tabular");
            server.Databases["AmoSample"].Process (ProcessType.ProcessFull);
            server.Disconnect();
        }
    }
}
```

Calling the *Process* method of the database object issues a command to the server that performs a ProcessFull process of the database. By changing the argument of the *Process* method, you can use other processing options, such as ProcessDefault.

Working with Partitions

Although processing an object is an easy task, working with partitions, which is the topic you learn in this section, is more difficult. First, you must learn what can be done with partitions and where partitions are stored.

In Tabular, a table can be partitioned. It does not matter whether it is a fact table or a dimension; any table can be partitioned. In Multidimensional, however, you have dimensions and measure groups, and dimensions cannot be partitioned. Partitions are objects that can belong only to measure groups in the AMO Multidimensional object model. Nevertheless, because of the way you have created the dimension and the measure group for your table, both data structures share the same storage. Thus, to partition a Tabular table, it is enough to create a partition in the measure group. The dimension will share the same data structure, resulting in the same partition strategy.

Partitions are represented by the *Partition AMO* object, which contains all the information needed to handle a partition. For example, if you want to add a partition to an existing table, execute the following lines of code.

```
string partitionID = "New Partition";
Partition currentPartition = newPartition(partitionID, partitionID);
currentPartition.StorageMode = StorageMode.InMemory;
currentPartition.ProcessingMode = ProcessingMode.Regular;
currentPartition.Source = new QueryBinding(newDatasource.ID, queryText);
modelCube.MeasureGroups[mgName].Partitions.Add(currentPartition);
```

You must pay attention to the query you use as the source of the new partition because SSAS will not check whether the source of the partition overlaps existing data. Data consistency is entirely in your hands.

By using AMO, you can delete a partition by calling the *Remove* method of the partition container, and you can merge two partitions by using the *Merge* method of a partition and passing the partition that needs to be merged as the parameter.

Whenever you want to merge two partitions, update the source of the newly merged partition if you plan to reprocess the partition later to include the data of the merged partition.

Using AMO with PowerShell

PowerShell is the command-line shell, available since 2007, which can be used to create scripts that automate many everyday tasks without the need to write Windows applications or services. It is useful to interact with SSAS because, in PowerShell, you can create and handle AMO objects by using very few commands. We will not describe in detail how PowerShell works; many books and sources are available that cover the topic in depth. In this section, you learn how to create simple scripts that might be useful. You can adapt the scripts provided in this section to fit your needs, but if you want to create more complex scripts, you must learn the PowerShell language.

First, to use AMO inside PowerShell, you must reference the AMO assembly inside a PowerShell script, create a server object, and connect it to your instance. These three lines perform these initial tasks.

```
[Reflection.Assembly]::LoadWithPartialName("Microsoft.AnalysisServices")
$Server=New-Object Microsoft.AnalysisServices.Server
$Server.connect("BISM\Tabular")
```

The first line loads the AMO assembly in memory; the second creates a variable (*ServerName*), which is a connection to the server; and the third connects the server to the BISM\Tabular instance. After these three lines have been executed, the *ServerName* variable can be used to manage the server.

If you want to get the list of databases in the instance, you can use the select-object cmdlet in the database properties of the server, as in the following example.

```
$Server.databases|select-object name
```

This command produces the list of the databases installed on the instance as the output.

```
Name
----
ManyToMany
BasketAnalysis
DirectQuery
CurrencyConversion
AmoTest
```

There is no reason to use PowerShell to retrieve the list of all the databases on a server unless you plan to use the output to perform further processing. This example is for educational purposes only.

Theoretically speaking, by using AMO inside PowerShell, you can perform any operation on the server, such as creating a database; setting up data sources; and creating tables, measures, and all the needed data structure to generate a complete database. However, these kinds of operations are too complex to be effectively handled by using scripts. PowerShell, however, can be used very effectively to attach or detach a database or to process the full database or a single table.

For example, to process the *AmoTest* database, you can use the following code.

```
$AmoTestDatabase = $Server.Databases.Item("AmoTest")
$AmoTestDatabase.Process()
```

You learn other processing techniques in Chapter 17, "Tabular Deployment," which is dedicated to Tabular deployment.

Using XMLA Commands

An easy and convenient way to issue commands to SSAS is to use XMLA commands. XMLA is an industry standard for data access in analytical systems, and it is a language based on XML that can be used to make SSAS perform specific operations. We will not describe XMLA in detail because it contains a huge number of commands and instructions and would require a book by itself. In this section, you learn how to get some basic XMLA commands and how to execute them against the server.

The easiest way to learn the XMLA command for a specific operation is to use the scripting capability of SSMS. If, for example, you right-click the table of a Tabular database and select Process, you open the Process Table(s) window from which you can choose the tables to process and the processing mode. Inside this window, there is a Script button (see Figure 16-8), which can be used to save the XMLA command that executes the selected operation.

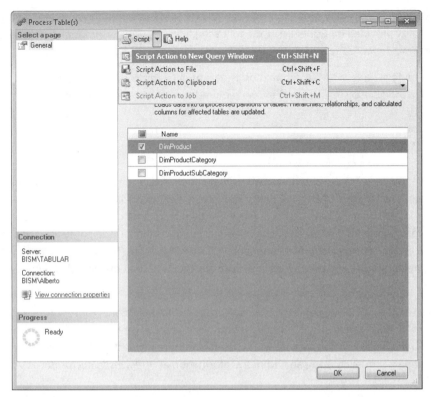

FIGURE 16-8 The Script command inside the Process Table(s) window creates XMLA commands.

When you use the Script Action To New Query Window command, SSMS opens a new query window containing the following XMLA command.

```
<Process xmlns="http://schemas.microsoft.com/analysisservices/2003/engine">
  <Type>ProcessDefault</Type>
  <Object>
    <DatabaseID>AmoTest</DatabaseID>
    <DimensionID>DimProduct</DimensionID>
  </Object>
</Process>
```

You can run the command as it is, or you can change some parameters inside to choose a different process type or dimension ID, for example.

The script option is available for most of the operations in SSMS, and it is useful to learn both XMLA and the structure of a Tabular data model. In fact, if you script the entire database as a *Create* statement, you obtain a very long and complex XMLA command that contains the entire database structure. By studying it, you can get many insights into the internals of Tabular.

If you want to execute an XMLA command, you can rely on SSMS when testing and debugging, or on the ASCMD utility provided on CodePlex at the following link: *http://msftasprodsamples.codeplex .com/wikipage?title=Katmai%21Readme%20For%20Command-line%20Utility%20Sample*.

ASCMD is useful to include in XMLA commands as part of batch processing or to perform automated tests of performance by measuring the time required to answer a batch of queries.

CSDL Extensions

The Tabular model is a set of tables and relationships that can be easily converted in other table-based data models. The Microsoft ADO.NET Entity Framework defines a conceptual application model that enables developers to create data access applications by programming on these abstraction layers instead of programming directly against a relational storage schema. The Entity Framework includes the Conceptual Schema Definition Language (CSDL), which is an XML-based language that describes tables, relationships, and data types in a more abstract way than the underlying physical data model does.

With Analysis Services 2012, you can use CSDL to represent a Tabular model for reporting by using CSDL Extension for Tabular Models. By using these extensions, you can represent Tabular entities and metadata in a more abstract format that will be useful in future products and that can integrate different tools for data modeling. You can find more information at *http://msdn.microsoft.com/en-us/ library/gg492114(v=SQL.110).aspxs*.

Summary

In this chapter, you learned how to interact programmatically with SSAS by using AMO and XMLA commands. To use AMO efficiently, you must understand the difference between Tabular and Multidimensional and how Tabular is translated into a Multidimensional model. AMO does not contain any objects that represent a Tabular entity; if you want to interact with AMO, you must have a good understanding of Multidimensional.

Tabular Deployment

After you create a Tabular model, you have to deploy it in a production environment, and this effort requires you to plan how you will partition data, how you will process data, and how you will handle DirectQuery mode. In this chapter, you see an extensive coverage of these topics, with particular attention given to design consideration to give you the knowledge to make the right decisions based on your specific requirements. You also find step-by-step guides to introduce you to the use of certain functions you see for the first time in this chapter. However, the chapter first discusses important considerations in defining the hardware requirements for a Tabular instance of Analysis Services.

Sizing the Server Correctly

When you plan a deployment, you usually have to provision the required hardware for the server. A server for a Tabular model can have very different requirements than a relational database server. There are also significant differences between servers optimized for Tabular or Multidimensional models. In this section, you see the techniques for sizing a server correctly for a Tabular instance of Analysis Services that manages a database deployed in-memory by using xVelocity. DirectQuery databases have different needs and minimal resource requirements for Analysis Services, as you see at the end of this section.

xVelocity Requirements

A Tabular model deployed in-memory uses the xVelocity in-memory engine, which offers excellent performance and has specific requirements for storage, memory, and processing power.

Disk and I/O

Consider I/O performance first. Assuming the server has only a Tabular Analysis Services instance, and the data sources for your Tabular models (such as Microsoft SQL Server) are on other servers, it is important to consider that disk access will be limited to service startup, first database access, and database process.

When you start the Analysis Services service, only metadata of attached databases are read from disk; then, at the first access to any object, the whole database is loaded in physical memory, accessing storage in a read-only way. In this case, elapsed time depends on sequential I/O performance and data transfer rate. The time required might range from a few seconds to a few minutes for very large databases (several GB of size with a slow disk subsystem). After the database has been loaded, it is never unloaded from memory unless it is detached. Note that connecting SQL Server Management Studio (SSMS) to a Tabular Analysis Services instance is sufficient to load all the databases in memory.

Processing a database requires only write operations to storage, and processing more tables can require concurrent write operations on several files. Both read and write operations are sequential for each file. There are no concurrent read operations on several files, and every file is read or written from the beginning to the end. Thus, the disk performances are not an important factor for a Tabular instance of Analysis Services, even if concurrent write operations occur during processing of multiple tables. Thus, it is better to allocate the hardware budget to the best processors and RAM instead of to expensive storage area networks (SANs).

I/O Operations in a Tabular Instance

Random I/O is not used in Tabular, and a good sequential I/O throughput can improve startup time, but there are no effects on query time, at least if you do not consider the first access to a database. During a process operation, if you have enough RAM, all the write operation will be sequential, but if you do not have enough available physical memory to store the data processed and the old data that you will replace, random I/O operations can occur to perform paging operations. However, with enough RAM available, files will always be accessed sequentially. The only reason for random access is the presence of many small files because different files might be accessed in an order that is not the order used to store them physically on the file system.

Memory

Memory is the most critical resource in a Tabular instance. All data have to be stored in physical memory, and SQL Server Analysis Services (SSAS) might also need RAM to create temporary structures answering to complex queries. In Chapter 9, "Understanding xVelocity and DirectQuery," you saw how to measure the storage size required for a Tabular model stored in xVelocity. As a rule, the memory available for a database should be at least 1.5 times the space required to store the database on disk. To process the model and avoid any paging operations, you need at least two to three times the space required to store the database on disk, at least if you run a Process Full operation on the whole database and you keep an old version of the database available for querying during process operations. With large databases, you can choose alternative strategies that lower the memory required to keep the database available for querying during process operations, as you will see later in this chapter.

Every query can require a temporary peak of memory usage to store partial results required to solve the complete query. Simple queries require minimal memory, but more complex queries might be expensive from this point of view. It is hard to estimate this cost, which also depends on the number of concurrent queries that Analysis Services receives. It is also difficult to provide a guideline for sizing memory, depending on concurrent users, and it is better to follow a heuristic approach, measuring memory consumption in the typical workload you expect to have, as you will see in Chapter 18, "Optimizations and Monitoring."

Memory size is an important requirement, but not all memories are the same, and in Tabular, the memory speed is more important than in many other types of servers. Memory bandwidth is a key factor for xVelocity performance and can cause a severe bottleneck of a query over a large database.

> **Note** The memory bandwidth is the rate at which data are transferred between RAM and CPU and is expressed in bytes/second, even if the common naming convention (such as DDR, DDR2, DDR3 . . .) provides a nominal MHz rating (that is, DDR2-1066), which corresponds to the number of transfers per second. The higher this number, the higher the memory bandwidth is. You can find more information at *http://en.wikipedia.org/wiki/ DDR_SDRAM.*

You can observe differences in performance with faster memory bandwidth that are more significant than those you can obtain by using a faster CPU clock. Thus, you should consider carefully the memory bandwidth of your system, which depends on RAM characteristics, CPU, chipset, and configuration. Considering that difference on a new server (in 2012) might range between 20 GB and 70 GB, you can understand why this could be a factor as important, if not more important, than CPU clock.

NUMA Architecture

When Non-Uniform Memory Access (NUMA) architecture is used, consider that NUMA is supported at an operating-system level (Windows), whereas Analysis Services in Tabular mode is not a NUMA-aware application. Thus, it might be better to run an Analysis Services Tabular instance on processors belonging to the same NUMA node, if multiple services run on the same server, and choosing a non-NUMA server for Analysis Services–dedicated machines. You can find a description of available methods to set processor affinity on a service at *http:// waynes-world-it.blogspot.com/2009/06/processor-affinity-on-windows-server.html.*

CPU

Even if Moore's law is still valid (see *http://en.wikipedia.org/wiki/Moore_Law*), modern CPUs are increasing the number of cores per socket without increasing clock speed. Performance improvements have been reached by optimizing the internal architecture of CPUs so that clock speed is not a key factor by which to compare different CPUs belonging to different architectures, but it is still an important discriminator between CPUs of the same family and is also important for xVelocity performance.

xVelocity uses multiple cores when a query reaches the storage engine, but parts of the query are still solved in a single-thread way (in the formula engine), and even with multiple cores involved, you can easily reach the bottleneck of memory bandwidth. Multi-core operations happen at the storage engine level, which usually performs large scans of memory, resulting in a high demand for memory bandwidth.

A key factor in CPU choice is the size of the L2 cache of the processor. The larger the cache, the better the xVelocity performance is. This is such an important factor that a more recent generation of CPU might be slower than an older one that has a larger L2 cache. If you consider only the xVelocity performance, using HyperThreading might also negatively affect performance because the L2 cache is shared between concurrent threads, lowering its efficiency. Thus, you might consider disabling HyperThreading if a server is completely dedicated to a Tabular instance of Analysis Services.

> **Note** Consider that HyperThreading usually offers a performance benefit to a wide range of applications, including SQL Server, as you can read at *http://www2.sqlblog.com/blogs/ linchi_shea/archive/2012/01/22/performance-impact-hyperthreading-on-intel-westmere-ep- processors-x5690.aspx*. Thus, if you disable HyperThreading, you benefit a Tabular instance of Analysis Services, but other services suffer, including Multidimensional instances of Analysis Services.

It is beyond the scope of this book to discuss the differences between CPUs. However, concerning xVelocity, a general rule is that with the same budget, it is better to look for performance by increasing L2 cache, CPU clock speed, and memory bandwidth than by increasing the number of cores, assuming you will get at least four to eight cores for your server. This usually does not result in more expensive hardware but, rather, in a different configuration with the same budget.

Fault Tolerance

You can obtain fault tolerance by storing the Analysis Services files in network-attached storage (NAS) and then by using clustering to fail over to another server if the primary server goes down. You can also use several active Analysis Services servers running in a load balancing configuration, as described in the following section.

Load Balancing

If you want to achieve load balancing, the best option is to duplicate the same database on multiple servers by using access with a load balancer system that also routes requests to a working server if one server is not available. Even if Analysis Services is a cluster-aware service, considering the memory requirements for xVelocity, it is usually not a good choice in view of the return on investment. You can find more information about complex configuration of load balancing in Analysis Services at *http://sqlcat.com/sqlcat/b/technicalnotes/archive/2010/02/08/aslb-setup.aspx* and a longer discussion about consolidation best practices for Analysis Services at *http://sqlcat.com/sqlcat/b/technicalnotes/ archive/2010/02/08/microsoft-sql-server-2008-analysis-services-consolidation-best-practices.aspx*.

DirectQuery Requirements

A Tabular model deployed in DirectQuery mode uses very few resources of the server, at least for the Analysis Services instance that runs it. All the queries are converted into SQL queries sent to SQL Server, so the workload is on the SQL Server machine. If the SQL Server machine queried is on the same machine as Analysis Services, its hardware must be sized according to SQL Server needs. Because almost all the operations made by answering queries sent to Analysis Services in DirectQuery mode are handled in a single thread, the most important factor is CPU speed to reduce the latency required to generate the SQL query. Memory bandwidth is much less important than working in-memory with xVelocity. However, when working in DirectQuery mode, most of the query time is probably spent awaiting results from SQL Server.

A Tabular instance can host databases in both DirectQuery and in-memory mode; you can also deploy databases in a hybrid way. Whenever you have databases that work with xVelocity, you should apply the xVelocity requirements to your server sizing process.

Automating Deployment to a Production Server

You can deploy a Tabular model to a production server in several ways:

- By deploying it directly from SQL Server Data Tools (SSDT), which deploys the model according to the Deployment Server configuration of your database. Visual Studio 2010 configurations, unfortunately, are not supported for Tabular projects. You can just change deployment server properties (such as server and database name) every time you want to switch from a development to a production environment. A workaround to that is using a custom MSBuild task, as described at *http://blogs.msdn.com/b/cathyk/archive/2011/08/10/deploying-tabular-projects-using-a-custom-msbuild-task.aspx*. This approach can work if you have access to all the servers from your development workstation, and you have administrative rights on every Analysis Services instance to execute the deployment operation by using MSBuild.

- By using the Analysis Services Deployment Wizard, which can generate a deployment XMLA script that you can forward to an administrator who can execute the script directly in SSMS, by ASCMD, or by scheduling it in SQL Server Agent, provided he or she has the required administrative rights. For further information about the wizard, refer to the documentation available on MSDN at *http://msdn.microsoft.com/en-us/library/ms176121(v=sql.110).aspx*.

- By using the Synchronize Database Wizard or by executing the XMLA script that this wizard can generate. This wizard copies the content of a database from the source server that you select to a target server. The server on which the wizard has been selected will be the target server and will receive the *Synchronize* command in an XMLA script. This option can be useful to move a database deployed on a development or test server to a production server, and is also useful when you want to duplicate the Tabular database in a server farm that is part of a scale-out architecture. You can find more information about synchronizing databases in Analysis Services at *http://msdn.microsoft.com/en-us/library/ms174928(v=sql.110).aspx*.

You can also automate the deployment from SSDT by using a custom post-build task that performs the deployment by using the MSBuild tool, as you can see at *http://blogs.msdn.com/b/cathyk/archive/2011/08/10/deploying-tabular-projects-using-a-custom-msbuild-task.aspx*.

Backup and Restore Operations

You can also back up and restore an Analysis Services database by using a procedure that is identical to the procedure used for a Multidimensional database. In fact, many of the management operations—such as synchronization, deployment, backup, and restore—use the same commands and procedures for both Multidimensional and Tabular models.

It is important to know that the backup of an Analysis Services database is just the copy of all the files in all the directories contained in the database folder, including both metadata and data. For this reason, the granularity of synchronize, backup, and restore operations is throughout the whole database. You can find more information about backup and restore of an Analysis Services database at *http://msdn.microsoft.com/en-us/library/ms174874(v=sql.110).aspx*.

Table Partitioning

An important design decision in a Tabular model using in-memory mode is partitioning strategy. Every table in Tabular can be partitioned, and the reason for partitioning is related exclusively to table processing. As you saw in Chapter 9, partitions do not give query performance benefits in Tabular and are useful only to reduce the time required to refresh data because you can update just the parts of a table that have been updated since the previous refresh. In this section, you learn when and how to define a partitioning strategy for your Tabular model.

Defining a Partitioning Strategy

Every table in Tabular has one or more partitions. Every partition defines a set of rows that are read from the source table. Every partition can be processed independently, but you cannot process multiple partitions of the same table concurrently, so you cannot use partitions to accelerate the processing of a single table. Another important consideration is that you define partitions related to the source table, but from the Tabular point of view, every table is made of several columns, and every column is a different object. Some columns are calculated and based on data of other columns belonging to the same or different tables. xVelocity knows the dependencies of each calculated column and, when you process a partition of a table, every dependent calculated column in the same or other tables has to be completely recalculated for the entire table to which it belongs. In other words, calculated columns are not partitioned even if they belong to a partitioned table. Moreover, other indexing structures exist for storing column dictionaries and relationships between tables. These structures are not partitioned and require recalculation for the whole table to which they belong if a column from which they depend has been refreshed, even if only for one partition.

Note In a Multidimensional model, only measure groups can be partitioned, and you cannot create partitions over dimensions. When a measure group partition is processed, all the aggregations have to be refreshed, but only for the partition. However, when a dimension is refreshed, it might invalidate aggregations of a related measure group. Dependencies between partitions and related structures such as indexes and aggregations in a Multidimensional model might seem familiar, but in reality, they are completely different, and the partitioning strategy can be very different between Multidimensional and Tabular models using the same data source. For example, processing a table in Tabular that is a dimension in a star schema does not require rebuilding indexes and aggregations on the measure group that corresponds to the fact table in the star schema. Relationships and calculated columns are dependent structures that must be refreshed in Tabular, but their impact is usually lower than that incurred in a Multidimensional model.

The reasons for creating more partitions for a table are:

- **Reducing processing time**   When the time required for processing the whole table is too long for the available processing window, you can obtain significant reduction by processing only the partitions containing new or modified data.

- **Easily removing data from a table**   A partition can be easily removed from a table. This can be useful when you want to keep the last *n* months in your Tabular model. By using monthly partitions, every time you add a new month you create a new partition, removing the older month by deleting the corresponding partition.

- **Consolidating data coming from different source tables**   Your source data is divided into several tables and you want to see all the data in a single table in Tabular. For example, you might have a different physical table in the source database for each year of your Orders, so you have one partition in Tabular for every table in your data source.

The most frequent reason is the need for reducing processing time. Consider that if you can identify only the rows added to the source table since last refresh, you might use the Process Add operation that implicitly creates a new partition and merges it with an existing one, as you see later in this chapter. However, Process Add can be used only when the existing data in the partition will be never modified. If you know that a row already loaded has changed in the data source, you should reprocess the corresponding partition containing that row.

Note An alternative approach to handling data change is inserting a compensating transaction by using Process Add, which is very common in a Multidimensional model. However, because a table can be queried in Tabular without aggregating data, this approach would result in showing all the compensating transactions to the end user.

Partitions do not give you a benefit at query time, and a very high number of partitions (100 partitions or more) can be counterproductive because all the partitions are considered during queries. xVelocity cannot ignore a partition based on its metadata, as Analysis Services does with a Multidimensional model containing partitions with a slicer definition. A partition should just define a set of data that can be easily refreshed or removed from a table in a Tabular model. You have the option to merge partitions, for example, by merging all the days into one month or all the months into one year. Merging partitions does not process data and therefore does not require accessing the data source. This can be important when data access is an expensive operation that occupies a larger part of the process operation. Other activities such as refreshing calculated columns and other indexes are still required in a merge, but they are done without accessing the data sources.

Finally, carefully consider the cost of refreshing indexing structures after you process one or more partitions. (See the "Process Recalc" section later in this chapter.) With complex models, this could be an important part of the process, and you have to lower the object dependencies to reduce the time required to execute a Process Recalc operation. Moreover, if you remove partitions or data changes in existing partitions that are refreshed, you have to plan a Process Defrag operation to optimize the table dictionary, reduce memory consumption, and improve query performance. Thus, implementing a partitioning strategy requires you to make a plan for maintenance operations. This maintenance is not required when you use the Process Full operation on a table because this operation completely rebuilds the table.

Defining Partitions for a Table in a Tabular Model

After you define your partition strategy, the first place in which you can create table partitions is the project of the Tabular model. This option is useful mainly if you have a fixed number of partitions, for example, because data comes from different tables or because the partitioning key is not based on time. If you have a more dynamic structure of partitions, you can change them by using SSMS or scripts, as you see in following sections. In this section, you learn how to create partitions by using SSDT.

You can edit the partitions for a table by selecting Table | Partitions and using the Partition Manager dialog box you see in Figure 17-1. In this case, the Customer table has just one partition (named Customer) with 18,484 rows.

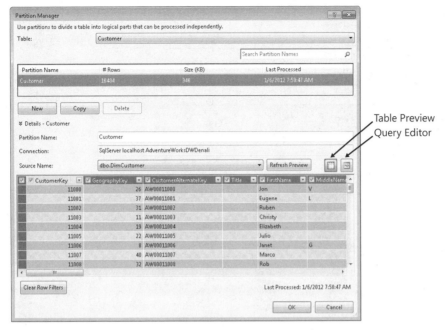

Table Preview
Query Editor

FIGURE 17-1 Partitions can be edited in the Partition Manager dialog box.

The Table Preview and Query Editor buttons enable you to choose the tool available in the Details area, below the Source Name combo box. In Figure 17-1, you see the Table Preview mode, which shows the columns and the rows that can be read from the table chosen in the Source Name combo box (dbo.DimCustomer in this case). If you select values for one column, you filter data in the table preview and implicitly define a query that applies the same filter when processing the partition. For example, in Figure 17-2, you see how to select just a few values for the *EnglishEducation* column.

> **Note** You should choose a column to partition that does not change over time. In fact, a customer might change its education over time, changing the partition to which it belongs. For this reason, this is just an example to show you the Partition Manager user interface, but it is not a best practice. A better partitioning column for Customer could be *Country of Birth* because it cannot change over time, but there is not have such a column in the sample database.

In this way, the Customer partition has a query you can view and edit by clicking the Query Editor button. The query that is generated depends on the sequence of operations that you perform through the user interface. For example, if you start from the default (all items selected) and clear the Partial College and Partial High School items, you obtain as a result the query you see in Figure 17-3, which includes all the future values, excluding only those you cleared in the list.

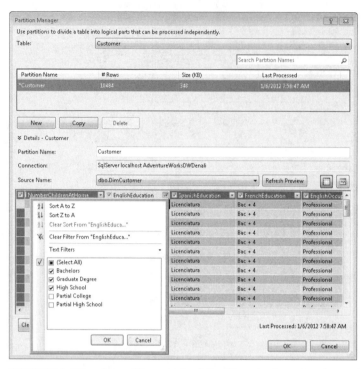

FIGURE 17-2 Filters for partitions can be defined by selecting values for a column.

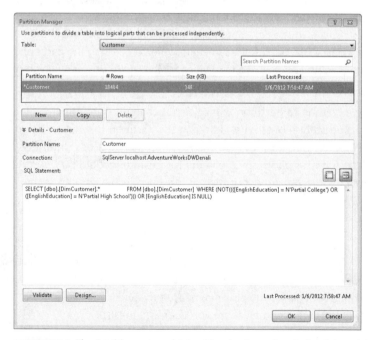

FIGURE 17-3 The Partition query obtained by clearing values in the list contains a *NOT* in the *WHERE* condition.

However, if you first clear Select All and then manually select Bachelor, Graduate Degree, and High School, you obtain a SQL statement that includes only the values you explicitly selected in the list, as you see in Figure 17-4.

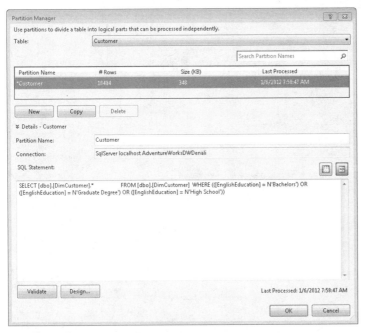

FIGURE 17-4 The Partition query obtained by selecting values in the list after clearing Select All only includes selected items in the *WHERE* condition.

You can edit the SQL statement manually by creating more complex conditions. If you do that, you can no longer use Table Preview mode without losing your query; the message shown in Figure 17-5 warns you about that when you click the Table Preview button.

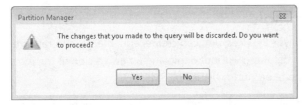

FIGURE 17-5 Manual changes to SQL Statement are lost by going back to Table Preview mode.

After you create a new partition or copy an existing one, you should change the filters in Table Preview or the SQL statement in the Query Editor to avoid the same data being loaded into more than one partition. You do not get any warning at design time about the potential for data duplication. Only if a column is defined as a Row Identifier and duplication occurs will the process operation fail.

Often, you must select a large range of values for a partition, and in these cases, you will probably choose to write a SQL statement similar to the one you see in the examples shown in Figure 17-6.

FIGURE 17-6 Table Preview mode cannot be used when a partition is defined by using a SQL statement.

Because one of the goals of creating a partition is to lessen the time required to process data, the SQL statement you write should also run fast on the source database, too. For this reason, you must check the SQL query performance, optimizing it if necessary.

Managing Partitions for a Table

After you deploy a Tabular model on Analysis Services, you can create, edit, merge, and remove partitions by directly modifying the published database without deploying a new version of the model itself. In this section, you see how to manage partitions by using SSMS.

If you browse the tables available in a Tabular model by using SSMS, you can right-click a table name and select Partitions in the context menu you see in Figure 17-7.

This menu displays a window that enables you to edit partitions of any table. You can choose the table through the combo box you see in Figure 17-8, which includes a description of the available operations through the buttons in the upper-left corner of the Partitions area. The list of partitions includes the number of rows and the size and date of the last process for each partition.

FIGURE 17-7 You can open the Partitions window through the Partitions context menu in SSMS.

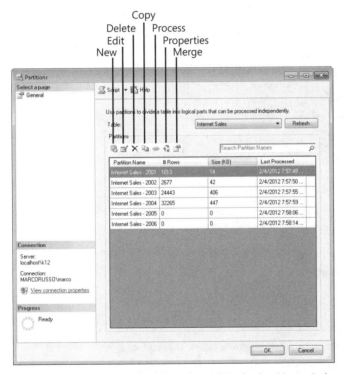

FIGURE 17-8 You can edit partitions of a table in the Partitions window.

The available commands are:

- **New**   Creates a new partition by using a default SQL statement that gets all the rows from the underlying table in the data source. You have to edit such a statement to avoid loading duplicated data in the Tabular table.

- **Edit**   Edits the selected partition and is enabled only when a single partition is selected.

- **Delete**   Removes the selected partition(s).

- **Copy**   Creates a new partition by using the same SQL statement of the selected partition. You have to edit such a statement to avoid loading duplicated data in the Tabular table. This command is enabled only when a single partition is selected.

- **Merge**   Merges two or more partitions. The first partition selected will be the destination of the merge operation; the other partition(s) selected will be removed after being merged into the first partition.

- **Properties**   Shows the properties of the selected partition and is enabled only when a single partition is selected. Properties are read-only and Estimated Rows (which is the only modifiable property) is not used by Tabular. (It is inherited by Multidimensional.)

The *New*, *Edit*, and *Copy* commands display the user interface you see in Figure 17-9, except that the window caption is New Partition for *New* and *Copy* commands and Edit Partition for the *Edit* command.

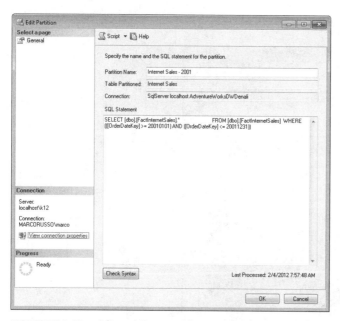

FIGURE 17-9 *New*, *Edit*, and *Copy* partition commands share the same user interface.

You do not have a table preview or a query designer in SSMS for editing a partition as you have in SSDT.

If you go back to the Partitions window shown in Figure 17-8 and select the first partition, Internet Sales – 2001, by pressing the SHIFT key, you select also Internet Sales – 2002 and Internet Sales – 2003. When you click the Merge button, you get the Merge Partition window that you see in Figure 17-10.

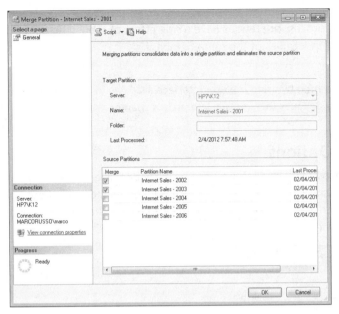

FIGURE 17-10 Partitions can be merged in the Merge Partition window.

The first partition you select will be the only partition existing after the Merge operation. The other partitions selected in the Source Partitions list will be merged into the Target partition and will be removed from the table (and deleted from disk) after the merge.

For any operation you make by using SSMS, you can generate an XMLA script that can be executed without any user interface, as you saw in Chapter 16, "Interfacing with Tabular." You can use such a script to schedule an operation or as a template for creating your own XMLA command, as you see in the Processing Automation section later in this chapter.

Processing Options

Regardless of whether you define partitions in your Tabular model, if you deploy the model by using the in-memory mode, you must define how the data is refreshed from the data source. In Chapter 9, you saw what happens during processing, and you should review that section before going further here. In this section, you learn how to define and implement a processing strategy for a Tabular model.

The process operation can be requested at three levels of granularity:

- **Database** The Process operation can affect all the partitions of all the tables of the selected database.

- **Table** The Process operation can affect all the partitions of the selected table.

- **Partition** The Process operation can affect only the selected partition.

Note Remember that certain process operations have a side effect of rebuilding columns and other internal indexes in other tables of the same database.

A Process operation can be executed by using the user interface available in SSMS or by using other programming or scripting techniques that you see later in this chapter.

Available Processing Options

You have several processing options, and not all of them can be applied to all granularity levels. The following table shows you the possible combinations, using Available for operations that can also be used in the SSMS user interface and Not in UI for operations that can be executed only by using other programming or scripting techniques.

Processing Option	Database	Table	Partition
Process Add			Not in UI
Process Clear	Available	Available	Available
Process Data		Available	Available
Process Default	Available	Available	Available
Process Defrag	Not in UI	Available	
Process Full	Available	Available	Available
Process Recalc	Available		

It is important to know what every operation does and what the side effects of each one are, as described in the following paragraphs.

Process Add

The Process Add operation adds new rows to a partition. It can be used only in a programmatic way, and you must specify the query returning only new rows that have to be added to the partition. Only the dictionaries are incrementally updated; all the other dependently related structures (calculated columns, relationships, indexes, and so on) are automatically recalculated. The Tabular model can be queried during and after a Process Add operation.

Process Clear

Process Clear drops all the data in the selected object (*Database*, *Table*, or *Partition*). The affected objects are no longer queryable after this command.

Process Data

Process Data loads data in the selected object (*Table* or *Partition*). Only the dictionary is computed, and dependently related structures (calculated columns, relationships, and indexes) are not updated. The affected objects are no longer queryable after this command. After Process Data, you should execute Process Recalc or Process Default to make the data queryable.

Process Default

The Process Default operation performs the necessary operations to make the target object queryable (except when it is done at Partition level). If the database/table/partition does not have data (that is, if it has just been deployed or cleared), it performs a Process Data first, but it does not perform Process Data again if it already has data (even if data in your data source has changed, because Analysis Services has no way of knowing it has changed). If dependent structures are not valid (because a Process Data has been executed implicitly or before the Process Default operation), it applies a partial Process Recalc to only those invalid dependent structures (calculated columns, relationships, and indexes). In other words, Process Default can be run on a table or partition, resulting in only Process Recalc on those specific objects, whereas Process Recalc can be run only on the database.

Process Default made at database level is the only operation that guarantees that the table will be queryable after the operation. If you request Process Default at a table level, you should include all the tables in the same transaction. If you request Process Default for every table in separate transactions, be careful of the order of the tables because lookup tables should be updated after tables pointing to them.

Processing Tables in Separate Transactions

Processing tables in separate transactions can be order-dependent because of calculated columns and relationships existing between tables. For example, if you have an Orders table and a Products table, and each order row is related to a product and the Products table contains a column that is calculated by using the Orders table, you should process the Orders table first and the Products table after it. If you do otherwise, you find that the Products Table cannot be queried until it runs a Process Default after this operation has been done on the Orders table. A better option is to perform this sequence of operations if you use separate transactions:

1. Execute Process Data on the Orders table.

2. Execute Process Data on the Products table.

3. Execute Process Default on the Orders table.

4. Execute Process Default on the Products table.

5. Execute Process Recalc on the database.

You should execute a Process Recalc operation after Process Default because Process Recalc recalculates only structures that have been invalidated by a Process Data operation and does not consume resources if calculated columns and other structures have already been updated. Thus, unless you want Orders-related columns to be available as soon as possible, before those related to the Products table, you can use this simpler sequence of operations because Process Recalc implies all the Process Default operation made on single tables:

1. Execute Process Data on the Orders table.

2. Execute Process Data on the Products table.

3. Execute Process Recalc on the database.

Including all these operations in a single transaction is also a best practice.

The Process Default operation made at the partition level does a Process Data operation only if the partition is empty, but it does not refresh any dependent structure. In other words, executing Process Default on a partition corresponds to a conditional Process Data, which is executed only if the partition has never been processed. To make the table queryable, you must still run either Process Default at database or table level or a Process Recalc operation. (Using Process Recalc in the same transaction is a best practice.)

Process Defrag

The Process Defrag operation rebuilds the table dictionary without the need to access the data source to read data again. It is exposed in the SSMS user interface only for tables. This operation is useful only when you remove partitions from your table or you refresh some partitions and, as a result, some values in columns are no longer used. These values are not removed from the dictionary, which will grow over time. If you execute a Process Data or a Process Full operation on the whole table, Process Defrag is useless because these operations rebuild the dictionary.

Tip A common example is a table that has monthly partitions and keeps the last 36 months. Every time a new month is added, the oldest partition is removed and, in the long term, the dictionary might contain values that will never be used. In these conditions, you might want to schedule a Process Defrag operation after one or more months have been added and removed.

If you use Process Defrag at the database level, data for unprocessed tables is also loaded. This does not happen when Process Defrag is run on a single table. (If the table is unprocessed, it is kept as is.)

Process Full

The Process Full operation at a database level is the easiest way to refresh all the tables and the related structures of a Tabular model inside a transaction so that the existing data is queryable during the whole process, and new data will not be visible until the process completes. All existing data from all partitions are thrown away, every partition is loaded, and after all the tables have been loaded, Process Recalc is executed over all the tables.

When Process Full is executed on a table, all the partitions of the table are thrown away, every partition is loaded, and then a partial Process Recalc is applied to all dependent structures (calculated columns, relationships, and indexes). However, if a calculated column depends on a table that is unprocessed, the calculation is performed by considering the unprocessed table as an empty table. Only after the unprocessed table is populated will a new Process Recalc compute the calculated column again, this time with the right value. Process Full of the unprocessed table automatically refreshes this calculated column.

 Note The Process Recalc operation that is performed within Process Full of a table automatically refreshes all calculated columns in other tables that depend on the table that has been processed. For this reason, Process Full over tables does not depend on the order in which it is executed in different transactions, distinguishing it from the Process Defrag operation.

If Process Full is applied to a partition, the existing content of the partition is deleted, the partition is loaded, and then a partial Process Recalc of the whole table is applied to all dependent structures (calculated columns, relationships, and indexes). If you run Process Full on multiple partitions in the same transaction, only one Process Recalc will be performed, but if Process Full commands are executed in separate transactions, every partition's Process Full will execute another Process Recalc over the same table. Therefore, it is better to include in one transaction multiple Process Full operations of different partitions of the same table. The only side effect to consider is that a larger transaction requires more memory on the server because data processed in a transaction is loaded twice in memory (the old version and the new one) at the same time, until the process transaction ends. Insufficient memory can stop the process or slow it down due to paging activity, according to the Memory\VertiPaqPagingPolicy server setting as discussed in *http://www.sqlbi.com/articles/ memory-settings-in-tabular-instances-of-analysis-services.*

Process Recalc

The Process Recalc operation can be requested only at the database level. It recalculates all the calculated columns, relationships, and other internal indexes that must be refreshed because underlying data in the partition or tables is changed. It is a good idea to include Process Recalc in the same transaction of one or more Process Data operations to get better performance and consistency.

> **Tip** Because Process Recalc performs actions only if needed, if you execute two consecutive Process Recalc operations over a database, the second one will perform no actions. However, when Process Recalc is executed over unprocessed tables, it makes these tables queryable and handles them as empty tables. This can be useful during development to make your smaller tables queryable without processing your large tables.

Defining a Processing Strategy

After you have seen all the Process commands available, you might wonder what the best combinations to use for the common scenarios are. Here you learn a few best practices and how transactions are an important factor in defining a processing strategy for your Tabular model.

Transactions

Every time you execute a Process operation in SSMS by selecting multiple objects, you obtain a sequence of commands executed within the same transaction. If any error occurs during these process steps, your Tabular model will maintain its previous state (and data). By using SSMS, you are not able to create a single transaction including different Process commands, such as Process Data and Process Recalc. However, by using XMLA script (that you can obtain from the user interface of existing Process operations in SSMS), you can combine different operations in one transaction, as you see later in this chapter.

You might want to separate process operations into different transactions to save memory usage. During process operations, xVelocity has to keep in memory two versions of the objects that are part of the transaction. When the transaction finishes, xVelocity removes the old version and keeps only the new one. If necessary, xVelocity can page out data if there is not enough RAM, but this slows down the overall process and might affect query performance if there is concurrent query activity during processing. Choosing the processing strategy should take into account the memory required and the availability of the Tabular model during processing. The following scenarios illustrate pros and cons of different approaches, helping you define the best strategy for your needs.

Process Full of a Database

Executing a Process Full operation over the whole database is the simpler way to obtain a working updated Tabular model. All the tables are loaded from the data source, and all the calculated columns, relationships, and other indexes are rebuilt.

This option requires a peak of memory consumption that is more than double the space required for a complete processed model, granting you complete availability of the previous data until the process finishes. To save memory, you can execute Process Clear over the database before Process Full. In this way, you will not store two copies of the same database in memory, but the data will not be available to query until Process Full finishes.

Tip You can consider Process Clear before Process Full if you can afford out-of-service periods. However, consider that in case of any error during processing, no data will be available to the user. If you choose this path, consider creating a backup of the database before Process Clear and automatically restoring the backup in case of any failure during the following Process Full operation.

Process Full of Selected Partitions and Tables

If the time required to perform a Process Full operation of the whole database is too long, you might consider processing only changed tables or partitions. Two approaches are available:

- **Include several Process Full operations of partitions and tables in the same transaction**   In this way, your Tabular model will always be queryable during processing. The memory required will be approximately more than double the space required to store processed objects.

- **Execute each Process Full operation in a separate transaction**   In this way, your Tabular model will always be queryable during processing, but you lower the memory required to something more than double the space required to store the largest of the processed objects. This option requires a longer execution time.

Process Data or Process Default of Selected Partitions and Tables

Instead of using Process Full, which implies a Process Recalc at the end of each operation, you may want to control when Process Recalc is performed because it could be a long operation on a large database and you want to minimize the processing-time window. You can use one of the following approaches:

- **Include Process Data of selected partitions and tables followed by a single Process Recalc of the database in the same transaction**   This way, your Tabular model will always be queryable during processing. The memory required will be approximately more than double the space required to store processed objects.

- **Execute Process Clear of partitions and tables to be processed in a first transaction and then Process Default of the database in a second transaction**   In this way, you remove from memory all the data in the partitions and tables that will be processed so that memory pressure will not be much higher than the memory originally used to store the objects to be processed. (Processing might require more memory than that required just to store the result.) By using this approach, data will be not queryable after Process Clear until Process Default finishes. The time required to complete the operation is optimized because only one implicit Process Recalc will be required for all the calculated columns, relationships, and other indexes.

- **Execute Process Data of partitions and tables to be processed in separate transactions and then Process Recalc in the last transaction**   In this way, you minimize the memory required to handle the processing to more than double the size of the largest object to be processed. With this approach, data will not be queryable after the first Process Data until the Process Recalc finishes. However, in case of an error during one of the Process Data operations, you can still make the database queryable by executing the final Process Recalc, even if one or more tables contain old data, whereas other tables will show refreshed data.

- **Execute Process Clear of partitions and tables to be processed in a first transaction, then Process Data of partitions and tables in separate transactions and Process Recalc in the last transaction**   This approach can be considered when you have severe constraints on memory. Data will be not queryable after Process Clear until Process Recalc executes. Because you immediately remove from memory all the tables that will be processed, the first table to be processed will have the larger amount of memory available. Thus, you should process the remaining objects by following a descendent sort order by object size. You can also consider using Process Full instead of Process Recalc to anticipate the calculation of larger objects that do not depend on tables that will be processed near the end. You should consider this approach only in extreme conditions of memory requirements.

Process Add of Selected Partitions

If you are able to identify new rows that have to be added to an existing partition, you can use the Process Add option. It can be executed in a separate transaction or included in a transaction with other commands. However, consider that Process Add implies an automatic partial Process Recalc of related structures. Thus, you should consider these two scenarios for using it:

- **Execute one or more Process Add operations in a single transaction**   In this way, your Tabular model will be always queryable during processing. Including more than one Process Add in the same transaction should be considered when the rows added in a table are referenced by rows added in another table; you do not want to worry about the order of these operations, and you do not want to make data visible until it is consistent.

- **Execute Process Add in the same transaction with Process Data commands on other partitions and tables, including a Process Recalc at the end**   You may want to do this when the rows you add point to or are referenced from other tables. Enclosing operations in a single transaction will show new data only when the process completes and the result is consistent.

Choosing the Right Processing Strategy

As you have seen, you must consider these factors to choose the processing strategy for your tabular model:

- **Available processing window**   How much time can you dedicate to process data?

- **Availability of data during processing**   Database should be queryable during processing.

- **Rollback in case of errors**   Which version of data do you want to see in case of an error during processing? Is it okay to update only a few tables? You can always do a database backup.

- **Available memory during processing**   The simplest and most secure processing options are those that require more physical memory on the server.

You should always favor the simplest and most secure strategy that is compatible with your requirements and constraints.

Executing Processing

After you define a processing strategy, you must implement it, and you probably want to automate operations. In this section, you see how to perform manual process operations, and in the following part of the chapter, you learn the techniques to automate the processing.

Process Database

In SSMS, you can open the Process Database window by right-clicking the name of the database in the Object Explorer window and selecting Process Database in the context menu you see in Figure 17-11.

FIGURE 17-11 The Process Database window can be opened through the Database context menu in SSMS.

Then you can select the processing mode in the Mode combo box in the Process Database window you see in Figure 17-12.

If you click OK, the database will be processed. You can generate a corresponding XMLA script by using the Script menu in the Process Database window. You see how to use XMLA in more detail in the "Using XMLA" section later in this chapter.

Note Even if you process a database without including the operation in a transaction, all the tables and partitions of the database are processed within the same transaction, and the existing database continues to be available during processing. In other words, a single *Process* command includes an implicit transaction.

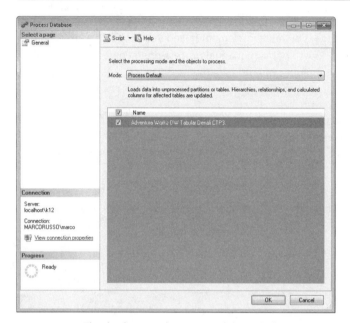

FIGURE 17-12 The database can be processed through the Process Database window.

Process Table

You can manually request to process one or more tables by using SSMS by selecting the tables in the Object Explorer Details window and selecting Process Table in the context menu that you see in Figure 17-13.

You can obtain the same Process Table item in the context menu by right-clicking a table in the Object Explorer window, but by doing that, you can select only one table. In any case, you can change the table to process in the Process Table(s) window, which will show the same selection you made before opening the window, as you see in Figure 17-14.

The process operation starts when you click the OK button. In this case, the tables selected will be processed in separate batches (and therefore in different transactions), by using the process mode you select in the combo box. However, the script that you can generate through the Script menu will contain the definition of a transaction if two or more tables have been selected, so all the tables will be processed within the same transaction.

 Note The script generated by the Process Table(s) window includes all the operations within a single transaction, whereas the direct command uses a separate transaction for every table.

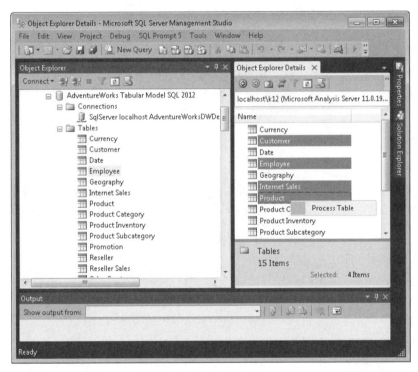

FIGURE 17-13 The Process Table(s) window can be opened through the Table context menu in SSMS.

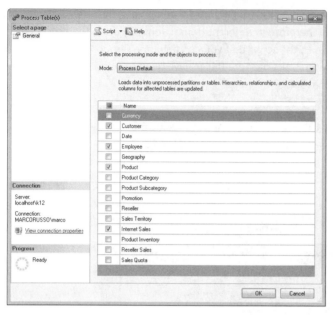

FIGURE 17-14 The Process Table(s) window can process one or more tables.

Process Partition

You can process one or more partitions by clicking the Process button in the Partitions window you saw in Figure 17-8. This command shows the Process Partition(s) window that you see in Figure 17-15.

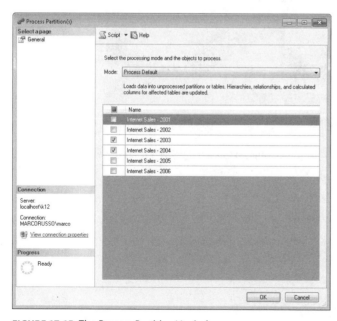

FIGURE 17-15 The Process Partition(s) window can process one or more partitions.

By clicking the OK button, all the partitions selected are processed as part of the same batch within a single transaction, by using the process mode you select in the combo box. The script that you can generate through the Script menu will also contain the explicit definition of a transaction if two or more partitions have been selected.

If you want to implement Process Add on a partition, you cannot rely on the SSMS user interface; you must manually write a script or a program that performs the required incremental update of the partition. You can find an example of Process Add implementation in the article at *http://www.sqlbi.com/articles/incremental-processing-in-tabular-using-process-add*.

Processing Automation

After you define partitioning and processing strategies, you must implement and probably automate them. You have several options available to do that and, in this section, you see an overview of all of them.

Using XMLA

XMLA stands for XML for Analysis and is an industry standard for data access in analytical systems. It is based on XML, and you can use some of these statements to send commands to Analysis Services. Every time you execute an administrative operation by using SSMS, such as processing an object or editing partitions, you can obtain an XMLA script that corresponds to the operation you intend to do, as you saw in Chapter 16. Such a script can be executed in several ways. For example, within SSMS, you can create an XMLA query window by using File | New | Analysis Services XMLA Query, as you see in Figure 17-16, or by right-clicking a database and selecting New Query | XMLA from the context menu.

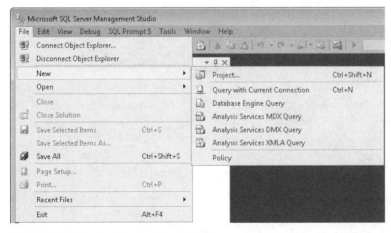

FIGURE 17-16 The Analysis Services XMLA Query window is in the File | New menu.

After you have an XMLA query window, you can write an XMLA command and then execute it by using Query | Execute. In Figure 17-17, you can see the result of a *Process Default* command on the Adventure Works database.

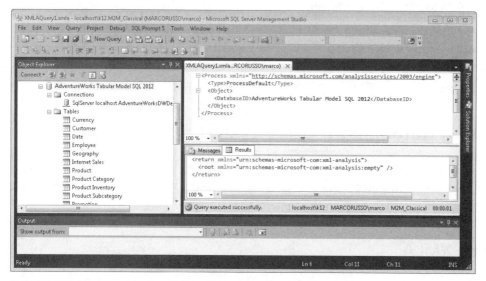

FIGURE 17-17 The execution of an XMLA script to process a database displays the result in the Results pane.

An important concept to mention is that you can group several XMLA commands into a single batch by using the *Batch* element, which enables you to specify whether several commands should be part of the same transaction. This can be an important decision, as you saw in the "Processing Options" section in this chapter. For example, the following XMLA command executes within the same transaction as the Process Data of two tables (Product and Internet Sales) and the Process Recalc of the database.

```
<Batch xmlns='http://schemas.microsoft.com/analysisservices/2003/engine'
Transaction='true'>
    <Process xmlns="http://schemas.microsoft.com/analysisservices/2003/engine">
      <Type>ProcessData</Type>
      <Object>
        <DatabaseID>AdventureWorks Tabular Model SQL 2012</DatabaseID>
        <DimensionID>Product_bd4ca113-593f-4dfd-98a2-8de806acb579
        </DimensionID>
      </Object>
    </Process>
    <Process xmlns="http://schemas.microsoft.com/analysisservices/2003/engine">
      <Type>ProcessData</Type>
      <Object>
        <DatabaseID>AdventureWorks Tabular Model SQL 2012</DatabaseID>
        <DimensionID>Internet Sales_78de3956-70d9-429f-9857-c407f7902f1e
        </DimensionID>
      </Object>
```

```
        </Process>
        <Process xmlns="http://schemas.microsoft.com/analysisservices/2003/engine">
            <Type>ProcessRecalc</Type>
            <Object>
                <DatabaseID>AdventureWorks Tabular Model SQL 2012</DatabaseID>
            </Object>
        </Process>
    </Batch>
```

The *Batch* command can include more than one *Process* command. The *Transaction* attribute in the *Batch* element determines the inclusion of the commands within the same transaction. The target of each Process operation is defined by the *Object* element, which identifies a table or a database. Because XMLA natively refers to the Multidimensional model, every table is identified as a dimension and, therefore, the *DimensionID* element is used. An important note is that the table is identified by its unique name, which contains a globally unique identifier (GUID) that is not part of the user-friendly name and is automatically generated when you create the object by using Microsoft Visual Studio. This is one of the reasons it is simpler to start an XMLA script by generating a similar statement from SSMS, which automatically uses the right name of every object. You can also obtain this unique name by looking at the ID property of a table deployed on a server by using the Table Properties window in SSMS.

If you want to group several commands in different transactions, you must create more *Batch* commands, which must be executed separately. For example, to run Process Clear on two tables and then a single Process Default on the database, you must run these two *Batch* commands.

```
<Batch xmlns='http://schemas.microsoft.com/analysisservices/2003/engine'
Transaction='true'>
    <Process xmlns="http://schemas.microsoft.com/analysisservices/2003/engine">
        <Type>ProcessClear</Type>
        <Object>
            <DatabaseID>AdventureWorks Tabular Model SQL 2012</DatabaseID>
            <DimensionID>Product_bd4ca113-593f-4dfd-98a2-8de806acb579
            </DimensionID>
        </Object>
    </Process>
    <Process xmlns="http://schemas.microsoft.com/analysisservices/2003/engine">
        <Type>ProcessClear</Type>
        <Object>
            <DatabaseID>AdventureWorks Tabular Model SQL 2012</DatabaseID>
            <DimensionID>Internet Sales_78de3956-70d9-429f-9857-c407f7902f1e
            </DimensionID>
        </Object>
    </Process>
</Batch>

<Batch xmlns='http://schemas.microsoft.com/analysisservices/2003/engine'
Transaction='true'>
    <Process xmlns="http://schemas.microsoft.com/analysisservices/2003/engine">
```

```
        <Type>ProcessDefault</Type>
        <Object>
            <DatabaseID>AdventureWorks Tabular Model SQL 2012
            </DatabaseID>
        </Object>
    </Process>
</Batch>
```

To run several commands in parallel, grouping Process commands into a single batch is not enough; you must also add a *Parallel* element inside the *Batch* element, as you see in the following example.

Note Only tables can be processed in parallel; different partitions of the same table will always be executed sequentially. Parallel processing can reduce the processing-time window and requires more RAM to complete.

```
<Batch xmlns='http://schemas.microsoft.com/analysisservices/2003/engine'
Transaction='true'>
  <Parallel>
    <Process xmlns="http://schemas.microsoft.com/analysisservices/2003/engine">
        <Type>ProcessFull</Type>
        <Object>
            <DatabaseID>AdventureWorks Tabular Model SQL 2012
            </DatabaseID>
            <DimensionID>Product_bd4ca113-593f-4dfd-98a2-8de806acb579
            </DimensionID>
        </Object>
    </Process>
    <Process xmlns="http://schemas.microsoft.com/analysisservices/2003/engine">
        <Type>ProcessFull</Type>
        <Object>
            <DatabaseID>AdventureWorks Tabular Model SQL 2012</DatabaseID>
            <DimensionID>Internet Sales_78de3956-70d9-429f-9857-c407f7902f1e
            </DimensionID>
        </Object>
    </Process>
    <Process xmlns="http://schemas.microsoft.com/analysisservices/2003/engine">
        <Type>ProcessRecalc</Type>
        <Object>
            <DatabaseID>AdventureWorks Tabular Model SQL 2012</DatabaseID>
        </Object>
    </Process>
  </Parallel>
</Batch>
```

It is beyond the scope of this book to provide a complete reference to XMLA commands. You can find a complete reference at *http://msdn.microsoft.com/en-us/library/ms187159(v=sql.110).aspx*. The best way to learn XMLA is by starting from the XMLA scripts that you can generate from the SSMS user interface and then looking in documentation for the syntax required to access other properties and commands not available in the user interface. You can generate an XMLA command dynamically from a language of your choice and then send the request by using the Analysis Management Object (AMO) API that we describe later in this chapter.

Executing from the Command Line (ASCMD)

You can execute an XMLA script file by using the ASCMD tool, which is provided as part of the product samples you can find at *http://msftdbprodsamples.codeplex.com*. Note that the ASCMD tool can split multiple batches or commands contained in a single file into multiple XMLA requests sent to Analysis Services without having to call ASCMD multiple times. This is particularly useful when you want to run a sequence of distinct batches to keep transactions separate.

Supposing you saved one of the previous XMLA scripts in a file named *process.xmla*, you can execute it by using the following command (assuming the server is an instance named Tabular on the local machine).

```
ASCMD -S localhost\tabular -i process.xmla
```

ASCMD also supports scripting variables that you can replace by using command-line parameters. You can find further information in the ASCMD Readme_ascmd.docx document included in the downloadable source code.

Executing from SQL Server Agent

You can schedule execution of an XMLA script in a SQL Server Agent job. You define a step of type SQL Server Analysis Services Command, and then you must write the XMLA script in the Command text box. You must also specify the Analysis Services instance name as Server and a proxy user in the Run As combo box that has the necessary rights to execute the specified XMLA script. (See Figure 17-18.)

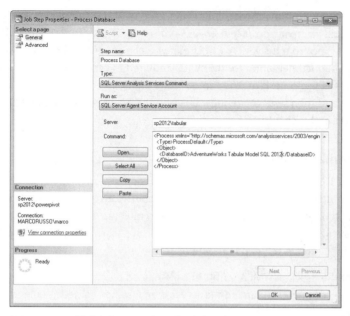

FIGURE 17-18 XMLA Command can be defined in a SQL Server Agent Job Step Properties window.

 Tip When SQL Server Agent runs a job, it does so by using the SQL Server Agent account. This account might not have sufficient privileges to run the process command on Analysis Services. To run the job step by using a different account, you must define a proxy account in SQL Server so that you can choose that account in the Run As combo box in the Job Step Properties window. You can find detailed instructions about how to do this at *http://msdn .microsoft.com/en-us/library/ms175834.aspx*.

Executing from SQL Server Integration Services (SSIS)

By using SQL Server Integration Services (SSIS), you can add an Analysis Services *Processing Task* control to the Control Flow of your package. Such a control, unfortunately, supports commands for Multidimensional models only and lacks the specific processing commands for a Tabular model. Thus, you cannot use Process Recalc, Process Defrag, and Process Add operations through this component. However, you can put an XMLA script into an Analysis Services Execute DDL Task.

Using AMO

In Chapter 16, you saw an extensive description of the object model provided by the Analysis Management Object (AMO) library and how you can use it to execute commands on an Analysis Services server. The AMO interface can be used by any .NET programming or scripting language. Thus, you can use it in a Script component in Integration Services because the AMO assembly is installed in the global assembly cache (GAC).

The following example shows how you can execute Process Data on Product and Internet Sales tables followed by Process Recalc in the same transaction. This code executes every process in a separate command in the same transaction without using an XMLA batch operation.

```
using System;
using Microsoft.AnalysisServices;

namespace AmoAutomation {
    class Program {
        static void Main(string[] args) {
            Server server = new Server();
            server.Connect (@"localhost\k12");
            server.BeginTransaction();
            Database db =
                server.Databases["AdventureWorks Tabular Model SQL 2012"];
            Dimension tableProduct = db.Dimensions.GetByName("Product");
            Dimension tableInternetSales =
                db.Dimensions.GetByName("Internet Sales");
            tableProduct.Process(ProcessType.ProcessData);
            tableInternetSales.Process(ProcessType.ProcessData);
            db.Process(ProcessType.ProcessRecalc);
            server.CommitTransaction();
            server.Disconnect();
        }
    }
}
```

If you prefer to execute the process commands in parallel, you can use batch execution, which is based on the CaptureXml property and the *ExecuteCaptureLog* command instead of the *BeginTransaction* and *EndTransaction* methods, as you see in the following code.

```
using System;
using Microsoft.AnalysisServices;

namespace AmoAutomation {
    class Program {
        static void Main(string[] args) {
            Server server = new Server();
            server.Connect(@"localhost\k12");
            server.CaptureXml = true;
            Database db =
                server.Databases["AdventureWorks Tabular Model SQL 2012"];
            Dimension tableProduct = db.Dimensions.GetByName("Product");
            Dimension tableInternetSales =
                db.Dimensions.GetByName("Internet Sales");
            tableProduct.Process(ProcessType.ProcessData);
            tableInternetSales.Process(ProcessType.ProcessData);
            db.Process(ProcessType.ProcessRecalc);
            server.CaptureXml = false;
            server.ExecuteCaptureLog(true, true);
            server.Disconnect();
        }
    }
}
```

See Chapter 16 for more details about how to work with AMO with partitions.

Using PowerShell

Microsoft Windows PowerShell is a useful command-line shell for automating processes and creating scripting because it can access AMO objects easily. You can find an introduction to PowerShell in Chapter 16.

The following PowerShell script shows how you can execute Process Data on the Product and Internet Sales tables followed by a Process Recalc in the same transaction. It is similar to the previous example written in Microsoft C# that calls the AMO library; there are just a few differences due to the PowerShell syntax.

```
[Reflection.Assembly]::LoadWithPartialName("Microsoft.AnalysisServices")
$server = New-Object Microsoft.AnalysisServices.Server
$server.connect("BISM\TABULAR")
$server.BeginTransaction()
$db = $server.Databases.Item("AdventureWorks Tabular Model SQL 2012")
$tableProduct = $db.Dimensions.FindByName("Product")
$tableInternetSales = $db.Dimensions.FindByName("Internet Sales")
$tableProduct.Process("ProcessData")
$tableInternetSales.Process("ProcessData")
$db.Process("ProcessRecalc")
$server.CommitTransaction()
$server.Disconnect()
```

Using SSIS

SSIS has limited support for Tabular in the Analysis Services *Processing Task* control, and the Analysis Services Execute DDL Task containing an XMLA script can be used as a workaround.

If you want to use the Analysis Services *Processing Task* control, you must consider that every table in a Tabular model corresponds to a dimension in a Multidimensional model. Thus, to process only a few tables, you must select only the corresponding dimension objects. For example, you can insert an Analysis Services *Processing Task* control in your package, as shown in Figure 17-19.

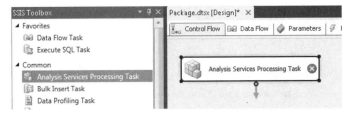

FIGURE 17-19 Insert an Analysis Services *Processing Task* control in an SSIS package.

Then you can open the Analysis Services Processing Task Editor and, by selecting Processing Settings, select an Analysis Services connection manager or create a new one. You must select a specific database with this control, and you must use a different connection in your package for each database you want to process.

> **Note** Integration Services puts DatabaseID in the XMLA command generated from the user interface of the Analysis Services *Processing Task* control. Thus, the connection manager might not control the target database in an effective way if you want to change the database on which the task has to operate.

In Figure 17-20, you see the Analysis Services Processing Task Editor window after you select the connection to a Tabular instance.

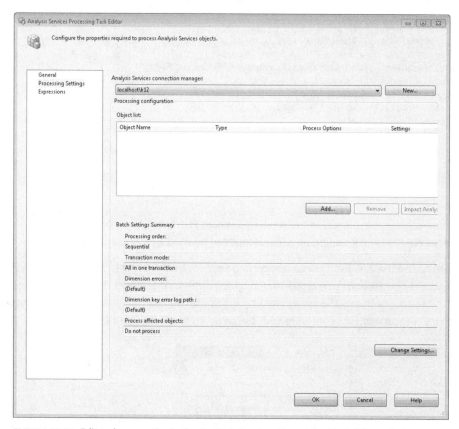

FIGURE 17-20 Edit task properties in the Analysis Services Processing Task Editor window.

By clicking the Add button, you can select the objects to process. To select the Product and Internet Sales tables, you must select the two corresponding dimensions, as you see in Figure 17-21. You do not have to select any cube or measure group, but you can include the database object if you want.

After clicking OK, go back to the Analysis Services Processing Task Editor window and select the two tables, represented as Dimension Type in the list. Then, by right-clicking, you can change the Process Options for all selected objects by choosing the corresponding item in the context menu you see in Figure 17-22.

FIGURE 17-21 Select tables to process in the Add Analysis Services Object window.

FIGURE 17-22 Change the Process Options in the context menu.

You can choose among all the processing options used by a Multidimensional model. However, Process Update and Process Index are not useful for table processing in Tabular. After you change the Process options of the Product and Internet Sales tables to Process Data, you can select the process operation for the Adventure Works database by using the combo box available in the Process Options column, which operates on only the object defined in the same row. In Figure 17-23, you see how to select Process Default for the Adventure Works database.

The Analysis Services *Processing Task* control configured in this way generates a single transaction containing a Process Data operation of Product and Internet Sales tables and a Process Default operation of the Adventure Works database. As noted before, you cannot specify Process Recalc for the database by using this component.

To avoid the limitations of this control, you can use the less sophisticated but more flexible Analysis Services *Execute DDL Task* control. You can insert this control in your package by choosing it from Other Tasks in the SSIS Toolbox, as you see in Figure 17-24.

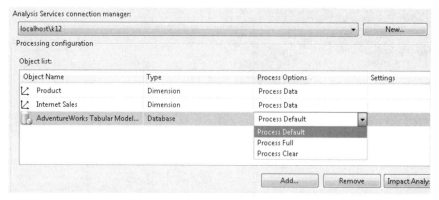

FIGURE 17-23 Select the process type in the Add Analysis Services Object window.

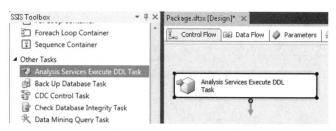

FIGURE 17-24 Insert an Analysis Services *Execute DDL Task* control in a SSIS package.

In the Analysis Services Execute DDL Task Editor shown in Figure 17-25, you must select a Connection to Analysis Services and, in the Source Direct property, you must paste the XMLA script you want to execute.

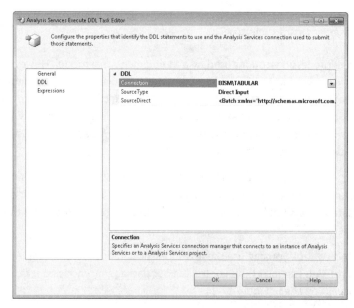

FIGURE 17-25 Configure task properties in the Analysis Services Execute DDL Task Editor window.

It is better to prepare the XMLA command by using the XMLA query window in SSMS because you have a minimal editor available instead than trying to modify the SourceDirect property directly in the DDL Statements editor, as you see in Figure 17-26.

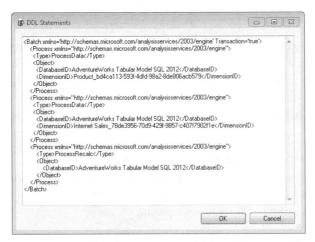

FIGURE 17-26 Edit the XMLA code in the DDL Statements window available to insert the SourceDirect property.

If you want to parameterize the content of the XMLA command, you must manipulate the SourceDirect property as a string. (For example, you can build the XMLA string in a script task by assigning it to a package variable and then using an expression to set the Source property of the task.) You do not have a built-in feature of parameterization for the XMLA script in this component.

DirectQuery Deployment

You saw in Chapter 9 how DirectQuery works, what limitations it has, and what the different options to deploy a model are. In this section, you learn how to choose between pure DirectQuery and hybrid modes, how to implement your decision, and how to manage security correctly in these scenarios.

Define a DirectQuery Partitioning Strategy

A Tabular model in DirectQuery mode uses just one partition, called DirectQuery partition. However, you can define multiple partitions on a table for hybrid modes, and you implicitly use a hybrid mode, at least during development, because the workspace database is automatically put in hybrid mode, even if you set it to DirectQuery only, to provide a responsive design experience. Three DirectQueryMode options involve the use of DirectQuery, and the following list presents a few common scenarios for their use:

- **DirectQuery** You can choose a pure DirectQuery model when your client generates only DAX queries, limiting its use to Power View and custom reporting (made by using Reporting Services, Report Builder, custom applications, or other relational reporting tools) containing queries written in DAX. The main reason to use this mode is to get real-time queries without the latency required to process the data model. In a future upgrade of Analysis Services, DirectQuery might be queryable with MDX also, enabling its use from existing clients generating MDX queries for a Multidimensional model, such as Microsoft Excel.

- **DirectQuery With In-Memory** In this hybrid mode, DirectQuery is the default choice made by the client. This is the right choice when you want to use both Excel (or any other MDX-based client tool) and Power View because Excel makes it possible to change the connection string by adding the DirectQueryMode=InMemory setting. Such a change in Power View requires you to use an RSDS connection instead of a BISM one (which is simpler to define for an end user). In an report server data source (RSDS) connection, you can specify the connection string by including the DirectQueryMode setting.

- **In-Memory With DirectQuery** This other hybrid mode is the right choice when you have only Excel or another MDX-based client tool, and you must use DirectQuery from only custom-made reports in which you can add DirectQueryMode=DirectQuery in the connection string. Again, in Power View you must use an RSDS connection instead of a BISM connection to specify the DirectQueryMode setting in the connection string.

By using one of the hybrid modes (those involving In-Memory), you can define more than one partition to be processed by the xVelocity in-memory engine. In such a case, you can apply all the guidelines you have seen previously in this chapter for defining a partitioning strategy that will be used for In-Memory modes. Please refer to Chapter 9 to see how you can set the DirectQueryMode property in your Tabular model.

> **Note** It is not possible to create hybrid models with a DirectQuery partition containing the most recent data (for example, the current month) and other In-Memory partitions with historical data, as you might be accustomed to doing in a Multidimensional model. DirectQuery uses only one partition and cannot produce a result obtained by mixing data from both DirectQuery and In-Memory partitions. In other words, a single query resolves from either DirectQuery or xVelocity but not from both.

Implementing Partitions for DirectQuery and Hybrid Modes

When you deploy a Tabular model supporting a DirectQuery or hybrid mode, you must consider how to manage partitions. Only one partition can be marked as a DirectQuery partition, and it will be the only partition that sends queries to SQL Server in DirectQuery mode. The simplest case is when your table has just one partition because it will also be the DirectQuery partition, and you do not have to choose. In Figure 17-27, you see the (DirectQuery) prefix in the *Partition Name* column that identifies the partition marked as DirectQuery.

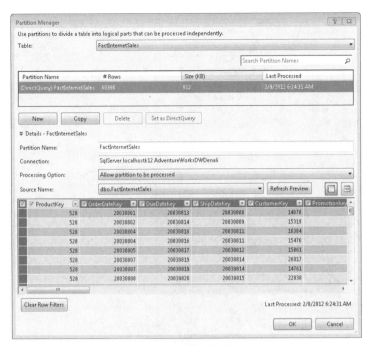

FIGURE 17-27 A single partition is always the DirectQuery partition.

If you copy this partition, you obtain two identical partitions that duplicate all the rows in the table. (Even if only one partition will be the DirectQuery partition, the data duplication affects only the In-Memory mode.) However, at this point, you can choose not to process the DirectQuery partition by selecting Never Process This Partition in the Processing Option combo box, as you see in Figure 17-28. This setting means that the partition will not be processed by xVelocity, so its content will be ignored when the Tabular model is queried by using the In-Memory mode.

> **Note** Usually, you will use the Allow Partition To Be Processed setting for Processing Option when the DirectQuery partition is the only partition in your table. If you have other partitions in your table, you might consider this setting whenever you want to offer real-time updates of recent data in DirectQuery mode, because other queries involving consolidated historical data require In-Memory mode.

Processing Option is available only in the DirectQuery partition and is not available in the other partitions. You see in Figure 17-29 that this option is not available in the partition named FactInternetSales – VertiPaq. Note that the # *Rows* and *Size (KB)* columns show values only for partitions that have been processed, whereas the DirectQuery partition no longer contains rows because it has been excluded from xVelocity processing.

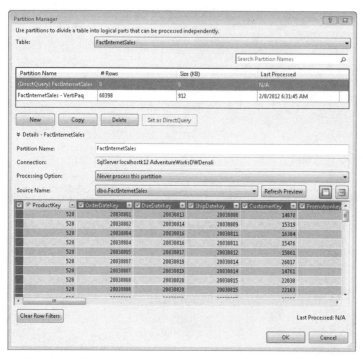

FIGURE 17-28 With more than one partition, one is for DirectQuery, others for In-Memory (xVelocity).

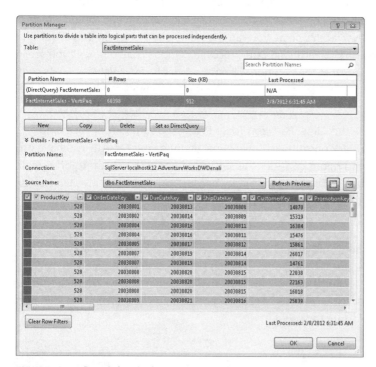

FIGURE 17-29 Processing Options are not available in non-DirectQuery partitions.

At this point, creating two identical partitions that will be used alternately between In-Memory and DirectQuery mode might not seem useful, considering that the result will be identical to what you obtain when a single partition for the table is used for both DirectQuery and In-Memory modes. In fact, it makes more sense to separate partitions when you want to process only a limited number of partitions by using xVelocity.

> **Tip** You might want to consider the configuration shown in Figure 17-29 whenever you have a pure DirectQuery model that will be never used with In-Memory mode. The configuration you use in this way can also be used to populate the table in SSDT during development. Thus, you might have a DirectQuery partition that corresponds to the whole table and a single xVelocity partition that processes a subset of the rows by either pointing to a view or using a query or a filter over the table. During development, you can process the xVelocity partition in the workspace database, but after deployment, you should never process the xVelocity partition if you do not want to deploy the database in hybrid mode.

In Figure 17-30, you see the partitions configuration of the FactInternetSales table that has been split into three xVelocity partitions (2001–2002, 2003, and 2004–Current) by defining a query for each one. Processing Option for the DirectQuery partition has been set to Never Process This Partition, as you can see from the lack of data in the corresponding row.

If you separate the xVelocity partitions from the DirectQuery partition, you will want to choose a hybrid configuration in the Database Property window, as you see in Figure 17-31, where the Query Mode has been set to DirectQuery With In-Memory.

If you want to select DirectQuery for Query Mode, the only effect of changing partition will be visible during the development because SSDT uses only xVelocity to show you table data.

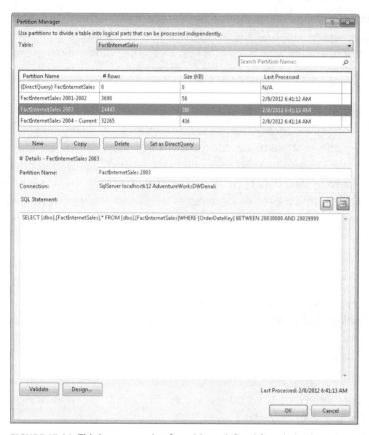

FIGURE 17-30 This is an example of partitions defined for a hybrid mode configuration.

FIGURE 17-31 A hybrid mode configuration requires proper selection in Query Mode.

Security and Impersonation with DirectQuery

When a Tabular model works in In-Memory mode, the row-level security is handled by Analysis Services, as you saw in Chapter 15, "Security." However, when you use DirectQuery mode, Analysis Services cannot provide any object-level or row-level security, which is delegated to SQL Server, as you see in this section.

The user who accesses a Tabular model in DirectQuery mode can either have access to the model itself or not. This is the only security check made by Analysis Services. If the user has access to the model, any DAX query is converted in a SQL statement that is sent to SQL Server, which is responsible only for security. In this scenario, it is important to look at the user who connects to SQL Server from Analysis Services. This is controlled by the Impersonation Settings property on the database, which can have one of two values:

- **Default**   Analysis Services connects to SQL Server to execute a query in DirectQuery mode by using the credentials specified in the data source connection, which are the same credentials used to process the tables in xVelocity.

- **ImpersonateCurrentUser**   When in DirectQuery mode, Analysis Services impersonates the current user's credentials to connect to SQL Server to execute the SQL query generated from the DAX query. If a hybrid mode is active and the model is processed by xVelocity, Analysis Services uses the credentials specified in the data source to connect to the data source.

If you impersonate the current user in DirectQuery mode, you must configure security on both Analysis Services and SQL Server. This gives you the ability to define row-level security in SQL Server by using this technique:

1. Assume you have the original table of the model created in the dbo schema. (If you do not, replace the dbo with the schema name in the following steps.) The user used in the data source connection in Analysis Services must use the dbo schema as a default schema.

2. Define a schema on SQL Server for every group of users.

3. Define a user on SQL Server for every user whom you will also enable on Analysis Services to access the Tabular model published in DirectQuery mode.

4. Assign to each user in SQL Server created in this way the corresponding schema (of the group to which he or she belongs) as a default schema.

5. Grant *SELECT* permission on each schema to all the users belonging to the same group (that is, users who see the same rows of data).

6. For every table in the dbo schema that you reference in the Tabular model, create a SQL view with the same name in each schema. This view must include a *WHERE* condition that filters only the rows that should be visible to that group of users.

7. In the Tabular model, assign to every DirectQuery partition a SQL statement instead of a direct table binding and remove any reference to any schema in the SQL query you use.

In this way, when the user queries the Analysis Services model, his or her credentials will be used by Analysis Services to connect to SQL Server. Because that user has a default schema that uses views with the same name as the original tables or views but with an additional *WHERE* condition that filters only the rows he or she can see, the SQL query generated by Analysis Services will use these views and return only the rows that the user can see. You can find another implementation of row-level security that is based on a more dynamic (data-based) approach at *http://sqlserverlst.codeplex.com*.

 Important Consider that every query assigned to the DirectQuery partition will be included in more complex SQL statements performing joins, subqueries, and other complex statements. It is up to you to filter the condition on every table and to monitor the resulting performance offered by SQL Server.

If you are interested in a deeper discussion about how DirectQuery impersonation works, more information is available at *http://blogs.msdn.com/b/cathyk/archive/2011/12/13/directquery-impersonation-options-explained.aspx*.

Summary

In this chapter, you saw how you should size the hardware correctly for a server hosting a Tabular instance of Analysis Services. After reading a list of the options available to deploy a model on a server production, you saw how to define and implement a partitioning strategy and a processing strategy. You also learned how the process operation can be automated by using several technologies. Finally, you saw how to handle partitioning and security in models deployed in DirectQuery mode.

Optimizations and Monitoring

Now that you have seen how to build a complete Tabular solution, this final chapter provides information about how to monitor its behavior and how to guarantee that your solution is running at its best.

In Chapter 9, "Understanding xVelocity and DirectQuery," you saw how the Tabular engine uses memory to process and query databases. This chapter shows how you can monitor the resources used by the system and how to change some parameters to optimize SQL Server Analysis Services (SSAS) and memory usage. It also provides some hints on how to write efficient DAX queries.

Finding the Analysis Services Process

Analysis Services is a process running as a service under the Microsoft Windows operating system. It starts as soon as the operating system starts, and it is normally waiting to receive commands, answer queries, process databases, and perform its work. The process name is MSMDSRV.EXE (Microsoft Multidimensional Server), and you can verify its existence by using the Windows Task Manager, as you see by looking at the Services tab in Figure 18-1.

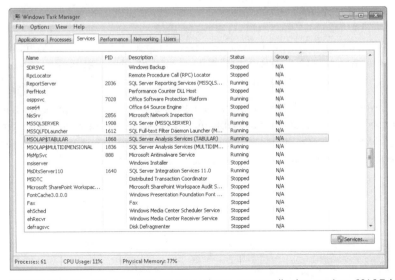

FIGURE 18-1 The Windows Task Manager shows, among all other services, SSAS Tabular.

You can see that there are two instances of SSAS, one running Tabular and one running Multidimensional. If you want to see the process running Tabular, right-click MSOLAP$TABULAR and choose Go To Process. Task Manager opens the Processes tab, highlighting the instance of MSMDSRV of Tabular that you see in Figure 18-2. Note that if the process is impersonating a different user, you must have the Show Processes From All Users check box selected.

> **Note** The name of an Analysis Services instance is chosen during the installation operation. In this book, we use Tabular and Multidimensional instance names to identify the corresponding roles of different SSAS instances, but you can choose different instance names during installation.

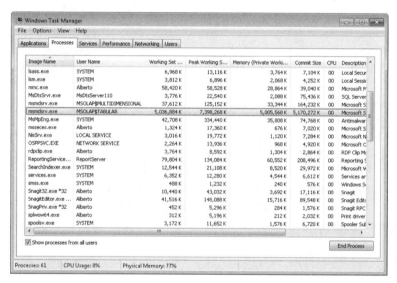

FIGURE 18-2 The Processes tab contains detailed information about the MSMDSRV.EXE process.

SSAS, like any other Windows process, consumes resources, asking for them from the Windows operating system, and it is important to monitor whether it has enough resources to run in an optimal way to ensure that the system is always responsive.

The easiest tool with which to monitor Tabular is the Task Manager. It already provides much information about memory and CPU usage, and it is available on any Windows installation to any user, without requiring special knowledge or administrative rights. Nevertheless, to fine-tune a solution, you will need more advanced tools and a deeper knowledge of SSAS internals.

> **Warning** Although it might seem obvious, remember that when you use the Task Manager to monitor SSAS, the server should not be running other time-consuming processes; otherwise, your observations will be contaminated by other tasks consuming the server resources.

Because it is an in-memory columnar database, SSAS Tabular is easy to monitor because it uses mainly two kinds of resources: memory and CPU. The disk usage of SSAS Tabular is not very important to monitor because disk activity happens only during processing, when the database is written to disk and when the database is being loaded when the first user accesses the database after the service starts. Both activities are sequential reads and writes, which are very fast operations on normal disk systems. Random I/O might happen during processing only if there is not enough memory to complete the operation and some data must be paged on disk.

Understanding Memory Configuration

Because memory is so important to Tabular, being able to monitor how much memory is used and learning how to configure memory usage is a very important topic. In this section, you learn the main tools available to configure and monitor memory used by a Tabular instance.

First, it is important to understand that SSAS uses memory during two phases:

- **Processing** During processing, SSAS needs memory to load data and create dictionaries and related data structures before it flushes them to disk. In addition, if the database being processed already contains some data, it must hold the previous version of the database until the transaction commits and the new database is ready to query. Refer to Chapter 9 for more information about internal structure and processing.

- **Querying** During a query, SSAS sometimes needs memory to hold temporary data structures that are needed to resolve the query. Depending on the database size and the query shape, these data structures might be very big, sometimes much bigger than the database itself. Later in this chapter, you see an example of a complex query using a lot of RAM.

Memory settings in Tabular are configured inside the *msmdsrv.ini* file, which contains the whole SSAS configuration. You can edit the file manually to change memory settings, but the easiest way to read or modify the content of the configuration is to right-click the server in the Object Explorer window of SQL Server Management Studio (SSMS) and choose Properties. The Analysis Services Properties window opens (see Figure 18-3) and, from there, you can configure most of the SSAS configurations.

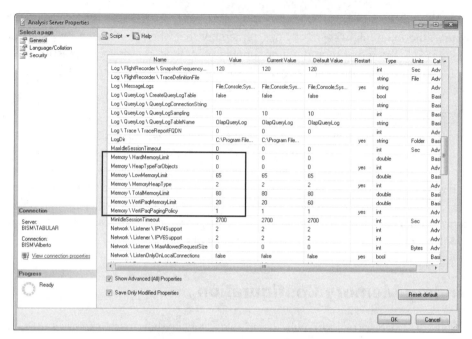

FIGURE 18-3 The Analysis Server Properties window contains all the configurations of SSAS.

In the highlighted box, you see the various memory settings for SSAS, which you learn about now. Note that to display all these settings, you must select the Show Advanced (All) Properties check box.

- **VertiPaqPagingPolicy**   The first setting you need to learn is VertiPaqPagingPolicy. It can have a value of *0* or *1*; we refer to its value as *mode 0* or *mode 1*. In *mode 0*, all xVelocity data is locked into memory, whereas in *mode 1*, data is not locked, and this allows the xVelocity in-memory engine to page data on disk if the system is running out of memory. More specifically, in *mode 1*, only hash dictionaries are locked; data pages can be flushed to disk, and this enables xVelocity to use more memory than is available. Keep in mind that if paging occurs, performances will suffer a severe degradation. The default value is *mode 1*.

- **VertiPaqMemoryLimit**   If you choose *mode 0*, the VertiPaqMemoryLimit defines the total amount of memory xVelocity is allowed to lock in the working set (hence the total that can be used for in-memory databases; remember that the Analysis Services service might use more memory for other reasons). In *mode 1*, it defines a limit for the physical memory that is used by xVelocity, allowing paging for the remaining memory (virtual committed memory) above this limit.

  The VertiPaqPagingPolicy setting provides a way to prevent xVelocity data from interacting badly with the memory-cleaning subsystem. In *mode 1*, it causes the cleaner subsystem to ignore memory allocated for xVelocity data beyond VertiPaqMemoryLimit when calculating the price of memory. In this mode, the server's total memory usage can exceed physical memory, and is constrained primarily by total virtual memory, paging data out to the system page file.

If you want to reduce memory for an instance of Analysis Services, it makes sense to set VertiPaqMemoryLimit to a number that is lower than LowMemoryLimit (see the following).

- **HardMemoryLimit** This is the maximum memory that SSAS can ever allocate. If SSAS exceeds the hard memory limit, the system aggressively kills active sessions to reduce memory usage. Sessions killed for this reason receive an error explaining the cancellation due to memory pressure. With a VertiPaqPagingPolicy in *mode 0*, it is also the limit for the maximum working set of the process. If HardMemoryLimit is set to *0*, it will use a default value midway between the high memory limit and total physical memory (or total virtual address space if you are on a 32-bit machine on which physical memory exceeds virtual memory).

- **LowMemoryLimit** This is the point at which the system starts to clear caches out of memory. As memory usage increases above the low memory limit, SSAS becomes more aggressive about evicting cached data until it hits the high/total memory limit, at which point it evicts everything that is not pinned.

- **TotalMemoryLimit** If memory usage exceeds the total memory limit, the memory manager evicts all cached data that is not currently in use. TotalMemoryLimit must always be less than HardMemoryLimit.

How aggressively SSAS clears caches depends on how much memory is currently being allocated. No cleaning happens below the LowMemoryLimit, and the aggressiveness increases as soon as the memory usage approaches the TotalMemoryLimit. Above the TotalMemoryLimit, SSAS is committed to clearing memory, even if the panic mode starts only after HardMemoryLimit.

All the limit values are expressed as numbers. If their value is less than 100, it is interpreted as a percentage of the total server memory. (On 32-bit systems, the maximum available memory can be up to 2 GB regardless of the memory installed on the system.) If it has a value greater than 100, it is interpreted as the number of bytes to allocate.

> **Important** Always remember that the value of these parameters, if greater than 100, is in bytes. If you use 8192, you are not allocating 8 GB; you are allocating 8 KB, which are not so useful. If you provide the wrong values, SSAS will not raise any warning but will try to work with the memory you made available to it.

When SSAS is working, it requests memory from the operating system to perform its tasks. It continues to use memory until it reaches TotalMemoryLimit. Nevertheless, as soon as LowMemoryLimit value has been reached, SSAS starts to reduce memory usage by freeing memory that is not strictly necessary. The process of reducing memory (which means cache eviction) is more aggressive as the system moves toward TotalMemoryLimit. If SSAS overcomes TotalMemoryLimit, it becomes very aggressive and, when it reaches HardMemoryLimit, it starts to drop connections to force memory to be freed.

Because cache eviction decisions and hard limit enforcement are normally done based on the process's total memory usage, it has been necessary to change that calculation when allowing databases to exceed physical memory in Tabular. (Remember that previous versions of Analysis Services supported only Multidimensional models.) Therefore, when VertiPaqPagingPolicy is in *mode 1*, indicating that memory can grow beyond total physical memory, the system will track the total memory used by xVelocity as a separate quantity (as reported in the MemoryVertiPaq* counters that you can analyze in Performance Monitor). If the total memory used by xVelocity exceeds VertiPaqMemoryLimit, the memory used by xVelocity in excess of the limit will be ignored for the purposes of determining what to evict.

The following example demonstrates these concepts. Say VertiPaqMemoryLimit is 100 GB, LowMemoryLimit is 110 GB, and TotalMemoryLimit is 120 GB. Now, assume that xVelocity data structures are using 210 GB of memory, and the process's total memory usage is 215 GB. This number is well above TotalMemoryLimit (and probably above HardMemoryLimit), so ignoring VertiPaqMemoryLimit, the cleaning would be very aggressive and would kill sessions. However, when PagingPolicy is *1*, the memory used by xVelocity in excess of the limit is ignored for the purpose of computing memory pressure. This means that the number used is computed according to the following formula.

```
 + <Total Memory>            + 215GB
 - <Total VertiPaq Memory>   - 210GB
 + <VertiPaqMemoryLimit>     + 100GB = 105GB
```

Because this value (105 GB) is below LowMemoryLimit, the cache is not cleaned at all.

> **Note** As you have noticed in this chapter, you are learning how the SSAS engine behaves with memory and how to configure it. This chapter does not talk about how to reduce the memory usage by using a correct database design. If you need some hints about this, refer to Chapter 9, where the topic is analyzed deeply.

Using Memory-Related Performance Counters

Now that you have learned how memory parameters can be set, you learn how to monitor them by using performance counters. To obtain a very useful graphical representation of the memory usage in SSAS, you can use Performance Monitor.

Performance Monitor is a utility available in Windows that can show you many counters that programs make available to monitor their behavior. SSAS offers many interesting and useful counters.

If you open Performance Monitor, you must add the SSAS memory-related counters to the graph. If the instance is called Tabular, as in our example, you can find the counters under the MSOLAP$TABULAR:Memory tree of the counters hierarchy. (If your instance is the default, the name will be MSAS11:Memory.) In Figure 18-4, you see the Add Counters dialog box with the interesting counters already selected.

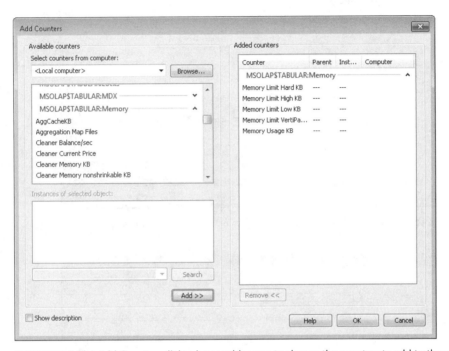

FIGURE 18-4 The Add Counters dialog box enables you to choose the counters to add to the graph.

Because the values are in KB, you must adjust the counter scale to make it fit into the chart and to make sure that all the counters use the same scaling. For these counters, a scale of 0.00001 is a good choice. The chart, immediately after a service restart, looks like Figure 18-5.

The chart has been drawn by using a machine with 8 GB of RAM, and we changed the default values for the parameters by setting HardMemoryLimit to 70, TotalMemoryLimit to 55, and LowMemoryLimit to 45. When values are smaller than 100, these numbers are used as percentages of the available memory (8 GB). The server has been configured in *mode 0*, so no paging will happen. Figure 18-6 shows what happens if you execute a query requiring a lot of memory.

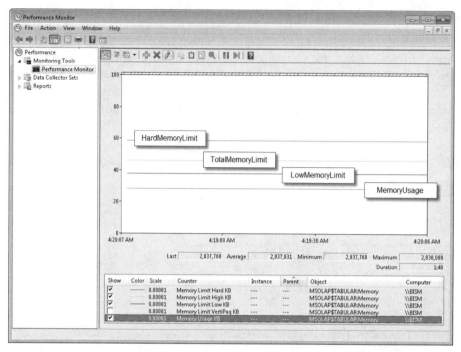

FIGURE 18-5 The counters on the chart clearly show the boundaries of memory usage.

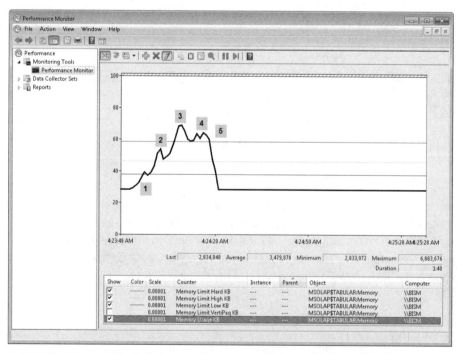

FIGURE 18-6 This analysis highlights some important steps during a complex query execution.

The query failed to execute. Here is an analysis of the five points highlighted in the chart:

1. The query started. Then, because LowMemoryLimit has been reached, the cleaner starts to clean some memory by using a graceful tactic because there is still plenty of memory available.

2. TotalMemoryLimit has been surpassed; the cleaner works aggressively to free memory because it is using too much memory. Cache is being cleared and the query starts to suffer in performance.

3. HardMemoryLimit has been surpassed. Note that this can happen because of the speed at which memory is requested during query execution. It takes some time for the cleaner to start. Nevertheless, now the cleaner is very aggressive and, in fact, after point 3, a large amount of memory is being cleared.

4. Even if the cleaner has tried its best to reduce memory usage, the query is still asking for memory, and the connection is closed because there is no option to give it the memory it needs because it is over the HardMemoryLimit.

5. The connection has been closed; all the memory requested by the query is being cleared, and SSAS can work normally.

Now, check the same query, on the same server, running in *mode 1*. In this mode, SSAS can page out memory to use more memory than the available one. You can see the first part of the chart in Figure 18-7.

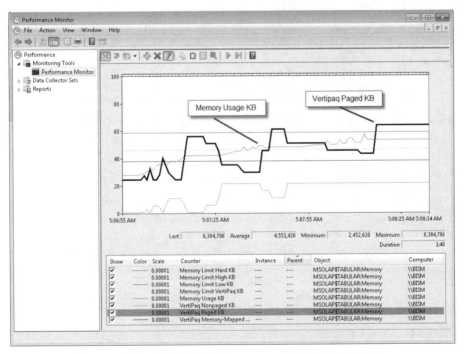

FIGURE 18-7 When *mode 1* is selected, xVelocity pages out data to free memory.

In the chart, the highlighted line is the VertiPaq Paged KB counter, which shows how many kilobytes of pageable memory are used by the engine. The other interesting line is Memory Usage. You can see that SSAS is not going over HardMemoryLimit, so the connection will not be dropped. Nevertheless, to avoid using RAM, xVelocity is using pageable memory, and the system is paging huge amounts of memory to disk, leading to poor performance. Moreover, during paging, the system is nonresponsive, and the whole server is suffering from performance problems.

This example is deliberately flawed; the query needed 15 GB of RAM for execution, and trying to make it work on an 8-GB server was not a very good idea. Nevertheless, it is useful to understand the difference between *mode 0* and *mode 1* and to learn how to use counters to check what is happening to the server under the cover.

Using *mode 1* has advantages and disadvantages. It lets the server answer complex queries even when it is running out of memory, but it can also cause severe performance problems not only to the complex query but also to all the users who are running much lighter queries. Using *mode 0*, the server is always very responsive, but as soon as it reaches HardMemoryLimit, it will close connections due to memory pressure.

Correctly setting the mode in a production server is a very complex task that requires a deep understanding of how the server will be used. Keep in mind that Tabular is very memory hungry; you need to check the memory usage of your queries carefully before correctly sizing memory for the production server.

Memory Usage Might Surprise You

If you are wondering how complex this query was and how important testing your queries correctly before going into production is, note that the query we used to produce these charts is the following.

```
EVALUATE
    ROW( "Distinct", COUNTROWS( SUMMARIZE( Numbers, Numbers[Num1], Numbers[Num2] ) ) )
```

This query runs on a database with 100 million rows and a distribution of Num1 and Num2, which guarantees that the result is exactly 100 million (that is, there are a hundred million combinations of Num1 and Num2), and it made the server run out of memory. The database size is 191 MB, yet the engine needed 15 GB to complete the query.

The reason the server ran out of memory is that the engine had to materialize (spool) the complete dataset to perform the computation. Under normal circumstances, the materialization leads to much smaller datasets because it is very unlikely that you want to compute a distinct count of a 100 million–row table, knowing that the result is exactly 100 million. Keep in mind that, in rare circumstances, spooling of temporary tables might consume quite a bit of memory.

Understanding Query Plans

In the previous sections, you saw how to configure memory for an SSAS Tabular instance and how a query, which may look simple, can create serious memory problems on the server. In the next section, you learn how to verify query performance by checking the query plan.

Every time you run a DAX query, the SSAS engine creates a plan to execute it and compute the results. The first thing to learn about query plans in DAX is that there are two types of them:

- **Logical query plan** This is created in advance very quickly and represents a first approximation of the query plan that will be executed.

- **Physical query plan** This is the query plan that has actually been executed and takes into account information that was not available when the logical query plan was determined. It does not use the same syntax and operators as the logical query plan; the two plans are different representations of the same algorithm.

If you are accustomed to the Microsoft SQL Server optimizer and its query plans, you know that SQL Server builds a query plan in advance by using statistics, and does not change it during execution. DAX has a different approach. After the logical query plan is built, it has the option to execute parts of it to gather very accurate information about the number of rows of intermediate steps and, based on this information, it can change the way the plan is executed, reaching an unprecedented level of optimization. In this chapter, we are not speaking about the physical query plan; our focus is on the logical query plan and how to monitor performance. A complete treatment of the physical query plan would be too complex to treat in a single chapter and is beyond the scope of this book.

 Note Note that the DAX optimizer is rule-based, whereas the SQL Server optimizer is cost-based. DAX does not use information gathered during query optimization to modify the query plan; it uses information to move predicates from one part of the tree to another, searching for the optimal filtering strategy. SQL Server, however, can modify the *JOIN* order and the query structure based on the cost of each operation.

The query plan determines how to compute values, but before values are computed, they must be retrieved from the database. Whenever the query plan requests information from the database, it must access the xVelocity in-memory analytics engine by using a VertiPaq SE query. In Figure 18-8, you see a diagram showing the steps needed to execute a DAX query.

As you can see, the *Logical Plan* event is fired after the simplification process has been completed and after some VertiPaq queries have already been executed. This means that sometimes you must wait for some time-consuming operations before you can see the logical query plan.

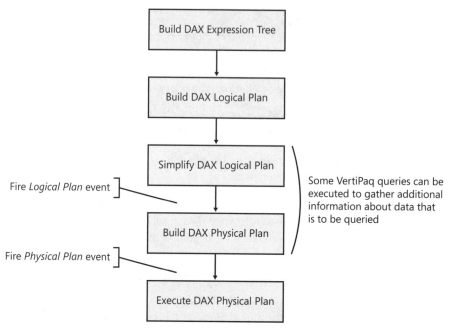

FIGURE 18-8 These are the steps needed to optimize and execute a DAX query.

To look at query plans, you must use the SQL Server Profiler. After you open it and create a new trace for the Tabular instance, select the events you are interested in monitoring. The *DAX Query Plan* event is located under the Query Processing tree and is visible only if you select the Show All Events check box. In Figure 18-9, you can see the Trace Properties dialog box with *DAX Query Plan* already selected along with some other interesting events such as *Query End* and *VertiPaq SE Query End*.

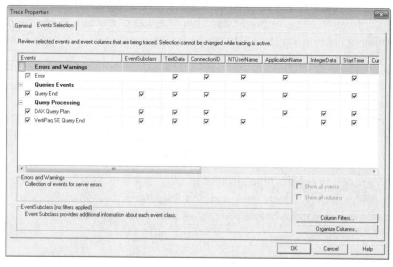

FIGURE 18-9 The *DAX Query Plan* event is visible if Show All Events is selected.

By using these events, you can catch the DAX query plans (the logical and the physical) and the VertiPaq queries needed to compute the final values. Now, look at this very simple query.

```
EVALUATE
CALCULATETABLE(
    SUMMARIZE(
        'Internet Sales',
        Geography[State Province Code],
        "Sales", SUM( 'Internet Sales'[Sales Amount] )
    ),
    FILTER(
        Customer,
        Customer[Last Name] = "Anand"
    )
)
```

If you run the query, the profiler will catch the events shown in Figure 18-10.

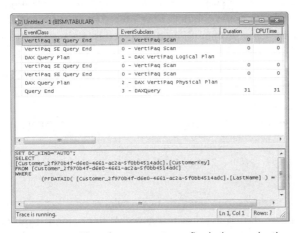

FIGURE 18-10 The relevant events are fired when evaluating a very simple query.

There are a couple of interesting points to note here:

- Some VertiPaq queries are executed before the logical query plan is shown. These are the queries that the engine requests to gather information that helps it optimize the query. Generally, these queries are normally *COUNT* of distinct values for the various columns involved in the query.

- After the optimization, other queries are executed to further optimize the physical query plan and to spool results in memory to speed up the following execution.

Now we will go into more detail to give you greater confidence with the various elements of this query.

Note The real syntax of the VertiPaq queries contains long names for the tables. In the book, we have slightly simplified the syntax by removing identifiers after the names to make them easier to read.

The first VertiPaq SE Query is the following one.

```
SELECT
    [Customer].[CustomerKey]
FROM
    [Customer]
WHERE
  ( PFDATAID( [Customer].[LastName] ) = 81 )
```

As you can see, the optimizer is interested in retrieving the different customer keys that have a last name equal to Anand. Because LastName is a string, the query requests the DataID of the string and not the string itself. After it gathers this information, the engine is now interested in understanding how many StateProvinceCode values exist for the customer it found. It finds this information by running the second VertiPaq query.

```
SELECT
    [Geography].[StateProvinceCode]
FROM [Internet Sales]
    LEFT OUTER JOIN [Customer] ON [Internet Sales].[CustomerKey] = [Customer].[CustomerKey]
    LEFT OUTER JOIN [Geography] ON [Customer].[GeographyKey] = [Geography].[GeographyKey]
WHERE
    [Customer].[CustomerKey] IN (11096, 11989, 17005, 22513, 28899, 15054, 19626, 20344, 25918,
27141...[74 total values, not all displayed]);
```

You can see that this pseudo-SQL query retrieves the values of StateProvinceCode that exist in the Internet Sales table for the customers gathered during the previous query. At this point, the optimizer has enough information to produce an optimal query plan, and it fires the *DAX Query Plan* event.

Note If you want to draw a parallel between the SQL Engine optimizer and the DAX Query optimizer, you can think of these steps as the ones carried out by the SQL Engine optimizer when it uses statistics to determine the optimal query plan. SQL Server must use statistics because it cannot spend precious I/O time loading the number of distinct values required to optimize the plan. Tabular, however, can compute these numbers accurately in a very small amount of time. Thus, the query optimizer of DAX always relies on correct data and does not make assumptions that might turn out to be incorrect when the query is executed.

The query plan is represented as a set of operators that must be executed. Each operator works on some parameters, and indentation shows the parameters of each operator. The syntax contains a rich set of information but makes the query difficult to read. Thus, you will read a very simplified version of the code here, from which many details have been removed. A graphical representation of the plan is shown in Figure 18-11.

```
CalculateTable
    AddColumns
        Scan_Vertipaq
        GroupBy_Vertipaq
            Scan_Vertipaq
        Sum_Vertipaq
            Scan_Vertipaq
            'Internet Sales'[Sales Amount]
    Filter_Vertipaq
        Scan_Vertipaq
        'Customer'[Last Name] = Anand
```

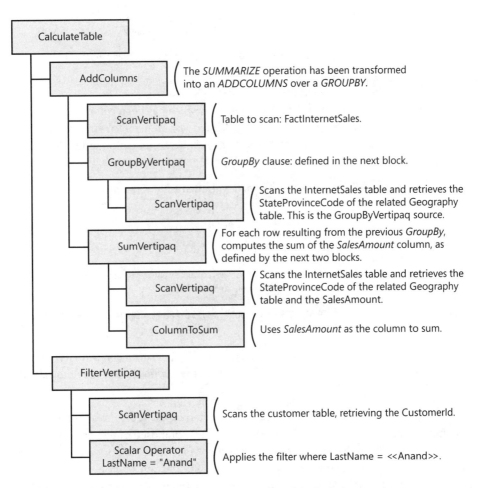

FIGURE 18-11 This chart shows a graphical representation of the logical query plan.

Looking at Figure 18-11, you see that the logical query plan is still very logical, meaning that the *AddColumns* operator seems to iterate over all the values returned by the *GroupBy* operator and, for each one, performs the sum of SalesAmount. In fact, this is the semantic of the query that has been created. Nevertheless, when the query plan becomes physical, some operations can be pushed to the xVelocity in-memory analytics engine. For example, xVelocity can perform the scan of the fact table and the sum of sales amount, grouping by state province code, in a single step.

For these reasons, the next statements executed by the server are VertiPaq queries. The first one is a single VertiPaq query that computes the following result.

```
SELECT
    [Geography].[StateProvinceCode],
    SUM([Internet Sales].[SalesAmount])
FROM
    [Internet Sales]
    LEFT OUTER JOIN [Customer] ON [Internet Sales].[CustomerKey]=[Customer].[CustomerKey]
    LEFT OUTER JOIN [Geography] ON [Customer].[GeographyKey]=[Geography].[GeographyKey]
WHERE
    [Customer].[CustomerKey] IN (11096, 11989, 17005, ...[74 total values, not all displayed])
VAND
    [Geography].[StateProvinceCode] IN ('VIC', 'BC', ...[21 total values, not all displayed]);
```

You can see that the query contains a *WHERE* condition, which has been computed due to the presence of *CALCULATETABLE* and its filter condition. SSAS does not need to retrieve the list of customers whose name is Anand again because it has already gathered that information during the plan optimization.

The result of this query will be spooled and joined with the result of the final query, which evaluates the table argument of *SUMMARIZE*.

```
SELECT
    [Geography].[StateProvinceCode]
FROM [Internet Sales]
    LEFT OUTER JOIN [Customer] ON [Internet Sales].[CustomerKey]=[Customer].[CustomerKey]
    LEFT OUTER JOIN [Geography] ON [Customer].[GeographyKey]=[Geography].[GeographyKey]
WHERE
    [Customer].[CustomerKey] IN (11096, 11989, 17005, 22513, 28899, 15054, 19626, 20344, 25918,
27141...[74 total values, not all displayed]);
```

This final query, because it is identical to the second one, hits the cache and does not require access to the database. The final step is to join the results of the queries to compute the *SUMMARIZE* result.

The interesting part of this plan is that it has been executed by using only two VertiPaq queries. Why is this important? As you might recall, the SSAS engine is composed of two engines: the formula engine (FE) and the storage engine (SE), also known as the xVelocity in-memory analytics engine (VertiPaq). The storage engine is very fast and works in a multithreaded environment, so it scales very well on multiple cores. When the xVelocity engine is working, the only bottleneck is the RAM speed because its task is to perform super-fast scans of big tables. Nevertheless, the storage engine is not capable of handling all the complexities of a DAX formula. The results of the storage engine must be interpreted and managed by the formula engine, which is in charge of using values returned by the storage engine and composing them to compute the result. The formula engine is single-threaded, and it cannot take advantage of multiple cores. Thus, the formula engine does not scale out.

If your formula runs, for the most part, in the storage engine, it will scale on multiple cores and run very fast. If, however, it spends time in the formula engine, your server will be underused because only one of the many cores will work. The SSAS engine contains many optimizations that are aimed to push the computation down to the storage engine whenever this is possible, but for very complex formulas, this cannot happen.

Understanding *SUMX*

As an example of how the SSAS engine is able to push calculations down to the xVelocity in-memory analytics engine, consider this simple query.

```
EVALUATE
    ROW("Sum", SUMX ( 'Internet Sales', 'Internet Sales'[Sales Amount] ) )
```

This query uses an iterator, but because the *[Sales Amount]* expression is a single column, it is optimized so that no real iteration occurs; the query is executed with a single VertiPaq SE query, which you can see in the following code.

```
SELECT
    SUM( [Internet Sales].[SalesAmount] )
FROM
    [Internet Sales]
```

This is the same plan that would have been executed if you used *SUM* instead of *SUMX*. But what happens for a more complicated query like this one?

```
EVALUATE
    ROW(
        "Sum",
        SUMX(
            'Internet Sales',
            'Internet Sales'[Sales Amount] / 'Internet Sales'[Order Quantity] )
    )
```

In this case, because the formula inside *SUMX* is a simple division, it is still pushed down to xVelocity. In fact, the (simplified) VertiPaq query executed to evaluate the formula is the following one.

```
SELECT
    SUM( [Internet Sales].[SalesAmount] / [Internet Sales].[OrderQuantity] )
FROM
    [Internet Sales];
```

Nevertheless, if the formula becomes too complicated, xVelocity will not be able to compute the values during its scan and will need to return the values to the formula engine, which will perform the aggregation. For example, the following query requires a real iteration.

```
EVALUATE
    ROW (
        "Sum",
        SUMX (
```

```
        'Internet Sales',
        IF (
            'Internet Sales'[Sales Amount] > 0,
            'Internet Sales'[Sales Amount] / 'Internet Sales'[Order Quantity]
        )
    )
)
```

You can see that the iteration has taken place because the format of the VertiPaq query is no longer a simple *SUM* but now contains a CallbackDataID invocation, as you can see in the corresponding VertiPaq query.

```
SELECT
    SUM(
        [CallbackDataID(
            IF (
                'Internet Sales'[Sales Amount]] > 0,
                'Internet Sales'[Sales Amount]] / 'Internet Sales'[Order Quantity]]
            )
        )]
        (
            PFDATAID( [Internet Sales].[OrderQuantity] ),
            PFDATAID( [Internet Sales].[SalesAmount] )
        )
    )
FROM [Internet Sales];
```

The presence of CallbackDataID means that, during the scan of the table, xVelocity needs to return each pair of values of OrderQuantity and SalesAmount to the formula engine, which evaluates the expression and computes the value that must be aggregated. This query, even if it looks like a simple VertiPaq query, is actually an iteration over a table, and performs much worse than the previous one.

What Is CallbackDataID?

When you see CallbackDataID, it means that the formula engine is pushing a filter condition or a computation down to xVelocity in a virtual way. To minimize the number of table scans during a single scan of the table, the xVelocity engine can call back the formula engine to check whether a specific row needs further processing that xVelocity cannot perform. In the case you have seen, the formula is too complex to be evaluated by xVelocity, and the storage engine relies on the callback to perform the real computation.

The same can apply to filters. Sometimes a filter is so complex that xVelocity cannot compute it, and in such a scenario, xVelocity calls back the formula engine to apply the filter.

You can think of each VertiPaq SE query as a single scan of a table. During the scan, the formula engine activates to perform some operation and uses callbacks to do so. Callbacks are expensive, but they are much better than a set of different table scans, one for each row processed by the *SUMX* operation.

Gathering Time Information from the Profiler

Up to now, you have used the profiler to catch the events and read query plans and VertiPaq queries to get more insight into the way SSAS executes queries. The SQL Server Profiler has many interesting features that you can use when profiling and optimizing a server—so many that we cannot cover them all in a Tabular book. Nevertheless, there are pieces of information that might prove useful and can be covered here, such as execution time.

In Figure 18-12, you see the trace of a simple query. The interesting columns are *CPUTime* and *Duration*.

FIGURE 18-12 Each event contains CPUTime and Duration information, useful to monitor the query duration.

Both CPUTime and Duration are expressed in milliseconds, and their value is meaningful in the *End* event. (A *Query Begin* event does not contain duration information.)

- Duration is the total time that was required to execute the query. In other words, the user waited that length of time before getting an answer.

- CPUTime is the time the CPU spent to solve the query. Because Tabular does not have any I/O time, it is normal for CPUTime to be greater than Duration because parts of the query can be executed in parallel, and a query requiring 3,000 milliseconds of CPUTime can be executed in about 550 milliseconds Duration if six cores are used together for the entire time.

If a query runs very fast, in less than 200 milliseconds, there is normally no need to try to optimize it because you won't get very far. If a query exceeds one second, it is likely that there are ways to optimize it, and you can start studying the query plan, reading the VertiPaq queries and figuring out what can be executed in a better way.

Clearly, the time needed to execute a query depends on the complexity of the calculations and on the size of the table that must be scanned; only experience will help you understand when something is going wrong and when, as a result, you need to dive deep into the query plan to optimize it.

Common Optimization Techniques

Covering all the relevant aspects of the xVelocity in-memory analytics engine would require at least half of this book because of the complexity of the topics, although it would be very interesting. In the remaining part of this chapter, you look at some optimization techniques without the full explanations we have given so far.

The goal of the next sections is not to give you practical hints; use the next part of this chapter as a series of exercises that you can try on your PC to get acquainted with the techniques used to analyze different query plans and obtain better performance as a result. We provide you with some considerations, but we don't show the full query plans because they would be too long and not very useful in a book.

Currency Conversion

The first example you analyze further is the currency conversion algorithm you learned in Chapter 12, "Using Advanced Tabular Relationships." In that chapter, you saw three formulas for currency conversion. This example will focus on the last two versions.

```
FirstCurrencyAmount :=
SUMX(
    DimCurrency,
    SUMX(
        DimDate,
        CALCULATE( VALUES( CurrencyRate[AverageRate] ) ) * SUM( FactInternetSales[SalesAmount] ) )
    )
)
```

```
SecondCurrencyAmount :=
SUMX(
    CROSSJOIN( DimCurrency, DimDate ),
    CALCULATE( VALUES( CurrencyRate[AverageRate] ) * SUM( FactInternetSales[SalesAmount] ) ) )
)
```

> **Warning** We suggest that you execute and monitor both queries, saving the various VertiPaq queries that are executed and comparing them before reading the conclusions that we draw in the next few paragraphs. It is an interesting exercise to test your new capabilities and will give you good insight into the process of optimizing a query.

Even if the two queries seem to be a simple syntax variation of the same algorithm, they are very different when analyzed by the SSAS engine. The FirstCurrencyAmount contains a first *SUMX* where the formula that needs to be computed is another *SUMX*, so it becomes a complex formula that cannot be easily simplified. Even if it is possible to execute the full computation inside the xVelocity in-memory analytics engine, the optimizer does not recognize this scenario. In fact, the xVelocity execution contains several iterations, meaning that the query will be executed mainly inside the formula engine. The query plan is actually a direct translation of the formula.

The SecondCurrencyAmount pattern is much easier to evaluate because it is a simple *SUMX* iteration with a subformula. Thus, the VertiPaq queries do not contain callbacks, and you might be tempted to think that the complete formula is evaluated inside the xVelocity in-memory analytics engine. However, studying the query plan a bit longer should show you that SSAS does the following:

- It spools (materializes) the *CROSSJOIN* of (DimCurrency x DimDate x AverageRate) in a temporary data structure.

- It spools the *SUM(SalesAmount)* grouped by *CurrencyKey* and *DateKey* from the fact table in a temporary table. This operation, which is probably the most complex for a production system, is executed completely inside the xVelocity in-memory analytics engine by using a single table scan. It will require memory for the temporary table, but it is very fast.

- It performs the join between the two tables inside the formula engine after both tables have been spooled. The time required depends solely on the size of the temporary tables.

Thus, even if no callbacks are present in the VertiPaq queries, the real implementation of SecondCurrencyAmount is still an iteration. Depending on the volume of your fact table and the number of dates that are present inside it, the SecondCurrencyAmount formula should perform better than the first one. It requires a single uninterrupted scan of the fact table, and the join, which is the only formula engine work, should be executed on fairly small tables because data will already have been aggregated.

Applying Filters in the Right Place

The next query you analyze is a very common pattern that you are likely to encounter often when querying Tabular. You want to get total sales, YTD sales, and QTD sales divided by year and month and, of course, you do not want blank values in the final result.

The query is straightforward.

```
DEFINE
    MEASURE 'Internet Sales'[Sales] =
        CALCULATE( ROUND( SUM( 'Internet Sales'[Sales Amount] ), 0 ) )
    MEASURE 'Internet Sales'[YTD Sales] = TOTALYTD( [Sales] , 'Date'[Date] )
    MEASURE 'Internet Sales'[QTD Sales] = TOTALQTD( [Sales] , 'Date'[Date] )
EVALUATE
FILTER(
    ADDCOLUMNS(
        CROSSJOIN(
            VALUES( 'Date'[Calendar Year] ),
            VALUES( 'Date'[Month] ),
            VALUES( 'Date'[Month Name] )
        ),
        "Sales", [Sales],
        "YTD Sales", [YTD Sales],
        "QTD Sales", [QTD Sales]
    ),
    NOT ISBLANK( [Sales] )
)
ORDER BY 'Date'[Calendar Year], 'Date'[Month]
```

Note that the internal *CROSSJOIN* contains both the month number and the month name because the *ORDER BY* clause requires the month number. Apart from that, the query seems straightforward, and if you execute it, you get very good results. On the Adventure Works Tabular data model, it takes 1,125 milliseconds to execute on a server with four cores and 8 GB of RAM.

The query plan is not simple to read because it is very long. These are the outermost operators.

```
Order
    Filter
        AddColumns
        ...

        Not
            IsBlank(''[Sales])
```

In the part that has been omitted a complex set of operators computes the numbers. Nevertheless, the overall structure is simple. The filter is the second-outermost operator, and the operator will filter the precomputed column *Sales*, which is exactly what we asked.

The point to note is that, inside AddColumns, all the values will be computed, including the YTD and QTD calculations, which are fairly expensive operations, because each one requires a scan of the fact table. However, if you look carefully at the query plan, you discover that the fact table is scanned very few times; it is spooled, and then the formula engine works on the spooled set of data, resulting in good performance. The YTD and QTD measures have been computed for rows that will never be returned to the user, due to the external filter on the Sales measure.

With these considerations in mind, you can remove the rows where the total sales value was empty earlier, during the query evaluation, and change the query this way.

```
DEFINE
    MEASURE 'Internet Sales'[Sales] =
        CALCULATE( ROUND( SUM( 'Internet Sales'[Sales Amount] ), 0 ) )
    MEASURE 'Internet Sales'[YTD Sales] = TOTALYTD( [Sales] , 'Date'[Date] )
    MEASURE 'Internet Sales'[QTD Sales] = TOTALQTD( [Sales] , 'Date'[Date] )
EVALUATE
ADDCOLUMNS(
    FILTER(
        CROSSJOIN(
            VALUES( 'Date'[Calendar Year] ),
            VALUES( 'Date'[Month] ),
            VALUES( 'Date'[Month Name] )
        ),
        NOT ISBLANK( [Sales] )
    ),
    "Sales", [Sales],
    "YTD Sales", [YTD Sales],
    "QTD Sales", [QTD Sales]
)
ORDER BY 'Date'[Calendar Year],
         'Date'[Month]
```

The only difference between this query and the previous one is that now *FILTER* is inside *ADDCOLUMNS* and not outside it. The expensive columns will still be computed, but only for the rows that are to be returned to the user. If the value of Sales is empty, neither YTD nor QTD will ever be returned.

The DAX query plan clearly reflects this new pattern; it now contains the following.

```
Order
    AddColumns
        Filter
            ...
```

If you look at it carefully, you discover that the Sales measure is computed twice: once to test the *ISBLANK* condition and once to add its value to the columns. That said, monitoring the query execution time shows you that this query executes in just 156 milliseconds. In other words, this latter query runs seven times faster than the previous one.

What lesson does this teach? Filter as soon as you can, because by doing so, you reduce the time needed to perform complex calculations on data that will never be used later. In this example, we have used YTD and QTD, which are not superfast, but you can apply the same pattern to many calculations. Moreover, changing the execution time from 1 second to 150 milliseconds might not seem a great result but, as numbers grow, the difference might be much more visible.

Using Relationships Whenever Possible

In Chapter 12, you learned that it is possible to use DAX to mimic relationships when the data model requires more-complex relationships than classical 1:N relationships handled natively by Tabular. Now that you are learning how to measure performance, we describe the difference between using DAX to mimic relationships and using existing ones. As you will learn, the engine works better with native relationships, and looking at the difference is an interesting exercise.

To use a simple test, you can load only DimProduct and FactInternetSales from the Adventure Works data warehouse in a new Tabular project. SSDT will create the relationship between the two fact tables automatically, but for this exercise, you must disable it (that is, do not delete it; keep it in the data model disabled). In Figure 18-13, you see this simple data model.

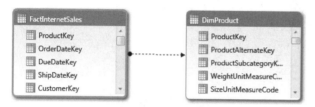

FIGURE 18-13 You will use this simple data model to test relationship performances.

On this data model, you want to run a query to retrieve all the products and, for each product, the total sold. There are two ways to express this query:

- You can use the existing relationship by using *USERELATIONSHIP* to activate it when needed.

- You can use standard filtering by using *FILTER* to create a filter over FactInternetSales to show only the sales of a single product.

The resulting query using the relationship is the following one.

```
EVALUATE
ADDCOLUMNS(
    DimProduct,
    "SumOfSales", CALCULATE(
        SUM( FactInternetSales[SalesAmount] ),
        USERELATIONSHIP( DimProduct[ProductKey], FactInternetSales[ProductKey] )
    )
)
```

If you do not use the relationship but only use *FILTER*, a possible solution is the following one.

```
EVALUATE
ADDCOLUMNS (
    DimProduct,
    "SumOfSales", CALCULATE(
        SUM( FactInternetSales[SalesAmount] ),
        FILTER (
            FactInternetSales,
```

```
            DimProduct[ProductKey] = CALCULATE( VALUES( FactInternetSales[ProductKey] ) )
        )
    )
)
```

Both queries, on Adventure Works, are so fast that you cannot use their execution time to make any sort of comparison. Nevertheless, the query plan shows a significant difference. Both queries require some VertiPaq scans, but the big difference is in the one that scans the fact table to get the sum of sales. The VertiPaq query using the relationship is the following one.

```
SELECT
    DimProduct.ProductKey,
    ...
    SUM (FactInternetSales.SalesAmount)
FROM FactInternetSales
    LEFT OUTER JOIN DimProduct
    ON FactInternetSales.ProductKey = DimProduct.ProductKey
WHERE
    ...
```

The query using the more complex *FILTER* is the following one.

```
SELECT
    FactInternetSales.ProductKey,
    SUM (FactInternetSales.SalesAmount)
FROM FactInternetSales
WHERE
    ...
```

The first query is resolved with a simple VertiPaq scan, which can, by using a single scan of the fact table, retrieve the complete dataset. The important fact is that columns from both DimProduct and FactInternetSales will be retrieved from xVelocity in the same dataset, leaving the formula engine only the work needed to return the data performing a very simple match.

The second query, however, performs a similar scan, but it retrieves values from FactInternetSales only. Even if the scans look very similar, a quick look at the physical query plan shows that after xVelocity has finished its work, the formula engine must still perform many difficult computations to match values from the DimProduct table with the values coming from FactInternetSales. In other words, the join is resolved by the formula engine in this case, whereas in the previous query, the join is resolved by the xVelocity in-memory analytics engine.

Because VertiPaq scans can run in parallel and scale on many cores, the first algorithm scales very well, and you can expect top performance from the first query. In contrast, the second one, on a big dataset, will probably use many cores during the initial scan but then last for a while, running a single core before returning the dataset.

Thus, the final lesson is simple: It is better to rely on standard relationships, even nonactive ones, than to use *CALCULATE* and *FILTER* to mimic relationships.

Monitoring MDX Queries

As you have learned, you can query a Tabular model by using both DAX and MDX. Thus, an interesting question might be, "What tools do we have to monitor MDX queries?" The answer is simple: The tools that monitor DAX queries can also monitor MDX queries.

The only problem is that the SSAS engine does not translate MDX into DAX on a 1:1 query basis. A single MDX query can generate tens of DAX query plans, which you can catch by using the profiler. As an example, take a look at this very simple query.

```
SELECT
    NON EMPTY Measures.[Internet Total Sales] ON COLUMNS,
    NON EMPTY CROSSJOIN (Date.[Calendar Year].Members, Date.[Month Name].Members ) ON ROWS
FROM
    [Internet Sales]
```

Following the query plan for this query is much more complicated than following a similar DAX query, mainly because there is no direct translation between the MDX code and the DAX algorithm used to answer it. In fact, this query creates three DAX logical plans. Each one of them is simple. The three query plans indicate that the SSAS engine is retrieving:

- SUM([Sales Amount])

- SUM([Sales Amount]) grouped by [Month Name]

- SUM([Sales Amount]) grouped by [Calendar Year], [Month Name]

Looking at the MDX query, it is clear that the three plans are used to compute the grand total, the subtotal at the month level, and the subtotal at the year and month level, which are the results required to answer the query.

It is interesting that a single MDX query is translated into many DAX query plans. This process happens behind the scene, and there is no way to learn how it happened or how to control its behavior. This fact makes the optimization of MDX over Tabular troublesome because, although it is easy to check what three simple query plans do, an MDX query of medium complexity can be translated into tens of different DAX query plans.

Note You might have noticed that we always speak about MDX being translated in DAX query plans and not in DAX queries. This is because no MDX/DAX translation is happening inside the engine. An MDX query is analyzed as MDX code and resolved, generating a DAX query plan. The query plan might not correspond to a DAX query. Thus, you can use the DAX query plan to understand the algorithm, but trying to translate into DAX code might not be feasible.

If you are accustomed to debugging MDX over Multidimensional, you already know that this is a difficult topic. Before SQL Server 2012, there was no logging concerning what the formula engine was about to perform to solve an MDX query. In SQL Server 2012, by using MDX over Tabular, you can at least understand what is happening behind what you can see. Remember that no MDX query plan exists for Multidimensional and, thus, there is no clear way to improve an MDX query unless you use your own experience and tools such as MDX Studio (*http://www.mosha.com/msolap/mdxstudio.htm*).

Monitoring DirectQuery

When SSAS executes a query in DirectQuery mode, what it really does is transform the DAX query into an equivalent SQL query, which is sent to SQL Server, which is in charge of computing the result. Thus, no DAX plan exists for DirectQuery; the plan is inside the SQL query.

If you must optimize a DirectQuery-enabled data model, you must catch the SQL code that is executed by the server and perform optimization on SQL Server, for example, by creating useful indexes.

To discover the SQL code that is executed for a query, you have two options:

- You can use SQL Server Profiler, connecting it to the instance of SQL Server that is holding the database and catch the queries from there.

- You can connect SQL Server Profiler to SSAS and enable tracing of the *DirectQuery End* event, which contains, in the TextData, the complete SQL query generated and sent to SQL Server.

The latter option is probably better because it does not require you to have administrative privileges on the instance of SQL Server; all you need is administrative privileges over the SSAS instance you are using.

Note, however, that the SQL code generated for DAX queries is complex and, thus, difficult to optimize. No matter how intricate the DAX query is, the engine will transform it into a single SQL query that the server must handle and, for complex DAX queries, the generated SQL can be complex. Remember: In DirectQuery, there is no formula engine and no xVelocity in-memory engine; DirectQuery is only a translation layer from DAX to SQL.

Gathering Information by Using Dynamic Management Views

SSAS makes available a set of Dynamic Management Views (DMVs), which are useful for gathering precise information about the status of a database or an instance of SSAS. The information provided by DMVs is reset at service startup, so it can show very interesting statistics about the usage of SSAS since its last restart.

There are many DMVs, and you can find a detailed description of each DMV at *http://msdn .microsoft.com/en-us/library/ms126221(v=SQL.110).aspx*. If you want to list all available DMVs, you can execute this query from inside an MDX query panel in SSMS.

```
SELECT * FROM $SYSTEM.DISCOVER_SCHEMA_ROWSETS
```

Although we will not provide a complete description of all the available DMVs, we can briefly discuss some queries to give you a better idea of the kind of information you can obtain by using DMVs.

As a first example, the following query retrieves the activity executed on different objects in the database since the service startup, and it is useful to see the objects in your instance on which the engine has spent more time.

```
SELECT TOP 10
    OBJECT_ID,
    OBJECT_CPU_TIME_MS
FROM $system.DISCOVER_OBJECT_ACTIVITY
ORDER BY
    OBJECT_CPU_TIME_MS DESC
```

The result is the set of the top 10 objects on which the SSAS instance has spent more time (expressed in CPU milliseconds).

Note Note that you cannot use the full SQL syntax when querying DMV. You have only a subset of SQL available, and features such as *JOIN*, *LIKE*, and *GROUP BY* are not available. DMVs are not intended to be used in complex queries; if you need complex processing, you should issue simple queries and then process the results further.

All the DMVs return many columns, most of which are useful for Multidimensional. (There are several columns that show numbers related to I/O which, in Tabular, are of no use.) This is a clear indication of the big difference between Tabular and Multidimensional. In Tabular, because all the data should be in memory, there should be no I/O at all, and the system maintenance and optimization are greatly reduced. All you need to do is optimize DAX queries and make sure that enough memory is available in the system.

Because memory is so important to Tabular, a very useful function of DMVs is gathering memory occupation by object. The DMV that returns this information is DISCOVER_OBJECT_MEMORY_USAGE. In the information you get with this DMV, there are both *SHRINKABLE* and *NONSHRINKABLE* memory usages. In the following query, there is an *ORDER BY* on the *NONSHRINKABLE* memory size. Note that in Multidimensional, the *SHRINKABLE* column is always empty; you must use the *NONSHRINKABLE* column to get meaningful values. If, for example, you run the following query

```
SELECT * FROM $system.DISCOVER_OBJECT_MEMORY_USAGE ORDER BY OBJECT_MEMORY_NONSHRINKABLE DESC
```

you will receive as a result the list of all objects currently loaded along with the amount of memory they are using, as you can see in Figure 18-14.

OBJECT_PARENT_PATH	OBJECT_ID	OBJECT_MEMO...	OBJECT_MEMORY_NONSHRINKABLE	OBJECT_VER:
BISM\TABULAR.Databases.Number02....	Segments	0	199962032	7667828
Global	Allocators	0	129998752	2949218
	Global	0	23388276	-1
Global	SystemHeap	0	22851808	778138424
Global	Tiny	0	7497728	4096
Global	Small	0	5554176	7209061
BISM\TABULAR.Databases.Adventure ...	Sandbox	0	2610748	4
BISM\TABULAR.Databases.Adventure ...	Segments	0	2038296	3211365
BISM\TABULAR.Databases.Adventure ...	Segments	0	2038296	-1
BISM\TABULAR.Databases.Adventure ...	Segments	0	2036208	-1

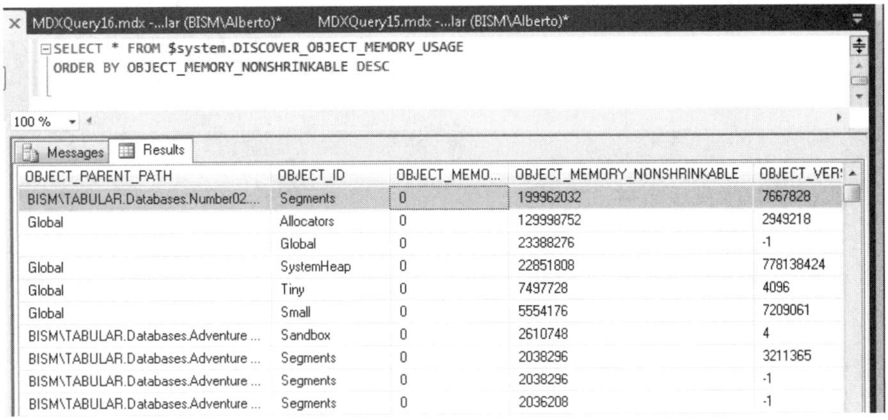

FIGURE 18-14 This result set shows the memory usage analyzed by using DMV.

As you might expect, the largest objects are the tables containing many distinct values. An interesting exercise you can perform to get a better understanding of how to reduce the memory footprint of your database is to use DMVs to get the memory usage of a table and then apply some of the techniques illustrated in this book to reduce the memory usage. Look at how memory decreases when you modify the table structure. For example, if you have a column containing DateTime with both date and time information, you can try to load it as it is in the database and then load the same column, extracting only the date information. This lowers the number of distinct values, so the dictionaries and memory required will also be reduced.

Summary

In this chapter, you learned the basics of SSAS memory handling, how to configure the memory options, and how to monitor memory usage of a running instance by using counters. The full topic is complex, and we had space to cite only the most relevant information and some links you can use to learn more about the topic.

It is important to remember that Tabular architecture is very different from Multidimensional architecture. In Multidimensional, you have to work hard to reduce I/O to a minimum, whereas in Tabular, no I/O occurs during query time and, thus, the whole process of server optimization is much easier because all you need to cover is memory usage.

Although this is a benefit, keep in mind that to reduce the response time of a database, you have only one option: optimizing DAX queries. In the second part of this chapter, you learned the basics of query optimizations by looking at some simple query plans, how to retrieve them by using the SQL Server Profiler, and how to read them by understanding query plans and operators. Optimizing DAX is a complex task because slow queries often show a complex plan (otherwise, they would be fast), and performing a deep analysis of a complex plan is a time-consuming operation that requires patience and attention.

DAX Functions Reference

THIS APPENDIX LISTS FUNCTIONS available in DAX along with their syntax.

Statistical Functions

Statistical functions aggregate and compute data, returning a scalar value. Usually, these functions operate on all the rows of the table containing the specified column, which has to be of numeric or date type. The A suffix identifies functions that also operate on any other type of columns. The X suffix identifies functions that allow aggregation of the result of an expression applied to each row of the specified table.

TABLE A-1 Statistical Numeric Functions Returning a Scalar Value

Function	Description
AVERAGE(<column>)	Returns the arithmetic mean of all the numbers in a column. <column> must be of date or number type.
AVERAGEA(<column>)	Returns the arithmetic mean of all the values in a column. It always returns 0 for text columns, and it returns the same value as *AVERAGE* for numeric columns. <column> can be of any type.
AVERAGEX(< table>, <expression >)	Returns the arithmetic mean of <expression> evaluated for each row of <table>. The <expression> must return a numeric type; otherwise, it returns an error.
COUNT(<column>)	Returns the number of values in a column containing numbers. <column> must be of a numeric type.
COUNTA(<column>)	Returns the number of values in a column that are not empty. It returns the same value as *COUNT* for numeric columns. <column> can be of any type.
COUNTAX(< table>, <expression >)	Returns the number of nonblank results of <expression> evaluated for each row of <table>. The <expression> can return any type.
COUNTBLANK(<column>)	Returns the number of empty cells in a column.
COUNTROWS(<table>)	Returns the number of rows in a table. <table> can be a table or an expression returning a table (such as *RELATEDTABLE*, *FILTER* and so on).
COUNTX(< table>, <expression >)	Returns the number of nonblank numeric results of <expression> evaluated for each row of <table>. The <expression> must return a numeric type; otherwise, it returns an error.

Function	Description
DISTINCTCOUNT(<column>)	Returns the number of different values in a column. <column> can be of any type.
MAX(<column>)	Returns the largest numeric value in a column. <column> must be of date or number type.
MAXA(<column>)	Returns the largest numeric value in a column. It always returns 0 for text columns, and It returns the same value as *MAX* for numeric columns. <column> can be of any type.
MAXX(< table>, <expression >)	Returns the largest numeric value of <expression> evaluated for each row of <table>. The <expression> must return a numeric type; otherwise, it returns an error.
MIN(<column>)	Returns the smallest numeric value in a column. <column> must be of date or number type.
MINA(<column>)	Returns the smallest numeric value in a column. It always returns 0 for text columns, and it returns the same value as *MIN* for numeric columns. <column> can be of any type.
MINX(< table>, <expression >)	Returns the smallest numeric value of <expression> evaluated for each row of <table>. The <expression> must return a numeric type; otherwise, it returns an error.
RANK.EQ(<value>, <column> [, <order>])	Returns the ranking of a value in a list of values. It works on any data type.
RANKX(<table>, <expression> [, <value> [, <order> [, <ties>]]] [, <expression> [, <value> [, <order> [, <ties>]]] [,...]])	Returns the ranking of <expression> evaluated for each row in <table>. Multiple expressions are considered in case of ties. The <expression> must be of a numeric data type.
STDEV.P(<column>)	Returns the standard deviation of the entire population.
STDEV.S(<column>)	Returns the standard deviation of a sample population.
STDEVX.P(<table>, <expression>)	Returns the standard deviation of <expression> evaluated for each row of <table>, which represents the entire population.
STDEVX.S(<table>, <expression>)	Returns the standard deviation of <expression> evaluated for each row of <table>, which represents a sample population.
SUM(<column>)	Adds all the numbers in a column. <column> must be of date or number type.
SUMX(<table>, <expression>)	Returns the sum of <expression> evaluated for each row of <table>. The <expression> must return a numeric type; otherwise, it returns an error.
VAR.P(<column>)	Returns the variance of the entire population.
VAR.S(<column>)	Returns the variance of a sample population.
VARX.P(<table>, <expression>)	Returns the variance of <expression> evaluated for each row of <table>, which represents the entire population.
VARX.S(<table>, <expression>)	Returns the variance of <expression> evaluated for each row of <table>, which represents a sample population.

Table Transformation Functions

Table transformation functions return a table, performing transformations over the columns and the rows of the table. These functions are explained in detail in Chapter 6, "Querying Tabular," and in Chapter 7, "DAX Advanced."

TABLE A-2 Functions Returning a Table

Function	Description
ADDCOLUMNS(<table>, <name1>, <expression1>, [<name2>, <expression2> [,...]])	Adds calculated columns to the given table or table expression.
CROSSJOIN(<table1>, <table2> [, <table3> [,...]])	Returns the Cartesian product of all rows from all tables in arguments.
GENERATE(<table1>, <table2>)	Returns the Cartesian product between each row in <table1> and the table that results from evaluating <table2> in the context of the current row from <table1>. Rows in <table1> that do not return rows from <table2> are excluded from the result.
GENERATEALL(<table1>, <table2>)	Returns the Cartesian product between each row in <table1> and the table that results from evaluating <table2> in the context of the current row from <table1>. Rows in <table1> that do not return rows from <table2> are included in the result.
ROW(<name1>, <expression1> [, <name2>, <expression2> [, ...]])	Returns a table with a single row containing values that result from the <expression> given to each column defined by <name>.
SUMMARIZE(<table>, <group_by_column1> [, <group_by_column2> [, ...]] [<name1>, <expression1> [, <name2>, <expression2> [, ...]]])	Returns a summary table for the requested totals over a set of groups. The <group_by_column> arguments define the grouping column. The <name> and <expression> arguments define the expression for each calculated column included in the resulting table. Every <expression> will be evaluated for each row in the result.
TOPN(<n_value>, <table>, <order_by_expression1>, [<order1> [, <order_by_expression2>] [<order2>] [,...]])	Returns the top <n_value> rows of the specified <table>, according to the value returned by <order_by_expression> (multiple expressions are considered in case of ties).

Logical Functions

Logical functions return information about the values or sets in the expression. These functions implement logical conditions in a DAX expression, for example, to implement different calculations depending on the value of a column or to intercept an error condition.

TABLE A-3 Logical Functions

Function	Description
AND(<boolean_expression1>, <boolean_expression2>)	Returns *TRUE* if both parameters are TRUE. Returns *FALSE* if any of the parameters are FALSE.
FALSE( )	Returns the logical value *FALSE* (a TRUE/FALSE type value).
IF(<boolean >, <value_if_true>, <value_if_false>)	Returns <value_if_true> parameter if <boolean_expression> is TRUE; otherwise, returns <value_if_false>. It always returns a single data type in a column. (Implicit conversion is used if the two values are of different types.)

Function	Description
IFERROR(<value>, <value_if_error>)	Returns <value_if_error> if <value> is an error; otherwise, it returns <value>.
NOT(<boolean_expression>)	Returns *TRUE* if <boolean_expression> is FALSE. Returns *FALSE* if <boolean_expression> is TRUE.
OR(<boolean_expression1>, <boolean_expression2>)	Returns *TRUE* if one of the parameters is TRUE. Returns *FALSE* if both parameters are TRUE.
SWITCH(<expression>, <value1>, <result1> [, <value2>, <result2> [, ...]])	Evaluates an <expression> against a list of values and returns the <result> of the expression corresponding to the first matching <value>.
TRUE()	Returns the logical value *TRUE*. (It is a TRUE/FALSE type value.)

Information Functions

Information functions analyze the type of an expression to look for a value in a table, to get information about current users and from connection strings, and to navigate parent/child hierarchies.

TABLE A-4 Information Functions

Function	Description
CONTAINS(<table>, <column1>, <value1> [, <column2>, <value2> [, ...]])	Returns *TRUE* if at least a row in <table> contains the <value> specified for every <column>; otherwise, it returns *FALSE*.
CUSTOMDATA()	Returns the content of the CustomData property in the connection string.
ISBLANK(<value>)	Returns *TRUE* if <value> is *BLANK* (empty cell); otherwise, it returns *FALSE*.
ISERROR(<value>)	Returns *TRUE* if <value> is an error; otherwise, it returns *FALSE*.
ISLOGICAL(<value>)	Returns *TRUE* if <value> is of TRUE/FALSE type (Boolean); otherwise, it returns *FALSE*.
ISNONTEXT(<value>)	Returns *TRUE* if <value> is not text; otherwise, it returns *FALSE*. A *BLANK* value (for example, an empty cell) is not text and returns *TRUE*.
ISNUMBER(<value>)	Returns *TRUE* if <value> is a number; otherwise, it returns *FALSE*. A *BLANK* value (for example, an empty cell) is not text and returns *FALSE*.
ISTEXT(<value>)	Returns *TRUE* if <value> is a text; otherwise, it returns *FALSE*. A *BLANK* value (for example, an empty cell) is not text and returns *FALSE*.
LOOKUPVALUE(<result_column>, <search_column1>, <value1> [, <search_column2>, <value2> [, ...]])	Returns the value in <result_column> for the row that matches for each <search_column> the corresponding <value>. If multiple values for <result_column> would be returned, the function returns an error.
PATH(<column_id>, <column _parent>)	Follows the parent/child hierarchy defined by <column_parent> that points to <column_id> and returns a delimited text string with the identifiers of all the parents of the current identifier specified, starting with the oldest and continuing until current.
PATHCONTAINS(<path>, <item>)	Returns *TRUE* if the specified <item> exists within the specified <path> (returned by *PATH* function).

Function	Description
PATHITEM(<path>, <position> [, <type>])	Returns the item at the specified <position> from a string resulting from evaluation of specified <path> (returned by the *PATH* function). The <type> argument defines the data type of the result and can be *TEXT* or *INTEGER*. Positions start from 1 and are counted from left to right.
PATHITEMREVERSE(<path>, <position> [, <type>])	Returns the item at the specified <position> from a string resulting from evaluation of specified <path> (returned by the *PATH* function). The <type> argument defines the data type of the result and can be *TEXT* or *INTEGER*. Positions starts from 1 and are counted backwards from right to left.
PATHLENGTH(<path>)	Returns the number of parents to the specified item in a given <path> (returned by the *PATH* function), including self.
USERNAME()	Returns the domain name and username from the credentials given to the system at connection time.

Mathematical Functions

The set of mathematical and trigonometric functions available in DAX is a subset of the mathematical functions available in Microsoft Excel. In particular, trigonometric functions such as *COS*, *SIN*, and *TAN* are missing, and only *PI* is available.

TABLE A-5 Math and Trigonometric Functions

Function	Description
ABS(<number>)	Returns the absolute value of <number>, which is the same value without the sign.
CEILING(<number>, <significance>)	Rounds <number> to the nearest integer or to the nearest multiple of <significance>. It differs from *ISO.CEILING* only for negative numbers of <significance>.
CURRENCY(<value>)	Evaluates the argument and returns the result as *currency* data type.
EXP(<number>)	Returns *e* (which is the base of the natural logarithm) raised to the power of <number>.
FACT(<number>)	Factorial of <number>. It is like 1 * 2 * 3 * ... * <number>.
FLOOR(<number>, <significance>)	Rounds <number> down to the nearest multiple of <significance>. Use 1 for <significance> if you want to round the number to the nearest whole integer, use 0.1 for rounding to one decimal, and so on.
INT(<number>)	Rounds <number> down to the nearest integer. It always removes the decimal part.
ISO.CEILING(<number>, <significance>)	Rounds <number> to the nearest integer or to the nearest multiple of <significance>. It differs from *CEILING* only for negative numbers of <significance>.
LN(<number>)	Natural logarithm of <number>.
LOG(<number>, <base>)	Logarithm of <number> to the specified <base>.
LOG10(<number>)	Base-10 logarithm of <number>.
MOD(<number>, <divisor>)	Remainder of <number> after it is divided by <divisor>.

Function	Description
MROUND(<number>, <multiple>)	Rounds <number> to the desired <multiple>.
PI()	Returns the value of pi, 3.14159265358979.
POWER(<number>, <power>)	Returns <number> raised to <power>.
QUOTIENT(<numerator>, <denominator>)	Returns the integer portion of the result of <numerator> divided by <denominator>.
RAND()	Random number greater than or equal to 0 and less than 1. The number changes on recalculation.
RANDBETWEEN(<bottom>, <top>)	Random integer number greater than or equal to <bottom> and less than or equal to <top>.
ROUND(<number>, <num_digits>)	Rounds <number> to the number of digits specified by <num_digits>. If <num_digits> is greater than 0, the number is rounded to the specified number of decimal places. If <num_digits> is less than 0, the number is rounded to the left of decimal point (for example, uses 2 to round on multiples of 100). If <num_digits> is 0, the number is rounded to the nearest integer.
ROUNDDOWN(<number>, <num_digits>)	Rounds <number> down to zero, using to the number of digits specified by <num_digits>. See *ROUND* description for the meaning of <num_digits>.
ROUNDUP(<number>, <num_digits>)	Rounds <number> up, away from zero, using the number of digits specified by <num_digits>. See *ROUND* description for the meaning of <num_digits>.
SIGN(<number>)	Returns *1* if <number> is positive, *0 if* <number> is 0 and *-1* if <number> is negative.
SQRT(<number>)	Square root of <number>.
TRUNC(<number> [,<num_digits>])	Truncates <number> to an integer by removing the decimal part of the number. The <num_digits> parameter is optional, and it is 0 by default. See *ROUND* description for the meaning of <num_digits>.

Text Functions

Text functions available in DAX to manipulate text strings are similar to those available in Excel 2010, with just a few exceptions.

TABLE A-6 Text Functions

Function	Description
CONCATENATE(<text1>, <text2>)	Concatenates <text1> and <text2> into a single string. Converts argument types to string if necessary. It is like writing <text1> and <text2>.
EXACT(<text1>, <text2>)	Compares two strings, returning *TRUE* if they are identical; otherwise returns *FALSE*. *EXACT* is case-sensitive.
FIND(<find_text>, <within_text> [,<start_num>])	Returns the initial position of <find_text> in <within_text> string. If <start_num> is specified, the search begins from character <start_num> in <within_text>. *FIND* is case-sensitive.

Function	Description
FIXED(<number> [,<decimals> [,<no_commas>]])	Rounds <number> to the specified number of <decimals> and returns the result as text type. If <decimals> is omitted, two decimals are used by default. The third optional parameter can be *TRUE* to eliminate commas in the returned text; by default, it is *FALSE* (so commas are included by default).
FORMAT(<value>, <format_string>)	Formats <value> according to <format_string>. Look for Custom Numeric Formats For The *FORMAT* Function in the DAX help. This function corresponds to the Excel *TEXT()* function.
LEFT(<text>, <num_chars>)	Returns the first <num_chars> characters from the start of <text> string.
LEN(<text>)	Number of characters of <text> string.
LOWER(<text>)	Converts all letters of <text> to lowercase.
MID(<text>, <start_num>, <num_chars>)	Returns the <num_chars> number of characters from <text> string, starting from position <start_num>, where the first character of <text> has position 1.
REPLACE(<old_text>, <start_num>, <num_chars>, <new_text>)	Replaces the part of <old_text> string starting at <start_num> position for <num_chars> character with the <new_text> string.
REPT(<text>, <num_times>)	Repeats <text> for <num_times> times.
RIGHT(<text>, <num_chars>)	Returns the last <num_chars> characters from the end of <text> string.
SEARCH(<search_text>, <within_text> [,<start_num>])	Returns the initial position of <search_text> in <within_text> string. If <start_num> is specified, the search begins from character <start_num> in <within_text>. *SEARCH* is not case-sensitive.
SUBSTITUTE(<text>, <old_text>, <new_text> [,<instance_num>])	Substitutes <new_text> for <old_text> in <text> string. If <instance_num> is specified, it indicates the occurrence of <old_text> to replace. By default, every instance of <old_text> is replaced.
TRIM(<text>)	Removes all the spaces from <text> except for single spaces between words.
UPPER (<text>)	Converts all letters of <text> to uppercase.
VALUE(<text>)	Converts <text> string that represents a number to a number. If the text does not contain a valid number, it returns an error. To convert a text column safely into a numeric one, converting all nonnumeric values into empty values, use *IFERROR*, as in this example: = IFERROR(VALUE(Table[Column]), BLANK())

Date and Time Functions

The basic date and time functions available in DAX operate primarily as converters between *text* and *datetime* types and are similar to corresponding functions in Excel. There are also other time intelligence functions that are specific to DAX, which are covered in Table A-9.

TABLE A-7 Date and Time Functions

Function	Description
DATE(<year>, <month>, <day>)	Returns a value of *datetime* type corresponding to the date defined by <year>, <month>, and <day>. Because the return is of *datetime* data type, hour, minute, and second are set to 0.
DATEVALUE(<date_text>)	Converts a date contained in <date_text> into a value of *datetime* type. Format of <date_text> depends on system settings.
DAY(<date>)	Day of month (number between 1 and 31) of <date>.
EDATE(<start_date>, <months>)	Returns the date that indicates number of <months> before or after the <start_date>. Positive values for <months> are considered after <start_date>; negative values are considered before <start_date>.
EOMONTH(<start_date>, <months>)	Returns the last day of the month before or after the <start_date> for a specified number of <months>. Positive values for <months> are considered after <start_date>; negative values are considered before <start_date>.
HOUR(<datetime>)	Hour (number between 0 and 23) of <datetime>.
MINUTE(<datetime>)	Minute (number between 0 and 59) of <datetime>.
MONTH(<datetime>)	Month (number between 1 and 12) of <date>.
NOW()	Returns current date and time.
SECOND(<datetime>)	Second (number between 0 and 59) of <datetime>.
TIME(<hour>, <minute>, <second>)	Returns a value of *datetime* type corresponding to the time defined by <hour>, <minute>, and <second>. Because the return is of *datetime* data type, year, month, and day are set to a reference date (which is December 30, 1899).
TIMEVALUE(<time_text>)	Converts a time contained in <time_text> into a value of *datetime* type. Format of <time_text> depends on system settings.
TODAY( )	Returns current date. Because the return is of *datetime* data type, hour, minute, and second are set to 0.
WEEKDAY(<date> [,<return_type>])	Day of week (number between 1 and 7) of <date>. The optional <return_type> parameter determines the return value: for Sunday=1 through Saturday=7, use 1; for Monday=1 through Sunday=7, use 2; for Monday=0 through Sunday=6, use 3. By default, it is 1.
WEEKNUM(<date> [,<return_type>])	Week number of <date>. The optional <return_type> parameter determines which day to consider as week beginning. With 1, week begins on Sunday; with 2, week begins on Monday. By default, it is 1. (See WEEKNUM help in Excel to get a complete list of possible values.)
YEAR(<date>)	Year (number between 1900 and 9999) of <date>.
YEARFRAC(<start_date>, <end_date> [,<basis>])	Calculates the fraction of the year represented by the number of whole days between <start_date> and <end_date> dates. The optional <basis> parameter defines the type of day count basis. (See YEARFRAC help in Excel to get a complete list of possible values.)

Filter and Value Functions

The functions that manipulate row context and filter context in DAX calculations are explained in detail in Chapter 5, "Understanding Evaluation Context," and in Chapter 7, "DAX Advanced."

TABLE A-8 Filter and Value Functions

Function	Description
ALL(<table_or_column>)	Returns all the rows in a table or all the values in a column, ignoring any filters that have been applied.
ALLEXCEPT(<table> [,<column1> [,<column2> [,...]]])	Overrides all context filters in the table except filters that have been applied to the specified columns.
ALLNOBLANKROW(<table_or _column>)	Returns all the rows, except for blank rows, in a table or column, and disregards any context filters that exist.
ALLSELECTED(<table_or_column>)	Removes context filters from columns and rows in the current query while retaining all other context filters or explicit filters. This function can be used to obtain visual totals in queries.
BLANK( )	Returns a blank.
CALCULATE(<expression> [,<filter1> [,<filter2> [,...]]])	Evaluates an expression in a context that is modified by the specified filters.
CALCULATETABLE(<expression> [,<filter1> [,<filter2> [,...]]])	Evaluates a table expression in a context modified by filters.
DISTINCT(<column>)	Returns a one-column table that contains the distinct values from the specified column.
EARLIER(<column> [,<number>])	Returns the current value of the specified column in an outer evaluation pass of the specified column.
EARLIEST(<table_or_column>)	Returns the current value of the specified column in an outer evaluation pass of the mentioned column.
FILTER(<table>, <filter>)	Returns a table that represents a subset of another table or expression.
FILTERS(<column>)	Returns the values that are directly applied as filters to the specified <column>.
HASONEFILTER(<column>)	Returns *TRUE* when the number of directly filtered values on <column> is one; otherwise, it returns *FALSE*.
HASONEVALUE(<column>)	Returns *TRUE* when the context for <column> has been filtered down to one distinct value; otherwise, it returns *FALSE*.
ISCROSSFILTERED(<column>)	Returns *TRUE* when <column> or another column in the same or related table is being filtered.
ISFILTERED(<column>)	Returns *TRUE* when <column> is being filtered directly. If there is no filter on the column or if the filtering happens because a different column in the same table or in a related table is being filtered, then the function returns *FALSE*.
RELATED(<column>)	Returns a related value from another table.
RELATEDTABLE(<table>)	Follows an existing relationship, in either direction, and returns a table that contains all matching rows from the specified table.
VALUES(<column>)	Returns a one-column table that contains the distinct values from the specified column. This function is similar to the *DISTINCT* function, but the *VALUES* function can also return *Unknown Member*.

Time Intelligence Functions

There are special functions to make complex operations on dates, such as comparing aggregated values year over year or calculating the year-to-date value of a measure. This set of functions is called Time Intelligence Functions and is described in Chapter 8, "Understanding Time Intelligence in DAX."

TABLE A-9 Time Intelligence Functions

Function	Description
CLOSINGBALANCEMONTH (<expression>, <dates> [,<filter>])	Evaluates the specified expression at the calendar end of the given month. The given month is calculated as the month of the latest date in the dates argument after applying all filters.
CLOSINGBALANCEQUARTER (<expression>, <dates> [,<filter>])	Evaluates the specified expression at the calendar end of the given quarter. The given quarter is calculated as the quarter of the latest date in the dates argument after applying all filters.
CLOSINGBALANCEYEAR(<expression>, <dates> [,<filter>] [,<year_end_date>])	Evaluates the specified expression at the calendar end of the given year. The given year is calculated as the year of the latest date in the dates argument after applying all filters.
DATEADD(<date_column>, <number_of_intervals>, <interval>)	Returns a table that contains a column of dates, shifted either forward in time or back in time from the dates in the specified date column.
DATESBETWEEN(<column>, <start_date>, <end_date>)	Returns a table of dates that can be found in the specified date column, beginning with the start date and ending with the end date.
DATESINPERIOD(<date_column>, <start_date>, <number_of_intervals>, <intervals>)	Returns a table of dates that can be found in the specified date column, beginning with the start date and continuing for the specified number of intervals.
DATESMTD(<date_column>)	Returns the subset of dates from <date_column> for the interval that starts at the first day of the month and ends at the latest date in the specified dates column for the month that is the corresponding month of the latest date.
DATESQTD(<date_column>)	Returns the subset of dates from <date_column> for the interval that starts at the first day of the quarter and ends at the latest date in the specified dates column for the quarter that is the corresponding quarter of the latest date.
DATESYTD(<date_column> [,<year_end_date>])	Returns the subset of dates from <date_column> for the interval that starts the first day of the year and ends at the latest date in the specified dates column for the quarter that is the corresponding quarter of the latest date.
ENDOFMONTH(<date_column>)	Returns the last day of the month in the specified date column.
ENDOFQUARTER(<date_column>)	Returns the last day of the quarter in the specified date column.
ENDOFYEAR(<date_column> [,<year_end_date>])	Returns the last day of the year in the specified date column.
FIRSTDATE(<date_column>)	Returns the first date in the current context for the specified <date_column>.
FIRSTNONBLANK(<column>, <expression>)	Returns the first value in the <column> filtered by the current context where the <expression> is not blank.
LASTDATE(<date_column>)	Returns the last date in the current context for the specified <date_column>.
LASTNONBLANK(<column>, <expression>)	Returns the last value in the <column> filtered by the current context, where the <expression> is not blank.

Function	Description
NEXTDAY(<date_column>)	Returns the next day date from <date_column>.
NEXTMONTH(<date_column>)	Returns the set of dates in the next month from <date_column>.
NEXTQUARTER(<date_column>)	Returns the set of dates for the next quarter from <date_column>.
NEXTYEAR(<date_column> [,<year_end_date>])	Returns the set of dates for the next year from <date_column>.
OPENINGBALANCEMONTH (<expression>, <dates> [,<filter>])	Evaluates the specified expression at the calendar end of the month prior to the given month. The given month is calculated as the month of the latest date in the dates argument after applying all filters.
OPENINGBALANCEQUARTER (<expression>, <dates> [,<filter>])	Evaluates the specified expression at the calendar end of the quarter prior to the given quarter. The given quarter is calculated as the quarter of the latest date in the dates argument after applying all filters.
OPENINGBALANCEYEAR(<expression>, <dates> [,<filter>] [,<year_end_date>])	Evaluates the specified expression at the calendar end of the year prior to the given year. The given year is calculated as the year of the latest date in the dates argument after applying all filters.
PARALLELPERIOD(<date_column>, <number_of_intervals>, <intervals>)	This function moves the specified number of intervals and then returns all contiguous full months that contain any values after that shift. Gaps between the first and last dates are filled in, and months are also filled in.
PREVIOUSDAY(<date_column>)	Returns the previous day date from <date_column>.
PREVIOUSMONTH(<date_column>)	Returns the set of dates in the previous month from <date_column>.
PREVIOUSQUARTER(<date_column>)	Returns the set of dates in the previous quarter from <date_column>.
PREVIOUSYEAR(<date_column> [,<year_end_date>])	Returns the set of dates in the previous year from <date_column>.
SAMEPERIODLASTYEAR (<date_column>)	Returns a table of dates that can be found in the specified <date_column>.
STARTOFMONTH(<date_column>)	Returns the first day of the month in the specified <date_column>.
STARTOFQUARTER(<date_column>)	Returns the first day of the quarter in the specified <date_column>.
STARTOFYEAR(<date_column> [,<year_end_date>])	Returns the first day of the year in the specified <date_column>.
TOTALMTD(<expression>, <dates> [,<filter>])	Evaluates the specified expression for the interval that starts at the first day of the month and ends at the latest date in the specified dates column after applying all filters.
TOTALQTD(<expression>, <dates> [,<filter>])	Evaluates the specified expression for the interval that starts at the first day of the quarter and ends at the latest date in the specified dates column after applying all filters.
TOTALYTD(<expression>, <dates> [,<filter>] [,<year_end_date>])	Evaluates the specified expression for the interval that starts at the first day of the year and ends at the latest date in the specified dates column after applying all filters.

Index

M

O

P

Y

X

About the Authors

MARCO RUSSO is a Business Intelligence (BI) consultant and mentor. His main activities are related to data warehouse relational and multidimensional design, but he is also involved in the complete development life cycle of a BI solution. He has particular experience and competence in such sectors as financial services (including complex OLAP designs in the banking area), manufacturing, gambling, and commercial distribution.

Marco is also a book author and, apart from his BI-related publications, has written books on .NET programming. He is also a speaker at international conferences such as PASS Summit, SQLRally, and SQLBits.

He has achieved the unique SSAS Maestro certification and is also a Microsoft Certified Trainer with several Microsoft Certified Professional certifications.

ALBERTO FERRARI is a BI consultant. His main interests are in two areas: the methodological approach to the BI development life cycle and performance tuning of ETL and SQL code.

His activities are related to designing and implementing solutions based on Integration Services and Analysis Services for the financial, manufacturing, and statistical markets.

A certified SSAS Maestro, Alberto is also a book author and a speaker at international conferences such as PASS Summit, SQLRally, and SQLBits.

CHRIS WEBB is a consultant specializing in Analysis Services, MDX, PowerPivot, and DAX. He is a coauthor of *Expert Cube Development with SQL Server 2008 Analysis Services* and *MDX Solutions: With Microsoft SQL Server Analysis Services 2005 and Hyperion Essbase*.

Chris is a certified SSAS Maestro and is a regular speaker at PASS Summit and SQLBits conferences.